The Women's Movement Today

The Women's Movement Today

An Encyclopedia of Third-Wave Feminism

Volume 2, Primary Documents

Edited by
Leslie L. Heywood

GREENWOOD PRESS
Westport, Connecticut • London

Library of Congress Cataloging-in-Publication Data

The women's movement today : an encyclopedia of third-wave feminism / edited by Leslie L. Heywood.
p. cm.
Includes bibliographical references and index.
ISBN 0–313–33133–2 (set: alk. paper)—ISBN 0–313–33134–0 (v. 1: alk. paper)—ISBN 0–313–33135–9 (v. 2: alk. paper)
1. Feminism—Encyclopedias. 2. Women—Social conditions—21st century—Encyclopedias. I. Heywood, Leslie.
HQ1115.W644 2006
305.42'03—dc22 2005019217

British Library Cataloguing in Publication Data is available.

Library of Congress Catalog Card Number: 2005019217
ISBN: 0–313–33133–2 (Set)
0–313–33134–0 (Vol. 1)
0–313–33135–9 (Vol. 2)

First published in 2006

Greenwood Press, 88 Post Road West, Westport, CT 06881
An imprint of Greenwood Publishing Group, Inc.
www.greenwood.com

Printed in the United States of America

The paper used in this book complies with the Permanent Paper Standard issued by the National Information Standards Organization (Z39.48–1984).

10 9 8 7 6 5 4 3 2 1

Contents

Part II Consumerism, Globalization, and Third-Wave Lives

PART I

Third-Wave Feminism: Definitions and Debates

The documents in this section include a range of voices weighing in on the question of what it means to be third wave. The pieces address generational divides, debates around race and class, and questions of what counts as feminist activism. The third wave is known for lively debate rather than consensus.

1. Rebecca Walker, "Becoming the Third Wave," from *Ms.* Magazine

Ms. 39 (January/February 1992): 41.

Here Rebecca Walker asserts that, "I am not a postfeminism feminist. I am the Third Wave." The movement is widely thought to have taken its name from this piece, which argues why feminism is still vital, necessary, and urgent.

I am not one of the people who sat transfixed before the television, watching the Senate hearings. I had classes to go to, papers to write, and frankly, the whole thing was too painful. A black man grilled by a panel of white men about his sexual deviance. A black woman claiming harassment and being discredited by other women.... I could not bring myself to watch that sensationalized assault of the human spirit.

To me, the hearings were not about determining whether or not Clarence Thomas did in fact harass Anita Hill. They were about checking and redefining the extent of women's credibility and power.

Can a woman's experience undermine a man's career? Can a woman's voice, a woman's sense of self-worth and injustice, challenge a structure predicated upon the subjugation of our gender? Anita Hill's testimony threatened to do that and more. If Thomas had not been confirmed, every man in the United States would be at risk. For how many senators never told a sexist joke—how many men have not used their protected male privilege to thwart in some way the influence or ideas of a woman colleague, friend, or relative.

For those whose sense of power is so obviously connected to the health and vigor of the penis, it would have been a metaphoric castration. Of course this is too great a threat.

While some may laud the whole spectacle for the consciousness it raised around sexual harassment, its very real outcome is more informative. He was promoted. She was repudiated. Men were assured of the inviolability of their penis/power. Women were admonished to keep their experiences to themselves.

The backlash against U.S. women is real. As the misconception of equality between the sexes becomes more ubiquitous, so does the attempt to restrict the boundaries of women's personal and political power. Thomas' confirmation, the ultimate rally of support for the male paradigm of harassment, sends a clear message to women: "Shut up! Even if you speak, we will not listen."

I will not be silenced.

I acknowledge the fact that we live under siege. I intend to fight back. I have uncovered and unleashed more repressed anger than I thought possible. For the umpteenth time in my 22 years, I have been radicalized, politicized, shaken awake. I have come to voice again, and this time my voice is not conciliatory.

The night after Thomas's confirmation I ask the man I am intimate with what he thinks of the whole mess. His concern is primarily with Thomas' propensity to demolish civil rights and opportunities for people of color. I launch into a tirade. "When will progressive black men prioritize my rights and well-being? When will they stop talking so damn much about 'the race' as if it revolved exclusively around them?" He tells me I wear my emotions on my sleeve. I scream "I need to know, are you with me or are you going to help them try to destroy me?"

A week later I am on a train to New York. A beautiful mother and daughter, both wearing green outfits, sit across the aisle from me. The little girl has tightly plaited braids. Her brown skin is glowing and smooth, her eyes bright as she chatters happily while looking out the window. Two men get on the train and sit directly behind me, shaking my seat as they thud into place. I bury myself in *The Sound and the Fury*. Loudly they begin to talk about women. "Man, I fucked that bitch all night and then I never called her again." "Man, there's lots of girlies over there, you know that ho, live over there by Tyrone's, Well, I snatched that shit up." The mother moves closer to her now quiet daughter. Looking at her small back I can see that she is listening to the men. I am thinking of how I can transform the situation, of all the people in the car whose silence makes us complicit. Another large man gets on the train. After exchanging loud greetings with the two men, he sits next to me. He tells them he is going to Philadelphia to visit his wife and child. I am suckered into thinking that he is different. Then, "Man, there's a ton of females in Philly, just waitin' for you to give 'em some." I turn my head and allow the fire in my eyes to burn into him. He takes up two seats and has hands with huge swollen knuckles. I imagine the gold rings on his fingers slamming into my face. He senses something. "What's your name, sweetheart?" The other men lean forward over the seat.

My instinct kicks in, telling me to get out. "Since I see you all are not going to move, I will." I move to the first car. I am so angry that thoughts of murder, of physically retaliating against them, of separatism, engulf me. I am almost out of body, just shy of being pure force. I am sick of the way women are negated, violated, devalued, ignored. I am livid, unrelenting in my anger at those who invade my space, who wish to take away my rights, who refuse to hear my voice. As the days pass, I push myself to figure out what it means to be a part of the Third Wave of feminism. I begin to realize that I owe it to myself, to my little sister on the train, to all of the daughters yet to be born, to push beyond my rage and articulate an agenda. After battling with ideas of separatism and militancy, I connect with my own feelings of powerlessness. I realize that I must undergo a transformation if I am truly committed to women's empowerment. My involvement must reach beyond my own voice in discussion, beyond voting, beyond reading feminist theory. My anger and awareness must translate into tangible action.

I am ready to decide, as my mother decided before me, to devote much of my energy to the history, health, and healing of women. Each of my choices will have to hold to my feminist standard of justice. To be a feminist is to integrate an ideology of equality and female empowerment into the very fiber of my life. It is to search for personal clarity in the midst of systemic destruction, to join in sisterhood with women when often we are divided, to understand power structures with the intention of challenging them. While this may sound simple, it is exactly the kind of stand that many of my peers are unwilling to take. So I write this as a plea to all women, especially the women of my generation: Let Thomas' confirmation serve to remind you, as it did me, that the fight is far from over. Let this dismissal of a woman's experience move you to anger. Turn that outrage into political power. Do not vote for them unless they work for us. Do not have sex with them, do not break bread with them, do not nurture them if they don't prioritize our freedom to control our bodies and our lives.

I am not a postfeminism feminist. I am the Third Wave.

2. Barbara Findlen, "Introduction," from *Listen Up: Voices from the Next Feminist Generation*

Excerpts from "Introduction," by Barbara Findlen, published in *Listen Up: Voices from the Next Feminist Generation* (Seattle: Seal Press, 1995), xi–xvi. Reprinted with permission.

Barbara Findlen's introduction to her influential third-wave essay collection, *Listen Up*, explored the idea that third-wave feminists had come of age in a very different set of historical circumstances than did feminists of the second wave. These were circumstances the second wave helped enable: "The legacy of feminism for me was a sense of entitlement ... during our early years, feminism was already a major social force." Findlen's piece also addresses the question of bringing all aspects of oneself to feminism, not just those associated with gender.

My feminism wasn't shaped by antiwar or civil rights activism; I was not a victim of the problem that had no name. Indeed, by the time I was discovering feminism, naming had become a principal occupation of feminists. Everywhere you looked feminists were naming things—things like sexual harassment, date rape, displaced homemakers and domestic violence—that used to be called, as Gloria Steinem pointed out, just life.

In fact, born in 1964, I became a part of a massive, growing, vibrant feminist movement at the age of eleven—something that literally had not been possible for Gloria Steinem, Kate Millett, my older sisters, my mother, or any of my other feminist role models. While feminism has been around for as long as patriarchy, I came of age during one of those moments in history when the feminist movement was becoming so large, so vocal and so visible that it could reach into and change the life of an eleven-year-old suburban girl.

It was a time of unlimited possibilities for women—or that was my impression, anyway. When I was eight, I cried as my father tried to explain to me why my brother could play Little League baseball, while I, who had just reached the age of eligibility, was still somehow ineligible. Two years later, my best friend Linda Brauer and I joined a nearby team, the ban on girls having magically disappeared. I knew that there was a feminist movement, but I hadn't learned about the grueling and sometimes humiliating struggle of the girl, Maria Pepe, two years older than me, who had sued Little League Baseball all the way to the New Jersey State Supreme Court in order to be allowed to play the game.

To me, feminism meant that women and men, girls and boys, were equal. Almost every woman has experienced the feeling of being mistreated, trivialized, kept out, put down, ignored, assaulted, laughed at or discriminated against because of her gender. To me, the existence of feminism—and a feminist movement—meant that the rage I felt was no longer impotent. When I was locked out of Little League, I didn't know what to do except cry. When I then was allowed to play, I realized that change was possible, although I didn't yet realize the struggles and risks inherent in making change.

The legacy of feminism for me was a sense of entitlement. The year after Linda and I joined our baseball team, we started to wonder why the "boys' yard" at our elementary school was the one with the basketball court, baseball field, football field and jungle gym, while the "girls' yard" offered only a hopscotch grid. We took our complaint to the principal, who eventually integrated recess.

A trivial matter? Perhaps, in the scheme of things. But the possibility of achieving redress, even if it starts on a small scale, is self-perpetuating. The more justice you think you can achieve, the more you try to achieve. If it had been 1955 instead of 1975, we wouldn't have questioned the unfairness, even if we resented it. In 1965, we may have asked for fair treatment, but we probably would have been laughed at. But because we were eleven at a time when there was a feminist movement creating awareness everywhere about sexism, we could not only identify an injustice in our world, we could right the wrong.

While this certainly is not the kind of experience every young woman, or even every young feminist, has had, the point is that it's the kind of experience *only* a woman of this generation could have had. We are the first generation for whom feminism has been entwined in the fabric of our lives; it is natural that many of us are feminists.

... Women of this generation in the United States ... have been shaped by the unique events and circumstances of our time: AIDS, the erosion of reproductive rights, the materialism and cynicism of the Reagan and Bush years, the backlash against women, the erosion of civil rights, the skyrocketing divorce rate, the movement toward multiculturalism and greater global awareness, the emergence of the lesbian and gay rights movement, a greater overall awareness of sexuality—and the feminist movement itself. During our early years, feminism was already a major social force. As we reached adolescence and adulthood, the feminist movement was challenging society's basic assumptions about gender. For the first time, there were significant numbers of girls and boys growing up in feminist families. But even those of us not lucky enough to be raised by feminists have found other avenues to discover and integrate feminism into our lives: women's studies, a huge body of feminist fiction and nonfiction, community- and school-based activist groups, the occasional sitcom.

Generation X, thirteenth generation, twenty something—whatever package you buy this age group in—one of the characteristics we're known for is our disunity. Maybe we're not as unified as the generation that preceded us. Maybe we're just not as categorizable. In any case, I wonder whether the famous unity of the baby boomers might not be a bit mythical. Even in eras that offer unifying forces more momentous than *The Brady Bunch*, each individual's personal experiences define the time for her. Women's *experiences* of sexism have always been an important basis for political action. And our experiences of sexism are far from universal; they have always been affected by race, class, geographic location, disability, sexual identity, religion and just plain luck. How patriarchy crosses our paths and how we deal with that can also be determined by our families, school systems, the degree and type of violence in our communities and myriad other factors. So what may appear to be a splintering in this generation often comes from an honest assessment of our differences as each of us defines her place and role in feminism.

... Young feminists write about the ongoing process of integrating their feminist identities with ethnic, racial, religious, sexual, regional, class and other identities. Many women of color in particular struggle to promote the visibility and concerns of feminists in communities of color and at the same time ensure that feminist scholarship, activism and institutions fully integrate the lives and realities of women of color.... We are determined, as Sonja D. Curry-Johnson writes, "to bring our whole selves to the table."

Young feminists are constantly told that we don't exist. It's a refrain heard from older feminists as well as in the popular media: "Young women don't consider themselves feminists." Actually, a lot of us do. And many more of us have integrated feminist values into our lives, whether or not we choose to use the label "feminist." This is an important barometer of the impact of feminism, since feminism is a movement for social change—not an organization doing a membership drive.

... Some young women do fear the feminist label, largely because of the stereotypes and distortions that still abound. If something or someone is appealing, fun or popular, it or she can't be feminist. Feminists are still often assumed to be strident, man-hating, unattractive—and lesbian. I continue to be amazed at the power of that final "accusation," even though as a lesbian, I am well accustomed to the depth of the homophobia that pervades this country. The idea that all feminists are lesbians is scary enough for some women to stay away from the feminist label *and* movement even when their beliefs are basically feminist. When a young woman decides to identify as a feminist—a woman who stands up for herself and other women—she soon discovers at least two things: that women of all sexual identities are feminists, and that, even so, she will now be subject to the same stereotypes and dyke-baiting that may once have scared her away. But simply denying that all feminists are lesbians is not the way to right this wrong. We need to take the harder road of challenging the homophobia that gives this image its power.

... There's no singular "young feminist" take on the world. But more to the point, there's no one "feminist" take on the world, and there never has been. And that's one of the many ways in which there's more common ground than differences between young feminists and older feminists.... It is clear that the kinds of experiences that lead young women to feminism are often similar to those that have always led women into feminism, even though the personal circumstances and social context may differ.

If there is a troublesome legacy from the feminism that has come before, it's the burden of high expectations—of both ourselves and the world. Many young feminists describe growing up with the expectation that "you can do anything," whether that message came directly from parents or just from seeing barriers falling. But there's a point where you realize that while you may indeed feel capable of doing anything, you can be stopped—because of sexism. Maybe you played Little League baseball but found yourself relegated to girls' softball at age thirteen. Maybe you were the smartest kid in your high school class, and were stunned the first time you heard a college professor say that women couldn't be great artists or mathematicians or athletes. Maybe your mother gave you *Our Bodies, Ourselves* and taught you to love your body, but that didn't stop you from being raped.

The moment when sexism steps into your path can be disappointing, humiliating, shocking. It can take away your breath, your hope, your faith in yourself, your faith in the world. The impact is even greater if you're not expecting it, if you have no framework for understanding that you are being mistreated because of your gender. Feminism is what helps us make sense of the unfairness by affirming that it's about political injustice, not personal failure. The feminist movement offers us strength to fight back.

This country hasn't heard enough from young feminists. We're here, and we have a lot to say about our ideas and hopes and struggles and our place within feminism.

3. Joan Morgan, "Hip-Hop Feminist," from *When Chickenheads Come Home to Roost*

In excerpts from this essay that pinpoint differences between second- and third-wave feminism in a humorous and accessible way, Morgan writes of "a feminism that would allow me to explore who we are as women—not victims. One that claimed the powerful richness and delicious complexities inherent in being black girls now—sistas of the post–Civil Rights, post-feminist, post-soul, hip-hop generation."

... When I told older heads that I was writing a book which explored, among other things, my generation of black women's precarious relationship with feminism, they looked at me like I was trying to re-invent the wheel. I got lectured ad nauseum about "the racism of the White Feminist Movement," "the sixties and the seventies," and "feminism's historic irrelevance to black folks." I was reminded of how feminism's ivory tower elitism excludes the masses. And I was told that black women simply "didn't have time for all that shit."

While there is undeniable truth in all of the above except the latter—*the shit* black women don't have time for is dying and suffering from exorbitant rates of solo parenting, domestic violence, drug abuse, incarceration, AIDS, and cancer—none of them really explain why we have no black feminist *movement*. Lack of college education explains why 'round-the-way girls aren't reading bell hooks. It does not explain why even the gainfully degreed (self included) would rather trick away our last twenty-five dollars on that new nineties black girl fiction (trife as some of it may be) than some of those good, but let's face it, laboriously academic black feminist texts.

White women's racism and the Feminism Movement may explain the justifiable bad taste the f-word leaves in the mouths of women who are over thirty-five, but for my generation they are abstractions drawn from someone else's history. And without the power of memories, these phrases mean little to nothing....

... At the heart of our generation's ambivalence about the f-word is black women's historic tendency to blindly defend any black man who seems to be under attack from white folks (men, women, media, criminal justice system, etc.). The fact that the brothers may very well be in the wrong and, in some cases, deserve to be buried *under* the jail is irrelevant—even if the victim is one of us. Centuries of being rendered helpless while racism, crime, drugs, poverty, depression, and violence robbed us of our men has left us misguidedly over-protective, hopelessly male-identified, and all too often self-sacrificing.

And yes, fear is part of the equation too, but I don't think it's a fear of the possible. Rather, it is the justifiable fear of what lies ahead for any black woman boldly proclaiming her commitment to empowerment—her sistas' or her own. Acknowledging the rampant sexism in our community, for example, means relinquishing the comforting illusion that black men and women are a unified front. Accepting that black men do not always reciprocate our need to love and protect is a terrifying thing, because it means that we are truly out there, *assed out* in a world rife with sexism and racism. And who the hell wants to deal with that?

... *Cojónes* became a necessary part of my feminist armature—but not for the reasons I would have suspected.... I used to fear the constant accusations—career opportunism, race treason, collusion with "The Man," lesbianism—a lifetime of explaining what I am not. I dreaded the long, tedious conversations spent exorcising others of the stereotypes that tend to haunt the collective consciousness when we think of black women and the f-word—male basher, radical literary/academic black women in their forties and fifties who are pathetically separated from real life, burly dreadlocked/crew cut dykes, sexually adventurous lipstick-wearing bisexuals, victims. Even more frightening were the frequent solo conversations I spent exorcising them from my own head.

In time, however, all of that would roll off my back like water.

Cojónes became necessary once I discovered that mine was not a feminism that existed comfortably in the black and white of things. The precarious nature of my career's origins was the first indication. I got my start as a writer because I captured the sexual attention of a man who could make me one. It was not the first time my externals would bestow me with such favors. It certainly would not be the last.

My growing fatigue with talking about "the men" was the second. Just once, I didn't want to have to talk about "the brothers," "male domination," or "the patriarchy." I wanted a feminism that would allow me to explore who we are as women—not victims. One that claimed the powerful richness and delicious complexities inherent in being black girls now—sistas of the post–Civil Rights, post-feminist, post-soul, hip-hop generation.

I was also looking for permission for ask some decidedly un-P.C. but very real questions:

Can you be a good feminist and admit out loud that there are things you kinda dig about patriarchy?
Would I be forced to turn in my "feminist membership card" if I confessed that suddenly waking up in a world free of gender inequities or expectations just might bug me out a little?
Suppose you don't want to pay for your own dinner, hold the door open, fix things, move furniture, or get intimate with whatever's under the hood of a car?
Is it foul to say that imagining a world where you could paint your big brown lips in the most decadent of shades, pile your phat ass into your fave micromini, slip your freshly manicured toes into four-inch fuck-me sandals and have not one single solitary man objectify—I mean roam his eyes longingly over all the intended places—is, like, a total drag for you?
Am I no longer down for the cause if I admit that while total gender equality is an interesting intellectual concept, it doesn't do a damn thing for me erotically? That truth be told, men with too many "feminist" sensibilities have never made my panties wet, at least not like that reformed thug nigga who can make even the most chauvinistic of "wassup, baby" feel like a sweet, wet tongue darting in and out of your ear.
And how come no one ever admits that part of the reason women love hip-hop—as sexist as it is—is 'cuz all that in-yo-face testosterone makes our nipples hard?
Are we no longer good feminists, not to mention nineties supersistas, if the A.M.'s wee hours sometimes leave us tearful and frightened that achieving all our mothers wanted us to—great educations, careers, financial and emotional independence—has made us wholly undesirable to the men who are supposed to be our counterparts? Men whose fascination with chickenheads leave us convinced they have no interest in dating, let alone marrying, their equals?
And when one accuses you of being completely indecipherable there's really nothing to say 'cuz even you're not sure how you can be a feminist and insist he "respect you as a woman, treat you like a lady, and make you feel safe—like a li'l girl."

In short, I needed a feminism brave enough to fuck with the grays. And this was not my foremothers' feminism.

Ironically, reaping the benefits of our foremothers' struggle is precisely what makes their brand of feminism so hard to embrace. The "victim" (read women) "oppressor" (read men) model that seems to dominate so much of contemporary discourse (both black and white) denies the very essence of who we are.

We are the daughters of feminist privilege. The gains of the Feminist Movement (the efforts of black, white, Latin, Asian, and Native American women) had a tremendous impact on our lives—so much we often take it for granted.

We walk through the world with a sense of entitlement that women of our mothers' generation could not begin to fathom. Most of us can't imagine our lives without access to birth control, legalized abortions, the right to vote, or many of the same educational and job opportunities available to men. Sexism may be a very real part of my life but so is the unwavering belief that there is no dream I can't pursue *and* achieve simply because "I'm a woman."

Rejecting the wildly popular notion that embracing the f-word entails nothing more than articulating victimization, for me, is a matter of personal and spiritual survival. Surviving the combined impact of racism and sexism on the daily means never allowing my writing to suggest that black women aren't more than a bunch of bad memories. We *are* more than the rapes survived by the slave masters, the illicit familial touches accompanied by whiskey-soured breath, or the acts of violence endured by the fists, knives, and guns of strangers. We are more than the black eyes and heart bruises from those we believed were friends.

Black women can no more be defined by the cumulative sum of our pain than blackness can be defined solely by the transgenerational atrocities delivered at the hands of American racism. Because black folks are more than the stench of the slave ship, the bite of the dogs, or the smoldering of freshly lynched flesh. In both cases, defining ourselves solely by our oppression denies us the very magic of who we are. My feminism simply refuses to give sexism or racism that much power.

Holding on to that protective mantle of victimization requires a hypocrisy and self-censorship I'm no longer willing to give. Calling rappers out for their sexism without mentioning the complicity of the 100 or so video-hos that turned up—G-string in hand—for the shoot; or defending women's reproductive rights without examining the very complicated issue of *male choice*—specifically the inherent unfairness in denying men the right to choose whether or not *they want* to parent; or discussing the physical and emotional damage of sexism without examining the utterly foul and unloving ways black women treat each other ultimately means fronting like the shit brothers have with them is any less complex, difficult, or painful than the shit we have with ourselves. I am down, however, for a feminism that demands we assume responsibility for our lives.

In my quest to find a functional feminism for myself and my sistas—one that seeks empowerment on spiritual, material, physical, and emotional levels—I draw heavily on the cultural movement that defines my generation. As post–Civil Rights, post-feminist, post-soul children of hip-hop we have a dire need for the truth.

We have little faith in inherited illusions and idealism. We are the first generation to grow up with all the benefits of Civil Rights (i.e., Affirmative Action, government-subsidized educational and social programs) and the first to lose them. The first to have the devastation of AIDS, crack, and black-on-black violence makes it feel like a blessing to reach twenty-five. Love no longer presents itself wrapped in the romance of basement blue lights, lifetime commitments, or the sweet harmonies of The Stylistics and The Chi-Lites.

Love for us is raw like sushi, served up on sex platters from R. Kelly and Jodeci. Even our existences can't be defined in the past's simple terms: house nigga vs. field nigga, ghetto vs. bourgie, BAP vs. boho—because our lives are usually some complicated combination of all of the above.

More than any other generation before us, we need a feminism committed to "keeping it real." We need a voice like our music—one that samples and layers many voices, injects its sensibilities into the old and flips it into something new, provocative, and powerful. And one whose occasional hypocrisy, contradictions, and trifeness guarantee us at least a few trips to the terror-dome, forcing us to finally confront what we'd all rather hide from.

We need a feminism that possesses the same fundamental understanding held by any true student of hip-hop. Truth can't be found in the voice of any one rapper but in the juxtaposition of many. The keys that unlock the riches of contemporary black female identity lie not in choosing Latifah over Lil' Kim, or even Foxy Brown over Salt-N-Pepa. They lie at the magical intersection where those contrary voices meet—the juncture where "truth" is no longer black and white but subtle, intriguing shades of gray.

4. Naomi Wolf, "Two Traditions," from *Fire with Fire*

In this controversial essay, Wolf defines the terms "power feminism" and "victim feminism" that she claims divide the third wave from the second. Criticizing what she sees as the second wave's exclusive focus on the ways in which women are victimized and oppressed, Wolf argues that the world has experienced a "genderquake" of social change and that women are now significantly better off and should embrace their power to achieve for themselves instead of focusing on what is wrong. Roundly criticized for describing conditions that often apply only to upper-middle class, white women, Wolf's essay got a great deal of media attention in the 1990s and was responsible for many of the competing ideas and misconceptions about third wave.

TWO TRADITIONS

While feminism was having trouble getting its message out, some of the problem had to do with the message itself. Over the last twenty years, the old belief in a tolerant assertiveness, a claim to human participation and human rights—power feminism—was embattled by the rise of a set of beliefs that cast women as beleaguered, fragile, intuitive angels: victim feminism.

Victim feminism is when a woman seeks power through an identity of powerlessness. This feminism takes our trousseau reflexes and transposes them into a mirror-image set of "feminist" conventions.

This feminism has slowed women's progress, impeded their self-knowledge, and been responsible for most of the inconsistent, negative, even chauvinistic spots of regressive thinking that are alienating many women and men. Victim feminism is by no means confined to the women's movement; it is what all of us do whenever we retreat into appealing for status on the basis of feminine specialness instead of human worth, and fight underhandedly rather than honorably.

One of the features of this feminism is its misuse of the reality of women's victimization. Right now, critics of feminism such as Katie Roiphe in *The Morning After*, and Camille Paglia just about anywhere, are doing something slick and dangerous with the notion of victimization. They are taking the occasional excesses of the rape crisis movement and using them to ridicule the entire push to raise consciousness about sexual violence. Roiphe, for instance, paints an impressionistic picture of hysterical "date-rape victims" who have made it all up, but she never looks squarely at the epidemic of sex crimes that has been all too indelibly documented by the Justice Department and the FBI. In her definition, victim feminism includes the acts of fearing rape, and of confronting the real scars that rape inflicts. In her eagerness to do away with the Dworkin/MacKinnon picture of systematic male brutality, she washes away the real differences in power that do exist between men and women—such as physical strength. In her world of Princeton eating clubs, when a man grabs a woman's breast, the woman dumps a glass of milk on his head. End of story. In real life, where the provosts might not be drinking sherry nearby, the spunky lass might find herself dragged into an alley and peremptorily sodomized.

Though these critics' view of how often rape is imaginary belongs in another solar system, we do need to talk about the victim problem in current victim feminism, but we need to define it in a completely different way. There *is* something wrong with the way some feminist attitudes approach the persona of the victim. But documenting or protesting a very real rape epidemic is not the problem.

No, there is nothing wrong with identifying one's victimization. That act is critical. There is a lot wrong with molding it into an identity. Here is a highly subjective comparison of the two different ways by which women can approach power.

Victim Feminism

Charges women to identify with powerlessness even at the expense of taking responsibility for the power they do possess.

Is sexually judgmental, even antisexual.

Idealizes women's childrearing capacity as proof that women are better than men.

Depends on influence or persuasion rather than on seeking clout in a straightforward way.

Believes women to be naturally noncompetitive, cooperative, and peace loving.

Sees women as closer to nature than men are.

Exalts intuition, "women's speech," and "women's ways of knowing," not as complements to, but at the expense of, logic, reason, and the public voice.

Denigrates leadership and values anonymity.

Is self-sacrificing, and thus fosters resentment of others' recognition and pleasures.

Sees money as contaminating.

Puts community first and self later, hence tends toward groupthink, as well as toward hostility toward individual achievement.

Is judgmental of other women's sexuality and appearance.

Believes it is possessed of "the truth," which must be spread with missionary zeal.

Projects aggression, competitiveness, and violence onto "men" or "patriarchy," while its devotees are blind to those qualities in themselves.

Is obsessed with purity and perfection, hence is self-righteous.

Casts women *themselves* as good and attacks men *themselves* as wrong.

Has a psychology of scarcity: There is only so much to go around, so one woman's gain is another's loss. If there is inequity, wants women to "equalize downward"—e.g., to give up "heterosexual privilege" by not marrying, instead of extending civil rights; to give up beauty, instead of expanding the definition.

Wants all other women to share its opinions.

Thinks dire: believes sensuality cannot coincide with seriousness; fears that to have too much fun poses a threat to the revolution.

Power Feminism

Examines closely the forces arrayed against a woman so she can exert her power more effectively.

Knows that a woman's choices affect many people around her and can change the world.

Encourages a woman to claim her individual voice rather than merging her voice in a collective identity, for only strong individuals can create a just community.

Is unapologetically sexual; understands that good pleasures make good politics.

Seeks power and uses it responsibly, both for women as individuals and to make the world more fair to others.

Knows that poverty is not glamorous; wants women to acquire money, both for their own dreams, independence, and security, and for social change.

Acknowledges women's interest in "signature," recognition, and fame, so that women can take credit for themselves and give generously to others.

Asks a woman to give to herself and seek what she needs, so she can give to others freely, without resentment.

Is tolerant of other women's choices about sexuality and appearance; believes that what every woman does with her body and in her bed is her own business.

Acknowledges that aggression, competitiveness, the wish for autonomy and separation, even the danger of selfish and violent behavior, are as much a part of female identity as are nurturant behaviors; understands that women, like men, must learn to harness these impulses; sees women as moral adults.

Seeks "bilingualism"—the joining together of what is best about women's traditional knowledge and commitments with traditionally male resources.

Has strong convictions, but is always skeptical and open, and questions all authority, including its own.

Hates sexism without hating men.

Sees that neither women nor men have a monopoly on character flaws; does not attack men as a gender, but sees disproportionate male power, and the social valuation of maleness over femaleness, as being wrong.

Has a psychology of abundance; wants all women to "equalize upward" and get more; believes women deserve to feel that the qualities of stars and queens, of sensuality and beauty, can be theirs.

Wants all women to express their own opinions.

Knows that making social change does not contradict the principle that girls just want to have fun. Motto: "If I can't dance, it's not my revolution."

Power feminism has little heavy base ideology beyond the overarching premise "More for women." The ideology it does uphold is flexible and inclusive. Its core tenets are these:

1. Women matter as much as men do.
2. Women have the right to determine their lives.
3. Women's experiences matter.
4. Women have the right to tell the truth about their experiences.
5. Women deserve more of whatever it is they are not getting enough of because they are women: respect, self-respect, education, safety, health, representation, money.

Those are the basics. No overdetermined agendas, no loyalty oaths, just the commitment to get those unmarked "power units"—health, education, the vote—to women, for women to use as adult individuals, with conflicting visions and wills. What women do with those units of potential is up to them.

My beliefs about what you should do with that power may contradict yours. Let us claim full representation, and fight our beliefs out in the public arena, as men who cannot be reduced to a group identity do. On this level of the definition of power feminism, the statement "I am a feminist" means only "I am a sentient, strong individual who objects to being held back—or having other women held back—on the basis of gender." It is the very beginning of the conversation about what a given woman believes, not the endpoint.

But doesn't opening up the definition risk making the term meaningless? I think we can lay that fear to rest. When women engage fully in the political process, they tend, as we are starting to see, to vote their interests. And we are safer in a country in which women feel empowered to promote a myriad of beliefs than in one in which all women share my views of what is best for the gender, or yours.

On one level all women should be able to own the word "feminism" as describing a theory of self-worth and the worth of other women. On this level, saying "I am a feminist" should be like saying "I am a human being." It is on this level that we can press for women who believe anything they want to to enter public life; this level wants the world thrown open to all women regardless of their goodness. On this level women should be free to exploit to save, give or take, destroy or build, to exactly the same extent that men are. This is the level of simple realization of women's will, whether we like the result or not. On this level Camille Paglia is certainly a feminist; Indira Gandhi was a feminist; Mother Teresa is a feminist. On this level "feminist" is a word that belongs to every women who is operating at her full speed; ideally, it includes wanting other women to operate at their full speed; but it recognizes that women have many opinions about the best ways to empower women, and Mother Teresa's are not going to be mine.

On another level, of course, feminism should be broadly understood as a humanistic movement for social justice. This definition excludes more people than the former one does, but it draws in far more people than the popular current image of feminism does. On this level, "I am a feminist" means "No one should stand in my way because of my gender, and no one should stand in anyone's way because of this race, gender, orientation." As a humanistic movement its parameters are these: no hate. It is illogical to claim one's rights as a woman yet deny them to others on the basis of their skin color or sexual orientation. It also sets a narrower focus than does "humanism": On this level, it is okay to work on behalf of women because female humans are oppressed in ways unique to their gender. But working on behalf of women does not allow one *ever* to deify them as better than, or cosmically separate from, their male counterparts. The "no hate" plank of the definition includes not hating on the basis of gender, including when it comes to men.

Before we go on to compare power and victim feminism, let us be clear what "the victim problem" in victim feminist is *not*. The idea of female victimization is tremendously muddled right now.

Feminists are currently under siege for allegedly creating a "cult of the victim." This wave of "it's all in your head" theory was inevitable, given the recent success of the victim's-rights movement in drawing attention to the widespread nature of sex crimes. Critics who charge this pursue a scorched-earth policy: if there are some unrepresentative excesses in the fight against sexual violence, demolish the whole, in spite of the fact of the suffering of millions. I too will be talking about some mistakes victim feminism has made in framing the theme of female victimization. But my intent is very different. I am calling for a recognition of female victimization that does not leave out autonomy and sexual freedom; I am calling on us to look clearly at the epidemic of crimes against women without building a too-schematic world view upon it.

I will insist that we talk about rape and sexual harassment with greater specificity so that crimes can be prosecuted with the utmost severity while we create more careful demarcations of harm that reflect the complexity of women's real experiences.

The "victim culture" critics attack even the act of analyzing real harm done to women. Critics attacked Anita Hill's testimony, the outcry over Tailhook, *Backlash*, and *The Beauty Myth*, for "having at their center ... the image of women as victims." But these critics seem to believe themselves that women have no will or critical intelligence. The act of documenting the way others are trying to victimize women is the very opposite of treating women as natural victims. The premise that guides such documentation is that women are not natural victims. The point of exposing the information is that women deserve to decide such cases for themselves. Critics condescend to women by suggesting that merely hearing allegations of harm will make women collapse into a jelly of quivering victim-consciousness. I have never heard the argument that informing men of how, say, the Federal Reserve controls the economy or PACs shape party platforms is bad for men because it makes them feel like "victims." Men presumably, can handle the information. Indeed, it is assumed that such information makes them better able to make informed choices.

Nor am I joining the chorus that calls women's objections to injustice "whining." Women's documentation of rape, child abuse, sexual harassment, educational discrimination, and domestic violence is called "the culture of complaint"; the art women make out of it is called "a fiesta of whining." But when white men fret in print about a paucity of contemporary Italian-American novelists, or the decline of baseball, that's not whining; that's cultural criticism. Women's desire to be included in the curriculum is called a frothy "self-esteem" issue; when white men object to reassessed history—as with Christopher Columbus revisionism—this is not a self-esteem problem but a "battle for tradition." When middle-class white men refuse to pay high taxes, they are not complaining but engaging in a "populist uprising," a "taxpayer revolt." And when it is real injustice that men object to, they are not producing a "victim culture" but the Magna Carta, the Declaration of Independence, and the "Marseillaise."

The problem in victim feminism that I object to is *not* the act of protesting harm. There is no way around it: Women are not natural victims, but they sure *are* victimized. Domestic violence is the number-one reason women seek medical attention; one third of all female murder victims are killed by husbands or boyfriends; up to 45 percent of abused women are battered during pregnancy; 60 percent of battered women are beaten when pregnant; half of all homeless women and children are fleeing domestic violence. Women are victims of violent intimates at a rate three times that of men. These are raw facts. And facing them is the first step toward changing them.

But it is not "blaming the victim" to issue the warning that people worn out with fighting are tempted to redefine victim status itself as a source of strength and identity. When ex-model Marla Hansen, who was slashed across the face by two thugs, underwent treatment to remove the scars, she was asked, "Will it make a difference in your life not to have a noticeable scar? ... Is it a psychological adjustment as well?" She replied, "I've been living with the scar as part of my identity. A lot of people have defined me as a crime victim. My doctor said I should be prepared to lose that. It is a loss, and you have to put something in its place." The women's movement as a whole is at exactly such a psychological juncture.

The focus of some feminists, like Andrea Dworkin, Catharine MacKinnon, and Adrienne Rich, on female victimization foreshadowed over female agency, derives from conditions that were once truer than they are now. During the early seventies women were indeed overwhelmingly silenced and negated; and during the Reagan-Bush administrations, the structures of power were indeed basically immovable. But the genderquake means that the core rationale of this kind of foreshadowing is becoming obsolete.

For power, we learned in the genderquake, is hardly unshakably male; we can make it female with ease: with votes, with voices, and with a little money from a lot of wallets. These writers should be read and understood. But grieving for the real victimization that women suffer must be a feminism that also teaches women how to see and use their enormous power so as never to be helpless victims again.

Virtually every women's political organization, and most grassroots groups, seek power feminist goals. But the language of victim feminism often dominates discussion of the movement in the mass media. Critics of feminism often cast feminists as extremists who are going too far and must temper or dilute their message for the mainstream. I am arguing the opposite—that women in the mainstream have gone much further in articulating an embrace of power than has this brand of feminism; and that victim feminism is not going remotely far enough to keep up with them. The unidentified power feminism of mainstream women has far outstripped the victim feminism of many insiders. But the power-feminist images and icons we have—from Roseanne Arnold to Queen Latifah to Janet Reno—are seldom "owned" by organized feminism. So mainstream women identify intensely with the power feminism that these women represent, but do not identify that vision with the movement.

5. Rebecca Walker, "Being Real: An Introduction," from *To Be Real: Telling the Truth and Changing the Face of Feminism*

Rebecca Walker coined the term "third wave" and was also one of the first to chart what it stood for and what was at stake. This essay, which introduces *To Be Real,* was the first to face the issue of generational conflict head on. What "being a good feminist" meant for second-wavers seemed to be "without contradiction and messiness": gender, unity between women, and solidarity based on gender seemed to characterize the world view of the second wave. This view does not make sense to third-wave feminists because third-wave lives are nothing if not messy, contradictory, and multifaceted, combining a number of identity factors (race, class, sexuality, ethnicity) that seem just as important as gender. Encouraging young women to craft their own definitions of feminism and feminist identity, this piece is important to third-wavers everywhere.

A year before I started this book, my life was like a feminist ghetto. Every decision I made, person I spent time with, word I uttered, had to measure up to an image I had in my mind of what was morally and politically right according to my vision of female empowerment. Everything had a gendered explanation, and what didn't fit into my concept of feminist was "bad, patriarchal, and problematic." I couldn't stay intimate with a male friend who called someone a "pussy" derogatorily and revealed an un-decolonized mind, I couldn't live with a partner because I would never be able to maintain my independence and artistic strength as a woman, I couldn't utter thoughts of dislike or jealousy for another woman because that would mean I was horribly unfeminist, and so, horribly bad.

My existence was an ongoing state of saying no to many elements of the universe, and picking and choosing to allow only what I thought should belong. The parts of myself that didn't fit into my ideal were hidden down deep, and when I faced them for fleeting moments they made me feel insecure and confused about my values and identity. Curiosity about pornography, attraction to a stable domestic partnership, a desire to start a business and pursue traditional individual power, interest in the world of S/M, a love for people who challenged and sometimes flatly opposed my feminist beliefs—these feelings in themselves were not terribly terrible, and I think that for most who consider them they seem terribly trivial, but for me and my sense of how to make feminist revolution, they represented contradictions that I had no idea how to reconcile.

Linked with my desire to be a good feminist was, of course, not just a desire to change my behavior to change the world, but a deep desire to be accepted, claimed, and loved by a feminist community that included my mother, godmother, aunts, and close friends. For all intents and purposes their beliefs were my own, and we mirrored each other in the most affirming of ways. As is common in familial relationships, I feared that our love was dependent upon that mirroring. Once I offered a face different from the one they expected, I thought the loyalty, the bond of our shared outlook and understanding, would be damaged forever.

The thought of exploring myself and the world and coming up with new questions and different answers was not half as terrifying as the thought of sharing these revelations with people I admired and loved. That moment of articulating my difference, when I imagined it in my mind, was not one of power, of me coming to voice about my own truths, it was one filled with the guilt of betrayal. If the Goddess didn't work for me, if I didn't think violence on TV translated into real-life violence, if I didn't believe in the essential goodness of women's culture, I thought I might be perceived as betraying "The Movement" rather than celebrating it. I feared that this betrayal, which was grounded in staying true to myself, could mean banishment from the community for questioning the status quo. Because feminism has always been so close to home, I worried that I might also be banished from there.

The ever-shifting but ever-present ideals of feminism can't help but leave young women and men struggling with the reality of who we are. Constantly measuring up to some cohesive fully down-for-the-feminist-cause identity without contradictions and messiness and lusts for power and luxury items is not a fun or easy task. As one woman said to me at a small Mid-western college where I was giving a lecture, "I feel I can't be a feminist because I am not strong enough, not good enough, not disciplined enough." At an all women's college in Virginia, another young woman expressed relief when I told the group that there was no one correct way to be a feminist, no seamless narrative to assume and fit into. This soft-spoken young woman told the group hesitantly, "I have always believed in equal rights and been involved in speaking up, but I didn't think I could call myself a feminist because I am also Christian." The concept of a strictly defined and all-encompassing feminist identity is so prevalent that when I read the section in my talk about all the different things you can do and still be a feminist, like shave your legs every day, get married, be a man, be in the army, whatever, audience members clap spontaneously. This simple reassurance paves the way for more openness and communication from young women and men than anything else I say.

Buried in these vibrant young women's words are a host of mystifications, imagistic idealizations, and ingrained social definitions of what it means to be a feminist. For each young woman there is a different set of qualifiers, a different image which embodies an ideal to measure up to, a far-reaching ideological position to uphold at any cost. Depending on which mythology she was exposed to, she believes that in order to be a feminist one must live in poverty, always critique, never marry, want to censor pornography and/or worship the Goddess. A feminist must never compromise herself, must never make concessions for money or for love, must always be devoted to the uplift of her gender, must only make an admirable and selfless livelihood, preferably working for a women's organization. She fears that if she wants to be spanked before sex, wants to own a BMW, is a Zen priest, wants to be treated "like a lady," prioritizes racial oppression over gender oppression, loves misogynist hip-hop music, still speaks to the father that abused her, gets married, wants to raise three kids on a farm in Montana, etc., that she can't be a feminist. That is, she can't join a community of women and men working for equality, and can't consider herself a part of a history of societal transformation on behalf of women.

From my experience talking with young women and being one myself, it has become clear to me that young women are struggling with the feminist label not only, as some prominent Second Wavers have asserted, because we lack a knowledge of women's history and have been alienated by the media's generally horrific characterization of feminists, and not only because it is tedious to always criticize world politics, popular culture, and the nuances of social interaction. Young women coming of age today wrestle with the term because we have a very different vantage point on the world than that of our foremothers. We shy from or modify the label in an attempt to begin to articulate our differences while simultaneously avoiding meaningful confrontation. For many of us it seems that to be a feminist in the way that we have seen or understood feminism is to conform to an identity and way of living that doesn't allow for individuality, complexity, or less than perfect personal histories. We fear that the identity will dictate and regulate our lives, instantaneously pitting us against someone, forcing us to choose inflexible and unchanging sides, female against male, black against white, oppressed against oppressor, good against bad.

This way of ordering the world is especially difficult for a generation that has grown up transgender, bisexual, interracial, and knowing and loving people who are racist, sexist, and otherwise afflicted. We have trouble formulating and perpetuating theories that compartmentalize and divide according to race and gender and all of the other signifiers. For us the lines between Us and Them are often blurred, and as a result we find ourselves seeking to create identities that accommodate ambiguity and our multiple positionalities: including more than excluding, exploring more than defining, searching more than arriving.

Whether the young women who refuse the label realize it or not, on some level they recognize that an ideal woman born of prevalent notions of how empowered women look, act, and think is simply another impossible contrivance of perfect womanhood, another scripted role to perform in the name of biology and virtue. But tragically, rather than struggling to locate themselves within some continuum of feminism, rather than upset the boat a little by reconciling the feminism they see and learn about with their own ideas and desires, many young women and men simply bow out altogether, avoiding the dreaded confrontation with some of the people who presently define and represent feminism, and with their own beliefs....

... Feminist writers grapple with some of the assumptions about who they are supposed to be, as people who believe in equal access, equal pay, an end to gender violence, and the right to privacy, and how they are supposed to interact with and respond to the world. As they struggle to formulate a feminism they can call their own, they debunk the stereotype that there is one lifestyle or manifestation of feminist empowerment, and instead offer self-possession, self-determination, and an endless array of non-dichotomous possibilities....

... By broadening our view of who and what constitutes "the feminist community," these thinkers stake out an inclusive terrain from which to actively seek the goals of societal equality and individual freedom they all share. At the same time, they continue to build upon a feminist legacy that challenges the status quo, finds common ground while honoring difference, and develops the self-esteem and confidence it takes to live and theorize one's own life....

... The people in the world who are facing and embracing their contradictions and complexities and creating something new and empowering from them are important voices leading us away from divisiveness and dualism. I hope that in accepting contradiction and ambiguity, in using *and* much more than we use *either/or*, these voices can help us continue to shape a political force more concerned with mandating and cultivating freedom than with policing morality. Rather than judging them as unevolved, unfeminist, or hopelessly duped by the patriarchy, I hope you will see these writers as yet another group of pioneers, outlaws who demand to exist whole and intact, without cutting or censoring parts of themselves: an instinct I consider to be the very best legacy of feminism.

These voices are important because if feminism is to continue to be radical and alive, it must avoid reordering the world in terms of any polarity, be it female/male, good/evil, or, that easy allegation of false consciousness which can so quickly and silently negate another's agency: evolved/unconscious. It must continue to be responsive to new situations, needs, and especially desires, ever expanding to incorporate and entertain all those who wrestle with and swear by it, including those who may not explicitly call its name....

6. Leslie Heywood and Jennifer Drake, "Introduction," from *Third Wave Agenda: Being Feminist, Doing Feminism*

Excerpts from "Introduction" by Leslie Heywood and Jennifer Drake, published in Leslie Heywood and Jennifer Drake, *Third Wave Agenda: Being Feminist, Doing Feminism* (University of Minnesota Press, 1997), 1–20. Reprinted with permission.

Although popular third-wave feminism had already been part of the cultural dialog for a couple of years, *Third Wave Agenda* was the first academic collection to join the conversation. In this introductory essay, the authors distinguish between third-wave feminism and postfeminism and try to theorize some of the issues most important to the third wave: engagement with consumer culture, coming of age in a time of multiculturalism and a focus on multiple identities, and the intellectual debts to and legacies from the second wave.

Recently much media attention has been given to writings about third wave feminism, often labeled "postfeminism." In the perpetual battle of representation and definitional clout, the slippage from "third wave feminism" to "postfeminist" is important, because many of us working in the "third wave" by no means define our feminism as a groovier alternative to an over-and-done feminist movement. Let us be clear: "postfeminist" characterizes a group of young, conservative feminists who explicitly define themselves against and criticize feminists of the second wave.

Not surprisingly, it is these conservative feminists who are regularly called upon as spokespersons for the "next generation." Writers such as Katie Roiphe, Rene Denfeld, and Naomi Wolf argue against feminist critiques of rape, sexual harassment, and abortion. They publish books, appear on op-ed pages, and write for popular young women's magazines such as *Glamour* and *YM*. Conservative postfeminism is in every way more visible than is the diverse activist work that terms itself "third wave." The one anthology that explicitly refers to a "third wave" of feminism, *The Third Wave: Feminist Perspectives on Racism*, cited in a *Genders* article in 1994, reflects on how the "third wave" is defined by the challenge that women-of-color feminists posed to white second wave feminism. This book, unlike the work of conservative white feminists, has seen a difficult road to publication. Perhaps because this book challenges easily assimilated feminist stereotypes and because it is being published by a small, independent house, the book's production has seen problems that rarely occur in the large, mainstream publishing houses to which conservative feminism has easier access....

Because our lives have been shaped by struggles between various feminisms as well as by cultural backlash against feminism and activism, we argue that contradiction—or what looks like contradiction, if one doesn't shift one's point of view—marks the desires and strategies of third wave feminists. Whereas conservative postfeminist thinking relies on an opposition between "victim feminism" (second wave) and "power feminism" (third wave), and suggests that "power feminism" serves as a corrective to a hopelessly outmoded "victim feminism," to us the second and third waves of feminism are neither incompatible nor opposed. Rather, we define feminism's third wave as a movement that contains elements of second wave critique of beauty culture, sexual abuse, and power structures while it also acknowledges and makes use of the pleasure, danger, and defining power of those structures. Conservative postfeminist Christina Hoff Sommers splits feminism into two camps only: equity feminists (power feminists) and gender feminists (victim feminists). She defines equity feminists as those who "stay within the bounds of traditional scholarship and join in its enterprise." She defines gender feminists as those who "seek to transform scholarship to make it 'women-centered'." For Sommers, and for postfeminists in general, anyone who speaks of "oppression" or is "woman-centered" is in the "victim" camp.

One group of feminists not accounted for by this polarity—ourselves among them—is young feminists who grew up with equity feminism, got gender feminism in college, along with poststructuralism, and are now hard at work on a feminism that strategically combines elements of these feminisms, along with black feminism; women-of-color feminism, working-class feminism, pro-sex feminism, and so on. A third wave goal that comes directly out of learning from these histories and working among these traditions is the development of modes of thinking that can come to terms with the multiple, constantly shifting bases of oppression in relation to the multiple, interpenetrating axes of identity, and the creation of a coalition politics based on these understandings—understandings that acknowledge the existence of oppression, even though it is not fashionable to say so. We know that what oppresses me may not oppress you, that what oppresses you may be something I participate in, and that what oppresses me may be something you participate in. Even as different strains of feminism and activism sometimes directly contradict each other, they are all part of our third wave lives, our thinking, and our praxes: we are products of all the contradictory definitions of and differences within feminism, beasts of such a hybrid kind that perhaps we need a different name altogether.

In the important second wave collection *The Feminist Papers*, Alice Rossi contests the position that feminism "died" after the suffrage movement and came to life again in the late 1960s. Instead, she argues, there is a continuity between feminist generations that doesn't seem like continuity:

> [T]he public heroines of one generation are the private heroines of the next.... [B]etween 1920 and 1960 ... [women] private[ly] consolidated ... gains made by their mothers.... [S]trong-minded descendants of the suffragists were pouring much of their energy into education and employment, and if they were married, they did double duty at work and at home; such a profile leaves little time and energy for political involvement.

Facing classrooms of young women and men who are trained by the media caricature of "feminazis," who see feminism as an enemy or say "feminist" things prefaced by "I'm not a feminist, but ...," finding little time in our own overextended, economically insecure lives for traditional public activism, we may be experiencing a repetition of the historical pattern Rossi documents.

In the current historical moment, then, third wave feminists often take cultural production and sexual politics as key sites of struggle, seeking to use desire and pleasure as well as anger to fuel struggles for justice. Those forms of third wave activism don't always look "activist" enough to second wave feminists. But, as Rossi argues, exploring different activist practices doesn't mean we're not feminists: "[T]he [less publicly activist] generation, unnoted by historians, may consolidate gains and provide the foundation on which the [next] generation takes off again into public and historical notice." Within the "generation" addressed in *Third Wave Agenda*, whose birth dates fall between 1963 and 1974, we can see this historical dialectic in operation. Those of us on the older end of this spectrum have tended to spend more time establishing our careers, whereas those of us on the younger end have had more experience with public activism. But, as *Third Wave Agenda* attempts to establish, we are all third wave feminists, bringing the specificity of our historical situation to our widely variable definitions of that term.

One public figure who demonstrates some of the contradictions that third wave feminism brings together is Courtney Love, the punk rock musician who bridges the opposition between "power feminism" and "victim feminism." She combines the individualism, combativeness, and star power that are the legacy of second wave gains in opportunities for women (which arrived in conjunction with cultural backlash against such gains), with second wave critiques of the cult of beauty and male dominance. Love is a prototype of female ambition and a sharp cultural critic of both the institutions that sustain that ambition and those that argue against it. Glamorous and grunge, girl and boy, mothering and selfish, put together and taken apart, beautiful and ugly, strong and weak, responsible and rebellious, Love bridges the irreconcilability of individuality and femininity within dominant culture, combining the cultural critique of an earlier generation of feminists with the backlash against it by the next generation of women, legacies of Reagan Republicanism who are busy reclaiming the province of beauty for female power in ways that can only fail because they have been critiqued too thoroughly.

Love's most famous song, "Doll Parts," contradictorily combines the second wave critique of "I am / doll eyes / doll mouth / doll legs" with the third wave postmodern individualism facilitated by the second wave—"I want to be the girl with the most cake / I fake it so real I am beyond fake"—but returns to the lived cost of female ambition: "[S]omeday, you will ache like I ache." Love's media persona combines the reality of female competitiveness with a feminist sensibility and a vocal support of other women: in conversation, Love often cites Susan Faludi's *Backlash* and raves about some women's performances at the same time that she defines herself competitively against others. Even in her mass media incarnation as Althea Flynt in Miloš Forman's *The People vs. Larry Flynt* and her January 1997 layout in *Vogue*, Love is still throwing an unfashionable feminism in the face of fashion, tongue in cheek. Love was "bossily laying into me," the *Vogue* reporter writes, "about anorexic models, the power of fashion magazines to determine national standards of body mass." "I can't stand it, that whole thing," Love says, "sitting around with your girlfriend and kvetching about weight. It takes all your confidence.... [T]hat's my big feminist lecture for today." Love is aware of the social context that now makes a "big feminist lecture" unhip, thus harming chances for individual success, yet does it anyway.

Love's star quality and personal ambition may be a legacy of the Reagan 1980s and a quality discouraged by the collective movement ethos of second wave feminism, but it was the second wave that made ambition a realizable possibility for women. Equity feminist, postmodern feminist, and victim feminist all at once, Love combines the contradictory aspects of these discourses in a way that recognizes and makes use of complications that young women working within dominant culture face today. For better and for worse, she may be our Gloria Steinem, in that she is a highly visible lightning rod for third wave issues. Stylistically, however, Love emerges more from the playful, parodic tradition of the late 1960s WITCH (Women's International Conspiracy from Hell) and women's liberation guerrilla theater movements.

African American hip-hop artist Me'shell Ndegéocello is another public figure who exemplifies third wave feminist hybridity, contradiction, and activism. With her deep voice, barely there hair, and sexily androgynous clothing, Ndegéocello plays the edges of boy and girl, masculine and feminine, while her music voices a bisexual feminist sensibility strongly grounded in African American culture and hip-hop's hybrid logic. Many of the songs on *Plantation Lullabies* (1993) call for love between black men and women, "a love that is essential to the loving of one's self," whereas on *Peace beyond Passion* (1996) Ndegéocello attacks homophobia in "Leviticus: Faggot" and speaks to a woman lover in "Who Is He and What Is He to You." In songs such as "Two Lonely Hearts (on the Subway)," gendered desire becomes less important than raced desire and connection. The lyrics addressed an unspecified "you" whose "lovely black face" the speaker wants to get to know, perhaps by reading Ntozake Shange or the *Village Voice* together. Collaborative escape into love and language, the speaker suggests, might provide an antidote to "singin' the blues on the subway." Ndegéocello's songs enact the pleasures of desiring and desirable blacknesses and show how love's necessary and healing power mingles with the outrage of "livin' in the midst of genocide." Loving Black men *and* Black women in such a world, and saying this out loud, is one way for Ndegéocello to live her whole, complex self.

The movement between love and outrage also characterizes Ndegéocello's take on religion, particularly evident in *Peace beyond Passion.* Taking Old Testament books as song titles, and collaging verses and images that recall Moses and Diaspora, human divinity, Mary Magdalene's prostitute beauty, racial uplift, and some Christians' biblical justification for condemning homosexuality, Ndegéocello seeks healing through a redefinition of Christian faith and tradition. Revising, hybridizing, and reclaiming a spirituality that can do what she needs it to, Ndegéocello also turns to other religions, naming one song "God Shiva" and dedicating another to Kahlil Gibran. As *Rolling Stone* writer Ann Powers observes, in this activist work Ndegéocello "joins the chorus of contemporary women—Tori Amos, Joan Osborne, Polly Jean Harvey, Jewel—re-imagining the mystical through the vehicle of pop, using music's power to challenge conceptions and build some myths of their own." Ndegéocello's engagements with spirituality also participate in a key aspect of black feminist praxis. Taken together, the various facets of her performances work the edges of contradiction in a powerfully feminist way.

In the introduction of *To Be Real*, Rebecca Walker lists contradiction as a generative force for her collection but sets third wave hybridity in opposition to what she describes as a rigidly ideological second wave feminism:

> Constantly measuring up to some cohesive, fully down-for-the-feminist-cause identity without contradictions and messiness and lusts for power

> and luxury items is not a fun or easy task.... For many of us it seems that to be a feminist in the way that we have seen or understood feminism is to conform to an identity and way of living that doesn't allow for individuality, complexity, or less than perfect personal histories.

Third Wave Agenda makes things "messier" by *embracing* second wave critique as a central definitional thread while emphasizing ways that desires and pleasures subject to critique can be used to rethink and enliven activist work. We see the emphasis on contradiction as continuous with aspects of the second wave....

... This politics is perhaps best expressed today in the inclusive feminist activist collective Third Wave, which Rebecca Walker founded. Third Wave is a good example of a coalition-politics activism that defines itself, and its politics, through the multiple subject positions and diverse community affiliations of its members. Third Wave's mission statement reads as follows:

> Third Wave is a member-driven multiracial, multicultural, multisexuality national non-profit organization devoted to feminist and youth activism for change. Our goal is to harness the energy of young women and men by creating a community in which members can network, strategize, and ultimately, take action. By using our experiences as a starting point, we can create a diverse community and cultivate a meaningful response.

Third Wave makes the inclusion of persons of various genders, sexualities, nationalities, and classes a top priority and combines elements of equity feminism and gender feminism in a grassroots feminism that still fights for equal access and equal pay for equal work but also seeks to transform the structures within which young people work.

The lived messiness characteristic of the third wave is what defines it: girls who want to be boys, boys who want to be girls, boys and girls who insist they are both, whites who want to be black, blacks who want to or refuse to be white, people who *are* white *and* black, gay *and* straight, masculine *and* feminine, or who are finding ways to be and name none of the above; successful individuals longing for community and coalition, communities and coalitions longing for success; tensions between striving for individual success and subordinating the individual to the cause; identities formed within a relentlessly consumer-oriented culture but informed by a politics that has problems with consumption. Although many third wave writings make provocative use of these contradictions, they often posit a cleaner break between the second and the third wave than *Third Wave Agenda*'s contributors are willing to advocate, and those writings often do not mention where these contradictions have previously been most powerfully voiced.

FROM THE THIRD WORLD TO THE THIRD WAVE: OUR DEBTS

Characterizing the "third wave" as a movement defined by contradiction is not new. In fact, the definitional moment of third wave feminism has been theorized as proceeding from critiques of the white women's movement that were initiated by women of color, as well as from the many instances of coalition work undertaken by U.S. third world feminists. As Kayann Short notes in an article in *Genders*, "[S]ome feminists of color use the term 'the third wave' to identify a new feminism that is led by and has grown out of the challenge to white feminism posited by women of color." As early as 1981, which saw the publication of the landmark anthology *This Bridge Called My Back: Writings by Radical Women of Color*, and 1983, the year of the publication of Barbara Smith's *Home Girls: A Black Feminist Anthology*, contradiction was claimed as a fundamental definitional strategy, a necessary, lived, embodied strategy. Why, then, has there been in mainstream media representation no "third wave" until the 1990s? What is the relationship between the self-named U.S. third world feminism of *This Bridge Called My Back* and the third wave feminism of the "next generation"? ...

... Chela Sandoval's important 1982 essay on U.S. third world feminism and white feminist racism, "Feminism and Racism: A Report on the 1981 National Women's Studies Association Conference," argues for a feminist movement defined by difference: "What U.S. third world feminists are calling for is a new subjectivity, a political revision that denies any one perspective as the only answer, but instead posits a shifting tactical and strategic subjectivity ... no simple, easy sisterhood for U.S. third world feminists." And what third wave feminists seek and find in the writing of hooks, Hazel Carby, Audre Lorde, Gloria Anzaldúa, Maxine Hong Kingston, Ntozake Shange, Patricia Hill Collins, Bharati Mukherjee, Patricia Williams, Ana Castillo, Coco Fusco, Toni Morrison, and so many others, is languages and images that account for multiplicity and difference, that negotiate contradiction in affirmative ways, and that give voice to a politics of hybridity and coalition. *Third Wave Agenda* acknowledges how fully third wave feminism comes out of this groundbreaking work, and how U.S. third world feminism changed the second wave of the women's movement for good.

In acknowledging the profound influence of U.S. third world feminism on the third wave, it is imperative to recognize the dangers of appropriation, as well as the ways that, as Hazel Carby argues, "feminist theory has frequently used and abused [the writing of black women] to produce an essential black female subject for its own consumption." For example, as important as hooks's work has been for U.S. third world feminism and third wave feminism, she is often read and taught as *representing* black feminist thought. And, as Patricia Hill Collins notes, "While black women's particular location provides a distinctive angle of vision on oppression, this perspective comprises neither a privileged nor a complete standpoint." A definitive aspect of third wave feminist movement, then, is negotiating multicultural and antiracist standpoints amid the ongoing tensions between borrowing and appropriating. As Vron Ware points out in *Beyond the Pale: White Women, Racism, and History*, "[T]he extent to which this borrowing, or appropriating, is acknowledged obviously varies a great deal, but I think it can potentially provide an important link between different types of struggles ... [leading] to forming alliances." White U.S. feminism has a long history of borrowing from, allying with, and betraying African American liberation movements, and a consciously multicultural third wave feminism must continuously work with and through these tensions. Perhaps this is where the concept to "feminist generations" is most useful: as an articulation of feminist *movement*, ongoing change, and struggle.

If "whiteness" has been assumed by white women to mean privilege, visibility, belonging, and sisterhood, many of the writers in *Third Wave Agenda* have spent their lives feeling the often inchoate failures of whiteness, white femininity, and competitive individualism. As James Baldwin argued so eloquently, there is no white community: "America became white—the people who, as they claim, 'settled' the country became white—because of the necessity of denying the Black presence, and justifying the Black subjugation. No community can be based on such a principle—or in other words, no community can be established on so genocidal a lie." And, as historian David Roediger writes, "Whiteness describes, from Little Big Horn to Simi Valley, not a culture but precisely the absence of culture. It is the empty and therefore terrifying attempt to build an identity based on what one isn't and on whom one can hold back." In a world whose population is expected to double in the next ten years, where social criticism and angst are treated by Prozac, and where Republicans and Democrats alike trumpet the vision of "family values" and nuclear, single-career families precisely when so many of us make alternative families and seek dual careers by choice *and* because we must—in this world, the old motivator of individual distinction, required and perpetuated by the lies of whiteness and assimilation and equal opportunity, often feels like the dustiest myth. In this historical moment we are motivated by "despair, uncertainty, and loss of a sense of grounding" to do something other than adopt "the ideology of individualism that assumes a competitive view of the individual."

Yet that oh-so-American ideology has been ingrained into our deepest senses of ourselves, an ironic legacy of the second wave feminist and civil rights struggles that fought for equal access to the opportunities of white men. Despite our knowing better, despite our knowing its emptiness, the ideology of individualism is still a major motivating force in many third wave lives. Further, our struggles to negotiate individualism's powerful seductions and betrayals provide the third wave with an odd form of common ground, linking us across our many differences. So many of us are panicked about our futures and places, or lack thereof, in the world. With hundreds or sometimes thousands of applications for every "good job"—that is, a job with benefits that is not temporary or part-time—it is hard to think in terms of joining together with others rather than competing against them. The specter of anonymity, linked as it is with the threat of un- and underemployment for all workers, is one of our generation's biggest fears. As David Wild writes in an article on MTV's *The Real World* for *Rolling Stone*,

> One senses *The Real World* speaks to an entire generation of viewers that can hardly wait to get a camera crew on its ass. An application in *The Real Real World* book led to 10,000 new young bodies anxious to sign on for house duty. One imagines packs of pushy twentysomethings lying in wait for a quick way out of the ghetto of obscurity.

In a time of radically diminished economic opportunity, the reality of this "ghetto of obscurity" generates an almost panicked impulse to escape, a panic that makes pushiness and ruthless competition easy. It is a panic that makes other bodies look, on certain mornings, like so many bowling pins to bump out of the way. It is a panic that fuels the current backlash against affirmative action programs, the tightening of border security and anti-immigration laws, and the legislation ending welfare as we know it. The powerful motivating force of this fear often bumps up against a more reasoned knowledge that this adversarial attitude only contributes to the sense of placelessness. Competition can appear to be the most readily available survival strategy even as we know it ensures our extinction. This is a contradiction that feminism's third wave has to face: an often conscious knowledge of the ways in which we are compelled and constructed by the very things that underline us.

This isn't just "Generation X" whining but, rather, a form of spiritual sickness that most compels generationally third wave men and women to activism and that most works as a galvanizing force for social change. Bell hooks writes in "Postmodern Blackness":

> The overall impact of postmodernism is that many other groups now share with black folks a sense of deep alienation, despair, uncertainty, loss of a sense of grounding even if it is not informed by shared circumstance. Radical postmodernism calls attention to those shared sensibilities which cross the boundaries of class, gender, race, etc., that could be fertile ground for the construction of empathy—ties that would promote recognition of common commitments, and serve as a basis for solidarity and coalition.

Although hooks points out that a longing for community is specific to middle-class white women who have been allowed to join the competitive fray of the dominant culture, it may be this longing that helps fuel white participation in third wave activism. Hooks writes that white feminism "did not question whether masses of women shared the same need for community.... [T]he focus on feminism as a way to develop shared identity and community has little appeal to women who experience community, who seek ways to end exploitation and oppression in the context of their lives." But it may be that the longing for community that is characteristic of some white feminists will serve as a motivation to form coalitions that seek to "end exploitation and oppression" affecting lives other than just their own. In addition, the concept of "equal rights," which obscures the complex ways that exploitation and oppression work and are normalized, is also a concept that, *because* most young Americans internalize it naively, can lead to coalition. While growing up, we take "equal rights" seriously, assuming that they apply to all Americans, and we are often horrified when we realize, sooner or later, that in practice, "equal rights" apply only to a few.

Shaped by hegemonic privileges, white women's paths to a coalition-based feminist consciousness have often been based in ignorance, contradiction, and confusion. In some fundamental ways many of us still don't "get it." Striving for the success and equality with white men that second wave feminism made possible, white women in particular often became so focused on individual achievement and success that we became wholehearted supporters of the very structures we most wanted to contest. Third wave women and men of color who have gained access to these kinds of "opportunities" also get caught in this bind. In short, many of us have been clueless, swallowing status quo gambits whole, not choking until we find they have eaten us up from the inside—our hearts, livers, stomachs, lungs—until we can't feel or eat or breathe. We once *could* eat and breathe, and because we could, others couldn't. Third wavers know in theory that, as hooks wrote in 1984, "[B]roader perspectives can only emerge as we examine both the personal that is political, the politics of society as a whole, and global revolutionary politics." But we don't always know how to accomplish this.

Perhaps these are some of the reasons that, for most women who are generationally third wave, the feminist-separatist, pro-woman "gynocriticism" and "goddess worship" of some feminisms, although they sometimes sounded nice, seemed all too wishful and frilly and arcane to make any sense of our lives. Although we also owe an enormous debt to the critique of sexism and the struggles for gender equity that were white feminism's strongest provinces, it was U.S. third world feminism that modeled a language and a politics of hybridity that can account for our lives at the century's turn. These are lives marked by the realities of multicultural exchange, fusion, and conflict, lives that combine blackness, whiteness, brownness, gayness, bisexuality, straightness. These are lives that combine male-identification and female-identification, middle-class status and staggering debt, lives that are hopeful and stressed and depressed, empowered and exhausted and scared. As Gloria Anzaldúa writes in her foreword to the second edition of *This Bridge Called My Back*, "[W]e have come to realize that we are not alone in our struggles nor separate nor autonomous but that we—white black straight queer female male—are connected and interdependent." We hope that in these pages we have begun—provisionally, slowly, making some dumb mistakes—to pay our debts to those women whose work has sometimes literally saved our lives.

7. Kimberly Springer, "Third Wave Black Feminism?" from *Signs: Journal of Women in Culture and Society*

Excerpts from Kimberly Springer, "Third Wave Black Feminism," *Signs* 27(4) (2002): 1059–1082. Reprinted with permission of University of Chicago.

In this landmark article, Kimberly Springer challenges the "wave" theory in U.S. feminism that associates first wave with the suffragist struggle for voting rights and the second-wave struggle for rights around questions of sexuality and the workplace, exposing the racism central to this formulation. She looks at the writing and activism of black women and locates the writing of "third-wavers" such as Lisa Jones and Joan Morgan in a long tradition of black women's thought and activism not amenable to the "wave" categorization. The third wave of black feminist theorizing, she argues, developed as an alternative to and critique of mainstream feminisms in the second wave, making black feminist theory a central point of departure for third-wave thinking.

BLACK FEMINISM: DROWNED OUT BY THE WAVE

Feminist activists and women's movement historians use the "wave" model to describe the women's movement in the United States. This model obscures the historical role of race in feminist organizing. If we consider the first wave as that moment of organizing encompassing woman suffrage and the second wave as the women's liberation/women's rights activism of the late 1960s, we effectively disregard the race-based movements before them that served as precursors, or windows of political opportunity, for gender activism.

In relationship to the first wave, the oration, organizing, writing, and agitation skills that white women gleaned from their work in the abolitionist movement, as well as the cues taken from Black women involved in antislavery, antilynching, and suffrage work, were instrumental to the evolution of the first wave. Consider these three examples. In Boston, Maria Stewart, a free Black from Connecticut, gave a public lecture to a racially mixed audience of men and women; she was the first woman of any race to do so. In the 1850s, Mary Shadd Cary, the first Black woman newspaper editor in North America, published the *Provincial Freeman*, which was an abolitionist paper with the motto, "Self-Reliance is the True Road to Independence." Anna Julia Cooper, author of *A Voice from the South by a Black Woman of the South* (1988), wrote the first book-length feminist treatise on the condition of African Americans. A pivotal text of Black feminist thought, Cooper argues for women's leadership in the Black community, as well as the need for Black women to work separately from white feminists because of racism experienced personally, political betrayals, and the strategic need for separatism. Inserting these women into the public record of feminist activism challenges the notion that "race women" were not also concerned about gender. African-American women, if inserted into this wave model, make the wave, shall we say, a much bigger swell. Remaining mindful of the links between the struggles for freedom from racism and sexism is critical as future social justice coalition work depends on accurate—for better or worse—historical memory.

More disruptive of the wave model is the work of scholars such as Angela Davis and Deborah Gray White on enslaved African women's forms of resistance to gendered violence. As Davis observes in her pioneering article "Reflections on the Black Woman's Role in the Community of Slaves" ([1971] 1995), and as White notes in *Ar'n't I a Woman: Female Slaves in the Plantation South* (1985), enslaved women actively resisted rape, forced pregnancy, and separation from their children on plantations. Through natural abortion methods and fighting back against nonconsensual sexual relations when they could, they enacted an early form of feminist resistance to distinctly gendered oppression aimed at women. Harriet Jacobs's (1987) emancipation narrative, for example, is one of the few historical documents written from a Black woman's perspective demonstrating early feminist resistance to slavery and sexual abuse. None of this is meant to discount the gendered atrocities that Black men faced in the slave economy (e.g., castration and other attempts at demasculinization), but it is meant to highlight the ways in which, early on, Black women enacted feminist politics that acknowledged the ways that they were oppressed as Blacks *and* women. This resistance to *gendered* violence predates that of the abolition movement, but it also happened while the movement emerged. Thus, we can make the case that the idea of a first wave beginning with suffrage excludes the fact that Black women resisted gendered oppression during the antebellum period.

In sum, as we learn more about women of color's feminist activism, the wave analogy becomes untenable. What might, for example, the inclusion of American Indian women's gendered resistance do to even my time line? Reexamining the wave model of the women's movement can only benefit the movement as we continue to expand the category of "women" and make sure that, as bell hooks asserts, "feminism is for everybody."

Another way that this critique of waves dismisses race is the evolution of the term *third wave* itself. My initial reading of writings labeled as third wave, such as the Barbara Findlen anthology *Listen Up! Voices from the Next Feminist Generation* (1995) and Rebecca Walker's volume *To Be Real: Telling the Truth and Changing the Face of Feminism* (1995), triggered memories of women of color using the term *third wave* in the late 1980s. Barbara Smith, founder of Kitchen Table, Women of Color Press and editor of, among other works, *Home Girls: A Black Feminist Anthology* (1983), confirms that Kitchen Table set out to publish a book on racism called *The Third Wave*. In this conceptualization of third wave that emerged in the late 1980s, the book was to describe an antiracist, women-of-color-led feminism for the coming decade. Smith notes quite logically that it is only common sense, based on the first wave and second wave analogies, for those seeking to define a new direction of feminism to call it the "third wave."

The term *third wave feminism* as we now know it signals a new generation of feminists. It came to public consciousness, or at least leftist consciousness, in the form of Rebecca Walker's founding of the Third Wave Foundation in 1992, which initially conducted a Freedom Summer-styled voter registration campaign that same year. This generation of third wave feminism credits previous generations for women-centered social and political advances. This acknowledgment, however, took the form of seeming ungratefulness and historical amnesia in Walker's anthology, *To Be Real*. Some contributors voiced a sense of feeling stifled by the previous generation's organizing style and seemed to reduce the third wave's argument to a gripe about feminism as lifestyle dogma. Yet, more recent writings about third wave feminism—particularly Jennifer Baumgardner and Amy Richards's recent book *Manifesta: Young Women, Feminism, and the Future* (2000)—attempt to define thirdwave politics and mend the generational rift that arose between some older and younger white feminists. Moreover, *Manifesta* at least gives lip service to the role of women of color, lesbians, and, to a lesser degree, poor women in the third wave women's movement.

The wave model perpetuates the exclusion of women of color from women's movement history and feminist theorizing. Still, as it is so deeply embedded in how we examine the history and future of the women's movement, it remains useful for internal critique. As it is used historically and today, it is too static. To serve a wide range of women's needs, it is imperative that the wave model includes women of color's resistance to gender violence.

WHAT TO DO WITH OUR MOTHERS' GARDENS?

If we proceed with this idea of third wave feminism in its most obvious form, that of denoting generations of feminism, what is the relationship between Black feminists of differing generations? Does a generational rift exist between them? One aspect of the generational tensions between feminists in general is the frustration that older feminists feel at watching younger women reinvent the wheels of social change. Michele Wallace, in retrospect, recognized the irritation of her mother and other women of her mother's generation. In her essay "To Hell and Back," Wallace writes of the late 1960s: "My thesis had been that I and my generation were reinventing youth, danger, sex, love, blackness, and fun. But there had always been just beneath the surface a persistent countermelody, … what I might also call my mother's line, a deep suspicion that I was reinventing nothing, but rather making a fool of myself in precisely the manner that untold generations of young women before me had done." Other than this autobiographical insight by Wallace, few sources speak of conflicts or distinctions between Black feminists of different generations.

In interviews with Black feminists who participated in 1970s feminist activism, some voiced a mix of disappointment and understanding at young Black women's seeming lack of interest in feminism. Their understanding came from intimate knowledge of the struggle, name-calling, and painful awakening around claiming feminism as a political stance. Simultaneously, older Black feminists also seemed disappointed that young Black women could appear to turn their backs on the foundations of Black feminist activism, which made possible, at the very least, a few societal gains for the next generation.

The few articles about Black feminism that have made it into the mainstream press either lament the lack of formal Black feminist organizations or pick up where *Essence* left off in the 1970s—questioning the need for feminism in Black women's lives. As an example of the questioning of the existence of Black feminism on the organizational level, the most recent, high-profile article is Kristal Brent Zook's (1995) essay "A Manifesto of Sorts for a Black Feminist Movement," which appeared in the *New York Times Magazine*. She calls Black women to task for their failure to organize on the behalf of Black women and for serving instead as auxiliaries to male-centered causes like the Million Man March or the "Endangered Black Male" crusades of figures such as O. J. Simpson, Tupac Shakur, and Mike Tyson. Zook also voices frustration with an older generation that continues to define leadership as male-centered and rooted in traditions such as NAACP conventions and benefit fashion shows.

Jones, Morgan, and Chambers all address the question of generation—along with the benefits and drawbacks of being born after the 1960s and 1970s social movements that drastically altered the sociopolitical landscape of racial and sexual politics. They give credit to the Civil Rights, women's, and Black nationalist movements for the place of privilege that those movements put some of us in, in terms of opportunities. Yet, they also recognize the complacency that such awe-inspiring heroes encouraged in Generation X. Chambers recalls being a fifth grader and watching documentaries about Black history:

> It seemed that all the big black battles were over by the time I was born.... Watching footage of the bus boycotts, the sit-ins, and the marches ... I would wonder if I would have been brave. My brother and I used to say, "No way were we sitting on the back of the bus!" but the look my mother would give us told me that we had no idea what we would or wouldn't have done. Deep down inside, I wondered. As bad as those times were, I wished sometimes that there was some sort of protest or something that I could get involved with.

Chambers lived with both parents until her father left the family when she was ten years old. At the time of Chambers's reminiscence, her parents had always provided the basics for her and her brother, and the fact that they had always lived in a house with a yard is a significant marker of the class security that she felt as a child. Chambers's parents instituted a "Black History Day" in their home before Black History Month came into existence, so their daughter had an early sense of the sacrifices they made, particularly her mother, but felt none of those barriers herself. Chambers's memories of contemplating what she would have done during the height of the Civil Rights movement is the luxury of a generation that benefited from that particular struggle.

Is contemplation of the past a luxury of middle-class ascendancy? Or do past struggles at least provide the room to dream about middle- or upper-class status? Morgan views successful social movements, in terms of the sometimes temporary gains of the Civil Rights movement, as having a lulling effect on Generation X. The introduction to Morgan's book is entitled "Dress Up." In it, she recalls envying her mother's generation of women, not because their lives were easy but because of the simultaneous emergence of the women's movement and dissemination of ideas about independence and self-fulfillment at that time. Women of her mother's generation also had the cultural explosion of Black women's literature to affirm their existence and the circumstances of "being black, female and surviving." Morgan was ten years old when Ntozake Shange's choreopoem *for colored girls who have considered suicide when the rainbow was not enuf* premiered in New York. When her mother refused to take her, a young Joan tried every trick in her arsenal—from whining, to singing "the Five Stairsteps' 'O-o-h child things are going to get easier' over and over again—attitudinal and loud—until I was two seconds shy of an ass whooping." But when she was older Morgan understood that "the play held crucial parts of her [mother]—parts she needed to share with her husband and not her ten-year-old daughter."

In this retelling we see a nod to the previous generation of women who, whether they identified as feminist or not, made possible Morgan's self-described position as a hip-hop feminist. When she attends the twentieth anniversary run of *for colored girls* in Manhattan, Morgan hopes that it will reveal "the secrets of black womanhood" that she thought her mother withheld when she saw the play. This was not the case. She says, "As a child of the post–Civil Rights, post-feminist, post-soul hip-hop generation my struggle songs consisted of the same notes but they were infused with distinctly different rhythms." In realizing that she was waiting for someone to write a *for colored girls* for her generation, Morgan calls to task her own complacency, as well as that of her generation. She cautions that "relying on older heads to redefine the struggle to encompass our generation's issues is not only lazy but dangerous. Consider our foremothers' contributions a bad-ass bolt of cloth. We've got to fashion the gear to our own liking." Linking generational style and politics, Morgan calls upon the hip-hop generation to create a language and culture that signifies more than a lifestyle but also a political stance worthy of definition.

By describing herself as "a child of the *post*–Civil Rights, *post*-feminist, *post*-soul hip-hop generation," Morgan is not implying that, as a society, we are somehow finished with the struggle for civil or women's rights. The popular press's use of the term *postfeminist* signifies a uniquely liberated, sexy, young woman who believes that feminism is dead or all the battles have been won. Morgan uses the prefix *post* to signal the end of a particular era of tactics and action. She in no way indicates that the goals or hopes of those movements were fulfilled or are no longer relevant to current generations. She does openly recognize that "we are the daughters of feminist privilege." The "we" means college-educated, middle-class Black girls who believe that there is nothing we cannot achieve because we are women, though sexism and racism might fight us every step of the way. Morgan attempts to craft a collective identity for a new generation of thinkers and organizers. This is a unifying move meant to reach out to women like Chambers who long for significant struggles like those of past eras, as well as to those who feel as though the movements of the 1960s were failures because of conservative backlash, without taking into account our own lack of political vigilance.

Jones issues a similar call to action for the post–Civil Rights, postfeminist generation. Though the subtitle of her book only mentions race, sex, and hair, she is also class-conscious, either explicitly or implicitly, in the forty-four essays that make up her book. About the differences between generations, Jones parallels Morgan in her observations of the cultural production of the 1970s:

> The renaissance of fiction by black women in the seventies, we caught that too. Those books made us feel less invisible, though their stories were far from our own lives as big-city girls; girls who took ballet and were carted off to Planned Parenthood in high school so as not to risk that baby that Mom, not Mama, warned would have "ruined our lives." College was expected. The southern ghosts of popular black women's fiction, the hardships and abuse worn like purple hearts, the clipped wings were not ours. We had burdens of our own. Glass ceilings at the office and in the art world, media and beauty industries that saw us as substandard, the color and hair wars that continued to sap our energy. We wanted to hear about these.

As young white feminists are seeking to step outside of what they consider rigid lifestyle instructions of their feminist foremothers (e.g., stylistic and political), young Black women are attempting to stretch beyond the awe-inspiring legendary work of women like Fannie Lou Hamer, Coretta Scott King, Ruby Doris Smith Robinson, Barbara Smith, bell hooks, and Angela Davis. Their work cannot be matched. When Jones poses the question, "Do you know who speaks through you?", she poses a rhetorical question that recognizes the significance of history in giving current struggles meaning.

Morgan and Jones exhort the post–Civil Rights, postfeminist, hip-hop generation to pay homage to past struggles but not to rest on our ivory tower degrees. Both recognize the class implications of being exposed to Black feminists' texts as assigned reading in college. Morgan, while recognizing historical reasons for Black women's lack of engagement with feminism—for example, racism in the women's movement, feminism's alleged irrelevancy to Black lives—believes that what it comes down to is that Black women are "misguidedly over-protective, hopelessly male-identified, and all too often self-sacrificing." She interprets home-coming parades for Tyson on his release from prison after serving a sentence for sexual assault and blind support for conservative Supreme Court Justice nominee Clarence Thomas as knee-jerk reactions to centuries of racist violence. However, jumping to the defense of Black men—even when Black *women* are the victims of male violence—does nothing for current and future generations struggling against gender bias within the Black community. Critiquing popular culture and writing openly from a Black feminist perspective in periodicals, such as the hip-hop magazine *Vibe* and the *Village Voice*, Morgan and Jones most likely reach a mix of middle-class Blacks and white readerships. Still, in their writings they reference a continuum of Black and women's struggle, overlaying historical context onto contemporary manifestations of racism and sexism, that can be useful for articulating a vision for attacking battering, rape, and gender violence in the Black community.

STRONGBLACKWOMEN/BULLETPROOF DIVAS

"Some writers write to tell the world things, others of us write to find something out," Jones commented to a reporter for the *Boston Herald*. Morgan writes that we, Black women, need to take an honest look at ourselves and then tell the truth about it. Jones, Morgan, and Chambers want to tell the truth about, in part, the myths that circumscribe the lives of Black women. Yet, similar to some Black Panther Party women's critique of feminism, Morgan raises the culpability of Black women in keeping these myths alive. All three women dissect external messages from white society about beauty and how these messages wreak havoc with Black women's self-esteem. These authors also pry apart the layers of self-hatred that work to smother Black women within the Black community. The solutions they offer all involve, to some degree, letting go of the past and opening up to a future as fallible human beings and not women of mythical proportions.

Morgan situates the standard of the strongblackwoman in the history of slavery and the ways that Black women were expected to persevere under any circumstances. Referencing Wallace's explanation of the myths of the superwoman, the mammy, the jezebel, and the sapphire, Morgan contends that these myths have metamorphosed into the contemporary figures of, among others, the "Ghetto Bitch ... Hoochie Mama ... Skeezer ... Too independent ... Don't need no man ... [and] Waiting to Exhale" women. She believes that the older myths justifying slaveowners' brutality against Black women metamorphosed into contemporary conservative welfare myths. We have internalized new myths and have been indiscriminate in crafting our identities from them. At one point in her life, Morgan begins to feel like she is suffocating under the burden of trying always to appear in control and strong. A friend diagnoses her as succumbing to "strongblackwoman" syndrome. The motto of the strongblackwoman? "No matter how bad shit gets, handle it alone, quietly, and with dignity."

Morgan writes "strongblackwoman" as one word and abbreviates it to SBW, signifying the transformation of a stereotype into an accepted and recognizable identity trait for Black women. This linguistic move solidifies the idea of "strong," "black," and "woman" as nonseparable parts of a seemingly cohesive identity. In this title, there is no room for being just one of the three identities at any given time. There is the expectation in the Black community that Black women will be all three, *at all times*. This is not a new concept. Nineteenth- and early twentieth-century crusaders trumpeted the strongblackwoman as a model for "lifting as we climb," but Wallace and contributors to Toni Cade Bambara's *The Black Woman* (1970) deconstructed this model in the 1970s. Morgan wants to take apart the strongblackwoman image for what it is: a way for Black women to deny emotional, psychic, and even physical pain, all the while appearing to keep it together—just like our mothers appeared to do.

Once when she was about thirteen years old, Chambers told her mother that she was depressed. Her mother gave her a scolding about being ungrateful for all that she had, and she let Veronica know that depression was a "white girls'" domain. Black women were strong and did not get depressed, and, her mother added, Veronica would not be able to count on the world to make her happy.

As much as Chambers's mother warns against the realities of a racist and sexist world, she can never fully explain *why* these realities exist. This is not a personal failure, but the inability of adult, Black Americans to explain a number of social realities to their children. The worsening of poverty in Black communities, the continued degradation of women, the rescinding of civil rights gained in the 1960s, and the lack of a clear course of action from Black leaders (or the lack of Black leaders, period) are equally incomprehensible to children, as well as to adults living in a so-called democracy.

After a series of struggles and achievements—including abuse at the hands of her father and stepmother, putting herself through Simon's Rock College (entering at the age of sixteen), recognition as one of *Glamour* magazine's Top Ten College Women of 1990, and several successful magazine internships—Chambers burns out. She goes through a period of not eating and not sleeping, though she is exhausted. She keeps this information from her mother because she believes "depression was absolutely not allowed." She likens Black women to magicians, "masters of emotional sleight of hand. The closer you get, the less you can see. It was true of my mother. It is also true of me."

Veronica lived with an aunt at the time of her depression, and it is she who reports to Veronica's mother that something is amiss with her daughter. When Veronica does open up to her mother about her exhaustion and depression, she learns that her mother always assumed that everything was fine. Her mother was so busy worrying about her brother, who was not doing well in school and would later deal drugs and end up in jail, that she was just happy not to have to worry about Veronica. This conversation, Chambers's "coming out" to her mother as *not* always strong, begins her process of letting go of the strongblackwoman image. She is aided in this process by a group of college sistah-friends with whom she can relax and speak freely, peppering her language with affectionate "chile, pleases," "girlfriends," "sis's," and "flygirls." Through them and a better relationship with her mother, Chambers is able to recapture a feeling that she had not had since her childhood days of playing double Dutch in Brooklyn, New York. Of those days she says, "There is a space between the two ropes where nothing is better than being a black girl. The helix encircles you and protects you and there you are strong. I wish she'd [Chambers's mother] let me show her. I could teach her how it feels."

The solutions that Morgan, Jones, and Chambers offer to fighting strongblackwoman syndrome are not unlike those that Black feminists in the 1970s offered. In addition to fighting the racist and sexist implications of this myth, Morgan and Jones call for redefinition. Morgan calls it her "Memo of Retirement." In it she addresses white people, people in her life who are overdependent on her to comfort them, and men who expect her to support them unequivocally without having needs of her own. She resolves, "The fake 'Fine' and compulsory smile? Gone. Deaded. Don't look for it.... Some days I really am an evil black woman." Ultimately, when Morgan has her bout with depression, she leaves New York and moves to San Francisco for the winter. There she allows herself to fall apart with people who are not afraid of her fragility and do not expect her to be a strongblackwoman.

Many women, particularly women of color, do not have the resources to take a winter sabbatical. Yet, the more accessible aspect of Morgan's cure for depression is "claiming the right to imperfections and vulnerabilities." Across classes, Black women are taught to hide their imperfections for fear of being a discredit to the race or vilified as welfare queens. Perhaps more challenging than finding the monetary resources to take a mental health break is finding those people, female or male, with whom a Black woman can be less than strong.

Jones, though more casual in her approach, calls for redefinition of self as key to recuperating an image of Black women that is not detrimental to our individual and collective well-being. She advocates the creation of the "Bulletproof Diva," defining not only what she is but also what she is *not*. I quote extensively from Jones to demonstrate the range of experience that she allows for in this redefinition:

> Consider this a narrative in which we invent our own heroine, the Bulletproof Diva. A woman whose sense of dignity and self cannot be denied; who, though she may live in a war zone like Brownsville, goes out everyday greased, pressed, and dressed, with hair faded and braided and freeze-dried and spit-curled and wrapped and locked and cut to a sexy baldie (so she is all eyes and lips) and piled ten inches high and colored siren red, cobalt blue, and flaming yellow. She is fine and she knows it.

> She *has* to know it because who else will.... A Bulletproof Diva is not, I repeat, *not* that tired stereotype, the emasculating black bitch too hard for love or piety. It's safe to assume that a Bulletproof Diva is whoever you make her—corporate girl, teen mom, or the combination—as long as she had the lip and nerve, *and as long as she uses that lip and nerve to raise up herself and the world.* (emphasis mine)

Morgan's "Memo of Retirement" and Jones's definition of the Bulletproof Diva do not advocate dropping out of politics or individualism. Rather they remind us of the road that Black women have traveled to get to this point in our collective history. They open up the possibility of self-preservation and community activism as intersecting, reinforcing objectives on the road to Black liberation.

Another aspect of Black women's relationships is how Black women relate to one another. Young Black women writers both highlight the support they feel from other Black women and bear witness to the misguided power that Black women, sharing similar experiences around racism and sexism, exert over one another to wound in unfathomable ways. Competition, vying for status, and degraded self-worth can be Black women's worst interpersonal enemies. Morgan, Chambers, and Jones heed Audre Lorde's call in her essay "Eye to Eye" (1984) for Black women to face how we treat one another and what that says about how we feel about ourselves.

Chambers recalls encounters with other Black girls that, while not unusual, emphasize the ways that African-American women try to hold one another back, from calling Chambers a "sellout" to accusing her of "talking white" because she takes her education seriously. Morgan, in her chapter entitled "Chickenhead Envy," cogently calls out the behavior of said Chickenheads. To her credit, she is also self-reflective, exploring what so-called Chickenheads reflect back to Black women who are independent and ambitious. Morgan is initiating much needed dialogue about Black women's culpability in our own oppression and how we oppress one another, especially in the areas of class, color, and sexual orientation. Morgan and Chambers, in fact, disrupt the notion that there is a unified Black sisterhood. While that may be the ideal, these authors point out how Black sisterhood is sometimes far from the reality of our relationships....

THE BROTHAS

The recurring point of contention that Black women have with feminism is its impact on Black male/female relationships. Many times, Black feminists in the 1970s spent so much time reaffirming their commitment to Black men and the Black community that their gender critiques and actions to end sexism fell by the wayside. Thus it is incumbent on young Black feminist writers to tread a line between—to apply the Combahee River Collective Statement to the present—struggling with Black men *against* racism but also struggling with Black men *about* sexism. Chambers, Jones, and Morgan do this to varying degrees by writing about Black men as fathers, as mothers' sons, as biological brothers, as spiritual/artistic brothers, as potential lovers, and as lifetime partners. In their personal and political examination of their lives, these writers show that the love Black women feel for Black men is sometimes diluted by the mutual disrespect and mistrust engendered by slavery and kept alive through women's and men's sustained patriarchal notions about gender.

Black fathers make brief appearances in these texts. Both Morgan's and Chambers's fathers left their families when they were young, and Jones's parents (writers Hettie Jones and Amiri Baraka, then LeRoi Jones) divorced. The emphasis that the Black community and media have placed on Black men's role in raising their sons has resulted, Morgan contends, in "precious little attention [being paid to] the significant role Black men play in shaping their daughters' ideas about themselves and love." More than a dismissal of the role of fathers, the pain these women experience around the father-daughter relationship slips in and out of their narratives. This pain is unresolved and, therefore, unspoken and untheorized. Morgan, in her chapter entitled "babymother," does attempt to address men's rights to choose, or not to choose, fatherhood as a reproductive rights issue with which feminists must deal if we desire equality. However, the reader is left to wonder how much of Morgan's anxiety about men's reproductive rights is linked to the emotional and political fallout of her own father's absence. Such a revelation would do much of the professed work of feminist theory by connecting theory and personal experience.

The physical or emotional absence of fathers in a number of Black homes allows both Chambers and Morgan to confront Black women about the significant differences in the ways that they rear girl children and boy children. Chambers knew from an early age that her mother and her mother's closest friends, also immigrants from Panama, prized their boy children while girls were an afterthought. "'And Veronica,' they would say eventually. 'She's fine. All A's as usual,'" her mother would say in a sad voice that Veronica interpreted as a display of her mother's overriding concern for her brother, Malcolm. Malcolm began exhibiting behavioral problems after their father left. Chambers is consistently aware of sexist ideologies and their impact on girls. However, when lamenting her brother's drug problem and incarceration, Chambers appears resistant to considering his problems to result from sexist and racist ideologies as well. The endangered Black male dialogue of the late 1980s and 1990s was problematic, but a broader political analysis of Black men's vulnerability and subsequent understanding of her brother's life under white supremacy are buried under Chambers's sibling rivalry.

Morgan offers a fuller analysis of the disparities in how Black women love their sons and raise their daughters, perhaps because her examination focuses more on the connections between sons and the lovers/partners/husbands they become. This is the closest that any of these authors comes to lobbing a generational grenade and assigning culpability for perpetuating the strongblackwoman and endangeredblackmale roles, which are compatible only in that they encourage an enabler/dependent relationship. Morgan wonders how older women can teach their daughters to be independent and ambitious and then comment that they are too strong willed to be acceptable to any man. Morgan also notes that these are the same women who loved their sons but did not teach young men about mutuality in relationships.

The doppelgänger to this portrayal of Black mothers is, according to Morgan, those women who maintain "all men are dogs." This might be a defensive stance to pass on to daughters, but what message does this impart to their sons about self-worth? And what behavior do mothers condone or abet if they think men are meant to have many girlfriends, to be "playas"? Women who believe their sons can *do* no wrong and those who believe their sons can only *be* wrong, and therefore need constant protection, pass along a fatalistic stance that ignores all the Black men who are, Morgan notes, "taking care of their kids, working and contributing to their communities."

The writers examined here clearly are conflicted about how Black women and Black men relate to one another. Jones recalls the Black men who responded to her feminist performance group's work as artistic and intellectual compatriots. Yet in her chapter "Open Letter to a Brother," she ponders the ways that sexual liberation enabled Black men to reinforce negative myths about themselves, resulting in what she calls "the Dog Syndrome." Offering much-needed critiques of Black masculinity, Jones seeks to delve deeper into how Black men's lack of access to political and economic power became so entrenched in obtaining sexual power. The Dog Syndrome is in fact, according to Jones, "black male impotence masquerading as power."

Jones's and Morgan's essays, read with Chambers's more personal backdrop, begin to offer a direction for open discussion in the Black community about Black masculinity and femininity, Black men and Black women. If generational politics come into play in Black feminist thought for these women, it is in putting contemporary tensions into historical perspective. Rather than blaming the past for the distrust that plagues Black women and men, younger Black feminists are, read in conjunction, asking Black men to forgo atonement for the past and take responsibility for male privilege in the present. Being a Black man in U.S. society is much more complex than adopting a pose and maintaining it. Yet, critically, these Black feminists, Morgan in particular, are offering complementary suggestions for Black women to check their behavior and expectations of men and relationships. How do we participate in our own oppression and that of future generations? What is our stake in maintaining gender relations that can only lead to continued trauma?

KEEPIN' IT REAL: OLD SCHOOL ANALYSIS AND NEW SCHOOL MUSIC

There is no guarantee that the work of Chambers, Morgan, or Jones will reach those young people who need it the most—young people who will not be exposed to Black feminist theory and thought in college classrooms. Though their writing appears in free publications in major cities, what guarantees that a young Black woman on her way to work or school in Manhattan will stop and pick up the *Village Voice* and find Black feminism within its pages? Moreover, these writers' regional focus—they all live and work in New York City—also raises questions about the reach of young Black feminist theorizing geographically.

Ideally, by even daring to write about gender and the Black community, these writers give organizers and educators a springboard. Certain modes of resistance have lost their power; for example, Washington, D.C., marches have become more of a C-SPAN spectacle than the powerful form of radical agitation that the March on Washington was in 1963. Moreover, as we see with some protests against globalization, the state apparatus has become quite adept at shutting down direct action before it even starts. One reason that young people focus on writing and music as forms of protest—not that these are new—is because we need fresh modes for developing collective consciousness.

It is up to those of us with resources and commitment to take these writings and synthesize them into programs that appeal to the next generation, which needs them the most. I propose a project fusing music and intellectualism in much the same way that Public Enemy and Bogie Down Productions did with the resurgence of Black cultural nationalism in the early 1990s. Music is one of the most accessible educational tools left untapped.

How might educators and those who work closely with young people use a compact disc containing hip-hop, R&B, and rap songs along with an educator's guide to readings and discussion questions about gender and African Americans? How many more people would Black feminism reach if, instead of defending against what Black feminism is *not*, we offered Black feminist visions for the future? In the appendix is a list of songs and readings that I propose for this purpose. For example, Lauryn Hill's song "Doo-Wop (That Thing)" from her album *The Miseducation of Lauryn Hill* persuasively takes to task men and women for ill behavior in relationships. With its refrain "How you gon' win when you ain't right within?" Hill's song, and others like it, are prime moments for discussion and education around gender in Black communities.

Another, more recent, example is India Arie's song "Video," from her album *Acoustic Soul*. In it she disavows the image of the "video ho" and makes the bold claim that she is the center of her own world: "I will always be the India Arie." This song could easily be paired with a reading and/or discussion of Morgan's "Hip-Hop Feminist" or "Flygirls, Bitches, and Hos" chapters to provoke debate about Black artists' political responsibilities, if they have any, and Black women's agency in participating in music video culture....

Young Black feminists are not uniform in political thought, so it would be dishonest to assert that Black women still feel the need to apologize for engaging feminist politics. Yet, in linking with the work of feminist foremothers, contemporary, young Black feminist writers continue to explain feminism's relevance to Black communities. Far from reinventing the feminist wheel, young Black feminists are building on the legacy left by nineteenth-century abolitionists, antilynching crusaders, club women, Civil Rights organizers, Black Nationalist revolutionaries, and 1970s Black feminists. They are not inserting themselves into the third wave paradigm as much as they are continuing the work of a history of Black race women concerned with gender issues. These three writers in particular also have in common with their ancestors the gift of literacy and the privilege of education.

Sheila Radford-Hill's *Further to Fly: Black Women and the Politics of Empowerment* advocates an "authentic feminism." This is not another brand of feminism but a call for Black feminism not to "fall in love with the sound of its own voice" and return to an applied feminism. Young Black feminist writers might, in fact, need to fall in love with the sounds of their own voices. In a discriminatory society that continues to marginalize the theorizing of women of color, who but ourselves will honor our words as we continue the legacy of struggle to end racism, sexism, heterosexism, ablism, and classism? The key to that honoring, as Chambers, Morgan, and Jones note in their writing and as the hip-hop generation insists, is to keep it real.

8. Chandra Talpade Mohanty, "Defining Genealogies: Feminist Reflections on Being South Asian in North America," from *Our Feet Walk the Sky: Writings by Women of the South Asian Diaspora*

In a key essay for understanding the third-wave commitment to questions of identity and hybridity, migration, immigration, expatriatism, and workers across the globe, Mohanty reflects on how she is categorized as a "foreign student" because she is from India, and the racism, sexism, and discrimination she experiences. These experiences form the basis for her political activity in grass roots organizations in India and the United States.

My local newspaper tells me that worldwide migration is at an all-time high in the early 1990s. Folks are moving from rural to urban areas in all parts of the Third World and from Asia, Africa, the Caribbean, and Latin America to Europe, North America, and selected countries in the Middle East. Apparently two percent of the world's population no longer lives in the country in which they were born. Of course, the newspaper story primarily identifies the problems (for Europe and the United States) associated with these transnational migration trends. One such problem is taking jobs away from citizens. I am reminded of a placard carried by black and Third World people at an antiracism rally in London: We Are Here Because You Were There. My location in the U.S.A., then, is symptomatic of large numbers of migrants, nomads, immigrants, workers across the globe for whom notions of home, identity, geography, and history are infinitely complicated in the late twentieth century. Questions of nationality, and of belongings (witness the situation of South Asians in Africa) are constitutive of the Indian Diaspora. This essay is a personal, anecdotal mediation on the politics of gender and race in the construction of South Asian identity in North America.

On a TWA flight on my way back to the U.S. from a conference in the Netherlands, the professional white man sitting next to me asks: (a) which school do I go to? and (b) when do I plan to go home?—all in the same breath. I put on my most professorial demeanor (somewhat hard in crumpled blue jeans and cotton t-shirt—this uniform only works for white male professors, who of course could command authority even in swimwear!) and inform him that I teach at a small liberal arts college in upstate New York, and that I have lived in the U.S. for fifteen years. At this point, my work is in the U.S., not in India. This is no longer entirely true. My work is also with feminists and grass-roots activists in India, but he doesn't need to know this. Being mistaken for a graduate student seems endemic to my existence in this country. Few Third World women are granted professional (i.e., adult) and/or permanent (one is always a student!) status in the U.S., even if we exhibit clear characteristics of adulthood like gray hair and facial lines. He ventures a further question: what do you teach? On hearing Women's Studies he becomes quiet and we spend the next eight hours in polite silence. He has decided that I do not fit into any of his categories, but what can you expect from a Feminist (an Asian one!) anyway? I feel vindicated and a little superior—even though I know he doesn't really feel put in his place. Why should he? He has a number of advantages in this situation: white skin, maleness, and citizenship privileges. From his enthusiasm about expensive ethnic food in Amsterdam, and his J. Crew clothes, I figured class difference (economic or cultural) wasn't exactly an issue in our interaction. We both appeared to have similar social access as professionals.

I have been asked the "home" question (when are you going home) periodically for fifteen years now. Leaving aside the subtly racist implications of the question (go home—you don't belong), I am still not satisfied with my response. What is home? The place I was born? Where I grew up? Where my parents live? Where I live and work as an adult? Where I locate my community—my people? Who are my people? Is home a geographical space, an historical space, an emotional, sensory space? Home is always so crucial to immigrants and migrants—I even write about it in scholarly texts, perhaps to avoid addressing it as an issue that is also very personal. Does two percent of the world's population think about these questions pertaining to home? This is not to imply that the other ninety-eight percent does not think about home. What interests me is the meaning of home for immigrants and migrants. I am convinced that this question—how one understands and defines home—is a profoundly political one.

Since settled notions of territory, community, geography, and history don't work for us, what does it really mean to be South Asian in the U.S.A.? Obviously I was not South Asian in India—I was Indian. What else could one be but Indian at a time when a successful national independence struggle had given birth to a socialist democratic nation-state? This was the beginning of the decolonization of the Third World. Regional geographies (South Asia) appeared less relevant as a mark of identification than citizenship in a postcolonial independent nation on the cusp of economic and political autonomy. However, in North America, identification as South Asian (in addition to Indian, in my case) takes on its own logic. South Asian refers to folks of Indian, Pakistani, Sri Lankan, Bangladeshi, Kashmiri, and Burmese origin. Identifying as South Asian rather than Indian adds numbers and hence power within the U.S. State. Besides, regional differences among those from different South Asian countries are often less relevant than the commonality based on our histories of immigration and our experiences in the U.S.

Let me reflect a bit on the way I identify myself, and the way the U.S. State and its institutions categorize me. Perhaps thinking through the various labels will lead me back to the question of home and identity. In 1977, I arrived in the U.S.A. on an F1 visa—a student visa. At that time, my definition of myself—a graduate student in Education at the University of Illinois—and the official definition of me (a student allowed into the country on an F1 visa) obviously coincided. Then I was called a foreign student and expected to go "home" (to India—even though my parents were in Nigeria at the time) after getting my Ph.D. Let's face it, this is the assumed trajectory for a number of Indians, especially the postindependence generation (mine) who come to the U.S. for graduate study.

However, this was not to be my trajectory. I quickly discovered that being a foreign student, and a woman at that, meant being either dismissed as irrelevant (the quiet Asian woman stereotype), treated in racist ways (my teachers asked if I understood English and if they should speak slower and louder so that I could keep up—this in spite of my inheritance of the Queen's English and British colonialism!), or celebrated and exoticized (you are so smart! your accent is even better than that of Americans—a little Anglophilia at work here, even though all my Indian colleagues insist we speak English the Indian way!).

The most significant transition I made at that time was the one from foreign student to student of color. Once I was able to read my experiences in terms of race, and to read race and racism as it is written into the social and political fabric of the U.S., I was able to anchor myself here: racism and sexism became analytic and political lenses. Of course, none of this happened in isolation—friends, colleagues, comrades, classes, books, films, arguments, and dialogues were constitutive of my political education as a woman of color in the U.S.

In the late 1970s and early 1980s feminism was gaining momentum on American campuses—it was in the air, in the classrooms, on the streets. However, what attracted me wasn't feminism as the mainstream media and white Women's Studies departments defined it. Instead, it was a very specific kind of feminism, the feminism of U.S. women of color and Third World women that spoke to me. In thinking through the links between gender, race, and class in their U.S. manifestations, I was for the first time enabled to think through my own gendered, classed postcolonial history. In the early 1980s, reading Audre Lorde, Nassal el Sadaawi, Cherríe Moraga, bell hooks, Gloria Joseph, Paula Gunn Allen, Barbara Smith, Merle Woo, and Mitsuye Yamada, among others, generated a sort of recognition that was very inspiring. A number of actions, decisions, and organizing efforts at that time led me to a sense of home and community in relation to women of color in the U.S. Home not as a comfortable, stable, inherited and familiar space, but instead as an imaginative, politically charged space where the familiarity and sense of affection and commitment lay in a shared collective analysis of social injustice, as well as a vision of radical transformation. Political solidarity and a sense of family could be melded together imaginatively to create a strategic space I could call "home." Politically, intellectually, and emotionally I owe an enormous debt to feminists of color—and especially to the sisters who have sustained me over the years. Even though our attempt to start the Women of Color Institute for Radical Research and Action fell through, the spirit of this vision, and the friendships it generated, still continue to nurture me. A number of us, including Barbara Smith, Papusa Molina, Jacqui Alexander, Gloria Joseph, Mitsuye Yamada, Kesho Scott, and myself, among others, met in 1984 to discuss the possibility of such an institute. The Institute never really happened, but I still hope we will pull it off one day.

For me, engagement as a feminist of color in the U.S. made possible an intellectual and political genealogy of being Indian that was radically challenging as well as profoundly activist. Racialization and gender and class relations and histories became the prism through which I understood, however partially, what it could mean to be South Asian in North America. Interestingly, this recognition also forced me to reexamine the meanings attached to home and community in India.

What I chose to claim, and continue to claim, is a history of anti-colonialist, feminist struggle in India. The stories I recall, the ones that I retell and claim as my own, determine the choices and decisions I make in the present and the future. I did not want to accept a history of Hindu chauvinist (bourgeois) upward mobility (even though this characterizes a section of my extended family). We all chose partial, interested stories/histories—perhaps not as deliberately as I am making it sound here. But consciously, or unconsciously, these choices about our past(s) often determine the logic of our present.

Having always kept my distance from conservative, upwardly mobile Indian immigrants for whom the South Asian world was divided into green-card holders and non-green-card holders, the only South Asian links I allowed and cultivated were with Indians with whom I shared a political vision. This considerably limited my community. Racist and sexist experiences in graduate school and after made it imperative that I understand the U.S. in terms of its history of racism, imperialism, and patriarchal relations, specifically in relation to Third World immigrants. After all, we were into the Reagan-Bush years, when the neoconservative backlash made it impossible to ignore the rise of racist, antifeminist, and homophobic attitudes, practices, and institutions. Any purely culturalist or nostalgic/sentimental definition of being "Indian" or "South Asian" was inadequate. Such a definition fueled the "model minority" myth. And this subsequently constituted us as "outsiders/foreigners" or as interest groups who sought or had obtained the American dream.

In the mid-1980s, the labels changed: I went from being a "foreign student" to being a "resident alien." I have always thought that this designation was a stroke of inspiration on the part of the U.S. State, since it accurately names the experience and status of immigrants—one's status as an "alien" is primary. Being legal requires identity papers. (It is useful to recall that the "passport"—and by extension the concept of nation-states and the sanctity of their borders—came into being after World War I.)

One must be stamped as legitimate (that is, not-gay-or-lesbian and not-communist!) by the Immigration and Naturalization Service (INS). The INS is one of the central disciplinary arms of the U.S. State. It polices the borders and controls all border crossings—especially those into the U.S. In fact, the INS is also one of the primary forces which institutionalizes race differences in the public arena, thus regulating notions of home, legitimacy, and economic access to the "American dream" for many of us. For instance, carrying a green card documenting resident alien status in the U.S. is clearly very different from carrying an American passport, which is proof of U.S. citizenship. The former allows one to enter the U.S. with few hassles; the latter often allows one to breeze through the borders and ports of entry of other countries, especially countries which happen to be trading partners (much of Western Europe and Japan, among others) or in an unequal relationship with the U.S. (much of the noncommunist Third World). At a time when notions of a capitalist free-market economy seem (falsely) synonymous with the values attached to democracy, an American passport can open many doors. However, just carrying an American passport is no insurance against racism and unequal and unjust treatment within the U.S. It would be important to compare the racialization of first-generation immigrants from South Asia to the racialization of second-generation South Asian Americans. One significant difference between these two generations would be between the experience of racism as a phenomenon specific to the U.S. versus the ever-present shadow of racism in which South Asians born in the U.S. grow up. This suggests that the psychic effects of racism would be different for these two constituencies. In addition, questions of home, identity, and history take on very different meanings for South Asians born in North America. But to be fair, this comparison is beyond the scope of this essay.

Rather obstinately, I have refused to give up my Indian passport and have chosen to remain as a resident alien in the U.S. for the last decade or so. Which leads me to reflect on the complicated meanings attached to holding Indian citizenship while making a life for myself in the U.S.A. In India, what does it mean to have a green card—to be an expatriate? What does it mean to visit Bombay every two to four years, and still call it home? Why does speaking in Marathi (my mother tongue) become a measure and confirmation of home? What are the politics of being a part of the majority and the "absent elite" in India, while being a minority and a racialized "other" in the U.S.? And does feminist politics, or advocating feminism, have the same meaning and urgency in these different geographical and political contests?

Some of these questions hit me smack in the face during my last visit to India in December 1992 post-Ayodhya (the destruction of the Babri Majid in Ayodhya by Hindu fundamentalists on 6 December 1992). In earlier, rather infrequent visits (once every four or five years was all I could afford), my green card designated me as an object of envy, privilege, and status within my extended family. Of course the same green card has always been viewed with suspicion by left and feminist friends who (quite understandably) demand evidence of my ongoing commitment to a socialist and democratic India. During this visit, however, with emotions running high within my family, my green card marked me as an outsider who couldn't possibly understand the "Muslim problem" in India. I was made aware of being an "outsider" in two profoundly troubling shouting matches with my uncles, who voiced the most incredibly hostile sentiments against Muslims. Arguing that India was created as a secular state and that democracy had everything to do with equality for all groups (majority and minority) got me nowhere. The very fundamentals of democratic citizenship in India were/are being undermined and redefined as "Hindu."

Bombay was one of the cities hardest hit with the waves of communal violence following the events in Ayodhya. The mobilization of Hindu fundamentalists, even paramilitary organizations, over the last half century and especially since the mid-1980s had brought Bombay to a juncture where the most violently racist discourse about Muslims seemed to be woven into the fabric of acceptable daily life. Racism was normalized in the popular imagination such that it became almost impossible to publicly raise questions about the ethics or injustice of racial/ethnic, religious discrimination. I could not assume a distanced posture toward religion any more. Too many injustices were being done in my name.

Although born a Hindu, I have always considered myself a non-practicing one—religion had always felt rather repressive when I was growing up. I enjoyed the rituals but resisted the authoritarian hierarchies of organized Hinduism. However, the Hinduism touted by fundamentalist organizations like the RSS (Rashtriya Swayamsevak Sangh, a paramilitary Hindu fundamentalist organization founded in the 1930s) and the Shiv Sena (a Maharashtsan chauvinist, fundamentalist, fascist political organization that has amassed a significant voice in Bombay politics and government) was one that even I, in my ignorance, recognized as reactionary and distorted. But this discourse was real—hate-filled rhetoric against Muslims appeared to be the mark of a "loyal Hindu." It was unbelievably heart-wrenching to see my hometown become a war zone with whole streets set on fire and a daily death count to rival any major territorial border war. The smells and textures of Bombay, of home, which had always comforted and nurtured me, were violently disrupted. The scent of fish drying on the lines at the fishing village in Oanda was submerged in the smell of burning straw and grass as whole bastis (chawls) were burned to the ground. The very typography, language, and relationships that constituted "home" were quietly but surely exploding. What does community mean in this context? December 1992 both clarified as well as complicated for me the meanings attached to being an Indian citizen, a Hindu, an educated woman/feminist, and a permanent resident in the U.S. in ways that I have yet to resolve. After all, it is often moments of crisis that make us pay careful attention to questions of identity. Sharp polarizations force one to make choices (not in order to take sides, but in order to accept responsibility) and to clarify our own analytic, political, and emotional topographies.

I learned that combating the rise of Hindu fundamentalism was a necessary ethical imperative for all socialists, feminists, and Hindus of conscience. Secularism, if it meant absence of religion, was no longer a viable position. From a feminist perspective, it became clear that the battle for women's minds and hearts was very much center-stage in the Hindu fundamentalist strategy. Feminists in India have written extensively about the appeal of fundamentalist rhetoric and social position to women. (The journals *The Economic and Political Weekly of India* and *Manushi* are good sources for this work.)

Religious fundamentalist constructions of women embody the nexus of morality, sexuality, and Nation—a nexus of great importance for feminists. Similar to Christian, Islamic, and Jewish fundamentalist discourses, the construction of femininity and masculinity, especially in relation to the idea of the Nation, are central to Hindu fundamentalist rhetoric and mobilizations. Women are not only mobilized in the service of the Nation, but they also become the ground on which discourses of morality and nationalism are written. For instance, the RSS mobilizes primarily middle-class women in the name of a family-oriented Hindu nation, much like the Christian Right does in the U.S., but discourses of morality and nation are also embodied in the normative policing of women's sexuality (witness the surveillance and policing of women's dress in the name of morality by the contemporary Iranian State). Thus, one of the central challenges Indian feminists face at this time is how to rethink the relationship of nationalism and feminism in the context of religious identities. In addition to the fundamentalist mobilizations tearing the country apart, the recent incursions of the International Monetary Fund and the World Bank with their structural adjustment programs which are supposed to discipline the Indian economy are redefining the meaning of postcoloniality and of democracy in India. Categories like gender, race, caste/class are profoundly and visibly unstable at such times of crisis. These categories must thus be analyzed in relation to contemporary reconstructions of womanhood and manhood in a global arena increasingly dominated by religious fundamentalist movements, the IMF and the World Bank, and the relentless economic and ideological colonization of much of the world by multinationals based in the U.S., Japan, and Europe. In all these global economic and cultural/ideological processes, women occupy a crucial position.

In India, unlike most countries, the sex ratio has declined since the early 1900s. According to the 1991 census, the ratio is now 929 women to 1000 men, one of the lowest (if not the lowest) sex ratios in the world. Women produce seventy to eighty percent of all the food in India and have always been the hardest hit by environmental degradation and poverty. The contradictions between civil law and Hindu and Muslim personal laws affect women—rarely men. Horrific stories about the deliberate murder of female infants as a result of sex determination procedures like amniocentesis, and recent incidents of sati (self-immolation by women on the funeral pyres of their husbands) have even hit the mainstream American media. Gender and religious (racial) discrimination are thus urgent, life-threatening issues for women in India. In 1993, politically conscious Indian citizenship necessitates taking such fundamentally feminist issues seriously. In fact, these are the very same issues South Asian feminists in the U.S. need to address. My responsibility to combat and organize against the regressive and violent repercussions of Hindu fundamentalist mobilizations in India extends to my life in North America. After all, much of the money which sustains the fundamentalist movement is raised and funneled through organizations in the U.S.

Let me now circle back to the place I began: the meanings I have come to give to home, community, and identity. By exploring the relationship between being a South Asian immigrant in America and an expatriate Indian citizen in India, I have tried, however partially and anecdotally, to clarify the complexities of home and community for this particular feminist of color/South Asian in North America. The genealogy I have created for myself here is partial, interested, and deliberate. It is genealogy that underlies my self-identification as an educator involved in a pedagogy of liberation. Of course, my history and experiences are far messier and not at all as linear as this narrative makes them sound. But then the very process of constructing a narrative for oneself—of telling a story—imposes a certain linearity and coherence. But that is the lesson, perhaps, especially for us immigrants and migrants: i.e., that home, community, and identity all fall somewhere between the histories and circumstances we inherit and the political choices we make through alliances, solidarities, and friendships.

One very concrete effect of my creating this particular space for myself has been my recent involvement in two grassroots organizations, one in India and the other in the U.S. The former, an organization called Awareness, is based in Orissa and works to empower the rural poor. Their focus is political education (similar to Paolo Freire's notion of conscientization), and they have recently begun to very consciously organize rural women. Grassroots Leadership of North Carolina is the U.S. organization I work with. It is a multiracial group of organizers (largely African American and white) working to build a poor and working people's movement in the American South. While the geographical, historical, and political contexts of these two organizations are different, my involvement in them is very similar, as is my sense that there are clear connections to be made between the work of the two organizations. In addition, I think that the issues, analyses, and strategies for organizing for social justice are also quite similar. This particular commitment to work with grass-roots organizers in the two places I call home is not accidental. It is very much the result of the genealogy I have traced here. After all, it has taken me over a decade to make these commitments to grass-roots work in both spaces. In part, I have defined what it means to be South Asian by educating myself about, and reflecting on, the histories and experiences of African American, Latina, West Indian, African, European American and other constituencies in North America. Such definitions and understandings do provide a genealogy, but a genealogy that is always relational and fluid as well as urgent and necessary.

9. Bushra Rehman and Daisy Hernández, "Introduction," from *Colonize This!: Young Women of Color on Today's Feminism*

Taking the events of September 11 as a catalyst for thinking about the complications of race and ethnicity and what these bring to third-wave feminist activism, in this essay Hernández and Rehman reflect on their "bittersweet experience with white feminism," and the "other kind of feminism" they learned about through "word of mouth from other women of color": "it was among these women that we both began developing a feminist way of looking at la vida that linked the shit we got as women to the color of our skin, the languages we spoke, and the zip codes we knew as home." A much-needed corrective to the tendency in some forms of third-wave feminism to take the white, middle class experience as the experience of all, this piece shows just how central the lives and thinking of women of color have been to anything definable as "third wave."

This morning I woke up to the news radio. Women were throwing off their veils in Afghanistan and I thought about how for years the women I have known have wanted this to happen. But now what a hollow victory it all is. I am disgusted by the us-and-them mentality. "We" the liberated Americans must save "them" the oppressed women. What kind of feminist victory is it when we liberate women by killing their men and any woman or child who happens to be where a bomb hits? I feel myself as a Muslim-American woman, as a woman of color fearing walking down the street, feeling the pain that my friends felt as they were beaten down in the weeks after September 11th. Solemnly, we counted as the numbers rose: two, five, seven ... My friend telling me: They told me I smelled—they touched me everywhere—and when I talked back, they made fun of me, grabbed me, held my arms back, told me to go back to my country, took my money and ran. My other friend telling me: they punched me, kicked me, called me queer—they had found the pamphlets in my bag, and I'm here on asylum, for being a queer activist—my papers were just going through—I'm not safe in this country as a gay man. My other friends telling me: We didn't want to report it to the police, why just start another case of racial profiling? They're not going to find the guys who did it. They're just going to use our pain as an excuse for more violence. Use our pain as an excuse for more violence. It's what I hear again and again in a city that is grieving, that is beginning to see what other countries live every day.

But where does women of color feminism fit into all of this? Everywhere. As women of color feminists, this is what we have to think about.

—Bushra Rehman

At first I think the teacups have fallen. Broken, they sit on a shelf in the attic apartment Bushra and her sister Sa'dia share. The teacups look antique, etched with thin lines that loop like the penmanship from old textbooks. I imagine they have been in the family for years, but then I find out they were created by Sa'dia for her art exhibit. She made the cups and inscribed each one with the name of a woman from her family. Each cup represents that woman and is broken to the degree of her rebellions. Some are cracked a little, others shattered. They are piled on top of each other, as if someone needs to do the dishes.

The teacups broken and the women broken. That's how it feels sitting on this thin carpet, editing these essays on feminism while Washington wages war against terrorism. Life feels like something broken on purpose. During the Spanish evening news, a man in Afghanistan says, "It was an enemy plane and a woman cried." His words stay with me as if they were a poem. It was an enemy plane and a woman cried. I think of that woman and TV cameras in Colombia, my mother's country. The footage shows bloodied streets and women crying. My mother refuses to look. I can't look away. Her eyes are sad and grateful: my American daughter who can just watch this on TV. My aunt gives us cups of tea and tells me to watch what I say on the phone. Rumors are spreading that the

> FBI is making people disappear. My aunt with the wide smile. She tapes an American flag to my window, determined to keep us safe.
>
> —Daisy Hernández

When we began ... we knew only a little about each other. We were two dark-haired women who moved in overlapping circles of writers, queers, artists and feminists. We had met in New York City through the collective Women in Literature and Letters (WILL), which organized affordable writing programs that were women of color-centered. It was while editing this book, however, that we realized how much a Pakistani-Muslim girl from Queens could have in common with a Catholic, Cuban-Colombian girl from New Jersey.

We both grew up bilingual in working-class immigrant neighborhoods. Our childhoods had been steeped in the religions and traditions of our parents' homelands, and at an early age, we were well acquainted with going through customs, both at home and at the airports. We followed our parents' faith like good daughters until we became women: At fifteen, Daisy left obligatory Sunday mass and Catholicism when a nun said the Bible didn't have to be interpreted literally and no, Noah's ark had never existed. At sixteen, Bushra discovered her body—and stopped praying five times a day.

Of course, there were also differences. Bushra had been raised knowing that violence was as common as friendship between people of color. Her family had moved from Pakistan to New York City to Saudi Arabia to Pakistan and then back to New York City. Daisy, on the other hand, had grown up with white European immigrants who were becoming white Americans, and her familia had only moved from one side of town to the other. We also broke with our families in different ways: Bushra left home without getting married; Daisy stayed home and began dating women.

Our personal rebellions led to a loss of family that took us on another path, where we met other not-so-perfect South-Asian and Latina women also working for social change. It felt like it had taken us a lifetime to find these spaces with women who gave us a feeling of familiarity and of belonging, something that had never been a given in our lives. With these women we could talk about our families and find the understanding that would help us go back home. We began to realize, however, that working with our own was only the groundwork. To make change happen we needed to partner up with other women of color. To work on this book we had to venture out of our safe zones.

And then 9/11 happened. People from our communities turned on each other in new ways. Girls wearing the hijab to elementary school were being slapped by other colored girls. Any mujer dating an Arab man was now suspect in her own community. People we considered friends were now suspicious of Middle Eastern men, Muslims and Arab immigrants, even if they were immigrants themselves. Living near Ground Zero, we watched people respond to their grief and fear with violence that escalated in both action and conversation, and we felt our own fear close to home: Daisy was afraid that, with the surge of pro-American sentiments, her mother would be mistreated for not speaking English, and Bushra feared for her mother and sisters who veil, and for her father and brothers with beards who fit the look of "terrorists."

In response to the war, we wanted to do "traditional" activist work, to organize rallies and protest on the street, but abandoning this book project didn't feel right. Darice Jones, one of our contributors, reminded us of Angela Davis's words: We are living in a world for which old forms of activism are not enough and today's activism is about creating coalitions between communities. This is exactly our hope for this book. Despite differences of language, skin color and class, we have a long, shared history of oppression and resistance. For us, this book is activism, a way to continue the conversations among young women of color found in earlier books like *This Bridge Called My Back* and *Making Face, Making Soul*....

As young women of color, we have both a different and similar relationship to feminism as the women in our mothers' generation. We've grown up with legalized abortion, the legacy of the Civil Rights movement and gay liberation, but we still deal with sexual harassment, racist remarks from feminists and the homophobia within our communities. The difference is that now we talk about these issues in women's studies classes, in classrooms that are multicultural but xenophobic and in a society that pretends to be racially integrated but remains racially profiled.

We have also grown up with a body of literature created by women of color in the last thirty years—Alice Walker's words about womanism, Gloria Anzaldúa's theories about living in the borderlands and Audre Lorde's writings about silences and survival. In reading the submissions for this anthology, we found that it was the books that kept young women of color sane through college, abortions and first romances with women. Many of us just needed the books: We needed another woman of color writing about her fear of loving a dark woman's body or about being black and pregnant and feeling the scarcity of her choices.

In working with the writers in this book, we often thought of Audre Lorde's words from her poem, "A Litany for Survival": *We were never meant to survive.* Who would think that we would survive—we, young girls prey to the hands of men, the insults of teachers, the restrictive laws of holy texts and a world that tells us "this is not your world." For the young women in this book, creating lives on their own terms is an act of survival and resistance. It's also a part of a larger liberation struggle for women and people of color....

We hope that this book will introduce some of the ideas of woman of color feminism to women who have thought that feminism is just a philosophy about white men and women and has nothing to do with our communities. We also want this book to deepen conversations between young women of color. We believe that hearing each other out about our differences and similarities is an important step toward figuring out how to work with whatever divides us....

... As shani jamila writes ... "The most important thing we can do as a generation is to see our new positions of power as weapons to be used strategically in the struggle rather than as spoils of war. Because this shit is far from finished."

10. Rebecca Hurdis, "Heartbroken: Women of Color Feminism and the Third Wave," from *Colonize This!: Young Women of Color on Today's Feminism*

Excerpts from Rebecca Hurdis, "Heartbroken," published in Daisy Hernández and Bushra Rehman, eds., *Colonize This!: Young Women of Color on Today's Feminism* (Seattle: Seal Press, 2002), 279–292. Reprinted by permission of Rebecca Hurdis.

In the following essay, Hurdis draws from the "life of multiplicity" she lives as an "adopted, woman of color feminist." Hurdis argues that third-wave feminism must examine "the intersection of race and gender" and finds in mainstream works of third-wave feminism such as *Manifesta* "the specific history of white (privileged) women.... It is as if their work is the master narrative of feminism, with women of color feminism as an appendage." True third-wave feminism, she argues, is "pushing, expanding and exploding ideologies of multiplicity and intersectionality" so that it will "be a living theory and a way to survive."

This essay isn't just about an adopted, woman of color feminist; rather, it is a story about how I came to believe that I was worthy of all of these identities. It isn't just a story about feminism or solely about adoption. It is an exploration of where the mind stops and the heart follows. It is too easy to distract myself with ideas about "deconstruction" and "critical analysis," terms that lack the emotional depth to explain my experiences. The struggle is not to find one place where I can exist, but to find it within myself to exist in all of these places, uncompromisingly. To live a life of multiplicity is as difficult as it is to write about it.

All of my life I have been told the story of when my mother held me in her arms for the first time. It was late at night at the airport in Newark, New Jersey. My mother, father and two brothers, along with my grandparents and uncle, were all waiting in the terminal lounge for my plane to arrive from Seoul, Korea. There were other families also waiting for their new babies to be brought off the plane. My mother tells me that she watched in anticipation as all the escorts walked off of the plane with small bundles of Korean babies. Each time they walked toward her, they would pass by, giving the babies to other families. My family grew anxious and nervous as the flow of people exiting the plane grew sparse. My chaperone and I were the last to deplane. The woman walked toward my family and placed me in the arms of my mother. I was six months old. I clung to her, put my head on her shoulder, patted her back and called her "mother" in Korean. The year was 1975. The day was Mother's Day.

Growing up in a transracial adopted family, I was often confused by the images of the "normal, nuclear families." We didn't look like any other family

I saw. I couldn't comprehend how I could love my family, feel accepted by them and believe that I belonged to them as much as my phenotypically white brothers. Yet every time I looked in the mirror, my reflection haunted me, because the face that stared back was not the same color as my family's. This awareness was reinforced by the sometimes brutal questions of others. I constantly had to explain that I really was my brother's sister. He was not my husband but truly my brother. I was not the foreign exchange student that just never left. Embarrassed by the attention, I tried to ignore the differences. I took the negativity and dissociation I felt and began to internalize the feelings. I fooled myself into thinking and acting the role of a "good little Asian saved from her fallen country and brought to the land of salvation." I began to believe the messages about being an Asian girl and about being adopted. This compliance was one of the only ways I learned to gain acceptance and validation as a child. I realized that my identity was being created *for* me not *by* me.

When I was ten years old, we moved from a progressive city in Maryland to a small town in Connecticut. Aside from the infamous New England fall foliage, the only color I saw was white. I suppose it wasn't such a radical change for the rest of my family, because they didn't need the difference and diversity I required for spiritual survival. I quickly realized the key to acceptance was to not be too ethnic, or ethnic at all. To be accepted, I had to grasp and identify with whiteness, completely denying my Asian self. I spent my teenage years running away from myself and rebelling from the stereotype of the "good, cute little Asian." The only images of Asian Americans that I saw came from the television. I accepted the misrepresentations as real and accurate because our town only had a few people of color to begin with. I always thought they were the exceptions to the stereotypes. We were the "fortunate ones" and we self-perpetuated the lies about ourselves and about our people.

I fooled myself into believing that life was so great. I was accepted and had all of the things that I thought made me just like everyone else, yet I couldn't understand why I still carried around a sadness. I was playing out the script that had been given to me, yet I kept feeling as though I was in the wrong play. When I would talk to my friends about it, they wouldn't and couldn't understand. I was told that I was making too big a deal out of being Asian and besides I *was* just like everyone else. They thought that I just worried too much. My friends went so far as to convince me by telling me that "I wasn't really Asian, I was white." But the truth couldn't be denied, just as the color of my skin couldn't either. They thought that because we were friends they were entitled or allowed to nickname me "Chinky." They tried to justify it by saying that it was only a joke. My boyfriends were ashamed that they had an Asian-American girlfriend. They assumed they had a right to physically, mentally and sexually abuse me because they thought they were doing me a favor by lowering their standards to be with a woman of color.

I came across feminism as a first-year student at Ohio State University. I was extremely depressed at the time. Everything—my created identity, the world of whiteness that I knew, the denial of my race—that I had worked so hard at repressing and ignoring throughout my life was finally surfacing and emerging. I no longer had the validation of whiteness to protect my false identity. The world that I had understood was changing, and I was confronted with defining myself without the associations of my family and friends. I was forced to step outside of my white world, shedding my blinders to find that I wasn't white and that I had never really been so. The only illusion was the one that I had created for myself, the one that had found acceptance. But I was beginning to realize the cost of this facade.

Yes, I had a large circle of white friends and boyfriends throughout high school. Despite their acceptance, however, I was simultaneously cast as the other. I was undeniably Asian. I was the subject and the object. I was the china doll and the dragoness. The contradictions and the abuse confused me. How could my friends and boyfriends love me, yet in a heated argument spit out "chink" at me? How could they respect me, yet sing the song that had been popularized from the movie *Full Metal Jacket*, "Me So Horny?"

My first women's studies course focused on the history of the women's movement, the social context and the contemporary issues facing feminism today. We looked at issues ranging from violence to sexual orientation to women-centered spirituality to representation in music and film to body image. I began to recognize my extensive history of sexual, mental and physical abuse with boyfriends, and I started to comprehend the cycle of abuse and forgiveness. I was able to begin to stop blaming myself and shift the responsibility back to those who had inflicted the abuse. Initially I had disconnected the abuse from racism, even though it was heavily intertwined and simultaneous. It was just too large for me to understand, and it was still too early for me to grapple with race. I still was thinking that I just needed to become the "right" kind of Asian American and then everything would make sense.

I know that for a lot of women of color, feminism is perceived as being a white woman's movement that has little space or acknowledgment for women of color. I understand how that is true, but back then this class became a catalyst for change and healing. It was a major turning point in my life, where I was able to break my silence and find empowerment within myself and for myself. Women's studies offered me a place where there was validation and reason. I was uncovering and understanding how my own internalization was tied to ideologies of racism and sexism. Although the analysis of racism was somewhat limited in these courses, it served as a lead for future interests. Women's studies and feminism was a steppingstone toward striving for a holistic understanding of myself.

Initially I identified my experiences as being part of a larger discourse and reality. I named the abuse and trauma of my past and could therefore heal from it. I proudly began calling myself a feminist. I viewed feminism broadly as the eradication of sexism, racism, ageism, ableism and heterosexism. It was a social and political commitment to a higher vision for society by resituating women from the margins into the center. I began recognizing and naming what I believed was sexism. The summer after my first women's studies course, I returned home and wrote a dramatic letter to the Congregational church of which I was a member. I earnestly asked them to remove my name from their list because "I did not want to support or be affiliated with a patriarchal institution such as a Christian church." I felt this act was a rite of passage, my initiation into the feminist movement.

But I left college feeling as though there was something missing to this feminism. Professors would talk about Black feminism or women of color feminism, but merely as another mark on their feminist timeline. Little time was dedicated to really examining the intersection of race and gender. Back home I went to my local new-age store (which also doubled as the feminist bookstore) and stumbled on *This Bridge Called My Back: Writings by Radical Women of Color* (edited by Cherríe Moraga and Gloria Anzaldúa). It was the first time I had found a book that had the words "women of color" as part of the title. It was as if I had found the pot of gold at the end of the feminist rainbow. Even though I didn't find myself completely represented in the book, specifically because none of the contributors had been an adopted child, I did find my thoughts, anger and pain represented through the eloquent voices of other women of color. Their writings incorporated race and sexuality.

Reading this anthology, I realized I was entitled to feeling something other than apologetic. I could be angry. I could be aggressive. I could be the opposite of this little china doll that everyone expected me to be. Given my background, this book was life-changing. It represented one of the first moments where I could claim something that was mine; something different from my parents, my friends, my community; something other than whiteness. I remember sitting at the town beach on a hot and humid August day, flipping through the book, my mind exploding and expanding. As I sat there frantically reading, I recall looking up at the sun, closing my eyes and thanking the goddess that I had found this work. Through this discovery I had found that I was not alone. Not only was I feminist, but I was a woman of color feminist.

What makes my relationship to women of color feminism different from most other women of color is how and why I entered the conversation. I began looking at race through gender, where most have the reverse experience. This idea of entry point is crucial. I call myself a woman of color before I call myself an Asian American. It reflects how I have come to see myself and how I understand my own identity. The term "women of color" seems broadly inviting and inclusive while "Asian American" feels rigid and exclusive. Women of color feminism took me from being a victim to being a warrior.

I am now in an ethnic studies graduate program trying to explore if women of color are within feminism's third wave, and if so, where. I began this project as an undergraduate but I had hit a wall. It was difficult locating voices that represented generation X or third wave women of color feminism. Not much had been written, as our voices were just beginning to emerge. I found women of color feminists in alternative places such as zines, anthologies, magazines and pop culture. I felt frustrated that our voices were deemed not "accredited" enough to be represented in the mainstream.

I held a certain expectation for Jennifer Baumgardner and Amy Richards's book, *Manifesta: Young Women, Feminism, and the Future*. This book markets itself as being *the* text for the third wave of feminism, and I had high hopes that it would address issues of race, gender and class sexuality. Instead, I found the specific history of white (privileged) women. This is a great book for the college white woman who has recently been inspired by feminism and wants to know about the past and how she should contribute for the future. Yet this history is complicated by the fact that the authors do not honestly acknowledge that this is their intention. Rather, they assert that this book is a history of all women, dropping the names of such women of color as Rebecca Walker and Audre Lorde.

I found it astounding that there is no extensive discussion of women of color feminism. This indicates that Baumgardner and Richards feel as though this is a separate issue, a different kind of feminism. It is as if their work is the master narrative of feminism, with women of color feminism as an appendage. I had hoped that they would have considered such books as *This Bridge Called My Back* and Audre Lorde's *Sister Outsider* as groundbreaking, as they are deemed by most generation X women of color. These books were life-changing to me not only because their critiques have historical value, but also because what these writers were saying in the 1980s was still relevant in the 1990s. *Manifesta* is successful in creating momentum for young white women's activism through the attempt to move feminism out of academia and back into a social and political movement. But the book's greatest contribution was that it raised a need for creating a lineage for women of color feminism.

Is it possible to construct a feminist genealogy that maintains inclusivity? Does feminism still exist for women of color or is it just a "white thing?" Are generation X women of color participating in feminism? These questions propelled me to further think about the connections as well as the separations between women of color and feminism. In the exploration of the third wave of women of color feminism, I talked to several women of color professors and students at the University of California at Berkeley. Their responses and our conversations together were incredibly helpful. These women challenged me to further think about my own conceptions surrounding feminism.

I had expected that as women of color, most of these students would also identify as women of color feminists. I believed the two terms to be synonymous. Instead, I found a rejection of the word "feminism." I hear many women of color refer to themselves as such, yet they make the distinction that they are not claiming a feminist identity. Although many of the women support and stand in alliance with women of color feminism, there is still a lapse in their chosen identity. Many report to have read the popular and pivotal texts within women of color feminism and have felt moved, but their "empowerment" only goes so far.

What is it about the word "feminism" that has encouraged women of color to stand apart from it? Feminism has been indoctrinated into the academy through the discipline of women's studies. It has moved out of the social and political spaces from where it emerged. Women's studies have collapsed the diversity that was part of the feminist movement into a discipline that has become a homogenous generality. For women in the third wave then, one needs to have the academic training of women's studies to be an "accredited feminist." Once race is added to the complexity, many women of color feel as though the compromise or negotiation is just too high a price to pay to be called a feminist. Women of color's participation in women's studies and feminism still causes splintering in our identities.

Many women believe that there is a certain required persona to be a feminist. In the ethnic studies course "Women of Color in the U.S." at Berkeley, for example, students expressed feeling that they didn't have enough knowledge or background to be able to call themselves feminists. The students' comments reflect how many women of color find difficulty in accessing feminism. Often the response is that "feminism is a white woman's thing." Whiteness in feminism comes to represent privilege, power and opportunity. It rarely positioned women of color as being as legitimate as the identities of white women. Women's studies has been accurately accused of treating race as a secondary oppression through offering courses about race that are separate from the central curriculum, while ethnic studies feel more comfortable as a place to discuss race and gender. But even in ethnic studies, women's experiences and histories still remain on the margins. Like women's studies, they too have had problems integrating gender into the analysis of race.

Women of color often feel women's studies is a battlefield when they are forced to defend their communities and themselves. Women's studies, the academic endeavor of feminism, has a history of relegating women of color as second. When women of color raise issues of race in these classrooms, the response from other students is often defensive and loaded with repressed white guilt. For young women of color, there is a sentiment that we must find a central identity that precedes all others. We are asked to find one identity that will encapsulate our entirety. We are asked to choose between gender, class, race and sexuality and to announce who we are first and foremost. Yet where is the space for multiplicity?

Although I am a self-proclaimed woman of color feminist, I struggle with being an "authentic" woman of color feminist. Even though I realize it is self-defeating, I worry that other women of color will look at my feminism and judge it as being socialized whiteness and an effect of adoption. The roots of my feminism are connected to my adopted mother, although I am uncertain whether she would identify as a feminist. She was a woman who wouldn't let us watch the *Flintstones* or the *Jetsons* because of their negative portrayal of women, yet she unquestionably had dinner on the table every night for her husband, sons and daughter. Most important, she raised me to believe I could be whoever I wanted to be and in that a strong woman. If feminism has been bestowed onto me from my adopted mother, then I choose not to look at it as another indicator of whiteness or of being whitewashed. Rather, I see it as a gift that has shown me not the limitations of mainstream feminism but the possibilities of women of color feminism. People sometimes question my attachment to feminism. Despite the criticisms, it has served as a compass that navigates me away from paralysis into limitless potential.

One of the reasons that my project is now at a standstill is that the conversation has changed. In the 1970s and 1980s women of color feminists seemed to be in solidarity with each other. Their essays showed the racism and classism within mainstream feminism, forcing mainstream feminism to be accountable. Today, however, women of color are focused on the differences that exist among us. When we try to openly and honestly acknowledge the differences between us, we become trapped in difference, which can result in indifference.

Women of color feminism has currently been reduced to a general abstraction that has flattened out difference and diversity, causing tension between women of color. Instead of collectively forming alliances against whiteness, women of color now challenge the opposing identities that exist under the umbrella term "women of color." It raises questions about entitlement and authenticity. It tries to suppress the heterogeneous composition of women of color feminism by trying to create a unifying term. Yet the differences of class, racialization and sexuality have arisen and persisted, challenging assumptions that all women of color are in solidarity with each other. We all come with backgrounds and histories that differ from one another, and despite knowing this, we still maintain this ideal and creation of authentic "women of color." The one that is the right class, the right race, the right sexuality. We must refuse being reduced to an abstraction. We must address the conflicts that have begun to fester paralysis instead of fostering change. But that also means that we need to revitalize women of color feminism so that those actions can begin to take place.

I see women of color feminism at this moment of indifference. I see the backstabbing. I hear the gossip. I feel the tension. We use our words like fists to beat each other down and beat each other silent. It is not pretty and certainly not productive. When do we recognize that the moment has come to move forward? I wish I had some solution of a way to "use our difference to achieve diversity instead of division." But we know that clichés are just clichés. They don't provide us with the fairy-tale endings. They don't make us feel better or more hopeful. More often than not, I think clichés just annoy us and leave us sarcastic.

It is crucial to explore and expose the problems of women of color feminism, but we also need to be weary of what we are willing to sacrifice. I think a new, third space is being created in women of color feminism. Those of us who are not easily recognized and acknowledged as women of color are coming to feminism as a place to discuss the implications of invisibility. We are pushing, expanding and exploding ideologies of multiplicity and intersectionality. We come as transracial adoptees, women of mixed race, bisexuals, refugees and hundreds of other combinations. For us, women of color feminism continues to be a living theory and a way to survive.

11. Deborah L. Siegel, "Reading between the Waves: Feminist Historiography in a 'Postfeminist' Moment," from *Third Wave Agenda: Being Feminist, Doing Feminism*

Excerpts from "Reading between the Waves" by Deborah L. Siegel, published in Leslie Heywood and Jennifer Drake, *Third Wave Agenda: Being Feminist, Doing Feminism* (Minneapolis, MN: University of Minnesota Press, 1997), 55–77. Reprinted with permission.

Siegel's chapter describes the tensions third-wave feminists feel in a cultural context where the media reports continually trumpet the end of feminism, and young women who are saying "I'm not a feminist, but...." Siegel explores the contradictory position of the third-waver, "endlessly indebted yet reluctant to claim certain aspects of second-wave legacies," feminists who disavow postfeminism and "power feminism," feminists rejected by the ideals of mainstream mass media, *and* by second wave predecessors who found the third wave "not feminist enough."

> *For it will not be time to speak of postfeminism until we can legitimately speak of post-patriarchy.* —Nancy Fraser

In the spring of 1995, Gloria Steinem came to my town. When I announced the lecture in my first-year composition class, my students looked at me blankly. "Gloria who?" asked a woman in the front row. At twenty-six, I was baffled to find that my assumption that Steinem mattered was not necessarily shared by a new generation of women. Waiting in line with the other ticket holders on the night of the event, I stared in disbelief as a number of protesters—grown men in baseball caps and plaid shirts—passed out flyers that read, "Take Back the Penis!" Fed up with the tired tactics of the penis gang, on the one hand, and dissatisfied with the number of polls that showed young women supporting feminist issues but rejecting the label, on the other, I took matters into my own hands.

On the morning after Steinem's visit, I headed for the stalls of the women's restroom in the undergraduate library. I scrawled the following question on the bathroom door: "*Is* feminism dead?" My survey has met with indignation. "Is the pope dead?" wrote the first respondent; "Hell no!" added a second; "It'll only die if we let it," scrawled a bird. In the lively debate that followed, anonymous scribbling women struggled with definitions of feminism, challenging assumptions about who can be one: "Can a woman who works at Hooters really be a feminist, as she claims she is?" "If I'm pro-life, can I be pro-feminist?" "What *is* a feminist, anyway?" For an exhilarating week during daily trips to the second stall, I watched as women of the third wave embraced the topic of feminism with the revolutionary fervor of public restroom philosophers. By Friday the bathroom door was covered with query and contradiction, qualification and commitment—a living testimony of feminism's future that would, I think, make Steinem proud. "Feminism," wrote one woman toward the end of the week, "the ability of a woman to transcend barriers of racism, classism, and sexism in order to intellectualize and experience life to the fullest." While this particular forum vanished with a swipe of the janitor's rag, I hope that the third wave will continue to find such unabashedly personal political spaces where we may intellectualize and experience our lives. To me, this is feminism's best legacy. We are not the first generation to contend with penis gangs and disbelievers. Nor will we be the last....

FEMINISM'S DISSENTING DAUGHTERS

In what follows, I will explore the epistemological, ontological, and ethicopolitical assumptions, or the meaning-making apparatus, that inform the works of some of feminism's prominent (published) daughters.... Ideas popularized by Camille Paglia, Naomi Wolf, and Katie Roiphe have contributed to individualistic and depoliticized portrayals of power and victimization. What has yet to be interrogated, however, are the ways in which historiographic discourse is used as a power play in such portrayals.

Positioning themselves as daughters of second wave feminist legacies, twentysomething "pop" authors Naomi Wolf, Katie Roiphe, and Rene Denfeld interrogate their inheritance and incite their age-peers to "reclaim" feminism for the 1990s. Though they differ in the tones they adopt, as well as in the strategies they advocate, these third wave historiographers share the common mission of reclaiming feminism by converting confused or otherwise misguided readers to "good" feminist practice. I have chosen to juxtapose these three populists of American feminism because their tracts are in many ways intertextual and because all three have received substantial media coverage. Denfeld's book *The New Victorians: A Young Woman's Challenge to the Old Feminist Order* has been dubbed the sequel to Roiphe's *The Morning After: Sex, Fear, and Feminism.* Both Denfeld's and Roiphe's texts echo, in some respects, Wolf's *Fire with Fire: The New Female Power and How to Use It.*

Though Wolf and Roiphe have sparred publicly on the pages of the *New York Times*, both are motivated by the desire to reinvent a viable feminism of their own. Dissenting feminist voices participate in a much needed intergenerational conversation at the very moment in which feminist discourses within and outside the academy have taken a self-reflexive turn. Yet the historiographic readings of a social movement that these particular authors produce are severely limited, in that the authors' desires for mastery overwrite any attempt to keep a dialogue moving. In their incorporation of a rhetoric of repossession, in their masterful articulation of "good" feminism, and in their righteous condemnation of a monolithic "bad" feminism, Wolf, Roiphe, and Denfeld make feminist history the story of a product rather than that of a process. In the interest of affirming the difference of the third wave, many third wave narratives assume a metonymic view of the second wave, in which a part of second wave activity is substituted for the whole. If intergenerational dialogue among feminists is to move forward, however, it must move beyond narrative scripts in which a monolithically constructed second wave necessarily becomes the bad mother, for such scripts can only result in paralysis....

... Wolf, Roiphe, and Denfeld ... self-consciously position themselves as authors of interventionist accounts of what and where feminism has been, where it is, and where it should be going. When I look up *wave* in my deskside *Roget's College Thesaurus*, I find myself drawn instead to the next word, *waver*, which means, "vacillate, fluctuate, hesitate, sway, tremble, totter. See DOUBT, OSCILLATION." Although many of us identify with the feminist label, other third wavers waver. To speak of, about, and to the feminisms of my generation, a third wave historiographer would need to ... acknowledge the feminisms of pro-woman women who, for whatever reason, do not identify with the "f" word. My understanding is that many women of my generation reject the "f" word for at least two reasons.

In 1983, Alice Walker coined the word *womanist* to refer to, among other identities, a feminist of color:

> Womanist 1. From *womanish.* (Opp. of "girlish," i.e., frivolous, irresponsible, not serious.) A black feminist or feminist of color. From the black folk expression of mothers to female children, "You acting womanish," i.e., like a woman. Usually referring to outrageous, audacious, courageous, or *willful* behavior. Wanting to know more and in greater depth than is considered "good" for one....
>
> 2. *Also*: A woman who loves other women, sexually and/or nonsexually. ... Traditionally universalists, as in: "Mama, why are we brown, pink, and yellow, and our cousins are white, beige, and black?" Ans.: "Well, you know the colored race is just like a flower garden, with every color flower represented."...
>
> 4. Womanist is to feminist as purple to lavender.

In this context the rejection of the label "feminist" is often code for a rejection of an elitist practice perpetuated by some of feminism's middle-class, heterosexual, white female founders (and their daughters). Here the refusal of the label is a politicized gesture critiquing a feminism that restricts itself to the discussion of a singular idea of oppression derived from the perception of sexual difference as its primary cause. In another context, however, the rejection of the label bespeaks a conservative or perhaps reactionary fear of the radical-lesbian-man-hating-militant stigma, as in, "I'm not a feminist, but I support women's right to social, political, and economic equality." Although there remain, no doubt, multiple and varied rationales for the rejection of the "f" word, Wolf, Roiphe, and Denfeld maintain that the primary reason young women flee from the term today is because the feminist movement has gone seriously awry. The problem? "We feminists" has come to mean, unilaterally and unequivocally, "we victims."

Armed with this explanatory device and inspired by the mission of recuperating feminist agency for the good of all, these three dissenting daughters set out to reclaim the label "for the majority." In their campaign against the "victim mythology" that they argue pervades current organized feminist activism, Roiphe and Denfeld appropriate the phrase "taking back" feminism, a parodic play on the "Take Back the Night" rallies organized by campus rape crisis centers in the 1980s. Although Wolf takes Roiphe to task for her ethically irresponsible coinage of the term "rape-crisis feminism" and for her shameless mockery of the feminist perspectives informing the "Take Back the Night" events, Wolf herself was one of the first to coin the now infamous term "victim feminism." Though they differ in the degree to which they see this "victim" paradigm at work within the ranks of establishment feminism, Denfeld, Wolf, and Roiphe maintain that the regressive obsession of today's feminist leaders with women's victim status is turning young women away from feminism in droves, as is evident in the following representative excerpts from their respective texts:

> Today's feminists are remarkably similar to Victorians in significant ways [such as the way they embark on a moral and spiritual crusade and advocate political helplessness], and not only in their vision of sexuality. This is clear through an examination of several different causes and trends in today's movement that, if anything, are a complete reversal of the movement's progress during the seventies. This is the New Victorianism. And this is why women of my generation are abandoning the women's movement. (Denfeld)
>
> In *Fire with Fire*, I will argue that we are at what historians of women's progress call "an open moment." Twenty-five years of dedicated feminist activism have hauled the political infrastructure into place, enough women in the middle classes have enough money and clout, and all women now have enough desire and determination to begin to balance the imbalance of power between the sexes. But three obstacles stand in our way: Many women and their movement have become estranged; one strand of feminism has developed maladaptive attitudes; and women lack a psychology of female power to match their new opportunities....
>
> I will also point out that victim feminism is obsolete because female psychology and the conditions of women's lives have both been transformed enough so that it is no longer possible to pretend that the impulses to dominate, aggress, or sexually exploit others are "male" urges alone. (Wolf)

> At the most uncharted moments in our lives, we reach instinctively for the stock plots available to our generation, as trashy and cliched as they may be. In the fifties it was love and marriage, or existentialism and Beat poetry in smoky bars. Now, if you're a woman, there's another role readily available: that of the sensitive female, pinched, leered at, assaulted daily by sexual advances, encroached upon, kept down, bruised by harsh reality. Among other things feminism has given us this. A stock new plot, a new identity spinning not around love, not marriage, not communes, not materialism this time, but passivity and victimhood. This is not what I want, not even as a fantasy. (Roiphe)

Call it "power feminism," call it "babe feminism," call it "feminism for the majority," today's populist feminists are rejecting the "obsolete" and "maladaptive," the "Victorian" and the "stock plot fantasies" of their feminist foremothers—and their progeny....

The final section of Wolf's *Fire with Fire*, for instance, bears the heading "What Do We Do Now? Power Feminism in Action." Denfeld includes her own recommendations for action (which, incidentally, include a recommendation to "dump women's studies programs") in a closing chapter entitled "The Final Wave: Reclaiming Feminism." Though I may (and do) profoundly disagree with many of the strategies and changes they advocate, I applaud these writers' efforts to incite a resurgence of feminist activism in an era that badly needs it. (Whereas Roiphe's and Denfeld's impassioned critiques are often uninformed and somewhat appalling, some of Wolf's recommendations are well researched and tremendously appealing.) What is immensely troublesome, however, is the way in which these historiographic diatribes are marketed and received as representative of an entire generation.

Never mind that Roiphe's book grew out of her experiences as a student at Harvard and Princeton, two of the nation's most elite academic institutions. One has only to look at the title of the paperback edition to understand that Roiphe's claim now extends the walls of campus culture. Whereas the original hardcover edition bears the subtitle *Sex, Fear, and Feminism on Campus*, the subtitle of the 1994 paperback edition (which also includes a new introduction) reads, *Sex, Fear, and Feminism*. Further, Roiphe translates her own transparent, "real" experience ("what I see") into historical evidence without genuinely acknowledging the ideological pitfalls of a historiography based on experiential evidence. She relies heavily on personal anecdote, and the result is an uneasy mix of research and reminiscence, a limitation to which she pays lip service in the introduction:

> This book is not a scientific survey of campus life, measuring the immeasurable with statistical certainty. This is not a comprehensive, encyclopedic sociological analysis. It is not a political polemic. I am not a camera.... I cannot offer the objective truth, unfiltered through my own opinion. I have written what I see, limited, personal, but entirely real. I have written my impressions.

In spite of this disclaimer (which is somewhat troubling in and of itself, as Roiphe goes on to generalize from her admittedly limited "real" experience to the Real of history), Barbara Presley Noble celebrates *The Morning After* as "one of the books that defines the Zeitgeist" in an interview with Roiphe published in the *New York Times*. As is evident in the new introduction, in public appearances, and in magazine interviews, Roiphe herself increasingly has come to see her dissenting position as representative of a majority silenced within a supposedly "liberal" feminist society virulently intolerant of dissent. Not surprisingly, Roiphe's celebrants include right-wing commentators such as George Will, who honors what he calls "a bombshell of a book" with a personal endorsement in the preliminary pages of the paperback edition....

... Whereas Wolf's recommendations for a continued feminist future may be genuinely "new" (albeit elitist—hence, old), there is nothing particularly new about Roiphe's and Denfeld's respective challenges to the "old feminist order." The issues may be different, but the condemnation of a burlesqued "feminist order" is the same. The rhetoric with which many of Denfeld's and Roiphe's advocates praise their work is boringly familiar: these two young soothsayers bravely condemn those "smug" (read shrill) "extremists" (read radicals), those "porn-mongering" (read bra-burning) "male-bashers" (read lesbians) who are perpetually angry and embarrassingly sexually repressed. Though today's scary demons have new names—the New Victorians, the victim feminists, the rape-crisis feminists (George Will, take your pick)—those speaking in the name of taking back feminism seem merely to be reproducing a stock antifeminist plot, one that would deliver us all back to a pre-feminist past.

GOOD FEMINISM, BAD FEMINISM

I might respond to the popular reception of and response to these self-identified feminist authors in any number of ways. Yet any response I might offer may be readily countered with the cry that I am merely arguing from the standpoint of an ideologically rigid advocate of victim feminism. Any attempt to engage genuinely and critically with the issues these authors raise may be met with the countercritique that I am merely a smug New Victorian crying backlash. Though these rebellious pundits declare that an entity called "the feminist establishment" is increasingly intolerant of dissent, we seem to be at a deadlock on all sides. Thus, in the hope of creating a space for a genuine intergenerational and *intra*generational dialogue in a moment when the status of feminism is being interrogated within and outside the academy, from the Left and from the Right, I would like to explore the contours of the new—yet old—terminology and rhetoric adopted by these "new" historiographers. Fighting the urge to be equally dismissive, that is, suppressing my desire to wander down to the proverbial riverbank and sling some not-so-proverbial mud, I am really quite interested in the names being called, for name-calling is never a neutral act—politically, ontologically, or epistemologically.

In their attempts to master (and bury) the would-be past of feminist history, Wolf, Roiphe, and Denfeld create sensational, fictional accounts of a demonized feminism to satisfy a "progressive" narrative structure that might be summarized (pace each author's respective rhetorical flourish) as, "Down with the 'bad' feminism and up with the 'good!'" Their critique of the "bad" is often based upon a presupposition of a preexisting ideal of a public sphere that claims to represent all women and thus can be criticized and made answerable for its failure to do so, as is evident in the following passages:

> There are, in essence, two different women's movements alive today. One is a cultural movement, reflected in women's magazines such as *Glamour* ... and expressed in the independent actions of thousands of feminist-thinking women who fight for equality in their lives—such as [Shannon Faulkner, of Citadel fame, and Dallas Malloy, an amateur boxer fighting for women's right to the ring].... But this movement lives primarily in the hearts and minds of women: It isn't organized, and most of its members do not call themselves feminists. That's because that word refers to the *other* women's movement—the organized, ideological form of feminism represented by groups such as NOW, women's studies courses, and feminist leaders. It is this organized women's movement—which defines the feminist label—that is the focus of this book. (Denfeld)

> I'll show that there are and have always been two different approaches within feminism. One—"victim feminism," as I define it—casts women as sexually pure and mystically nurturing, and stresses the evil done to these "good" women as a way to petition for their rights. The other, which I call "power feminism," sees women as human beings—sexual, individual, no better or worse than their male counterparts—and lays claim to equality simply because women are entitled to it. Victim feminist assumptions about universal female goodness and powerlessness, and male evil, are unhelpful in the new moment for they exalt what I've termed "trousseau reflexes"—outdated attitudes women need least right now. (Wolf)

> When I got to Harvard in the fall of 1986 ... I found something called feminism that was unfamiliar to me. The feminism around me in classrooms, conversations, and student journals was not the feminism I grew up with. The Take Back the Night marches and the sexual harassment peer-counseling groups were alien, and even sometimes at odds with what I thought feminism was. All of a sudden feminism meant being angry about men looking at you in the street and writing about "the colonialist appropriation of the female discourse." (Roiphe)

In their reconstruction of a precritically conceived past (and present), Wolf, Roiphe, and Denfeld compose cartoonish caricatures of contemporary feminists and reduce the terms of contemporary feminist debate to the old rhetoric of equality versus difference.

The major flaws of these books, and their greatest danger, is that they set up an image of an atomistic difference-feminism as their straw woman, and although they cogently argue against that image, they fail to realize that what they are advocating in its place is a straw woman with a new hat marked, "Agency! Power! Equality!" (Hey, grrrls—isn't it about time we all get out of the cornfield?) All three argue against what Denise Riley has termed the effeminization or over-feminization of feminism, that is, the emphasis on women's essential weakness or victim status. Writes Michelle Green, for example, in her review of *The New Victorians*, "Like Naomi Wolf in her book *Fire with Fire*, Ms. Denfeld maintains that her contemporaries are weary of being cast as maidens in distress."

Repackaging Wolf's "victim feminist" by dressing her up in Victorian garb, Denfeld argues that an "antimale sentiment has led to what amounts to victim mythology, a set of beliefs that promote women as the helpless victims of masculine oppression." As both Victorianist scholar Gertrude Himmelfarb and feminist commentator Katha Pollitt suggest in their respective analyses of Denfeld's book, Denfeld's representation of Victorian culture is historically inaccurate (Himmelfarb) and politically out of vogue (Pollitt). Similarly, Denfeld's descriptions of what she repeatedly refers to as "the feminist school of thought" are, like many popular descriptions of feminist positions, simplified and overstated. Caricaturing feminism (in the singular) as a naïve movement that has not much changed since the early 1970s, Denfeld and her cohorts fail to note the complexity and the diversity of current feminist modes of thinking.

It seems odd, given their search for an alternative to "victim feminism," that these authors do not more carefully acknowledge and build on the work of feminist theorists such as Linda Gordon, a historian known for her resistance to a "victim" paradigm of women's history and for her advocacy of a complicated notion of social control that promotes the analysis of ways in which women maneuver within the specific constrictions they face. It seems equally odd, given their commitment to reclaiming feminism for the majority, that they do not acknowledge and build upon the work of African American historians and literary critics such as Hazel Carby and Barbara Christian, who document ways in which African American women historically have retained a tremendous sense of agency from within multiple matrices of oppression. These omissions are not surprising, however, given the fact that all three historiographers are eager to differentiate their work from a demonized straw woman named feminist theory.

Attacking academic feminisms, which she lumps together under the nicknames "club feminism" and "insider feminism," Wolf blames feminist academics for being irresponsibly irrelevant:

> The prose style of the best feminist academic thinking ensured that the most fashionable and influential ideas would be drained of relevance

> to the real world of politics and action, and would be couched in what, to the millions of women and men outside the ivied gated who had not incentive to master an exclusive and elaborate professional jargon, amounted to pig Latin.

Whereas Denfeld clumsily blames New Victorians for having "climbed out on a limb of academic theory that is all but inaccessible to the uninitiated," Roiphe parodically nicknames her feminist seminars "The Mad Hatter's Tea Party." According to all three, theory is the refined instrument of feminist fascism; theory exists in, of, and for itself; theory exists independently from actual feminist movements and causes; that is, feminism rallied around specific, "real-world" actions and claims.

It is, of course, misleading for Wolf, Roiphe, and Denfeld to market their historiography as free of "theory" and "ideology." Yet they do. In the promotional blurb from the *National Review* that graces Roiphe's book, the reviewer markets the book as "Unpretentious [read theory-free] ... a fast, entertaining read. Hooray for Katie Roiphe!" Like Roiphe, Denfeld dispenses the obligatory disclaimer to those who would take her observations as "scientific" analysis, but she then proceeds to generalize from her experience and to theorize about the needs and wants of a generation: "Throughout this book, you will hear voices from other women of my generation.... I sought these women out in a variety of places, and I make no claim that I conducted anything even remotely resembling a scientific survey. But I do think these women speak for many." Though these authors may claim otherwise, science-free does not mean theory-free or methodless.

In defense of the multiple sites, forms, and functions of theorizing, as bell hooks and Katie King argue from their different academic contexts, theory (pretentious and unpretentious) takes many forms. In her analysis of how academic machinery often privileges theory made by certain individuals and leaves others uncredited or unacknowledged, King theorizes a warning against a metonymic view of the production of theory that seems relevant to the discussion at hand, and thus worth repeating in full:

> An error feminists make over and over is to mistake the *part* of a particular theoretical reading, especially a published reading, for the *whole* of the many forms theorizing takes: active thinking, speaking, conversation, action grounded in theory, action producing theory, action suggesting theory, drafts, letter, unpublished manuscripts, stories in writing and not, poems said and written, art events like shows, readings, enactments, zap actions such as ACT UP does: or for that matter, incomplete theorizing, sporadic suggestiveness, generalizations correct and incorrect, inadequate theory, images and actions inciting theoretical interventions, and so on. It's not that all human actions are equivalent to theorizing, but rather that a particular product of many forms of theorizing should not be mistaken for the processes of production itself.

Though they voice a genuine (and justified) concern that theory, as a democratic tool, should be accessible to many, by engaging in the unilateral and ever popular sport of theory-bashing, Wolf, Roiphe, and Denfeld play into an anti-intellectualism that banishes theory as something "they"—not "we"—do.

In an essay entitled "Theory as Liberating Practice," hooks argues that critical thought predicated upon "lived theorizing" closes the gap between theory and practice. Though she acknowledges that not all theory is "inherently liberatory, or revolutionary" and that theory "fulfills this function only when we ask that it do so and direct our theorizing towards this end," she nevertheless acknowledges the possibility that theory can function as (lived) critical intervention. According to hooks, theory can be the act of "making sense out of what [is] happening," a sanctuary where one might "imagine possible futures, a place where life could be lived differently." Theory takes multiple forms and often transpires in unlikely places. In their passionate embrace of my question on the back of the restroom door, for instance, the women of the undergraduate library were practicing—and living—theory.

Although Wolf, Roiphe, and Denfeld profess an interest in thinking and living the feminist life differently, it seems that the energy behind these texts is deconstructive (in the sense of destructive) rather than reconstructive, with Wolf's how-to manual being an important exception. Roiphe closes the body of her text on a note of rejection: "This is not what I want, not even as a fantasy." If Roiphe spends 180 pages denouncing rape-crisis feminists, Denfeld devotes a full 279 (not counting the last 14 pages of recommendations for action) to a full-force demonization of the New Victorians. In the introduction to *The New Victorians*, Denfeld specifies the "organized women's movement," the one that "defines the feminist label," as the focus of her book, yet one wonders why she does not foreground instead the exemplary actions of the so-called silenced majority; that is, "the independent actions of thousands of feminist-thinking women who fight for equality in their lives," the unorganized movement that "lives primarily in the hearts and minds of women." In the closing paragraph of her book, Denfeld (smugly?) pouts, "If there were a movement that addressed [young women's] concerns, we would gladly call ourselves feminists." To this I might reply, there exists such a movement. Young women, adding their voices to those of their foremothers, are continuing to imagine feminist futures—on restroom doors and elsewhere....

In June 1994, a review of five recently published books assessing and critiquing women's movements in the United States, playfully entitled "Sisterhood Was Powerful," is published in the widely distributed newsmagazine *Newsweek*. On December 22, 1994, PBS airs William F. Buckley Jr. hosting an edition of *Firing Line* wishfully entitled "Resolved: The Women's Movement Has Been Disastrous." Popular feminists appear on TV talk shows responding to the question "Is feminism dead?" The publication of *Fire with Fire*, *The Morning After*, and *The New Victorians*, then, roughly coincides with the pronouncement by the mainstream media and by conservative pundits that we are living in a "postfeminist" era.

I place the term "postfeminist" in quotation marks intentionally, for I am afraid of the popular connotations, and the ideological implications, of this trendy little neologism. When invoked in the popular press, "postfeminist" most often describes a moment when women's movements are, for whatever reasons, no longer moving, no longer vital, no longer relevant; the term suggests that the gains forged by previous generations of women have so completely pervaded all tiers of our social existence that those still "harping" about women's victim status are embarrassingly out of touch. Like Friedman, who notes that "The Montreal massacre of fourteen women gunned down as 'feminists' because they were women in an engineering class hammered home the message that women, as women, are not safe, because they are women," I insist that this world is emphatically not beyond the need for feminisms.

In an October 1993 interview published in *Glamour*, reporter Judith Stone asks Roiphe whether she sees the oppression of women as part of the fabric of American life. Roiphe responds, "No. I don't choose to, maybe. I don't think it's constructive. There are parts of this society in which it is true, but I'm talking about the people I know." Aside from the fact that Roiphe's sense of social justice and equity is unconstructively elitist and devastatingly naïve, she is not alone in her adoption of a classist historiographic method. Roiphe's statement echoes Wolf's claim that "enough women in the middle classes now have enough money and clout," that "all women now have enough desire and determination to begin to balance the imbalance of power between the sexes," that "twenty-five years of dedicated feminist activism have hauled the political infrastructure into place," and that "power feminism" is the way to go. Although Wolf's model of "power feminism" may be a hope for the future that can be readily practiced by privileged women today, I find myself questioning Wolf's belief that a feminist infrastructure is currently firmly in place. Is it really time to say "enough"? The tone of current debates about welfare reform, teenage pregnancy, and affirmative action would suggest that there is still quite a long way to go before we can ethically say "enough."

Denfeld echoes both Roiphe and Wolf when she argues that because some gains have been institutionalized for the already enfranchised, we no longer have a need for the word *victim*; what the matter really comes down to, according to Denfeld, is choice:

> We have it much better now than our mothers ever did....
>
> For women of my generation, feminism is our birthright. While sexism may still permeate society, we know what it is to live without excessive confinement. We are the first generation to grow up expecting equal opportunity and equal education, as well as the freedom to express our

> sexuality. We are the first to assume what feminists had to force society to accept against its deeply ingrained prejudice: that we are the equals of any man. This belief may translate into the pursuit of a career or it may mean demanding respect for raising children—women of my generation believe in the right to choose.

To whom, I ask, are "we" referring?

Desperately needing to read beyond these premature (and presumptuous?) calls (and wishes?) for "the end" of "victim feminism," I find myself in the position of wanting to reclaim the term "victim." Although Wolf, Roiphe, and Denfeld would drain claims to victimhood of any semblance of agency, the radical act of pronouncing oneself victim to systemic inequity does not necessarily amount to a defeatist confession of utter weakness. In many instances, to name oneself "victim" is an articulation of strength, for to give a name to the injustices that continue to oppress is to adamantly refuse victim status. A feminist philosophy or theory that advocates such naming actions is not operating from the confines of a victim paradigm. In my desire to break through the racist, classist, sexist, heterosexist, ageist ties that continue to bind, I am not a "victim feminist." I am a feminist activist who actively refuses to be a victim.

I cannot tolerate the thought of those purporting to "take back" feminism taking it back from me, for feminism was never mine alone to begin with. Feminists of different stripes must stop jockeying for control and ownership, must cease mistaking each other for the enemy, must begin to forge links with their feminist predecessors, if movement is to continue moving forward. As a young woman committed to the continuation of feminist revolution within and outside the academy, I am both inspired and burdened by the knowledge that there is so much moving left to do, so much history left to make. I feel the weight of generations upon me, and I wonder, with increasing urgency, just how "we" are going to find the words, and the movements, to make it.

12. Candis Steenbergen, "Talkin' 'bout Whose Generation?!," from *Turbo Chicks: Talking Young Feminism*

Excerpts from "Talkin' 'bout Whose Generation?!" by Candis Steenbergen, published in Allyson Mitchell, Lisa Bryn Rundle, Lara Karaian, eds., *Turbo Chicks: Talking Young Feminism* (Toronto: Sumach Press, 2001), 256–271. Reprinted with permission.

Tackling the vexing question of feminist "generations," in this essay Steenbergen discusses how generational labels reduce the complications of feminism and unnecessarily divide feminists against each other. Although she argues that there is a specific third-wave sensibility, especially as feminism is under so much attack in the larger culture, she calls for solidarity and dialog between Boomers and Gen-Xers, the second wave and the third.

I was born in 1972. Over the course of the last decade, that date has bestowed upon me an almost instant identity: cohorts based on population data; a supposed apathy towards inequality, injustice, politics, economics and culture; overeducation; underemployment; an inclination to navel-gaze; and a bleak outlook on the future. I was also born female. The result of that genetic lottery expanded my prescribed selfhood even more. I am a beneficiary of a still-rigid sexual code, successor of the women's movement; a daughter of the Sexual Revolution; a "modern woman." At some time between my birth and right now, I had my feminist "click." Since that moment, I have watched—largely in amazement—my identity augment even more. At twenty-seven, if popular rhetoric is to be believed, I am already an elder member of the new feminism. Power-feminism. Career feminism. "Do-me" feminism. Lipstick feminism. Babe feminism. Dissident feminism. Capitalist feminism. Consumer feminism. Post-modern feminism. Millennium feminism. According to mainstream media over the last few years, these tags, and variations on them, define members of my feminist cohort. These labels characterize the "new faces" of feminism and, in effect, popularly identify "the next generation" of the women's movement.

Sweeping generalizations based on demographic affiliation are nothing new. The number of babies born from 1946 to 1964 is North America has held the interest of futurists, historians and journalists alike, and the aging, influence and affluence of the "baby boom" continues to receive public attention. The "Woodstock generation," the "revolutionaries," the "radical" counterculture of the 1960s successfully transformed popular culture and rapidly became the focus group of virtually every institution: from government and education, to advertising and television programming. Due, in part, to the enormity of the baby boom's size and also to the tumultuous political environment (manifested both at home and abroad), the decade of the 1960s has come to be known as one of the great mythological eras of modern times. In retrospect, the baby boom grew to fulfill "a special historical destiny," and the social, cultural and economic experiences of an entire group of North Americans were branded into history.

By the early 1990s, the generation born after the baby boom—mine—received its very own label: Generation X. Douglas Coupland's best-seller, *Generation X: Tales for an Accelerated Culture* (published in 1991), launched a media catch phrase that swiftly and effectively classified an entire group of people born in the late 1960s and early 1970s. Remarkably different from their predecessors in size and (apparently) values, the generation entering adulthood in the midst of an economic recession and a neoconservative environment seemed to be plagued by contradiction, and mainstream media scrambled to define them. Speculation and analysis of the new generation abounded, and popular understanding of the successors of the baby boom was illustrated through the application of even more dubious tags: the Baby Busters, the Lost Generation, the 13th Generation, Generation Redux, twentynothings, Generation Why?, Generation After (after the 1960s, after it all happened), Generation Ecch!, The Recycled Generation, and the like.

Nine years and an equal number of publications later, Coupland's epithet has endured the media bombardment of features and editorials concerning the plight of an entire generation destined to be little more than apathetic slackers; a group of people with "no identity, standing for nothing, and going for nothing." While media fascination with the "Baby Boom vs. Generation X" phenomenon has long since evaporated into little more than a marketing tool for financial investors, the generational descant surrounding feminism and the women's movement seems to be picking up speed. Announcing the arrival of a young, independent, confident, sexually free and aggressive generation of women into the public sphere, popular discourse has exalted the victory of women's liberation and, consequently, professed the imminent death of feminism. At first gloss, it appears as though North America, at the turn of the new century, has entered a "post-feminist" era.

In the summer of 1998, the cover of *TIME Magazine* featured black and white photos of the antiquated faces (and, in effect, perspectives) of Susan B. Anthony, Betty Friedan and Gloria Steinem next to the fresh, full-colour visage of the fictional prime-time television character Ally McBeal. Under McBeal lay the question "Is Feminism Dead?" The cover story by Ginia Bellafante announced that a new generation of "enlightened" women has emerged, actively promoting a new version of "female empowerment":

> ... feminism at the very end of the century seems to be an intellectual undertaking in which the complicated, often mundane issues of modern life get little attention and the narcissistic ramblings of a few new media-anointed spokeswomen get far too much.... What a comedown for the movement.... But if feminism of the 60s and 70s was steeped in research and obsessed with social change, feminism today is wed to the culture of celebrity and self-obsession.

Ginia Bellafante argued that the next generation of feminists is concerned with little more than individual gain, the consumption of material goods and the exertion of their own "enlightened" power and concluded that the insurgence of young self-absorbed women has contributed to the "flightiness" of feminism at the millennium. Critics argued that *TIME* failed to look at the larger picture and that Bellafante consciously selected very particular written materials as "proof" of the current apolitical, post-feminist climate. According to Marcia Ann Gillespie, editor of Ms. *Magazine*, the failure to mention the activism and written work of young feminists was intentional, and that the lack of interviews with "any of the many women of that generation who are doing righteous work" was another indication of the media's misunderstanding and misrepresentation of the women's movement itself.

My Definition of Feminism

To me, feminism means so many things. It is the theoretical framework I unknowingly adopted in an undergraduate politics class remarkably

> low on other women; it is the still-evolving history that continues to teach me about the intersections of sexuality, age, race, class and ability; it is my language, my politics and the cause of some of the most heated discussions I've ever had. It is the internal wince reacting in situations where it's probably best to keep my mouth shut; a pejorative tag stuck to my forehead; an often contradictory, complicated and downright frustrating paradigm, a fluid and flexible (and often context-specific) praxis that encompasses the bizarre multiplicity of things I've felt, seen, learned, purchased, listened to, wrote, read and still hope to experience.

Heterosexual, white, able-bodied, well-educated, financially successful, aggressive and overtly sexual women have received an enormous amount of print space and air time for their assertions that women in the 1990s have "made it." Emerging in mass-market books, works of fiction, in glossy magazines and on television, such women (even the fictitious ones) have been touted as the heirs of the sexual revolution and, more often than not, the new faces of feminism. Post-feminist texts present the women's movement as the mastermind behind stringent sexual and moral codes, as the promoter of a villain-versus-victim mythology, and as antiquated protectors of "political correctness." Feminists (on the whole) are portrayed as anti-men, anti-sex and obsessed with notions of women as hapless victims. The post-feminist herself, however, is the antithesis of the second-wave stereotype: she is "successful and independent, and less likely to espouse 'dangerous' feminist ideals."

By way of particularly (and often personally) nasty criticisms of feminism and its proponents and the clever manipulation of celebrity, power and the authority to speak publicly (bestowed by mainstream media), post-feminism has chic, inoffensive, commercial qualities. It is an easily absorbed, painless product for the public to consume. As bell hooks has commented, "like any other 'hot' marketable topic, feminism has become an issue that can be opportunistically pimped by feminists and non-feminists alike." Post-feminist ideology has been, to date, analytically weak but, surprisingly, rhetorically persuasive. Based on the presumption that equal opportunities for all women are a reality, their texts celebrate the successes of certain women in previously male-dominated realms. In doing so, post-feminists render the oppression of marginalized women even more invisible and undermine the ongoing history of the women's movement as a whole. As Maglin and Perry have noted, "while their individual messages vary ... the overall effect of their work is to suggest that because some women have prospered, the systematic inequalities facing all women have vanished into history."

In the spring of 1999, Germaine Greer, one of western feminism's more noted spokespersons, published *The Whole Woman*, the book she had said she would never write. Presenting a harsh critique of the current state of the women's movement, Greer thrashed contemporary feminists and feminisms:

> The future is female, we are told. Feminism has served its purpose and should now eff off. Feminism was long hair, dungarees and dangling earrings; postfeminism was business suits, big hair and lipstick; post-post-feminism was ostentatious sluttishness and disorderly behaviour. We all agree that women should have equal pay for equal work, be equal before the law, do no more housework than men do, spend no more time with children than men do—or do we?

Greer devoted a small portion of her text to young women's misguided (non) participation in the women's movement. In less than ten pages, the feminist icon added her perception of the latest generation of young women to a list of what she called "false starts and blind alleys" in feminism's history. Greer erroneously correlated Riot Grrrl activism in the 1990s and the Girl Power of the Spice Girls and discarded both as mediocre facsimiles (corrupted by corporate media) of 1970s-style rockers Vivienne Westwood and Chrissie Hynde. Independent pro-feminist zines were mentioned with nostalgia, and Greer stated that the "fossilized remains of the feminist fanzines" can only be found buried deep (or in an appropriated commercial form) in the pages of glossy fashion magazines and on television. Young women's activity in cyberspace was limited to one Internet site: Australia's "Geekgirl." Essentially, Greer negated the struggles of young feminists with her own mainstream feminist privilege: the power to dictate feminist membership, the control over deciphering "good" feminism and "bad" feminism, and the ability to captivate a popular audience. Consequently, young feminist attempts at activism were dismissed as a "cultural phenomenon" amounting to little more than the recycled work of "kinderwhores."

Similar, more subtle sentiments can be found in Canada as well. In October of 1999, prominent feminist journalist and social commentator Michele Landsberg wrote an article on a progressive young woman who was earnestly involved in the eradication of child labour in Nepal. Landsberg characterized this woman and her colleagues as "liv[ing] outside the anxious clatter of consumer culture," and contrasted them with youths who more often capture the attention of the mainstream media: youths who party at "all-night raves," those with "tongue-piercing," and users of "illicit drugs." With a sweeping generalization of an entire generation in her opening line, Landsberg discounted the work of young feminist activists who have been vigorously engaged in complex critiques of popular culture and consumerism. Because they do not fit the description of "clear-eyed, bright activist youths," women who work outside the realm of a prescribed definition of "feminist activism" remain invisible.

Both Greer and Landsberg expressed (explicitly and implicitly) their frustration with the seemingly unsympathetic and apolitical generation of women following in their wake. The "parent generation," which Greer labels herself and her contemporaries, has not (as yet) recognized that a younger, activist and unmistakably feminist generation of women has emerged in recent years. To many, they exist solely as spotlight-hungry post-feminists. To others, they simply do not exist at all. Greer asserts that women at the millennium are in crisis and expresses her distress over the prevalence of apathy in contemporary feminism. She declares that "it's time to get angry again." But young feminists *are* angry. And vocal. And active. The problem, as many self-described third-wave feminists would attest, is that no one has been listening.

It is plain to see why post-feminists have received more mainstream visibility and public attention than the diverse struggles and accomplishments of third-wave feminists. Glamourous, media-friendly icons are more fitting illustrations for items reporting the women's movement's "cat-fights," and declarations of feminism's decline make far better copy than accurate representations of burgeoning activism among young women. Although it is easy and trendy (and very tempting) to blame the media for the mass promulgation of post-feminism, a more realistic assessment of the current circumstances would also recognize that pop culture reflects (with a heavily distorted lens) the ever-changing ideological climate of its host. A new generation of young feminists has emerged in recent years—and the tension that often marks relationships between generations is alive and well—but the true "generation gap" in the contemporary women's movement has eluded both mainstream and feminist commentators to date.

The intergenerational hostility within the ranks of the women's movement at the current time is indeed grounded in the successes of feminism itself. I certainly grew up in an environment remarkably different than my feminist foremothers. In many ways, I am a "daughter of feminism": mine is the first generation of women able to benefit directly from the accomplishments of the contemporary women's movement (to put this into perspective: I was born exactly eleven months after the birth of Ms. *Magazine*). Access to and participation in previously male-dominated realms and a broad spectrum of legal rights were facets of my growth that I've taken for granted, not battles that I have fought. I enrolled in courses in established (but impoverished) Women's Studies departments, learned the theories and the histories, and actively sought to fit a feminist framework into my work in other disciplines and in my everyday world. In many ways, feminism is my birthright, and I do feel a sense of entitlement as a result. However, my reality has also been shaped by a multitude of other concerns; some new, others persistent: HIV/AIDS, date rape drugs, neo-conservatism, advancements in information and communication technology, increased commercialism, post-feminism, racism, homophobia, poverty and the spread of pop culture influences. The world has changed immensely in the last quarter-century, and young feminists like myself have inherited a complex social environment, an increasingly complicated women's movement and an unfinished sexual revolution.

The third wave is still very much in the process of emerging, but it is nevertheless an active, if amorphous, group. After all, third wavers are writing zines, publishing on-line ezines, contributing to magazines of the mainstream and alternative varieties, geurilla stickering, postering, graffiti writing, boycotting, critiquing both mass media generally and popular culture specifically, negotiating and re-negotiating relationships, contemplating the contradictions of sexuality, challenging paradigms, questioning dogma and resisting, resisting, resisting in their own innumerable private and public ways. While there are few organizational structures surrounding them as a "wave" (outside of the National Action Committee's Young Women's Caucus or the Third Wave Foundation in the US), there is a shared concern for the agency, rights and status of women at this transitional moment in history. In many ways, they are an ideological generation.

But that doesn't make the third wave any less legitimate or any more apathetic; it simply translates into the development of a movement that looks markedly different than what has come before. A movement that is resisting both in reaction to and in conjunction with the confused and confusing world in which we currently live. But common threads can still be found in the feminist work of younger women. Their written work to date has indicated an ardent interest in sexuality, body politics and pop culture. An ever-increasing number of young scholars, writers, artists, activists and critics of the mass media have attempted to link the allure of (and their participation in) the hyper-sexualized culture of consumerism and consumption with their identities as women, sexual beings and feminists. Jennifer Drake writes:

> Third Wave women talk a lot about pleasure. This could be because we're young or because we're such well-trained consumers or because we're into some kind of playful postmodern aesthetic or because we watched too much TV growing up, but I can't dismiss this, for it's such a hunger and a joy in Third Wave texts ... clearly, the pleasure seeking impulse makes its unruly way through the personal and political play with sex/uality, but it also consistently informs Third Wave claims to feminism itself.

That focus, I would argue, has contributed to their invisibility as legitimate members of the women's movement. Reviewing and critiquing the shortcomings of the so-called "Sexual Revolution" of the 1960s has only been part of that analysis; another has been to respond to and attempt to counter the post-feminist persona, and yet another has been to demystify the power of the popular media. Although representations of sexually confident, seemingly "empowered" women hold considerable allure, third-wavers would agree that "a sexualized society does not guarantee sexual pleasure for individuals." As such, the realities of women's lived experiences must be acknowledged:

> Consumption does not simply represent "the power of hegemonic forces in the definition of women's role as consumer," but rather "is a site of negotiated meanings, of resistance and of appropriation as well as of subjection and exploitation." Along with this concern with consumption, there is the related attempt to analyze gender in the context of other dimensions of power such as class and race, thereby building upon the foundations laid by socialist feminism.

That negotiation process, between the alluring, pre-packaged, advertised and purchased version of femininity and the difficulties of translating it into a lived reality in our current cultural climate, is paramount to the future of feminism. To many third wavers, those pursuits have revolved around continual self-analysis and personal negotiation, an attempt to reconcile a desire to create their own version of "femininity" and their fear of betraying their allegiance to feminism and the struggle for female empowerment.

While "some second-wave feminist angst has fixed itself on what 'younger feminists' are doing (or not doing) to and with the achievements of the 1970s and 1980s," the third wave is struggling with the task of defining feminism for themselves. That has necessitated not only the deconstruction of stereotypes, traditional assumptions and strategies, but also the active redefinition and renaming of women's disparate conditions in the process of expanding the meaning of feminism to include and bring together diverse perspectives. Many young women have attempted to incorporate differences, tackle inconsistencies of thought and modes of activism, and confront the seemingly irreconcilable paradoxes of what constitutes feminism today. Having their ideas recognized, validated or legitimized, however, has been an even tougher challenge. Fenella Porter explains how this has affected her as a daughter:

> This is clearly because their experience and the way in which they see their identity as women does not fit into the linear structure of the women's movement as it has been defined by our mothers. Nor does it fit into the definition of "feminism" as it has been defined and lived by our mothers. Feminism, if it is to include the experience of all women, needs to be much more diverse and complicated—uncontrollable even.

Charges by the second wave that younger women are "reinventing the wheel" and comments suggesting that there is "nothing new" about young feminist approaches have become almost commonplace. Although the "mainstreaming" of feminist thought and the "professionalization" of feminist organizations affirms the accomplishments of the movement as a whole, authority structures within its ranks have been created that must be acknowledged. As self-described third waver Devoney Looser asserts, "younger feminists are not counterfeits in the face of the older and more genuine article. We are not the badly manufactured copies of second-wave originals." We are only doing our feminism the way we have learned: by questioning, critiquing and challenging what we know.

Young feminists exist as a new wave within the ongoing history of the women's movement; a generation addressing, in various ways, the complexities of young women's everyday experiences and the personal and structural relations affecting them. Their comments and criticisms are intended to improve the status of women and to move feminism forward, not to slander the movement or its proponents. Nonetheless, solidarity (in any form) with their predecessors has been difficult to attain. As Rebecca Walker notes, third wavers "have a very different vantage point on the world than that of our foremothers. We shy away from or modify the label in an attempt to articulate our differences while simultaneously avoiding confrontation." But perhaps confrontation is precisely what is needed. One of the distinguishing features of feminism has been the synergy of the personal and the political, the connection between women's personal experience and the political context within which it is organized. Members of the early women's liberation movement took pride in "listening to each woman's experience and respecting her decisions." Dialogue—open, mutually-respectful discussions conducted with strong, shared objectives between and among the waves—stands as one possibility of bridging feminism's generation gap. As Imelda Whelehan suggests, "the legacy of radical feminist politics provides, perhaps, the strongest potential for both defense and counter-attack."

Threats to contemporary feminism have been aggressive and insidious, and the public demonstration of a strong women's movement, one which supports the interests of women of all sexual orientations, ages, colours, ethnicities, abilities, education, and economic backgrounds, has become an important and immediate endeavour. The decade preceding the millennium has experienced persistent calls for a re-evaluation of the last thirty years of feminism. At present, as Vicki Coppock, Deena Haydon and Ingrid Richter have noted, "feminism is learning to reconstitute itself as a social force that takes account of women's differences rooted in experiential identities." The time has come, strategically, for feminists to reexamine both the accomplishments and setbacks that have occurred over time. That will require in-depth investigations of the challenges facing contemporary feminism: those of privilege, participation and control.

The generation known as the baby boom assumed epic proportions largely, in retrospect, through the oversimplification of events by the mainstream media and grandiose accounts of "the decade of the sixties" by members of the cohort. The "Baby Boom v. Gen X" war has, in actuality, been waged by a limited number of people. Anecdotal descriptions of "the way it was" and historical accounts of the "Swingin' Sixties" have generally been created, perpetuated and maintained by those with a voice: frequently white, well-educated, heterosexual, middle-class scholars and media. Generation X, a smaller and infinitely less influential generation in terms of broad structural change, has been besieged with simple descriptions and unjust comparisons to their large predecessor. Some members of the younger generation like Kiké Roach, have responded swiftly to such condemnations:

> People of my age have been branded "Generation X" and accused of apathy and indifference. But our realities, anxieties, and accomplishments cannot be summarized or symbolized by a letter in the alphabet. Activism is not unique to any generation. It is not the property of the sixties, although there are a lot of important lessons to be drawn from that time. Progressive young people do exist, and there is still reason for us to organize.

And others remain silent and invisible, resisting, organizing, waiting for time to pass and for new histories to be written. Until thorough re-evaluations of our current moment in time occur, narratives on post-feminism, the decline of feminism and the apolitical tendencies of my generation will undoubtedly remain "truths" within the pages of history texts and people's minds. I suspect that the real story has not yet been told, and that we will see, years from now, the beginnings of a strong, unprecedented, revolutionary movement rooted in the "untraditional" mobilizing and activism happening at the turn of the twenty-first century.

Never thought I'd say this, but I can't wait to get older.

13. Anita Harris, "Not Waving or Drowning: Young Women, Feminism, and the Limits of the Next Wave Debate," from *Outskirts: Feminisms along the Edge*

Excerpts from "Not Waving or Drowning: Young Women, Feminism, and the Limits of the Next Wave Debate," *Outskirts* 8 (May 2001): 1–9. Reprinted with permission.

In this key article, one of the first to theorize differences in second- and third-wave activism, Harris argues that global consumer technoculture has profoundly affected activist strategies. Harris argues that young women's ways of conducting political organization, protest, debate, and agitation have been shaped in response to "the co-optation of left politics as merely a marketable style.... The trend toward an increased surveillance of youth, the re-discovery of young women in particular as the new consumers, and the cultural fascination with girlhood, have all resulted in a deep suspicion of overt activism as the best method for protest and the creation of social change." Instead, third-wave activism uses and resists mainstream by creating its own media sites and networks, and the constitution of third wave as a dispersed and diverse movement, as opposed to a single-leader and single-issue movement, is necessary for survival in global technoculture. Third-wave feminism, by necessity, is part of these struggles that go beyond gender because our world—our very beings—have been shaped not by patriarchy but by transnational, economic forms: the WTO, the IMF, NAFTA. What looks like the disappearance of feminist activism is really its reformulation.

Debate over the 'next wave' has contributed to particular representations of young women and their relations to feminism. This debate has framed competing discourses about young feminists as 'power feminists' fighting 'victim feminism', girl-powered Do-It-Yourselfers developing a new style of sassy, in-your-face feminism, or the 'third wave' simply grasping the baton from the previous generation. Young women are primarily constructed (and many construct themselves) through these discourses as rejecting victimhood and instead seizing power. Here I argue that these kinds of claims about the nature of young feminism emerge out of a context within which girls have become cultural symbols of change, risk and danger. The desire to frame young feminism around the concept of power is in part a consequence of the overdetermination of girlhood as a container for cultural anxieties about social change. However, these (competing) claims about the ways young feminism rejects victimhood, and the attempt to homogenise young feminism into a single and identifiable 'wave' around the idea of power tends to obscure this context within which young women's lives have taken on new cultural meanings.

Further, the diversity of young women's political engagements, particularly those for whom the terms of this debate lack immediacy and meaning, can be lost in the process. This paper thus also seeks to map out the complexity, diversity and dynamism both within the category of young women and in terms of their feminist politics beyond the terms of the next wave debate. I suggest that the feminism lived by many young women is constituted in diverse, networked, global, and interconnected praxis. To move out of the victim/power framework of the next wave debate, I would argue that young women are not necessarily 'waving', but nor are they therefore 'drowning' as a consequence. Although their feminisms cannot be contained within the terms of a singular 'next wave' movement, young women, in their diversity and through a range of strategies, are passionately engaged with improving the lives of girls and women globally. However, it is only by acknowledging the limitations of a closed category such as the 'next wave' that this engagement, and perhaps the future of feminism, can be recognised.

CONSTRUCTIONS OF YOUNG WOMEN, CONSTRUCTIONS OF YOUNG FEMINISM

Since the early to mid 1990s, young womanhood has become a topic central to debates about culture and society. At this time, two discourses about girlhood took hold as key explanatory devices for understanding young women's lives. These were the stories of 'girlpower' on the one hand, and girls 'at risk' on the other. The story of girlpower, of girls as sassy, confident and sometimes dangerous, has seen a phenomenon whereby 'young women have replaced youth as a metaphor for social change'. The counter-story of girls at risk, which has seen a rising concern with young women's risk taking behaviours (drugs, sex, crime), has resulted in more elaborate 'regimes of youth regulation' directed specifically at girls. The debate about young women's relationship to feminism thus has taken place within a broader context of cultural fascination with girlhood, and against a framework which constructs young women as either 'having everything' or being in serious trouble.

To explore how young women became a 'problem' for feminism, we need to take this wider context into account. Specifically, young women were deemed to be silent on key feminist issues, either because they felt they already had everything, or because they were too deeply troubled to find a feminist voice. If they were perceived as articulating feminist principles, they did not express their feminist convictions in appropriate ways, being either too absorbed in risk and victimhood, or mistaking feminism for simply reversing sexual objectification and having a laugh. This power/risk image was and continues to be bolstered by other popular contemporary moral panics around young women, for example, debates about either their increased 'sexiness' or sexual vulnerability, concerns about their apparently increasing tendencies toward violence and criminality, and discussions about their disaffection and disengagement from civic life more generally.

It was along with these broader concerns about young women that this debate about the shape of young feminism emerged. In response to the image of young women as apathetic and selfish, or sociopathic and at risk, many have sought to challenge this binarism and demonstrate the ongoing feminist activism of a new generation. The identification of the 'next wave' of feminism became critical, not least on the part of young women themselves, many of whom felt maligned by their critics. In particular, young women urgently felt the need to explain what it meant to have some power and some rights, but to still see the need for feminist work; that is, to move forward as a generation for whom 'the legacy of feminism was a sense of entitlement'. What quickly occurred, however, was the introduction of distinctive 'styles' of young feminism, which came with labels ('power feminism', 'DIY/girlpower', the third wave), leaders (Naomi Wolf, Courtney Love, Rebecca Walker) and, I would suggest, little in the way of elaborated theory and sometimes politics. The construction of these styles of new feminism lay somewhere between well-intentioned young women themselves, good marketing by publishing companies, and multinational corporations piggy-backing on new images of girlhood to gain access to potential consumers. Further, I would argue that the predominantly reactive nature of these elaborations has seen new feminisms also trapped in a power/risk framework, obliged to claim young feminism as primarily concerned with celebrating young women's power whilst seeking to outline the challenges facing them without resorting to 'victimhood'. Further, as I will go on to argue, in the hurried attempt to name, classify and own a new form of young feminism, the distinctive features of the range of young women's feminist politics of the 1990s and today—diversity, dispersion, leaderlessness, and so on—were lost. However, before exploring this idea further, I will briefly work through three major ways young feminism is commonly represented.

Power Feminism

One of the most significant ways in which the young woman's approach to gender inequality is categorised is through the concept of 'power feminism'.

Power feminism represents itself as a completely new approach that breaks dramatically with the tradition of the previous two women's movements. It argues that the gains of the second wave have been underestimated, and that the key issues facing young women are those few lingering formal barriers to equality. It makes a clear distinction between the personal and the political, and tends to display commitment to either individual empowerment or single issue groups rather than a women's 'movement'. A key proponent is Natasha Walter (1998), who argues for a power-based approach in her book *The New Feminism*. She claims that this kind of feminism focuses on increased power and equality for women, is celebratory and optimistic, and is integrated into mainstream society rather than part of a radical fringe. It is made up of a large collection of allied organisations, with a focus on what she deems to be political rather than personal issues; that is, material inequities rather than private concerns, such as sexuality and body image. She says, 'Rather than concentrating its energy on the ways women dress and talk and make love, feminism must now attack the material basis of economic and social and political inequality'. For Walter, this kind of feminism sees and celebrates the transformation in men, and has no ambivalence about women taking on power.

Naomi Wolf (1994), who actually coins the term 'power feminism' in *Fire With Fire*, also advocates a feminism that focuses on women's power rather than subordination or victimisation, and that distinguishes itself from 'gloomy' feminism by being sexy and fun. She believes that women are very close to equality, and should use their powers as consumers, tax payers and voters to fight for equality. Rene Denfeld (1995) in *The New Victorians* picks up on these themes, articulating the characteristics of power feminism as being against 'male-bashing', or believing that sexual violence, pornography and heterosexuality are modes of men's power, and focussing instead on issues such as childcare, political representation, abortion, and contraception. We could also include here Katie Roiphe's (1993) *The Morning After* as another example of an articulation of new young feminism that seeks to restore women's status from victim to agent, and positions itself against previous waves of overzealous, 'anti-sex' feminism. What characterises power feminism is the rejection of what is deemed to be the 'victim feminism' of the second wave. That is, power feminists are concerned that feminism has become too focused on men's power versus women's oppression, and the ways these are played out in the realm of the sexual and the personal. They are concerned about young feminists getting caught up in this interpretation whereas they should see themselves as strong, sexual, and powerful, and should focus on women's individual strengths.

DIY and Grrrlpower

A rather different definition of young feminism is offered through the framework of Do-It-Yourself/grrrlpower. Grrrlpower is generally seen to have originally emerged from a combination of punk and feminism in the early 1990s. There are few formal texts that lay out the DIY/grrrlpower agenda, but there are many examples of this approach in less mainstream publications such as fanzines, web pages and music, and these have come to the attention of academics and journalists. These interpretations are found in books such as Karen Green and Tristan Taormino's (1997) *A Girl's Guide to Taking Over the World*, Hillary Carlip's (1995) *Girlpower*, Kathy Bail's (1996) *DIY Feminism*, and Marcelle Karp and Debbie Stoller's (1999) *Bust Guide to the New Girl Order*, which all focus on girls as capable, tough, articulate, and reflective. DIY/grrrlpower draws on previous women's movements but argues for a new, 'girl-centred' feminism. It reclaims the word 'girl' and sometimes focuses on young women's anger as a feminist tool. It sees that many major issues still face young women, especially regarding the body and sexuality. At the same time, it emphasises autonomy, sassiness, and is sometimes depicted as sexy and aggressive.

Unlike power feminism, it is committed to a view of the personal (sexuality, body image, relationships, the impact of cultural representations) as political. However, it seeks to represent young women as angry, in charge, and taking action. For example, Flea writes in her zine *Thunderpussy*, 'Feminism isn't over, it didn't fail, but something new happened—grrrl power. Next time a bloke feels your arse, patronises you, slags off your body, generally treats you like shit—forget the moral highground, forget he's been instilled with patriarchy and is a victim too, forget rationale and debate. Just deck the bastard'. In a slightly different take on girlpower and DIY, Kathy Bail argues that young women have embraced this form of 'in your face' feminism because they 'don't want to identify with something that sounds dowdy, asexual or shows them to be at a disadvantage. They don't want to be seen as victims.' Thus both 'power feminism' and 'grrrlpower/DIY' share a desire to mark out a new young feminism that is not based in victim images of girls.

While I would take issue with some of the rather stereotyped basic assumptions about previous waves of feminism that are held by versions of each of these new young feminisms (power feminism in particular), I believe this attempt to reclaim 'power' is worth looking at closely. In the context of the cultural dichotomisation of girls as either tough or hopeless, choosing the strong and powerful option makes some sense. To blame second-wave feminism for emphasising the other is to my mind wrongheaded. But if generational divide is perceived as partially responsible for the construction of youth as an 'at risk' problem, it is easy to see how older feminists have become implicated. This sense of complicity is only fueled by observations by high profile second wavers such as Beatrice Faust, who believes that 'many young women are so naïve that if you spit in their face they'll say it's raining', or Germaine Greer, who claims that 'the career of the individual bad girl is likely to be a brief succession of episodes of chaotic drinking, casual sex, venereal infection and unwanted pregnancy, with consequences she will have to struggle with all her life'. In constructing a new young feminism that is sassy and smart, tough and in control, some young women are attempting to answer back to these images of girls' feminist principles as ingenuous, misguided, and self-harming. In the process, however, the oppositional positions of 'powerful girl' versus 'victim' that are currently circulating only become further entrenched.

The Third Wave

The third example of an elaborated 'style' of young feminism includes those who actively embrace the term 'Third Wave' to mark their place as the next 'wave' in the tradition of the previous two women's movements. This category perhaps offers the most in terms of working outside the power/victim framework to complicate the picture of young feminism. Some specific examples of those whose work could be classified as Third Wave would include Rebecca Walker, who founded the Third Wave Direct Action Corporation in 1993 and edited *To Be Real* (1996). In this text she proclaims third wave feminism to be more individual, complex, and 'imperfect' than previous waves. It is not as strictly defined or all-encompassing as the second wave, less punitive and rigid, especially about personal choices (fashion, sexuality), and is keen to avoid easy polarities in identifying forces of oppression in women's lives. Further, she claims it is more ethnically, sexually, and economically diverse. Leslie Heywood and Jennifer Drake's (1997) *Third Wave Agenda* follows similar lines. They argue that the Third Wave elaborates and complicates the second wave critique of beauty, sexuality, and power, is diverse in its membership, and focuses on the cultural field as a site of feminist activism (for example, music, TV, magazines).

As an Australian example, Virginia Trioli's (1996) *Generation f* is consistent with this kind of approach. She identifies this generation as highly pragmatic (that is, they implement their feminism in workplaces, law courts, and on the street), and particularly wise about using the law to fight sexism. She claims that they take feminist principles for granted as part of their world, and apply these both unashamedly and subtly. We could also include under this category Rosamund Else-Mitchell and Naomi Flutter's (1998) *Talking Up*, and Barbara Findlen's (1995) *Listen Up: Voices from the Next Feminist Generation.*

Third Wave feminism thus places itself in an historical sequence, seeing itself as building on and expanding previous waves of feminism for contemporary times. It is particularly careful to acknowledge and thank second wave feminists, but argues that there are new issues facing young women today. These are generally associated with either the problems faced by women as they attempt to put second wave gains into action (for example, 'going to the cops', using new laws and policies), or with obstacles that are less obvious but just as real, for example, ideological barriers. The third wave considers the politics of issues such as beauty, sexuality, fashion and popular culture to be more complicated than is sometimes presented by earlier feminist analyses. In their debates, they attempt to explain what it means to enjoy some previously gained achievements but still fight for others in a world where both the state and political activism have changed radically. They talk about being 'the first generation for whom feminism has been entwined in the fabric of (their) lives', who 'live their feminism each day'; that is, with an ongoing sense of both entitlement and injustice. Consequently, they walk a fine line between displaying their strengths and working on what must still be done....

THINKING BEYOND POWER FEMINISM, DIY AND THE THIRD WAVE

To think beyond power feminism, DIY/Girlpower or the Third Wave as the only categories of young feminism is to see that the young feminist membership is much larger than may be initially imagined, and further, is concerned with a feminism beyond merely claiming girls' power. Central to this perspective are two tasks. First, it is necessary to look at girls' issues and activism beyond the familiar, and especially beyond the West. The kinds of issues raised by young women outside the Western world draw attention to the limited focus of the 'young feminism' debate and its inability to account for a range of girls' voices. Second, it is critical to look in places often disregarded as sites for feminist work. The role of cultural productions such as zines, web pages, creative writing, and performance in allowing 'ordinary' young women to express their views must not be underestimated. As I have argued elsewhere, amidst the current flurry of interest in girlhood, real sites and complex discourses for young women's own political articulations have diminished or gone 'underground'. Listening to 'other' voices and looking in 'other' places can help to open up the debate about the next wave and identify some of the features of young feminisms that press beyond the limitations of the existing categories. I would suggest that in attending to these tasks, it becomes possible to see an enormous potential in new feminist praxis as diverse and open to a range of viewpoints; as exploiting the resources of contemporary societies (technology, popular culture, the media) in important ways; and as focussing on dispersed activism rather than a single leader or movement. Here I will offer some brief examples of these three features.

Diversity and Multiplicity

Much contemporary research finds that young women are keen to offer a critique of the standard categorisations of young feminism, or even feminism itself. Primarily, this is due to a perception of these categories as limited. I would argue that this demonstrates that young women are much more attentive to diversity and to the need for feminisms that are grounded in multiplicity than they are given credit for in categorisations of young women, or than feminists have perhaps been in the past. For example, Maria Pallotta-Chiarolli has found in her research with 'ordinary' girls that young women's feminist praxis is marked by the following features. They acknowledge differences within and between groups of people, understand racism, homophobia and sexism as interconnected, acknowledge shift and flux in definitions and identities, and uphold self-ascriptive meanings as opposed to assigned labels. A small example of the ways these features are informing young feminisms can be found in the

UNICEF online forum on girls' rights (http://www.unicef.org/). An interest in diversity, difference, and holding complexity manifests itself here in a range of young women's debates around the issues of race, religion and culture. The following discussion takes place amongst young women from Nigeria, the United Kingdom, and China, who share their insights about the uses and abuses of religion and culture in the treatment and experiences of girls, and what this means for feminist theory and practice.

> The work done in the past and being done now by UN on women and girls is commendable. I am a muslim woman living in the West, and any work on my gender to improve my life must take my belief system into consideration. Any work done on gender issues pertaining to the Muslim Women cannot ignore "religion"—otherwise, the project is doomed to failure. (girl, UK)

> In my country, Nigeria, boys are favoured (more) than the girls, in the area of education, boys are allowed to go to school while girls are thrown to one trade or the other, most times they are not allowed to learn any trade but stay at home and do all the work at home and later sent to an old man's house as a wife. This is done in the northern part of Nigeria where they are mostly muslims. This is very bad because this innocent girls end up having V.V.F [HIV] and end up being dumped by the so called husband who has about four of them as wives. Men don't allow their wives to work. I think we children should try to do something about it. (girl, Nigeria)

> I think that most of the traditional religions are still imposing some unfair limit and "rules" on women. In addition, they give the men many privileges! Since those ideas are already brainwashed in everyone's brain, most of the people, especially the women, is just going to bear them. I am not challenging any religions, which may be worshiped by many people, but it is the time to think of it and ask WHY—why two sexes are not equal in front of most of the gods! To many women in some Asian countries, the beliefs of the local religion is really a great obstacle to their development. Changing such kind of ideas is difficult, and also, females are always taught to be "accepting" of anything, no matter it is fair or not. (girl, China)

While this discussion does not itself seek to resolve these different perspectives, or suggest ways activism might emerge out of the differences, we can see here that a range of views is opened up without any one being defended as 'more feminist' than another. The three perspectives build up a picture of the complexity of a feminist take on girls, religion, nation, and culture. None of this fits easily into pre-constructed categories of young feminism, but to my mind suggests an important move forward in feminist analysis. In this example, these young women are expanding the concept of feminism to enable, as a matter of course, very careful and sophisticated analyses of the meanings of culture and religion. These analyses do not deny difference and the complexity of contradictory grounded experience that complicates fixed notions of privilege and discrimination. Raised here is the careful use of personal knowledge, as well as the potential for understanding the different meanings of, for example, living as a poor girl under Sharia law in the northern Islamic states of Nigeria, or as a second generation middle class women of Malaysian origin in London, or the degree to which 'traditionalism' dictates the repressive capacity of any religious belief.

The ways this translates into political practice, whilst this is not evidenced directly here, are also significant. In this next example, the US organisation *Blackgrrrlrevolution* offers some insights into how diversity and alliances work in their experience. They say

> [T]here's like 20 areas on which we advocate for black grrrls, meaning all girls of colour and many languages—we stand on so many radical frontlines, so I think we're re-focusing our expectations of alliances.... We're not going to ally ourselves with the people everyone thinks that we would naturally ally ourselves with (interview, 2001).

This organisation advocates for a wide diversity of young women but eschews what might be typical alliances, for example, with some other Black or girls' organisations, because they are perceived to be too rigid and limited in their focus. The fact that their platform is diverse and represents a range of differences in lived experience has led them to, as they say, 'shifting paradigms in terms of political organising and doing business' (for more details, see their webpage at blackgrrrlrevolution.org). However, the subtleties and complexities of this interest in diversity, change, and multiplicity are not often attended to in the official versions of young feminism. In particular, they are not often addressed beyond individual grappling with difference. Neither are they addressed in terms of their implications for feminist praxis, the role and efficacy of women's programmes (for example, within the UN), and the capacity for a range of women to debate, disagree, and work together.

Other Sites

The fact that these debates about culture, religion, feminism, and alliances take place in cyberspace is significant. We can see this as just one example of the contemporary sites and strategies for feminism developed or used by young women around new technology, as well as popular culture and the media. Young women who do not have access to publishers and cannot get their voices heard in the mainstream have been responsible for creating new feminist activism and networks through alternative media. Henry Giroux argues that 'when youth do speak, the current generation in particular, their voices generally emerge on the margins of society—in underground magazines, alternative music spheres, computer hacker clubs and other subcultural sites'. This is certainly the case for much young feminist debate, for example, as evidenced in the creation of grrrlzines, girls' webpages and chat rooms. 'Zines', short for fanzines, are independently produced informal newsletters, which usually include reviews, information sharing, editorials, and creative writing around issues relevant to young women. They are distributed through wide networks for the purposes of sharing information and building a community of young feminists. Stephen Duncombe argues that zines have become an important new locale for young people's political debate and resistance in the wake of the decline of old style social movements. He says 'throughout the 1980s while the Left was left behind, crumbling and attracting few new converts, zines and underground culture grew by leaps and bounds, resonating deeply with disaffected young people ... (constituting) perhaps ... the next wave of meaningful political resistance'. Many young women also use the Internet as a place for political action through listservs and chatrooms.

These kinds of cultural politics—zines, e-zines, comics, and Web pages—have often been misinterpreted as girls just 'having fun'. Rather, I would argue that they hold real promise for feminist work precisely because they constitute 'other spaces' for politics. The three 'next wave' categories tend to concentrate on either demonstrating young women's continued engagement with old style political activism (lobbying government, holding protests, campaigning, civil disobedience, and so on), or on their lack of need for this. What is lost in the two sides of this argument is the possibility (and indeed, the very real evidence) that young women have developed quite new ways of conducting political organisation, protest, debate and agitation. These new ways are a response to the perceived co-option of left politics as merely a marketable style, and appropriation of their resistant voices when expressed through traditional protest modes. The trend towards an increased surveillance of youth, the re-discovery of young women in particular as the new consumers, and the cultural fascination with girlhood, have all resulted in a deep suspicion of overt activism as the best method for protest and the creation of social change. Young women have repeatedly seen their politics sold back to them as products, and consequently seek other modes for debate and agitation.

Movements without Leaders

Finally, another feature of an uncategorised young feminism is that there is not a single leader heading up a single movement. (Of course, this is not to suggest that the second wave was a uniform dictatorship!). This trend away from the organised, hierarchised movement is a key feature of many forms of social justice action under postindustrialisation. As Naomi Klein (2000) argues, these new practices of resistance respond 'to corporate concentration with a maze of fragmentation, to globalization with its own kind of localization, to power consolidation with radical power dispersal'. The dispersion of the feminist movement is consistent with this broader shift. This has become an important way to enact feminist change within particular communities on specific issues relevant to that place. Young women are engaged in both specific issues that affect them in their own communities and in wider concerns that reach across the world. These include anti-sweat shop and other labour-related campaigns, raising awareness about health, sexuality, and disease, environmental and animal rights activism, pro-education and anti-sex slavery work, and so on. All of this is feminist. As *Blackgrrrlrevolution* claims in their case, but arguably in the case of many forms of young feminism, feminism as a framework has become broader. They say:

> [F]eminism is a necessary tool for human liberation, freedom and empowerment: that's broad.... What that essentially is saying is that pro black girl feminism, the pro black girl movement is a queer movement, it is a Marxist movement, it is a social movement, it is a labour movement, it is a civil rights movement, it is a gay rights movement, it is every movement. (interview, 2001)

There is no requirement put on them to choose any one or the other, or to try to homogenise issues into one big movement that might involve silencing or excluding some over others. The three next wave categories have tended to articulate this move away from the movement by at times denying it or by overstating young women's desire to express individual needs. None has contextualised this change in terms of the wider trend of left politics, where it can be most easily understood as a reorganisation rather than disintegration of feminist alliances.

CONCLUSION

The purpose of offering these notes towards other kinds of feminisms enacted by young women is to push open the categories currently competing for preselection as the 'real' next wave. I have argued that the three most common representations of this next wave are stylised versions of 'feminism as girls' empowerment'. These have emerged in response to the construction of contemporary girlhood as at risk, and contemporary young women as troubled, naïve, or selfish. However, in this race to colonise the terrain of young feminism, some of the most exciting, if uncategoriseable, girls' activism and politics are being lost. The same circumstances which have seen girlhood become a receptacle for social anxieties about change have also seen new possibilities, places, and modes for their feminist theory and practice. It is in these other spaces and through these other expressions that may emerge 'a "new feminism" we do not yet know'.

As a concluding thought, I would proffer the idea that where the activism is happening today is where it hasn't been seen to happen in feminism for years. In Australia at least, we are perhaps seeing some kind of hearkening back to the forgotten feminism between the wars that was heavily concentrated on Aboriginal rights, ideas of nation, citizenship and equality, union issues, and migrant labour debates. While I have not had room here to explore specific issues addressed by young women working beyond the categories of the next wave, I would just note that it is possible to document a kind of resurgence of these sorts of concerns today. These are of course also inflected by new developments in the lives of young women, and new technologies and changing socioeconomic circumstances—for example, changes brought about by the internet, globalisation, and the forces of postindustrialisation. To look at the YWCA 'yGALS', who are non-Aboriginal young women working on reconciliation, the involvement of young women in anti-sweatshop campaigns and broader anti-globalisation movements, the anti-Hanson high school walkouts, and the anti-capitalist and anti-corporate feminist politics of many contemporary young women, is to see some interesting parallels with 'between the waves' Australian feminism. Interestingly, this older period in feminist history has remained unlabelled and is remembered as a time when young women deserted feminism. Further, it was also a period in which enormous social, economic, and cultural changes were taking place that saw young women become a cultural presence in unprecedented ways. During this period, also, younger women were at times blamed by older women for being unfeminist and too concerned with themselves and having sold out to frivolity, image, and self-interest. I would suggest that today, as in the past, there is another story to be told about young women and feminism. This story does not fit neatly into texts or labels; it presses both the borders of generational feminist debates and the constitution of girlhood as a carrier for cultural anxieties about change. It is a story that responds to the particular and complex social worlds within which young women live.

14. Sarah Gamble, "Postfeminism," from *The Routledge Critical Dictionary of Feminism and Postfeminism*

Excerpts from "Postfeminism" by Sarah Gamble, published in Sarah Gamble, ed., *The Routledge Critical Dictionary of Feminism and Postfeminism* (New York: Routledge, 2000), 43–54. Reprinted with permission.

Gamble's fundamental definitional essay serves to distance the third wave from the postfeminism with which it is often confused, thus articulating what third-wave feminism *is* as well as what it is not.

> *Currently, feminism seems to be a term without any clear significance. The "anything goes" approach to the definition of the word has rendered it practically meaningless.*
>
> —bell hooks, *Feminist Theory: From Margin to Center* (1984)

'Postfeminism' is a term that is very much in vogue these days. In the context of popular culture it's the Spice Girls, Madonna, and the *Girlie Show*: women dressing like bimbos, yet claiming male privileges and attitudes. Meanwhile, those who wish to maintain an allegiance to more traditional forms of feminism circle around the neologism warily, unable to decide whether it represents a con trick engineered by the media or a valid movement. In books such as Tania Modleski's *Feminism Without Women: Culture and Criticism in a 'Postfeminist' Age* (1991) and Imelda Whelehan's *Feminist Thought: From the Second Wave to 'Post-feminism'* (1995) the term is barricaded between inverted commas, thus keeping both author and reader at a properly sceptical distance.

Much of this distrust is to do with the fact that, outside of its infinitely flexible media definition, exactly what postfeminism constitutes—even whether it exists at all as a valid phenomenon—is a matter for frequently impassioned debate. As Vicki Coppock, Deena Haydon and Ingrid Richter put it in the *The Illusions of 'Post-feminism'* (1995), 'post-feminism has never been defined. It remains the product of assumption.' It is a characteristic postfeminism shares with its semantic relative, post-modernism, which has been similarly described as 'an amorphous thing'.

Indeed, even the most cursory reading of texts tagged with the 'postfeminist' label reveals that there is little agreement among those with whom it is popularly associated as to a central canon or agenda. Very generally speaking, however, postfeminist debate tends to crystallise around issues of victimisation, autonomy and responsibility.

Because it is critical of any definition of women as victims who are unable to control their own lives, it is inclined to be unwilling to condemn pornography and to be sceptical of such phenomena as date-rape: because it is skewed in favour of liberal humanism, it embraces a flexible ideology which can be adapted to suit individual needs and desires. Finally, because it tends to be implicitly heterosexist in orientation, postfeminism commonly seeks to develop an agenda which can find a place for men, as lovers, husbands and fathers as well as friends.

The term 'postfeminism' itself originated from within the media in the early 1980s and has always tended to be used in this context as indicative of joyous liberation from the ideological shackles of a hopelessly outdated feminist movement. This is the view which has reached the ninth edition of *The Concise Oxford Dictionary*, where 'postfeminism' is defined as 'of or relating to the ideas, attitudes, etc., which ignore or reject feminist ideas of the 1960s and subsequent decades'. However, those to whom the postfeminist label is most often attached by the media do not generally regard themselves as part of any kind of anti-feminist movement, as Justine Picardie's 1996 article for the *Independent on Sunday* on a TV show called *Pyjama Party* testifies:

> There has been much feverish talk in the press about these programmes ... do they represent the snarling face of the postfeminist babe – 'the new ladette' – or is this just a pre-feminist excuse for titillating the viewers with a great deal of cleavage? The girls on their way to *Pyjama Party* ... couldn't care less about this debate ('postfeminist what?' says one, while her friends look equally blank: 'never heard of it!').

The source of such confusion, for postfeminism as much as for postmodernism, is at least partially due to the semantic uncertainty generated by the prefix. Turning again to the *Concise Oxford Dictionary*, 'post' is defined as 'after in time or order', but not as denoting rejection. Yet many feminists argue strongly that postfeminism constitutes precisely that—a betrayal of a history of feminist struggle, and rejection of all it has gained. Tania Modleski's dismissal of postfeminist texts as 'texts that, in proclaiming or assuming the advent of postfeminism, are actually engaged in negating the critiques and undermining the goals of feminism—in effect delivering us back to a prefeminist world' is typical of such attacks.

The assertiveness of Modleski's rhetoric here makes the issue appear beyond dispute, but it is possible to argue that the prefix 'post' does not necessarily always direct us back the way we've come. Instead, its trajectory is bewilderingly uncertain, since while it can certainly be interpreted as suggestive of a relapse *back* to a former set of ideological beliefs, it can also be read as indicating the *continuation* of the originating term's aims and ideologies, albeit on a different level. This more positive interpretation is certainly, however, complicated in postfeminism's case, given that it lacks both an agreed-upon set of ideological assumptions and any prominent figureheads. This latter statement may seem rather odd, since postfeminism abounds in 'personalities'—glamorous Naomi Wolf; the swaggering self-publicist Camille Paglia; Rene Denfeld, the streetwise amateur boxer. It is telling, however, that most—if not all—of the women who are widely identified with postfeminism have not claimed the term for themselves, but had it applied to them by others; nor does a great deal of solidarity exist between them as a group.

POSTFEMINISM AND THE BACKLASH

The notion that postfeminism, to paraphrase Modleski's words quoted above, 'delivers us back' to some kind of prefeminist state is an argument frequently deployed by its critics. The most influential definition of postfeminism through reference to a rhetoric of relapse is Susan Faludi's, who in *Backlash: The Undeclared War Against Women* (1991) portrays postfeminism as a devastating reaction against the ground gained by second wave feminism.

> Just when record numbers of younger women were supporting feminist goals in the mid-1980s (more of them, in fact, than older women) and a majority of all women were calling themselves feminists, the media declared that feminism was the flavour of the seventies and that 'postfeminism' was the new story—complete with a younger generation who supposedly reviled the women's movement.

For Faludi, postfeminism *is* the backlash, and its triumph lies in its ability to define itself as an ironic, pseudo-intellectual critique on the feminist movement, rather than an overtly hostile response to it. In a society which largely defines itself through media-inspired images, women are easily persuaded that feminism is unfashionable, *passé*, and therefore not worthy of serious consideration. 'We're all "post-feminist" now, they assert, meaning not that women have arrived at equal justice and moved beyond it, but simply that they themselves are beyond even pretending to care.'

While most critics date the inception of postfeminism from about the mid-1980s onwards, Faludi claims that 'postfeminist' sentiments appeared much earlier, 'not in the 1980s media, but in the 1920s press'. In her identification of it as merely the most recent label for a much older phenomenon—a knee-jerk reaction on the part of the mainstream in defence of the *status quo*—Faludi attempts to unmask postfeminism as a wolf in (albeit trendy) sheep's clothing....

POSTFEMINISM AND POSTMODERNISM

In fact, to accept the inherently theoretical nature of the postfeminist project perhaps offers the most convincing way in which the term can be used. In this context, postfeminism becomes a pluralistic epistemology dedicated to disrupting universalising patterns of thought, and thus capable of being aligned with postmodernism, poststructuralism, and postcolonialism.

One example of this approach is provided by Ann Brooks in *Post-feminisms: Feminism, Cultural Theory and Cultural Forms* (1997). She argues that second-wave feminism bases its claims on an appeal to 'the liberal humanism of enlightened modernity': for example, it assumes that a simple reversal of the hierarchical dualism of 'man/woman' will effect the liberation of the female half of the equation. A feminist approach indebted to postmodernist thought, however, will tend to question the ideological process by which 'man' and 'woman' are placed in separate, oppositional, categories, and may, indeed, seek to destabilise the notion of the autonomous subject (gendered or otherwise) altogether, thus rendering the development of any kind of overarching metatheory impossible.

According to Brooks, therefore, postfeminism replaces dualism with diversity, consensus with variety, and thus 'establish[es] a dynamic and vigorous area of intellectual debate, shaping the issues and intellectual climate that has characterised the move from modernity to post-modernity in the contemporary world'. Brooks's analysis does not mention Wolf, Roiphe, or any of the other women popularly defined as postfeminists within the media. Instead, she appropriates theorists such as Julia Kristeva, Hélène Cixous, Laura Mulvey, and Judith Butler for postfeminism, claiming that such writers 'have assisted feminist debates by providing a conceptual repertoire centred on "deconstruction", "difference" and "identity".'

Interesting though Brooks's argument is, however, certain aspects of it are problematic, since in transforming postfeminism into another theoretical movement, she runs the risk of removing it from the 'real' world of political agency and social activism. Although she may maintain that postfeminism 'facilitates a broad-based, pluralistic conception of the application of feminism, and addresses the demands of marginalised, diasporic and colonised cultures for a non-hegemonic feminism capable of giving voice to local, indigenous and post-colonial feminisms', it remains difficult to see how these theoretical debates can be translated into concrete action. For some, indeed, her approach may bear out the claims of some of the popular postfeminists that the development of feminism as an academic discipline has limited its appeal outside the universities. Rene Denfeld, for example, accuses academic feminists of having 'climbed out on a limb of academic theory that is all but inaccessible to the uninitiated', while Naomi Wolf complains that it has adopted 'an exclusive and elaborate professional jargon' which amounts to no more than 'pig-Latin'.

POSTFEMINISM OR THIRD WAVE?

In 1970 Germaine Greer published *The Female Eunuch*, which became one of the founding texts of second-wave feminism: 1999 has seen the publication of its sequel, *The Whole Woman*, a book which places Greer once again at centre stage in the feminist debate. In her introduction, Greer makes it quite clear she has written this book as a reaction against postfeminist ideology: "The future is female, we are told. Feminism has served its purpose and should now eff off. Feminism was long hair, dungarees and dangling earrings; postfeminism was business suits, big hair and lipstick; post-postfeminism was ostentatious sluttishness and disorderly behaviour.' As Greer defines it, postfeminism is little more than a market-led phenomenon, for 'the most powerful entities on earth are not governments, but the multi-national corporations that see women as their territory'. Its assurance to women that they can 'have it all'—a career, motherhood, beauty, and a great sex life—actually only resituates them as consumers of pills, paint, potions, cosmetic surgery, fashion, and convenience foods. Greer also argues that the adoption of a postfeminist stance is a luxury in which the affluent western world can indulge only by ignoring the possibility that the exercising of one person's freedom may be directly linked to another's oppression. In such a situation, she asks, how can a woman believe that she has passed beyond feminism?

> If you believe, as I do, that to be a feminist is to understand that before you are of any race, nationality, religion, party or family, you are a woman, then the collapse in the prestige and economic power of the majority of women in the world as a direct consequence of western hegemony must concern you.

Whether one agrees with Greer or not—and her love of inflammatory rhetoric should not be forgotten—the publication of this book makes clear that the debate concerning the future of feminism is not over. Second-wave feminism isn't dead, and a triumphant postfeminist world is still far from being imaginable, let alone a reality. While it is certainly true that feminism, like all other ideologies, must adapt to respond to the exigencies of a changing world—and any failure to address younger women must certainly be addressed—the postfeminist phenomenon, which was always primarily a media-led movement anyway, has reached an impasse out of which a coherent solution cannot be developed.

But perhaps there is another way for feminism to accommodate itself to changing times. Increasingly feminists in their twenties and thirties are distancing themselves from the problematic politics of postfeminism by describing themselves as participating in a 'third wave'; a term in which the twin imperatives of continuity and change are neatly entwined. A number of third-wave women's groups have sprung up in the US, including the Women's Action Coalition and Third Wave (founded by Rebecca Walker, daughter of the novelist Alice Walker). The editors of *Third Wave Agenda*, Leslie Heywood and Jennifer Drake, maintain that the primary difference between third-wave and second-wave feminism is that third-wave feminists feel at ease with contradiction. Because they have been brought up within competing feminist structures, they accept pluralism as a given.

> We know that what oppresses me may not oppress you, that what oppresses you may be something I participate in, and that what oppresses me may be something you participate in. Even as different strands of feminism and activism sometimes directly contradict each other, they are all part of our third wave lives, our thinking, and our praxes: we are products of all the contradictory definitions of and differences within feminism, beasts of such a hybrid kind that perhaps we need a different name altogether.

Heywood and Drake make absolutely clear, however, that that 'different name' will not be postfeminism, which is something third-wave feminists define as fundamentally conservative and reductive in its thought.

At the beginning of this chapter, I traced postfeminism back to its origins in the eighties media and have argued that it is through the media that it has, to a great extent, maintained its cultural presence. Intriguingly, the term 'third wave' was born at about the same time, but found its way to public notice by a rather different route. Heywood and Drake identify its moment of origin in 'critiques of the white women's movement that were initiated by women of color, as well from the many instances of coalition work undertaken by U.S. third world feminists'. It is this, they say, which has led to the third wave's innate acceptance of hybridity, its understanding that no account of oppression is true for all women in all situations all of the time. Moreover, its links with political activism should ensure that the third wave is more than just a theory, but an approach that will actively work against the social injustices which still form part of the everyday experience of many women.

It's no coincidence that one of the women predominantly identified with a feminist 'third wave' is the black theorist and writer bell hooks, whose work has persistently challenged white bourgeois women's unthinking assumption of an oppressed subject position. As early as 1984, hooks was arguing against a homogenized feminism which was seen 'as a lifestyle choice rather than a political commitment'—a statement which could be seen as a rather prescient description of popular postfeminism. Instead, she proposes a position from which feminism is 'advocated' rather than assumed.

> A phrase like 'I advocate' does not imply the kind of absolutism that is suggested by 'I am'.... It implies that a choice has been made, that commitment to feminism is an act of will. It does not suggest that by committing oneself to feminism, the possibility of supporting other political movements is negated.

It is this combination of commitment with flexibility which is now being claimed by the third wave....

15. Rory Dicker and Alison Piepmeier, "Introduction," from *Catching a Wave: Reclaiming Feminism for the 21st Century*

Claiming a more direct affiliation with the second wave than some third-wave thinkers, Dicker and Piepmeier argue for a return to strategies of consciousness raising to help fight the widely disseminated media idea that equality has already been won. The steps to claiming a feminist consciousness are (1) recognizing that sexism exists and that feminism is still necessary, (2) identifying as a feminist despite the backlash that demonizes the term, (3) noticing a range of feminist activities in what seem unlikely places, (4) examining, critiquing, and redefining feminism to account for all axes of identity, and (5) practicing activism, "taking a feminist awareness and using it to effect change in the larger world."

> *As far as I can tell, the third wave is just the second wave with more lip gloss.*
>
> —Young woman at the National Women's Studies Association Conference (June 2001)

We are tired of waiting. Sick and tired.

At Vanderbilt University's graduation ceremony in 2002, the top students in each of nine schools received awards. These were exceptional students whose accomplishments in scholarship service and leadership distinguished them from thousands of their peers who were also graduating on this day. Of these nine honorees, six were women. Presenting the awards were the deans of the students' schools. Of these nine deans, two were women—unsurprisingly they were deans of the education and nursing schools. The remaining seven deans were men.

"So what?" you might say. If you'd been there you might not even have noticed. Scenes such as this are so commonplace that they seem unremarkable, perhaps because, even thirty years after the start of the women's movement, we are still used to seeing men in positions of power. Although the presence of these six talented achieving female students reveals the success of feminist efforts, the scarcity of highly placed women in university administrations, corporate America, and government—to name only the most obvious institutions—demonstrates our very real need for continued feminist activism. Young women today have more options available to them than at any other time in history, and because of these options they feel, as we ourselves have felt, that not only can they accomplish anything they want to but there are no gender-based barriers: sexism, these young women are sure, is a thing of the past. Yet, as the above example illustrates, in spite of these beliefs, societal structures have not changed as much as feminists might have hoped or expected.

When we point out these kinds of structural inequalities, we generally receive one of two responses. Some people dismiss us as hyper-analytical, oversensitive "feminists with a capital F" who are only wallowing in victimhood. To these people, there's really no need for feminism, anyway, so the subject of inequality seems irrelevant. Other people, those who are more sympathetic to the idea of women's empowerment, try to assuage us by telling us that things are getting better and have changed so much already. If we wait twenty years, they say, things will be much more equal.

This is what they were saying twenty years ago. We are tired of waiting.

In fact, if we were to be as patient as our sympathetic listeners, we might be waiting a long time. Although women have now entered traditionally male professions with such regularity that it may appear that there are no barriers to women's success, the fact remains that women are dramatically underrepresented in decision-making, power-brokering positions. To look at only one professional realm, top management: "Twenty-five years ago, graduating business school classes included 20 to 25 percent women; today, 99.94 percent of the CEOs, and 97.3 percent of the top earners are men." These statistics reveal that women entered the corporate world in reasonably large percentages and with competitive educational backgrounds a generation ago. These women should be in the pipeline, assuming or being ready to assume significant leadership roles. They should be university deans, bank presidents, and members of Congress, but they are not. The solution to this lack of women in power is not to continue to wait. Indeed, as Susan Estrich informs us, if we keep waiting, "at the rate we're going, it will be another 270 years before women achieve parity as top managers in corporations and 500 years before we achieve equality in Congress."

We can't wait that long. The alternative to waiting is waking up, recognizing the inequalities that surround us, and figuring out what we can do to redress the balance. To do these things, we need feminism, a social philosophy aimed at eradicating the pervasive sexism of our culture. The point is not that all women need to be CEOs or senators (as if they could) or that female leaders would necessarily have the interests of women at heart; instead, the point is that the lack of women in the pipeline is one sign of a deeply patriarchal culture that perpetuates sexist ideologies and systems. To combat this sexism, *Catching a Wave* contends that this generation needs a politicized, activist feminism that is grounded in the material realities and the cultural productions of life in the twenty-first century. We need a feminism that is dedicated to a radical, transformative political vision, a feminism that does not shy away from hard work but recognizes that changing the world is a difficult and necessary task, a feminism that utilizes the new technologies of the Internet, the playful world of fashion, and the more clear-cut activism of protest marches, a feminism that can engage with issues as diverse as women's sweatshop labor in global factories and violence against women expressed in popular music.

Though we often refer to our feminism as the third wave, we want to render problematic an easy understanding of what the third wave is. Typically, the third wave is thought of as a younger generation's feminism, one that rejects traditional—or stereotypical—understandings of feminism and as such is antithetical or oppositional to its supposed predecessor, the second wave. The feminism we claim, however, aligns itself with second wave strategies for recognizing and addressing structural inequalities. One such strategy is consciousness-raising, developed in the 1960s and 1970s. In their heyday, consciousness-raising (CR) groups offered a space for women to discuss their life experiences and feelings. What women often discovered in these groups was that problems that they thought were particular to them were shared by many others and were, in fact, part of a larger system of sexist practices. These groups launched much feminist activism and social change. We wanted to continue this activist tradition by using a consciousness-raising format in this book....

If you think that there's no need for feminism because the world is basically equal, consider this: women are 51 percent of the U.S. population, but only 13 of 100 U.S. senators and only 59 of 435 representatives are women. This means that women occupy only 13.8 percent of the seats in Congress. Only 2 of the 9 Supreme Court justices are women, and we have never had a female president or vice president.

Our lack of political power translates into economic inequality. Today, nationwide, when you control for factors such as age, experience, education, occupation, and industry, women earn around seventy-three cents on a man's dollar. In fact, although we like to believe that we're making progress, the wage gap between women and men in managerial positions actually widened between 1995 and 2000. As of 2002, only six women are CEOs of Fortune 500 companies. Worldwide, when a woman does a job, even if that job is virtually identical to one performed by a man, the man's work is more valued and better compensated. Women tend to be concentrated in the lowest occupational sectors; as a result, women and children constitute 70 percent of the world's impoverished people. In the United States, "welfare reform" in the 1990s disproportionately affected women, shunting them into low-paying "women's" jobs—even when they were qualified for other kinds of work.

Just as women's economic inequality reveals their low status, so does their treatment in personal relationships. Violence against women is a worldwide epidemic, affecting the health and well-being of countless women. In fact, according to the United Nations Population Fund, at least 1 in 3 women in the world has been physically or sexually abused by a man at some time in her life. Every year, 700,000 women are raped in the United States, a country that claims to value women and provide for their safety; in this allegedly civil society, a woman is more likely to be killed at the hands of a man she loves than by anyone else.

Worldwide, women's and girls' bodies are prey to abuse. More than 130 million women globally are affected by female genital mutilation (FGM), which involves the excision of the clitoris without anesthesia, and sometimes the slicing and sewing up of the entire vaginal area, leaving only a small hole for the elimination of urine and menstrual blood. In some cases, the exploitation of female bodies becomes part of global economic strategy. For instance, many Western men travel to Thailand to participate in the thriving "sex tourism" industry there, paying to have sex with girls as young as six. The World Bank and the International Monetary Fund encourage this tourism as part of Thailand's "development." Up to 4 million women and girls around the world are bought and sold into marriage, prostitution, or slavery every year.

Our bodies are under attack in other ways as well. Reproductive rights for women in the United States are more threatened now than they've been in thirty years. Although abortion is technically legal, its availability is severely limited, with 86 percent of U.S. counties providing no access to abortion. This is only going to get worse if the Supreme Court overturns *Roe v. Wade*, which seems likely if President Bush gets to nominate a new justice. The right to abortion is under attack, and, ironically, so is contraception: insurance companies in the United States cover half of the prescriptions for the erection-inducing drug Viagra, but only one-third of the prescriptions for birth control pills.

Although the United States likes to tout its "family values," it has the worst parental leave policy of any industrialized nation. Only 50 percent of new parents in the United States are guaranteed parental leave—and legally they're guaranteed only twelve weeks, unpaid. Compare that to eighteen weeks in Great Britain, ten months in Italy, and almost a full year of paid parental leave in Norway and Sweden. Given its policies, it comes as no surprise that the United States is the only industrialized nation in the world that has not signed the United Nations' Convention on the Elimination of All Forms of Discrimination Against Women (CEDAW), putting it in the company of countries such as Saudi Arabia and Sudan.

Being confronted with such sweeping inequalities may be surprising, given that many of us view injustice as something that happened in the past: if injustice does occur in the present, we assume it is an aberration, not a widespread or systemic problem. The facts we've just listed would suggest otherwise.

We present these facts because a recognition that inequality not only exists but is indeed pervasive is necessary to an understanding of feminism. So is anger. Feminists have often been ridiculed for their anger, but this anger comes from an acknowledgment of social problems and a desire to improve the world. If we don't identify the ways in which women and girls are exploited globally—if we don't realize the reasons for feminist anger—then feminism, a movement concerned with eradicating inequality, will seem irrelevant, irrational, or even passé. Yet this movement is not at all out of date ... we can create a world we want to live in only with the help of a feminist consciousness.

The anger and passion that feminists express on behalf of women lead many people to label them man-haters. However, most feminist praxis operates not out of hatred of men but out of a deep commitment of women's lives and to redressing the injustices that they face. In its most basic sense, feminism calls for the social, political, and economic equality of women. While feminists have traditionally sought equality for women, more recently they have realized that the term "woman" is an inadequate category because of the many differences among women; to be effective, feminist practice must take these differences into account. The influential black feminist writer Barbara Smith encapsulates the multiethnic, multi-issue approach that must define feminism: "Feminism is the political theory and practice to free all women: women of color, working-class women, poor women, physically challenged women, lesbians, old women—as well as white economically privileged heterosexual women. Anything less than this is not feminism, but merely female self-aggrandizement." As Smith notes, feminism is not simply about women's issues but is a broad-based political movement that seeks freedom for all those who are oppressed....

THE WAVES: UNDERSTANDING FEMINIST HISTORY

The history of feminism in the United States is often explained by using the metaphor of waves. According to this language, the first wave of the women's movement began in 1848 at the women's rights convention in Seneca Falls, New York, where Elizabeth Cady Stanton and her colleagues wrote the "Declaration of Sentiments." The central goal of this wave was gaining a legal identity for women that included the right to own property, to sue, to form contracts, and to vote. Although this wave is widely assumed to have ebbed with the ratification of the Nineteenth Amendment in 1920, feminist historians such as Sheila Ruth remind us that women from the 1920s to the 1960s simply channeled their energies into other social justice and activist work. Spurred by the civil rights movement, countercultural protests, and the publication of crucial texts, including Betty Friedan's *The Feminine Mystique* (1962), feminist awareness and activism gained momentum in the 1960s. This heightened activity, referred to now as the second wave, focused on gaining full human rights for women: some of its central demands were equal opportunities in employment and education, access to child care and abortion, the eradication of violence against women, and the passage of the Equal Rights Amendment. Second-wave activists critiqued the notion of biological or inherent differences between the sexes, contending instead that these differences are socially constructed.

In the 1970s and 1980s, U.S. women of color and lesbians, responding to their marginalization by the mainstream white, middle-class women's movement, extended the insights of second wave feminism by theorizing about their experiences. They called for a recognition that identity is intersectional—in other words, that gender, race, ethnicity, class, and sexuality are interlocking and that oppression is not experienced simply along one axis. These women, who labeled themselves U.S. third world feminists, questioned the tendency within the second wave to reduce the category of "woman" to its essence. In their writings, U.S. third world feminists moved the concepts of difference and diversity to the foreground, reminding us that even if sisterhood is global, not all women's lives and experiences are identical. As Leslie Heywood and Jennifer Drake have asserted, U.S. third world feminism created the space for the emergence of a third wave of feminism: "[T]he definitional moment of third wave feminism has been theorized as proceeding from critiques of the white women's movement that were initiated by women of color, as well as from the many instances of coalition work undertaken by U.S. third world feminists." The third wave thus recognizes that the differences among women are as substantial as the differences between women and men: the category of "woman" is no longer the only identity worth examining.

Third wave feminism represents a reinvigorated feminist movement emerging from a late twentieth-century world. Many of the goals of the third wave are similar to those of the second wave, though some, such as its insistence on women's diversity, are new. *Catching a Wave* contends, however, that third wave feminism's political activism on behalf of women's rights is shaped by—and responds to—a world of global capitalism and information technology, postmodernism and postcolonialism, and environmental degradation. We no longer live in the world that feminists of the second wave faced. Third wavers, who came of age in the late twentieth century and after, are therefore concerned not simply with "women's issues" but with a broad range of interlocking topics—topics ... ranging from protests of the World Economic Forum and welfare reform to activism on behalf of independent media outlets. Just as it is interested in a multiplicity of issues, the third wave operates from the assumption that identity is multifaceted and layered. Since no monolithic version of "woman" exists, we can no longer speak with confidence of "women's issues"; instead, we need to consider that such issues are as diverse as the many women who inhabit our planet. Although third wave feminists have a reputation for sexiness and frivolity—a reputation voiced in our epigraph—this doesn't represent the heart of the third wave as we see it. At its best, the third wave engages with a diverse spectrum of issues in ways that are passionate as well as playful, inclusive as well as rigorous, making use of the best of second wave theory and strategy as well as critiques of second wave feminism. . . .

THE SECOND AND THIRD WAVES: CONFLICT OR COMMUNITY?

Although claiming the presence of the third wave has been an exuberant act for young feminists, it has been seen by many in the second wave as profoundly alienating, an act of amputation. This perception is not entirely inaccurate; many third wave feminists perceive the second wave as a movement to which they don't want to belong, and they are not quiet about these feelings. According to many third wavers, second wave feminism is repressive and restrictive, and this is one reason that the third wave has had to break away and formulate new ways of being feminist. As Rebecca Walker explains in the introduction to *To Be Real*:

> For many of us it seems that to be a feminist in the way that we have seen or understood feminism is to conform to an identity and way of living that doesn't allow for individuality, complexity, or less than perfect personal histories. We fear that the identity will dictate and regulate our lives, instantaneously pitting us against someone, forcing us to choose inflexible and unchanging sides, female against male, black against white, oppressed against oppressor, good against bad.

Walker goes on to describe a feminism that is "simply another impossible contrivance of perfect womanhood." Walker's characterization of the second wave rehearses the story told by Katie Roiphe in *The Morning After* (1993) that second wave feminists hate sex and perpetuate Victorian sexual ideals. In these stories, second wave feminists are cold figures with an agenda more than a personality; they seem somewhat like the often-invoked "feminazis."

Descriptions like Walker's and Roiphe's are echoed at feminist and women's studies conferences, in third wave books, on feminist listservs, and even in popular media. In all these venues, the relationship between the second and third waves of feminism is characterized as confrontational and uncooperative, even hostile. This emphasis on intergenerational conflict has certainly captured the media's attention: typically, the media describe one generation as the victim and the other as the perpetrator, with frequent role reversals, depending on the cultural climate. Though there's no denying that this makes a good story, it's really just the latest incarnation of the feminist catfight. For example, an episode of *Oprah* in 2002 featured younger and older feminists in conversation. Instead of using this hour to educate Oprah's 6 million viewers about violence against women, pay equity, and the myriad other issues on which feminists of both generations collaborate, the show depicted family dysfunction and culminated in the younger feminists obsequiously thanking the older ones. This staging of conflict and reconciliation ultimately works to dissipate feminist energies and to trivialize the real work being done in the movement.

Instead of focusing on the alleged conflict between the generations, we see many strands of continuity between the second and third waves. After all, the goals set by the second wave have not yet been accomplished, and thus the current generation of feminists is—and should be—working on many of the same issues as the second wave, often alongside older feminists. Indeed, in "Please—Stop Thinking about Tomorrow: Building a Feminist Movement on College Campuses for *Today*," Sarah Boonin describes not just her frustration with the antagonism she sees between older and younger feminists but also the intergenerational collaboration between the second wave Feminist Majority Foundation and third wave campus leaders. Boonin's essay shows that, while some third wave writers may depict older feminism as puritanical, repressive, and homogeneous, such a picture is a distortion that relies on a reductive rendering of an incredibly varied social movement. The second wave feminists we've met and worked with—women such as Robin Morgan, Gloria Steinem, Susan Douglas, and Katha Pollitt, as well as our own personal mentors—aren't strict disciplinarians monitoring our feminism for its allegiance to their agenda. They aren't puritanical figures who shy from anything sexy or fun, either. Although there are conflicts between the generations—second wavers may see third wavers as more concerned with image than with material realities, and younger feminists may see older feminists as essentializing gender and unconcerned with diversity—there is far more continuity than discord between the two waves.

Nonetheless, there are certainly some differences. One way that the third wave distinguishes itself from the second wave is through its emphasis on paradox, conflict, multiplicity, and messiness. This generation's feminism is often informed by postmodern, poststructuralist theories of identity; as a result, we are able to see the constructed nature of identity as well as the ways in which gender may be a performance that can be manipulated and politically altered as it is performed. Because this theoretical framework calls into question the very idea of a unified self, it allows for a playful incorporation of performed identities, even when they contradict one another. This contradiction and multiplicity of identities plays itself out especially in third wavers' love/hate relationship with the media and pop culture. For instance, in "Do the Ladies Run This … ? Some Thoughts on Hip-Hop Feminism," Gwendolyn D. Pough describes her problematic relationship to hip hop: as a feminist, she deplores its sexism, but as a music lover, she enjoys its soul and rhythm. Another kind of multiplicity important to the third wave has less to do with performance and more to do with reality: third wavers themselves are multiracial, multiethnic, and multi-issued.

Although we see efforts to embrace diversity as a valid and important theoretical contribution, we are troubled by the ease with which scholars, writers, and activists lay claim to multiplicity in third wave discourse. That is, sometimes it seems as if everything and everyone can fit within the third wave—it doesn't matter what they actually think, do, or believe. We call this the "feminist free-for-all": under this rubric, feminism doesn't involve a set of core beliefs that one shares or goals that one works for, but instead involves claiming beliefs and ideas one day and discarding them the next, as they go in and out of fashion or as they become personally or intellectually difficult to sustain. This is the worst interpretation of bell hooks's edict that "feminism is for everybody": it implies that anybody can be a feminist, regardless of her or his actions.

The seduction of the "feminist free-for-all" is evident in much third writing. For instance, in an essay in the perceptive and hard-hitting collection *Jane Sexes it up* (2002), a book that explores third wave feminism and heterosexuality, Merri Lisa Johnson challenges some views of the feminist theorist bell hooks. In an earlier essay (1984), hooks argued that lifestyle choices must not undercut feminist politics. To that end, she asserted that feminists concerned with eradicating violence against women must not perpetuate violent models of sexuality in their own lives; in particular, hooks demanded that feminists relearn desire so that they would not be turned on by hypermasculine, oppressive men. Although Johnson agrees with hooks's goal of ending violence against women, she takes issue with hooks's agenda. Almost as if she is echoing Rebecca Walker's complaint about the difficulty of conforming to a rigid second wave identity, Johnson notes hooks's "old-school feminist style" and suggests that her demand is "daunting in the discipline it would require." She goes on to say, "I won't do it. I am not that feminist, not that kind of feminist." Rather than exploring why hooks's ideas upset her, she simply backs away.

This moment in an otherwise-probing essay is emblematic of a key conflict between second and third wave feminists: many in the third wave—in their attempt to complicate and broaden feminism, in their attempt to bring postmodern and poststructuralist theoretical concepts to bear on feminist theory and praxis—run the risk of abandoning feminist politics. In other words, Johnson seems to be just on the verge of saying, "I don't want to change my desires because it's just too hard." And the unspoken assumption behind this statement is that "feminism's not supposed to be that hard." It's one thing to examine hooks's demand and conclude that it isn't theoretically sound; it's another to reject it because it would demand too much work from us.

Granted, there are many ways of going about changing the world, and one of the theoretical contributions of third wave feminism is the notion that politics isn't that simple—and neither are identities, desires, or the intersections of our internal and external landscapes. Johnson's interrogation of the congruence between feminist identity and performed desire represents a theoretical contribution of the third wave; Johnson questions whether one's desires need to conform to one's politics. We think that the third wave impulse to challenge certain perceptions of what feminism is or how is should be performed is valid, as is the impulse to make feminism as inviting as possible to a broad range of people. However, we contend that this invitation to feminism must be politically rigorous; rather than emptying feminism of its political content, we must embrace feminism's potential to transform our lives and our world. And if someone's challenge to feminism simply rests on the difficulty feminist ideology poses, then she runs the risk of making feminism nothing but a posture.

16. Stacy Gillis and Rebecca Munford, "Genealogies and Generations: The Politics and Praxis of Third Wave Feminism," from *Women's History Review*

Excerpts from "Genealogies and Generations: The Politics and Praxis of Third Wave Feminism" by Stacy Gillis and Rebecca Munford in *Women's History Review* 13(2) (2004): 165–178. Reprinted with permission.

This article looks at how postfeminism and third-wave feminism are used interchangeably, within both popular and academic conversations. Because the third wave has to some extent tried to establish itself as a popular, non-academic feminism, this has created tensions for third-wavers. Popular components of third-wave feminism have been criticized as "not feminist," including girl culture, the Grrrl movement and *Bust* magazine, and icons such as Courtney Love, Madonna, and the Spice Girls. But the focus on these icons and movements within the third wave also points to the ways postfeminism—when informed by postmodern theory and understood as a "radical conceptual shift within feminism from debates around equality to a focus on debates around difference"—can be a viable alternative to second-wave feminism. However, unlike postfeminism, third-wave feminist politics allow for *both* equality and difference. The main problem with third-wave feminism is with the wave paradigm itself, which paralyzes feminism, pitting generations against one another.

> *[T]here have always been, and will always be, differing versions of what feminism is about, with the 'new' or latest trajectories invariably keen to mark their distance from the 'old'.*
>
> —Lynne Segal, *Why Feminism? Gender, Psychology, Politics* (1999)

In 1999 Lynne Segal published *Why Feminism?*, both a summary of feminist debates over the previous twenty years and an outline of ways to move the debates forward. Asking herself 'why feminism?', she answered that '[t]he special legacy of feminism lies in its striving to keep relating the personal and the cultural to the economic and political, however forbidding and precarious that enterprise might be'. *Why Feminism?* provides a cogent argument for feminism, whilst pointing up the dilemmas contained within the movement today.

> Most have seen the dilemmas of feminism to be a result of the confusions generated between competing objectives. The first is its struggle to improve the lives and status of the majority of women, especially where they have appeared most vulnerable when classed as a sex—whether in

> their sexual, reproductive, working or social lives. It is campaigning for gender justice or equality that feminism presents itself in its decisively activist mode, most reminiscent of the 1970s. The second objective is to reinvent the meanings of womanhood, to imagine the feminine in ways which radically subvert existing symbolic binaries of sex, gender, and sexuality. This is the declared stance of a 'nineties' feminist post-structuralism (confusingly also often labelled 'post-modern').

Segal positions these objectives as competing discourses that should be reconciled in both academic and non-academic feminism. But she dismisses another competing discourse: 'the post-structuralist theorizing of phallogocentrism and women's nomadic, multifarious but ineluctable "otherness" (the bedrock of those young women "Doing Feminism, Being Feminists" in the 1990s, some of whom call themselves "the third wave")'. What is this third wave that can be summarily dismissed, labelled in quotations, and shored up against a bedrock of ineluctable otherness?

In so far as any notion of a 'third wave' implies that second-wave feminism is over, it has too often been conflated with 'post-feminism'. Post-feminism is itself an ambiguous and contested term that has been seized upon by a media all too eager to declare the demise—and failure—of feminism. As Susan Faludi describes in her study of anti-feminism, *Backlash* (1991):

> Just when record numbers of younger women were supporting feminist goals in the mid-1980s (more of them, in fact, than older women) and a majority of all women were calling themselves feminists, the media declared that feminism was the flavour of the seventies and the 'post-feminism' was the new story—complete with a younger generation who supposedly reviled the women's movement.

In 1982, the *New York Times Magazine* featured an article, 'Voices from the Post-Feminist Generation', which positioned feminism as passé, its aims met or unnecessary to the lives of everyday women. Post-feminism has since become the keyword for mainstream media representations of feminism, where it most frequently describes:

> a movement when women's movements are, for whatever reasons, no longer moving, no longer vital, no longer relevant; the term suggests that the gains forged by previous generations of women have so completely pervaded all tiers of our social existence that those still 'harping' about women's victim status are embarrassingly out of touch.

Associated with the arguments of the media-friendly conservative feminists Naomi Wolf, Katie Roiphe, Christina Hoff Sommers and Camille Paglia, this version of (post)feminism is underpinned by a binarised distinction between 'victim feminism' and 'power feminism'. Power feminism has been positioned, by these writers, as the only viable way in which to counteract the supposed lack of agency in victim feminism. The victim vs. power paradigm was and is a largely US-based phenomenon. In the United Kingdom, a more fluid understanding of feminist discourse—one which initially ignored the seduction of the antagonism implicit in US feminist debates—was heralded by the publication of Natasha Walter's *The New Feminism* in 1998. Similar criticisms have been made of both this 'new' feminism in the United Kingdom and conservative feminism in the USA:

> In Britain in the late 1990s, widespread publicity accompanied the appearance of a book declaring the dawn of a "New Feminism': this time as a mainstream, majority movement in which women—from the Spice Girls to Cherie Blair and her husband's hundred new women MPs—can celebrate their own sudden power and achievements (in part thanks to Margaret Thatcher for normalizing female success) ... [This feminism is] a form of power-feminism, applauding women's growing success, identification with their jobs and their ability to help each other.

The generational divide between second wave feminism and the new forms of feminism—whether it be a third wave or not—is one of the defining characteristics of the movement. Despite, or perhaps because of, these criticisms against it, this new generation of feminist voices is increasingly demanding to be heard, to be given credence and to claim a place in a feminist genealogy.

It is this generation of feminists which identifies as the third wave but which is labelled, more often than not, post-feminist. The slippage between the two terms may explain the caution with which the academy regards the possibility of a new 'kind' of feminism. Whereas second wave feminist activism introduced feminism to the academy, the academy is only just beginning to acknowledge the possibility of a third wave. In the 1990s, third wave feminism's academic presence was confined to *Third Wave Agenda: being feminist, doing feminism* (1997) and a special issue of *Hypatia* (1997). In July 2002, one of the first academic conferences on third wave feminism took place at the University of Exeter, bringing together theorists and activists, second wave feminists and third wave feminists. The conference identified the ambiguous relationship between those who identify as third wave feminists and those who identify their work as belonging to a field informed by post-structuralist and postmodern theories of identity and subjectivity. These tensions are explored in the special issue on third wave feminism and women's studies of the *Journal of International Women's Studies* (2003), as well as in *Catching a Wave: reclaiming feminism for the 21st century* (2003). *Third Wave Feminism: a critical exploration* (2004) is the first collection to address third wave feminism as an academic subject—moving from feminist popular culture to new constructions of sex and gender—rather than as a subject that belongs only to those who identify as 'third wavers'.

Even a cursory reading of these texts indicates that third wave feminism does not have a comfortable position within the academy. This can be partly ascribed to academic feminism's quick embracing of post-feminism rather than third wave feminism. This post-feminism is not the 'after the fact' post-feminism of the media; rather, it is understood as feminism within post-structuralist theory. Ann Brooks's *Postfeminisms: Feminism, Cultural Theory and Cultural Forms* (1997) defines academic postfeminism as 'an expression of a stage in the constant evolutionary movement of feminism ... [its] "coming of age", its maturity into a confident body of theory and politics, representing pluralism and difference and reflecting on its position in relation to other philosophical and political movements similarly demanding change'. *The Routledge Companion to Feminism and Postfeminism* (1998) likewise links post-feminism with postmodernism in its desire 'to destabilise fixed definitions of gender, and to deconstruct authoritative paradigms and practices'. The academic split between post-feminism and third wave feminism is actualised in the companion's identification of the third wave as 'characterised by a desire to redress economic and racial inequality as well as "women's issues" ... [it] has been viewed with scepticism by many as merely a short-lived fashion rather than a genuine indication that women have reached the next stage in the feminist struggle'. Thus, the theoretical designation of post-feminism versus third wave feminism is fought across the equality/difference divide. Post-feminism, within the academy, has been positioned as a radical 'conceptual shift within feminism from debates around equality to a focus on debates around difference' informed by post-structuralist and postmodernist theorising. However, as will be shown, third wave feminist politics allow *for both* equality and difference....

Some of the strongest, and most self-consciously clamorous, voices of third wave feminism are those emerging from 'girl' culture. In spite of its homogenised media representation—and second wave reception—'girl' culture is an extremely eclectic phenomenon which includes the Riot Grrrls of the punk movement, the Hello Kitty-accessorised and lipglossed Girlies exemplified by the writers of zines such as *Bitch* and *BUST*, as well as the more anodyne mainstream proponents of 'girl power' identified with the Spice Girls. Although these various groups are not always politically aligned, they do have in common a vigorous reclamation and recuperation of the word 'girl' as no longer a simply derogatory and disrespectful term but one that captures the contradictions shaping female identity for young women whose world has been informed by the struggles and gains of second wave feminism. Centred on music and zines, girl culture foregrounds the relationship between feminism and popular culture that had been positioned by many second wave feminists as unavoidably antagonistic. Heywood and Drake, for example, identify the third wave more generally as a generation of feminists who 'often take cultural production and sexual politics as key sites of struggle, seeking to use desire and pleasure as well as anger to fuel struggles for justice'. But the extent to which girl culture provides a site of resistance to patriarchal structures has been contested by many second wave feminists. In *The Whole Woman* (1999), Germaine Greer decries what she describes as the 'depressingly durable' cultural phenomenon of '"girls", "girls behaving badly", "girls on top"'. In many respects, it is not surprising that the very notion of girl culture has received scathing criticism from second wave feminists who had challenged the application of 'girl' to adult women because of its implications of infantilisation and belittlement.

Yet girl culture has been too easily positioned as a depoliticised and dehistoricised product of the 'backlash' against feminism. Mainstreamed under the media-friendly 'girl power' slogan, largely associated with the Spice Girls, and couched in the rhetoric of a popularised post-feminism, girl culture has been deprived of its radical and activist history. For example, Rosalind Coward erroneously describes how the Spice Girls 'coined the phrase [girl power] as a bit of promotional fun but is passed quickly into the wider culture as a good label to use in any situation in which girls might be putting themselves forward in new, brash, and "unfeminine" ways'. The emergence of girl culture in the early 1990s, however, was less a post-feminist manifestation of the backlash than it was an outraged—and organised—response from young women to the designations of post-feminism. Kay Ebeling's article, 'The Failure of Feminism', in the 19 November 1990 issue of *Newsweek* motivated Kathleen Hanna and her all female band Bikini Kill along with other Riot Grrrl bands in Olympia and Washington, DC, to express their anger at the allegations of feminism's demise by calling for 'revolution, girl-style now'. While co-opting its angry and noisy rebellion, Riot Grrrl bands such as Bikini Kill, Bratmobile and Babes in Toyland censured the fundamentally patriarchal structures of the punk scene, in much the same way as Queen Latifah intervened in the 'hip-hop phallo-universe'. In addition to concerts, the Riot Grrrls organised weekly meetings to discuss issues of sexual abuse, eating disorders and sexual harassment, as well as self-defence and skill-sharing workshops. Through zines and girl-only moshpits, the Riot Grrrls forged a unique feminist space for young women (usually aged between fourteen and twenty-five) that was not structurally dissimilar to that sustained by the second wave consciousness-raising groups and support networks. The weekly meetings in Olympia and Washington spread around the country and, along with the Riot Grrrl Convention in Washington, DC in July 1992 and the burgeoning of guerrilla zines such as *Bikini Kill*, *Riot Grrrl*, *Girl Germs* and *Girl Power!*, called attention to the energy and presence of a network of young feminists in the face of the backlash rhetoric that feminism had petered out and failed.

Identifying the underground music community as a vital place of feminist activism, Melissa Klein aptly highlights the extent to which by reconfiguring consciousness-raising groups in the girl-only moshpits, Rio Grrrls often deployed 'second wave activist techniques but applied them to third wave forms'. While acknowledging the extent to which third wave feminism, and specifically its Riot Grrrl configuration, 'owes much to the struggles of the second wave,' Klein moves on to claim that such third wave forms are defined by 'a postmodern focus on contradiction and duality, on the reclamation of terms. S-M pornography, the words *cunt* and *queer* and *pussy* and *girl*—are all things to be re-examined or reclaimed'. With their dishevelled vintage dresses, short dyed hair, luminescent red lipstick, and heavy combat boots, the Riot Grrrls re-present rather than reject conventional ideas about 'femininity' in order to create models of contradiction and conflict: 'We want not to get rid of the trappings of traditional femininity or sexuality so much as to pair them with demonstrations of strength or power'. Although the use of a 'traditional' femininity could bear out Segal's 'ineluctable otherness', the explicit foregrounding of a transgressive sexual and political agency ironically underscores the Riot Grrrls' desires.

It is this acceptance of hybridity and contradiction that similarly underlies the feminist philosophy of the self-proclaimed Girlies. While the Riot Grrrls voiced their anger and protest through punk rock, the Girlies, an older group of young women, focused on popular culture, similarly forging a space of social agency and resistance through zines such as *Bitch* and *Bust*. Baumgardner & Richards offer the following definition of 'Girlie':

> A Girlie-girl can be a stereotypically feminine one—into manicures and hairstyles and cooking and indoorsy activities. Girlie is also a feminist philosophy ... Girlies are adult women, usually in their mid-twenties to late thirties, whose feminist principles are based on a reclaiming of girl culture (of feminine accoutrements that were tossed out with sexism during the Second Wave), be it Barbie, housekeeping, or girl talk.

Like the Riot Grrrls, the Girlies foreground a celebration of the paraphernalia of 'femininity'—of makeup, fashion, etc.—that had previously been censured by second-wave feminists as inextricably caught up in patriarchal definitions of female identity. For the Girlies, 'femininity' is no longer at odds with 'feminism', but at the very center of an ideology of agency, confidence, and resistance. Marcelle Karp and Debbie Stoller, the editors of *BUST*—of which a selection of articles are collected in *The BUST Guide to the New Girl Order* (1999)—claim that the zine captures 'the voice of a brave new girl: one that is raw and real, straightforward and sarcastic, smart and silly, and liberally sprinkled with references to our own Girl Culture—that shared set of female experiences that includes Barbies and blowjobs, sexism and shoplifting, *Vogue* and vaginas'. Where early feminist engagement with popular culture had largely focused on the oppressive ideology underlying media representations of women, the writers of zines such as *Bitch* and *Bust* built on the innovations of the mainstream *Sassy* magazine of the late 1980s to forge a space which combined a critique of dominant constructions of femininity and a reclamation and celebration of girlhood.

Bitch's mission statement claims that '[t]he much-touted "girl power" and "girl culture" have the potential to counteract the now-documented plunge in girls' self-esteem during their pubescent years ... *Bitch* is about formulating replies to the sexism that we see every day. It's about critically examining all the images of femininity and feminism that are thrown at us'. Demystifying some of those second wave feminist stereotypes that functioned to 'fix' female identity, Girlie culture questions definitions of what it means to be a feminist by foregrounding the contradictions and conflicts shaping young women's experiences. Rebecca Walker captures the tensions and contradictions shaping the self-positioning of young feminists who are uncomfortable with what they see as the inflexibility of second wave identity politics:

> For many of us it seems that to be a feminist in the way that we have seen or understood feminism is to conform to an identity and way of living that doesn't allow for individuality, complexity, or less than perfect personal histories. We fear that the identity will dictate and regulate our lives, instantaneously pitting us against someone, forcing us to choose inflexible and unchanging sides, female against male, black against white, oppressed against oppressor, good against bad.

Debates around the contradiction and conflict crucial to configurations of third wave feminist identities have been centred on one of the most prominent and public grrrl heroines: Courtney Love. The lead singer of [the] punk rock band Hole and proponent of the kinderwhore aesthetic, Love has been positioned as a mouthpiece for both the Riot Grrrls and the Girlies and embraced by third wave feminists more generally for her dramatic subversion of the polarity between 'power' and 'victim' feminisms. Heywood and Drake posit that Love is a third wave feminist icon who:

> [C]ombines the individualism, combativeness, and star power that are the legacy of second wave gains in opportunities for women (which arrived in conjunction with cultural backlash against such gains), with second wave critiques of the cult of beauty and male dominance ... Love bridges the irreconcilability of individuality and femininity within dominant culture, combining the cultural critique of an earlier generation of feminists with the backlash against it by the next generation of women.

Still, Love's claim to be the postmodern feminist who harnesses contradiction and conflict for the politics of girl culture is difficult to reconcile with her own 'bad girl' philosophy that 'we like our dark Nars lipstick and LaPerla panties, but we hate sexism, even if we do fuck your husbands/boyfriends'. Love's ironic 'postmodern feminism' might confound the dichotomisation of Madonna and Whore, empowerment and victimhood, but does it really dismantle these binaries?

Of course, we have been here before. These arguments have been well rehearsed in relation to the 'representational industry' surrounding Madonna, the postmodern icon and material girl *par excellence*. Calling attention to female pleasure and sexual agency through endlessly recasting her public identity, Madonna reinvented the 'significance of dyed blonde hair, dark lipstick, padded bras, polka-dot bikinis or fishnet tights ... with female-to-female laughter and irony'. More so than Love, feminist debates around Madonna have highlighted configurations of female identity and subjectivity across the intersection of postmodernism and consumerism. Third wave feminism posits youth music culture as a productive site for activism: '[b]ecause contemporary rap, rock, and alternative music is produced and consumed primarily by persons in the third wave, music has emerged as a site for activist coalition and community building like no other'. But to what extent does commodification neutralise feminist politics? Madonna may be reinventing herself, but the question of whether she 'offer[s] a mockery of conventional femininity, or just another way to be fashionable and "sexy"' that remains attractive to the patriarchy needs further consideration. The politics of subjectivity need to incorporate an understanding of the agency within self-representation as well as the appropriation of that agency. In short, the 'power' and the 'girl' in girl power need to be interrogated rather than dismissed outright. What Love and Madonna—and even Britney Spears—foreground is a shift from the second wave focus on the politics of representation to an emphasis on the politics of self-representation....

Katherine Viner is amongst those who have dismissed the individualism of girl power: '[s]uddenly feminism is all about how the individual feels right here, right now, rather than the bigger picture. The idea of doing something for the greater good—or, indeed, because the reasons behind the action might be dangerous or insecure or complex—has become an anachronism'. How far can the 'Jell-O-shot versions of feminism'—this celebration of Barbies and blow jobs—offered by zines like *BUST* really take us? While recognising the extent to which they have 'created a joyful culture that makes being an adult woman who calls herself a feminist seem thrilling, sexy, and creative', Baumgardner wishes that the Girlies discussed in *Manifesta* 'would organize as well as they onanize'. Similarly, in spite of its early commitment to direct action and social change at the beginning of the 1990s, by the end of the decade the Riot Grrrl movement had neither consolidated a clear agenda nor a programme for activism—in this respect, the girl-style revolution promised by the largely white and middle-class Riot Grrrls and the New Girl Order is a far remove from the carefully considered programme of political activism propounded by Baumgardner and Richards in *Manifesta*. Moreover, there is a very real danger that while third wave feminists, as exemplified by Walker, have expressed their discontent with the inflexibility of second wave identity politics, the insularity of Grrrl and Girlie culture risks instituting another set of conventions.

Viner attributes this reactionary response to second wave identity politics as symptomatic of a broader misunderstanding of that axiom of the second wave by pointing up that '[t]he personal as the political was never meant to be a prescription of how to live your life. It was never meant to be a rallying cry to shave off your hair or take up with the lady next door. But what it was really meant to do was create an awareness of how our personal lives are ruled by political factors'. The phrase 'the personal is political'—invented by members of New York Radical Women—endorsed a politics sustained by concrete personal experiences of male domination. One of the tenets of third wave feminism is its insistence and reliance upon the confession as a tool of empowerment, one that is privileged over other models of empowerment (including academic theory). *Third Wave Agenda* claims to fuse the confessional mode with the more analytic mode of the academy whereas *To Be Real* is predicated upon an equation of third wave feminist practice with anecdote, the personal providing the example for political action. But what alienates the academic from the activist are these sorts of claims: 'testimony is where feminism starts. Historically, women's personal stories have been the evidence of where the movement needs to go politically and, furthermore, that there is a need to move forward'. Although this has its strengths—for example, Amy Richards and Rebecca Walker founded the *Third Wave Foundation* (see www.thirdwavefoundation.org), a national organisation to get young feminists voting—this is a particularised understanding of politics as democratic action. Baumgardner & Richards can thus claim that the personal testimonies in *To Be Real* and *The* Bust *Guide to the New Girl Order* (the latter including such essays as 'The Mysterious Eroticism of MiniBackpacks' and 'More than a Blow Job: It's a Career') are 'the foundation of the personal ethics upon which a political women's movement will be built' and comparable with such events as the Anita Hill/Clarence Thomas hearings in 1991. The unquestioning conflation of the personal and the political focuses on personal freedom, but at the expense of political equality, as Ally McBeal and Bridget Jones demonstrate. Third wave feminism lacks an acknowledgement of the tensions in 'the personal is political'. Of course, positioning feminism as a politics that emerged out of personal experiences had its origin in the consciousness-raising groups of the 1970s. These consciousness-raising groups brought women together and encouraged them to share experiences, allowing them to realize that they were not alone. However, the metonymic gap between the personal and the political is what allowed post-feminism to emerge as a 'viable' alternative to feminism—the confusion between personal accounts and politicising the personal. Segal has pointed up 'the espousal of a new type of "feminized", personalized or therapeutic rhetoric ... borrowing the feminist consciousness-raising discourses of disclosure and shared pain'. The widespread emotional equation in the West of the personal and the political destabilises its (re)appropriation by third wave feminists.... Feminist history is traditionally understood as a succession of waves. However, the trouble with this model is that generations are set up in competition with one another and definitions of feminism are positioned around the 'leaders' of these generations, whether it be the Pankhursts, Gloria Steinem or Germaine Greer. Current feminist figures are compared incessantly (and unfavourably) with these past 'leaders'. The wave paradigm also means that figures who write 'outside' of it—for example, Mary Wollstonecraft or Simone de Beauvoir—are regarded as anomalies at best or ignored at worst. This competitive generational model does not allow for a collective memory of female-based thought, empowerment and activism:

> The fuzzy sense of where we've been plays out when something like *Bust* or Bikini Kill or the phrase 'girl power' turns masses of females on to feminism—and then peters out after the first rush. Having no sense of how we got here condemns women to reinvent the wheel and often blocks us from creating a political strategy.

The wave paradigm not only ensures that each generation must 'reinvent the wheel' but also lends power to backlash politics and rhetoric. Faludi has foregrounded, in minute detail, the ways in which the Reagan and Thatcher years were marked by a backlash against feminism. She identifies the way in which the wave metaphor is used against feminist thought and activity.

> In times when feminism is at a low ebb, women assume the reactive role—privately and most often covertly struggling to assert themselves against the dominant cultural tide. But when feminism itself becomes the tide, the opposition doesn't simply go along with the reversal: it digs in its heels, brandishes its fists, builds walls and dams. And its resistance creates countercurrents and treacherous undertows.

The irony is, of course, that backlash rhetoric points up the supposed irrelevance and powerlessness of feminism—the same feminism which requires such a strong backlash to 'contain' it. The internecine and cross-generational arguments contribute to the potency of the wave paradigm and, ultimately, to the potency of backlash politics. Thus, the question surrounding third wave feminism is not so much 'what is it?' but 'how does another wave contribute to the future of feminism?'

That it was only in 1998 that an international court denounced rape as a form of torture in prison and that nearly twice as many women as men are illiterate testify to the overwhelming necessity for engaged, politicised and active feminism(s). As tired as this seems, and as obvious as it is to those of us who think about feminism, these statements of fact need to be made, and to be made repeatedly in the face of the generational divides that mark feminist theory and practice. The third wavers are keen in their assertion that they are doing something different from the second wave feminists—and second wave feminists are equally keen to dismiss this new form of feminism: 'In the interest of affirming the difference of the third wave, many third wave narratives assume a metonymic view of the second wave, in which a part of second wave activity is substituted for the whole'. Similarly, second wave feminists also use metonymic configurations of the 'third wave' (for example, the Spice Girls or Naomi Wolf) in order to dismiss its power (as demonstrated by Segal in the opening paragraph). The politics of the fairy tale—with successive mother figures threatened by the sexual agency of their daughters—have been analysed by numerous feminists. This model could be usefully deployed as a way of understanding and interrogating feminist history, rather than being simply a method of feminist analysis. The generational account of feminism—which third wave feminism is perpetuating—should be understood as merely another tool of the backlash. As Misha Kavka notes in *Feminist Consequences: Theory for the New Century* (2001), '[f]eminism is not ... the object of a singular history but, rather, a term under which people have in different times and places invested in a more general struggle for social justice and in so doing have participated in and produced multiple histories'. The lack of attention to multiple histories is evidenced by the fact that while tremendous work has been accomplished by activists and theorists since second wave feminism, third wave feminist texts still only provide a largely white Anglo-American perspective, with the occasional article on hip-hop. One way forward in constructing these multiple histories is to build on the work of US third world feminists who have 'moved the concepts of difference to the foreground, reminding us that even if sisterhood is global, not all women's lives and experiences are identical'. The lessons of the first and second waves need to be more fully learned—both as history and as warning—so feminism can break the wave paradigm.

17. Astrid Henry, "Daughterhood Is Powerful: The Emergence of Feminism's Third Wave," from *Not My Mother's Sister*

Excerpts from Astrid Henry, *Not My Mother's Sister* (Bloomington, IN: Indiana University Press, 2004): 16–51. Reprinted with permission.

Exploring the mother/daughter metaphor and the problem of generational conflict within feminism, in this chapter Henry argues that the emergence of third-wave feminism was related to shifts in consciousness around women's issues provoked by events such as the Clarence Thomas/Anita Hill testimonies, the Clinton presidency, "fighting women" films such as *Thelma and Louise,* and the declaration of feminism's "death" in the media. Henry looks at prominent third-wavers such as Rebecca Walker and Naomi Wolf and reads in both a contradictory desire to "suggest a breaking away from second wave feminism even as it disavows this break." A complicated account of different articulations of "third wave," this essay is a must-read for the way it situates third-wave thinking.

THE DAWNING OF THE THIRD WAVE

The term "third wave" has been attributed to Rebecca Walker, who first used it in a 1992 Ms. essay; later that same year, Walker co-founded a national organization called Third Wave Foundation devoted to young women's activism. In fact, however, the term "third wave" originally surfaced, to my knowledge, five years earlier in an essay titled "Second Thoughts on the Second Wave," by Deborah Rosenfelt and Judith Stacey. In describing the ebbs and flows of feminism throughout the late 1970s and 1980s, Rosenfelt and Stacey write that "what some are calling a third wave of feminism [is] already taking shape." Naomi Wolf, in her 1991 *Beauty Myth*, first imbued the term with a specifically generational meaning, referring to the "feminist third wave" as women who were in their twenties in the early 1990s.

During the late 1980s and early 1990s, the term "third wave" was also being used by some feminists "to identify a new feminism that is led by and has grown out of the challenge to white feminism posited by women of color." The text which is often cited as making this claim is an anthology which never materialized in book form, due to financial problems at Kitchen Table: Women of Color Press. Though never actually published, *The Third Wave: Feminist Perspectives on Racism* continues to inform the way some feminists employ the term "third wave," using it to signal a new wave of feminism led by women of color that is specifically anti-racist in its approach. As Lisa Albrecht, one of this text's editors, reports, however, within the context of this anthology, the term "third wave" was not meant to be understood as a generational term.

> Third wave feminism as we used it was NOT about young feminists or generational feminism. It was/is about a movement beyond the first two waves of feminism, which we saw as [focused on] white women.... We defined third wave feminism as emerging with *This Bridge Called My Back* and the rise of vocal women of color challenging white women.

Albrecht's use of "third wave" to indicate a challenge by women of color to white feminists and the racism within the second wave continues to shape contemporary uses of the term. However, by the mid- to late 1990s, the term "third wave" had become synonymous with younger feminists and with stressing generational differences from the second-wave feminists of the 1970s.

The use of the term "wave" long predates its use in the 1990s. Women involved in the women's liberation movement of the late 1960s and early 1970s adopted the term "second wave" in order to signify their connection to the feminism of the nineteenth and early twentieth centuries, which from that moment on became known as the first wave of feminism. The term "wave" served to indicate a resurgence of a previously existing movement. However, the second wave's use of the term "first wave" to mark the earlier period in feminist activity frequently carried with it an assumption about the superiority of their own movement, using the numerical delineation of a "second wave" to signify feminism's progress.

The wave metaphor signals both continuity and discontinuity; in fact, both are essential to its rhetorical effectiveness. Continuity is suggested in the very notion of a wave, which is inevitably followed by successive waves cresting on the shore. The term "wave" is rarely used to stress the singularity of something but rather emphasizes the inevitability of—and connection to—other such waves. Discontinuity—and often progress and improvement—is highlighted by the numerical delineation of a new, in this case second, wave. While waves may inexorably be connected to other waves, and thus never stand alone in isolation, the announcement of a new wave is typically meant to stress the *evolution* of ideas and political movements. The wave metaphor, then, manifests the same contradictory take on the earlier women's movement that I have been emphasizing: it allows one both to identify and disidentify with the past.

In her 1992 article "Becoming the Third Wave," written in response to the Clarence Thomas hearings, Rebecca Walker uses the term to emphasize both that feminism is not dead and that a new generation of feminists is beginning to mobilize. As she states, "I am not a postfeminism feminist. I am the Third Wave." In defining herself as not post-feminist, Walker insists that she has not moved beyond the space created by the second wave; she is not beyond feminism. Her denunciation of the category post-feminist can be read as an indictment of the media's labeling of all women who chronologically follow the second wave as such. Moreover, Walker's claim can also be read as a way to distance herself from the group of women—whether organized generationally or not—who have embraced the term "post-feminism." Her claiming of the title "feminist" maintains a link with second-wave feminists while simultaneously enabling her to distance herself from the generation that immediately precedes her.

Yet the fact that Walker's "I am not a postfeminism feminist" is immediately followed by "I am the Third Wave" suggests that, for her, merely adopting the label "feminist" is not sufficient. As she later notes, third-wavers "modify the label [feminism] in an attempt to begin to articulate our differences." Walker's use of the term "third wave," like the second wave's self-baptism two and a half decades earlier, represents a desire to be a part of something new, a movement distinct from the previous wave. In fact, the term "third wave" can only be understood within the context of its two preceding waves, the first and, more important, the second wave of U.S. feminism. In the move from second to third, the naming of a new wave relies upon the connotation of progress implied by the metaphor of the wave. The bravado behind Walker's claim—"*I am* the Third Wave"—would further seem to suggest a breaking away from second-wave feminism even as it disavows this break.

Like Walker, Naomi Wolf's 1991 description of the then-burgeoning third wave is concerned with remaining within an ongoing feminist tradition—that is, she does not describe herself as beyond or "post" feminism—while simultaneously breaking away from second-wave feminism.

> I have become convinced that there are thousands of young women ready and eager to join forces with a peer-driven feminist third wave that would take on, along with the classic feminist agenda, the new problems that have arisen with the shift in Zeitgeist and the beauty backlash.... While transmitting the previous heritage of feminism intact, it would need to be, as all feminist waves are, peer-driven: no matter how wise a mother's advice is, we listen to our peers. It

> would have to make joy, rowdiness, and wanton celebration as much a part of its project as hard work and bitter struggle, and it can begin all this rejecting the pernicious fib that is crippling young women—the fib called postfeminism, the pious hope that the battles have all been won.

Within this relatively short passage from *The Beauty Myth*, a number of the distinguishing characteristics of the "new" feminism called the third wave are evident, ideas that would be explored in greater detail by a wide range of young feminists as the 1990s rolled on. This generation enters into feminism through both rejecting the imagined postfeminism of their immediate predecessors (and some of their peers) and reclaiming the feminism of the early second wave.

The identificatory relationship established between second- and third-wave feminists, however, has as much to do with disidentifying as it does with identifying. Like the relationship constructed by second-wave feminists to their first-wave predecessors, in this relationship it is the ambivalence or tension between acceptance and rejection—moving closer and breaking away—that is most interesting. In Wolf's text, while it is not particularly zealous in trying to break free from second-wave feminism, one can see tendencies that point toward this disidentifying trend within third-wave writing. Wolf writes that "along with the classic feminist agenda," third-wave feminism would also need to address "the new problems that have arisen with the shift in Zeitgeist." Thus, while this feminism would need to transmit "the previous heritage of feminism intact," it would also need to go beyond that heritage and offer something new. But what exactly would be new about this feminism, and what would it look like?

Wolf does not explore this question in much detail in *The Beauty Myth*, but she does offer us some clues. In defining this new wave as peer-driven, she unequivocally divides coexisting generations of feminists into age-based camps. Furthermore, the way she describes this generational division—"No matter how wise a mother's advice is, we listen to our peers"—stresses that it is predicated on the difference between the familial and the non-familial, mothers and peers. Within this structure, second-wave feminists become the mothers of the new wave. Their feminism is reduced to advice which, "no matter how wise," can, and perhaps should, be rejected in favor of what non-familial cohorts have to offer.

In describing second-wave feminism as a figurative mother figure to the third wave, Wolf provides an early example of what was to become a ubiquitous trope within subsequent writing on feminist generational relationships. The reliance on the mother-daughter trope to describe the relationship between the second and third waves may have been inevitable given that the age difference between each wave's representatives is roughly the equivalent of one familial generation. The effectiveness of this metaphoric familial relationship is compounded by the fact that for some third-wave writers and activists, their real mothers are, in fact, second-wave feminists: this is the case for both Rebecca

Walker and Naomi Wolf, for example. Second-wave feminists, then, are literally mother figures to the third wave, even as they are given this figurative role in their writing.

Central to this imagined mother-daughter relationship, however, is the absence of the generation of women who came of age in the late 1970s and 1980s: the so-called post-feminist generation. This generation has slipped through the cracks of the current generational structure being used to talk about feminism, feminist generations, and feminist waves. Its disappearance is no accident. This generation cannot be a branch on feminism's family tree if the wave structure and the family structure are to be mapped onto one another. Had Wolf included this missing generation into her description of feminism, her easy characterization of second-wave feminists as mothers would never have been possible. The overwhelming preference for talking about feminist generations in terms of second and third waves—a generational structure modeled on the familiar structure of the mother-daughter relationship—has meant that women who were in their twenties and early thirties in the 1980s must be metaphorically exiled from feminism's imagined family.

In her attempt to visualize the possible feminism of a third wave, Wolf provides the following image of pleasure, which would become central in defining generational differences between the two waves: "It would have to make joy, rowdiness, and wanton celebration as much a part of its project as hard work and bitter struggle." Wolf did not set these contrasting images of how feminism *feels* to those who engage with it in opposition in this passage; in fact, she argues that both must be central to the third-wave project. As the 1990s continued, however, "joy, rowdiness, and wanton celebration" would increasingly come to define third-wave feminism, while "bitter struggle" would be almost exclusively attributed to the second wave, with the emphasis on bitterness....

The third-wave feminism represented in ... more recent texts paints a very different portrait of contemporary feminism that the one offered by third-wave writers such as Katie Roiphe and Naomi Wolf, most specifically because these latter writers rarely engage with feminism that isn't produced by and about white women. The intense media focus given to Roiphe and other white "dissenter" feminists has tended to obscure one of the most exciting aspects of this burgeoning movement: namely, that the third wave is truly a multiracial, multiethnic coalition of young activists and writers. At least, that is how many third-wave writers have tried to describe this new wave. As Catherine Orr notes:

> [T]he contradictory character of the third wave emerged not from the generational divides between second wavers and their daughters, but from critiques by Cherríe Moraga, Gloria Anzaldúa, bell hooks, Chela Sandoval, Audre Lorde, Maxine Hong Kingston and many other feminists of color who called for a "new subjectivity" in what was, up to that point, white, middle-class, first world feminism. These are the discourses that shaped, and must continue to shape, third wave agendas in the years to come.

An early example of this conceptualization of the third wave is found in Sandoval's 1991 essay, "U.S. Third World Feminism: The Theory and Method of Oppositional Consciousness in the Postmodern World." In it she writes, "the recognition of differential consciousness" coming out of U.S. Third World feminism "is vital to the generation of a next 'third wave' women's movement and provides grounds for alliance with other decolonizing movements for emancipation." As seen in much third-wave writing by writers of all races, the central insight of U.S. Third World feminist thought regarding the interlocking nature of identity—that gender, race, ethnicity, sexuality, and class never function in isolation but always work as interconnected categories of oppression and privilege—has been described as the second wave's most influential and vital lesson. For many third-wavers, critiques of feminism's racism, its homophobia, and its inattention to other forms of oppression among women have been at the center of what they have learned as feminist theory and the history of the women's movement. As Ednie Kaeh Garrison noted in 2000, "It is clear now that feminist critiques of feminism are part of the very origins of Third Wave feminism rather than trailing behind an already unitary model of the movement."

While Garrison is correct to note that these critiques are "part of the origins" of the third wave—at least for many of the writers included in the more recent anthologies noted above—a "unitary model of the movement" still circulates within third-wave writing: namely, a unitary second wave in which women of color are relegated to the sidelines. Even when second-wave feminists of color are recognized as foundational to the third wave, such feminists seem unable to represent feminism itself. On one hand, depicting the second wave as primarily white can be read as an acknowledgment of the secondary status given to feminists of color during the last forty years of feminist theory and movement. On the other hand, this gesture enables third-wave feminists to position themselves as superior to the feminists of the past in their seeming ability to make *their* feminism anti-racist from its inception. An emblematic example of this gesture can be found in *Colonize This!*, where one contributor writes:

> The predominantly white and racist feminist movement of the 1970s ignored the relationship between racism, classism and homophobia. This pervasive feminist thinking has denied the complexities of the oppression I fight everyday [*sic*]. In the growing emergence of "third wave" feminism, feminism isn't reduced to one English-speaking white face from North America.

While I don't mean to suggest that the feminist movement of 1970s was not "predominantly white and racist," I am interested in how repeating this representation enables younger feminists to present their new wave as more progressive and inclusive than that of their second-wave predecessors. As Lisa Marie Hogeland rightly points out, "It's become a truism that the second wave was racist, for instance, no matter that such a blanket argument writes out of our history the enormous and important contributions of women of color in the 1970s." For feminism to truly be transformed from within, as the most optimistic third-wave writers argue it has been, it must incorporate a history of the struggles that got us next-generation feminists to where we are today. Feminism's history cannot be reduced to a simple narrative in which the "bad" white racist second wave was replaced by the "good" racially diverse and antiracist third wave.

As it has developed over the last decade, the third wave has been given variety of meanings, particularly with regard to what makes it new or different from second-wave feminism. As of this writing, third-wave feminism refers to at least three distinct, albeit interconnected, concepts: generational age, ideological position, and historical moment. In its primary use, "third wave" signifies the age of its adherents; that is, "third wave" refers to the feminism practiced and produced by women and men who were born after the baby-boom generation. In its earliest formulation, "third wave" was frequently conflated with Generation X (those born 1961–1981) because Gen X feminists were in their twenties and early thirties when the third wave first emerged in the early 1990s. By the turn of the twenty-first century, however, segments of Generation X had moved into their late thirties and (gasp!) early forties, raising interesting questions about the ways in which "third wave" denotes age and generational location. In *Manifesta*, Baumgardner and Richards claim that "third wave" refers to feminists "under thirty-five," while Third Wave Foundation, the organization co-founded by Richards and Rebecca Walker, describes its mission as "support[ing] the leadership of young women 15 to 30." While Generation X ages, the third wave remains young, unhinging the relationship between the two terms. It would appear, then, that "third wave" remains a signifier of youth rather than of a particular generation. Like the 1960s slogan "don't trust anyone over 30," this meaning of third wave suggests that a particular politics is the province of the young. This understanding of the term radically alters our use of the wave metaphor in describing feminist generations. Just as Baby Boomers remain within their demographic category even as they age, second-wave feminists remain "second wave" even as they grow older. (One could even say that this aging has been central to the third wave's representation of the second wave.) However, if Generation X feminists are no longer third wave once they reach thirty-five, what wave are they a part of? Does aging make one second wave? No matter what their year of birth or demographic generation is, will feminists under thirty-five own the third wave?

A second understanding of "third wave" stresses its value as an ideology independent from a demographic generation. In this understanding of the term, the third wave represents a shift within feminist thought, moving it in a new direction by blending aspects of second-wave feminism with other forms of contemporary critical theory, such as queer, postcolonial, and critical race theories. As Heywood and Drake describe this ideological shift, third-wave feminism "contains elements of second wave critique of beauty culture, sexual abuse, and power structures while it also acknowledges and makes use of the pleasure, danger, and defining power of those structures." This ideological understanding of third-wave feminism leads to a third meaning which sees it as developing out of the realities of the current historical moment, "a world of global capitalism and information technology, postmodernism and postcolonialism, and environmental degradation," as Dicker and Piepmeier write in *Catching a Wave*. "We no longer live in the world that feminists of the second wave faced." Third-wave feminists, they continue, "are therefore concerned not simply with 'women's issues' but with a broad range of interlocking topics."

The ways in which historical moment, ideology, and age are frequently conflated within third-wave discourse complicates any easy separation of the term's meanings. In fact, if the third wave's ideology is seen as an *inevitable* by-product of either this current historical moment or the age of its practitioners, there seems to be little difference between the terms. Yet, if the term "third-wave feminism" is meant to describe a particular ideological stance in relation to contemporary social and political realities, it could, of course, be adopted—or rejected—by feminists of all ages. Writing as a, generationally speaking, second-wave feminist, Carol Siegel notes: "Lately, among some of the self-described third-wave feminists, I have finally started to feel, once again, at home in feminism. Could feminism's third wave be my wave?" Siegel's comments point to the possibilities of cross-generational identification, cautioning us against permanently affixing ideologies to people simply because of their chronological age.

In none of these various understandings, however, is the term "third wave" used to describe a political movement in the 1960s sense; rather, the third wave functions more like "an ideology without a movement." As Ednie Kaeh Garrison argues, "In the Third Wave, feminist collective consciousness may not necessarily manifest itself in a nationalized and highly mobilized social movement unified around a single goal or identity. At the moment, this hardly seems imaginable." In fact, in its current manifestation, third-wave feminism is more about textual and cultural production, local forms of activism, and a particular form of feminist consciousness than it is a large-scale social justice movement....

FEMINISM AS BIRTHRIGHT AND THE IDEOLOGY OF INDIVIDUALISM

"For anyone born after the early 1960s," write Jennifer Baumgardner and Amy Richards, "the presence of feminism in our lives is taken for granted. For our generation, feminism is like fluoride. We scarcely notice that we have it—it's simply in the water." Put another way, "feminism is our birthright," as Denfeld writes in *The New Victorians*. This ubiquitous phrase within third wave discourse highlights the third wave's unique and historically unprecedented relationship to feminism, one that grants women my age a noticeably different experience of feminism than that of our mothers' generation. Particularly for those of us who were raised by feminist parents to be feminists, feminism is a given, handed to us at birth. It is often not something we need to seek out or fight for. "I didn't spend much time thinking about feminism," writes Roiphe. "It was something assumed, something deep in my foundations." Roiphe's description of feminism as that which is "deep in her foundations"—like Rebecca Walker's statement that feminism "has always been so close to home"—suggests that feminism is indeed "our birthright," a kind of genetic inheritance, passed down at birth. (One critic went as far as describing Roiphe as a woman "who could be said to have imbibed feminism with her mother's milk.")

Handed to us at birth, feminism no longer requires the active identification that it once did. We often don't need to get to feminism through some means—whether consciousness-raising, activism, or reevaluating our personal relationships—because feminism is already there for us. As Barbara Findlen writes in *Listen Up*, "My feminism wasn't shaped by antiwar or civil rights activism; I was not a victim of the problem that had no name." We don't need to create feminism, it already exists. We don't need to become feminists, we already are. Because women of my generation often do not experience feminism as a process—that is, as something we actively choose or help to create—we have a much more ambivalent identification with it. Even for those of us who see ourselves as aligned with second-wave feminism, our sense of owing feminism can still feel tenuous. We own feminism in the sense that it is our birthright, yet in other ways it is not ours. It belongs to another generation, another group of women: second-wave feminists. They were the ones who went through the heady experience of *creating* feminism; we just get to reap the benefits.

In order to get a sense of how different feminism felt for second-wave feminists, one need only look at Gloria Steinem's introduction to Walker's anthology, *To Be Real*. In it, she writes, "Because I entered when feminism had to be chosen and even reinvented, I experienced almost everything about it as an unmitigated and joyful freedom—and I still do." When one compares Steinem's "unmitigated and joyful freedom" with the depressing sense of confinement and curbed independence found in some third-wave texts, it is clear that there has been a definite generational shift in the way that women experience feminism. Perhaps the third-wave complaint that feminism feels constricting—as opposed to feeling like "unmitigated freedom"—should be read as a lament for what we missed out on: entering feminism when it had to be chosen and reinvented.

The tendency within much third-wave writing toward making a clean break with the past, rather than maintaining a sense of connection, may be inevitable given the language used to describe the third wave's relationship to feminism. Conceiving of feminism as a birthright passed from mother to daughter undoubtedly influences the third wave's understanding of and relationship to feminism. It may be that something inherited from one's mother is likely to be rejected, no matter what it is. It may be that a birthright, bound up as it is with one's mother, is unable to produce individuality. Defining what she terms "matrophobia," Adrienne Rich writes of "the womanly splitting of the self, in the desire to become purged once and for all of our mother's bondage, to become individuated and free." Given this matrophobia, identifying with one's mother and with her feminism may ultimately incite rebellion, a desire "to move away," as Denfeld calls for.

In fact, I would argue that the excessive focus on individualism by many third-wavers reveals more than just a preference for liberal feminism. In their descriptions of what this individuality is set in opposition to, one gets the sense that individuality provides a means of resisting the group identity implied by the terms "feminists" and "women." Beyond simply disidentifying with these two identity categories, this resistance might also suggest a desire to break away from their mothers, both real and figurative. In *Fire with Fire*, for example, Wolf describes power feminism, the feminism she advocates, as that which "[e]ncourages a woman to claim her individual voice rather than merging her voice in a collective identity." Wolf gives us a clue about what individuality represents for many third-wave feminists: it is the antithesis of "merging her voice in a collective identity." What is to be resisted is staying (sub)merged in collectivity. Wolf's description suggests that in order to retain—or even to gain—one's identity and autonomy, one must unmerge, move away, break free.

In psychoanalytic terms, the notion that one achieves autonomy and individuality through making a clean break from the mother has traditionally been ascribed to the male experience. As part of the individuation process, girls must also separate from their mothers, but because of the gender identification between a girl and her mother, this process is often more difficult, more confusing, and more incomplete. It has been argued that the inability to make such a clean break from the mother—which is, of course, itself an impossible fantasy—leads women to experience their identity as relational. That is, self-identity is always interconnected with the identity of the other, causing girls and women to have less investment in the defensive clean-break model of autonomy exhibited by many boys and men. While this theory has been adopted by many feminists in order to stress the positive psychological traits produced by such identity formation, in general, it has not been able to account for the more negative—or perhaps less idealized—aspects of the female individuation process. In particular, feelings such as ambivalence and even outright hostility toward the mother have gone relatively unexplored.

In the third wave's relationship to the second wave, I believe we see signs of the difficulty that individuation poses for women, particularly in the face of a powerful mother figure: in this case, feminism. As one third-wave writer notes, "A daughter fears that she will somehow be co-opted by her mother's desires, drives, and idiosyncrasies and will become the mother at the expense of the self." In both their retaining of the identity "feminist" and in the rare moments when they champion second-wave feminism, third-wavers maintain a connection to their mothers' generation—and often to their real mothers. Like the shared gender identity between mother and daughter, they are not easily able to extricate themselves from the shared identity of feminist. In their frequent attempts to radically break free from the feminism of the past, however, their desire for autonomy and their own individual identity is revealed. They want a shared connection through feminism, but they want their freedom and individuality too.

In her introduction to *To Be Real*, Walker describes a new generation of feminists that seeks to challenge many of the second wave's perceived orthodoxies; she argues for a feminism that includes contradictions and an ability to go beyond political correctness. As she describes the feminism of the previous generation: "For many of us it seems that to be a feminist in the way that we have seen or understood feminism is to conform to an identity and way of living that doesn't allow for individuality, complexity, or less than perfect personal histories." Challenging the perceived dogmatism of second-wave feminism, third-wavers have steered clear of prescribing a particular feminist agenda and instead have chosen to stress individuality and individual definitions of feminism. As Heywood and Drake note, "[T]he ideology of individualism is still a major motivating force in many third wave lives." Individualism as a shared ideology makes for a political paradox, of course, since historically women's liberation movements, like other civil rights movements, have required some sense of collectivity to pursue political goals. Yet this collectivity—or what a previous generation may have termed "sister-hood"—no longer seems available or even desirable. "The same rights and freedoms feminists won for us have allowed us to develop into a very diverse generation of women, and we value our individuality," writes Denfeld. "While linked through common concerns, notions of sister-hood seldom appeal to women of my generation."

Third-wave feminists' preference for defining feminism in their own terms—that is, for each individual feminist to define feminism *for herself individually*—can be seen in the original declaration of the third wave, Rebecca Walker's 1992 statement, "*I am* the Third Wave." In calling for a new wave, Walker does not speak in a collective voice. There is no "we" in this statement, just an "I." An early expression of what was to become a common theme within third-wave discourse, Walker's essay does not attempt to speak in the name of the other women. Rather, she writes about her own, individual desire to devote her life to feminism.

The third wave's "ideology of individualism" has found its perfect form in the autobiographical essay, the preferred writing genre of third-wavers and one that shares little with the group manifestos of a previous generation. The majority of third-wave anthologies published since the mid-1990s have been structured around such personal essays and, correspondingly, personal definitions of feminism. Such essays can be seen as the first step in the consciousness-raising process developed from the earlier women's liberation movement. That is, they provide a means by which to express individual experiences and to analyze those experiences in larger social and political terms. Where the third wave has often appeared stuck, however, is in moving from this beginning consciousness-raising stage of self-expression to developing a larger analysis of the relationship between individual and collective experience, culminating in theory and political action.

The third wave's individualistic form of feminism also has an interesting relationship to another second-wave concept: identity politics. As it was conceived by second-wave feminists, as well as other groups from the period, identity politics posits a relationship between one's gender, racial, and class experience and one's political interests. While these identity categories are also routinely stressed in third-wave texts, there is little sense that they can provide a coalescing structure to bring people together, nor are claims in the name of any one group, such as "women," likely to be found in these texts. A good example of how identity categories are stressed in order to further individual expression, as opposed to a collective political agenda, can be found in Barbara Findlen's introduction to *Listen Up*, where she describes the authors in her collection:

> Women in this book call themselves, among other things, articulate, white, middle-class, college kid; wild and unruly; single mother; Asian bisexual; punk; politically astute; active woman; middle-class black woman; young mother; slacker; member of the Muscogee (Creek) Nation; well-adjusted; student; teacher; writer; an individual; a young lady; a person with a visible disability; androgynous; lapsed Jew; child of professional feminists; lesbian daughter; activist; zine writer; a Libra; an educated, married, monogamous, feminist, Christian African American mother.

In its attention to speaking from an embodied and particular position, one that is always inflected by race, class, sexuality, religion, and educational status, this litany of identity categories reveals the influence of second-wave feminism. Yet unlike the second wave, the third wave does not move beyond these individual assertions of identity to a larger collective political identity. The Asian bisexual can only speak for herself, not for other Asians, nor other bisexuals. For the third wave, identity politics is limited to the expression of individual identity.

Within this "ideology of individualism," feminism has frequently been reduced to one issue: choice. In its most watered-down version, this form of third-wave feminism is appealing to many since it rarely represents political and social issues in ways that suggest the need for collective action or change other than on the individual level. As Elspeth Probyn has noted, it is a "choice freed of the necessity of thinking about the political and social ramifications of the act of choosing." Feminism thus becomes an ideology of individual empowerment to make choices, no matter what those choices are.

For the more conservative of this new breed of feminists, this focus on choice and individualism is conceptualized as a return to "the original ideal of feminism," in which "women have ultimate responsibility for their problems, happiness, and lives." As Karen Lehrman argues in advocating what she terms "real feminism," "The personal, in other words, is no longer political." In its worst form, this feminism marks its progress by the status of white middle-class women; as long as this group is doing well, there's clearly no longer a need for a mass movement. This position is the main thesis of Lehrman's 1997 *The Lipstick Proviso: Women, Sex and Power in the Real World*, where she argues that "discrimination is not as bad as it's made out to be," adding, "Women are not 'oppressed' in the United States, and they're no longer (politically at least) even subjugated." In this narrow view, feminism is exclusively concerned with gender equality and fails to recognize the interconnectedness of race, class, and sexuality, let alone connect feminism to other social and economic justice movements. In an essay entitled "Betty Friedan's Granddaughters: *Cosmo*, Ginger Spice & the Inheritance of Whiteness," Jennifer Harris argues that economic and racial privilege enable white, middle-class feminists to solipsistically explore their own identities. These "granddaughters," she argues, "must move beyond reading the 'problems' of contemporary women, as well as the concerns of feminism and the freedom of women, in particularly narrow ways." If the third wave has been schooled in the lessons of the second wave, as some third-wavers argue it has been, then it must conceive of feminism as more than just a movement to empower white economically privileged women. Yet clearly the various articulations of feminism's next generation suggest that there are as many competing narratives of the third wave as there are of the second....

18. Lisa Jervis, "The End of Feminism's Third Wave: The Cofounder of *Bitch* Magazine Says Goodbye to the Generational Divide," from *Ms.* Magazine

Excerpts from "The End of Feminism's Third Wave," by Lisa Jervis, published in *Ms.* Magazine (Winter 2004). Reprinted with permission.

In this article, *Bitch* magazine publisher Lisa Jervis addresses the usefulness (or lack thereof) of the term "third wave," arguing that the wave language has resulted in divisive, unproductive stereotyping on both sides. "Here's what we need to recognize so that we can all move on: those in their 20s and 30s who don't see their concerns reflected in the feminism of their elders are ignorant of history; those in their 50s and beyond who think that young women aren't politically active—or active enough, or active around the right issues—don't know where to look." Jervis argues that the generational divide is an illusion.

"Are you in the third wave?"

"When did the third wave start?"

"What's the most important issue to third wavers?"

I get asked this a lot—at campus lectures, during radio interviews, at publishing conferences. I hate these questions. There are so many ways to answer, none of them entirely satisfactory.

I always want to pepper my interlocutor with questions instead:

Do you want to know how I identify, or how others would label me? Are you asking when the term was coined? When the first feminists who are considered part of the third wave became politicized? When the first riot grrl zine was published? What makes you think it's possible to elevate one issue over all others? Which definition of the third wave are we talking about here, the chronological or the ideological?

This reluctance isn't just me being cranky and not wanting to answer any hard questions. Here is the reality: we've reached the end of the wave terminology's usefulness. What was at first a handy-dandy way to refer to feminism's history and its present and future potential with a single metaphor has become shorthand that invites intellectual laziness, an escape hatch from the hard work of distinguishing between core beliefs and a cultural moment.

Using the simplest and most straightforward definition, I am, indisputably, a member of the third wave: I was born in 1972, right smack in the demographic that people think about when they think about the third wave. But discussions of the waves are only nominally about demographics. The metaphor wraps up differences in age, ideology, tactics, and style, and pretends that distinguishing among these factors is unimportant.

Even the more nuanced discussions of third-wavers tend to cast them (or, given my birthday, should I say "us"?) as sex-obsessed young thangs with a penchant for lip gloss and a disregard for recent history, or sophisticated identity politicians who have moved past the dated concerns of their predecessors.

It's no mystery why the discourse that has developed around the waves is divisive and oppositional. Writers and theorists love oppositional categories—they make things so much easier to talk about. Similarities are much more difficult. So, naturally, much has been said and written about the disagreements, conflicts, differences and antagonisms between feminists of the second and third waves, while hardly anything is ever said about our similarities and continuities.

The rap goes something like this: Older women drained their movement of sexuality; younger women are uncritically sexualized. Older women won't recognize the importance of pop culture; younger women are obsessed with media representation. Older women have too narrow a definition of what makes a feminist issue; younger women are scattered and don't know what's important.

Stodgy versus frivolous. Won't share power versus spoiled and ignorant.

Nothing on this list is actually true—but, because this supposedly great generational divide has been constructed out of very flimsy but readily available materials, the ideas persist in the face of overwhelming evidence to the contrary.

It's just so much easier to hit on the playful cultural elements of the third wave and contrast them with the brass-tacks agenda—and impressive gains—of the second wave: It's become the master narrative of feminism's progression (or regression, as some see it).

But when has it ever been a good idea to trust a master narrative? After all, the oft-repeated notion among self-described third-wavers that those labeled as hopelessly second-wave reject humor, fashion, sex, or anything else that might be fun is just a slightly—and only slightly—more nuanced and polite version of the stone-faced, hairy-legged manhater whom we all know to be a myth that originated in the sexist culture at large and was cultivated and amplified by conservative, anti-feminist, and/or just plain clueless journalists and pundits.

The image of the frivolous young pseudofeminist has the same provenance. Take *Time*'s infamous June 29, 1998, cover story, "Is Feminism Dead?" for instance. In lambasting young women for being more interested in celebrity than the wage gap and seeing vibrators as more important than protests, writer Ginia Bellafante had to carefully ignore the vibrant anti-sweatshop movement spawning on college campuses at the time, or organizations like the Third Wave Foundation, feminist.com, SOUL, Home Alive, or many of the other activist projects founded and run by women born in the '70s and after.

When feminists engage in this kind of nuance-deprived conflation of age and ideology, we're doing little more than reinscribing the thoroughly debunked notion that we need to agree with each other all the time.

As we all know, feminism has always held within it multitudes of ideologies, tactics, and priorities. The movement's two current generations have come to be painted as internally monolithic, but they are each as diverse philosophically as feminism itself—they have to be; they *are* feminism itself.

There are elements of both that are playful and take pop culture as both their medium and their subject matter: the 1968 Miss America protests defined the very start of the second wave, and their lineage extends to guerrilla theater groups like Ladies Against Women in the '80s and the Radical Cheerleaders today.

There are elements of both that are relentlessly—and appropriately—serious: Combating rape and domestic violence was a key issue 35 years ago; its importance has not changed. Affordable, accessible child care is no less a concern now than it was in the '70s.

Chronologically thirdwave publications such as *Feminista!* share their ideologies about pornography and sex work with Catharine MacKinnon and Andrea Dworkin. The riot grrls groups that sprang up in the early '90s have clear connections to consciousness-raising groups. Last April's hugely successful and inspiring March for Women's Lives was intergenerational in both planning and attendance.

There's certainly no shortage of disagreements both large and small within feminism. There are those who see transgender folks as interlopers in feminist spaces, and those who see genderqueers as the frontline soldiers against sexist systems of power.

There are those who would like to see "feminine" values replace "masculine" values as the defining characteristics of our society, and those who reject the very notion that these values have any gender apart from what's been assigned by a sexist culture.

There are those who see gender as the overarching factor that shapes women's oppression, and those who think that raising the minimum wage would achieve more feminist goals in one fell swoop than any other single act.

The issues motivating both sides of the '80s sex wars are very much still with us. Even if some views are more common among one generation than another, at their roots these are ideological disagreements—but they can't be discussed productively while in disguise as generational issues. That disguise keeps us distracted from the real work before the movement today.

Here's what we all need to recognize so that we can move on: Those in their 20s and 30s who don't see their concerns reflected in the feminism of their elders are ignorant of history; those in their 50s and beyond who think that young women aren't politically active—or active enough, or active around the right issues—don't know where to look.

We all want the same thing: To borrow bell hooks' phrase, we want gender justice.

We may not all agree on exactly what it looks like or how to get it. We should never expect to agree. Feminism has always thrived on and grown from internal discussions and disagreements. Our many different and often opposing perspectives are what push us forward, honing our theories, refining our tactics, driving us toward a more thorough dismantling of the white-supremacist, capitalist patriarchy (to borrow another phrase from hooks).

I want to see these internal disagreements continue. I want to see as much wrangling over them as ever. But I want them articulated accurately. And that means recognizing the generational divide for what it is—an illusion.

PART II

Consumerism, Globalization, and Third-Wave Lives

The globalization of economics, populations, and cultures has had a profound effect on the context for third-wave lives. Essays in this section address these issues, from the tyranny, power, and pleasure of the mass media, to the illusions of "girl power" produced by neoliberalism, to the effects of immigration on racial identities to the growing economic inequalities that structure third-wave lives, both within the United States and worldwide.

19. Susan Bordo, "In the Empire of Images: Preface to the Tenth Anniversary Edition," from *Unbearable Weight: Feminism, Western Culture, and the Body*

Excerpts from Susan Bordo, *Unbearable Weight: Feminism, Western Culture, and the Body* (Berkeley: University of California Press, 2003), xiii–xxxiii.

Bordo is a second-wave feminist theorist who is much-loved by many feminists in the third wave. This essay, Bordo's preface to the tenth anniversary edition of her landmark collection *Unbearable Weight,* describes with great power and detail the empire of images that shape subjectivity in the third wave and in the future generations that will follow it. There has been some positive change, Bordo argues, in the variety of images, but the ideals they create still set up prescriptions that are hard to follow.

In our Sunday news. With our morning coffee. On the bus, in the airport, at the checkout line. Sharing our day off from work, from school, illicit and delicious with us under the quilt. Or domestic company, out of the corner of the eye as we fold the laundry in front of the television. It may be a 5 A.M. addiction to the glittering promises of the infomercial: the latest in fat-dissolving pills, miracle hair restoration, make-up secrets of the stars. Or a glancing relationship while waiting at the dentist, trying to distract from the impending root canal. Or a luscious, shiny pile, a deliberate splurge, a can't-wait-to-get-home-with-you devotion. A teen magazine tips on how to dress, how to wear your hair, how to make him want you. A movie seen at the theater, still large and magical in the dark. The endless commercials and advertisements we believe we pay no attention to.

Constant, everywhere, no big deal. Like the water in the goldfish bowl, barely noticed by inhabitants. Or noticed, but dismissed: "Eye Candy"—a harmless indulgence. They go down so easily, in and out, digested and forgotten. Hardly able anymore to rouse our indignation.

Just pictures.

"NO ONE GETS SICK FROM LOOKING AT A PICTURE": CROSS-CULTURAL SNAPSHOTS

The young girl stands in front of the mirror. Never fat to begin with, she's been on a no-fat diet for a couple of weeks and has reached her goal weight: 115 pounds, at 5-foot-4—exactly what she should weigh, according to her doctor's chart. But goddamnit, she still looks dumpy. She can't shake her mind free of the "Lady Marmalade" video from *Moulin Rouge*. Christina Aguilera, Pink, L'il Kim, and Mýa, each one perfect in her own way: every curve smooth and sleek, lean-sexy, nothing to spare. Self-hatred and shame start to burn in the girl, and other things too. When the video goes on, the singers' bodies are like magnets for her eyes; she feels like she's in love with them. But envy tears at her stomach, is enough to make her sick. She'll never look like them, no matter how much weight she loses. Look at that stomach of hers, see how much weight she loses. Look at that stomach of hers, see how it sticks out? Those thighs—they actually jiggle. Her butt is monstrous. She's fat, gross, a dough girl.

Frontline asked Alexandra Shulman, editor of British *Vogue*, if the fashion industry felt any responsibility for creating the impossible-to-achieve images that young girls measure themselves against. Shulman shrugged. "Not many people have actually said to me that they have looked at my magazine and decided to become anorexic."

Is it possible that Shulman actually believes it works that way?

In Central Africa, ancient festivals still celebrate voluptuous women. In some regions, brides are sent to fattening farms, to be plumped and massaged into shape for their wedding night. In a country plagued by AIDS, the skinny body has meant—as it used to mean among Italian, Jewish, and Black Americans—poverty, sickness, death. "An African girl must have hips," says dress designer Frank Osodi. "We have hips. We have bums. We like flesh in Africa." For years, Nigeria sent its local version of beautiful to the Miss World Competition. The contestants did very poorly. Then a savvy entrepreneur went against local ideals and entered Agbani Darego, a light-skinned, hyper-skinny beauty. (He got his inspiration from M-Net, the South African network seen across Africa on satellite television, which broadcasts mostly American movies and television shows.) Agbani Darego won the Miss World Pageant, the first Black African to do so. Now, Nigerian teenagers fast and exercise, trying to become "lepa"—a popular slang phrase for the thin "it" girls that are all the rage. Said one: "People have realized that slim is beautiful."

Brenda Richardson and Elane Rehr, authors of *101 Ways to Help Your Daughter Love Her Body*, tell the story of newly arrived Russian immigrants Sasha, thirty-two, and her fourteen-year-old sister. Sasha, who immediately lost twenty pounds, became disgusted with her little sister's upper arms and thighs. "My little sis has fleshy arms and thighs ribboned with cellulite," she told Richardson, and complained that their mother was dressing her in short-sleeved dresses. When her mother did this, Sasha tried to stop her, telling her sister to "cover up her fat."

Rent a Russian movie made before the doors to U.S. culture were flung open; look at the actresses' arms. You'll see just how extraordinary—and how illuminating—this one little anecdote is.

I was intrigued when my articles on eating disorders began to be translated, over the past few years, into Japanese and Chinese. Among the members of audiences at my talks, Asian women had been among the most insistent that eating and body image weren't problems for their people, and indeed, my initial research showed that eating disorders were virtually unknown in Asia. But when, this year, a Korean translation of *Unbearable Weight* was published, I felt I needed to revisit the situation. I discovered multiple reports on dramatic increases in eating disorders in China, South Korea, and Japan. "As many Asian countries become Westernized and infused with the Western aesthetic of a tall, thin, lean body, a virtual tsunami of eating disorders has swamped Asian countries," writes Eunice Park in *Asian Week* magazine. Older people can still remember when it was very different. In China, for example, where revolutionary ideals once condemned any focus on appearance and there have been several disastrous famines, "little fatty" was a term of endearment for children. Now, with fast food on every corner, childhood obesity is on the rise, and the cultural meaning of fat and thin has changed. "When I was young," says Li Xiaojing, who manages a fitness center in Beijing, "people admired and were even jealous of fat people since they thought they had a better life.... But now, most of us see a fat person and think, 'He looks awful.'"

Because of their remote location, the Fiji islands did not have access to television until 1995, when a single station was introduced. It broadcasts programs from the United States, Great Britain, and Australia. Until that time, Fiji had no reported cases of eating disorders, and a study conducted by the anthropologist Anne Becker showed that most Fijian girls and women, no matter how large, were comfortable with their bodies. In 1998, just three years after the station began broadcasting, 11 percent of girls reported vomiting to control weight, and 62 percent of the girls surveyed reported dieting during the previous months.

Becker was surprised by the change; she had thought that Fijian cultural traditions, which celebrate eating and favor voluptuous bodies, would "withstand" the influence of media images. Her explanation for the Fijians' vulnerability?

They were not sophisticated enough about media to recognize that the television images were not "real."

"REALITY" IN THE EMPIRE OF IMAGES

Are we sophisticated enough to recognize that the images are not "real"? Does it matter?

In the charming *L.A. Story*, Steve Martin asks Sarah Jessica Parker why her breasts feel so funny to the touch. "Oh, that's because they're real," she replies. It's funny. But it's also no longer a joke—because real breasts are the anomaly among actresses and models nowadays, with consequences that extend beyond the wacky culture of celebrity-bodies. Many young men can't get aroused by breasts that don't conform to Hollywood standards of size and firmness. Do they care that those centerfold breasts aren't "real"? No. Nor do the more than 215,000 women who purchased breast implants in 2001. Breast enhancement is one of the most common surgical procedures for teenagers. These girls are not superficial creatures who won't be satisfied unless they look like goddesses. More and more, girls who get implants feel that they need them in order to look normal in a culture in which "normal" is being radically redefined, not only by the images but by the surgeons. A cosmetic surgeon's ad in the *Lexington Herald Journal*: "Certainly, models and entertainers have breast augmentation, but the typical patients are women that you see every day. Your neighbors. Your co-workers. They could even be you."

In *Unbearable Weight*, I describe the postmodern body, increasingly fed on "fantasies of rearranging, transforming, and correcting, limitless improvement and change, defying the historicity, the mortality, and indeed, the very materiality of the body. In place of that materiality, we now have cultural plastic."

When I wrote these words, the most recent statistics, from 1989, listed 681,000 surgical procedures performed.

In 2001, 8.5 million procedures were performed.

They are cheaper than ever, safer than ever, and increasingly used, not for correcting major defects, but for "contouring" the face and body. Plastic surgeons seem to have no ethical problem with this. "I'm not here to play philosopher king," says Dr. Randal Haworth in a *Vogue* interview; "I don't have a problem with women who already look good who want to look perfect." Perfect. When did "perfection" become applicable to a human body? The word suggests a Platonic form of timeless beauty—appropriate for marble, perhaps, but not for living flesh. We change, we age, we die. Learning to deal with this is part of the existential challenge—and richness—of mortal life. But nowadays, those who can afford to do so have traded the messiness and fragility of life, the vulnerability of intimacy, the comfort of human connection, for fantasies of limitless achievement, "triumphing" over everything that gets in the way, "going for the gold." The Greeks called it hubris. We call it our "right" to be all that we can be.

What Haworth isn't saying, too, is that the bar of what we consider "perfection" is constantly being raised—by cultural imagery, by the surgeon's own recommendations, and by eyes that become habituated to interpreting every deviation as "defect." Ann, a prospective patient described in the same *Vogue* article, has a well-toned body of 105 pounds but is obsessed with what she sees as grotesque fat pockets on her inner thighs. "No matter how skinny I get, they get smaller but never go away," she complains. It's unlikely that Ann, whom Haworth considers a perfect candidate for liposuction, will stop there. "Plastic surgery sharpens your eyesight," admits a more honest surgeon. "You get something done, suddenly you're looking in the mirror every five minutes—at imperfections nobody else can see."

Where did Ann get the idea that any vestige of fat must be banished from her body? Most likely, it wasn't from comparing herself to other real women, but to those computer-generated torsos—in ads for anti-cellulite cream and the like—whose hips and thighs and buttocks are smooth and seamless as gently sloping sand dunes. No actual person has a body like that. But that doesn't matter—because our expectations, our desires, our judgments about bodies, are becoming dictated by the digital. When was the last time you actually saw a wrinkle—or cellulite—or a drooping jowl—or a pore or a pucker—in a magazine or video image? Ten years ago *Harper's* magazine printed the invoice *Esquire* had received for retouching a cover picture of Michelle Pfeiffer. The picture was accompanied by copy that read: "What Michelle Pfeiffer needs ... is absolutely nothing." What Pfeiffer's picture alone needed to appear on that cover was actually $1,525 worth of chin trimming, complexion cleansing, neck softening, line removal, and other assorted touches.

That was then.

Now, in 2003, virtually every celebrity image you see—in the magazines, in the videos, and sometimes even in the movies—has been digitally modified. Virtually every image. Let that sink in. Don't just let your mind passively receive it. Confront its implications. This is not just a matter of deception—boring old stuff, which ads have traded in from their beginnings. This is perceptual pedagogy, How to Interpret Your Body 101. These images are teaching us how to see. Filtered, smoothed, polished, softened, sharpened, re-arranged. And passing. Digital creations, visual cyborgs, teaching us what to expect from flesh and blood. Training our perception in what's a defect and what is normal.

Are we sophisticated enough to know the images are not "real"? Does it matter? There are no disclaimers on the ads: "Warning: This body is generated by a computer. Don't expect your thighs to look this way." Would it matter to Ann if there were? Who cares about reality when beauty, love, acceptance beckon? Does sophistication have anything to do with it?

A SAD CONFIRMATION

When I wrote *Unbearable Weight*, it was widely believed that privileged white girls had the monopoly on eating and body-image problems. The presumption was a relic of the old medical models, which accepted the "profile" presented by the typical recipient of therapy—who was indeed largely white and upper middle class—as definitive, and which failed to recognize the central role of media imagery in "spreading" eating and body-image problems across race and class (and sexual orientation). Like the Black Africans and the Fijians and the Russians (and lesbians and Latins and every other "subculture" boasting a history of regard for fleshy women), African Americans were believed "protected" by their alternative cultural values. And so, many young girls were left feeling stranded and alone, dealing with feelings about their bodies that they weren't "supposed" to have, as they struggled, along with their white peers, with unprecedented pressure to achieve, and watched Janet Jackson and Halle Berry shrink before their eyes.

Many medical professionals, too, were trapped in what I'd call the "anorexic paradigm." They hadn't yet understood that eating problems take many different forms and inhabit bodies of many different sizes and shapes. Binge eating—a chronic problem among many African American women—is no less a disordered relation to food than habitual purging, and large women who don't or won't diet are not necessarily comfortable with their bodies. Exercise addiction is rarely listed among the criteria for eating problems, but it has become the weight control of choice among a generation emulating Jennifer Lopez's round, tight buns rather than Kate Moss's skeletal collarbones. Just because a teenager looks healthy and fit does not mean that she is not living her life on a treadmill—metaphorically as well as literally—which she dare not step off lest food and fat overtake her body.

Until recently, most clinicians were not receptive to the arguments of feminists like Susie Ohrbach (and later, myself) that "body image disturbance syndrome," binge/purge cycling, "bulimic thinking," and all the rest needed to be understood as much more culturally normative than generally recognized. They wanted to draw a sharp dividing line between pathology and normality—a line that can be very blurry when it comes to eating and body-image problems in this culture. And while they acknowledged that images "play a role," they clung to the notion that only girls with a "pre-disposing vulnerability" get into trouble. Trained in a medical model which seeks the cause of disorder in individual and family pathology, they hadn't yet understood just how powerful, ubiquitous, and invasive the demands of culture are on our bodies and souls.

Families matter, of course, and so do racial and ethnic traditions. But families exist in cultural time and space—and so do racial groups. Thus, no one lives in a bubble of self-generated "dysfunction" or permanent immunity—especially today, as mass media culture increasingly has provided the dominant "public education" in our children's lives. The "profile" of girls with eating problems is dynamic, not static; heterogeneous, not uniform. Therapists now report treating the anorexic daughters of anorexics and are coming to realize the role parents play, not just in being "over-controlling" or overly demanding of their children, but in modeling obedience to cultural norms. And the old generalizations about race and "fat acceptance," while perhaps valid for older generations of Black Americans, do not begin to adequately describe the complex and often conflicted attitudes of younger people, many of whom are aware of traditional values but constantly feel the pull of contemporary demands. While working on *Unbearable Weight*, I called up organizations devoted to Black women's health issues, asking for statistics and clinical anecdotes, and was told: "That's a white girl's thing. African American women are comfortable with their bodies." For twenty-something Tenisha Williamson, who suffers from anorexia, such notions are almost as oppressive as her eating disorder: "From an African American standpoint," she writes, "we as a people are encouraged to 'embrace our big, voluptuous bodies.' This makes me feel terrible because I don't want a big, voluptuous body! I don't ever want to be fat—ever, and I don't ever want to gain weight. I would rather die from starvation than gain a single pound. [This makes me feel like] the proverbial Judas of my race ... and so incredibly shallow."

In fact, the starving white girls were just the forward guard, the miners' canaries warning of how poisonous the air was becoming for everyone. I could see it in the magazines, the videos, and in my students' journals. I could see it, as I write in "Material Girl," in the transformations of Madonna and other performers of Italian, Jewish, and African American descent who seemed, at the start of their careers, to represent resistance to the waifs and willows but who just couldn't hold out against what, indeed, had begun to look like a tsunami, a cultural tidal wave of obsession with achieving a disciplined, normalized body.

It became a central argument of *Unbearable Weight* that eating disorders, analyzed as a social formation rather than personal pathology, represented a "crystallization" of particular currents, some historical and some contemporary, within Western culture. Western philosophy and religion, to begin with, have a long history of anxiety about the body as a source of hungers, needs, and physical vulnerabilities always threatening to spin out of control. But maintaining some zone of comfort with the body's needs is especially difficult in our own time. Consumer culture continually excites and encourages us to "let go," indulge in our desires—for sugar, fat, sex, mindless entertainment. But at the same time, burgeoning industries centered on diet, exercise, and body enhancement glamorize self-discipline and code fat as a symbol of laziness and lack of willpower. It's hard to find a place of moderation and stability in all this, easy to fall into disorder. For girls and women, the tensions of consumer capitalism are layered, additionally, with the contradictions of being female in our time. These contradictions, I argued, are succinctly embodied in the slenderness ideal. On the one hand, the lean body represents a rejection of the fifties ideal of cuddly, reproductive womanhood, and an assertion of a postfeminist, nondomestic identity. On the other hand, the steadily shrinking space permitted the female body seemed expressive of discomfort with greater female power and presence.

One of the hardest challenges I faced, in presenting these ideas at conferences and public lectures, was getting medical professionals and academics to take cultural imagery seriously. Most clinicians, unaccustomed to viewing images as anything other than "mere fashion," saw cultural interpretation as somehow minimizing the seriousness of eating disorders. I insisted—an argument I laid out explicitly in a later book, *Twilight Zones*—that images of slenderness are never "just pictures," as the fashion magazines continually maintain (disingenuously) in their own defense. Not only are the artfully arranged bodies in the ads and videos and fashion spreads powerful lessons in how to see (and evaluate) bodies, but also they offer fantasies of safety, self-containment, acceptance, immunity from pain and hurt. They speak to young people not just about how to be beautiful but about how to become what the dominant culture admires, how to be cool, how to "get it together." To girls who have been abused they may speak of transcendence or armoring of too-vulnerable female flesh. For racial and ethnic groups whose bodies have been marked as foreign, earthy, and primitive, or considered unattractive by Anglo-Saxon norms, they may cast the lure of assimilation, of becoming (metaphorically speaking) "white."

Academics, on their part, were not hostile to interpretation but to what they saw as my suppression of racial and ethnic "difference." As I saw my argument, I was calling attention to a discernable historical development—the spread of normalizing imagery across race and nationality. "Difference" was being effaced, indeed. But it was mass popular culture that was effacing it, not me. Today, the evidence of this is indisputable. There is no denying that there are still racial differences in attitudes toward eating, dieting, body aesthetics. But even more dramatic are the generational differences, which show that "comfort with the body" is fast becoming a relic of another era, irrespective of race or nationality. The mythology persists, of course; it's a big ingredient in a certain kind of ethnic pride. So, Jennifer Lopez and Beyoncé Knowles insist they are happy with their bodies, bragging about their bodacious bottoms. "Us sisters have padding back there," says Beyoncé. "Being bootylycious is about being comfortable with your body." But sexy booty is okay, apparently, only if it's high and hard, and if other body-parts are held firmly in check. Beyoncé is comfortable with her body because she works on it constantly. On the road, she does five hundred sit-ups a night, and Jennifer ("One of the most driven people I've ever seen," according to her personal trainer) does ninety minutes of hard training "at least" four times a week. Her truly voluptuous *Selena* body is a thing of the distant past. J.Lo and Beyoncé are "full-figured" only if Lara Flynn Boyle is your yardstick.

And then there are the men and boys, who once seemed so immune. If ever there was confirmation that eating and body image problems are products of culture, they are surely it. Women, studies always showed, are chronically dissatisfied with themselves. But ten years ago men tended, if anything, to see themselves as better looking than they (perhaps) actually were. Straight guys were proud of their beer bellies. "Do I look like I care?" was the manly way to be. Body-sculpting? Very sexually suspect. Dieting? The average, white, heterosexual guy would no more be seen at Weight Watchers than in a feather boa. The "one" in "Pepsi One" was created to sell men a diet drink without having to call it that.

And then, as I chronicle in *The Male Body*, the diet industries, the cosmetics manufacturers, and the plastic surgeons "discovered" the male body. With so much money to be made, why did it take so long? Arguably, manufacturers and advertisers feared that anxiety about being seen as gay would prevent heterosexual men from showing too obvious an interest in their bodies. African American athletic superstars like Michael Jordan and hip-hop performers like Puff Daddy (Sean P. Diddy) Combs did a lot to change that. They made jewelry, high fashion, strutting one's stuff into a macho thing. But designer Calvin Klein broke the biggest barrier. He brought the sinuous, sculpted male body out of the closet, and made everyone, gay and straight, male and female, succumb to its classic, masculine beauty. I remember the first time I saw one of his underwear ads. No male waif, the model's body projected strength, solidity. But his finely muscled chest was not so overdeveloped as to suggest a sexuality immobilized—like Schwarzenegger's, say—by the thick matter of the body. He didn't stare at the viewer challengingly, belligerently ("Yeah, this is an underwear ad and I'm half-naked. But I'm still the one in charge here. Who's gonna look away first?"). No, this model's languid body-posture, eyes downcast but not closed, offered itself nonaggressively to the gaze of another. Feast on me; I'm here to be looked at.

Today, men no longer think of personal care or taking pleasure in one's clothing, one's body, one's beauty in the eyes of another as feminine things. But basking in the admiration of the gaze, as men are finding out, requires committed bodily upkeep. This is consumer culture, after all. It can never have too much of a good thing. It thrives on our capacity for excess; it wants us to not be able to stop. Today, the athletic, muscular male body that Calvin first plastered all over buildings, magazines, and subway stops has become an aesthetic requirement, for straights as well as gays. "No pecs, no sex," is how the trendy David Barton gym sells itself: "My motto is not 'Be healthy'; it's 'Look better naked,'" Barton says.

And now, young guys are looking in their mirrors, finding themselves soft and ill defined, no matter how muscular they are. Now they are developing the eating and body image disorders that we once thought only girls had. Now they are abusing steroids, measuring their own muscularity against the oiled and perfected images of professional athletes, bodybuilders. *Men's Health* models. Now the industries in body enhancement—cosmetic surgeons, manufacturers of anti-aging creams, spas and salons—are making huge bucks off men, too.

Now, too, that boys and men are developing body-image problems, feminist cultural arguments—unacknowledged—seem to have finally won the day. Psychologists are producing pictures demonstrating the increasing lean, muscular proportions of toys like G.I. Joe, illustrating their studies with photos of "steroided" centerfolds, and reassuring readers that even the most "well-adjusted men" are at risk. Say the authors of *The Adonis Complex* (all medical professionals): "Men could be relieved of much suffering if they could only be liberated from society's unrealistic ideals of what they should look like."

I agree, of course. But I can't help but think of all the guilt and shame that girls, women, and their families have suffered, as our body disorders have been trivialized and pathologized over the years. It's time we made it decisively clear that "well-adjusted" girls and women are at risk, too. That no racial or ethnic group is invulnerable. That body insecurity can be exported, imported, and marketed across the globe—just like any other profitable commodity.

AGING IN THE EMPIRE OF IMAGES

They carded me until I was thirty-five. Even when I was forty-five, people were shocked to hear my age. Young men flirted with me, even at fifty. Having hated my face as a child—bushy red hair, freckles, Jewish nose—I was surprised to find myself fairly pleased with it as an adult. Then, suddenly, it all changed. The women at the make-up counter no longer compliment me on my skin. Men don't catch my eye with playful promise in theirs.

I'm fifty-six. The magazines tell me that at this age, a woman can still be beautiful. But they don't mean me. They mean Cher, Goldie, Faye, Candace. Women whose jowls have disappeared as they've aged, whose eyes have become less droopy, lips grown plumper, foreheads smoother with the passing years. They mean Susan Sarandon, who looked older in 1991's *Thelma and Louise* than she does in her movies today. "Aging beautifully" used to mean wearing one's years with style, confidence, and vitality. Today, it means not appearing to age at all. And—like breasts that defy gravity—it's becoming a new bodily norm.

Greta Van Susterin: former CNN legal analyst, forty-seven years old. When she had a face-lift, it was a real escalation in the stakes for ordinary women. She had a signature style: no bullshit, down-to-earth lack of pretense. (During the O.J. trial, she was the only white reporter many Blacks trusted.) Always stylishly dressed and coiffed, she wasn't really pretty. No one could argue that her career was built on her looks. Perhaps quite the opposite. She sent out a subversive message: brains and personality still count, even on television.

When Greta had her face lifted, another source of inspiration and hope bit the dust. The story was on the cover of *People*, and folks tuned in to her new show on Fox just to see the change—which was significant. But at least she was open about it. The beauties never admit they've had "work." Or if they do, it's vague, nonspecific, minimizing of the extent. Cher: "If I'd had as much plastic surgery as people say, there'd be another whole person left over!" Okay, so how much have you had? The interviewers accept the silences and evasions. They even embellish the lie. How many interviews have you read which began: "She came into the restaurant looking at least twenty years younger than she is, fresh and relaxed without a speck of make-up."

This collusion, this myth, that Cher or Goldie or Faye Dunaway, unaltered, is "what fifty-something looks like today" has altered my face, however—and without benefit of surgery. By comparison with theirs, it has become much older than it is.

My expression now appears more serious, too (just what a feminist needs), thanks to the widespread use of botox. "It's now rare in certain social circles," a *New York Times* reporter observed, "to see a woman over the age of 35 with the ability to look angry." This has frustrated some film directors, like Baz Luhrman (who did *Moulin Rouge*). "Their faces can't really move properly," Luhrman complained. Last week I saw a sign in the beauty parlor where I get my hair cut. "Botox Party! Sign Up!" So my fifty-six-year-old forehead will now be judged against my neighbor's, not just Goldie's, Cher's, and Faye's. On television, a commercial describes the product (which really is a toxin, a dilution of botulism) as "botox cosmetic." No different from mascara and blush, it's just stuck in with a needle and makes your forehead numb.

To add insult to injury, the rhetoric of feminism has been picked up to help advance and justify the industries in anti-aging and body alteration. Face-lifts, implants, and liposuction are advertised as empowerment, "taking charge" of one's life. "I'm doing it for me"—the mantra of the talk shows. "Defy your age!"—Melanie Griffith, for Revlon. We're making a revolution, girls. Get your injection and pick up a sign!

Am I immune? Of course not. My bathroom shelves are cluttered with the ridiculously expensive age-defying lotions and potions that constantly beckon to me at the Lancome and Dior counters. I want my lines, bags, and sags to disappear, and so do the women who can only afford to buy their alpha-hydroxies at K-Mart. There's a limit, though, to what fruit acids can do. As surgeons develop ever more extensive and fine-tuned procedures to correct gravity and erase history from the faces of their patients, the difference between the cosmetically altered and the rest of us grows more and more dramatic.

"The rest of us" includes not only those who resist or are afraid of surgery but the many people who cannot afford basic health care, let alone aesthetic tinkering—not even of the K-Mart variety. As celebrity faces become increasingly more surreal in their wide-eyed, ever-bright agelessness, as *Time* and *Newsweek* (and *Discover* and *Psychology Today*) proclaim that we can now all "stay young forever," the poor continue to sag and wrinkle and lose their teeth. But in the empire of images, where even people in the news for stock scandals or producing septuplets are given instant digital dental work for magazine covers, this is a well-guarded secret. The celebrity testimonials, the advertisements, the beauty columns all participate in the fiction that the required time, money, and technologies are available to all.

GROWING UP FEMALE IN THE EMPIRE OF IMAGES

Here's how I can tell the ages of audience members at the talks I give: My generation (and older) still refers to "air-brushing." Many still believe it is possible to "just turn off the television." They are scornful, disdainful, sure of their own immunity to the world I talk about. No one really believes the ads, do they? Don't we all know these are just images, designed to sell products? Scholars in the audience may trot out theory about cultural resistance and "agency." Men may insist that they love fleshy women.

Fifteen years ago, I felt very alone when my own generation said these things; it seemed that they were living in a different world from the one I was tracking and that there was little hope of bridging the gap. Now, I simply catch the eye of a twenty-year-old in the audience. They know. They understand that you can be as cynical as you want about the ads—and many of them are—and still feel powerless to resist their messages. They know, no matter what their parents, teachers, and clergy are telling them, that "inner beauty" is a big laugh in this culture.

In their world, there is a size zero, and it's a status symbol. The chronic dieters have been at it since they were eight and nine years old. "Epidemic of eating disorders" is old stuff; being preached to about it turns them right off. Their world is one in which the anorexics swap starvation diet tips on the Internet, participate in group fasts, offer advice on how to hide your "ana" from family members, and share inspirational photos of emaciated models. But full-blown anorexia has never been the norm among teenage girls; the real epidemic is among the girls with seemingly healthy eating habits, seemingly healthy bodies, who vomit or work their butts off as a regular form of anti-fat maintenance. These girls not only look "normal" but consider themselves normal. The new criterion circulating among teenage girls: If you get rid of it through exercise rather than purging or laxatives, you don't have a problem. Theirs is a world in which groups of dorm girls will plough voraciously through pizzas, chewing and then spitting out each mouthful. Do they have a disorder? Of course not—look, they're eating pizza.

Generations raised in the empire of images are both vulnerable and savvy. They snort when magazines periodically proclaim (about once every six months, the same frequency with which they run cover stories about "Starving Stars") that in the "new Hollywood" one can be "Sexy at Any Size." They are literati, connoisseurs of the images; they pay close attention to the pounds coming and going—on J.Lo, on Reese, on Thora, on Christina Aguilera, on Beyoncé. They know that Kate Winslett—whom director James Cameron called "Kate Weighs-a-lot" on the set of *Titanic*—was described by the tabloids as "packing on," "ballooning to," "swelling to," "shooting up to," "tipping the scales at" a "walloping," "staggering" weight—of 135. That slender Courtney Thorne Smith, who played Calista Flockhart's friend/rival on *Ally McBeal*, quit the show because she could no longer keep up with the pressure to remain as thin as David Kelly wanted them to be. That Missy Elliott and Queen Latifah are not on diets just for reasons of health.

I track the culture of young girls today with particular concern, because I'm a mother now. My four-year-old daughter is a superb athlete with supreme confidence in her body, who prides herself on being able to do anything the boys can do—and better. When I see young girls being diminished and harassed by the culture it feels even more personal to me now. I'm grateful that there's a whole new generation of female athletes to provide inspiration and support for girls like Cassie. That our icons are no longer just tiny gymnasts, but powerful soccer, softball, and tennis players, broad-shouldered track stars. Mia Hamm, Sarah Walden, Serena Williams, Marion Jones. During a recent visit to a high school, I see how the eyes of a fourteen-year-old athlete shine as she talks about what Marion Jones means to her. In this young girl I see my own daughter, ten years from now, and I'm filled with hope.

But then, I accidentally tune in to the *Maury* (Povich) show, and my heart is torn in two. The topic of the day is "back-to-girl" makeovers. One by one, five beautiful twelve-, thirteen-, and fourteen-year-old "tomboys" (as Maury called them) are "brought back to their feminine side" (Maury again) through a fashion makeover. We first see them in sweatshirts and caps, insisting that they are as strong as any boy, that they want to dress for comfort, that they're tired of being badgered to look like girls. Why, then, are they submitting to this one-time, on-air transformation? To please their moms. And indeed, as each one is brought back on stage, in full make-up and glamour outfit, hair swinging (and in the case of the Black girls, straightened), striking vampy supermodel "power" poses, their mothers sob as if they had just learned their daughters' cancers were in remission. The moms are so overwhelmed they don't need more, but Maury is clearly bent on complete conversion: "Do you know how pretty you are?" "Look how gorgeous you look!" "That guy in the audience—he's on the floor!" "Are you going to dress like this more often?" Most of the girls, unsurprisingly, say yes. It's been a frontal assault; there's no room for escape.

As jaded as I am, this *Maury* show really got to me. I want to fold each one of the girls in my arms and get her out of there. Of course, what I really fear is that I won't be able to protect Cassie from the assault. It's happening already. I watch public television kids' shows with her, and can rarely find fault with the gender-neutral world they portray. We go to Disney movies and see resourceful, spirited heroines. Some of them, like the Hawaiian girls in *Lilo and Stitch*, even have thick legs and solid bodies. But then, on the way home from the movies, we stop at McDonald's for a Happy Meal, and—despite the fact that Cassie insists she's a boy and wants the boy's toy, a hot wheels car—she is given a box with a little mini-Barbie in it. Illustrating the box is Barbie's room, and my daughter is given the challenging task of finding all the matching pairs of shoes on the floor.

Later that day, I open a Pottery Barn catalogue, browsing for ideas for Cassie's room. The designated boy's room is all in primary colors, the bedspread dotted with balls, bats, catching mitts. The caption reads: "I play so many sports that it's hard to pick my favorites." Sounds like my daughter. On the opposite page, the girls' room is pictured, a pastel planetary design. The caption reads: "I like stars because they are shiny." That, too, sounds like my daughter. But Pottery Barn doesn't think a child can inhabit both worlds. If their catalogues were as segregated and stereotyped racially as they are by gender, people would boycott.

I rent a video—*Jimmy Neutron, Boy Genius*—for Cassie. It's married as a kids' movie; it's on that wall at Blockbuster. And the movie is okay, for the most part. But then we get to the music video, which follows the movie, unaccompanied by any warnings. It's a group I've never heard of, singing a song called "Kids in America." Two of the girls are thirteen. Two are fifteen and one is sixteen. I know this because their ages are emblazoned across the screen, as each makes her appearance. They are all in full vixen attire, with professionally undulating bodies, professionally made-up, come-hither eyes.

Why are we told their ages, I wonder? Are we supposed to be amazed at the illusion of womanhood created by their performance? Or is their youth actually supposed to make it all right to show this to little kids? A way of saying "It's only make believe, only a dress-up game"? How long ago was it that an entire culture was outraged over clips of Jon Benet Ramsey, performing femininity in children's beauty pageants? In 2002, toddler versions of Britney Spears were walking the streets on Halloween night. Can it really be that we now think dressing our daughters up like tiny prostitutes is cute? That's what Sharon Lamb, author of *The Secret Lives of Girls*, thinks. She advises mothers to chill out if their nine-year-old girls "play lovely little games in high heels, strip teasing, flouncing, and jutting their chests out," to relax if their eleven-year-olds go out with "thick blue eye shadow, spaghetti straps and bra straps intertwined, long and leggy with short black dresses." They are "silly and adorable, sexy and marvelous all at once," she tells us, as they "celebrate their objectification," "playing out male fantasies ... but without risk."

Without risk? I have nothing against dress-up. But flouncing is one thing; stripteasing is another. Thick blue eye shadow in mommy's bathroom is fine; an eleven-year-old night on the town is not. Reading those words "without risk," I want to remind Sharon Lamb that 22 to 29 percent of all rapes against girls occur when they are eleven and younger. We might like to think that these rapes are the work of deranged madmen, so disconnected from reality as to be oblivious to the culture around them. Putting vast media energy into a so-called epidemic of girl-snatching, such as we witnessed during the summer of 2002, helps sustain that myth and lets us believe that we are doing all we need to do to protect our daughters if we simply teach them not to take candy or go into cars with strangers.

The reality is, however, that young girls are much more likely to be raped by friends and family members than by strangers and that very few men, whether strangers or acquaintances, are unaffected by having a visual culture of nymphets prancing before their eyes, exuding a sexual knowledge and experience that preteens don't really have. Feminists used to call this "rape culture." We never hear that phrase anymore, do we?

HOPE AND FEAR

Still, progressive forces are not entirely asleep in the empire of images. I think of *YM* teen magazine, for example. After conducting a survey which revealed that 86 percent of its young readers were dissatisfied with the way their bodies looked, *YM* openly declared war on eating disorders and body-image problems, instituting an editorial policy against the publishing of diet pieces and deliberately seeking out full-size models—without "marking" them as such—for all its fashion spreads. I like to think this resistance to the hegemony of the fat-free body may have something to do with the fact that the editors are young enough to have studied feminism and cultural studies while they got their B.A.'s in English and journalism.

Most progressive developments in the media, of course, are driven by market considerations rather than social conscience. So, for example, the fact that 49 million women are size twelve or over is clearly the motive behind new, flesh-normalizing campaigns created by "Just My Size" and Lane Bryant. These campaigns proudly show off unclothed *zaftig* bodies and, unlike older marketing to "plus-size" women, refuse to use that term, insisting (accurately) that what has been called "plus size" is in fact average. It's a great strategy for making profits (I know they've got my ten bucks), but a species of resistance nonetheless. "I won't allow myself to be invisible anymore," these ads proclaim, on our behalf. "But I won't be made visible as a cultural oddity or a joke, either, because I'm not. I'm the norm."

The amorality of consumer capitalism, in its restless search for new markets, new ways to generate and feed desire, has also created a world of racial representations that are far more diverse now than when I wrote *Unbearable Weight*. This is another issue that has required special meaning for me, because my daughter is biracial, and I am acutely aware of the world that she sees and what it is telling her about herself. Leafing through current magazines, noting the variety of skin tones, noses, mouths depicted there, I'm glad, for the moment, that Cassie is growing up today rather than in the seventies, when Cheryl Tiegs ruled. It's always possible, of course, to find things that are still "wrong" with these representations; racist codes and aesthetics die hard. The Jezebels and geishas are still with us, and although Black male models and toddlers are allowed have locks and "naturals," straight hair—straighter nowadays than I ever thought it was possible for anyone's hair to be—seems almost a mandatory aesthetic for young Black women.

It's easy, too, to be cynical. Today's fashionable diversity is brought to us, after all, by the same people who brought us the hegemony of the blue-eyed blonde and who've made wrinkles and cellulite into diseases. It's easy to dismiss fashion's current love affair with full lips and biracial children as ethnic chic, fetishes of the month. To see it all as a shameless attempt to exploit ethnic niches and white beauty-tourism. Having a child, however, has given me another perspective, as I try to imagine how it looks through her eyes. Cassie knows nothing about the motives of the people who've produced the images. At her age, she can only take them at face value. And at face value, they present a world which includes her, celebrates her, as the world that I grew up in did not include and celebrate me. For all my anger and cynicism and frustration with our empire of images, I cannot help but be grateful for this.

On good days, I feel heartened by what is happening in the teen magazines and in the Lane Bryant and "Just My Size" ads. Perhaps advertisers are discovering that making people feel bad about themselves, then offering products which promise to make it all better, is not the only way to make a buck. As racial representations have shown, diversity is marketable. Perhaps, as Lane Bryant and others are hoping, encouraging people to feel okay about their bodies can sell products too. Sometimes, surveying the plastic, digitalized world of bodies that are the norm now, I am convinced that our present state of enchantment is just a moment away from revulsion, or perhaps simply boredom. I see a twenty-something woman dancing at a local outdoor swing party, her tummy softly protruding over the thick leather belt on her low-rider jeans. Not taut, not toned, not artfully camouflaged like some unsightly deformity, but proudly, sensuously displayed, reminding me of Madonna in the days before she became the sinewy dominatrix. Is it possible that we are beginning to rebel against the manufactured look of celebrity bodies, beginning to be repelled by their armored "perfection"?

These hopeful moments, I have to admit, are fleeting. Usually, I feel horrified—and afraid for my daughter, I am sharply aware that expressing this horror openly nowadays is to run the risk of being thought a preachy prude, relic of an outmoded feminism. At talks to young audiences, I try to lighten my touch, celebrate the positive, make sure that my criticisms of our culture are not confused with being anti-beauty, anti-fitness, or anti-sex. But I also know that when parents and teachers become fully one with the culture, children are abandoned to it. I don't tell them to love their bodies or turn off the television—useless admonitions today, and ones I cannot obey myself. But I do try to provide a disruption, if only temporary, of their everyday immersion in the culture. For just an hour or so, I won't let it pass itself off simply as "normalcy."

The lights go down, the slides go up. Much bigger than they appear in the magazines, but also, oddly brought down to size. For just a moment, we confront how bizarre, how impossible, how contradictory the images are. We laugh together over Oprah's head digitally grafted to another women's body, at the ad for breast implants in which the boobs stick straight up in the air. We gasp together as the before and after photos of Jennifer Lopez are placed side by side. We cheer for Marion Jones's shoulders, boo the fact that WNBA Barbie is just the same old Barbie, but with a basketball in her hand. For just a moment, we are in charge of the impact the faked images of "perfect" bodies have on us.

We look at them together and share—just for a moment—outrage....

20. bell hooks, "Global Feminism," from *Feminism Is for Everybody*

Excerpts from bell hooks, *Feminism Is for Everybody* (Cambridge, MA: South End Press, 2000), 44–47. Reprinted with permission.

A key thinker whose work the third wave continually draws upon, hooks argues for the importance of examining racism, sexism, and class elitism together in a global perspective whenever one is speaking in terms of feminism. Hooks emphasizes the need for a global rather than regional, national, or class-based feminism.

Individual female freedom fighters all over the world have single-handedly struggled against patriarchy and male domination. Since the first people on the planet earth were nonwhite it is unlikely that white women were the first females to rebel against male domination. In white supremacist capitalist patriarchal Western culture neocolonial thinking sets the tone for many cultural practices. That thinking always focuses on who has conquered a territory, who has ownership, who has the right to rule. Contemporary feminist politics did not come into being as a radical response to neocolonialism.

Privileged-class white women swiftly declared their "ownership" of the movement, placing working-class white women, poor white women, and all women of color in the position of followers. It did not matter how many working-class white women or individual black women spearheaded the women's movement in radical directions. At the end of the day white women with class power declared that they owned the movement, that they were the leaders and the rest of merely followers. Parasitic class relations have overshadowed issues of race, nation, and gender in contemporary neocolonialism. And feminism did not remain aloof from that dynamic.

Initially when feminist leaders in the United States proclaimed the need for gender equality here they did not seek to find out if corresponding movements were taking place among women around the world. Instead they declared themselves liberated and therefore in the position to liberate their less fortunate sisters, especially those in the "third world." This neocolonial paternalism had already been enacted to keep women of color in the background so that only conservative/liberal white women would be the authentic representatives of feminism. Radical white women tend not to be "represented," and, if represented at all, they are depicted as a fringe freak element. No wonder then that the "power feminism" of the '90s offers wealthy white heterosexual women as the examples of feminist success.

In truth their hegemonic takeover of feminist rhetoric about equality has helped mask their allegiance to the ruling classes within white supremacist capitalist patriarchy. Radical feminists were dismayed to witness so many women (of all races) appropriating feminist jargon while sustaining their commitment to Western imperialism and transnational capitalism. While feminists in the United States were right to call attention to the need for global equality for women, problems arose as those individual feminists with class power projected imperialist fantasies onto women globally, the major fantasy being that women in the United States have more rights than any group of women globally, are "free" if they want to be, and therefore have the right to lead feminist movement and set feminist agendas for all the other women in the world, particularly women in third world countries. Such thinking merely mirrors the imperialist racism and sexism of ruling groups of Western men.

Most women in the United States do not even know or use the terms colonialism and neocolonialism. Most American women, particularly white women, have not decolonized their thinking either in relation to the racism, sexism, and class elitism they hold towards less powerful groups of women in this society or the masses of women globally. When unenlightened individual feminist thinkers addressed global issues of gender exploitation and oppression they did and do so from a perspective of neocolonialism. Significantly, radical white women writing in *Night-Vision: Illuminating War and Class on the Neo-Colonial Terrain* emphasize the reality that "to not understand neocolonialism is to not fully live in the present." Since unenlightened white feminists were unwilling to acknowledge the spheres of American life where they acted and act in collusion with imperialist white supremacist capitalist patriarchy, sustained protest and resistance on the part of black women/women of color and our radical white sisters was needed to break the wall of denial.

Yet even when large numbers of feminist activists adopted a perspective which included race, gender, class, and nationality, the white "power feminists" continued to project an image of feminism that linked and links women's equality with imperialism. Global women's issues like forced female circumcision, sex clubs in Thailand, the veiling of women in Africa, India, the Middle East, and Europe, the killing of female children in China, remain important concerns. However, feminist women in the West are still struggling to decolonize feminist thinking and practice so that these issues can be addressed in a manner that does not reinscribe Western imperialism. Consider the way many Western women, white and black, have confronted the issue of female circumcision in Africa and the Middle East. Usually these countries are depicted as "barbaric and uncivilized," the sexism there portrayed as more brutal and dangerous to women than the sexism here in the United States.

A decolonized feminist perspective would first and foremost examine how sexist practices in relation to women's bodies globally are linked. For example: linking circumcision with life-threatening eating disorders (which are the direct consequence of a culture imposing thinness as a beauty ideal) or any life-threatening cosmetic surgery would emphasize that the sexism, the misogyny, underlying these practices globally mirror the sexism here in this country. When issues are addressed in this manner, Western imperialism is not reinscribed and feminism cannot be appropriated by transnational capitalism as yet another luxury product from the West women in other cultures must fight to have the right to consume.

Until radical women in the United States challenge those groups of women posing as feminists in the interest of class opportunism, the tone of global feminism in the West will continue to be set by those with the greatest class power who hold old biases. Radical feminist work around the world daily strengthens political solidarity between women beyond the boundaries of race/ethnicity and nationality. Mainstream mass media rarely calls attention to these positive interventions. In *Hatreds: Racialized and Sexualized Conflicts in the 21st Century*, Zillah Eisenstein shares the insight:

> Feminism(s) as transnational—imagined as the rejection of false race/gender borders and falsely constructed "other"—is a major challenge to masculinist nationalism, the distortions of statist communism and "free"-market globalism. It is a feminism that recognizes individual diversity, and freedom, and equality, defined through and beyond north/west and south/east dialogues.

No one who has studied the growth of global feminism can deny the important work women are doing to ensure our freedom. No one can deny that Western women, particularly women in the United States, have contributed much that is needed to this struggle and need to contribute more. The goal of global feminism is to reach out and join global struggles to end sexism, sexist exploitation, and oppression.

21. Michelle Tea, "Introduction," from *Without a Net*

Excerpts from *Without a Net* by Michelle Tea (Seattle: Seal Press, 2003), xi–xiv. Reprinted by permission of Seal Press.

One criticism often made of third-wave feminism is that it is more about middle-class consumption and the concerns of middle-class girls and women than it is about any wider economic issues. Michelle Tea's introduction to *Without a Net* serves as a refutation of that charge, showing how fully economic stratification is part of a third-wave feminist approach. Especially since third wave was conceptualized in a time of economic globalization and corporate downsizing in the United States, and there is an increasing disparity between "haves" and "have nots" both within the United States and worldwide, this piece articulates the experience of "living without a net" that characterizes the lives of so many today.

When I was in fifth grade I came upon the book *The Outsiders* and it split my world open. That it was written by both a girl and a poor person was clear to me, because here was a raw and sensitive look at the reality of being poor. In *The Outsiders*, all the protagonists are poor, and there is much tragedy. But the tragedy isn't their poverty, it's what happens to them *because* of their poverty, the way the world judges and despises them, fights and blames them, makes their lives plenty hard. The book displays the joys of being poor, the physicality of fighting, the closeness of being in a gang, the tiny triumph of shoplifting. And in the end, the bad kids don't turn good, turn middle-class. In the end, resolution comes when the main character links his struggle as a "greaser"—a poor kid—to the struggles of all the other poor kids out there, struggling to be understood and to survive, and he decides to tell his story. He writes a book, and the book is *The Outsiders*. Transcendent, it turns in on itself, the book eating its own tail. It made me want to write my own books, and I have. I can feel the influence of S. E. Hinton's Ponyboy on my own words, and in the spirit of the story I want to tell, the story of growing up a girl on the margins of the world, where the poor people are. The particulars of how poverty impacts females—their bodies, their sense of themselves, their options. And how it marks you for your whole life, how even if you decide to pass as a middle-class person in the world (and manage to pull off such a feat), you're still carrying that poor little child around somewhere inside you, in your heart or your gut, or in your mind, where she has spun herself into fearful notions of scarcity and less-than.

I love to read the stories of the working class. It's my home, and I like to see it represented. It always feels like a tiny bit of justice when a poor person manages to get their stories published. For years I've been going to literary readings and poetry open mics, I've been reading zines and self-published chapbooks, and I've been collecting, in my head, the working-class writers I've heard and read. I've wanted them all in one place, together, in the pages of a book I can selfishly pick up and enjoy whenever I want. I've wanted them all together in a book as another piece of justice, to correct the cultural misunderstanding that poor people don't have voices because they don't have anything to say. The misunderstanding that we're comfortable letting well-meaning middle-class writers speak for us. The misunderstanding that our writing isn't out there because we don't write. So many misunderstandings and so many underestimations! One little book isn't going to create the drastic change in perception that our society needs, but it's something. A united force of fierce truth-telling to entertain, educate, and attempt to even the score.

I was talking recently to a friend of mine, a guy who grew up in the same lousy, disadvantaged city I was raised in. He was talking about the freedom he felt as a working-class teenage boy in that town, how fun it was to run the streets, feeling like you owned the place, swiping hub caps, indulging in petty vandalism, no doubt terrorizing the females they tromped past with their simple presence. He stopped for a minute and said, as if thinking it for the first time, "I guess girls didn't really have the freedom we did, huh?" I wanted to smack him in the head. Um, no, not really. Most poor places are tough and most tough places are violent and in violent places females are easy targets. As tough and wild as poor girls might have looked held up against our better-off sisters, we're probably not as tough or wild as the boys we had to share our neighborhoods with. What's it like to grow up receiving messages from the dominant culture that to be a female is to behave in a way that will get you eaten for lunch in your roughneck city? What's it like to be viewed as dirty, stupid, or promiscuous simply because you're broke? Where are the females in *The Outsiders*? Even Ponyboy, our bookish, sensitive, only-fights-when-he-has-to narrator disses the greaser girls every chance he gets. The upper-class "Soc" girls are smart and classy; Cherry Valance, the only girl in the book, is a Soc but a greaser ally, a sort of dream girl. No greaser girls speak, they're written off as tough and trashy, wearing too much makeup. Sounds depressingly familiar. I wanted, of course, to know their stories....

... I wanted to capture the breathtaking, exhilarating, and scary experience of going through life knowing that there is no safety net to catch you should you fuck up and fall. There is no trust fund, no parents with cash on hand to cover a month's rent; the way the stress of being poor or working class can rip apart a family or destroy its members often means there's no family to call, period. Sometimes the net you're surviving without is that simple emotional support. I like to imagine that our lives are dazzling athletic feats, our survival graceful and artistic. It's a romantic way of looking at it, but you can't fault me for wanting to highlight our strengths, the brilliant flare of our collective defiance. When poor and working-class people are written about—and usually we are written *about*, rarely telling our own stories—it's always the tragedy that is documented. The incessant struggle, the rampant injustice.

Barbara Ehrenreich's smash bestseller *Nickel and Dimed: On (Not) Getting By in America* is a great example of this: fainting Merry Maids! Overworked, underpaid Wal-Mart workers! I try, I really do, to keep the cynicism and general bad attitude I have toward Ehrenreich's book in check. Truly her intentions were noble—to sink into the world of the minimum-wage worker, emerge with first-hand proof that it is a rough world, an impossible, soul-slaughtering existence. The problem, perhaps, is not her project itself, or even the fact that she was terribly well paid to be poor for a while. Perhaps the reason I found my cracked teeth gritting and my stomach scrambling with frustration while I read is that I couldn't believe this was news, a big hit, a bestseller. *Duh*, I thought, again and again, leafing through the book. Of course minimum-wage work is bone-crushing drudgery, difficult to live on, even more difficult to get out of. Why did it take a middle-class woman on a well-paid slumming vacation to break this news to the world? Where are the voices of the poor people who don't get to leave these lives when the story is completed? The people whose stories generally don't get completed? I knew that these stories were out there, and the image they'd present of the working-class experience in the U.S. would be deeper and more complicated than the tragic view the middle class always takes on our lives. There's tragedy, for sure there's tragedy, but there are also kick-ass survival skills to be proud of, so many ingenious approaches to surviving poverty—everything from the focused, determined march out from under it via college and hard work to a gleeful, defiant, dumpster-diving exultation in the freedom that can accompany living at the bottom. There is joy in poor people's lives, and humor and camaraderie. Girls who grow up working class grow up tough and clever. There is hope in our lives, whether it's the pure potential of a Lotto ticket and a bingo card, or the deep faith that things are gonna get better 'cause they sure as hell can't get any worse. We know the world is vast and complicated, our responses to our situations are often contradictory, counterintuitive, but we get by. We are all survivors, and have no use for the pity and condescension that often accompany discussions about our lives.

Discussions, incidentally, that we're rarely a part of. Poor people are always left out of the intellectual conversation, despite being the subjects of entire books. In *Nickel and Dimed*, Ehrenreich, a successful middle-class woman, speaks directly to other middle-class people. This happens frequently in books and articles about working-class people—it is assumed that none of us will be reading the text. It's a decidedly creepy experience to read about your life like this, passed from one middle-class perception to another. It's like being talked about in a room where you sit, invisible. It's a game of intellectual keep-away, the words lobbed over your head, but worse—no one even knows you're trying to get in on the game. It doesn't even occur to them that you could play....

22. Daisy Hernández, "My Father's Hands," from *Without a Net*

Excerpts from "My Father's Hands" by Daisy Hernández, published in Michelle Tea, ed., *Without a Net* (Seattle: Seal Press, 2004), 49–57. Reprinted with permission.

A beautiful personal history focused on issues of transnationalism, immigration, multiculturalism, and the effects of economic policies such as NAFTA, "My Father's Hands" vividly captures the consequences of deindustrialization, downsizing, and a culture based on consumption in the United States for third-wave feminists not born to privilege. Through image and narrative, Hernández provides a moving critical portrait of the dialog between mainstream consumer culture and the lives produced within it.

My father is in his sixties. He is a tall, thin man with an almost bald head. He has a small beer belly beneath his white cotton T-shirt. His hands are never empty. There is always a cigar, cigarette, or beer can in them. He's handsome, and he's an alcoholic.

Years before the Cuban revolution, my father, then a teenager, saw a soldier in the hills where he and his family picked coffee beans, cut sugar cane, and raised pigs. He liked the soldier's matching jacket and pants, the uniform's sense of purpose. My father didn't want to be a farmer. He wanted something more. He wanted to be on the side that won.

Some years later, he got the uniform and fought against Fidel Castro. Unfortunately, he only talks about it now when he's drunk, slurring the words and his history into a number of possibilities. But this much is true, he says: It isn't easy to switch sides in a war. So he left the island along with the United States embassy workers and came to New Jersey, where he cut hair, opened a bakery, painted houses, closed the bakery, and cut wood. By the early 1970s, he had settled into factory work and married my Colombian mother.

He returned to visit Cuba once before NAFTA and told his cousins how good work was in the north. His job was to stay up through the night with a textile machine. He'd replace needles that broke and alert the bosses to any problems. It was he and the night and the deafening sound of the machines. He didn't need more than a few English phrases. On weekends he made extra money helping with plumbing, electricity—those many jobs where a man is always useful.

Then, in the nineties, factories began closing. My father's work hours were cut from twelve a day to eight, and then six. I began finding him home at all hours of the day and night and after awhile I slopped asking why, because all he would say was, "*Se terminó el trabajo* (the work ended)." The work ended like a novel, its mournful last page close at hand.

When he wasn't on the clock, my father drank. His hands would point at me and remind me to study hard because "you don't want to end up at a factory like your mother and me." Even before I understood words and phrases like "manual labor," "working class," and "alcoholism," I knew how they felt: like my father's hands.

Parts of my father's hands are dead. The skin has protected itself by hardening, turning his large hands into a terrain of calluses and scars, the deep tines scattered on his palms like dirt roads that never intersect. His hands are about power and survival, my first lessons about class. The dreaded question comes on Wednesday afternoons when my father drags the trash cans to the curb. That's when the Colombian lady across the street pushes her screen door open. She's noticed my father at home lately and asks him about his job. When he tells her the factory is closed *por ahora*, she tilts her head like she already knew. "*Y estás colectando?*"

What she really wants to know is if he's collecting unemployment benefits.

"There's no work to be found," my father answers. His pants are falling from his narrow hips and he yanks them up with his left hand.

"*Pero, estás colectando?*"

My father shrugs his shoulders. "*Es la mísma basura.*" It's the same garbage.

He wishes the Colombian lady well. From my bedroom window, I watch him walk into the two-family house he and my mother bought with years of savings. In the basement, he finishes a six-pack of Coors beer and listens to Radio WADO. He's found a store down Bergenline Avenue where the price of beer drops when unemployment rises.

At Catholic Mass on Sunday, the collection basket makes the rounds. The Cold War is over, but the world is still divided into good and evil, democracy and communism, Catholics and others, the ones who give and the ones who collect. It is a simple arrangement. One ill-spoken word could damn you to hell, communism, and poverty.

There is some comfort in knowing even God has to collect. But still the church's collection basket makes me anxious. I'm afraid we don't have money to give because, when it comes to Strawberry Shortcake stickers, my mother says we don't have the money. In church, my eyes rarely turn to her. Instead, I listen carefully to hear whether her pocketbook will join the others to interrupt the church's silence. It does.

The collection baskets crawl down each pew and swallow the sounds of crinkled dollars and jingling coins. I hold two, sometimes four quarters, excited to throw them into the basket. The tap dancing of those coins into the basket makes me feel we are as good as any of the families here with five-dollar bills in their hands.

Spanish is a Romance language except when you're trying to make ends meet. The Spanish we speak is a language in which life is reduced to talking about what you need, what's working and what isn't. *No hay trabajo. Media libra de chuletas. Basta ya. Van pal'iglesia. Estás colectando?*

Are you collecting? The rest of that sentence, the words "unemployment benefits," never makes it into Spanish. There is no need for it, because everyone here knows what is meant when the question is asked. No one says we're "receiving" or "getting," because no one here really believes we have a right to that money. You're "collecting" because you don't have work. You're one step away from *la gente en* welfare and two steps away from the old lady at Port Authority who's collecting pennies from commuters. Even in English, we call it "unemployment *benefits*," thinking it's a benefit to get something back from the work we do.

I live with Spanish, with coming home to find my mother watching a *telenovela*. Her factory shut down for a few days and her Spanish words are to the point. "Your father's in the basement. They called from work, said to not come today."

In the basement, my father talks to Elegua, an Afro-Cuban god without hands who lives in a clay dish and opens doors. He has only a face, sculpted into a round pointy crown. When my father is collecting unemployment, he feeds Elegua more candy and espresso so the god will open the door to another job.

Elegua is better than learning English. He's the god of trickery and journeys; you can trust him more than English words that change tenses, don't sound the way they look, and get turned on you at the factory.

As a child, I am drawn to Elegua and his candy dish. The Cuban women explain to my Colombian mother that Elegua loves children and that's why I'm spending time with him. But they are wrong. I am a practical child. Elegua's the god who opens doors and I am desperately trying to get away from my father's angry, drunk hands, and the feeling that our destinies are scribbled in the square opaque windows of my father's factory. Because Elegua is the god of crossroads, I imagine he understands the contradiction of my growing up: that I want to escape from my father and also take him with me, that I want to flee my life without leaving Papi behind.

I am meant to escape. Everyone tells me so at the barbecue for my mother's birthday. "Girl, you're going to be something some day. You're going to make it. Irma, will you look at this thing the *nena* wrote for the school paper, her name and everything. Girl, you're going places." No one ever says where I am going, but they are sure that a place is waiting for me.

By the time I am nine and translating my report card for my father, I know he is not going with me.

In elementary school, I hear that Americans are trying to keep up with a family named Joneses. The Joneses are a mystery of the English language. My mother says she's never heard of "*la famîlia Yoneses*" and I should quit worrying about what everybody else is doing.

In our part of the world, no one is keeping up. We belong to a community based on the fact that we are all doing bad. When someone does a little better, there is an unspoken betrayal. You smile at them and when they leave, you talk about how they are lying to get welfare checks, working *por la izquierda*, putting on airs. When you are the one doing better, you sit at your kitchen table and say, "It's incredible but true. Any little good thing you got, somebody else wants." You talk about how *celoso*, jealous, people can be. It is easier to say that people are jealous than admit they have a right to want something better.

It takes years for me to understand that the Joneses happen only in English, in houses where people cook in one room and eat in another. The Joneses don't happen where people are called "white trash" and "spics," "welfare queens" and "illegals." And no one ever asks the Joneses if they are collecting.

When someone asks my father how he is doing, he looks at his hands, studies the scattering of black scars and the dryness of the skin. His answer is always the same, "*Ahi, caballero, en la mísma lucha.*"

When I ask him what it means to say you are in the same *lucha*, my father says it means you are doing the same old thing. Years later in community activism, that's all I hear, that we're in this *lucha* together. *Lucha* means struggle, someone tells me. The same old thing, *la lucha*. I sit at a lesbian collective meeting, my hand clasping my pen tightly. It's hard to explain how in one moment, someone can translate a word and your understanding of your family and your history can be turned around.

In the mid-nineties, the *lucha* changed. Neighbors began talking about working as home attendants. The closed factories began outnumbering the ones that stayed open, and the new jobs were in cleaning floors and baby diapers and serving food. Men from Central America arrived, renting the first floor of our home, eight men, two bedrooms. The whites who could moved out. People came from all parts: Mexico, Pakistan, Brazil, India. The men waited at the street corner for construction work that barreled down the street in blue pickup trucks. In our basement, the Spanish newspaper was marked in red ink with circles and X's.

My father survived the onset of NAFTA because of the Cuban revolution. A political refugee, he was entitled to citizenship and the unemployment benefits that carried us between his jobs. The newer immigrants and those who came from other countries didn't have his privileges.

At the unemployment agency, he sat alongside African Americans, Pakistanis, Dominicans, and Nigerians, and they learned the English words for the work they did, and how to spell them. "Embroidery." "Seamstress." "Machine operator."

Factories closed for a week, a month, forever, and we waited for the phone to ring. The calls came randomly. At first the voices were Pure American English, a language that rarely falters. It begins with a "hey, your dad home?" and ends with a "thanks."

I was never to say that my father was out looking for another job or that he'd found one, part-time. I was never to reveal anything over the phone. Just take the message.

Sometimes the factory had not closed but "tell your dad to come at eight, not five, tonight." Or, "Tell him we need him tonight." "Tell him to call us next week." "Tell him he can file for unemployment."

As the years passed, the factories changed hands and the callers changed. The American voices disappeared and were replaced by an English that stumbled all over itself. "Halo, Ignacio?" No, he's not home. "Eh, tell him, no work, eh, come ehere efriday."

Even the unemployment agency changed to a new dial-in system to collect unemployment benefits. The brochure came in Spanish and English.

My mother studied it carefully. My father made the money and my mother handled it. She wrote the checks, paid the bills, and completed the forms for unemployment with me. My father's hands could do many things, but handling money was not one of them. Making phone calls was not one of them, either. His hands would wake me up with a gentle shake. He'd still be sober. "Your mother called unemployment and couldn't get through. Come on, get up, call them."

The dial-in system was fabulously efficient. Much more so than the factories that closed.

If your social security number ends on an odd number, call on Tuesday. If it ends on an even number, call on Thursday. Enter the weeks for which you're claiming.

The dial-in system was clever. They said it was to help us, to avoid waiting at the agency for a long time. I suspect it was the best way to handle a possible riot as the economy switched from the manufacturing to the service sector. Not making a trip to the agency meant you wouldn't have to see in one room how many other people were going through the same thing. When you did show up (because the phone system didn't work), there were fewer people, even though back on your street you knew it was more people than that. You began to doubt yourself. Maybe it wasn't so bad.

Not going to the agency meant you could avoid seeing the pain of other people. You didn't need to know English to understand the agency man telling someone on the line that "no, sir, according to this you have nothing left to collect." You didn't need a translation for the immigrant man's English words, "But I no find job." And then came that dreaded English word—"welfare." "Sir, I'm gonna need for you to get off this line because we can't help you here. Get on the line at window four and you can talk to someone there about welfare."

Calling in, you could avoid that man's eyes, the way his brown body, sheltered under five layers of clothes against the winter storm, turned away and left. You could avoid looking at his empty hands. You could avoid thinking about what would happen one day when none of us could collect.

The only thing I feared more than my father not being able to collect was time spent collecting. At least when there was work he wasn't around drinking and yelling at me as much. The world was cruel to him, yes, but it was hard for me to be angry and afraid of an abstract idea like "world." It was easier to be afraid of my father's hands. Easier to be angry when the blistered and swaying drunk hands slapped me on the back of my head. And there were other emotions that came more easily than anger: fear and guilt. Fear that life would always be like this—at the mercy of a factory closing, a paycheck arriving. Guilt because I—with my English words and schooling—would one day lead a different life than his. I just had to get there.

For about a year, I worked at McDonald's. I worked the register and got free meals. My job meant that if I set my mind to it and flirted with the right managers, I could become a manager too, with paid vacation, paid sick time, and a steady paycheck. So I watched my classmates play softball, run for student council, and drive their new Nissans. I'd get home and change from my Catholic uniform to my McD's one. If I worked enough hours, I made as much as my mother did at the factory.

On Saturdays, the manager created competitions to make us work faster. "The register that makes the most money before noon gets two tickets to Loews movie theater!" It was the first time anyone had ever referred to me as a machine. But I just smiled politely. I was proud of learning the register, its grid of prices. Big Macs, Large Fries, Apple Pies. But the manager was right. In a matter of months, I had become a machine. You had to shut down some part of yourself to the sexist jokes, to your hours cut when a new manager took over the schedules and didn't like you. The job was like walking on a tightrope without a net. You are up in the air alone. Interacting with other people is an act of acrobatics. You never know who will start talking shit about you. You never know what will piss off your boss. You never know why they sent you home but not the others. A wrong word could mean your hours the next week were reduced from forty to thirty-two.

It's hard to write this part of the story. It's the part of the story I never talk about with my New York friends, writer friends, community activist friends, with anyone. We act the same—like we never worked with our hands.

Sometimes we mention in conversation that we worked menial jobs, we stripped, we waited tables, we worked fast-food jobs, we cleaned diapers. We use those middle-class words to describe experiences that are not middle-class. But we don't know how else to talk about them.

It's hard to write about how quickly I moved that Saturday, how jealous and ashamed I was when I came in a close second for those tickets. It's hard to write about burning my fingers at the fry machine, how the grease of the place sticks to your skin, how you take the money you earn to the nail salon and get long acrylic tips and for a moment forget you are at a job that slowly turns your hands to cardboard. And it's harder still to know that a good number of people don't work and live like this. Harder still to know those people are your teachers, your friends who live in towns where McDonald's aren't even allowed to open.

In college and after, there are other jobs, the ones you really talk about over dinner with friends. The job at the library, the newspaper, the publishing house. But after years of numbing myself to working-class life, an alcoholic father, a fast-food job, it isn't easy to make myself feel something. I am too used to a world where trips to museums are something you do on class trips in high school. Our passions weren't work, but what we saw on the Spanish news, our romantic lives, losing weight, getting pregnant, waiting to love, wanting to be loved, the specials on Bergenline, the freebies at the Macy's Clinique counter with a purchase of $19.95. We talked about dreams, where we'd go if we had all the money in the world, who we would marry if we could pick anyone.

Those office jobs after college meant walking into a place where people didn't dream like that. They had jobs they liked, money-market accounts, paid vacation time. Dreams were something that actually happened. No one talked about buying a Lotto ticket.

More than anything now I am trying to feel something rather than numbing myself to the gap between my father and me, between the past and the present. I get a paycheck for writing newspaper articles about unemployment, while he works part-time as a janitor. Friends tell me to feel accomplished, that my résumé is a reflection of him, his sacrifices and triumphs. That's probably true, but it doesn't resonate.

The only things that do make me feel something are art, writing about him, loving him, taking pictures of his hands, listening to him tell me I should photograph this one scar on his index finger. He can't remember how he got it.

23. bell hooks, "Women at Work," from *Feminism Is for Everybody*

Excerpts from bell hooks, *Feminism Is for Everybody* (Cambridge: South End Press, 2000), 48–54. Reprinted with permission.

In this essay, hooks argues that feminism must address the question of the economic plight of women, and that this issue might serve as a collective platform for organizing and uniting women.

More than half of all women in the United States are in the workforce. When contemporary feminist movement first began the workforce was already more than one-third female. Coming from a working-class, African-American background where most women I knew were in the workforce, I was among the harshest critics of the vision of feminism put forth by reformist thinkers when the movement began, which suggested that work would liberate women from male domination. More than 10 years ago I wrote in *Feminist Theory: From Margin to Center*: "The emphasis on work as the key to women's liberation led many white feminist activists to suggest women who worked were 'already liberated.' They were in effect saying to the majority of working women, 'Feminist movement is not for you.'" Most importantly I knew firsthand that working for low wages did not liberate poor and working-class women from male domination.

When reformist feminist thinkers from privileged class backgrounds whose primary agenda was achieving social equality with men of their class equated work with liberation they meant high-paying careers. Their vision of work had little relevance for masses of women. Importantly the aspect of feminist emphasis on work which did affect all women was the demand for equal pay for equal work. Women gained more rights in relation to salaries and positions as a result of feminist protest, but it has not completely eliminated gender discrimination. In many college classrooms today students both female and male will argue that feminist movement is no longer relevant since women now have equality. They do not even know that on the average most women still do not get equal pay for equal work, that we are more likely to make seventy-three cents for every dollar a male makes.

We know now that work does not liberate women from male domination. Indeed, there are many high-paid professional women, many rich women, who remain in relationships with men where male domination is the norm. Positively we do know that if a woman has access to economic self-sufficiency she is more likely to leave a relationship where male domination is the norm when she chooses liberation. She leaves because she can. Lots of women engage feminist thinking, choose liberation, but are economically tied to patriarchal males in ways that make leaving difficult if not down-right impossible. Most women know now what some of us knew when the movement began, that work would not necessarily liberate us, but that this fact does not change the reality that economic self-sufficiency is needed if women are to be liberated. When we talk about economic self-sufficiency as liberating rather than work, we then have to take the next step and talk about what type of work liberates. Clearly better-paying jobs with comfortable time schedules tend to offer the greatest degree of freedom to the worker.

Masses of women feel angry because they were encouraged by feminist thinking to believe they would find liberation in the workforce. Mostly they have found that they work long hours at home and long hours at the job. Even before feminist movement encouraged women to feel positive about working outside the home, the needs of a depressed economy were already sanctioning this shift. If contemporary feminist movement had never taken place, masses of women would still have entered the workforce, but it is unlikely that we would have the rights we have, had feminists not challenged gender discrimination. Women are wrong to "blame" feminism for making it so they have to work, which is what many women think. The truth remains that consumer capitalism was the force leading more women into the workforce. Given the depressed economy white middle-class families would be unable to sustain their class status and their lifestyles if women who had once dreamed solely of working as housewives had not chosen to work outside the home.

Feminist scholarship has documented that the positive benefits masses of women have gained by entering the workforce have more to do with increased self-esteem and positive participation in community. No matter her class the woman who stayed at home working as a housewife was often isolated, lonely, and depressed. While most workers do not feel secure at work, whether they are male or female, they do feel part of something larger than themselves. While problems at home cause greater stress and are difficult to solve, those in the workplace are shared by everyone, and the attempt to find solutions is not an isolated one. When men did most of the work, women worked to make home a site of comfort and relaxation for males. Home was relaxing to women only when men and children were not present. When women in the home spend all their time attending to the needs of others, home is a workplace for her, not a site of relaxation, comfort, and pleasure. Work outside the home has been most liberating for women who are single (many of whom live alone; they may or may not be heterosexual). Most women have not even been able to find satisfying work, and their participation in the workforce has diminished the quality of their life at home.

Groups of highly educated privileged women previously unemployed or marginally employed were able through feminist changes in job discrimination to have greater access to work that satisfies, that serves as a base for economic self-sufficiency. Their success has not altered the fate of masses of women. Years ago in *Feminist Theory: From Margin to Center* I stated:

> If improving conditions in the workplace for women had been a central agenda for feminist movement in conjunction with efforts to obtain better-paying jobs for women and finding jobs for unemployed women of all classes, feminism would have been seen as a movement addressing the concerns of all women. Feminist focus on careerism, getting women employed in high-paying professions, not only alienated masses of women from feminist movement; it also allowed feminist activists to ignore the fact that increased entry of bourgeois women into the work force was not a sign that women as a group were gaining economic power. Had they looked at the economic situation of poor and working-class women, they would have seen the growing problem of

unemployment and increased entry of women from all classes into the ranks of the poor.

Poverty has become a central woman's issue. White supremacist capitalist patriarchal attempts to dismantle the welfare system in our society will deprive poor and indigent women of access to even the most basic necessities of life: shelter and food. Indeed a return to patriarchal male-dominated households where men are providers is the solution offered women by conservative politicians who ignore the reality of mass unemployment for both women and men, and the fact that jobs simply are not there and that many men do not want to provide economically for women and children even if they have wages.

There is no feminist agenda in place offering women a way out—a way to rethink work. Since the cost of living in our society is high, work does not lead to economic self-sufficiency for most workers, women included. Yet economic self-sufficiency is needed if all women are to be free to choose against male domination, to be fully self-actualized.

The path to greater economic self-sufficiency will necessarily lead to alternative lifestyles which will run counter to the image of the good life presented to us by white supremacist capitalist patriarchal mass media. To live fully and well, to do work which enhances self-esteem and self-respect while being paid a living wage, we will need programs of job sharing. Teachers and service workers in all areas will need to be paid more. Women and men who want to stay home and raise children should have wages subsidized by the state as well as home-schooling programs that will enable them to finish high school and work on graduate degrees at home. With advanced technology, individuals who remain home should be able to study by watching college courses on videos augmenting this with some period of time spent in classroom settings. If welfare not warfare (military spending) was sanctioned by our government and all citizens legally had access to a year or two of their lives during which they received state aid if they were unable to find a job, then the negative stigma attached to welfare programs would no longer exist. If men had equal access to welfare then it would no longer carry the stigma of gender.

A growing class divide separates masses of poor women from their privileged counterparts. Indeed much of the class power elite groups of women hold in our society, particularly those who are rich, is gained at the expense of the freedom of other women. Already there are small groups of women with class power working to build bridges through economic programs which provide aid and support to less privileged women. Individual wealthy women, particularly those with inherited wealth, who remain committed to feminist liberation are developing strategies for participatory economics which show their concern for and solidarity with women who lack class power. Right now these individuals are a small minority, but their ranks will swell as their work becomes more well known.

Thirty years ago contemporary feminists did not foresee the changes that would happen in the world of work in our society. They did not realize that mass unemployment would become more of a norm, that women could prepare themselves for jobs that would simply not be there. They did not foresee the conservative and sometimes liberal assault on welfare, the way that single mothers without money would be blamed for their economic plight and demonized. All these unforeseen realities require visionary feminist thinkers to think anew about the relationship between liberation and work.

While much feminist scholarship tells us about the role of women in the workforce today and how it changes their sense of self and their role in the home, we do not have many studies which tell us whether more women working has positively changed male domination. Many men blame women working for unemployment, for their loss of the stable identity being seen as patriarchal providers gave them, even if it was or is only a fiction. An important feminist agenda for the future has to be to realistically inform men about the nature of women and work so that they can see that women in the workforce are not their enemies.

Women have been in the workforce for a long time now. Whether we are paid well or receive low wages, many women have not found work to be as meaningful as feminist utopian visions suggested. When women work to make money to consume more rather than to enhance the quality of our lives on all levels, work does not lead to economic self-sufficiency. More money does not mean more freedom if our finances are not used to facilitate well-being. Rethinking the meaning of work is an important task for future feminist movement. Addressing both ways women can leave the ranks of the poor as well as the strategies they can use to have a good life even if there is substantial material lack are vital to the success of feminist movement.

Early on, feminist movement did not make economic self-sufficiency for women its primary goal. Yet addressing the economic plight of women may ultimately be the feminist platform that draws a collective response. It may well become the place of collective organizing, the common ground, the issue that unites all women....

24. Peggy Orenstein, "Afterword: Thriving in a Time of Flux," from *Flux*

In this moving account of women's struggles in the "half-changed world" that third-wave feminists inherited, Orenstein presents and analyzes the conditions that inform those struggles, including the "anything is possible" model that third-wavers grew up with, and how the unrealistic nature of that mantra affects women's daily lives. She argues for the need for men to take on more responsibility at home if women are to reach their full potential, and that women need to give up the mythology of "the good mother."

On a rainy fall afternoon my phone rings. "Peggy!" says a familiar voice. "It's Abbey Green."

It has been over two years since I've spoken with Abbey, though I've thought about her frequently. I'd felt an especially visceral connection with her during our interviews: so often she'd reminded me of my own younger self. Last I'd heard, Abbey had left New York to attend graduate school in the Midwest. Now, she tells me, she's working in the marketing department of an Internet company, a place that fosters the kind of open, visionary management style of which she once dreamed. I mention that I'm just a few weeks shy of finishing my book. "Really?" she says with characteristic enthusiasm. "Well, what did you find out?"

I hesitate briefly. What could I tell Abbey—or any of the women I met—that could help them in making future choices, challenge their thinking, inspire them to effect change? The nature of flux is that it is dynamic, ever-shifting; that's what makes this moment in history both exciting and frustrating—and nearly impossible to sum up. Women's lives have become a complex web of economic, psychological, and social contradictions, with opportunities so intimately linked to constraints that a choice in one realm can have unexpected consequences (or benefits) ten years later in another.

After four years of talking to women, though, a few things have become clear. The first is fundamental: there's a critical connection between sexual agency and a lifelong sense of self. As Abbey herself attested, it's imperative that girls feel a strong sense of sexual self-determination from the outset, that they understand that sex is not about pleasing boys or competing with friends but ought to grow from authentic desire, feelings of intimacy, mutual respect, as well as an innate right to pleasure. "It's absolutely key to esteem issues for me," she had insisted when we first met. "If you're comfortable with your body, you're comfortable with yourself. If you feel like you deserve all this pleasure in bed, you start to feel like you deserve it other places too." Like Abbey, many of the young women I interviewed had struggled to overcome dehumanizing early experiences, encounters which teach them that men's desires supersede their own. As they grow older, that lesson fuels a more general reluctance to articulate (and in some cases, to even recognize) their own needs, particularly in their relationships with men and children.

For most of the young women I met, part of the Promise was attaining a marriage of equals, one in which intimacy and responsibility—both in and outside the home—were reciprocal. They believed that the most satisfying life would be one in which independence combined with interdependence, in which they contributed to the world through work as well as nurturing their families. Yet, the images of the Perfect Wife and the Good Mother cast surprisingly long shadows over their lives. Even as they dreamed of equality they were tracking themselves into lower-paying, more flexible jobs than their male peers under the assumption that, when the time came, it would be up to them to make most of the sacrifices at home. They viewed that strategy as pragmatic, a compromise between dueling expectations, but, in addition to potentially decreasing their engagement with work, it ensures that they will have less leverage in negotiating chores and childcare, that their future husbands will feel less accountability at home, and, over time, that the prospect for the kind of partnerships they envision will be vastly reduced.

The fact remains that in order for women to fulfill their potential as individuals, separate from their roles as wives and mothers, men—at least more men—have to take on full responsibility at home. Some do. The couples I met who had avoided the Near-Peer slide, such as Emily and Dan Sorenson in Chicago, were more satisfied with the balance of their lives than anyone else I interviewed. Those couples had several things in common. The wives earned at least half of their family's income. The husbands had flexible jobs, worked regular hours, or were self-employed—the same circumstances that typically free women to handle emergencies, stay home with sick kids and, generally, devote more time to family life. Often something unexpected had happened—the woman needed to travel for her job, for instance, or a man was temporarily downsized—that had disrupted traditional gender roles, allowing the husband to develop his own sense of parental authority.

Sometimes among these couples the men had faced the kind of no-win trade-offs that typically befall women: men in dual-career marriages receive fewer promotions than their single-earner peers. (They also take a salary hit—a "Daddy penalty"—earning up to nineteen percent less for the same job.) Still, just as for women who make similar compromises, the payoff is a closer relationship to their children. Nor does father-nurturing subtract from mothering: The amount of time women spend with their children remains the same regardless of how much time Dad puts in. Men who share childcare more equally also report more positive feelings about their wives' employment and the wives themselves are less likely to be depressed. "Dan likes that we're both experiencing things and we're both trying to balance similar things," Emily told me. "And I think we don't tend to take each other for granted as much as we might otherwise. You start living in separate worlds if one is staying at home and one is working. So while it's difficult sometimes, it balances our marriage. Not to say your finances dictate the balance of power in your marriage, but it sure has a big influence, don't you think?"

I thought of what Emily had said when I read an article in *The Wall Street Journal* about how young women, much like the ones I'd met, were preparing for motherhood years in advance, "arm[ing] themselves to the teeth" by laying the groundwork for flexible careers. Unsurprisingly, few young men were doing the same. The writer seemed to be admiring the women's savvy in avoiding "the painful work-family conflicts of older women." Yet, anticipating the Near-Peer slide and reinforcing the Good Mother mythology may be precisely the wrong tactics: it appears that the more roles are reversed, the less stressful family life will become. Perhaps, then, all those well-intentioned seminars on work-life balance that are offered to young women in college and graduate school should be rethought: we all might be better off if they were targeted at men.

Men may have to do more, but women also have to let them. Mother management among the women I interviewed kicked in early. Recently I joked with a friend that every time she felt the urge to correct her husband's handling of their newborn, every time she was about to snatch the baby from him because Mother Knows Best, she should consider whether she wanted to *have* to do that when the child is ten. Stepping in made her feel a rush of competence, but it also reinforced that he was just her sidekick, not really responsible for their child's basic needs.

Micromanaging family life makes women feel in control, makes them feel like Good Mothers. It's also a very real source of power in a world where women can still feel powerless. That's not so easy to give up, but until we're free from the Good Mother's psychological grip, with its unattainable standards and sweet sense of authority, we can never fully address the external barriers to a more satisfying life. Perversely, though, as women's opportunities have grown outside of the home, Perfect Mother martyrdom seems to have grown more extreme, even glorified. For instance, there's the e-mail I received last March, telling the story of a couple watching TV. "I'm going to bed," the wife says, then proceeds to perform a long list of household tasks: throwing a load of clothes in the wash, setting out the breakfast dishes, checking the kids' homework, feeding the dog. Every few minutes her husband looks up and says, "I thought you were going to bed." "In a minute," she replies, then continues with her chores. This goes on and on. The punch line? Eventually the husband says, "I think I'll go to bed too." And he does. The letter ended with the suggestion: "Send this to five phenomenal women in celebration of women's history month." I was stunned. Since when is it "phenomenal" for a woman to resign herself to such imbalance? Since when is it cause for celebration?

It's a simple equation: if you're doing it all, you do not have it all. Mother management, driven by the fear of being judged by others as well as by their own harsh internal judgment, reinforces both the Near-Peer slide and the Second Shift. It also makes children—how they dress, how they comport themselves, how mentally healthy they appear—a reflection of a mother's self-worth, an extension of her identity. Giving up mother management is no small challenge. To do it requires that women get down in the psychological mud and wrestle with their deepest convictions about female silence and deference, about motherly self-denial and identity. It requires the courage to stand up to society censure and a great deal of faith that an alternative is possible. It also requires banishing, once and for all, the Good Mother.

Even when traditional roles seem the most desirable—or the most practical—course, they can be undertaken with egalitarian ideals in mind. That's especially important for women who decide to stay home full-time. The couples I met who had made the most conventional choices were least likely to discuss their implications. Periodically during my research, I recalled an early conversation in

New York with a twenty-seven-year-old, pregnant financial analyst who was planning to quit her job after her child was born. "I don't worry about divorce," she'd told me defiantly. "If that came about, it would be so horrible, let the whole world fall in on me. If it's compounded by the fact that I don't have a career, who cares." It was such an extreme response, and, given the statistics on divorce and widowhood, so foolhardy.

Perhaps more than anyone, women who follow the most traditional path need to clarify their roles with their spouses in advance: How, while staying home, can they still strive for intellectual and economic equality as partners, and how will they assure some equity in parenting? The women I spoke with who were home full time complained just as much—perhaps more—than working women about lack of time as a couple, lack of time for themselves, unfair division of labor, and a stagnant sex life. Given that, it seems imperative for a woman to consider before committing to at-home motherhood how she can adapt traditional patterns to have a stronger sense of autonomy within them. Aside from the childcare, how much housework will she be expected to do? How much will her husband do? How will she build skills for eventual reentry into the workforce? If they agree that her domestic labor contributes as much to their partnership as his wage-earning, would he expect to hand over half of his income, his pension, his company stock options, even his business to her if they divorce? (According to a *Business Week*/Harris Poll of households earning $100,000, the answer is no, perhaps offering the most honest assessment of men's beliefs about women's unpaid labor. Only 41 percent felt that an estate should be divided evenly when one spouse has generated most of the wealth; most believed the higher earner deserved the larger slice of the pie.) Over the short term, how will a couple assure that the woman has free time, that she has room for self-development? "What do I want for *myself* now?" was the typical question of midlife—but, really, women need to ask it all along the way, for their own well-being as well as for the good of their relationships with husbands, children, employers, and friends.

Women can't lead fuller lives until men are equal partners in the home, but men can't be true partners at home until there's further change in the workplace. Most of the employers I visited, like women's husbands, were more accommodating than in generations past, but, they, too, hadn't come far enough. Three of the women I profiled—Emily, Denise Littleton, and Mira Brodie—worked for corporations that have been cited by publications such as *Working Woman* and *Working Mother* as among the most supportive of women. Despite that, they had each encountered barriers to advancement and believed that the only way to reach the uppermost tiers of their professions was to conduct themselves as men traditionally have—but without the luxury of a stay-at-home spouse. Some, like Mira, were willing to remain single and childless if that's what it took. That's a valid choice when freely made, and it may well be the right one for her, but it shouldn't be a prerequisite of success. When I first met Mira, she argued that the workplace wouldn't really change until there was a critical mass of women at the highest levels of power. She's right: According to a Families and Work Institute report, having a few token women in top positions doesn't affect the culture of an institution. It's not until women fill half or more of upper-level jobs that companies become more likely to provide near-site day care, elder care resource and referral programs, and that options such as flextime can be pursued without penalty. But here's the rub: Until those humanizing factors are in place, women will have a hard time achieving the numbers necessary to make change. That's partly why, although women have flooded formerly male-dominated professions for decades, they make up only 13 percent of law partners, 26 percent of tenured professors, and 12 percent of corporate officers.

That means that until men fully understand what it means to straddle two worlds, women who pursue "life balance" will continue to sacrifice career advancement. Take the case of Lewis Platt, who was, until recently, CEO of the Hewlett-Packard Company. Under his leadership, HP became known as a bastion of enlightened, egalitarian thinking. Why? Because Platt's wife, who had stayed home with their daughters, died of cancer in 1981. Until then, according to *The New York Times*, he felt that women essentially created their own problems. Juggling a demanding job as a single parent, though, he had a conversion experience. When he became CEO, Platt not only instituted but *encouraged* HP employees—from upper-level executives on down, men as well as women—to use flexible scheduling, share jobs, work from home, and take sabbaticals, all without sacrificing advancement opportunities. The turnover rate among women at the company, which had been twice that of men's, is now the same, and women are well seeded along the pipeline to top-level positions. It's no coincidence that when Platt moved on to become the company's chairman in 1999 (he subsequently left the corporation), he was replaced by a woman, one of just three female CEOs of Fortune 500 companies. Platt's story shows that radically redefining the workplace—the very meaning of work—is possible, although his example is not without irony: Do women really have to *die* in order for men to see the light?

I thought about Platt during a recent conversation with an old high school buddy who is now an AIDS researcher at a prestigious university, married, with one child. "So many of my female colleagues really struggle to balance everything," he told me. "I really feel for them. A lot of them just drop out once they have kids."

"Well," I snapped back, "my goal is to make it just as hard for you as it is for them." He laughed. "No, I'm serious," I said, glaring. He'd irked me, so my response wasn't quite what I'd meant. My goal, really, was for men to reckon with the same conflicts as women do, as well as have the same choices: They should be as willing and able as women to choose low-paying, personally fulfilling professions, to marry a high-earning spouse and be primary caretakers of their children. As for those women who were forced to choose between work and family obligations, what if they could have made progress toward finding a cure for AIDS? Until that level of transformation happens, there will continue to be a loss of talent and a tremendous social cost to the contradictions we all face.

Women don't need corporations or even men to change to expand their own vision of what it means to be female. The lives of the single and childless women were especially valuable in that regard. Recall that Roseanne Peretti, the divorced account executive in Brooklyn, had consciously created meaningful multigenerational ties to community, family, and children. Her experience (which was not unique among the never-married, divorced, and childless women I interviewed) illuminated the opportunities for nurturing, creative expression, social contribution and self-development outside traditional boundaries. It also belied a culture that depicts single women, even the glamorous ones, as emotionally stunted, desperate, or victims of their own ambition. In fact, research consistently shows that single women grow happier as they age and are more independent, more assertive, and more interested in personal growth than their married peers. Nor does childlessness affect a woman's long-term well-being. Childless couples are as happy as parents who have good relationship with their children—and happier than those whose relationships are distant.

Most young women I met agreed that a woman could lead a full life without a husband and children, but they weren't eager to try it. As long as marriage and motherhood feel compulsory, though, they risk compromising themselves in their choice of partners, in their decisions about when and whether to have children, and in how those children are cared for. They will also be encouraged to act against their own best interests when trying to balance their needs with their families, and they'll be less equipped to hang on to an essential sense of self in the largely selfless relationship of a parent to a child.

The gap between the relative contentment of midlife single women and younger women's perceptions of them was alarming—particularly since, with a lower marriage rate, later marriage, divorce, and widowhood, today's women will spend more of their lives alone than in any previous era. Perhaps young women should look more closely at the statistics on women's health in marriage and their satisfaction in divorce, not to dissuade them, but to inspire them to find an approach to marriage—its beginning, its middle, and its potential end—that would be more flexible, airier, that would leave more room for a female self that is both distinct and connected.

The need for women to share such experience with one another, to talk across lines of age and circumstance, came through most emphatically in my interviews. Women tended to cluster with those most like themselves—working mothers with working mothers, single women with single women, forty-year-olds with forty-year-olds. That's not surprising: In an unstable time, someone else's choices and accommodations can feel like a reproach. My own hunger for that kind of honest, multigenerational discussion was part of what drove me to write this book. When I began, I was tormented by a deeply personal question: Should I have children? I ended up answering so much more. I'm a different woman than I was four years ago—more open, more optimistic, less judgmental of others and of myself. Talking with younger women like Abbey, Mira, and Shay, for instance, I reflected on how I, too, had struggled with the contradictions of the Promise, and how that confusion shaped my subsequent choices. Too often, I realize, I made decisions based on what I *didn't* want to be rather than what I hoped to become.

In retrospect, I suspect I was searching for my own perfect role model among the mothers I met, someone whose life could act as a blueprint to guide me through the Crunch. I didn't find her, but that turned out to be okay: Each conversation gave me new ideas about how I'd like to define, or perhaps redefine, motherhood for myself, and that was far more valuable. The single midlife women I met, both those who were never married and those who were divorced, were a revelation. They inspired me to contemplate how I've changed since becoming a wife, the parts of myself I needed to relinquish to truly share my life with Steven, and the parts, perhaps, I shouldn't have. Along with the childless women, they taught me that there are many ways beyond motherhood to build a meaningful, connected life. As the months have gone by and I have not yet become pregnant again, I have had some dark days, but, overall, I've retained my equanimity. I have the single and childless women I interviewed to thank for that. The relationships they had with siblings' and friends' children, their volunteer work, and the advantage they took of their freedom gave me a true alternative to which I can aspire.

Reporting this book was not always easy. Sometimes I bumped up against my own biases; sometimes I confronted my own regrets. As a result of that process, though, I feel more prepared to consciously construct the life I want and better able to accept the times when I fall short of that mark. I'm grateful to have had the opportunity to learn so much from my interviews but also a little disheartened: I wish such conversations were the norm in women's lives, that they didn't have to be so artificially and elaborately created. I hope, someday, they can be.

There are so many interviews I'd still like to do, so many questions I'd like to ask. I wonder how caring for sick and aging parents will affect women's choices, how it will shape the next phase of their lives. Is there a "Good Daughter" icon that correlates to the Good Mother and Perfect Wife? I would've liked to have pressed further on issues of widowhood too, which need to be front and center of the next feminist agenda. How is it that, after a lifetime of being caretakers themselves, elderly women are more likely than men to be neglected by their families? How can we better protect ourselves from poverty? In the end, there is no single path to a textured, satisfying life—nor should there be. But there are decisions we can make more consciously, strategies we can employ more usefully, consequences we can understand more fully as we assemble the pieces of our professional and personal dreams. Through that process women can move a little further, come a little closer, to reaching the promise of our half-changed world.

25. Elizabeth Wurtzel "Introduction: Manufacturing Fascination," from *Bitch: In Praise of Difficult Women*

An example of popular feminism that uses strategies of reappropriation to fight stereotypes of women, Wurtzel's introductory chapter to her book *Bitch* established her clearly as a third-wave feminist. Wurtzel looks at the representation of complicated, assertive women in popular culture, the so-called bitch, and concludes that "the world simply does not care for the complicated girls, the ones who seem too dark, too deep, too vibrant, too opinionated ... most men in the end don't quite have the stomach for that much person." Wurtzel argues that the "bitch" is really the fully developed person in charge of herself and her own feelings, that not being a "bitch" means to sacrifice oneself, and that so-called bitches should be reevaluated and loved for being themselves, not derided.

For a woman it is never enough to be just an artist, just a talent: our art in our life, carrying on with charisma, all that counts. I don't mean that a woman has to be a great beauty to matter—Janis Joplin was far from anything of the sort, but she had great possession, great élan, she wore lame and feathers and wiggled a lot, and the intensity of release in her soul singing all adds up to great style, and in that a great fight against the invisibility that would be hers because she is a woman and she is not a beauty. That's how Madonna came to be: she is the triumph of style alone, talent more in mise-en-scène than elsewhere. She reduces the requirements of visible femaleness so that all that is left *is* visible femaleness. And it is not surprising that she is the leap between Patti and Chrissie and eventually Courtney and Liz (in the rock world, there was nothing in between—Quarterflash and Pat Benatar don't count).

But woman's ability to use her sexuality to express liberation—which Madonna's whole career is so stylishly symbolic of—resulted paradoxically in her body's increased availability as an object of oppression. Since the sixties, the commodities of temptation and desire have been put on display in both a blatant and sidelong sense more now than ever: sex lines, the videocassette market that has made pornography a $5 billion a year industry, Victoria's Secret catalogues as a softer substitute, the Playboy channel, the virtual-reality sex sites that are the only real moneymakers on the Internet—all of these things are actually born of women's newfound freedom, and all of them serve monthly the interests of men. There is so much sex available in so many purchasable, perishable, inconsequential, and trivial ways, so much that it practically *demands* that men focus on their sexual needs and ignore everything else. This has made for a lonelier world that gives the impression that it is more free. "I had come of age at a time when sexual liberation did not yet mean groupies and massage parlors, when it was still a potent metaphor for liberation in general," wrote

Ellen Willis in 1975, in a *Rolling Stone* article about her brother's conversion to fundamentalist Judaism while visiting Israel. "Though I hated the way this vision [of sexual freedom] had been perverted, co-opted and turned against women, I believed no less in the vision itself."

As feminism has charged forward—and no one can deny the leaps and strides it has made—so has the invention of the overeager hyper-sexualized female body. Nowadays you pay for sex not because you are lonely and miserable and can't get laid, or [are] married and looking for cheap thrills, but because sex as a commodity is not distasteful; it's *interesting*. The recent best-seller by three Hollywood call girls, *You'll Never Make Love in This Town Again*, essentially chronicles the availability for money of just about anything. The women write about their experiences servicing major Hollywood movie stars, men who presumably don't "have to" pay for sex, but like to be able to control the action, or like the absence of any emotional involvement, or just plain think it's cool. In the midst of all this, it seems hard to talk about date rape or anything else, because as much as women may try to be seen not as sex objects there is a countervailing force in which many women collaborate—mostly out of financial need—to turn women into nothing but sex objects.

Which is why the good-time liberated lady whose sexual bravado could be celebrated by Germaine Greer and Helen Gurley Brown alike has metastasized over time into a harsh, hard force of flat, canned sexuality whose most protuberant and pertinent metonymy is the obvious and bulbous silicone breast implants that caricature a sexual reality that is already a cartoon, that don't even try to mimic mammarian nature.

I think the choices become whether you will use it for yourself or against. Look, I think many people have rescued themselves from this game, but pretty girls, girls who learned to manipulate, girls whose hearts always belonged to daddy—they just can't help it. And the world rewards it at the same time it condemns it. On the whole, one lesson of a book like *You'll Never Make Love in This Town Again* is that sex is really not much of a weapon in the end. You need to have some talent and brains or nothing will work. Most men who sleep with some girl won't want to give her a job since they'd prefer never to deal with the situation again. I think that's the main thing that's missing from any discussions of this subject—the complexities of date rape, the way strip clubs have become feminist enterprise zones while ignoring the degrading damaging nature of the work. For a woman to do just as she pleases and dispense with other people's needs, wants, demands, and desires continues to be revolutionary. Men pretty much do as they will, and women pretty much continue to pick up the slack. That's why books like *The Rules* and *Men Are from Mars, Women Are from Venus* succeed. It remains to this day, even after feminism, a woman's chore to close the gap. Time is not on our side, our youth and beauty is brief, tick-tock the biological clock, and that message is thrown at us over and over again. In *Manhattan Nocturne*, an unusually perspicacious noir novel with the genre's usual theme of the good man brought down by a beautiful bad girl, the author Colin Harrison muses at one point on what a short shelf life a pretty girl in New York City has: "I would say the most determined people are the young women who arrive in the city from America and around the world to sell, in one way or another, their bodies: the models and strippers and actresses and dancers who know that time is running against them, that they are temporarily credentialed by youth."

Of course, we are meant to understand that this is the lot of glamour girls, that those of us who put brains before beauty need not worry about this stuff. But to paraphrase Rosie O'Donnell once again: It *feels* as if it's true for us all. And while there are commitment-phobic women, the story you always hear when there is a troubled relationship—when the balance of power is off—for the most part it's always the one of women trying to get men to tie the knot. Now, I personally know a number of women who are putting off their boyfriends who are eager to get married—but those relationships are not the ones that seem in constant crisis, they are not the ones where somebody is always complaining, because for any number of reasons, the focus on commitment still only assumes a desperate cast when the woman is the injured party.

And the fact that all this relationship anxiety marks a regression of sorts is not lost on pioneers of the women's movement who thought it would be better by now. London eating disorders expert Susie Orbach, author of *Fat Is a Feminist Issue*, is the founder of the Women's Therapy Centre, where among her patients was Princess Diana. "I see all sorts of young confident women around," she told *Mirabella* in late 1996. "But when they're in my consulting room, they talk about the same bloody issues we had thirty years ago. They're afraid. Women in the most oppressive relationships are trying to manage them rather than get out of them. Only now, with no women's movement, if you have problems you feel like a freak. All the problems are internalized."

That's why *The Rules* is a runaway best-seller and may well be a perennial hit.

But it is wrong to see that book as a setback to feminism in any way, or to be mad at the authoresses for their Aunt Edna-like advice because the book is completely nonideological: feminism is beside the point in a list of what is probably fairly sound advice for learning to behave like a woman who is about to embark on some serious, goal-oriented dating. It tells women how to act so as to compensate for the fact that while feminism has changed the way many of us think and behave, while it has made men change diapers and do dishes and spend quality time with children while women perform neurosurgery and direct movies and trade Eurodollars, it has failed to truly change the way we *feel*. As Ellen Willis put it, most succinctly: "Feminism had transformed women's consciousness without, as yet, transforming society, leaving a gap between what many of us demanded of a relationship and what most men were willing to give." The proof: Go to any bookstore and there are hundreds of titles in the self-help section about how to overcome love addiction and fear of abandonment and the like, and while there are plenty of books for women about how to deal with commitment-resistant, impossible men—*Smart Women, Foolish Choices* and the like—there is not one book addressed to men about how to work out their own damn problems with relationships. No book for men about how to get over fear of commitment, how to learn to open one's heart, how to stop running from emotional involvement—I know, because I searched high and low for such a thing for my last boyfriend and it doesn't exist.

Do you know why?

Because it doesn't need to. Men don't have to change the way they sexually assess women, the way certain triggers and indications of female power or feminine weakness may frighten them off. They don't have to change the psychic messages inculcated into their brains from way back in their preverbal, pre-Oedipal days. They don't have to because we women will learn to behave. We could all enact, by collective will, an emotional *Lysistrata* of sorts, we could all walk out, like Meryl Streep in *Kramer vs. Kramer*, like the woman in Mary-Chapin Carpenter's song "He Thinks He'll Keep Her," like the women in a zillion country songs—we could all say that we abdicate all responsibility for the emotional well-being of our relationships, let the men learn to cope with it all. But we don't. And there's no indication it would do any good anyway. So we'll "adjust"—the word Betty Friedan used over thirty years ago in *The Feminine Mystique* to describe how intelligent Seven Sisters types learned to accept the notion that Mop & Glo was intellectually stimulating—and if we're from Venus and they're from Mars, we'll learn to speak Martian. We'll follow *The Rules*: We won't call them, we won't ask them out, we won't talk about ourselves, we won't make snide comments, we'll be good.

Well, I for one am sick of it. All my life, one person or another has been telling me to behave, saying don't let a guy know you're a depressed maniac on the first date, don't just be yourself, don't show your feelings. And the truth is, this is probably good advice, men probably don't like overbearing, hotheaded women who give blow jobs on the first date. In all likelihood the only man who will ever like me just as I am will probably need to believe I'm somebody else at first. I probably *do* need to learn to behave. But I don't like it. It seems like, all this, all these years of feminism, Mary Wollstonecraft, Charlotte Perkins Gilman, Simone de Beauvoir, Virginia Woolf, Gloria Steinem, Susan Faludi—all that smart writing all so we could learn to behave? Bra burning in Atlantic City—so we could learn to behave? *Roe v. Wade*—so we could learn to behave? *Thelma & Louise*—so we could learn to behave? The gender gap—so we could learn to behave? Madonna, Sally Ride, Joycelyn Elders, Golda Meir, Anita Hill, Bette Davis, Leni Riefenstahl—all those strong, indefatigable souls so we could learn to behave? What good really have any of those things done if we still get the feeling that we have to contain our urges and control ourselves in the interest of courtship and love? Did Germaine Greer importune us so long ago with the words "Lady, love your cunt," and did Anka Radikovich regale us with her tales of the sexual picaresque in *The Wild Girls Club* so we could be told never to succumb to sexual abandon on the first date? After all this agitation, along comes *The Rules* to tell us that we're not even allowed to accept a date for a Saturday night after Wednesday.

Here's my point: I have no quarrel with *The Rules* or the advice it gives—it actually seems pretty sound to me—but if we had really come a long way, baby, if men's perceptions of women had transformed fundamentally and intensely so that we were accepted as full-fledged sexual creatures and romantic operatives who were free to chase or be chased, and if this expanded dimension of women's sexual personal were not frightening or overwhelming to them, then we would not need *The Rules*. We would be truly free.

So of course the bitch persona appeals to us. It is the illusion of liberation, of libertine abandon. What if you want to be large in world that would have you be small, diminished? You don't want to diet, you don't want to say *no, thank you,* and pretend somehow that what is there is enough when always, always, you want more. That has been your defining characteristic: You have appetites, and only if you are truly shameless will you even begin to be sated because nothing is ever really enough. Not because you are greedy or insatiable but because you can't help it, you can't go along with the fiction that the world would have you believe and adhere to: that you ought to settle and be careful and accept the crumbs that are supposed to pass for a life, this minimized self you are supposed to put up with, that feminism and other political theories of woman cannot really begin to address because this is about something else entirely.

This is about what has become the almost monstrous notion of female desire. This is not about making demands of other people or wearing down those who have their own screams for MORE! to address: You'd be amazed at how often we are reluctant to indulge ourselves by our own means. It is amazing that the smallness of the space we've been told to squeeze into has meant that we don't even know how to ask or what to want. Everything tells us to stop, to not talk to that guy first, to not have a thousand lovers if that's what feels right because one husband is supposed to be enough. Everything says we don't need another piece of chocolate cake, we don't need another Gucci bag, another dime-store lipstick, another Big Mac, another night on the town, another spin on the Rainbow Room dance floor. Well, this is meant to be a story about people who are so beyond need, who want and have figured out that it's never too soon to make demands of this life, this world, this everything. It's about how nice it must be to just decide I will not be nice, I am never sorry, I have no regrets: what is before me belongs to me.

I think for men this attitude is second nature, it's as much in their atmosphere as snow is in an Eskimo's. They don't even *know* how much they assume.

But for a woman, to assume she has to be not nice, it puts her outside of the system, outside of what is acceptable. She can be a deeply depressive Sylvia Plath, a luxuriating decadent Delilah, a homicidal adolescent Amy Fisher, she can be anyone who decides that what she wants and needs and believes and must do is more important than being nice. She may, in fact, be as nice as can be, but as soon as she says *catch me if you can I'm so free this is my life and the rest can fuck off and die*—as soon as she lays down the option of my way or the highway, it's amazing how quickly everyone finds her difficult, crazy, a nightmare: a bitch....

26. bell hooks, "Our Bodies, Ourselves: Reproductive Rights," from *Feminism Is for Everybody*

Excerpts from bell hooks, *Feminism Is for Everybody* (Cambridge, MA: South End Press, 2000), 25–30. Reprinted with permission.

In this essay hooks argues that reproductive rights are a central issue for all women and that the recent ground lost on this issue is a major rallying point for feminists today.

When contemporary feminist movement began the issues that were projected as most relevant were those that were directly linked to the experiences of highly educated white women (most of whom were materially privileged). Since feminist movement followed in the wake of civil rights and sexual liberation it seemed appropriate at the time that issues around the female body were foregrounded. Contrary to the image the mass media presented to the world, a feminist movement starting with women burning bras at a Miss America pageant and then later images of women seeking abortions, one of the first issues which served as a catalyst for the formation of the movement was sexuality—the issue being the rights of women to choose when and with whom they would be sexual. The sexual exploitation of women's bodies had been a common occurrence in radical movements for social justice whether socialist, civil rights, etc.

When the so-called sexual revolution was at its peak the issue of free love (which usually meant having as much sex as one wanted with whomever one desired) brought females face to face with the issue of unwanted pregnancy. Before there could be any gender equity, around the issue of free love women needed access to safe, effective contraceptives and abortions. While individual white women with class privilege often had access to both these safeguards, most women did not. Often individual women with class privilege were too ashamed of unwanted pregnancy to make use of their more direct access to responsible health care. The women of the late '60s and early '70s who clamored for abortions had seen the tragedies of illegal abortions, the misery of forced marriages as a consequence of unwanted pregnancies. Many of us were the unplanned children of talented, creative women whose lives had been changed by unplanned and unwanted pregnancies; we witnessed their bitterness, their rage, their disappointment with their lot in life. And we were clear that there could be no genuine sexual liberation for women and men without better, safer contraceptives—without the right to a safe, legal abortion.

In retrospect, it is evident that highlighting abortion rather than reproductive rights as a whole reflected the class biases of the women who were at the forefront of the movement. While the issue of abortion was and remains relevant to all women, there were other reproductive issues that were just as vital which needed attention and might have served to galvanize masses. These issues ranged from basic sex education, prenatal care, preventive health care that would help females understand how their bodies worked, to forced sterilization, unnecessary cesareans and/or hysterectomies, and the medical complications they left in their wake. Of all these issues individual white women with class privilege identified most intimately with the pain of unwanted pregnancy. And they highlighted the abortion issue. They were not by any means the only group in need of access to safe, legal abortions. As already stated, they were far more likely to have the means to acquire an abortion than poor and working-class women. In those days poor women, black women included, often sought illegal abortions. The right to have an abortion was not a white-women-only issue; it was simply not the only or even the most important reproductive concern for masses of American women.

The development of effective though not totally safe birth control pills (created by male scientists, most of whom were not anti-sexist) truly paved the way for female sexual liberation more so than abortion rights. Women like myself who were in our late teens when the pill was first widely available were spared the fear and shame of unwanted pregnancies. Responsible birth control liberated many women like myself who were pro-choice but not necessarily pro-abortion for ourselves from having to personally confront the issue. While I never had an unwanted pregnancy in the heyday of sexual liberation, many of my peers saw abortion as a better choice than conscious, vigilant use of birth control pills. And they did frequently use abortion as a means of birth control. Using the pill meant a woman was directly confronting her choice to be sexually active. Women who were more conscientious about birth control were often regarded as sexually loose by men. It was easier for some females just to let things happen sexually then take care of the "problem" later with abortions. We now know that both repeated abortions or prolonged use of birth control pills with high levels of estrogen are not risk-free. Yet women were willing to take risks to have sexual freedom—to have the right to choose.

The abortion issue captured the attention of mass media because it really challenged the fundamentalist thinking of Christianity. It directly challenged the notion that a woman's reason for existence was to bear children. It called the nation's attention to the female body as no other issue could have done. It was a direct challenge to the church. Later all the other reproductive issues that feminist thinkers called attention to were often ignored by mass media. The long-range medical problems from cesareans and hysterectomies were not juicy subjects for mass media; they actually called attention to a capitalist patriarchal male-dominated medical system that controlled women's bodies and did with them anything they wanted to do. To focus on gender injustice in these arenas would have been too radical for a mass media which remains deeply conservative and for the most part anti-feminist.

No feminist activists in the late '60s and early '70s imagined that we would have to wage a battle for women's reproductive rights in the '90s. Once feminist movement created the cultural revolution which made the use of relatively risk-free contraceptives acceptable and the right to have a safe, legal abortion possible women simply assumed those rights would no longer be questioned. The demise of an organized, radical feminist mass-based political movement coupled with anti-feminist backlash from an organized right-wing political front which relies on fundamentalist interpretations of religion placed abortion back on the political agenda. The right of females to choose is now called into question.

Sadly the anti-abortion platform has most viciously targeted state-funded, inexpensive, and, when need be, free abortions. As a consequence women of all races who have class privilege continue to have access to safe abortions—continue to have the right to choose—while materially disadvantaged women suffer. Masses of poor and working-class women lose access to abortion when there is no government funding available for reproductive rights health care. Women with class privilege do not feel threatened when abortions can be had only if one has lots of money because they can still have them. But masses of women do not have class power. More women than ever before are entering the ranks of the poor and indigent. Without the right to safe, inexpensive, and free abortions they lose all control over their bodies. If we return to a world where abortions are only accessible to those females with lots of money, we risk the return of public policy that will aim to make abortion illegal. It's already happening in many conservative states. Women of all classes must continue to make abortions safe, legal, and affordable.

The right of women to choose whether or not to have an abortion is only one aspect of reproductive freedom. Depending on a woman's age and circumstance of life the aspect of reproductive rights that matters most will change. A sexually active woman in her 20s or 30s who finds birth control pills unsafe may one day face an unwanted pregnancy and the right to have a legal, safe, inexpensive abortion may be the reproductive issue that is most relevant. But when she is menopausal and doctors are urging her to have a hysterectomy that may be the most relevant reproductive rights issue.

As we seek to rekindle the flames of mass-based feminist movement reproductive rights will remain a central feminist agenda. If women do not have the right to choose what happens to our bodies we risk relinquishing rights in all other areas of our lives. In renewed feminist movement the overall issue of reproductive rights will take precedence over any single issue. This does not meant that the push for legal, safe, inexpensive abortions will not remain central, it will simply not be the only issue that is centralized. If sex education, preventive health care, and easy access to contraceptives are offered to every female, fewer of us will have unwanted pregnancies. As a consequence the need for abortions would diminish.

Losing ground on the issue of legal, safe, inexpensive abortion means that women lose ground on all reproductive issues. The anti-choice movement is fundamentally anti-feminist. While it is possible for women to individually choose never to have an abortion, allegiance to feminist politics means that they still are pro-choice, that they support the right of females who need abortions to choose whether or not to have them. Young females who have always had access to effective contraception—who have never witnessed the tragedies caused by illegal abortions—have no firsthand experience of the powerlessness and vulnerability to exploitation that will always be the outcome if females do not have reproductive rights. Ongoing discussion about the wide range of issues that come under the heading of reproductive rights is needed if females of all ages and our male allies in struggle are to understand why these rights are important. This understanding is the basis of our commitment to keeping reproductive rights a reality for all females. Feminist focus on reproductive rights is needed to protect and sustain our freedom.

27. Lisa Jones, "Is Biracial Enough? (Or, What's This about a Multiracial Category on the Census?: A Conversation)," from *Bulletproof Diva*

For the third wave, which is characterized by an increasingly multicultural, multiethnic, and multiracial dynamic, old categories of identity simply do not hold. Jones argues in this essay that political alliances now are between "a multitude of communities" and highlights the way that third wave has had to rethink feminist activism in these terms.

Who are you, what are you, where are you from, no, where are you really from, where are your parents from, are your grandparents Americans? Are you from here, what's your background, what's your nationality, where do you live? Are you black, are you white, do you speak Spanish? Are you really white, are you really black? Are you Puerto Rican, are you half and half, are you biracial, multiracial, interracial, transracial, racially unknown, race neutral, colorless, colorblind, down with the rat race or the human race? Who are you? Where are you coming from? Who are your people?

THE IDENTITY FAIRY: Excuse me, before you get all up in my business, don't you want to know my name?

Should we keep it simple or run the extended-play version? I hail from the Afro-rainbow tribe. Papa's black by way of Newark and South Carolina, Mom's Jewish by way of Brooklyn and Eastern Europe. Ethnically I'm African American. Politically I'm a person of color. My résumé: Womanist-theater producing circa the eighties; day jobbing at an alternative newspaper, looking to define the role of race woman in the multiculti nineties. My faith is strictly rhythm and blues. Still hung up on soul music, poetry and jazz, sixties girl groups. Air guitar to the Isley Brothers and Living Colour. Marley heals my soul. Al Green and Sting wake me up in the morning. I go to Aretha and Joni Mitchell when I need to cry.

I know a Panamanian-American computer technician who is deep brown as a Senegalese and ethnically Latino. He speaks Spanish and Brooklyn-Italian blue-collar English. Ask him what he is, he'll tell you black Hispanic. I know a Caribbean-American architect who has lived on three continents, calls soccer football, and has a white great-grandfather and a Chinese great-grandfather, though he himself is gingerbread brown. This guy is from Grenada originally, though he identifies politically as African American. I also know a music promoter, black, who was raised by his mother, Jewish, in the suburbs of San Francisco. But from the way this guy swaggers and curses you'd think he was gangsta straight out of Compton. Trust me, all three guys are cute.

Say I marry one of these guys, will our children be multiracial, multiethnic, African American, black, people of color? Will they be called "niggers," "cocos," or "spics"? Will they live in an America where race, as Cornel West reports, still matters? Will they live in a war zone like Bosnia, where ethnicity, culture, and religion still matter? Or will AIDS and toxic waste cut their lives short before they can begin their pontificating, philosophizing, awfulizing, agonizing, rejoicing, preachifying, and signifying over just who they are in this shaky home we call the Americas?

Last night I had dinner with a group of friends who are Asian, Latino, and African American, and combinations of the above mixed with European. I love us dearly. We take David Dinkins's gorgeous mosaic quite literally and we aren't alone. We value the ethnic histories, rituals, stories passed down to us from our families of origin, from our families of choice, and from our book learning. We swap these traditions, make up new ones. At home, we identify each other by turf: Peter is Miss Mott Street, I'm Miss Bowery, Miss Dorado Beach is Maria. Yet we'd probably be more comfortable with the public monikers black, Latino, or Asian, than with "biracial" or "multiracial."

Most of us just hit the big three-oh. We saw the sixties as grade-school lads. We memorized TV pictures of dogs sicced on black folks in Mississippi and stories our grandparents told of Japanese internment camps out West. We can tell you about the years before English-as-a-second-language programs, when little girls María, Margie, and Gladys were thrown into English-only classrooms and left to sink or tread water. We got to Ivy League colleges thanks to affirmative action programs. Corporate America hired us under diversity initiatives.

The idea of a "multiracial" category on the census fills us with ambivalence. Is this just one more polite, largely academic game of identity hopscotch folks are playing while Los Angeles burns? Still, we're keeping our ears open.

What do you know about the groups that are behind this census movement? Are they a multiracial, interracial Mafia? Biracial Rambos and contras? Are they white parents of mixed-race bambinos bartering for a safety zone for their café-au-lait kids? Or are they regular folks searching for a new way to identify their families?

THE IDENTITY FAIRY: This is what I know so far. There's the Association of MultiEthnic Americans (AMEA), a nationwide confederation of interracial/multiethnic support groups based in San Francisco. And there's Project RACE (short for Reclassify All Children Equally), a lobbying organization out of Atlanta that campaigns on the local level. As of May 1993, due to the labors of Project RACE, three states have passed and two are reviewing legislation that adds the category "multiracial" to school forms.

AMEA and Project RACE are at the forefront of the census movement. This June these groups and several others will converge on Washington at hearings before a subcommittee on the census. If their efforts pay off, "multiracial" will replace "other race" on census forms in the year 2000. What this will mean, no one's sure. Could there be a massive flight from the categories Hispanic and black? Will the 9.8 million Americans who checked "other race" in 1990 switch over without a hitch to "multiracial"? By the turn of the new century, will the numbers in the "other race," now "multiracial" category, have multiplied dramatically? Will America have become the brown stew pot that *Time* and *Newsweek* have been warning us about since the mid eighties? And call them black, multiracial, or Hispanic (another ethnic appellation concocted by politics), will the majority of these brown ones still be poor folks? Or might all Americans check "multiracial," finally recognizing their heritage for what it is?

Give us your off-the-cuff take on this census movement.

THE IDENTITY FAIRY: I haven't been to any meetings, but I did speak at length with several organizers and foot soldiers, including, among others, Carlos Fernandez, president of AMEA, Susan Graham, executive director of Project RACE, Kendra Wallace, Project's vice president in California, and Michelle Erickson of Chicago. Erickson pulled her five-year-old son out of the public school system rather than choose between existing racial categories. (She identifies Andrew, her son, as biracial.) Instigated by Erickson's letter-writing campaign and the lobbying of Project RACE, the state of Illinois is now considering the "multiracial" category.

Many in the census movement see the bottom line of their crusade as a fight for the self-esteem of their children. Graham of Project RACE, who is a white mother of two, as she calls them, "multiracial kids," says children are psychologically healthiest when they have accurate racial labels at their disposal. But what on earth constitutes an accurate racial label? And if the census movement is ultimately out to do away with such sacrosanct labels, will creating new ones accomplish this?

Beyond the children's self-esteem issue, the movement's larger agenda and philosophical goals registered blurry. Race is configured as choice, as a category on a school form. Race is not seen as a political/economic construct, a battleground where Americans vie for power and turf, but a question of color, a stick-on, peel-off label. If there *is* an end goal to the census movement's efforts, it appears to be assimilation. I don't mean this in the didactic sense of chiding others for wanting their piece of American pie; I mean it as finding a place to fit in, creating a space of comfort for self, away from the choke hold of race.

The business as usual of discrimination, against the have-nots, who are usually shades of brown, and in favor of the have-sos, who are usually shades of pink, is left undisturbed.

When I heard that all state legislation for school forms would remain symbolic until the Congress and the Office of Management and Budget vote to add multiracial to the list of official categories, I scratched my head. And when I heard that the activists couldn't agree on whether those who checked the "multiracial" box would be considered a disadvantaged minority deserving of federal protections under the Voting Rights Act, I scratched some more. Why was this movement—potentially a vital movement for the acknowledgment of hybrid cultures/lives—being tied to a kite that no one could steer?

Do you have other concerns about the census movement?

THE IDENTITY FAIRY: Let's look at a few:

Is race (and racism) left intact? Instead of fighting for a new racial category, if the end goal is, as census activists say, to do away with the biological pseudoscience of race, why aren't they in the trenches casting stones at institutional racism? Anna Deavere Smith's *Fires in the Mirror* quotes an interview the playwright did with Angela Davis. Davis says she feels tentative about the meaning of race these days, but not tentative at all about racism. People of color, whether they call themselves biracial, Swirls (as they do in Fostorio, Ohio), or zebra Americans, are disproportionately members of America's underclass. Here's a meaningful contrast: Ohio became the first state last year to adopt the multiracial category on school forms. This year, Ohio saw a bloody uprising at the Lucasville state prison. Almost 60 percent of prisoners there are black men, though African Americans make up barely one quarter of the state's population. Will the symbolic recognition of multiracial identity reverse numbers like these?

I was struck that the census movement had no alliances with progressive organizations representing other people of color. None of these organizations had staged a teach-in or protested over the miscarriage of justice in the Rodney King case. Was biraciality being constructed as a less progressive stance than identifying as a "person of color," that catchphrase invented in the eighteenth century, then popularized in the seventies, as an expression of solidarity with other p.o.c.s worldwide?

Cape Town, U.S.A.? It's been asked before, and until I hear a good comeback, the question stands: Would "multiracial" be akin to South Africa's "colored" caste created under apartheid? Carlos Fernandez of AMEA believes that an "in-between" racial category isn't racist in itself, it is how such a category is used. Yet why wouldn't multiracial/colored by mythologized or positioned politically any differently in America?

Are we special? The census movement and its "interracial/biracial nationalists," as I refer to them playfully, claim biraciality as a mark of "racial" singularity, one that in America (where most racial groups are multiethnic and multicultural) has little grounding. Their insistence on biraciality's unique status borders on elitism. They marvel at the perks of biraciality: That biracials have several cultures at their disposal. (Though don't we all as Americans?) They say things like "biracial people are free of bias because they embody both black and white." Can you fight essentialism with essentialism? Are we to believe that all biracials are chosen people, free of prejudice, self-interest, and Republican Christian fundamentalism?

By proclaiming specialness aren't biracials still clinging to the niche of exotic other? "How could we not love them, they're so cute," boasted one white mother active in the census movement of her biracial children. Minus butter-pecan skin and Shirley Temple curls would they be less of an attractive proposition?

The nationalist vibe. The writer Kristal Brent-Zook calls nationalism a search for home, for family, and for sameness. Young movements of any kind are prone to nationalism, yet it's hard to forgive the biracialists for indulging. A large part of why they disassociate themselves from traditional ethnic communities is just *because* of their hybridity, their lack of purity.

Is there now to be a biracial party line to tow and a biracial lifestyle to upkeep? *Interrace*, a magazine chronicling the census movement and interracial and biracial social life, called the actress Halle Berry's choice *not* to marry interracially a "cop-out." (One guesses they made this judgment about the race of Berry's husband, baseball star David Justice, based on photographs. A few issues later, *Interrace* pronounced Justice to be "Afro-European," and laid out the biracial carpet.) Are those of us who marry the same, "mono-race" partners now retro, antiprogressive? Have the interracial/biracial police determined that the only way to change the world is to breed a "new race?" "Like it or not," read a letter to *Spectrum*, the newsletter published by Multiracial Americans of Southern California (MASC), "racially mixed people are the most beautiful people of all." The new Stepford people.

What's history got to do with it? As black/white biracials, when we distance ourselves from the African-American freedom struggle, from aging, though historically critical, ideas like "black power" and "block community," do we fail to honor a history that brought us to where we are today? Is biraciality political sedition? And if it feels that way, and it shouldn't, how can we make it feel less so? Are there ways to be responsible to a history that we are indebted to without being imprisoned by it?

I found the generalizations the census movers made about African Americans disturbing. Resistance from some blacks to the multiracial category was translated into resistance from the entire African-American population. Aren't some of the parents involved in the census movement African Americans? The bills to add the "multiracial" category on the state level have all been introduced by African-American legislators. The census initiative has garnered support from local chapters of the NAACP. *Essence* magazine and other black publications spread the word about AMEA and fellow interracial groups long before their white counterparts.

To say that biracials have been cold-shouldered by African-Americans throughout history, as some activists suggested, is selective ignorance. Black communities have always been shelter to multiethnic people, perhaps not an unproblematic shelter, yet a shelter nonetheless. Black folks, I'd venture, have welcomed difference in their communities more than most Americans.

Nothing but a photo-op? Watching biraciality gobbled up so eagerly on the Donahue and Oprah circuit makes me pause. If it weren't such a fashionable and marketable identity these days would so many folks be riding the bandwagon? (And like the hip-hop club, media darlings of the late eighties, the biracial lobby comes across on television as having no agenda other than its own pride politics.)

Are biracial people being offered up as the latest market ripe for exploitation? *Interrace* magazine sells T-shirts inscribed with Webster's definition of biracial. The ads urge buyers to "Wear the Right Thing" or to "end racism ... advertise in *Interrace*." *New People: The Journal for the Human Race* hawks ceramic wedding figurines in your choice of complexions. Not unlike trade or hobby magazines, both publications look at the world through one prism: biracialism.

Are we family? Shouldn't we ask what makes biracial people a community? What holds us together other than a perceived sense of our own difference from the ethnic mainstream? Consider if the Mexican-Samoan kid in San Diego has the same needs as the black-Jewish kid from New York's Upper West Side? Maybe politically as people of color, but do they share a definitive mixed-race culture? And if they do, should we call it "biraciality" or should we call it "American culture"?

Does blackness remain a stigma? As my telephone travels made clear, the census camp is not minus attitudes of: "If you had a choice you'd be anything but black." Biraciality was posited by some as an escape from the "blemish of blackness." Chicago mother Michelle Erickson asked me quite innocently if I knew how degrading it was "to be attached to categories like black or Hispanic." Kendra Wallace, a biracial woman in her early twenties, pronounced rules of membership in the black community to be too stiff—based, she feels, on such criteria as "hair texture and whether one speaks proper English or not." (Is African-American diversity still that invisible to the world? One could have come away with a picture far more complex by watching a week's worth of sitcoms.)

A moment of cruel and unusual irony took place in a conversation with Project RACE's Susan Graham. During Black History Month, Graham's son returned home with some materials on Langston Hughes. Graham was disappointed that the school had failed to focus on "Langston Hughes's biraciality." I reminded Graham that African Americans as a whole were a multiethnic and multiracial folk, and that Hughes never hid the fact that he had white family, yet he "cast his lot," as the expression went back then, with his darker kin. Hughes's writing, one can safely say, celebrates, if not romanticizes

African-American culture. Graham seemed irritated. The one-drop rule was the only thing that kept him in the black community, she insisted. If Hughes were alive today, he would choose to be multiracial, he would identify first with mixed-race people and the work of her lobbying group.

People of all races and cultures should feel free to claim Hughes as an idol, but wasn't Graham aware of a rather painful history? One where black people have had their every gift confiscated and attributed to others? Would this now happen in the name of multiracialism?

Seems like you've exhausted the critical tip. Did you happen upon anything constructive in your telephone encounters with the biracial movement?

THE IDENTITY FAIRY: Carlos Fernandez said something that made sense. Official recognition of multiracial identity may not end racism; it is, however, a necessary step. If we refuse to recognize that any material reality exists between black and white, we do nothing except enshrine these social boundaries—and enshrine the political divide that upholds them.

Certainly the daguerreotype of mixed-race people as freaks of nature could use a long overdue slashing. If the biracial lobby can help in this regard, bless them. Says Kendra Wallace: "We're invisible or our identities are always problematized and sexualized." Our "bloods" are at war inside of us. If mixed race were made normal, we could look forward to the comic mulatto, the introspective, the slovenly. We might one day come to miss ye olde tragic mulatto, the world's pet mule.

As much as I found myself resisting the biracial nationalists, to deny a group the right to identify as they wish to seems equally reactionary. In October last year the San Diego Unified School District, known for its conservatism, balked at admitting a little boy to grammar school until his mother, Patricia Whitebread, who is black, assigned him an "appropriate race." (Unlike many school forms nationally, San Diego's has no "other" designation.) Whitebread refused. The school district admitted the child anyway. Later the district classified her son as black without Whitebread's permission.

The activists I spoke to framed their cause as a civil rights movement. Perhaps one not as transparently vital as a movement for equal opportunity in employment or fair access to housing, but certainly one consummate with religious freedom or freedom of expression. In *Interrace*, psychologist Francis Wardle, director of the Center for the Study of Biracial Children, a clearinghouse in Colorado, makes a passionate appeal for interracial family networks not to been seen as a threat to African Americans:

"We are so aware of the need to improve conditions for so many blacks in this country that we are very puzzled some high profile blacks spend time and energy fighting us."

"We are not the enemy.... Don't insist we must raise our children to belong to a distinctive (and arbitrary) racial or ethnic category. Don't say that history and society must define who we are and what we want our children to become."

Perhaps the arrival of the biracialists might finally drive home to traditional ethnic communities the need for more proactive coalition politics. Kendra Wallace thought biracial organizing would allow people to leave racial enclaves, build bridges, and in time, return. In the lore of the passing novels, those who "passed for white" (or in this case "stood for colored") always found their way back to the black hearth. Of course the black hearth, as we approach the twenty-first century is more fragmented and scattered than ever.

At the dinner table last night we gathered, not to discuss the dainties of identity politics and the census, but to remember a close friend who died a year ago from AIDS. I could tell you that AIDS is an equal opportunity killer and I'd be telling the truth. I could also tell you that more and more of those who die from AIDS are people of color; that would be true too. This speaks reams about race and the very real equation of power, poverty, and privilege.

I like to think of Eduardo Mejia, the friend we lost, as a multiculturalist and global citizen cut from the cloth of a W.E.B. Du Bois. To Eddie, unlike Kendra Wallace, *black* embraced every ethnic community that wished to claim it (a belief he shared with the Pan-Africanists of the sixties and the British Asian-Caribbean-African coalitions of the seventies). Would it surprise you that Eddie was a fair-complexioned Puerto Rican? A gay man and nurse, "the Queen," as we called him, was a street-shrewd philosopher who studied race all his life. He identified as a black, as a person of color, as Latino, as Puerto Rican, as a New Yorker. No one identity canceled out the other. Knowing Eddie, "biracial" would have been a label either too precious or sterile. He would have told you in one breath that he was "a Puerto Rican from a Haitian block in Brooklyn, who stands for gay rights and the freedom struggles of people of color around the world" before he would describe himself as biracial. It wouldn't have been fierce enough, specific enough, or ultimately progressive enough for Eddie in his day. But that would've been Eddie's choice; you may decide otherwise. Eddie, I'm sure, would have loved you and claimed you just the same.

What's your idea of art and scholarship that politicizes multiracialism?

THE IDENTITY FAIRY: Certainly the visual art and writings of Adrian Piper provides keen example. Piper works genius at demystifying the political economy of what she tags "racial classification." Her call to American whites to face up to their black heritage (and to blacks to do the reverse) takes multiracialism/multiculturalism beyond politically correct arts programming and into the realm of configuring a new American identity.

The work of writers and media artists Guillermo Gómez-Peña and Coco Fusco also stands out. In her contribution to the anthology *Black Popular Culture* Fusco tells us that in Cuba, where the black people in her family come from, there's an expression that goes "*Chivo que rompe tambor con su pellejo paga*," which translates literally, "The goat who breaks the drum will have to pay with his skin." The phrase has another meaning as well: "The troublemaker turns him- or herself into the instrument to continue the music." Fusco argues that "black popular cultures, especially musical cultures, have generated an abundance of archetypes that embrace dissonance and contend with internal difference; these [are] semantic residues of histories of contradiction and conflict. Maybe one of these days our intellectual debate will catch up with our popular cultural ability to engage dissent, without the defensiveness that continuously rears its head."

Gómez-Peña's work takes on America in the "intercultural crisis." Writes critic Richard Schechner: "Interculturalists [such as Gómez-Peña] refuse utopian schemes, refuse to cloak power arrangements and struggles. Instead, interculturalists probe the confrontations, ambivalences, disruptions, fears, disturbances, and difficulties when and where cultures collide, overlap or pull away from each other. Interculturalists explore misunderstandings, broken messages, and failed translations—what is not pure and what cannot successfully fuse. These are seen not as disasters, but as fertile rifts of creative possibilities."

Any last words of advice to those swimming in the identity pool?

THE IDENTITY FAIRY: As you get older, chances are you will define yourself by your alliances with a multitude of communities. No one community will speak for you completely and no one community should be so static as to not let you share in others.

As for the biracial nationalists and their movement: Check them out, debate them, start your own. Don't accept any position—be it biracial/multiracial/interracial/African/Asian/or Latin American—as a political catchall.

Challenge all your communities to live up to you. The late poet Audre Lorde, African American, Caribbean American, feminist, gay, and supporter of the global causes of people of color, always spoke as a member of all her many homes.

In coming to self, balance individual identity with a responsibility to and critical eye on history. I'll never forget visiting the Afro-American Cultural Center at Yale as a prefreshman. I wandered around the building looking at the posters and murals, remnants of the late sixties, of the days when black students were admitted to mainstream universities in sizable numbers, of student protest for admission and retention initiatives, of sit-ins for ethnic studies departments. Alone, I walked the rooms of the House, as we call it, and felt the spirits of those students. A priceless moral and intellectual inheritance was being passed to me. On the train back home, I wept all kinds of tears: angry tears, tears of pride, gratitude tears. Later I would move away from the House and find other homes, but I always took the House and that inheritance with me.

Welcome to America. It ain't as airbrushed as a Benetton ad, but it's a happening place. Hope you brought your Rollerblades *and* your Air Jordans.

28. Cristina Tzintzún, "Colonize This!" from *Colonize This!: Young Women of Color on Today's Feminism*

Excerpts from "Colonize This!" by Cristina Tzintzún, published in Daisy Hernández and Bushra Rehman, eds., *Colonize This!: Young Women of Color on Today's Feminism* (Seattle: Seal Press, 2002), 17–28. Reprinted with permission.

The essay from which *Colonize This!* took its name, Tzintzún's story of her multiracial family and the racial politics on which it is based is a classic example of third-wave thinking. It accounts for the complications of an increasingly multiracial, multicultural world that is not beyond colonialist thinking and stereotypes. She bravely explores the contradiction of a white father who, supposedly "liberal, feminist, antiracist, and anticlassist," "instilled the basic principles of feminism in me," but who in his actions was the opposite of these things. Tzintzún articulates an experience of self increasingly common for third-wavers: "I am mixed. I am the colonizer and the colonized, the exploiter and the exploited. I am confused yet sure. I am a contradiction."

I worry about dating whites, especially white men. I worry that even though my skin is white like theirs, they will try and colonize me. I see what a white man did to my beautiful, brown, Mexican mother. He colonized her. It is not love that drew my father to my mother, as I used to think; rather, it was the color of her skin, her impoverished background, her lack of education, her nationality, her low self-esteem, her submissiveness. In his mind these qualities reinforced his superiority. Instead of recognizing the differences between him and her as beauty, my father saw them as a means for exploitation.

My father met my mother in Morelos, Mexico. She was working at a store when he came and asked her for change. He told her that he was from the States and that he would be back for her. She just thought he was a crazy, gringo hippie, and she paid no attention to him. Later that day he came back for her. He told my mother that he and his friend Zauza, named after the Tequila brand, were going to take her to their place. My mother naïvely thought that they were kidnapping her—she had never seen gringos dressed so oddly. So she went with them fearing for her life. They took her to their house where the rest of their roommates were tripping on acid. My mother was doubly frightened by this, not only were they kidnapping her, but they were going to turn her into a drug addict. After a few hours they took my mother home, and after that they came to visit her regularly.

Two years later my parents got married. They raised my older sister in Mexico for her first year. Then they came to the States to "visit" but never returned to Mexico to live. If my mother could have returned to Mexico safely with us, her children, she would have. She feared that my father would kidnap us—not an unrealistic fear considering my uncle did the same thing to my aunt when she left him for the first time. Also, the economic possibility of raising three children in Mexico as a single parent was unrealistic. My mother was no longer in her early twenties and therefore considered undesirable for employment in machista Mexican culture. Her only choice was to raise us in the United States.

Both my father and my mother raised us to be proud of who we were. Shame was not part of my vocabulary. As a child I was proud to identify myself with brown, with poor, with Indian, with "other." I specifically remember my father teaching me the avenues to fight my oppressors. He was the one who taught me feminist theory. He taught me about systemic racism. I listened to my father's advice. I was not like most girls. I always spoke my mind. I had no reservations about acting "unfeminine." I was raised with such fire. I was aggressive. I spoke like the boys did and never gave it a second thought. I was not worried about it if they would like it or disagree, or if they would like me.

I worry about dating white men because of my father. He is a "progressive" man, or so people think. Only those close to him realize his hypocrisy. Most consider him to be a liberal, a feminist, an anti-racist, an anticlassist, but I know he is not. He is the wolf in sheep's clothing. He disguises himself as a humanitarian, but this deception makes him the worst offender of them all.

I was told never to submit to any man, but I was only demonstrated submission by my mother and domination by my father. I was raised with eyes closed but ears open. I heard my father tell me that as a womon, a Mexican, I should not let anyone degrade me because of my race or gender, yet this is exactly what he did to my mother. When he made fun of her accent, when he forced her to have sex with him, when he beat her, when he cheated on her, when he told her that she was stupid, when he told her that without him she was nothing.

I saw the contradictions between my father's actions and words, but I had trouble processing it all. I did not realize what it meant that my father only cheated on my mother with African-American, Asian and Latina womyn. But the flashing lights became harder to ignore when I would hear my father tell other white American men that they should go to Mexico and marry a nice Mexican girl. So that she could take care of him, that they are such good cooks and so submissive that they would make anyone the perfect wife. I heard him only encourage my brother to date Mexican girls. They would be so grateful to go out with a gringo. To my father it did not matter whether my brother liked them or not.

When I would hear these comments I'd tell my father that he is a racist. That just because he is white and American does not mean that every brown womon wants him. I'd tell him that just because they are poor and Mexican, he thinks he is better than they are. That they are people too, people with emotions not to be toyed with, that they are not his brown dolls! My father rolls his eyes. I'm too damned PC, he says.

I remember the first time I saw sex. It wasn't on TV, or catching my parents. It was my father with another womon, and I was three. My parents used to sell jewelry door to door. Sometimes there would be deliveries to be made, and on such an occasion I accompanied my father while my brother, sister and mother waited in the car. I remember a petite African-American womon answering the apartment door and my father locking me in the bathroom, telling me to stay in there. I was frightened but also curious why I was not supposed to open the door. When I did, I saw the answer: my father naked having sex with another womon. I quickly shut the door, my stomach churning, knowing that something was wrong. When I went back to the car and told my mother what I had seen, my father called me a liar and my mother chose to believe him, too hurt to admit the truth to herself.

My father never did try hard to hide the other womyn. My mother, however, did try hard to deny and forgive. It was difficult for her to accept the truth. In the beginning, she not only became angry with my father but with the other womyn. She blamed them for "making" my father cheat. My mother felt worthless. She, like many other Mexican womyn, fell into the trap of thinking that without her man, she could not do or be anything. Not until my mother was able to see the value in herself was she able to face reality. She finally saw the truth behind the other womyn's situations: that these womyn were the same as her.

When I think of colonization, I think of my father's "conquests." I think back to all the faces that he has colonized. I think back to Dow, the womon from Thailand; Denise, the long-time girlfriend; Guadalupe, his soon-to-be new wife in Mexico. And I think back to all the faces which I never saw. The girls in the whore houses from here to Mexico to Thailand. I see faces as young as mine. I remember the note I left my father with a package of condoms, before his business trip to Thailand, begging him to think of his actions, begging him for once to think of the lives of these girls. I noticed it, he did not; this was rape. Sex with a thirteen-year-old girl. My father is a rapist. She was forced to work in the brothel; she is not a prostitute—she is a slave. And I want to hold her hand and beg a million apologies. I want to cry with her. I want to look into her eyes, for I can only imagine her pain; she is my sister. We are both human, both equal, but my father does not acknowledge this. For my father even has the audacity to claim that he knows what it is to be a womon of color, because he used to have long hair in the sixties.

As long as I can remember, my father has always been fascinated with womyn of color. He likes to flaunt money and power in front of these womyn. He thinks this makes him superior, more powerful, and more intelligent. So he chooses to date only womyn of color—these are the womyn he feels he can exploit. Black, brown or yellow, my father loves them all—he is so multicultural.

When I think of all the womyn my father has used, I feel sick. My father exploits their poverty, their desperation, their need to eat. And for me it is not some far-off image of who these womyn are, or of their economic situations. No, these womyn are my close relatives—my mother, my aunts, my grandmother. You see, my father is not the only person I know who "colonizes" womyn of color. No, it runs in the family. My grandfather is also married to a Mexican womon (my father's stepmother). She married my grandfather so that her daughter would have economic stability, so she would have a father, but what kind of father calls his daughter "his little spic"? My uncle has been married to three different Costa Rican womyn. He smugly says to me, "Any womon can be bought." I just smile and nod. While he thinks he is fucking these womyn, they fuck him. Like Raquel, his second wife, who left him black-eyed and bruised when he raised his hand to her, or Guiselle, who stole $10,000 from him. I admire these womyn—they could never be colonized.

I know that my brother is going to help me stop the circle of colonization. He refuses to partake in my father's racist, sexist, exploitative games. And for him like me, it is an internal struggle. One that requires me to question what I feel and most of all my memory. I must make sure again and again that my father's superiority complex has not seeped into me subconsciously. I have met other mutt/colonized children like myself, but instead of overcoming their colonization they succumb to it. They become internally conquered. They shame themselves into believing that half of them is inferior. They choose to deny their culture and heritage. They make such claims that their brown skin originated from their French background. And sometimes they become the worst type of colonized people, those who try and hide their feelings of inferiority by persecuting those like them.

It took me till the age of eighteen to connect the dots of why I exist, of why my family was and no longer is. I saw something amiss, something foul in my father's actions and words. I knew there was a lie. I knew the truth was deep and painful. When I found it, I was left confused. I did not know what to do with it. My whole existence is based on things I cannot tolerate. I was raised with eyes closed because I did not see my family for what it was. It was based on the ideals of "isms." It was there to soothe my father's ego. I often wonder if my father even sees anyone as his equal. I wonder if he knows that when he demeans other womyn of color that he demeans me. His actions and words pierce me to the core. This is not just any man who is saying these things, this is my father. This is half of me. This is where I come from.

I am careful to learn from other people's mistakes as well as my own. I know that in the past I have let comments slide. My first boyfriend (white) found it funny to tell me to go get him a Coke so that he could pretend I was his Mexican maid. His friends called me spic and told me I smelled of tacos. Back then I didn't know how to challenge their discrimination. I kicked the boy who called me spic but I had no words. For the first time I could not speak. My "friends" then thought such words were not racist, that the only hate word that existed was "nigger." Their definition of racism was so rigid, pseudo-liberal, and white. I knew I was faced with racism, yet my peers could not see this through my brown eyes.

It was my mother's mistake not to challenge my father; it was my mistake not to do the same to the people I dated. I know I will not make these same mistakes twice. I know I cannot be colonized. I realize now that I can't be with anyone who wants to pat me on the head and tell me how neat it is that I am Mexican but never actually wants to hear me talk about it. Far too many times I have tried to speak of my struggles or those of my people to be met with bored or un-understanding eyes. It leaves me frustrated and isolated. When one friend learned what I was writing this piece about, she replied, "Blah, blah.

Heard it all before. Nothing new." My body goes numb when she says these things. I want to punch her, slap her. Instead I just call her an asshole. When I am done with this essay, I will make her read it. Her lack of emotion and understanding makes it next to impossible to speak to her. She is as sensitive and caring as an electroshock. I see her words as self-absorbed ignorance, resentful and dismissive of a culture she does not even try to understand. I struggle to make my voice heard so that she and people like her will learn that there is more than just a white experience.

In my parents' relationship, my mother constantly struggled for equality. She fought to be seen as my father's equal. In many aspects she succeeded; in my eyes and my siblings' eyes she was equal if not *more* than my father. Her unconditional love and support gave us the strength and independence we needed. When my mother became tired of my father controlling the family money, she became self-employed. With the small amount she earned working, selling jewelry at local festivals, she would buy us the fast food my father wouldn't let us eat. She would take us to dollar movies and bus trips downtown to the children's science museum. Around my mother I could always be myself. I never had to live up to any false expectations, unlike with my father.

My mother is the strongest womon I know, she stayed with my father so that my siblings and I could have an education, so that my sister and I would have the means to take care of ourselves, so we would not need to depend on any man as she had. She felt she had no escape from my father, she was not from this country, she did not speak the language, nor did she have anyone to turn to. So my mother did the best she could. My mother hid her tears, cried in her pillow, and I slept soundly. This was her sacrifice. She did not want us to feel her inferiority. She put her feelings of inadequacy aside and raised us to be proud. And for this I am absolutely grateful to my mother. In fact, I feel fortunate that I was raised with such true contrasts. It helped me find balance. My mother now tells me that her biggest fear when my sister and I were growing up was that we would be submissive. We laugh about her worries now. My mother says that she could not have hoped for more feisty, self-assured daughters.

I do not hate my father. I love my father. I respect him as a father but not as a person. If it were not for him, I would not be as proud and outspoken as I am today. If it were not for him, I would not be passionate about womyn's issues. I look at my father and I see the best example of what not to be. He preached one thing but did another. This taught me to question not only him but the world around me. This helped me see through the lies society fed me. It also made me take action. My father always spoke of the injustice in the world, the racist war on drugs, factory farms, homophobia, free trade. He taught me so much, but he left so much out. He spoke and spoke but never did a damn thing about these injustices. He saved his activism for reading books and preaching to those he could feel more intelligent than. It is because of my father that I am a vegan, even though he eats meat. It is because of my father that I don't tolerate homophobia, even though he says "dyke." It is because of my father that I teach English classes to undocumented immigrants, even though my father calls them "wetbacks" and tells me I should charge them for my services. If it were not for him, I would not be committed to a life of activism. I see his true colors, and I am glad he is my father. I do not wish to change what I cannot, my father or the past. Yet, I choose not to speak to him. He is too sad and pathetic to know how to love. To him love is something to manipulate. And my love is far too precious to be treated in such a manner. I know that to continue speaking with him only hurts me. So I must keep severed ties with this man that I still call daddy. I have hope for my mother. After twenty-one years she has signed divorce papers. She was ready—her three children out of high school, her sacrifice complete. I, like her, have been waiting for her freedom for some time now. And at last it will soon be here.

It was my father who instilled the basic principles of feminism in me, but it was feminism that taught me who I was as a womon. During my high-school years I felt isolated from my peers. They seemed shallow, spoiled and sheltered. I was uninterested in their idea of weekend fun, of football games, and catering to the needs of rich white boys. I found no relief in the alternateen scene; skipping school to do drugs and secretly wishing to be "popular" bored me. Instead, I opted to be the outcast. I wanted to analyze the culture that maintained my middle-class white neighborhood. I wanted to know why their system seemed to be so afraid of me. Why when I questioned something, my new name became dyke or bitch. I made the decision to confront every homophobic, racist or sexist word I heard. Sometimes it seemed like I never got a chance to shut up. When I wasn't challenging my peers and teachers, I spent my time reading. I read all the feminist literature I could get my hands on. They gave me the support I needed. They made me feel less alone. They made me proud to call myself a feminist and queer. Those books taught me more than my school ever could.

I appreciate the outlet those books created for me. Although they gave me something to identify with, they never gave me anything to identify with as a Latina. I remember reading *Listen Up: Voices from the Next Feminist Generation* and being angry that the book contained only one Latina contributor, who I was only able to tell was Latina, not by what she had written but by her Spanish surname. I felt the book had represented many other minority groups well, but I felt invisible. I find it frustrating that when most books mention womyn of color, "color" and "gender" are presented as something separate. I am not just a womon or just a person of color—I am a womon of color.

In the past year a new part of myself has awoken, my history. And I don't know how to say it or what to do with it. I have lived my whole life until now away from reality. I am based on my father's superiority complex. I stand here before you because of racism. I look into the mirror and wonder, who am I? What does being based on white superiority make me? This is a question that I will have to answer, and I know there is no easy answer. I am mixed.

I am the colonizer and the colonized, the exploiter and the exploited. I am confused yet sure. I am a contradiction.

29. Lisa Weiner-Mahfuz, "Organizing 101: A Mixed-Race Feminist in Movements for Social Justice," from *Colonize This!: Young Women of Color on Today's Feminism*

Excerpts from "Organizing 101" by Lisa Weiner-Mahfuz, published in Daisy Hernández and Bushra Rehman, eds., *Colonize This!: Young Women of Color on Today's Feminism* (Seattle: Seal Press, 2002), 29–39. Reprinted with permission.

The daughter of an Arabic mother and a Jewish father, Weiner-Mahfuz takes her "mixed class, mixed race, mixed religion" background as a starting point for her essay about the "understanding of injustice," an understanding that only a "feminist framework for understanding the interconnectedness of oppression" can contribute to. Some forms of feminism force Weiner-Mahfuz to "check her whole self at the door," and those forms, she believes, are not feminist. A striking example of thinking that starts from looking at all the axes of identity as interconnected and contradictory, this piece articulates what it means to be third wave.

I have vivid memories of celebrating the holidays with my maternal grandparents. My Jido and Sito ("grandfather" and "grandmother," respectively in Arabic), who were raised as Muslim Arabs, celebrated Christmas rather than Ramadan. Every year, my Sito set up her Christmas tree in front of a huge bay window in their living room. It was important to her that the neighbors could see the tree from the street. Yet on Christmas day Arabic was spoken in the house, Arabic music was played, Arabic food was served and a hot and heavy poker game was always the main activity. Early on, I learned that what is publicly communicated can be very different from what is privately experienced.

Because of the racism, harassment and ostracism that my Arab grandparents faced, they developed ways to assimilate (or appear to assimilate) into their predominantly white New Hampshire community. When my mother married my Jewish father and raised me with his religion, they hoped that by presenting me to the world as a white Jewish girl, I would escape the hate they had experienced. But it did not happen that way. Instead, it took me years to untangle and understand the public/private dichotomy that had been such a part of my childhood.

My parents' mixed-class, mixed-race and mixed-religion relationship held its own set of complex contradictions and tensions. My father comes from a working-class, Ashkenazi Jewish family. My mother comes from an upper-middle-class Lebanese family, in which—similar to other Arab families of her generation—women were not encouraged and only sometimes permitted to get an education. My mother has a high-school degree and no "marketable" job skills. When my father married her, he considered it an opportunity to marry into a higher class status. Her background as a Muslim Arab was something he essentially ignored except when it came to deciding what religious traditions my sister and I were going to be raised with. From my father's perspective, regardless of my mother's religious and cultural background, my sister and I were Jews—and only Jews.

My mother, who to this day carries an intense mix of pride and shame about being Arab, was eager to "marry out" of her Arabness. She thought that by marrying a white Jew, particularly in a predominantly white New Hampshire town, she would somehow be able to escape or minimize the ongoing racism her family faced. She converted to Judaism for this reason and also because she felt that "eliminating" Arabness and Islam from the equation would make my life and my sister's life less complex. We could all say—her included—that we were Jews. Sexism and racism (and their internalized versions) played a significant part in shaping my parents' relationship. My father was never made to feel uncomfortable or unwelcome because he had married a Muslim Arab woman. He used his white male privilege and his Zionistic point of view to solidify his legitimacy. He created the perception that he did my mother a favor by "marrying her out" of her Arabness and the strictness of her upbringing.

My mother, however, bore the brunt of other people's prejudices. Her struggle for acceptance and refuge was especially evident in her relationship with my father's family, who never fully accepted her. It did not matter that she converted to Judaism, was active in Hadassah or knew all of the rituals involved in preparing a Passover meal. She was frequently made to feel that she was never quite Jewish enough. My Jewish grandmother was particularly critical of my mother and communicated in subtle and not so subtle ways that she tolerated my mother's presence because she loved her son. In turn, I felt as if there was something wrong with me and that the love that I received from my father's family was conditional. Many years later this was proven to be true: when my parents divorced, every member of my father's family cut off communication from my mother, my sister and me. Racism and Zionism played a significant (but not exclusive) role in their choice. My father's family (with the exception of my Jewish grandfather, who died in the early seventies) had always been uncomfortable that my father had married an Arab woman. The divorce gave them a way out of examining their own racism and Zionism.

Today my mother realizes that her notions about marrying into whiteness and into a community that would somehow gain her greater acceptance was, to say the least, misguided. She romanticized her relationship with my father as a "symbol of peace" between Jews and Arabs, and she underestimated the impact of two very real issues: racism within the white Jewish community and the strength of anti-Semitism toward the Jewish community. At the time she did not understand that her own struggle against racism and anti-Arab sentiment was both linked to and different than anti-Semitism.

For me the process of grieving the loss of the Jewish side of my family after the divorce led me to realize that their choice was a painful recognition and rejection of my mother and ultimately our Arabness. I needed to figure out how to not reject my Jewishness, while at the same time learning how to embrace my Arabness on my own terms rather than on those of the adults around me. Today I do not consider myself to be "less" of an Arab because I did not grow up with a direct and explicit understanding of myself as one. I also do not consider myself to be "less" of a Jew because I am half Arab. I consider myself a woman who is working to understand how spoken and unspoken messages have shaped my experiences and political perspective.

MAKING THE CONNECTIONS

My understanding of injustice started with a series of visceral reactions. As a child I remember feeling a pit in my stomach when I sat in temple listening to stories about the Holocaust or when my mother and her siblings used to talk about being beat up in school because of their "funny" names and hair. I later experienced that same reaction in high school when I learned about slavery in the United States and then again in college, when I took my first women's studies class and began to understand the impact of heterosexism on my life and the lives of all women. Despite these reactions, however, I did not have the language to articulate why these feelings were so personal to me until I started exploring feminism. Feminism awakened my commitment to fighting injustice. Feminism challenged me to see how deeply I had internalized my own assimilation. Feminism taught me that one can experience privilege and oppression simultaneously and that using my white privilege to try and hide my Arabness was not an honest way to live in the world, nor did it guarantee me safety—after all, being Jewish provides no refuge in an anti-Semitic culture.

Audre Lorde's book *Sister Outsider* provided me with a feminist framework for understanding the interconnectedness of oppression and my own identity as a Jewish/Arab-American, mixed-race, mixed-class, lesbian feminist. This book made a particular impact on me because Lorde was making visible and political her perspective as a woman with multiple identities. Before reading this book, I did not understand that my power and my commitment to fighting oppression lay in finding those places where my experiences of privilege and oppression seem to be at odds with one another. Lorde's work and life taught me that I must not be afraid to go to those complex and "messy" places to understand myself, the history of my people, and to learn how to use my identities in a clear and subversive way. Reading *Sister Outsider* was just the first step in helping me to see that this was possible. Figuring out the strategies and politics involved in *how* to do this at the intersections of my own identities has been and will continue to be a lifelong process.

Although feminism has shaped my personal and political perspective, it has also been a sharp double-edged sword in my work as an organizer. Time and again I have experienced being in a "feminist space" where I have been asked or forced to check my full self at the door—my Arabic words, my lesbian ideas or my Jewish experience. This, to me, is not feminism. I now focus on understanding the interconnectedness of my own identities and the role that oppression and privilege play in my life and work as an antiracism activist. This has been particularly difficult because many on the "left" uphold the mythology that since we work against "the evils of the world," we are somehow free of racism, sexism, classism, anti-Semitism, ableism, and adultism (the institutional power adults have to oppress and silence young people). After years of antioppression training and organizing work, however, I now know that many "progressive" people and organizations are just as invested in either/or dichotomous thinking and in perpetuating oppression in the world.

Six years ago I attended a conference in Boston entitled "Race and Racism in the Nineties." I participated in a workshop about women, spirituality and antioppression work. During the workshop the facilitators, a white woman and an African-American woman, divided the group into two caucuses: a white caucus and a woman of color caucus. Before breaking up the group, I raised my hand and asked where mixed-race people were to go. This question opened up a flood of questions and challenges toward me. The white women in the room, including the white facilitator, said they felt I should caucus with them because I could pass for white. Most of the women of color concurred with this. I recall feeling confused and vulnerable because I did not anticipate what I would be opening up by calling attention to the dualism that was at play. I also felt angry and hurt because I felt the women in the room responded to me based on my light skin rather than on my experiences or the politics of what I was trying to raise. The discussion proceeded with the facilitators spending ten minutes talking to the group about the privileges of being able to choose—as if I were not in the room. The level of tension in the room was palpable. Bodies stiffened and voices raised a notch.

I was frustrated with myself because I did not know how to handle the "logistics" of putting complex racial issues out in a group in a way that clearly demonstrated in word and deed that I was taking responsibility for my privilege while simultaneously taking an uncompromising stand against white supremacy. Although I had Audre Lorde's words floating around in my mind, I had not yet learned how to apply her teachings to my own experience. Finally, the group resolved that I could "choose" where to go. The feeling in the room was that the situation had been resolved. But it was not resolved for me. I felt alone. I felt that regardless of where I chose to go, it would be the wrong choice. I felt like the illegitimate bastard child that no one wanted or knew what to do with. Many of the women of color were angry with me. Many of the white women felt as if they had made an "antiracist" intervention by challenging me on my racism. Still as the group broke up into two, I made a choice and walked toward the room that the women of color were to meet in. As I approached the door, it quickly slammed in my face.

On this day "feminism" was extremely painful for all of us in the workshop. Everyone was angry and upset because I did not neatly fit into either the white or the colored framework. No one, including myself, knew how to grapple with the complexity in a constructive way. I struggled to articulate that taking responsibility for my white privilege did not mean I was "admitting" to being white. It meant I was recognizing my privilege and trying to establish my accountability. But in this case this difference and its complexity were not honored; they were not seen as something necessary to explore. It was also a hurtful experience because I had hoped that I could turn to other women, especially activists, to mentor and challenge me around how to bring my whole self to my work as an organizer. I learned that receiving that kind of support depended on two things: getting clarity about how my experiences of oppression and privilege overlap and challenging my own assumption that all women activists were automatically going to approach their work with an antioppression analysis.

RESISTING CLASSIC SCRIPTS

In talking with other mixed-race activists about their experiences, I have discovered that this is a classic script. This is how racism and internalized racism are often directed toward mixed people. In many activist circles it has become easier to delegitimize and shut us out, rather than to take on the challenge and opportunity that mixed-race people with antioppression politics can present. Our multiple perspectives and commitment to challenging oppression can deepen the discussions about and sharpen our tools for challenging white supremacy.

Yet the presence and voices of mixed-race people are often deeply feared. We are feared because interracial relationships are still taboo in our culture. We are feared because our mere existence calls into question the status quo and the way that race is constructed in our society. We are feared even by people on the "left" who propose to be working to challenge these deeply rooted beliefs and constructs. We live in a white supremacist culture that banks on dichotomous thinking to keep people divided and fragmented within themselves. Those of us who do not fit into either/or boxes therefore experience an enormous amount of pressure to choose one "side" of ourselves over another. We are not considered whole just as we are. We are taught that these are dualisms: Jewish/Arab, public/private, visible/invisible, Black/white, privilege/oppression, pride/shame. But these are false separations that don't exist. They are imposed. My struggle and that of other mixed-race people is to not internalize these dualisms and become paralyzed by a society that rejects our complexity in the name of keeping things simple and easy to categorize.

I have learned many lessons about how important it is to be accountable to those that experience oppression in ways that I do not. Being accountable does not mean that I allow my legitimacy to be freely debated by individuals or groups. From my perspective the question of who is a legitimate person of color (based on their skin color) is misguided. Rather, what is important to me is how individuals and groups use their privileges to challenge oppression. This means that where I experience oppression, I resist it alongside those who experience that same oppression. Where I experience privilege, I stand in solidarity with those whose lives are being impacted by challenging others who benefit from that same privilege.

Maintaining my accountability is not a choice, but it is certainly fluid. Each situation that I am in calls me to assess myself in relation to the time, place and company. For example, when I am with a group of darker-skinned people of color, I am very conscious of my privilege and actively take steps to acknowledge it. When I am in the company of white people, I am conscious of my privilege in a different way. I am prepared to challenge the assumption that my light skin makes me an ally in perpetuating racism.

I have come to define accountability in a complex way, one that both takes in account and challenges identity politics. Identity politics have given me the opportunity to define and claim myself as a complex and whole person and to build community with those who share common experiences in the struggle for justice. Yet identity politics, when narrowly defined and used as a tool to divide, have made my ability to maintain accountability a treacherous experience. I often feel pressure to choose one community over another, one part of myself over another. As mixed-race people with multiple identities, this pressure to choose can cut deeply and painfully into our souls. More often than not, I find identity politics to be defined narrowly in progressive circles. This can limit our work to build coalitions and solidarity across communities and movements because this leads us to simply replicate all that we want to eradicate in the world.

For personal and political reasons this essay on feminism covers racism and other forms of oppression. I have had to make sense of and to develop the tools for challenging why I, as a mixed-race, mixed-class, Jewish/Arab-American lesbian, have been shut out of so many "feminist" spaces. Developing and practicing antioppression politics is not just about my own survival, it is about creating a feminist movement that speaks to and represents the experiences of all women. I refuse to be shut out and I refuse to allow other women who do not fit into the mainstream feminist movement to be shut out. Being an antiracist activist is the best way that I know how to honor my mother's experience, to honor my own identities and to honor women, such as Audre Lorde, who paved the way before me to work for justice.

30. Gwendolyn Pough, "Bringing Wreck: Theorizing Race, Rap, Gender, and the Public Sphere," from *Check It While I Wreck It*

Excerpts from Gwendolyn Pough, "Bringing Wreck," published in Gwendolyn Pough, ed., *Check It While I Wreck It* (Boston: Northeastern University Press, 2004).

In an essay that addresses many crucial third-wave feminist concerns, Pough argues for a necessary redefinition of the public sphere and public culture to include black women involved in hip-hop culture, who are doubly marginalized by the dominant culture that marginalizes hip hop

and anti-feminist, homophobic aspects of hip-hop culture that marginalize women and homosexuals. Pough argues that Black women, who have always shaped the Black public sphere throughout history, need to be more fully represented and discussed today.

> Wreck: 1) fight. 2) recreation.
> Wrecking Crew: 1) boast of rap groups who say one can destroy or "wreck" the other lyrically. They call themselves "wrecking crews." 2) gang of violent thugs.
> Wrecking Shop: winning an MC Battle.
>
> —Alonzo Westbrook, *Hip Hoptionary: The Dictionary of Hip-Hop Terminology*

... Here, I will interrogate notions of the public sphere, as defined by Jürgen Habermas, and of the Black public sphere, as defined by various theorists of Black public culture, in order to fully understand how intersections of race, class, gender, and sexuality further complicate understandings of the public sphere. I explore issues of spectacle, representation, and the public/private split in relation to Black public culture, and maintain that—as a result of Black history in the United States—these concepts have to be rethought when applied to Black participation in the larger U.S. public sphere. In order to highlight the legacy that Hip-Hop culture builds on, I provide some brief historical examples of how Blacks have negotiated and navigated the larger U.S. public sphere. I also provide examples of the ways that Black people, once they gained access to certain segments of the larger public sphere, sought to disrupt commonly held beliefs about Blacks by bringing wreck to negative images and stereotypes. They did so by claiming control of the public's gaze and a public voice for themselves. *Wreck*, as seen in the epigraph to this chapter, is a Hip-Hop term that connotes fighting, recreation, skill, boasting, or violence. The Hip-Hop concept of wreck sheds new light on the things Blacks have had to do in order to obtain and maintain a presence in the larger public sphere, namely, fight hard and bring attention to their skill and right to be in the public sphere.

Bringing wreck, for Black participants in the public sphere historically, has meant reshaping the public gaze in such a way as to be recognized as human beings—as functioning and worthwhile members of society—and not to be shut out of or pushed away from the public sphere. I make comparisons and connections between past instances of Black public culture in order to explore the implications for spectacle and representation in Hip-Hop culture and Black women involved in Hip-Hop culture. I maintain that a reworking of Habermas's concept of the public sphere is key to an expanded understanding of the political potentialities of Hip-Hop as a youth movement.

Habermas defines the bourgeois public sphere as "the sphere of private people come together as a public" who use "the public sphere regulated from above against the public authorities themselves, to engage them in a debate over the general rules governing relations in the basically privatized but publicly relevant sphere of commodity exchange and social labor." Because he is describing a particular moment in eighteenth-century Europe, the "private people" Habermas describes are homogeneous in regard to race, class, and gender; there are no women or people of color represented. This does not mean that they were not there, as many scholars of color and feminist scholars have pointed out. Rather, they did not have access to the public sphere in the same ways that white male property holders did.

Therefore, when we apply the notion of "commodity exchange" to Blacks in the United States (specifically Black women), the term takes on a different significance because of the history of slavery. For centuries black people themselves were a commodity, and they provided much of the labor that built the country. They are entering the public sphere after a significant period of being excluded from it; the "general rules governing relations" at one point worked to keep them out. The concept of the public sphere, as Habermas defines it, must be renegotiated in order to fit the specific needs of Black public culture in the United States....

If people of color and women are to be represented in the public sphere, Habermas's model has to be altered. A variety of experiences have to be taken into consideration, and those experiences have to be open to differences between and within the various groups. For example, the idea that citizens do not carry their "particularities" into the public sphere would necessarily have to be retheorized. Black women, for example, cannot opt to leave their particularities at the door. They are physically marked as Black and female, and these are two sources of their oppression. Thus their particularities would necessarily inform their very participation in the public sphere. Particularities matter, therefore, when they work as markers that inhibit access to the public sphere. Indeed, it might be more fruitful in contemporary discussions concerning people of color and the public sphere to think in terms of multiple publics. As Nancy Fraser writes in *Justice Interrupts*, in order for a theory of the public sphere to be adequate it must encompass the multiplicity of public spheres that exist, distinguish between them, and show how some of the spheres marginalize others.

Unlike Habermas's public sphere, Fraser's multiplicity of public spheres cannot be confined to a single model. She recognizes not only media and government public spheres but also everyday, informal public spheres. Fraser recognizes there is not only one way to be political; rather, multiple spheres interact with and even marginalize each other. This opens the door for a consideration of the way Hip-Hop culture functions as a counter-public sphere and the way Black women in particular experience that sphere. For example, today rappers suffer marginalization from official governmental offices—via police harassment, harsh restrictions on concert venues, censorship, and strict copyright laws that affect sampling—because of the themes that they choose to speak about in their lyrics. Some mass-media representations of Hip-Hop cast the culture in a negative light, simultaneously vilifying it and granting it a public voice. This vilification leads to moral panic and public outcry that serves to alienate the Hip-Hop generation from other members of Black communities. The alienation highlights not only the generation gap but also the class schisms that divide Black communities.

Even as the Hip-Hop generation is vilified, alienated, and marginalized, certain elements within Hip-Hop work to vilify, alienate, and marginalize others. For example, while some rappers claim to be the new voice for the marginalized group of Black youth they claim to represent, they oppress and marginalize women and homosexuals. The rap lyrics that make constant references to "bitches" and "hos," "punks" and "faggots," work to create hostile environments for some women and homosexual participants in Hip-Hop culture. This hostility is evident not only in the lyrics but also in the attitudes that some rappers exhibit toward women and homosexuals, marginalizing and oppressing anyone who is not Black, straight, male, and dripping with testosterone. Even though Hip-Hop culture suffers state oppression, it can and does in certain instances act as an oppressor....

Unlike Habermas's model, in which the bourgeoisie ideally was able to use the regulated public sphere against the public authorities that sought to suppress and squelch their public voice, today's rappers do not have access to the regulatory aspects of the public sphere in the same ways. Bearing Black history in mind, we can see a pattern in which whenever Black dissident voices enter the public space, variables of containment and severe oppression—sometimes from outside forces and sometimes from inside mistakes and misjudgments—go into play that inhibit the strength and forcefulness of their message. Examples of these kinds of dynamics can be found throughout Black history in the United States, but the most recent example prior to the explosion of Hip-Hop can be seen in how the Black Panther Party functioned as a counter-public sphere in the United States during the late 1960s and early 1970s.

The Black Panther Party used spectacle and representation in the larger U.S. public sphere to grab national attention and claim a public voice. The black leather jackets, black berets, and guns contributed to their revolutionary image. Their rhetoric of the gun—of killing and being willing to die for the people—also contributed to their ability to navigate the spectacle. Before Hip-Hop, then, we have the Black Panther Party making use of spectacle and controlling the national gaze. However, unlike what we find in most of contemporary Hip-Hop, the Black Panther Party used spectacle and representation with a social and political goal: power for the people. In this way, the Black Panther Party and Black groups that came before and after them renegotiated the public sphere in order to claim power for themselves.

Examinations of Black history in the United States show that while Habermas's model can be useful, it has to be reconfigured to fit Black experiences. Habermas begs to be reread with the lens of inclusion and difference firmly in place and with a special emphasis on race, class, gender, and sexuality. Because the space for such difference does not exist in Habermas's original work—due to the period in which he wrote it and the specific historical period he deal with—one has to be created through a method of reinterpretation. I find a useful model for reinterpretation in the feudal period which Habermas also addresses.

For example, *representative publicity* is a term that needs to be looked at in terms of race, class, gender, and sexuality. Representative publicity and the "publicness" of lords is characteristic of the period prior to the development of the public sphere, in Habermas's model. Habermas describes the publicness of lords, kings, and noblemen as a display or embodiment that presented them as higher power—higher than the people they presented themselves to. He goes on to suggest that such representation is an aura—something that pretends to make something invisible visible. It something staged and "wedded to personal attributes such as insignia (badges and arms), dress (clothing and coiffure), demeanor (form of greeting and poise), and rhetoric (form of address and formal discourse in general)—in a word, to a strict code of noble conduct." For Habermas, representative publicity, because of the power arrangements of the era, is something that is placed before the people, a form of spectatorship that lacks political possibilities because there is no participation. However, when one moves forward to the late-twentieth-century United States and considers a minority group that historically has not had access to the public sphere, spectacle takes on an entirely different role.

For Black people in the United States specifically, their role has historically been one of invisibility. This invisibility in the eyes of the governing body and the society at large—represented by creative minds such as Ralph Ellison in *Invisible Man* and theorists such as Michele Wallace in *Invisibility Blues: From Pop to Theory*—calls for a certain amount of spectacle on many levels. This invisibility is one reason Habermas needs to be reread to fit Black experiences in the U.S. public sphere. The spectacle becomes the key; one has to be seen before one can be heard. Spectacle and cultural representation (when more direct political access is not available) are the first step in creating a disruption, the first steps in bringing wreck. When Black bodies and Black voices lay claim to public spaces previously 120 denied to them, that space necessarily changes on some level due to their very presence.

When representation becomes possible, it takes on a new role in that minority leaders are often called on to represent the race. Kobena Mercer calls the phenomenon of one Black person who has managed to obtain a public presence being constantly called upon by the larger society and the communities from which he or she comes to represent the entire race the "burden of representation." Although he discusses it predominantly in terms of Black artists and artistic freedom, the concept is relevant for any Black person who enters a place of prominence in the larger public sphere. As Mercer notes, the task of speaking for an entire marginalized group is impossible, and creates in the representation a sense of urgency because the call to speak for and represent is itself a cultural reproduction of a racism that requires regulation of Black visibility in the public sphere. Mercer's views on the burden of representation illuminate the ways representations and representatives of the race function as tools of a racist society bent on gatekeeping and allowing only a few marginalized voices a public presence. However, the question of representation and representatives needs to be broadened in order to consider the strategic and political uses of representation by marginalized voices.

Systemic regulation and exclusion force the minority to go to great lengths to claim public space—even if it means becoming a representative. At least as representatives, they have access to a public voice. In fact, some use their role as representative to correct wrongs and replace stereotyped representations of Blacks in the United States with more positive images. They use their position as representative to bring wreck and counter stereotypes. For example, the image of the illiterate, untrainable Black brute is challenged by the intelligent, well-spoken Black public intellectual poised to represent the race. Also, for some Blacks—both historically and currently—their role as representative is not viewed as a burden. They pride themselves on being the voice of the people.

Some historical examples of this kind of representation are evident in the examination of early-twentieth-century African American clubwomen, W.E.B. Du Bois's "talented tenth," and the Black Panther Party. African American clubwomen in the late 1800s and early 1900s sought to influence the images of Black womanhood prevalent in the larger U.S. public sphere. They used literacy and social outreach projects to reshape and combat negative images of Black womanhood. African American clubwomen saw themselves as "race women" and viewed the work they did as "race work." They also saw themselves as working toward women's progress. As Angela Davis notes in *Women, Culture, and Politics*, the clubwomen's motto, "Lifting as We Climb," highlighted their dedication to a tradition of struggle and politically linked them to crucial progressive causes. For the clubwomen of the day, this meant influencing the ways Black womanhood was represented in the larger public. They made use of both spectacle and representation to accomplish their goals. They carried themselves with the utmost respectability and subscribed to middle-class virtues of womanhood. Thus they enacted a form of spectacle that surfaced, for example, in the shroud of silence surrounding Black women's sexuality. In order to combat stereotyped public images of Black women as sexually promiscuous, some Black women developed what Darlene Clark Hine calls a "culture of dissemblance" surrounding sexuality. This silencing was a spectacle in that they consciously decided what they would show of themselves in public and crafted the presentable and respectable public image of Black womanhood.

They also thought it was their duty not only to help Black women of the lower classes but also to speak for them and represent their needs to the larger public. This form of representation surfaced in what Hazel Carby calls the "policing of the Black woman's body." The clubwomen were vigilant in their efforts to control the public images of Black womanhood—so much so that they sought to control recent Black women immigrants in the North, who were seen as a threat to both the progress of the race and the "establishment of a respectable urban black middle class." As proper race women, the clubwomen used their own visibility and action in the public sphere to ensure that Black womanhood was represented in ways that uplifted the race.... [Clubwomen's] use of spectacle and representation helped them to combat negative images of Black womanhood. And on some level, their very presence in the public sphere as speakers, activists, and writers brought wreck to commonly held beliefs not only about Black women's capabilities but also about the proper place in the public sphere for women in general. They used their position as race women to advocate for the race and to show the larger society all that the race could accomplish given the right opportunities. Similar interactions can be seen in Du Bois's concept of the "talented tenth."

W.E.B. Du Bois coined the phrase "talented tenth" in his 1903 essay by the same title and maintained that Black people should be led by "exceptional men"—"the best of their time." He wrote that "the Talented Tenth of the Negro race must be made leaders of thought and missionaries of culture among their people. No others can do this work and Negro colleges must train men for it. The Negro race, like all other races, is going to be saved by its exceptional men." What is perhaps most interesting about Du Bois's concept is the way it took shape within Black communities. He sets up a tradition—from slavery until the time he wrote—of stellar men and stellar acts. But it is his call for a talented tenth, his urging, that brings forth a kind of representation that some would say continues today.

The talented tenth—groomed for leadership and deemed proper—is also the group allowed to speak for the race. Like the clubwomen, this group too felt it knew what was best (an attitude that continues to exist today). There is also a certain element of spectacle, a spectacle that exudes a certain sense of class and by extension a certain element of respectability. It is not simply enough to be educated. It is just as important to appear educated—one would be no good without the other. The talented tenth, as it became embodied in Black communities, represented the best foot forward. They represent the best and brightest and therefore the ones allowed to have a public presence and voice in matters concerning the race. Even though Du Bois renounced the concept years later, it had already taken root. Traces of it can be seen in certain aspects of the civil rights movement and even today's public intellectual displays, showcased on CNN and elsewhere, with huge panels at all-day symposiums devoted to the best and brightest of Black America, whose participants are prepared to talk about and give advice to Black Americans.

During the civil rights movement, Black people created a form of spectacle in order to gain entry into the public sphere and attract the media. Men marched in suits and ties. Women marched in dresses, stockings, and high heels. They were a vision of respectability—marching and singing, not rioting and shouting. They wanted mainstream America to see that they were good people, respectable citizens who deserved civil rights. Their clothing and the manner in which they conducted themselves showcased this attempt at respectability and no doubt encouraged many mainstream white Americans to join the struggle, but it did not stop the fire hoses and dogs.

The exceptional-men mentality and the notion of a talented tenth will no doubt continue. But it was reshaped and altered for a brief moment with certain elements of the Black Power movement, specifically the Black Panther Party.

The Black Panther Party had to attract the attention of the media before it could be given any serious consideration. While the Black Panther Party did consider itself to be the vanguard of the revolution, its members did not feel that they were sent to lead the people in the same ways as the talented tenth was meant to. They insisted instead that they were taking their lead from the people. Their use of spectacle was twofold: their uniform of black beret, black leather jacket, and gun was meant not only to capture the mainstream American imagination but also to attract the masses of Black people, specifically the brothers on the block. They too used spectacle and representation to control gaze and as such bring wreck to what the larger public thought it knew about Black people. The Black Panther Party, instead of taking its cue from a talented Black elite, felt that the revolution would come from a group that the larger U.S. public had all but written off. In trying to move the masses of Black people, the Panthers went a step beyond standard Marxism's notion of the proletariat rising to power. They attempted to move the Black *lumpenproletariat*. Former Panther leader Elaine Brown writes:

> The Black "lumpen proletariat," unlike Marx's working class, had absolutely no stake in industrial America. They existed at the bottom level of society in America, outside the capitalist system that was the basis for oppression of Black people.... At their lowest level, at the core, they were the gang members and the gangsters, the pimps and the prostitutes, the drug users and dealers, the common thieves and murderers.

The Panthers wanted the lumpen proletariat to rise. They have in fact been criticized for celebrating and idealizing the lumpen. In this regard, some comparisons can be made between Hip-Hop culture's glamorization of the ghetto and their reinterpretations of 1970s blaxploitation cult figures such as gangsters, pimps, and big-time drug dealers. Even Hip-Hop's fascination with Glocks and Uzis can be connected to the Black Panther Party's rhetoric of the gun and ultimately their celebration of the lumpen and glamorizing of the ghetto. Before Hip-Hop, the Black Panther Party gave the United States its greatest nightmare. Although there was always a strain of the fear of Blackness running through the country, the Black Panther Party boldly reconfigured the nightmare's gaze. Where the United States once had its lies and stereotypes about Black brutes given by films such as *The Birth of a Nation* (1915), the country now had to contend with a gaze controlled by the spectacle. The Black Panthers not only presented a menacing picture themselves, but—speaking for the people, as representatives of the people—promised to ignite the lumpen proletariat, thus increasing the Panthers' numbers and by extension their threat. The Black Panther Party offers, then, a twentieth-century example of Black rage and a less-than-respectable representation in the larger U.S. public sphere. They set the stage for what we would see later in Hip-Hop culture.

Hip-Hop as a youth movement grew out of the rubble of a dying Black Power movement. Just as the Black Power movement was taking its last breath in the mid-1970s in America's inner cities, Hip-Hop was being created by Black and Latino youth in the South Bronx. It is therefore not much of a leap to see the Hip-Hop generation as direct descendants of the legacy left by Black Power groups such as the Black Panther Party. Certain segments of the Hip-Hop generation, in fact, can be seen as bringing to fruition the Black Panther Party's hopes of giving those voiceless members of the masses of Black people a voice. Rap music and Hip-Hop culture bring elements of spectacle and representation to higher levels in the larger U.S. public sphere than many aspects of Black public culture did in the past. Hip-Hop journalist Bakari Kitwana concurs: "Rap marked a turning point, a shift from practically no public voice for young Blacks—or at best an extremely marginalized one—to Black youth culture as the rage in mainstream popular culture. And more than just increasing Black youth visibility, rap articulated publicly and on a mass scale many of the generation's beliefs, relatively unfiltered by the corporate structures that carried it." Rap music and Hip-Hop culture offer a space in the public sphere and a chance to voice the concerns of this generation.

For example, in response to the public outrage and debate caused by accusations that some rap promotes and glorifies violence, many rappers have spoken out against the blame society places on rap music by claiming to be the voices of the Black people in America's inner cities. In interview after interview, rappers can be counted on to claim that they are "representin'" for the Black people left behind in their respective neighborhoods. Many rappers argue that they bring the stark reality of life in American ghettos to public attention. The fact is, some of the most humanizing and accurate accounts of life in impoverished ghettos come from rap songs and not the network news. Thus rappers bring wreck: they disrupt their way into and make themselves visible in the public sphere with the goal of not only speaking for disenfranchised Black people but also claiming both a voice and a living for themselves in a society bereft of opportunity for them. In making these disruptions, the rappers and other participants in Hip-Hop culture bring wreck to the common (mis)representations of Black youth. Much like the Black Panther Party did in the 1970s, these youths bring wreck by redirecting the gaze and controlling the images the larger public sees. In this they are representing the exact opposite of late-nineteenth- and early-twentieth-century notions of Black respectability.

They do so by making use of spectacle in ways that tell—in public—the stories that were once hidden from the larger public. Rap lyrics display gritty descriptions of sexual acts that the early clubwomen would no doubt disapprove of, especially coining from the mouths of women rappers barely out of their teens. Depictions of Black-on-Black crime, drug deals, drive-bys, and pimping are not necessarily the leadership of Blackness that the talented tenth wanted to foster and highlight. However, contemporary rappers are not shying away from the starker realities of life in America's inner cities. Rap music and Hip-Hop culture provide a spectacle of Black manhood not seen since the Black Power movement. The Hip-Hop generation has captured the American imagination, and that of the world. They have done so by making creative use of spectacle.

Rappers, with their bold use of language and dress, also use image and spectacle as their initial entry into the public sphere. In this instance, spectacle functions dually as both style and a plea to be heard, to be allowed to represent. They view representation or "representin'"—speaking for the people and voicing their concerns—as their role. In a talk given at Brown University titled "Material Witness: Race, Identity and the Politics of Gangsta Rap," Michael Eric Dyson describes the Hip-Hop generation's use of representation:

> At their best rappers shape the torturous twist of urban fate into lyrical elegies. The act of representing that is much ballyhooed in hip-hop is the witness of those left to tell the afflicted's story. They represent lives swallowed by too little love or opportunity. They represent themselves and their peers with aggrandizing anthems that boast of ingenuity and luck in surviving.

Although Dyson's view that rappers are speaking for the people may sound a bit naive to some, he no doubt arrives at this stance by taking into consideration the numerous rappers who have gone on record in interviews as saying that they are the voice of their respective "hoods." Whether they actually perform this task or not can be disputed; the same argument can be made in relation to the Black Panther Party and the impact it had on the Black community. Some felt that the Panthers were self-serving in the same ways the rappers are seen as self-serving—due to the money they receive at their manipulation of media attention. Rappers do bring issues and concerns, via their lyrics, to public attention that might not otherwise be heard. For example, while the government and the media pay a certain amount of lip service to the rising unemployment rate and the impact of poverty and crime on Black communities, rappers give narrations of Black experiences with these issues and so represent the concerns of some segments of their communities. For rappers, speaking for the people means representing the people. They are self-designated tellers of the people's suffering. But unlike the representative publicity of nobility and lords prior to the development of the public sphere Habermas describes, they are not simply a show placed in front of the people. And they do not have power already.

The show, the spectacle, is the first step toward change—the first part of getting heard. For a historically marginalized and invisible group, the spectacle is what allows them a point of entry into a public space that has proved to be violent and exclusionary. In fact when we take into consideration the many marches, protests, and demonstrations—all grand displays of spectacle—that the Black public cultures prior to the Hip-Hop movement had to develop in order to gain civil rights, the necessity of spectacle to Black political action becomes clear. As stated earlier in relation to the civil right movement, after a legacy of slavery and being labeled as three-fifths human, Blacks had to create a spectacle that allowed them to be seen as respectable citizens. And when that display was met with violence and exclusion, the logical next step would necessarily be the types of spectacle created by the Black Power movement, with guns, rage, and riots. All of these attempts are ways in which Blacks have tried to negotiate their freedom with the tools and power allowed them in this racist country. And while some methods worked better than others, when we move to the present and see how the gains of these past movements are being taken away one by one and how society as a whole has regressed in terms of race issues, should we be surprised that Black youths involved in Hip-Hop find themselves left with spectacle yet again as a way to gain entry into the public sphere? What has really changed?

Before Hip-Hop grabbed the national imagination, the Black and Latino youth who created it were neglected and unseen except for token guest spots in the nightly news as the criminal threat. With Hip-Hop culture sweeping the country and the world, these same youth now enjoy a form of publicity once denied to them. Spectacle, however, becomes a double-edged sword, because while without it rappers would have no vehicle to represent to the public at large or themselves, with only spectacle and no semblance of the political projects inherent in other forms of Black public culture the rappers risk becoming stuck in forms of publicity that have limited usefulness. Spectacle is limited because it works only as long as the group attempting to impact the public sphere controls the gaze. As soon as the spectacle is co-opted, it ceases to be effective. For example, while guns and menacing public images catapulted the Black Panther Party into the larger public sphere, once the media took control of the images and the U.S. government used them to launch an all-out attack on the Black Panther Party, the group not only suffered repression but also lost the support of the masses they had hoped to lead to revolution.

While exceptional representations of Blackness, as seen with the talented tenth and Black clubwomen, initially gave the larger U.S. public sphere images of Blackness that contradicted negative stereotyped images, these failed when they became co-opted by the larger public sphere. The exceptional few stand out as just that, leaving the rest of the group in the same position—marginalized and invisible—that they previously held. Representation is limited in similar ways: even though the person or group doing the representing is voicing the genuine needs of the community, they can represent the entire community to only a limited extent. Someone's needs will always be left out. Yet even with the limited usefulness of representation and spectacle, the gains made by the Black public sphere could not have happened without them....

In his book *What the Music Said: Black Popular Music and Black Public Culture*, Mark Anthony Neal establishes a timeline for the Black public sphere that begins after slavery. Only after emancipation was it possible for a true Black public sphere with an active and recognized citizenship—albeit a marginalized citizenship—to be formed. However, that citizenship was extended only to men. Thus Neal finds that the traditional Black public sphere was dominated by Black male discourse. He further notes two early public spheres that were crucial to the establishment of a functioning Black public sphere: the Black church and the blues. According to Neal, the Black church was the more visible and produced and distributed the majority of Black critical discourse. The blues, "as the primary musical text of informal public institutions like the jook, rent parties, and after-hours clubs," became a second source for the dissemination of Black critical discourse. Neal complicates the notion of the Black public sphere by extending its space to include not only expressive culture but also the public spaces that celebrate the culture. By including the counterpublic spaces of the jook joint and the rent party, he is moving away from liberal bourgeois notions of what constitutes a public sphere. He recognizes that Black critical discourse can take place in a variety of media, including Black music. This recognition is especially fruitful as we move to the Hip-Hop generation and begin to think about the political and cultural relevance of Hip-Hop culture and the possibilities it creates for change in the larger public sphere.

Neal also recognizes that women were present in these public spaces. He notes the centrality of Black female voices in the blues and references Elsa Barkley Brown and Evelyn Brooks Higginbotham's work on the ways in which Black communities—both men and women—used the church to debate, discuss, and disseminate information. Likewise, Houston Baker, in *Critical Memory: Public Sphere, African American Writing, and Black Fathers and Sons of America*, articulates the fact that women were always present in the Black public sphere, using as an example his own mother's activities. His mother co-led the campaign to raise funds for the hospital of which his father was superintendent, wrote speeches for his father, and was the financial consultant for the campaign. Baker views his mother's actions as continuing the legacy of Black womanist activism. He knows that his mother and women like her contributed to the building of Black institutions. And even though the focus of his project is the work and presence of Black men in the Black public sphere, he does make mention of notable women such as his mother. In fact, after a lengthy discussion of all that Black men have done, he posits a rhetorical question: "but by now, you are surely asking: 'Have the mothers, sisters, daughters, nieces, no part in all of this?' And the answer is, of course they do." Of course they do. They always have and they always will.

In ways that we have yet to fully recognize and acknowledge Black women have helped to shape and build the Black public sphere as we know it. They have shaped the public sphere so much that I would add the caveat that we can no longer simply say that the women were present. We need to articulate fuller accounts of their voices and their work. It is no longer acceptable to note Black male dominance in public discourse in ways that dismiss or write off any detailed discussion of women. We need to extend our interrogations and discussions in ways that validate not only the presence of women in the Black public sphere but women's roles in shaping that sphere. Instead of commenting on the strength of the Black male presence in the public discourse, we need to ask what Black women were doing to enable that presence. We will no doubt find women like Baker's mother writing speeches, raising funds, and building institutions. Instead of simply noting the dominance of the Black church as a public sphere and attributing this to the charismatic leadership of Black men preachers, we need to look at the women who make up the majority of the congregation members in the Black churches of today and of the past. As Alice Walker rightly notes when reflecting on the civil rights movement in the documentary *A Place of Rage*, if it were not for the Black church, then the civil rights movement as we know it could not have happened. And if it were not for the women, then the Black church would not have been able to support the movement, because they made up the majority of church members. These kinds of realizations push our interrogations further than "the women were also present." We already know that women were there. What we need to explore is how they used their influence and how they shaped the Black public sphere.

I maintain that we will not know exactly what the Black public sphere is or what it can be until we fully examine Black women's roles in it. For example, even when Black women were disenfranchised, they had a say in where the Black vote went. Elsa Barkley Brown documents such women in her study of Black Richmonders in the 1800s. These women saw Black men's votes as community property. They gathered in Black churches with Black men and children to discuss major issues, and here everyone voted. Brown maintains that "in Richmond and throughout the South exclusion from legal enfranchisement did not prevent African American women from shaping the vote and the political decisions." The Richmond women that Brown writes of guarded guns in order to keep the meetings safe. They took Election Day off from work in order to have large groups of Black people attend the polls together. By contributing to the numbers, they hoped to ensure that Black men would not be turned away and that they would be able to protect the voters and each other. Brown highlights the ways the Black women of Richmond helped to shape the Black public sphere in that city and by extension effect change in the larger public sphere. No doubt there are countless stories throughout history of women like those in Richmond, Houston Baker's mother, and the Black churchwomen and blues women that Mark Anthony Neal mentions. However, we will not hear their stories or know how they influenced and shaped the Black public sphere if we do not begin to rethink the Black public sphere. As Brown states:

> African American collective memory in the late twentieth century often appears partial, distorted, and dismembered. The definitions and issues of political struggle which can come from that partial memory are limited. Before we can construct truly participatory discussions around a fully democratic agenda where the struggles of women and men are raised as issues of general interest necessary to the liberation of all, we have some powerful lot of reremembering to do.

Half stories and half histories are no longer satisfactory, not if we want to realize the fullness of the Black public sphere's potential. We can start by noting that the discourse of the Black public sphere has historically and currently been dominated by the voices of Black men. But if we truly want to know what the political struggle has been and what the possibilities for freedom are, we must look at the women surrounding the men. When we simply say the women were there, we miss the full account. They were there shaping and molding the public in ways that ensured that we would have a Black public sphere to speak of.

The reremembering of Black historical events Brown mentions needs to occur. However, we also need a whole lot of reenvisioning of contemporary happenings as well. Like the Black women of Richmond, Black women took part in the Black public sphere throughout history and continue to do so today. Black women were major players through Reconstruction, the civil rights movement, and the Black Power movement. They were also very present and very active in the founding of the Hip-Hop movement. Refusing to explore the ways in which Black women contributed and continue to contribute gives us at best partial pictures of the Black public sphere. Understanding women's involvement and learning from and duplicating what worked for them, however, might just help us to enact change today. And as Black public sphere scholars have noted, if the Black public sphere is not ultimately about the business of evoking change, then we are wasting time.

31. Anita Harris, "Introduction," from *Future Girl: Young Women in the Twenty-First Century*

Excerpts from Anita Harris, *Future Girl: Young Women in the Twenty-First Century* (New York: Routledge, 2004), 1–9. Reproduced by permission of Routledge/Taylor & Francis Books, Inc.

Focusing on the production of girls' subjectivities in wealthy nations, Harris describes a corporate culture that, to make itself look progressive and full of economic opportunity for all, categorizes girls as "can do" or "at risk," investing in girls as a major source of both work and consumption. Although many of the representations of girls seem more positive, this categorization shifts the focus away from structural explanations of inequality and failure to "make it" and squarely onto the shoulders of each individual girl, obscuring the real determinants of girls' lives.

This book explores the idea that in a time of dramatic social, cultural, and political transition, young women are being constructed as a vanguard of new subjectivity. They are supposed to offer clues about the best way to cope with these changes. Power, opportunities, and success are all modeled by the "future girl"—a kind of young woman celebrated for her "desire, determination and confidence" to take charge of her life, seize chances, and achieve her goals. The abundance of books about girls' voices, webpages for their issues, and goods and services geared to a girl market indicates how young women are made visible in more and more places to exemplify this new way of being. Such a proliferation of sites to see and hear young women suggests that we are very interested in applauding but also scrutinizing their lives and that we have created more ways for this to happen. I suggest that this new interest in looking at and hearing from girls is not just celebratory, but is, in part, regulatory as well. There is a process of creation and control at work in the act of regarding young women as the winners in a new world. In holding them up as the exemplars of new possibility, we also actively construct them to perform this role.

What does it mean to say that young women and girlhood itself are constructed or regulated to demonstrate how we all might prevail today? In *Act Your Age!*, her brilliant study of the cultural construction of adolescence at the end of the nineteenth century, education scholar Nancy Lesko argues that

> adolescence became a social space in which to talk about the characteristics of people in modernity, to worry about the possibilities of ... social changes, and to establish policies and programs that would help create the modern social order and citizenry.

Lesko suggests that a new modern political and civic order was being created in the United States and the United Kingdom at the time, one that was preoccupied with nationalism, "civilization," and racial progress. The behavior, attitudes, and development of adolescents were all monitored closely in the interests of producing rational, patriotic, and productive citizens for a modern nation-state. In the late nineteenth century, therefore, the state, scientists, and the community paid considerable attention to young people's social and moral development because they were meant to embody the ideals of national progress. If educators "got it right" with youth, then nations themselves would have their futures secured. Young people were expected to personify modern civic values, such as responsibility, strength, and sacrifice, and model the new style of nation-defending citizenship.

I suggest here that this kind of attention to and construction of youth as integral to the successful transition to a new social order has reemerged in important ways. However, it is young women, rather than youth in general, who are now the subjects of this scrutiny and regulation. Displaying, extolling, and inquiring into young women and girlhood, rather than adolescence, serves many of the same purposes in a contemporary context. Young women today stand in for possibilities and anxieties about new identities more generally. At the beginning of the twenty first century, the creation of the contemporary social order and citizenship is achieved in part within the space of girlhood. That is, the appropriate ways to embrace and manage the political, economic, and social conditions of contemporary societies are demonstrated in the example of young women, through the ideal of the future girl. She is imagined, and sometimes imagines herself, as best able to handle today's socioeconomic order.

The focus on adolescents at the *fin de siècle* and the attention paid to young women today thus serve similar interests. Girlhood operates now as adolescence functioned then, as a space for "worries about unknown futures, about ability to succeed and dominate in changing circumstances, about maintenance of ... hierarchy in changing social and cultural landscapes." While these anxieties also confront contemporary social orders, what is different today is the kind of state/civil society relation that is constructed in this space. In the modern period of the late nineteenth century, youth were disciplined directly by the state and its agents so that they would develop slowly, under close supervision, to serve a unified and progressive nation. Late modern times, however, are characterized by dislocation, flux, and globalization, and demand citizens who are flexible and self-realizing. As we shall see, direct intervention and guidance by institutions have been replaced by self-governance; power has devolved onto individuals to regulate themselves through the right choices. The social and economic logic of late modernity compels people to become self-inventing and responsible citizens who can manage their own development and adapt to change without relying on the state. To understand this shift and its implications for youth in general and young women in particular, we need to explore the socioeconomic features of late modernity more closely. First, I want to provide some description and definitions of *late modernity*, focusing especially on the concepts of risk and individualization, as they are central to understanding the world in which future girls live. Although there are many national and cultural differences, I want to make some general claims about what late modernity means for young women across a range of Western nations.

LATE MODERNITY

Before exploring how young women and girlhood in contemporary Western societies are represented as the future, it is important to understand the circumstances and characteristics of late modernity that have given rise to anxieties about the direction of social and economic life. Only then can we interpret the significance of investments in young women as both carriers of and defenders against social change. Put briefly, as youth sociologists Andy Furlong and Fred Cartmel argue in their book *Young People and Social Change*,

"Young people today are growing up in a different world to that experienced by previous generations—changes which are significant enough to merit a reconceptualization of youth transitions and processes of social reproduction." This "different world" is marked by both social and economic characteristics that have forced a fundamental reassessment of the material with which young people are able to craft their identities and forge their livelihoods. Put simply, the late modern era is distinguished by its economic and social break with industrial modernity. This previous era was characterized by a system of industrial capitalism built around manufacturing; strong centralized government; enduring social ties based on shared identifications with community, class, and place; and, in the post-war era, the development of both liberal welfare states and robust social justice movements.

By contrast, late modernity is defined by complex, global capitalist economies and a shift from state support and welfare to the private provision of services. The key feature of late modern economies is deindustrialization—the contraction of large-scale manufacturing and the expansion of global communications, technology, and service industries. Across these and other industries, full-time ongoing employment has been replaced by part-time, casual, temporary, and short-term contract work. Markets, corporations, and production are increasingly globalized, a process fueled by the information revolution, the capacity to move capital and information around the world instantaneously, and changes in national regulations about trade, ownership, movement of capital, and offshore production. Along with this trend nation-states have retreated from industrial regulation of both transnationals and small businesses, and public policy often employs the language of individual responsibility and enterprise bargaining to fill the gap left by deregulation. The economic impact of these conditions has been an increase in family and child poverty, and greater polarization between rich and poor, both within states and between the North and the South.

The new focus on enterprise, economic rationalism, and individualization has social as well as economic effects. These include a sense of change, insecurity, fragmentation, and discontinuity within communities and nations, as well as a new emphasis on the responsibilities of individuals. Economic rationalism has been accompanied by a shift to a new brand of competitive individualism, whereby people are expected to create their own chances and make the best of their lives. The social theorists Ulrich Beck and Anthony Giddens suggest that the idea of predictability that was a feature of modern times has been replaced by a new sense of danger and contingency. Late modernity has been defined by Beck in his groundbreaking book *Risk Society: Towards a New Modernity* as generating the foundational conditions of what he describes as "risk society," wherein global insecurities and economic unpredictability are combined with weakening collective ties and identities. This feeling of risk, and a sense of the loss of what was known and enduring, are generated by real or perceived broader global trends towards a world sped up and in flux. Mass movements of migrants and refugees; the visibility of civil, religious, and ethnic conflicts; worldwide health threats; economics whose fortunes appear dependent on arbitrary and foreign forces; and global human security concerns all contribute to a real sense of living in a risk society. Alongside these experiences late modern individuals may also feel they have lost significant connections with others, for example, through the diversification of the family unit, the transience of neighborhood populations, and the fragmentation of social movements.

With the falling away of collective ties and longstanding social relationships that helped us know our place and identity, risks must be negotiated on an individual level. This means that people are required to make choices and create life trajectories for themselves without traditional patterns or support structures to guide them. They must develop individual strategies and take personal responsibility for their success, happiness, and livelihood by making the right choices in an uncertain and changeable environment. From one perspective this process of individualization creates opportunities for forming oneself independently of the traditional ties that have previously been so instrumental in structuring life trajectories. It carries with it the promise of choice, freedom, and real autonomy. However, apparent opportunities for self-invention and individual effort exist within circumstances that remain highly constrained for the majority of people. Sociologist Steven Miles suggests that the image of subjectivity generated by risk society is

> one of increased independence, self-determination and self realization. But as discussions of risk illustrate, the conditions within which these apparently positive developments are occurring are actually taking place in a world which in some respects is quite possibly less secure than it has ever been.

This insecurity is manifested in unpredictable chances for employment and other avenues for livelihood, the shift from production to consumption as a framework for making meaning and identity (which in turn depends on the capacity to generate income), the rollback of nation-states' accountability for the social rights of their citizens, and the replacement of strong social bonds with momentary identifications. Furthermore, whereas once obstacles to maximizing one's life chances could be understood through analyses of structured social inequality and addressed through political collectivities, the collapse of these collectivities means that today these can only be remedied through more strenuous self-invention and self-transformation.

These conditions and the requirement of individuals to now "make themselves" in order to survive and perhaps even flourish have generated considerable anxiety about the future of youth, who are imagined as the inheritors of this somewhat frightening world. It is young people who must try to forge their futures by mastering the anxieties, uncertainties, and insecurities conjured up by unpredictable times. As youth studies theorist Peter Kelly argues, "Processes of individualization … visit new forms of responsibility on young people and their families to prudently manage individual 'reflexive biographical projects' in increasingly uncertain settings." In other words, young people are newly obliged to make good choices for themselves and set themselves on a path toward success with little support or security outside the private sphere. In a risk society their circumstances and opportunities seem more precarious than ever. However, as the future-girl phenomenon suggests, youth are also imagined as those who may be best able to prevail, having grown up with unpredictability as their only reality. After all, young people are taking up the opportunities of late modernity, particularly in technology and communications, in ways that many of an older generation find admirable.

In the late nineteenth century youth were constructed as highly dependent and were expected to take guidance from experts to become citizens in the development of a larger social plan for national homogeneity and progress. The features of the ideal young person were clearly prescribed. Today, they are supposed to become unique, successful individuals, making their own choices and plans to accomplish autonomy. The benchmark for achieving a successful identity is no longer adherence to a set of normative characteristics, but instead a capacity for self-invention. This means that they are the focus of a different kind of attention from the state, service providers, educators, and advertisers. Young people in modern times were governed by experts who would overtly direct and then reward or punish appropriate behavior. The new watchfulness in youth research, policy, and popular culture seeks to shape conduct through perpetual everyday observation and to elicit self-monitoring in youth themselves. They are not only obliged to manage their own life trajectories, but are enticed to display this management for the scrutiny of experts and observers. The obligation for youth to become unique individuals is therefore constructed as a freedom, a freedom best expressed through the display of one's choices and projects of the self. The current focus on placing young people in school, workplaces, and appropriate recreational centers, and in hearing from them, for example, in youth citizenship debates, can be understood as related to this trend toward exhibition of one's biographical project.

WHY YOUNG WOMEN?

Young women have taken on a special role in the production of the late modern social order and its values. They have become a focus for the construction of an ideal late modern subject who is self-making, resilient, and flexible. But why is it young women and not youth in general who have been invested in, symbolically and materially, in these ways? I answer this question in two ways. First, changed economic and work conditions combined with the goals achieved by feminism have created new possibilities for young women. Successful campaigns for the expansion of girls' education and employment have coincided with a restructured global economy and a class/gender system that now relies heavily on young women's labor. Second, new ideologies about individual responsibility and choices also dovetail with some broad feminist notions about opportunities for young women, making them the most likely candidates for performing a new kind of self-made subjectivity.

The transformations in women's status throughout the Western world have been strongly felt in the sectors of education and employment. Women's participation in both areas has increased significantly since the 1960s and 1970s. Changes in laws, policies, and social mores have all made this participation possible and desirable for women. State-sanctioned discrimination which once privileged men in education and at work has been largely eliminated, and the assumption that women do not need careers because they derive their livelihood from a man, as well as a complete identity from the heterosexual nuclear family, has been fundamentally challenged. Young women have been promised equal access to all educational programs and are encouraged by educators and others to pursue meaningful work that aligns with their interests and skills.

At the same time that feminism was ensuring these entitlements, the world of education and employment was changing dramatically for young people, and young women in particular. With the collapse of the full-time youth job market, the rise of the service and communications sectors, and the fragmentation of both workplaces and work trajectories, young people are now expected to stay in education longer to train for flexible, specialized work in a constantly changing labor market. There has been an enormous increase in part-time work for women in the flourishing industries, as well as a departure of men from some professional and managerial spheres in favor of better-paying options in the new finance or technology sectors of the global economy. These conditions create opportunities (although not always good ones) for young women's work participation. Thus, the feminist push to dismantle the barriers keeping women out of education and employment has coincided with a broader socioeconomic need for young women to take up places in the new economy. As education scholar Jill Blackmore argues, "The new global work order has offered girls the types of opportunities that feminism and their education have well prepared them for, giving them both the skills and desire to take up new subject positions."

Further, education and employment have become increasingly important to the standing of young women in terms of the new class/gender structure of late modernity. This is particularly so for the middle classes. Whereas once a comfortable middle-class position was attained or sustained through marriage, today this process is much less assured. The family wage that was once paid to men on the assumption that they had a wife and children to support has largely disappeared. Regulations and protections around pay rates are no longer the norm, and men's incomes are less secure, particularly in the industries employing the lower and middle classes. In addition, the expansion of consumer capitalism and the connection between consumption and middle-class status mean that two incomes are required to sustain a family's appropriate class lifestyle. Finally, the changing nature of the labor market has seen an expansion of "women's work," such that there is sound economic logic for middle-class families to depend on women's wages. Middle-class young women can no longer rely on marriage to secure their economic status or social standing. These young women must become successful and income generating in their own right, and this means doing well academically and professionally.

Along with changes to education and employment have come reforms to legislation and a shift in attitudes regarding relationships, marriage and divorce, reproduction and sexuality, harassment and sexual assault, and many other dimensions of what had previously been seen as the realm of the personal. Feminism has often been described as a program for change to allow women freedom of choice regarding their bodies, work, family, and relationships—and personal, autonomous responsibility for these choices. These changes have enabled the current generation of young women to see themselves, and to be seen, as enjoying new freedoms and opportunities. They are far more at liberty to make choices and pursue lifestyles independently of their families, the state, and men in general. Young women have been encouraged to believe that "girls can do anything" and "girls are powerful."

These ideas about choice and freedom are central to contemporary notions of individuality. In today's risk society individuals are expected to be flexible, adaptable, resilient, and ultimately responsible for their own ability to manage their lives successfully. One's own life becomes a personal project much like a do-it-yourself assemblage or what Ulrich Beck calls a "choice biography" that can be crafted as one desires, rather than a fixed set of predictable stages and experiences. These are key ideas in differentiating late modern young people's identities from modern, late-nineteenth-century adolescence. As Peter Kelly argues, today, "youthful subjects are constructed as responsible for future life chances, choices and options within institutionally structured risk environments.... The subject is compelled to prudently manage ... his or her own DIY [Do-It-Yourself]-project of the self." These features of the late modern self pick up on key elements of some general feminist principles about young women's new opportunities for choice, individual empowerment, personal responsibility, and the ability to "be what you want to be." Young women are thus doubly constructed as ideal flexible subjects; they are imagined as benefiting from feminist achievements and ideology, as well as from new conditions that favor their success by allowing them to put these into practice.

By interrogating the new visibility of young women and focusing specifically on the idea of girls' success as a publicly displayed, mainstream experience, we can see how "making it" in new times appears to be contingent on personal responsibility and effort, the kind of effort best illustrated by the way all girls are now apparently leading their lives. The popular story is that girls as a whole are performing brilliantly and are the great example and hope for the future. Educated, young, professional career women with glamorous consumer lifestyles appear to be everywhere. This scenario is a reality for a small number, but the image also functions as a powerful ideal that suggests that all young women are now enjoying these kinds of lives and that this is what it means to be successful.

There are, however, many young women who are not living in ways that match the image of success. Their situation results from the same conditions that produce the future girl, that is, a changed labor market, economic rationalization, and a devolving of responsibility—a "responsibilization"—onto individuals. In order for the popular story to prevail, however, the consequences of the sexual and economic exploitation of these young women are not confronted, and the socioeconomic benefits delivered by them are not acknowledged. Instead, their circumstances are labeled "failure," and this is attributed to poor choices, insufficient effort, irresponsible families, bad neighborhoods, and lazy communities. In the move to cultivate young women as the new success story for our times, the struggles, disappointments, and barriers experienced by many young women are put to one side as the aberrant experiences of a minority of youth. Set in the context of the late modern Western world, this book therefore argues that there is another story behind the representation of young women as the winners in rapidly changing societies. I suggest that young women are living more complex lives than the dominant images of girls' freedom, power, and success suggest and that class and race inequalities continue to shape opportunities and outcomes. Because young women are supposed to embody the new flexible subjectivity, analyzing their experiences, practices, and political engagements can illustrate more broadly the dangers and opportunities of late modernity for its self-inventing subjects....

32. Leslie Heywood and Jennifer Drake, "'It's All About the Benjamins': Economic Determinants of Third Wave Feminism in the U.S.," from *Third Wave Feminism: A Critical Exploration*

Excerpts from Leslie Heywood and Jennifer Drake, "'It's All About the Benjamins'," published in Stacy Gillis, Gillian Howie, and Rebecca Munford, eds., *Third Wave Feminism: A Critical Exploration* (London: Palgrave, 2004), 13–21. Reprinted with permission.

Extending Barbara Findlen's and Astrid Henry's identification of the different historical circumstances that shaped third-wave perspectives, the article "It's All About the Benjamins" concentrates on the economic forces that most affect third-wavers—such as the fact that "the majority of young Americans have experienced relative gender equality in the context of downward mobility." This fact makes young Americans "identify as much with generation as with gender," and in a time of shifting demographics, makes them identify with race, ethnicity, or religion as much or more than gender. The third wave, Heywood and Drake argue, came of age in a time when economic restructuring such as downsizing, privatization, and globalization contributed to the economic insecurity, making gender one axis of inquiry among other struggles such as "environmentalism, anti-corporate activism, and struggles for human rights."

Although conversation and debates about third wave feminism have been ongoing since the nineties, there has been a lack of theory that delineates and contextualises third wave feminist perspectives, especially in the US. This chapter provides a partial redress of this through illustrating how third wave perspectives are shaped by the material conditions created by economic globalisation and technoculture, and by bodies of thought such as postmodernism and postcolonialism. Since writers usually identified as the 'third wave' are most likely to be part of a generation that has come of age in these contexts, the chapter outlines some of the economic variables that have heavily impacted the current generation in the US, and demonstrates how they have resulted in a feminist movement that is not focused on narrowly defined 'women's issues,' but rather an interrelated set of topics including environmentalism, human rights, and anti-corporate activism. While discussions of third wave feminism have tended to limit themselves to the context of North American consumer culture—and have thus largely been identified with writers living in the US—these discussions can only have theoretical and practical value if they are set within the larger frames of globalisation and technoculture, and do not prioritise the US.

THE ECONOMICS AND DEMOGRAPHICS OF POST-BOOMER GENERATIONS IN THE US

The following are definitional criteria that delineate the economic and demographic determinants of a generational perspective, a perspective that influences critical strategies employed by women and men who identify as third wave feminists in the US. This perspective is not monolithic and it does not exclude persons of other generations, but most third wave feminists (although not all who identify as such) were born after the baby boom. Transnational capital, downsizing, privatisation, and a shift to a service economy have had a drastic impact on the world these generations have inherited.

The shift away from the public works philosophy of the Roosevelt years to the free market fundamentalism of the Reagan/Thatcher years clearly contextualises the third wave tendency to focus on individual narratives and to think of feminism as a form of individual empowerment. In collections such as Barbara Findlen's *Listen Up*, Rebecca Walker's *To Be Real*, Marcelle Karp and Debbie Stoller's *The* Bust *Guide to the New Girl Order*, and Ophira Edut's *Adios, Barbie*, third wave writers took the second wave feminist mantra of 'the personal is political' seriously, using their own experiences to help name and situate their own feminist views. This valuation of the personal as a theoretical mode has led to charges that the third wave is 'a youthful continuation of individualist, middle-class liberal feminism,' and that its preoccupation with popular culture and media images is 'not serious enough.' These charges misunderstand third wave work, which can be understood through an examination of how the lives of post-boomer women and men in the US have been impacted by economic globalisation and technoculture.

Gender-based wage and education gaps are closing, especially in younger age groups, and this relative gender equality has shaped third wave perspectives.

The 1994 US census provides evidence that the wage gap has closed to within five percent for women and men aged 20–24, and that more women now earn BA and MA degrees than do men. While women only make 78 cents overall for every dollar that men make, this varies widely depending on the group of women. The United States Department of Labor's report *Highlights of Women's Earnings in 2001* states that

> [t]he women's-to-men's earnings ration varies significantly by demographic group. Among blacks and Hispanics, for example, the ratios were about 87 and 88 percent, respectively, in 2001; for whites, the ratio was about 75 percent. Young women and men had fairly similar earnings; however, in the older age groups, women's earnings were much lower than men's.

However, gender inequality persists on the highest levels of the economic ladder. The article 'Women Relatively Scarce in Realms of Top Earners' makes the case that

> far more men are earning high salaries than women, with the gap narrowing only in the lowest income categories, according to a report in the *New York Times* on a study by the Internal Revenue Service. The IRS examined wages reported by employers in 1998 and found that 43,662 men had annual salaries of $1 million or more, while 3253 women had top earnings; a 13 to 1 ratio. Men outnumbered women 10 to 1 in the $500,000 to $1 million category, and 9 to 1 in the $250,000 to $500,000 range. The gap closed as salary range decreased, with women and men roughly equally represented in the $25,000 to $30,000 category.

This data reveals the feminisation of poverty. It also reveals a blind spot in standard feminist analysis of women's wages. According to the United States Congress Joint Committee on Taxation, 90 percent of American families make less than $100,000 a year, and, according to Bernie Sander, the annual income per person in the US is $28,553. This makes the $25,000–30,000 category—in which women's and men's wages are largely equal—very close to the national average. However, feminist analyses of these numbers often emphasise the fact that men comprise the vast majority of top wage earners, despite the fact that the majority of women are not 'topped' in this particular manner. For example, Rory Dicker and Alison Piepmeier refer to the data that '97.3 percent of top earners are men' to help make their valid point that there is still very much a need for feminism today. Yet, as is characteristic of much feminist work on the gender wage gap, they fail to mention the situation of men who are not 'top earners,' and the relatively equal wages of men and women at lower income levels. If feminist analysis is truly differentiated for class, it becomes clear that for the majority of American women, especially in post-boomer generations, there is more gender parity in terms of wages except for the richest ten percent of the population.

Even *Newsweek* has emphasised the fact that, increasingly, women earn more of the family income. Peg Tyre and Daniel McGinn note that women who make more money than men is 'a trend we had better get used to.' In 2001, in 30.7 percent of married households with a working wife, the wife's earnings exceeded the husband's. A 2002 report from the US Bureau of Labor Statistics indicated that women now make up 46.5 percent of the labour force. However, the highest debt-to-income ratio in history undermines real wages and the progress that many women have made. People coming of age after the baby-boom generation have attained middle-class status only with both women and men in the labour market working longer hours; setting up dual or multiple income homes; going into debt; postponing marriage and children; and/or having fewer children. In *Nickel and Dimed: On (Not) Getting By in America* (2001), Barbara Ehrenreich pointed out that, according to the Economic Policy Institute, the living wage for one adult and two children is $30,000 a year. But 60 percent of American workers earn less than the $14 hourly wage that this standard of living requires. The economic situation may look better in terms of gender equality, but in terms of overall economic well-being, the situation is worse for both women and men with the exception, again, of the very top wage earners.

Third wave feminist thinking, then, is informed by the fact that the majority of young Americans have experienced relative gender equality in the context of economic downward mobility. It has also been shaped by the social and ethnic diversity of post-boomer generations. According to the 2000 US census, non-Hispanic whites account for 73 percent of baby boomers and an even larger proportion of older Americans, but they account for only 64 percent of Generation Xers and 62 percent of the Millennial Generation (United States Census Bureau). These post-civil-rights generations were raised on a multicultural diet, and their attitudes about racial, cultural and sexual diversity have continued to be shaped by the increasing globalisation of entertainment and image-based industries, including the import of Asian cultural products such as anime and kung-fu films; the national dissemination of grassroots cultural practices like grunge, hip hop, and car culture; the increasing visibility of gays and lesbians in the media; and the normalisation of porn imagery.

The economic and demographic determinants of third wave feminist thinking can be catalogued as follows. First, women are *as* likely or *more* likely to identify with their generation as with their gender. Because post-boomer men and women have substantially narrowed the wage gap, because they are likely to occupy similar entry-level to mid-level positions in workplace power structures, and because these realities mean economic struggle, women now often have more in common with men of their own age group than they do with women of previous generations. Secondly, codes for 'good' and 'bad' as well as gender ideals are no longer polarised. This shapes the third wave's simultaneous endorsement and critique of media representations, particularly sexual imagery. It also shapes third wave cultural production. For example, various aspects of girlie culture use the humorous reappropriation of traditions and symbols to craft identities in the context of structural disempowerment, such as reclaiming words like girl, bitch, and cunt. This playful reappropriation of stereotypes is often interpreted as marking a lack of seriousness, but such play is a serious part of the third wave's critical negotiations with the culture industries. Thirdly, women and men of the third wave tend not to locate meaning and identity in one place, particularly not in a job or profession. Owing to corporate downsizing and the shift to the service sector that occurred just as the oldest post-boomers reached their full-time employment years, these generations cannot expect to spend their entire lives in one workplace accruing benefits and advancing over time. While women in this demographic expect to work, the satisfaction that work offers is most often diminished. As is necessary in a global economy and workforce, workers' identities tend to be flexible and multifaceted, even contradictory. Finally, worldwide globalisation has contributed to a further concentration of wealth at the very top of the pyramid, shifting venues of political struggle from patriarchy to the World Trade Organization. The 'enemy' has been decentralised. While feminist perspectives are still valuable in what Peggy Orenstein calls 'this era of half-change,' an economic and demographic analysis has shown that these perspectives cannot fully describe the lived conditions experienced by post-boomer generations.

Thus, it is clear that third wave feminists are not simply daughters rebelling for rebellion's sake. Third wave lives have been and will continue to be profoundly shaped by globalisation and the new economy it fosters. What is common to the diversity of third-wave thinking is a complicated legacy; the third wave is torn between the hope bequeathed by the successes of the civil rights movement and second wave feminism, and the hopelessness born of generational downward mobility and seemingly insurmountable social and political problems worldwide. Of necessity, the third wave locates activism in a broad field that includes the kinds of issues often called 'women's issues,' but that also encompasses environmentalism, anti-corporate activism, human rights issues, cultural production and the connections between these. In this era of half-change, when it is clear how global events intersect local lives, here is what the third wave knows: women's issues—and women activists—cannot and do not stand in isolation.

TECHNOCULTURE AND THIRD WAVE FEMINISM

Although third wave thinking can be understood in the context of post-boomer economics and demographics, it must be acknowledged that many women and men choose to identify with third wave feminist perspectives whether or not they are part of a post-boomer generation. The third wave, then, refers *both* to a feminist generation *and* to emerging forms of feminist activism. These uses of the term overlap but are not the same. They both, however, emphasise that feminism takes shape in relation to its time and place. As feminists of all generations craft responses to our current context of technoculture, new forms of activism are emerging. A discussion of feminism and technoculture demonstrates how feminist activism has shifted and why that shift cannot be wholly attributed to generational difference.

Jodi Dean describes technoculture as an economic-political-cultural formation characterised

> by the rise of networked communication [such as] the Internet, satellite broadcasting, and the global production and dissemination of motion pictures; by the consolidation of wealth in the hands of transnational corporations and the migration and immigration of people, technologies, and capital; [and] by the rise of a consumerist entertainment culture and the corresponding production of sites of impoverishment, violence, starvation, and death.

This is a familiar litany of the changes wrought by globalisation. However, Dean raises the question of individual rights, a concept that marks a fundamental contradiction in feminisms generally. Dean argues that 'technoculture is marked by the end of patriarchalism,' since the conditions of women's lives changed substantially in the last half of the twentieth century. Women now make up a substantial percentage of the paid global workforce, and although working conditions are often appalling, as major wage earners for their families they have increasingly had some modicum of control in relation to sexual partners, marriage, and childbearing. For many women, Dean suggests, the patriarchal family has become 'one option among an increasingly diversified set of living and working relations'. This is increasingly true of women in developing countries. According to Perdita Huston, the concept of individual rights contained within globalisation breaks down traditional notions of male superiority and privilege, thereby improving women's status. Further, globalisation has made it necessary for women to work as providers for their families, which improves women's status since the provider function is seen as most valuable.

This sets up a difficult dilemma. According to John Cavanaugh *et al.* in *Alternatives to Economic Globalization*, globalisation has radically contributed to the concentration of wealth and inequality in terms of income distribution to the extent that 475 people now have fully half the world's wealth, which impacts upon women, who are disproportionately poor. But globalisation has also brought about an erosion of the gendered division of labour that traditionally denied women opportunities for education and independence. This is a question that feminism must face: if individual rights come at the price of the negative aspects of globalisation, to what extent should that concept of rights define feminist praxis? This is complicated by the fact that, according to Dean, the twin tiers of globalisation and the end of the patriarchy are linked with a 'decline of symbolic efficiency'. This means that 'arguments and authorities that might be persuasive in one context may have no weight in another one, [and] the identity we perform in one setting might have little to do with the one we perform in another'.

There are three distinctions to be made here. First, the de-authorisation of patriarchy might be claimed as one of the victories of second-wave feminism, but because that de-authorisation is part of a larger breakdown of master narratives, second-wave feminism itself is understood by the third wave as offering perspectives that are persuasive or useful only in some contexts. Secondly, the third wave must negotiate the profound contradiction that the collapse of central authority in postmodern global capitalism, which has given women greater authority, visibility, and cultural importance, is the same collapse that reinforces 'the vigor of global capital'. There has been a shift from a top-down hierarchical culture of power to a power focused in multinational corporations and dependent upon global flows. In this context, power understood as possessed by individuals has become inaccessible to almost everybody, so second-wave feminism's promise to obtain more power for women is impossible. Thirdly, the decentralisation that has enabled some women in the First World to access education and better jobs, that has helped to narrow the wage gap, and that has facilitated the construction of empowered women as a consumer demographic, is the same decentralisation that supports globalisation and the inequities it creates between nations, as well as the environmental destruction it perpetuates. Consequently, women's increasing visibility within American culture may have given women greater cultural capital, but at the expense of developing countries and the environment, in a contracting national economy. Women have made gains at great cost and may not have gained much at all—bitter realities that can be glossed over through a narrow (and much more pleasurable) focus on the expanded possibilities for racial and sexual minorities in consumer culture—a focus that has tended to characterise third wave writing until recently. Neither is this focus irrelevant. Both cultural and economic dimensions must be taken into consideration simultaneously. As Michael Hardt and Antonio Negri note, a strictly economic analysis 'fails to recognize the *profound economic power of the cultural movements*, or really the increasing indistinguishability of economic and cultural phenomena' (emphasis in original).

Through its celebratory and critical engagement with consumer culture, the third wave attempts to navigate the fact that there are few alternatives for the construction of subjectivity outside the production/consumption cycle of global commodification. Cornel West asks how we can speak of the 'profound sense of psychological depression, personal worthlessness, and social despair so widespread' in black America, a question worth considering in relation to the situation of post-boomer generations more generally. Because the nihilism West invokes has been particularly attributed to 'the hip-hop generation,' rap music and hip-hop culture can be read as providing a powerful perspective on the economic and demographic determinants shaping post-boomer lives, and as expressing the complex emotions created by struggling to survive. In this view, it is also significant that second-wave feminists and members of the civil rights generation—all baby boomers—share a sometimes patronising concern over the state of the next generation. African American Generation X scholars such as

Mark Anthony Neal articulate the importance of generational difference in shaping worldview as well as artistic and activist strategies. The attraction of large segments of the contemporary youth market to rap music and hip-hop culture cannot be merely understood as a pathological interest in violence or a 'White Negro' appropriation of black male cultural expression. It also indicates a strong post-boomer identification with rap's harsh representation of economic struggle and its obsessive fantasies of economic success. These identifications occur because young women and men of all races have come of age in a contracting economy. It is interesting, then, that the primary third wave feminist texts have tended to avoid the kinds of harsh economic truths found in rap, instead favouring stories of successful sex-gender rebellion and emphasising the pleasures of girl-culture consumption enroute to cultural critique.

However, as third wave feminists grow up and out of youth culture, having come of age through claiming power, the problems created and perpetuated by technoculture must be addressed. As Dean puts it, 'if this is post-patriarchy, something is definitely missing'. A paradox for the third wave is that this 'something' is missing when it seems like alternative images are part of dominant culture like never before. Multicultural fashion models, images of female athletes like Mia Hamm and Marion Jones, the commodified male body, lesbian chic—as corporate America searched for new markets in the 1990s, difference was glorified and on display. But in this brave new world of niche marketing, everyone is valued as a potential consumer, and no one is valued intrinsically. What looked like progress was a fundamental incorporation into the global machine. As Naomi Klein points out in *No Logo*, a documentation of the rise of anti-corporate activism, 'for the media activists who had, at one point not so long ago, believed that better media representation would make for a more just world, one thing had become abundantly clear: identity politics weren't fighting the system, or even subverting it. When it came to the vast new industry of corporate branding, they were feeding it'. Third wave approaches to activism, and the third wave suspicion of traditional forms of activism, have been forged in this crucible of empowerment and exploitation. Australian third wave feminist Anita Harris argues that young women's alternative ways of conducting political organisation, protest, debate, and agitation have been shaped in response to

> the co-optation of left politics as merely a marketable style ... The trend towards an increased surveillance of youth, the re-discovery of young women in particular as the new consumers, and the cultural fascination with girlhood, have all resulted in a deep suspicion of overt activism as the best method for protest and the creation of social change.

As such, the third wave is a movement committed to local action and characterised by dispersal and diversity, as opposed to a single-leader and single-issue movement, a strategy that resists co-optation and supports survival in global technoculture. Committed to cultural production as activism, and cognizant that it is impossible for most Americans to wholly exit consumer culture, third wave feminists both use and resist the mainstream media and create their own media sites and networks, both of which are key components of successful activism in technoculture. As Harris argues, 'these new practices of resistance respond to corporate concentration with a maze of fragmentation, to globalization with its own kind of localization, to power consolidation with radical power dispersal'.

As socialist feminists have long argued, feminism is an integral part of larger social justice struggles that are framed by global capitalism. The hip-hop phrase 'It's all about the Benjamins' titles this chapter because it signals that the global markets that have made difference visible only value difference for its carriers' ability to consume. This has necessitated the reconceptualisation of 'feminism as a movement to end all forms of oppression'. Therefore, anti-corporate activism like the 1999 Seattle protests has of necessity become part of feminism's focus, which makes feminism as a movement less visible than it once was—less visible and more widely dispersed simultaneously, part of multiple social struggles. To think about third wave feminism globally is to understand that 'young feminist membership is much larger than may be initially imagined, and ... is concerned with a feminism beyond merely claiming girls' power'. Feminism has become part of a global struggle for human rights that incorporates women's and gender issues. Third wave theory is a theory broad enough to account for various axes of difference and to recognise multiple forms of feminist work, including environmentalism, anti-corporate activism, and struggles for human rights. While gender play and cultural production are important parts of a third wave approach to feminist action, they are only one part of the third wave and they take place in only one site. Third wave perspectives recognise these forms of activism and place them alongside many other kinds of work....

33. Winifred Woodhull, "Global Feminisms, Transnational Political Economies, Third World Cultural Production," from *Third Wave Feminism: A Critical Exploration*

Excerpts from Winifred Woodhull, "Global Feminisms," published in Stacy Gillis, Gillian Howie, and Rebecca Munford, eds., *Third Wave Feminism: A Critical Exploration* (London: Palgrave, 2004), 252–260. Reprinted with permission.

In this article, Woodhull argues that in an age of globalization, third-wave feminism must be "conceived and enacted in global terms." Especially because third-wave feminism emerged in an era of "information technology and transnational finance ... deindustrialization, corporate downsizing, and underemployment" in which "postindustrial Western countries [were able to] dominate the rest of the world more effectively than before," Woodhull argues that "thinking through the mutually constitutive relations between Western feminism and feminism in other parts of the world should be key issues for twenty-first-century feminists of this 'new wave.'" Third-wave feminism must necessarily go beyond a focus on problems faced by women in the Western world to a focus on how these issues are directly connected to the problems faced by women elsewhere, and how the growing gap between the rich and poor undermines all but the most privileged women.

THIRD WAVE FEMINISM AND THE WIDER WORLD

Third wave feminism claims—rightly so—that new modalities of feminism must be invented for the new millennium. But is it enough to generate new conceptions of feminism and new forms of activism that pertain almost exclusively to people in wealthy countries, as the third wave has generally done so far? This chapter will argue that in an increasingly globalised context, it is crucial that feminism be conceived and enacted in global terms and that Western feminists engage with women's movements the world over. Feminism's third wave emerged in the late 1980s and early 1990s when information technology and transnational finance became the most powerful economic forces in the postindustrial Western countries, enabling those nations to dominate the rest of the world more effectively than ever before. Two aspects of this development fundamentally shaped Western feminism of the 1990s: the erosion of the Left's long-standing bases for political solidarity with the Third World; and the growing importance of information technologies in mobilising feminist political constituencies as well as linking women with common interests and concerns, and thus creating new forms of community. Owing to the deindustrialisation in the 1980s, this period was characterised by corporate downsizing, underemployment, and high unemployment, especially in Europe. Western democracies were failing to fulfill their post-World War II promise to provide a decent life to all members of their societies. Economic recession intensified racial strife and fuelled xenophobia directed at two groups of Third World peoples labourers who 'accepted' grossly exploitative wages and working conditions in the industrial plants that relocated overseas, and non-European immigrants in Europe and the US who were employed mainly in low-wage itinerant positions ('stealing our jobs'). Immigrants and 'foreign' labour, however, were not the only scapegoats in an economic shift that resulted in the collapse of the relatively stable and favourable terms of employment that had prevailed in the West since World War II. Women, too, became targets, for as employment prospects disappeared along with a living wage, angry white men in the 'Moral Majority' charged women not only with 'stealing our jobs' but also with abandoning their husbands and children in their selfish pursuit of their own goals, and thus undermining the bedrock of social stability: the patriarchal nuclear family. A powerful anti-feminist backlash eventually prompted both mainstream and extreme right-wing media pundits to declare the demise of feminism.

In the face of these developments, a key mandate of third wave feminism was to prove that feminism was alive and well. The most comprehensive reflections on third wave feminism that appeared in the US—Leslie Heywood and Jennifer Drake's *Third Wave Agenda*, Jacqueline N. Zita's special issue of *Hypatia*, and Rory Dicker and Alison Piepmeier's *Catching a Wave*—attest to feminism's capacity to adapt to historical change and to confront the issues currently affecting women and others subject to sexual domination and harassment. Other modes of expression by 'third wavers' showed that feminism was not only adapting in the 1990s but was assuming vibrant new forms, not least by renewing its efforts to move beyond the walls of the academy into arenas of everyday life. In the overlapping realms of culture and activism, there was a particularly striking manifestation of the third wave's determination and inventiveness in the concerts of the Riot Grrrl musicians. The Riot Grrrls tied their 'in-your-face feminism' to assertions of their own desires and pleasures as well as to grassroots political movements against racism and class exploitation ... The Riot Grrrls railed against the corporate power that was invading every realm of experience in order to commodify it and capitalise on it. Corporations, they said, were co-opting expressions of opposition to the status quo in order to neutralise their subversive potential and, at the same time, to profit financially from their popular appeal, as with the Spice Girls.

The Riot Grrrls continue to attract huge audiences and to generate a broad base of fans not only in North America and Europe but in venues such as Jakarta. Their activism is one of the most potent expressions of third wave feminism. Yet despite their engagement in real-world conflicts and their international appeal, the Riot Grrrls' politics focus on the situation of women in the global North. In this respect, they are typical of third wavers, who appear to have forgotten second wave feminism's roots not only in the US Civil Rights Movement but also in Third World liberation movements as well, in which radical feminists of the 1960s and 1970s considered their own struggles to be inextricably implicated. In those decades, there was an acute consciousness of radical feminism's links to Gandhi's non-violent resistance to British domination, Vietnam's anti-imperialist struggle against the US, and Algeria's anticolonial war against France, whose sexual torture of female freedom fighters like Djamila Boupacha was publicly denounced by Simone de Beauvoir and other French feminists. The awareness of these links seems to have faded, despite the third wave's emergence in tandem with the processes of globalisation. Globalisation involves the globally binding technologies of satellite communications and the Internet as well as other *potentially* democratising technologies such as video and CDs, fax machines and cell phones, alternative radio and cable television. Given the global arena in which third wave feminism emerged, it is disappointing that new feminist debates arising in the first-world contexts mainly address issues that pertain only to women *in* those contexts, as if the parochialism and xenophobia of the economically depressed 1980s were still hanging over feminism like a dark cloud.

At their best, third wave feminists attend to issues of race and class as they shape the politics of gender and sexuality in the global North—hence the myriad community groups, websites, zines, and scholarly publications devoted to economic inequality and the gender struggles of minority women in North America and Europe. Not surprisingly, many third wave feminist websites promote women's empowerment in and through computer technologies. The latter include sites such as DigitalEve and Webgrrrls International: The Women's Tech Knowledge Connection which celebrate women's involvement in the field of information technology and encourage all women to make use of it in any way that may be helpful to them and to feminist causes. Symptomatically, however, most of these sites either unabashedly promote capitalist self-advancement in the name of feminism or else mistakenly assume that their sincere appeal to feminist action, self help, and solidarity really addresses a worldwide audience. For example, Girl Incorporated, which 'designs Web sites and online marketing strategies that make sense,' passes itself off as feminist simply by virtue of being a women's business that markets to women in business. DigitalEve, on the other hand, which is feminist in a more meaningful sense insofar as it aims to broaden women's access to a masculinist domain and to put information technology in the service of feminism, characterises itself as a 'global' organization—by which it means that it has chapters in the US, Canada, the UK, and Japan. Thus it seems that in third wave (cyber)feminism, the First World, perhaps unwittingly, is synecdochally the whole world. At their worst, third wavers use new technologies, as well as more traditional ones such as the print media, to proffer glib commentaries about the supposed 'elitism' of second wave feminism. Throwing out the baby with the bath water, they summarily dismiss intellectuals' hard-to-read reflections on the politics of feminism ostensibly with a view towards making feminism less intimidating and more widely accessible. In the process, many of the most audible third wavers depoliticise feminism altogether. In a web interview, the co-author of the well-known third wave *Manifesta*, Jennifer Baumgardner, opines, for instance: 'Name an issue, if that's what you're interested in, then it's the most important whether it's eating disorder, sexual harassment, child care, etc.... Feminism is something individual to each feminist.' This is consumerism, not politics.

My analysis of this dynamic might risk the charge of elitism from those third wavers who applaud the accessibility of pleasure-affirming work and who see established feminist academics and their theories as oppressive and exclusionary. Nevertheless, it must be acknowledged that political theory plays a crucial role in feminist politics; that it plays as crucial a role in the analysis of popular cultural forms as it does in the analysis of elite ones; and that it is unhelpful to oppose theory to activism (or to personal needs and interests), as if the one were ethereal and the other real. Only theory can enable us to distinguish, for example, between meaningful modes of participatory democracy made possible by mass communication. Similarly, only theory can allow us to grasp, for example, the political implications of mass-mediated representations of gender, sexuality, and power ... or the new sexualities, pleasures, and forms of embodiment that are coming into being through human interaction in the new media.... Pleasure is an issue for the third wave, but it is certainly not a simple one: theory can cast light on the subjective processes, bodily experiences and social bonds that generate pleasures and assign value to them. It can also promote an understanding of the links between Western women's pleasurable play with affordable fashions in clothing and make-up, and the sweatshops in which Third World women and immigrants labour to produce those sources of middle-class (and largely white) enjoyment. Finally, only theory can enable us to grasp how the relation between elite and popular culture has been radically reconfigured in recent decades by global media networks. As Peter Waterman points out, the publishing industry that disseminates elite literature and scholarship 'can hardly be isolated from the more general electronic information, media, and advertising conglomerates into which publishing is increasingly integrated.' Theories of the political economy of global media are especially important for third wave feminism, since it is so heavily invested in mass-mediated forms of political affiliation, feminist solidarity, and pleasurable, politically engaged subjectivity. The crucial role of theory *in* and *as* politics, as well as the importance of thinking through the mutually constitutive relations between Western feminisms and feminisms in other parts of the world, should be key issues for twenty-first-century feminists of this new 'wave.'

THE TRANSNATIONAL/COSMOPOLITAN PUBLIC SPHERE AND GLOBAL FORMS OF CITIZENSHIP

For more than a decade, scholars in the humanities and social sciences have been investigating the globalisation process with the purpose of determining the extent to which it fosters the development of a transnational public sphere and global forms of citizenship. A transnational public sphere is considered to be important because it is rooted in civil society, that is a social space that is controlled neither by the market nor by national governments, and that promotes a sense of involvement with the affairs of other unknown, nonkin citizens. As flows of capital and labour alter national and ethnic landscapes worldwide, and as global media networks facilitate new forms of rapid communication, it becomes conceivable that a transnational public sphere could be expanded to include parts of the Third World (and for that matter the First World) that have so far been excluded, resulting in new freedoms for many people. Of course fundamental questions remain regarding the possibility that the mere existence of electronic linkages could guarantee meaningful political participation for ordinary citizens, and that new public 'spaces' would work to the benefit of women, ethnic and religious minorities, and others who have traditionally been excluded from effective involvement in the public sphere: '[i]n situations in which there is (as yet?) no civil society, can transnational news media, exile publishing, and the Internet really help in the creation of such a space?' Despite these basic questions, the possibility of a transnational public sphere that empowers the disenfranchised is an enticing prospect. The counterpart of a transnational public sphere is global citizenship, which involves both deepening democracy and expanding it on a global scale, so that 'issues such as peace, development, the environment, and human rights assume a global character.' Indispensable elements in global citizenship include inter governmental politics (as in the UN), international solidarity movements independent media, and grassroots democracy. In addition, cultural expression is crucial since it alone encourages sensuous and affective investment in social arrangements, both real and imagined. As such, it has greater power to generate progressive change and sustain egalitarian relationships than do rational calculations of shared interest.

For example, given the scattering of African writers and intellectuals across the globe, as well as new modes of political and cultural expression that bear witness to the sweeping economic and social changes of the past 20 years, it is important to consider the political activism and cultural production of African feminists in a global frame. To adopt a global frame surely means taking into account, as all Third World feminists are obliged to do, the neo-liberal economic forces driving globalisation, a process characterised by cross-border flows of finance capital and commodities, as well as by unprecedented migrations of cultures, ideas, and people, the majority of them poor labourers or refugees. It means taking seriously the repressive effects of that process, which stem from the operations of exploitative multinational corporations and transnational institutions such as the World Bank and the IMF, as well as the power plays of the world's wealthiest nation states, the US being at the top of the pyramid of those that call the political shots on the international stage at the same time as exercising daunting control over flows of information and culture through vast media networks spanning the entire planet. Finally, adopting a global frame suggests examining the ways in which feminist projects the world over are inevitably being shaped by the growing disparities of wealth, power, and well being not only between the North and the South, but between the rich and the poor in both those arenas.

Yet while it acknowledges the harm inflicted by globalisation, the interpretive frame I propose considers its potentially liberatory dimensions as well. David Rodowick defines the media state as 'a virtual information territory' which, in conjunction with the 'deterritorialized transnational communities' spawned by hegemonic forces, produces a 'cosmopolitan public sphere'—another term for the transnational public sphere. This new public sphere is said to be capable of fostering innovative forms of political activism despite its genesis by the very communication technologies and migratory flows that make possible state-of-the-art modes of domination. A transnational space fraught with contradiction, it is noticeably eroding the traditional functions of the state, sometimes in progressive ways. Echoing many earlier theorists of globalisation, Rodowick argues that one dimension of this space concerns the transnational concept of human rights, which is increasingly being defended on the ground by interstate and non-governmental organisations in situations where states fail to protect the rights of their citizens. He demonstrates too that, like human rights, citizenship is now a concept that is meaningful and effective beyond the frontiers of individual nation states. Owing in part to the communication networks linking individuals and communities in different parts of the world, growing numbers of citizens are in a position to put direct democracy into practice with respect to 'issues that are increasingly global and local at the same time.'

The other dimension of the cosmopolitan public sphere is 'defined by the global reach of electronic communication and entertainment networks.' While global media forms may themselves elude state regulation and restrict both the content and the dissemination of information in ways that undermine democracy the world over, they are not monolithic; rather 'they are heterogeneous and contradictory with respect to their source (print, film, television, video, radio, and the varieties of computer-mediated communication) and to modes of reception.' Media conglomerates create networks (e.g., satellite communications, cellular phones, and the Internet), the velocity and global range of which offer myriad possibilities for political intervention on the part of activists operating independently of repressive states. They provide technological resources that can be taken up by alternative media and channelled into new circuits. Once they have been 'recontextualised in *inunigré* and activist communities', they can help to generate new modes of identification and forms of collective action that are consonant with democratic politics worldwide.

AFRICAN FEMINISM IN THE WIDER WORLD: WOMEN'S RIGHTS/HUMAN RIGHTS

How is African feminism conceived and enacted in global terms? How is the concept of human rights being defended by the most democratic, independent African nongovernmental organisations in the transnational public sphere that is being created by progressive users of global media networks? How do these efforts affect African women? There are multiple examples: in Algeria, which has been in a violent civil war since 1991, feminists of the older generation—notably Khalida Messaoudi—continue to defend women's rights, legitimising and strengthening local grassroots movements through reference to the UN Convention to Eliminate Discrimination Against Women. Messaoudi's democratic activism on the world stage works for oppressed citizens in the name of human rights, independently of control by any state; as such it implicitly contests the presumption of wealthy countries to embody democracy and to define it for the rest of the world, even as the US and other first-world powers impose economic policies that undermine democratic forces in countless venues across the globe. Another example of a genuinely progressive African NGO defending human rights as a transnational concept is the group Women in Nigeria (WIN). The WIN collective is a grassroots African feminist organisation, one that sees women's liberation as inextricably linked to the liberation of poor urban workers and peasants in Nigeria, and that aims to 'merge the concern for gender equality into popular democratic struggles.' WIN works actively, through direct democracy in its own activities and through 'conscientisation,' to overcome hierarchies and conflicts not only of gender and class but also of language, region, ethnicity, and religion in its promotion of all Nigerian women's interests.

Women in Nigeria necessarily focuses much of its effort on dealing with the socioeconomic fallout of IMF- and World Bank-inspired structural adjustment policies (SAPs) imposed in Nigeria, as well as in much of the rest of sub-Saharan Africa since the late 1970s. These policies, which are intended to stabilise economies in order to make them attractive to lenders and foreign investors, require governments of poor nations to ensure that their people produce mainly for export, which often has the effect of requiring that most consumer goods be imported and purchased at inflated prices. Moreover, in the name of an 'open economy,' price controls and protective tariffs are abolished, with the result that local small- and medium-sized businesses are forced to fight a losing battle against multinational giants. Finally, in order to direct all possible elements in a nation's economy towards servicing the debt, the SAPs also impose radical reductions in public spending, which may cover everything from roads and transportation that do not directly serve foreign investors, to civil service jobs and pensions, as well as education, health, and other social services.

Ayesha M. Imam demonstrates that since the SAPs have been in place in Nigeria, the macroeconomic effects have been devastating. The rate of growth of the GDP has fallen precipitously (7.9 per cent in 1990 to 4.3 per cent in 1991); the value of the local currency, the Naira, has fallen dramatically against the US dollar, and the external debt has increased exponentially. At the social level, the effects of SAPs have been almost uniformly negative, with a general decrease in the standard of living and purchasing power. Contributing factors are growing unemployment, wage freezes, and delays of several months in payment of wages and/or benefits, if payments are made at all. As employment shrinks in the public sector, there is increasing pressure on the informal economy, which translates into greater competition and lower returns on labour there. Other factors include staggering levels of inflation and the effects of the cuts in social services, which disproportionately affect women and children. There have been marked decreases in the number of girls attending school at all levels, marked increases in infant mortality, and alarming increases in the numbers of people infected with HIV and AIDS. For feminist groups like WIN, a key concern in all of this is the dramatic increase in rape and domestic violence that has resulted from the combination of rising economic hardship, declining opportunities for meaningful political action, a burgeoning of misogynist fundamentalisms of all kinds, and the fact that in many African cultures, woman-beating is seen as the right of husbands and male relatives.

Unfortunately, the situation in Nigeria—the terrible effects of the SAPs, the repressive government, official and unofficial violence against women—exists, in various forms, all over sub-Saharan Africa. And while democratic and feminist NGOs *are* doing invaluable work in the defence of human rights in both national and international arenas, I am sceptical not so much about the liberatory *potential* of the transnational public sphere and grassroots democratic politics in Africa, but about their liberatory effectiveness in the here and now. As Imam points out, already in the mid-1990s, the SAPs had taken such a toll that it was almost impossible for WIN to raise funds for its operations by selling books and T-shirts, as it had done in the past, as a means of resisting state control and state appropriation. It could no longer even rely on donated meeting space because the economic crisis was so acute. In order to support its 'projects, campaigns, research, meetings, and publishing activities,' it was increasingly relying on grants from external sources. And while its policy in the mid-1990s was to accept outside funding only for projects that WIN had designed independently, it is hard to imagine that the organisation has been able to remain as autonomous as it once was.

CONCLUSIONS

Nigerian feminists have, since the late 1990s, expanded their means of political organising to include email networks and websites. Yet even as we take seriously the possibilities opened up by the newest forms of mass communication, we would do well to explore the ways in which groups like WIN might benefit, or do benefit, from more established media networks such as the forms of piracy that enable Africans to circulate videos outside official channels, with row after row of subtitles in Wolof, Arabic, and other African Languages. WIN has reported some success in using popular theatre for consciousness raising; could it also make use of mass-circulated popular cultural forms such as romance novels, as writers and publishers are doing in Nigeria and Ivory Coast? Could other African feminist organisations adjust the romance formulas to appeal to particular ethnic or national audiences, drawing on local traditions that provide a point of entry for raising questions about the gender politics of intimate relationships, work, and cosmopolitan modes of identification? Could they do so in a critical way that does more than to market print commodities profitably? We must also continue to give due attention to the ways in which older forms of cultural production, such as 'elite' literature, still enjoy considerable prestige and the power to shape people's thinking in many parts of the world, including Africa. However 'elite' it may be, a good deal of the literature published by well-known African writers since the mid- 1990s takes up many of the same issues that concern activist groups, such as the WIN collective. That is, the writings of Buchi Emecheta (Nigeria/UK), Lília Momplé (Mozambique), Nuruddin Farah (Somalia/UK), Nadine Gordimer (South Africa), and many others address the ways in which today's global economies adversely affect Africa. They promote feminist and other grassroots democratic struggles while enjoining readers to imagine and embrace new forms of political subjectivity. The questions concerning the accessibility and political effectiveness of these different modes of communication, within the transnational public sphere, are pressing ones: not just for Africans and Africanists, but for everyone if indeed we live in a globalised world. The larger issue is that reflections on the emancipatory possibilities of both the new and traditional media need to incorporate a serious consideration of the parts of the world that are not wealthy, that is most of the world. This issue is especially acute for third wave feminism, since the latter is defined by the historical moment of its emergence, a moment of unprecedented interrelation between the local and the global, and between the West and 'the rest.'

PART III

Resisting Culture

The documents in this section examine how third-wave feminism has made resistance to dominant cultural ideals a big part of its activism, from resistant performances in music to the production of zines, comics, and books that use terms such as "bitch" and "slut" against themselves to the use of the Internet to create positive spaces for third-wave activism and identity.

34. Ednie Kaeh Garrison, "U.S. Feminism—Grrrl Style! Youth (Sub)Cultures and the Technologies of the Third Wave," from *Feminist Studies*

Excerpts from Ednie Kaeh Garrison, "U.S. Feminism—Grrrl Style! Youth (Sub)cultures and the Technologies of the Third Wave," *Feminist Studies* 26(1) (2000): 141–170, by permission of the publisher, Feminist Studies, Inc.

A seminal account of Riot Grrrl and the third-wave feminist subcultures that sprung up around it, in this influential essay Garrison explores the way third-wave feminism takes shape in cultural activism. The essay articulates a convincing framework for understanding third-wave feminism and some of its methodologies, aspirations, and ideals.

"Grrrl," a word coined by Bikini Kill singer and activist Kathleen Hanna, is a spontaneous young-feminist reclamation of the word "girl." It has proud analogies among many groups of women; in fact, "grrrl" was at least partially derived from a phrase of encouragement popularized by young American black women in the late 1980s: "You go, guuuurlll!" As we all know, when it is not being used to describe a woman under sixteen, the word "girl" often takes on pejorative, infantilizing overtones, suggesting silliness, weakness or insubstantiality.

"Grrrl" puts the growl back in our pussycat throats. "Grrrl" is intended to recall the naughty, confident and curious ten-year-olds we were before society made it clear it was time to stop being loud and playing with boys and concentrate on learning "to girl".... Riot Grrrl is a

> loosely affiliated group of young, generally punkish, take-no-prisoners feminists who publish zines, play in bands, make art, produce radio shows, maintain mailing lists, create Websites and sometimes just get together and talk about our lives and being women in contemporary society. . . .
>
> We chose the title *Surfergrrrls* as a counter to the "nice girls don't hack around with computers" message that society (still!) sends out, despite the educational system's extensive lip service to getting girls involved with math and science. *Surfergrrrls* also acknowledges the great grrrl/girl presence already on the Net, from Stephanie Brail's *Digital Amazons* and Aliza Sherman's *Cybergrrl Website* to the searchable feminist database *Femina* and the Web zines *Foxy* and *Fat Girl.*
>
> —From *Surfergrrrls: Look Ethel! An Internet Guide for Us,* by Laurel Gilbert and Crystal Kile, 1996

I've opened with this lengthy passage from Laurel Gilbert and Crystal Kile's book because it suggests something of the contemporary milieu that creates the cultural geography of the Third Wave. By cultural geography I mean the material, political, social, ideological, and discursive landscapes that constitute the context, base, or environment of Third Wave feminism: Young women who come to feminist consciousness in the United States in the late twentieth century (from the mid-1980s to the present) haven't gone through Second Wave feminism themselves. Rather, they experience and are affected by it in historicized, narrativized form. As something other than "Second Wave," the "Third Wave" can be defined by a different set of historical events and ideological movements, especially the (fundamentalist, Moral Majority, neoconservative, Focus on the Family, antifeminist) backlash that emerged in response to the women's movement in the 1970s and so-called postfeminist feminism. As part of a larger project explaining why the name "Third Wave feminism" is so attractive to myself and others, this article considers specifically the role of democratized technologies, the media, subcultural movements and networks, and differential oppositional consciousness in the formation of feminist consciousness among young women in the historical/cultural milieu of the United States in the 1990s.

Like Gilbert and Kile, I am compelled by the many different invocations possible with the word "grrrl" and appreciate their spirited appropriation and contextualization of the term. Yet my purpose is not to extend their elaborations so much as to note the rhetorical play of signified and signifier as a discursive device in young women's cultural tool kits. I then turn my attention to the subject of the third paragraph: Riot Grrrl. Riot Grrrl is a recent young feminist (sub)cultural movement that combines feminist consciousness and punk aesthetics, politics, and style. Recognizing youth (sub)cultures as political spaces and refusing to separate political consciousness from subcultural formations, I argue that the convergence of music, print, and information technologies, the historical specificities of backlash and post-civil rights movements, and feminist consciousness raising multiplies the cultural locations where political activities can occur in the Third Wave. I focus here on Riot Grrrl because it has been viewed by many who study U.S. girls'/young women's cultures as exemplary of what's being called "youth feminism." And, although I do not think Riot Grrrl is the quintessential example of "youth feminism," or "Third Wave feminism," or that the two are synonymous, I do believe there is a lot of value in studying them.

Riot Grrrl is an alternative subculture built around opposition to presuppositions that young (usually white) U.S. girls and women are too preoccupied with themselves and boys to be interested in being political, creative, and loud. The tensions between this expectation and the political desires of members offers a powerful opportunity to learn different ways of resisting in a consumer-oriented culture. For more and more subcultures (youth or otherwise), the ability to intertwine politics and style is a risky and necessary tactic in a cultural-historical period marked by "the logic of late capitalism" in which the commodification of resistance is a hegemonic strategy. The hybrid political texts and distribution networks produced by feminists like Riot Grrrls are significant in the formation of Third Wave movement cultures; they are both "popular" and subcultural, they provide spaces for youth-controlled conversations, and they can operate as an interface between different Third Wave cohorts (they connect Riot Grrrls to one another but also to other feminists and women). How do young women in the United States claim feminist agency for themselves and each other by making use of a historically situated repertoire of cultural objects and images, codes, and signs in self-consciously political ways?

Some of the tools that constitute this repertoire include print and visual media; music genres, technologies, and cultures; girl-positive and woman-positive expressions; revolutionary and social justice discourses; shock tactics; nonviolent actions; and the Internet. I use the word "repertoire" following Ruth Frankenberg to recognize all these objects and practices as parts of the "tool kit" available to cultural subjects as instruments and objects that provide a context and space for analysis and reflection. "Tool kit" is also the image invoked by Ann Swidler to describe "culture" as the "habits, skills, and styles from which people construct 'strategies of action,'" as an alternative to traditional sociological and anthropological understandings of "culture" as providing "the ultimate values" that motivate action. This repertoire is utilized by Third Wave feminists to raise consciousness about, provide political commentary on, and resist and educate against racism, child abuse, rape, domestic violence, homophobia and heterosexism, ablism, fatism, environmental degradation, classism, the protection of healthcare rights, reproductive rights, and equity. It is a tool kit designed for providing access to and transformations of traditionally masculinist cultural institutions. The larger project from which this article is drawn attempts to examine, theorize, and provide some practical suggestions for comprehending and developing this kind of transformative tool kit.

In this article, I concentrate on some of the ways young, mostly white, and middle-class women in the United States use and manipulate the repertoire of cultural-technological spaces and activities such as feminism and punk so they can voice their dissonances and participate in making change. I consider how these young women make use of low-end—or "democratized"—technologies and alternative media to produce hybrid political texts such as zines and music through which they disseminate knowledge and information about subjects such as (but not limited to) feminism in local-national distribution networks. I do not assume that activists in the Second Wave didn't also use grassroots forms of communications technologies but, rather, argue here that the Third Wave has a different relationship with these technologies. Not only is there a difference in quality (copiers are not *quite* the same as mimeograph machines), but we also have a distinctly symbiotic—an interfaced—connection to technology. As Donna Haraway has suggested: "The machine is us, our processes, an aspect of our embodiment." This blurring of the boundaries between humans and machines constructs a technologics through which we shuttle back and forth constantly, disrupting "the maze of dualisms [through] which we have explained our bodies and our tools to ourselves."

A NOTE ON THE PRESUMPTION THAT "THIRD WAVE" DESIGNATES AN AGE-GENERATION COHORT

This article does focus on young women in the Third Wave; however, I have specific reasons for not believing it is restricted to an age cohort. As a product of a particular cultural moment, "Third Wave feminism" is historically situated or bound. The name "Third Wave" acknowledges that feminism has changed substantially in the late-capitalist and postmodern world but still references a longer movement history. Although frequently used to categorize a generational cohort—those who "came of age" during or after the height of the Second Wave—I believe the question of who counts as the Third Wave is much more complicated and layered; there are important differences between historical specificity and generational specificity. The "third" is the mark of historical specificity, and like the marker "second" in the Second Wave, it is not simply a sign of generational descendence. When we automatically assume "third" refers to a specific generation, we actually erase the significant presence and contributions of many overlapping and multiple cohorts who count as feminists, and more particularly, of those who can count as Third Wave feminists. Further, "Third Wave feminism" resonates in different ways for different people; for young women the resonances may be particularly strong because our historical consciousness is very much attached to the same historical conditions out of which Third Wave feminism surfaces and takes shape. And because many generational and age cohorts share this historical moment, to limit a Third Wave to "young women" alone suggests that no other feminists can claim Third Wave politics. Even more importantly, the emergence of a "Third Wave" owes a great deal to critiques of the homogenization of the category "women" articulated most directly in the political and intellectual work by radical women of color, poor women, and lesbians dating from at least the Second Wave. Their opposition to the perceived dominance of white feminism in the Second Wave is linked to critiques of racism, classism, and heterosexism within the 1960s and 1970s women's movement as well as in other groups, movements, and social formations. It is clear now that feminist critiques of feminism are part of the very origins of Third Wave feminism rather than trailing behind an already unitary model of the movement.

The shift from speaking about "women" as a unified subject to a recognition that women are not all the same, nor should they be, is something most feminists, young and not as young, take for granted in the 1990s. This isn't to say the issue of difference has been solved, but difference is a core component of Third Wave consciousness. Chela Sandoval—theorizing what she calls "U.S. Third World Feminism"—reminds us that there are still racial divides but also new possible racial coalitions within contemporary women's movements. I am not suggesting an easy or homologous correlation between "U.S. Third World Feminism" and "Third Wave feminism." Sandoval uses the former term to refer to feminists of color who problematize the gender category "women" and the binary "male/female," and for whom race, culture, class, and sexuality are not social categories separable from or less significant than gender. She names a particular constituency as well as a hoped-for coalition. Although I have encountered repeated slippages between "U.S. Third World," "Third World," and "Third Wave" in many conversations about Third Wave feminism, the distinctions are important and at no time do I want to either collapse or confuse these terms.

POSTMODERNITY, OPPOSITIONAL CONSCIOUSNESS, AND FEMINIST NETWORKING

> I prefer a network ideological image, suggesting the profusion of spaces and identities and the permeability of boundaries in the personal body and in the body politic. "Networking" is both a feminist practice and a multinational corporate strategy—weaving is for oppositional cyborgs.
>
> —Donna Haraway, "A Cyborg Manifesto," 1991

> The praxis of U.S. third world feminism represented by the differential form of oppositional consciousness is threaded throughout the experience of social marginality. As such it is also being woven into the fabric of experiences belonging to more and more citizens who are caught in the crisis of late capitalist conditions and expressed in the cultural angst most often referred to as the post-modern dilemma. The juncture I am proposing, therefore, is extreme. It is a location wherein the praxis of U.S. third world feminism links with the aims of white feminism, studies of race, ethnicity, and marginality, and with postmodern theories of culture as they crosscut and join together in new

> relationships through a shared comprehension of an emerging theory and method of oppositional consciousness.
>
> —Chela Sandoval, "U.S. Third World Feminism," 1991.

Images of weaving or threading together apparently disparate modes of consciousness, constituencies, ideologies, and practices tie these two passages to one another and suggest a relationship between the concept of networking advocated by Haraway and the kind of junctures Sandoval advocates as a mode of resistance necessary in our particular historical and political moment. To see and recognize such forms of resistance we often have to look "into the fabric of experiences" outside, beyond, and maybe even underneath the places that we are told have mattered. Kathleen Hanna, lead singer of Bikini Kill, intimately familiar with domestic violence, and an ex-stripper, writes: "Resistance is everywhere, it always has been and always will be. Just because someone is not resisting in the same way you are (being a vegan, an 'out' lesbian, a political organizer) does not mean they are not resisting. Being told you are a worthless piece of shit and not believing it is a form of resistance." Hanna goes on to list some other examples that challenge conventional (and hence "recognizable") forms of resistance....

... According to Sandoval, differential oppositional consciousness is a mode of "ideology-praxis" rooted in the experiences of U.S. Third World feminists. Modernist conceptions of oppositional politics center on mutually exclusive and essentialized identities. This ideology is perpetuated, she argues, by white feminists who construct histories of the Second Wave as consisting of four distinct categories: liberal, Marxist, radical, and socialist. In contrast, the differential mode of consciousness offers a strategic politics wherein modernist oppositional identities become tactical poses. In other words, a differential oppositional ideology-praxis makes possible a "tactical subjectivity" in which multiple oppressions can be confronted by shifting modes of consciousness as various forms of oppression are experienced.

Crucial to Sandoval's project is an understanding of the differential mode of oppositional consciousness as a "survival skill" that U.S. Third World women have been enacting, even though it has not been recognized as a legitimate ideology of political activity. This "survival skill" is, for Sandoval, a form of affinity politics, something quite different from more conventional notions of "identity politics." As Sandoval explains:

> Differential consciousness requires grace, flexibility, and strength: enough strength to confidently commit to a well-defined structure of identity for one hour, day, week, month, year; enough flexibility to self-consciously transform that identity according to the requisites of another oppositional ideological tactic if readings of power's formation require it; enough grace to recognize alliance with others committed to egalitarian social relations and race, gender, and class justice, when their readings of power call for alternative oppositional stands. Within the realm of

> differential consciousness, oppositional ideological positions, unlike their incarnations under hegemonic feminist comprehension, are tactics—not strategies.

Distinguishing what Sandoval means by tactics and strategies is crucial to understanding the kind of move she is suggesting in her rearticulation of oppositional consciousness. To be tactical means to be in service as necessary; but tactics can be changed, altered, shifted. Strategy is an informing ideology brought to one's engagement with an oppressor or opposing power; tactics are the moves one makes while engaged with the opposition. "Identity politics," as a modernist mode of oppositionality, has essentialist requisites which result in the production of unproblematic essentialized identities as the basis of oppositional consciousness. In Sandoval's framework, however, identity politics becomes a tactical maneuver rather than a single informing strategy; this move allows for the possibility of constructing social movement coalitions built on less-essentialized or strategically essentialized affinities. Recognizing U.S. Third World feminist praxis makes possible another kind of gender, race, class, sexual, cultural, political, and historical consciousness—a differential consciousness which multiplies what counts as feminist politics and consciousness. Sandoval claims this mode of oppositional consciousness as a praxis grounded in the experiences of women of color, lesbians, and poor women inside the United States, but she argues as well that it is becoming a form of consciousness "threaded throughout the experience of social marginality." Because of "an historically unique democratization of oppression," this form of consciousness "is also being woven into the fabric of experiences belonging to more and more citizens who are caught in the crisis of late capitalist conditions and expressed in the cultural angst most often referred to as the postmodern dilemma."

I think what can be seen in many of the sites of the formations of a Third Wave of feminism is precisely what Sandoval suggests. This Third Wave is as much a product of "postmodern cultural conditions" as it is a product of the First and Second Waves, or of women's studies, or the media backlash, or violence. Perhaps it is more appropriate to say it is a product of postmodern cultural conditions because it is a product of the First and Second Waves; the media backlash; violence; and other kinds of historical remnants, products and monsters. Therefore, the theories of culture that are useful to analyzing the Third Wave are those that help us to comprehend how young women are claiming feminist identities for themselves in spite of the backlash and the discomfort many feel about popular conceptions of what "feminism" connotes. This discomfort arises in part from the way many Second Wave white feminists (and later the media) defined feminism to suit their particular historical-cultural circumstances, definitions which are frequently at odds with the behaviors, politics, criticisms, and apparent irreverences of younger women. This may help us to understand how a historical moment called "postmodern" contributes to distinctions between the Third Wave and the First and Second Wave women's movements. For instance, the simultaneous confidence and uncertainty about what constitutes feminism doesn't have to be conceptualized as a "problem."...

Another indicator of the "postmodern" nature of the Third Wave is its reliance on networking among different cohorts of women who compose a movement culture that is disparate, unlikely, multiple, polymorphous. These are cohorts who remain indebted to their predecessors but who are simultaneously irreverent. They all share an interest in exploring what it means to be "women" in the United States and the world in the 1990s, as well as how to resist identification with the object "Woman." Unlike many white feminists in the early years of the Second Wave who sought to create the resistant subject "women," in the Third Wave, this figure "women" is rarely a unitary subject. As JeeYeun Lee writes at the end of her essay, "Beyond Bean Counting":

> These days, whenever someone says the word "women" to me, my mind goes blank. What "women"? What is this "women" thing you're talking about? Does that mean me? Does that mean my mother, my roommates, the white woman next door, the checkout clerk at the supermarket, my aunts in Korea, half the world's population? I ask people to specify and specify, until I can figure out exactly what they're talking about, and I try to remember to apply the same standards to myself, to deny myself the slightest possibility of romanticization. Sisterhood may be global, but who is in that sisterhood? None of us can afford to assume anything about anybody else. This thing called "feminism" takes a great deal of hard work, and I think this is one of the primary hallmarks of young feminists' activism today: We realize that coming together and working together are by no means natural or easy.

Lee, like other young feminists, has learned from the Second Wave, from critiques made by women of color, lesbians, and poor women, from the backlash of the 1980s, her own experiences, and the neo-, post-, and anti-feminist rhetorics that proliferate in the media today. And the lesson she emphasizes is that gender is not a mutually exclusive category; a feminist politics has to take into account the many differences that make up the category "women" and to recognize that these differences are all part of a feminist politics.

Networking is a critical concept in describing the movement, epistemology, and geography of Third Wave feminism. Besides incorporating Sandoval's important theorizing of oppositional praxis, this usage also draws upon Donna Haraway's theorizing of cyborg feminism and feminist networks and on Bruno Latour's use of this concept to describe "a new topology that makes it possible to go almost everywhere, yet without occupying anything except narrow lines of force and a continuous hybridization between socialized objects and societies rendered more durable through the proliferation of nonhumans." Networking as I conceptualize it involves a "technologic," a particular practice of communicating information over space and time, a creation of temporary "unified" political groups made up of unlikely combinations and collectivities (i.e., affinity groups or even anthologies), the combining of diverse technologies to construct powerful cultural expressions of oppositional consciousness (i.e., music, lyrics, zines, musical instruments, videos, production technology, CD booklets, the Internet), and the construction of feminist politics of location (weaving between and among the spaces of race, class, sexuality, gender, etc., that we inhabit).

"Technologics" also involves a particular way of articulating one's awareness of the ways information travels and the ways our cultural repertoire of discourses, objects, ideas, and modes of resistance merge and regroup in a cultural milieu that is proliferatively technologically saturated and mediated. Not only are we comprised of and surrounded by technological networks of the kind Haraway and Latour describe, but the feminist praxis we comprehend increasingly references technological rhetorics as well. I find this to be especially true among younger folks who have grown up in the webs of computers and the Internet. One trace of this technologics is the rhetorical word games used by young women and feminists that merge identity, politics, and technology (remember Gilbert and Kile's term "cybergrrrl"). The term "lesbionic," used by Jody Bleyle at Candy-Ass Records, invokes for me a half-machine, half-lesbian (or perhaps a les-bi) figure—maybe a lesbian six million dollar woman—one who makes lesbian-positive music through, from, and for her body/instrument as a form of survival and resistance. Bleyle is also a member of an all-lesbian queerpunk band called Team Dresch, named for Donna Dresch, the group's leader and inspiration. The group marks its various changes and transformations by employing the rhetoric of software companies who mark advancements in their products by using numerical designations such as 3, 3.1, 3.3. The group has also fondly referred to itself as Team Dresch Version 2 and Team Dresch Version 6.2 Beta. I would also situate within this notion of technologic rhetorics my own efforts to theorize the "wave" in "Third Wave" as radio waves rather than ocean waves—a move that my mother finds counter-intuitive for a water sign.

"Oppositional technologics" are the political praxis of resistance being woven into low-tech, amateur, hybrid, alternative subcultural feminist networks that register below the mainstream. The term "oppositional technologics" fuses together Haraway, Sandoval, and Latour with my own investments in the relationship between subjectivity formation and political consciousness (in the context of U.S. culture) and the proliferation of communications and visual technologies. I want to argue that this "movement" called the Third Wave is a network built on specific technologics, and Riot Grrrl is one node, or series of nodes, that marks points of networking and clustering. I like the way Latour describes a similar notion: "To shuttle back and forth, we rely on the notion of translation, or network. More supple than the notion of system, more historical than the notion of structure, more empirical than the notion of complexity, the idea of network is the Ariadne's thread of these interwoven stories."

THE TECHNOLOGICS OF THIRD WAVE CONSCIOUSNESS RAISING

> RIOT: (verb) 1. to take part in a tumult or disturbance of the peace; 2. [Now Rare] a) to live in a wild, loose manner, b) to engage in unrestrained revelry.
>
> —Annalee Newitz, "Riot Grrrls!" available from http://garnet.berkeley.edu/~annaleen/riot.online.html, Internet, accessed March 1997

In a 1993 essay, "The Female Bodywars: Rethinking Feminist Media Politics," Patricia Zimmerman discusses the production of low-cost video documentaries as an emerging feminist strategy in reproductive rights activism that places women and camcorders in a symbiotic relationship, one that allows the construction of cyborg identities. Like Sean Cubit, she argues that "the proliferation of video technologies multiplies the number of sites for cultural struggles." Similarly, in the production of music and zines, the proliferation and "democratization" of music technologies (underground and small, local recording companies), print technologies (Kinko's et al., and the increasing availability of computers to young people in school), and Internet technologies (especially as more programs designed for the computer "alliterate" web-page creator become available, and as the cost of the technology reaches levels low enough for mass consumption), sites of political praxis are expanded. Democraticized technologies become a resource enabling young women to get information to other young women, girls, and boys, a means for developing political consciousness, and a space that can legitimate girls' issues. Technology that is accessible to young people alters the controlling role of adults and other authority figures in the production of youth cultures and in the selection of political issues in which young people become involved. Beyond its use of these democratic technologies, the production of such hybrid texts as zines or girl music frequently resists and critiques the commodification of politically charged youth (sub)cultures by mass media.

Riot Grrrl, an alternative feminist movement emerging out of the alternative punk scene, provides one critical expression of youth (sub)cultures. Because I live in Washington State, I tend to associate Riot Grrrl with music cultures in Portland, Tacoma, Olympia, and Seattle; but this movement is as much national as it is local. This is due in part to media coverage during the early 1990s, which exposed many more people to an emerging "new" feminist political movement, challenging popular media insistence that "feminism" was a label rejected by all young women. But it also watered down the political content of the movement by focusing almost exclusively on commodifying the image of "the Riot Grrrl." However, the mainstream media has not been as important in the formation of Riot Grrrl as a local, national, and transnational movement as has the effective and sophisticated networking of girls involved in consciousness raising and information distribution. As one girl, Spirit, writes: "Our networking through mail, the Internet, through music, through zines and through the punk scene keeps us closely knit and strong." In fact, more and more of what I learn about Riot Grrrl comes from playing on the Internet. Putting in a net search for "riot grrrl" brings up hundreds of sites somehow linked to those two words. In this way the Internet serves as one place of clustering, a nodal point, for a movement that does not appear collective or unified.

But what is this thing "Riot Grrrl"? Spirit learned about Riot Grrrl in a local entertainment newspaper in San Jose, California. She says she was attracted to the movement because it seemed to reflect her own beliefs, which she describes as "generally anarchistic, anti fascist, anti sexist, and anti homophobic." She came to understand Riot Grrrl as "punk rock girls having the [same] beliefs [as I], creating a scene alternative to the one that they found themselves rejected by." For Spirit, the punk scene in San Jose "isn't very political or issue oriented," which she explains has made her feel alienated and isolated. Riot Grrrl helped to give her a sense of belonging. She describes it as a powerful force for girls and for punk music cultures:

> Riot Grrrl—the idea, the movement, the non localized group, whatever—inspired literally hundreds of girls to do zines, start bands, collectives, distributions, have meetings etc. The uprising of riot grrrl has been the only activity in the scene most of us have seen in years yet most of you probably don't know what a riot grrrl is and does, why we face so much opposition or who started it.

Spirit is especially critical of the media coverage Riot Grrrl has received since the early 1990s, noting that, in response, many of the most productive chapters (she names Olympia and D.C.) went into a kind of hiding pattern in order to prevent the possibility of colluding with "exploitation, misquoting, and such." In her estimation, "The mainstream media—what seemed like the best medium for communication, the best way to spread 'girl love'—had failed us." Yet she also recognizes that this exposure inspired many more girls "to question, challenge, create, demand."

The attention the Riot Grrrl movement and its media-appointed "leaders" have received in the popular press has been fought by those who claim to be Riot Grrrls and those who have been labeled without consent as such. They don't take out full-page ads in the *New York Times* or the *Seattle Post-Intelligencer.* They respond to media distortions by making use of more grassroots tactics. For instance, refusing to be identified as the voice of Riot Grrrl, Tobi Vail, the drummer for Bikini Kill, uses both the liner notes accompanying *The C.D. Version of the First Two Records* and her zine, *Jigsaw,* to proclaim:

> We are not in anyway "leaders of" or authorities on the "Riot Girl" movement. In fact, as individuals we have each had different experiences with, feelings on, opinions of and varying degrees of involvement with "Riot Girl" and tho we totally respect those who still feel that label is important and meaningful to them, we have never used that

> term to describe ourselves *AS A BAND*. As, [sic] individuals we respect and utilize and subscribe to a variety of different aesthetics, strategies and beliefs, both political and punk-wise, some of which are probably considered "riot girl."

In another location, Mimi has a heading on her Bikini Kill Homepage called "riot grrrl stuff" under which appears, in bold-type: "bikini kill aren't necessarily associated with all aspects of riot grrrl. As with any pseudomovement, stances vary widely from individual to individual so please check your newsweek fed paranoid attitude at the door please."

For me, it isn't so important whether individual Bikini Kill members call themselves Riot Grrrls or if they reject the label. What I am interested in is how they use the resources they have available to them as tools for grassroots girl-positive activism. They are actively invested in a punk and feminist cultural repertoire of music production, technology, performance, instruments, and underground distribution networks. They adopt punk DIY (Do It Yourself) philosophy to encourage women and girls to take the initiative to create art and knowledge, to change their cultural and political landscape, rather than waiting for someone else to do it for them. They work with fans and friends who maintain Internet homepages and various other print technologies used to make zines (members of the group have been involved with different zines, i.e., *Fuck Me Blind, Jigsaw, Girl Power, Riot Grrrl*). Bikini Kill is a band—like Bratmobile, Team Dresch, Heavens to Betsey, Sleater-Kinney (to name just a few local examples based in and around Olympia, Washington)—very much invested in issues identified as significant by many Third Wave feminists. A survey of the topics covered in their songs include racism, sexism, child abuse, domestic violence, sexuality, classism, privilege, sex industries, media spectaclization, AIDS, apathy, girl power, consumer pacifism, rock star elitism, and the commodification of coolness....

For Spirit ... Riot Grrrl is a punk-oriented form of feminism, with all the attendant stereotyping, antagonism, challenges, and fire; but she is also careful to point out that "riot grrrl didn't invent punk rock feminism." Rather, girls and women who consider themselves, their politics, and their issues part of their punk orientation "are simply reclaiming our place/voice in punk rock—a voice we've always had that's been trampled on."...

An important aspect of "reclaiming our place/voice" is the formation of collectivities or groups that share common objectives and goals. The formation of Riot Grrrl, one might say, is a "reflexive impulse," a response of young women who recognize that within punk, as well as in other cultural sites, they are "serialized" as women in particular ways that are demeaning and inhibiting. As Iris Marion Young explains in "Gender as Seriality: Thinking about Women as a Social Collective," "as a series woman is the name of a structural relation to material objects as they have been produced and organized by a prior history.... Gender, like class, is a vast, multifaceted, layered, complex, and overlapping set of structures and objects." This Riot Grrrl movement actively confronts these structures and objects by claiming them: their bodies, music and its objects, information technologies, language, anger and violence, even punk culture. In these acts of resistance and subversion many young women produce critiques that address their own and others' experiences as women as well as their experiences of race, sexuality, class, and other forms of embodiedness....

Patricia Zimmerman's analysis of the interface between reproductive rights activists and low-end video technology that opened this section demonstrates how the convergence of music, print, and information technologies, young women, and feminist consciousness raising multiplies the cultural spaces where political activities can occur. In issue #4 of *Girl Germs*, one young woman, Rebecca B., gives an account of her experience at "Girl's Night" at the International Pop Underground on August 20, 1991. Girl's Night, she explains, was originally suggested as a way to provide an "opportunity to demarginalize the role of girls in the convention and punk rock." For Rebecca B., the event proved to be a radicalizing moment even though, ironically, she only attended because guys were finally allowed in, which meant her boyfriend could go. And, she states, "wherever he went, I followed." And yet, Girl's Night ended up (to paraphrase her own words) shattering her securities and making her think. In a way, Rebecca's story is about the interaction between two worlds—a "post-feminist" one in which following a boy doesn't seem downgrading and the one created by Girl Night organizers, apparently modeling themselves after Second Wave women's music festivals. This interaction becomes the point of emergence for a third kind of "world," or "reality," in Rebecca's language.

Rebecca's account of Girl's Night includes a description of how girls/women can and do use musical instruments, microphones, stages, their bodies and voices, and performance as "a forum" for "female expression." By appropriating the objects, spaces, and aesthetics of a culture generally dominated and determined by men and male issues, Rebecca argues, a new "reality" is being formed, a "reality" in which "stands the new girl, writing her dreams, speaking her will, making her music, restructuring the very punk rock world you reside in." Rebecca describes girl bodies filling up the stage and the consciousness of being embodied girls filling up a room (the barroom, concert hall, sound room, bedroom) with sound and words and movement. Girl's Night served as a moment of feminist consciousness formation for Rebecca:

> Girl's night will always be precious to me because, believe it or not, it was the first time I saw women stand on a stage as though they truly belonged there. The first time I had ever heard the voice of a sister proudly singing the rage so shamefully locked in my own heart. Until girl's night, I never knew that punk rock was anything but a phallic extension of the white middle class male's frustrations.

The voice at the microphone, the people and machines that put together the text of a CD or tape, the performance event, the women at the keyboard creating homepages and filling in information, the women at Kinko's or at work putting together her/their zine(s) to distribute to girlfriends and other girls who write for copies all represent moments of convergence between democratized technologies and a networked, fractured form of Third Wave feminist differential consciousness. Girls like Rebecca may have the opportunity to experience such moments of consciousness raising in cultural sites created and institutionalized by the Second Wave (i.e., women's studies classrooms, progressive book-stores, rape crisis centers, or domestic violence shelters, to name a few). But instead, she experiences it inside a space and event she was not taught to see as coded "hers." Her last claim should not go underremarked. During Girl's Night, Rebecca realizes that a space coded white, middle-class, male, and frustrated does not innately have to reflect such narrow interests. It matters who takes up the tools, and it matters how those tools get used. Although such a moment of coming to consciousness is not in itself uniquely Third Wave, the historical, (sub)cultural, and technological specificity of the moment constitutes this event within the cultural geography of Third Wave feminism.

"IT'S MINE, BUT IT DOESN'T BELONG TO ME"

For these "punk rock girls," and for other girls and women who produce zines and music that aren't necessarily punk, the production of a new movement space and its objects is politically powerful. And, although it may not seem like the most effective space in which to bring about social change, many of these women recognize their work as extensions of, influenced by, and interconnected with other historical social justice movements. The conscious use of the word "revolution" after "Riot Grrrl" indicates this connection. As one of my favorite Riot Grrrls, Nomy Lamm, says:

> This is the revolution. I don't understand the revolution. I can't lay it all out in black and white and tell you what is revolutionary and what is not. The punk scene is a revolution, but not in and of itself. Feminism is a revolution; it is solidarity as well as critique and confrontation. This is the fat grrrl revolution. It's mine, but it doesn't belong to me. Fuckin' yeah.

There is no finality in this ending. The "Fuckin' yeah" is more like a pause after which Lamm or anyone else can take up the threads of thought and keep the conversation moving and weaving. Revolution here is change, radical intervention, rearticulating the interrelations of punk, feminism, fat consciousness, class, race, and ability as they meet on the body and in the voice of Nomy Lamm. Even her language expresses the complexity: just as race is not as simple as the binary "black and white," "the revolution" cannot be described in either/or oppositional statements. It is about who and how one fills in the spaces; it is about how a girl can make her feminism punk and her punk feminist; and how, for Lamm, all of this has to be articulated around fat, media representations of the female body, and self/girl-love.

Lamm's proclamation: "It's mine, but it doesn't belong to me," like Rebecca Walker's statement, "I'm not a postfeminism feminist. I am the Third Wave," claims the right to name and construct her consciousness without becoming the sole owner of what counts as feminism or feminist consciousness. They call out their issues, locate themselves, make feminism work for them, and conclude by opening up the conversation to others, taking what they need and passing it on. Walker's rejection of postfeminism and Lamm's embrace of a polymorphous feminism connects these two women not only historically and generationally, but also in their insistence that feminism provides a context and language from/with which they can articulate their issues. This is a consequence of the post-civil rights recognition of difference as a positive thing and represents another (postmodern) distinction between the Second and Third Waves.

The refusal to claim ownership of feminism allows these Third Wavers to maintain a sense of their own and other feminist-identified individuals' tactical subjectivity. When we understand that feminism is not about fitting into a mold but about expanding our ability to be revolutionary from within the worlds and communities and scenes we move around and through, then collective action becomes possible across the differences that affect people differently. This is not an argument for making feminism so expansive as to include absolutely anyone on the basis that she is a woman (something that seems quite popular in our culture); it is, instead, an attempt to point out how feminism enables revolutionary forms of consciousness when it is understood as ideology-praxis that strategically invokes the experiences of women across different locales and identities....

Although this task is painful and daunting (who really wants to have to deal with the ramifications of being both oppressor and oppressed?), the move toward this level of consciousness raising among some Riot Grrrls is worth further study. Just as Lamm challenges the idea that feminism is a subject/object/label owned by specific people/groups, Doza and Hanna challenge us to see that we are in and of "the system of abuse" and that we have complicated relationships to oppressor/power and oppressed/powerlessness. For young, mostly white and middle-class, women in the United States who turn to Riot Grrrl—even now when so many of its founders view it as "so '92"—to learn that being a feminist involves thinking about oneself as both oppressed and as oppressor is revolutionary. In the wake of the successes of the 1960s and 1970s, girls/young women in the United States today already know they are at a disadvantage. But rather than claim a position of total victimhood, isn't it more expedient to try to understand how the slipperiness of sexism, racism, classism, and other modes of domination are interwoven into the various and sundry privileges they are aware they have?...

Young feminists today, as well as older feminists and other social justice activists (advocates), recognize that political activity is always being subverted by the media—just as painted Volkswagen buses have come to represent some nostalgic sign of authenticity for neo-hippies, however devoid of antiwar and counterculture politics. Our historical moment (post-1960s, bordering the twenty-first century, late capitalist) precipitates particular kinds of political, cultural, aesthetic, and ideological consciousness; and like Zimmerman, I believe we need to look to other cultural and subcultural spaces for signs of activist politics. As Angela McRobbie has noted: "Subcultures are aesthetic movements whose raw materials are by definition, 'popular,' in that they are drawn from the world of the popular mass media." Like the major recording labels who "plunder" music subcultures and "indies" (independent bands and labels) for "talent and trends," subcultures "plunder" mainstream media, but their purposes are different: one is geared to profit margins and sustaining markets; the other to finding constructive meaning in a time of crisis and uncertainty. At a time when the mainstream mass media scripts politics as bumper stickers, soundbites, and tabloid sensationalism, it seems especially important to look for and foster (sub)cultural spaces that insist on political content and intent in members' activities and in the objects they create. These include the tactical subjectivities employed to counter and subvert the depoliticized politics of conspicuous consumption. Although youth (sub)cultures like punk and Riot Grrrl are often represented by the media as a trend (and a passing one at that), I insist that we make a mistake when we disregard apparently "aesthetic" movements as nonpolitical. The working-class connections to punk culture in England and the white working-class/urban-middle-class/suburban associations of much punk culture in the United States (including Riot Grrrl) attests to the significance of the political in these (sub)cultural aesthetic movements.

In the Third Wave, feminist collective consciousness may not necessarily manifest itself in a nationalized and highly mobilized social movement unified around a single goal or identity. At the moment, this hardly seems imaginable. Perhaps occasionally groups will come together to accomplish a specific purpose—such as the protection of reproductive rights for all women and men; protesting environmental injustices in poor and racially segregated communities and Third World countries; combating anti-immigration and racist xenophobic movements; or endorsing the right of all people, regardless of sexuality, to love whom they want, how they want, and to have their rights to do so legally recognized—but I think it is also important to look at Third Wave feminist activist politics in spaces that cross over and between what is called the "mainstream" or what is recognized as "a social movement." We need to consider the potent political movement cultures being generated by feminists (like the young women I write about) who are producing knowledge for each other through the innovative integration of technology, alternative media, (sub)cultural and/or feminist networks, and feminist consciousness raising. Such dispersed movement culture spaces are vital, as are the networks constantly being formed and reformed among them.

35. Lisa Jervis, Mission Statement for *Bitch* Magazine

Excerpts from "Bitch," by Lisa Jervis, published in *Bitch*, Vol. 1, No. 1 (Spring 1996). Reprinted with permission.

In this definitional third-wave feminist piece, the mission statement for the popular third-wave feminist magazine *Bitch*, Lisa Jervis, the magazine's publisher, discusses why it is important for third-wavers to think critically about the mass media and to create it themselves, thereby transforming popular culture.

So why *Bitch*? Because—*regardless of those who still think it's an insult—it's an action*. Because a confrontational stance is powerful. Because *Bitch* connotes anger, and I agree with bell hooks when she says, "Confronting my rage, witnessing the way it moved me to grow and change, I understood intimately that it had the potential not only to destroy but to construct. Then and now I understand rage to be a necessary aspect of resistance struggle."

This magazine is about thinking critically about every message the mass media sends; it's about loudly articulating what's wrong and what's right with what we see. This magazine is about speaking up. Will that make us bitchy? Yeah.

You wanna make somethin' of it?

I've always been a media junkie. Magazines, movies, television—I love them all and tend to consume them voraciously. But indiscriminate media consumption, maybe more than any other binge, can make you sick. When I was twelve years old I was looking for something to reflect who I thought I was. I wanted to confirm that I was not a freak, that my feelings and desires were normal. Unfortunately, in the mass media I found affirmation only for my I-desperately-need-to-be-skinny and I-need-to-have-a-"boyfriend" longings. And those weren't even mine, they were just the charred remains of I-really-want-to-like-myself and what-are-these-urges-and-what-can-I-do-to-satisfy-them? I couldn't identify my desires accurately because so many sources had already told me what they were supposed to be. None of my sources said that it was ok—hell, even possible—for girls to want sex just for the sake of pleasure; none of them said that a woman's brain is her most important body part. None of them said that I wasn't crazy for feeling like I was under assault from all the directives being tossed at me. I've continued to read magazines that tell me, both implicitly and explicitly, that female sexual urges are deviant. I've continued to watch tv programs that tell me I should care more about what I'm wearing than what I'm thinking. I've continued to see movies where the only women onscreen get ogled or killed without even speaking a word.

This magazine is about speaking up. Because when we hear, over and over again, without responding, what the mass media has to say—that women are stupid, shallow, incapable—we will believe it. Too much of the time we're told to shut up, to calm down, to take a joke. Well, we won't. Because it's not a joke, and what we have to say is too important to leave unsaid.

This magazine is about speaking up. It's about formulating replies to the sexism that we see every day. It's about using those replies to maintain our sanity. It's easy to point a finger at the most egregious of what we see and say simply, "This is bad." But we also need to recognize the more subtle assaults; they're more pernicious. We need to talk about what they're saying and why. We need to find and make girl-friendly places in the mass media. Where are the things we can see and read and hear that don't insult our intelligence? How can we get more of them? *This magazine is about theorizing and fostering a transformation of pop culture.*

36. Lisa Jervis and Andi Zeisler, "Barbie Can Just Bite Me," from *Bitch* Magazine

Excerpts from "Barbie Can Just Bite Me," by Lisa Jervis and Andi Zeisler, published in *Bitch*, Vol. 1, No. 3 (Fall 1996). Reprinted with permission.

In a humorous, biting look at the replication of traditional gender stereotypes seen in children's toys, Jervis and Zeisler use virtuoso third-wave feminist style showing how the acquisition of clothes and boys seems to be the primary goal taught to girls.

We've been doin' a lotta thinkin' about childhood lately.

It was so great, wasn't it, before we knew what the wage gap was, what street harassment felt like, before anyone told us we couldn't do something 'cause we were girls and that we had to do something else for the same reason. Oops, we slipped into fantasyland for a minute there. There was never a time like that. The traditional dichotomy equating maleness with action and femaleness with nurturance is alive and well in toy manufacturing and advertising. What gives? Do Mattel execs think they'll lose money if brothers and sisters share toys? Are they stuck in the Dark Ages? Nostalgic for the '50s? Or do they just not know any better?

We headed over to our local corporate toy emporium to see how the toy situation has changed since we rode our Big Wheels around the driveway of childhood. If an entire aisle glowing pink with Barbie and her ilk wasn't enough to clue us in to the fact that things have not changed for the better and may in fact have gotten worse, there was a seemingly infinite parade of examples to continue our study. This goes way beyond dolls that pee.

Toys are stuck in the land of the separate and unequal; gender neutrality is a nebulous, sparsely populated area where the only thing to play is Gator Golf. If you can get your kicks by putting into a plastic alligator head, well, more power to ya. Unfortunately, if you can't—well, you've got no choice but to have your leisure time defined by your gender.

AISLE 1, BOARD GAMES: GET STUFF AND THEN BOYS WILL LIKE YOU

You might expect board games to be kinda innocuous. After all, you just roll the dice and move around collecting things that help you win. I don't remember any icky girly board games from my childhood—we played Monopoly and Sorry just like everyone else. In board games, winning means getting more money than anyone else, or knocking other players off the board, right?

Apparently not. There's a whole slew of games out there where winning means getting a boy, some clothes, or both.

Take, say, Dream Phone. You "call on the phone, get clues, and find out which boy really likes you." These clues come via the phone, which spews pearls of wisdom like, "He's not at the beach," and "He's wearing a hat." When you figure it out, you dial his number and a male voice says, "You're right. I really like you." The only conclusions that can be drawn from this are that a) it's a great use of girls' time and deductive skills to figure out which pimply-faced boys like them, and b) girls should be so thrilled when boys like them that whether or not they like the boy in question is pretty irrelevant. Ack.

Then there are the materialistic games, the ones where the whole point is to get stuff. In Pretty Princess, you gather jewelry and a crown as you travel around the board. You win when you acquire some set amount of stuff plus the crown; then you become a princess. As the ad sing-songs, "Every Pretty Princess has sparkly things to wear and a pretty, pretty crown to place upon her hair."

Worse than the cloying Pretty Princess is Mall Madness, which pits girls against each other in a high-pressure shopping frenzy, using cardboard credit cards emblazoned with phrases like "EZ Money." What's the message here? Live to shop, girls, shop to live, and max out your credit cards? Please. As if teenage boys never hang out at the mall; as if shopping is something only girls do. Boys are equally rabid consumers and yet are never shown in the kind of frivolous, shopping-crazed way in which girls are portrayed in almost all teen media. (Does Brandon ever shop like Brenda did? The sister on *The Fresh Prince*, those *Sweet Valley High* girls ... the list goes on.) Of course, the notion that we're training a generation of girls to see credit cards as "EZ Money" is even more horrifying.

Worst of all, though, are the games that combine boy chasing with fanatical acquisitiveness. "Help your Barbie doll find just the right shoes, handbag, necklace, hair clips, and complete the outfit with a super bouquet!" reads the text on the pink box of the Barbie Dress-Up Game. "Along the way, stay away from the broken heart; it keeps Barbie from going out—and you from winning!" Okay, so Barbie is an obvious scapegoat in this small-scale gender war, but this is one very telling element of the whole big bad picture. The bouquet (read: marriage) is essential for victory. What good are all of Barbie's "independent woman" trappings (The 'Vette! The office! The pink business suits!) if she's trapped in the fucking Dream Townhouse waiting for a husband? Maybe the most disturbing element of these seemingly trivial games is that they encourage girls to compete against each other for the implied attentions of men. Not only is coupling supposed to be your goal, but you're supposed to beat out your friends to get it.

Would you expect a board game called Dream Girl, in which boys get cards clueing them in to which fourth-grade hottie wants them bad? No, of course not. Toys and games for the young male do not focus their energy on anxiety about their attractiveness to the opposite sex. Why not? Because that would be silly. Boys have their own bad selves to worry about. Girls' toys, on the other hand, seem to focus either directly or indirectly on boys, teaching them male-identification long before they are able to forge a complete sense of self.

AISLE 2, ACCESSORIES AND DRESS-UP ITEMS: PRACTICE FOR THE MOST IMPORTANT DAY OF YOUR LIFE

Dress-up is a great thing; no argument there. Putting on oversized, musty-smelling, loud, unidentifiable garments pulled from someone's Aunt Agatha's attic and then smearing lipstick across your forehead just for the hell of it—staples of childhood fun. Uh, that's not what's happening here. Instead, dress-up is for girls to practice for the future.

Pretty Girl and The Salon offer the trappings of womanhood—fake nails, "real" cosmetics, a carrying case (pink, duh), and of course, a mirror. The target group for this immersion in vanity? For Pretty Girl, ages 5 and up. For The Salon, ages 3 and up. Then there's Day Dream's Blushing Bride Fantasy, "the dress-up set that dreams are made of." This would be a tiny white lace dress, veil, and bouquet of flowers; it even includes a how-to role-playing book, so girls can start practicing early for that all-important event of marriage before they even know the difference between boys and girls. Ickiest of all is Baby's First Purse, which gives newborn girls an opportunity to revel in all their frivolous feminine glory with a lipstick rattle and compact mirror. Lordy.

We could go on and on—Magic Glamour Party, Fantastic Fingernails—but I think we've all had enough.

AISLE 3, ACTIVITIES: BOYS DO, GIRLS LOOK

Girls get Barbie Bridal Fashions Rub 'N' Color and the Fashion Plates Wedding Set. Boys get welding sets, tool shops, chemistry sets, model sets. Notice a theme, little ones? Even activities without any traditional gender connotations at all—magic tricks, for example—tend to picture boys front and center on the box, with little girls in the background oohing and ahhing over those oh-so-masculine 8-year-old shoulders.

The one exception: sports equipment. A gratifyingly large number of packages actually show little girls playing alongside little boys. It's kind of itty-bitty, especially in the face of everything else, but I find it cockle-warming that 7-year-old girls can buy baseball mitts that come in boxes emblazoned with figures who actually look like them.

AISLE NOWHERE, GENDER-NEUTRAL TOYS: NO, JANE DEAR, YOU CAN'T RIDE THE SAME TRIKE AS LITTLE TIMMY

Basketball hoops aside, even traditionally unisex toys now come in two different versions. The beloved primary-colored Big Wheel has been replaced with gender-specific models like the Lil' Galaxy Explorer Trike and its sister, the Lil' Sweetheart, which is a lavender affair with lots of foofy decals and color-coordinated handlebar streamers. We also get the Big Wheel Police Cycle and the Big Wheel Sunflower Cycle, both testament to the gender rift that toy companies help create.

You can't buy something that doesn't exist—and sadly, that means kids can't have toys that don't indoctrinate them into the pink/blue, passive/active dichotomy. When little girls beg for plastic kitchen sets and boys crave dump trucks, it's not because of some innate desire, some chromosome-linked instinct. But when they go to the store and are hit over the head with messages about what they're supposed to want and what's appropriate for them to have—well, what's a kid to do?

37. Ophira Edut, "Introduction," from *Adiós, Barbie*

Excerpts from "Introduction" by Ophira Edut, published in Ophira Edut, ed. *Adiós, Barbie* (Seattle: Seal Press, 1998), xix–xxiv. Reprinted with permission.

In exemplary third-wave feminist style, Ophira Edut takes on the Barbie image of beauty and looks at the cracks in the plastic: the body image crisis that so many girls face and the reductiveness and restrictiveness of that particular standard of beauty. "Everything is up for questioning today," Edut claims, "the media, our identities, each other, the very concept of beauty."

Ah, Barbie. Hard to believe the old girl's pushing forty. I mean, look at her. She has thighs like number-two pencils. Her tan lasts all winter. And that pink Corvette has dropped some serious mileage. Then there's the fancy wardrobe, the townhouse, the swimming pool ... and she hasn't worked a day in her life.

Okay, I know she has problems like the rest of us. Her boyfriend, I hear, can't perform too well. She had to have two ribs removed back in the '70s in order to retain that trademark hourglass figure. And she hasn't used the bathroom once in four decades.

But you're busted, Babs. You've been found guilty of inspiring fourth-grade girls to diet, of modeling an impossible beauty standard, of clinging to homogeneity in a diverse new world. Welcome to the dollhouse, honey. Your time is up. Pack your bags and be outta the Dreamhouse by noon.

At the turn of the millennium, body image is a national crisis among young women. Until now, there hasn't been a forum where women of diverse cultures and identities could gather to chronicle their experiences, to usher out the Barbie Era with pink champagne and a triumphant "adiós."

And the current national discussion of body image reflects this. To date, most literature continues to popularize the myth that distorted body image is merely a symptom of vanity suffered by bored, middle-class white girls. In 1995, *Newsweek* published results from a University of Arizona study that compared the body satisfaction of black and white adolescent girls. The gap in results was wider than the one between Barbie's thighs: 70 percent of the African-American subjects reportedly liked their bodies, while 90 percent of their white peers did not. While the black girls in the study described an ideal body as "full hips and thick thighs," perfection, according to the white girls, came in waifishly impossible dimensions: five-foot-seven and 100 to 110 pounds. The study's implied conclusion? Black girls have better body image than white girls do.

That didn't sit right with many women I knew. We wondered what would have happened if the study had polled subjects on whether they liked their hair texture, their skin and eye color, their facial features. Moreover, what if the study had asked girls whether they felt safe or powerful in their bodies? The focus on weight failed to connect body image to racism and sexism—to power. Class differences were not mentioned, nor was the history that may have shaped the subjects' varying ideals.

But women's struggle with body image *is* about power. Body image goes far beyond weight, and it runs deeper than skin color. Our bodies have become arenas for feelings we don't deal with, for unresolved traumas and injustices. Scratch away the surface of "I'm so fat" and "I hate my hair," and you'll find a sister treading water in a melting pot simmering with every "ism" imaginable.

This is difficult to articulate today, at a time when society has taken on the rosy blush of progressiveness. Are we empowered young women, or aren't we? Our inability to answer this question definitively is a natural offshoot of a capitalist, media-driven society that serves young people a daily diet of mixed messages. Society adopts the "girl power" mantra but refuses to arm girls with the tools to achieve it. Textbooks glorify violence and war, but schools won't properly educate students about safe sex, reproductive health, self-defense, and abuse. Multiculturalism is the new media buzzword, but laws upholding it are dismantled while we watch *Yo! MTV Raps* and read *Vibe* magazine. Young women are encouraged to follow rather than to lead, to become passive consumers rather than active creators of our culture and our destinies.

Our bodies—and our convoluted relationships with them—tell the real story. In a world that offers women challenges along with choices, compromise along with control, our bodies may seem the only realm where we can claim sovereignty. So we focus our power there. We start with what we can control—sorta. Our bodies. Our hair. Our weight. Our breasts. Our clothes. When this control inevitably eludes us, our feelings of powerlessness solidify.

Too often, the endless body chase becomes a distraction from a painful reality. Trauma survivors talk about "leaving their bodies" as a survival tactic during violation. For some women, feeling like we're "in our bodies" convinces us we exist. In a twisted way, intense body focus is the one thin thread connecting us to the material world. But gaining a sense of place in our bodies should ultimately build our sense of place in the world. It should be a means of healing, rather than escaping from pain. We need to feel connected to our bodies, to understand what they can do. Sometimes, this even means pushing them to new comfort zones. Can we do this with balance? That's the big question.

Young women are attempting to answer this question with a resounding "yes" by showing that our bodies can be our allies. Rather than simply shun the idea of being defined by our appearances, young women today include our bodies as part of our multilayered self-definitions. In a world that still tries to assume our identities, we rebel with an outward expression of self. Our passion for the truth, in all its messy complexity, compels us to visibly defy easy categories and sweeping labels, even if they were created from within. Rather, we rush to show the world who we are, instead of allowing it to paint us as one-dimensional characters. So instead of declaring "black is beautiful," a young African-American woman today is more likely to ask, *Why does this world assume I'm "too black" or "not black enough"? Who defines blackness anyway?*

Everything is up for questioning today—the media, our identities, each other, the very concept of beauty. The answer to the body image dilemma can't simply be to allow all women a place in the beauty structure. Sure, it's important to tell women of every size and color that they're beautiful and worthwhile people. But it's also fundamental to offer them a world where they are safe, valued and free from oppression. A world that values healing more than destruction, that seeks balance over domination....

... We are entitled to love our bodies at any size. We are entitled to speak, act, create and feel safe wherever we ago. We are entitled to resources, and to a real place in this culture. We are entitled to take off the rose-colored glasses: the world ain't always pink and pretty. And we are entitled to say so—out loud.

So take an about face, if you will, and confront head-on whatever you're running from. Start at the mirror. Take a good, hard look at the part of your body you fear the most, and tell it who's boss. Then give it all the love you've got. Instead of putting all your resistance into the leg press machine, focus some on the culture that directs our best energies into body-hating pursuits. Life is an opportunity for joy and celebration. How can our lives be full if our stomachs aren't? How can we understand life's gifts when we're too blinded by our own perceived inadequacies to appreciate them?

... Self-acceptance is not defeat. It's a way of plugging ourselves into the organic process of life. It's the entrance ramp to discovering our true power, which is rooted in who we are. When our bodies and identities are in tune, they reflect each other. This beautiful synchronicity hums with an energy that affects everything and everyone it touches. It changes the culture. And *that* is true girl power.

Hasta la vista, Barbie.

38. Heather M. Gray and Samantha Phillips, "The Beauty Standard: Wasting Our Time on Perfection," from *Real Girl/ Real World*

Excerpts from *Real Girl/Real World* by Heather M. Gray and Samantha Phillips (Seattle: Seal Press, 1998), 3–33. Reprinted by permission of Seal Press.

In this essay, two young feminist women offer their own critique of beauty culture and a guide to help girls become more critical of that culture, less pressured by it, and more accepting of themselves "as they are." The essay incorporates the voices of many young women and comes with many sidebars to illustrate their points. It covers all aspects of beauty culture from its history to models, Barbie, and plastic surgery.

> "Every society has its idea of beauty, and it teaches it to every generation in whatever way necessary."
>
> When you're a baby, people tell you that you are pretty, or they don't. People tell you who else is pretty, like, "Look at that pretty lady!" They are talking to a baby, and it never stops.
>
> —Rebecca, seventeen years old

From the moment we're born, girls are greeted with, "Ooh, how pretty, delicate and lovely." Our brothers, meanwhile, are told, "What a slugger! What a grip—he'll be an athlete!" Goo-goo. From day one we are taken for a ride about prettiness and beauty. So fasten your seatbelts—it's a bumpy trip. Bows are scotch-taped to our baby-bald heads. We're given dolls to primp and dress up and frilly party dresses that we can't party in. Even if we are tomboys and never play with dolls or wear dresses, we can't escape the pretty culture. We grow up among pictures of waif-like supermodels, fairy tales of beautiful princesses who live happily ever after, buxom, blonde Barbie dolls with permanently arched "high-heeled" feet, and adults who point out what's pretty and what's ugly.

> "I'd like to think that beauty is defined as being a good person, but I don't think it works out that way in our society."
>
> Basically, the beauty that everyone thinks they should be is what they see on TV, in movies and in magazines. Personally, I like people who look a little different.
>
> —Keisha, seventeen years old

> i think pretty is nice
> but i'd rather see something new
> all those plastic people
> got their plastic surgery
> but we got a big big beautiful
> we got it for free
> who you gonna be
> if you can't be yourself
> you can't get it from tv
> you can't force it on anybody else
>
> —Ani DiFranco, "Pick Yer Nose," *Puddle Dive*

THE IMPORTANCE OF BEAUTY: WHAT A HEADACHE

> What else do they want in life but to be as attractive as possible to men? Do not all their trimmings and cosmetics have this end in view? And all their baths, fittings, creams, scents, as well—and all those arts of making up, painting, and fashioning the face, eyes and skin? Just so. And by what other sponsor are they better recommended to men than by folly?
>
> —Erasmus, 1509

Beauty is made out to be a girl's greatest achievement. Our looks are judged as much or more than our actions. Sportscasters comment on how pretty or cute girl ice skaters and gymnasts are. Can you imagine them complimenting football players on their uniforms or wrestlers on their hairstyles? We get a sinking feeling that it is more important to be beautiful than to be creative, talented, or intelligent. Beauty: the ultimate source of power for women? That stinks. Fine if I am an accomplished pianist, great writer, adept athlete, or math wiz, but more important, *How do I look?* How we look shouldn't matter so much. It *is* possible to throw away the notion that beauty is our most important quality. We can start by reading fashion magazines with a grain of salt and realizing that beauty does not have to be our chore. We can critique what we don't like in the media and choose alternatives to mainstream images.

"We learn to be beautiful as the way to get a powerful guy."

> Men have so many more chances in life if they are not good-looking. It's universal, isn't it? There is a saying for young girls: "Just be beautiful and shut up." People often say, "Oh, the man is rich, that is why he has such a beautiful woman." But sometimes she has everything: the looks, the career; yet she chooses an ugly man, and it's not an issue. Yet if it's the other way around, you think, "That ugly woman must have a lot of money," or "What happened???" In Haiti we would wonder, "Did she do some voodoo to get him?" We are all so conditioned. We learn to be beautiful as the way to get a powerful guy, but who wants someone who's just interested in how we look?
>
> —Marie, eighteen years old

"It's like you're not even a real woman if you don't look beautiful."

> I think men have more leeway. Even though they are supposed to be built, it is not stressed nearly as much as it is for women. Sure, attractive men get attention, but it isn't like all men have to look attractive to be accepted. But for women, I think it's like you're not even a real woman if you don't look beautiful. Look at Woody Allen.
>
> He is a total nerd, but he is sexy. That is great, but it saddens me that it isn't that way for women. You have to live up to so much—it's really frustrating.
>
> —Morgan, seventeen years old

FEELING UGLY: BEAUTY AND SELF-ESTEEM

I don't look at faces
I look at my feet
I'm all alone when I walk down the street
I'm in the kitchen 'cause I can't take the heat
I want to live but I stay in my seat
Because I'm ugly with a capital "U"
and I don't need a mirror to see that it's true

—Juliana Hatfield, "Ugly," *Hey Babe*

On a good day, I can see dark brown eyes, long lashes, a sensual mouth, smooth skin and an endearing nose. On a bad day these are eclipsed and only the bags under my eyes, wrinkles, kinky hair, fat lips and a pug nose are visible. On a terrible day, there's almost nothing to see at all except a blur of indefensible humanity as I avert my gaze. And on a glorious day, the beautiful eyes behold me, full of love, humor and intelligence.

—Kathrin Perutz, *Beyond the Looking Glass*

How we feel about ourselves and how we feel about our looks are often tangled together. One day everything is going swell, and we look in the mirror and think, "No problem." Another day nothing is going right, and we look at ourselves and think, "Yuck."

We may put our lives on hold while we chase after a slippery beauty ideal that is not based on who we are: "As soon as I lose these couple pounds, then my life will work out," "Once my acne clears up, I'll have the perfect boyfriend," or "When I get my hair smooth and straight, everything will be great." Rather than striving to fit the beauty images we are presented with, we can choose to appreciate ourselves right now. We can celebrate our own ethnic look, our unique height and shape and our own dear hair color.

"I learned you don't have to look at the pictures."

When you look at magazines and you see those models, sometimes you feel bad about yourself. If you're a little bit overweight, you think, "Wow, I'm fat." That's the way I looked at it, but I learned you don't have to look at the pictures. If you don't like yourself it's okay to try to change it, but you have to realize you can't change much. You have to *deal* with how you look.

—Tanisha, fourteen years old

"I find I'm really not okay if I don't feel pretty."

If I don't feel I look good, then I don't approach people as easily. I've always envied people who could just be themselves no matter how they looked and be outgoing all the time. But I find I'm really not okay if

I don't feel pretty that day. I shouldn't feel that one day I look good and the next I don't. I'm the same person.

—Valerie, seventeen years old

Here She Comes, Miss America

Stories about competitions to find the most beautiful woman have been around for thousands of years. According to the Book of Esther, more than two thousand years ago the king of Persia created a beauty contest to find a queen, and beautiful young virgins from far and wide were paraded in front of him for his approval. The girls had spent a year preparing for the contest—six months softening their skin with oils and six months practicing applying perfumes and cosmetics. Queen Esther gained her crown by winning the contest.

The first Miss America beauty contest was held in Atlantic City in 1921. A group of businessmen thought they could boost tourism past Labor Day by holding a beachfront bathing beauty contest. There were eight contestants, and it was called a "National Beauty Tournament." The winner was Margaret Gorman, a sixteen-year-old blonde. Samuel Gompers (president of the American Federation of Labor) said this about the winner: "She represents the type of womanhood America needs. Strong, red-blooded, able to shoulder the responsibilities of homemaking and motherhood. It is on her type that the hope of the country rests." All for a sixteen-year-old who was considered the "prettiest"! The beauty-contest idea took off. By 1954, the Miss America pageant was broadcast live from coast to coast. Today it is broadcast to over eighty million viewers around the world.

The Miss America pageant was chosen as the site of one of the first modern-day feminist protests in 1968. The protest was based on the belief that the contest reflected women's role as "passive decorative object."

Fairy Tales: Pretty Little Princesses

In kindergarten, we cuddled up to our teachers at story time and listened to tales of beautiful princesses who lived "happily ever after." We learned that beauty is the key to a happy life. In fairy tales there are two types of female characters: the evil ones who are ugly, and the good ones who are beautiful. The heroines of these tales—whether Cinderella, Snow White, Sleeping Beauty or Ariel of the *Little Mermaid*—are the "prettiest in the kingdom" or the "fairest of them all." And they all have long, luxurious hair. (Try to imagine a fairy princess with a nice crew cut!) What does their magnificent beauty get them? Why, Prince Charming himself, and the chance to live "happily ever after." There is never much action on the heroine's part; in fact, she is often suspended in a kind of limbo, waiting for her prince to rescue her. The moral of the story always seems to be: Be beautiful, and it will all work out. If we were to believe these tales, we should all be sitting in front of the mirror waiting for our prince to ride in on his white horse.

Luckily, some modern fairy tales give the female heroine more active and diverse roles than the traditionally passive and pretty princess. Let's visit a classic prototype, and then an excerpt from the hip tale. *The Paper Bag Princess* by Robert Munsch.

> Once upon a time there was a princess who was the prettiest creature in the world. Her hair glittered, waved and rippled nearly to the ground, her dresses were embroidered with diamonds, and everybody who saw her fell in love with her. A prince called Charming came to the kingdom and decided he must have her hand. He was very brave and strong. One day Charming and Princess Lovely went for a walk in the woods. A giant tried to attack them, so Charming pulled out his shining sword while Lovely trembled in fear. With one fell swoop, Charming cut the giant's head off and saved the day. Upon their return to the kingdom, the two got married and lived happily ever after.

> [Elizabeth] was going to marry a prince named Ronald.
>
> Unfortunately, a dragon smashed her castle, burned all her clothes with his fiery breath, and carried off Prince Ronald.
>
> Elizabeth decided to chase the dragon and get Ronald back.
>
> She looked everywhere for something to wear, but the only thing that she could find that was not burnt was a paper bag. So she put on the paper bag and followed the dragon....
>
> [With her own cunning Elizabeth tired out the dragon, and he fell sound asleep.]
>
> Elizabeth walked right over the dragon and opened the door to the cave.
>
> There was Prince Ronald. He looked at her and said, "Elizabeth, you are a mess! You smell like ashes, your hair is all tangled and you are wearing a dirty old paper bag. Come back when you are dressed like a real princess."
>
> "Ronald," said Elizabeth, "your clothes are really pretty and your hair is very neat. You look like a real prince, but you are a bum."
>
> They didn't get married after all.

> "I see that life is not just about, 'If I looked beautiful then I'd be happy.'"
>
> My roommate is a model, and she is the embodiment of my concept of beauty. It is hard to deal with her without being jealous or resentful or in awe. A lot of times I feel intimidated by her and don't want to get close to her because she is not an equal, she is this gorgeous untouchable. It's hard for me not to feel less than beautiful around her. At times I can see her as a person—she is a nice person that I get along with and have things in common with. It helps to know she has problems too—she's

not entirely confident about what she looks like, she has bad days too. I see that life is not just about, "If I looked beautiful then I'd be happy."

—Kelly, eighteen years old

"Sometimes I'll wish my eyes were bigger, and my nose was narrower, and that I just looked more white in general."

But now I try not to compare myself to non-Asians; I just compare myself to other Asians. Ideally, I wouldn't compare on looks at all, but just on personality.

—Yun, seventeen years old

"I realized that there are also some advantages to not being that beautiful."

When I was fifteen, almost all the girls in my grade were very beautiful. All the boys in high school wanted to get to know them. I was not considered beautiful because I didn't dress up, and I have a big face and my body is round. I didn't feel like an attractive girl that people would like. This feeling of insecurity took a huge effort to surpass. It was really a crisis, and I had to find some confidence. One of the things I gained from this experience is I am not so fragile. I don't need to feel beautiful.

When two friends came to visit me, everyone said they were such pretty girls. But I realized that there are also some advantages to not being that beautiful. One of the girls, who is dating this popular guy, told me that she feels lonely. She thinks it might be because she has had too much success with men. She says she feels more sad than happy when everyone likes her because she doesn't like herself. What I like the most in my relationships with people is not whether they consider me beautiful or ugly but that they like me as a person.

—Anya, seventeen years old

Train to be a model or ... just look like one Gain popularity!
Confidence! Poise!

—Barbizon

Our dreams came true ... and yours can too!

—Supermodels of Tomorrow

MODELS OF BEAUTY: A SPLIT SECOND CAPTURED ON FILM

"She has a perfect body."

I admire the model Nikki Taylor because she's very pretty; she has a perfect body. She has really nice hair, and I like her beauty. Nope, there's no one else I admire.

—Nina, fourteen years old

When 552 girls in grades five through twelve were asked in a 1991 Harvard School of Public Health survey which women they admired most, the majority chose models above writers, actresses, singers, politicians, and their own mothers. This is frightening, because we are admiring a moment in time, a split-second captured on film.

> Our readers will not embrace an overweight model with zits. We don't give them exactly who they are. They [the readers] are aspiring to something.
>
> —Sally Lee, former editor at YM

What a joke. It's insulting to be handed such a narrow definition of beauty to "aspire to," especially since we live in a world stuffed with diversity. It would be a different story if magazines showed us hundreds of looks and body types, of which the white, skinny, tall type was just one. Then everything would be groovy. It's a drag that those glamorous, touched-up faces and bodies are nearly the only images of beauty presented. We are fooled into wishing we could transform ourselves into a fashion model.

Some agents report receiving four hundred phone calls a day and five thousand pieces of mail a week from girls wanting to be the next Naomi Campbell or Claudia Schiffer. These hopefuls are in for a rude shock, however, because statistically, it would be easier to be elected to the U.S. Congress than to become a supermodel! If we're not white, the odds may even be worse: Though 20 percent of Americans are not white, only a handful of supermodels are women of color. Another bitter truth is that the average female model is five feet, nine and a half inches tall and weighs 123 pounds, whereas the average American woman is five feet, four inches tall and weighs 144 pounds.

> cindy, oh cindy
> you've sold your soul
> to be that girl next door
> that sexy unattainable thing.
> squashing more young female hearts
> than you can imagine
>
> poet laureates?
> quantum physicists?
> daring philosophers?
> no. we need to be pretty.
> then things are cool.
> then old farts will ogle us,
> ridiculous studs will prey on us.
>
> be aloof. be mysterious.
> smile, always smile.
> don't reveal too much.
> that's the ticket.

give us some more makeup tips, cyn.
wink, wink. girlfriend.

yeah, well this chick has always
wanted more.
to scale the mountains,
live through the depths,
speak with god,
touch life ...

—Heather Gray

Picture Perfect: More than Meets the Eye

What can be changed in retouching film? "You can shrink heads, change eye color, skin color, add people, add clothes—any special effect that you can do in the movies you can do with stills; it's just a question of how much money the art director or photographer wants to spend," says David Terban, a digital artist and an expert in creating those images we all see as we turn the pages of any fashion or beauty magazine. According to Terban, readers should look at all these glamorous pics in good fun because "no one really looks that way. The only crazy part is a lot of the models really *are* that skinny."

The fashion industry likes to argue that fashion magazines are like the movies: one big fantasy with exotic locations that allow the photographer to be an artist and create an ideal look—something to strive for. But isn't it irresponsible to create standards that are essentially unattainable, except through the "magic" of film and computers?

So next time you check out the cover of a women's magazine and the model's skin is a bit *too* perfect, even for a fashion model, remember—it just ain't real! Take comfort in this, and love your own *natural* look...

"I want to see magazines that reflect what I see on the street and at my school."

Magazines think that the public doesn't want to see *real* people. The typical teen magazines only show their definition of beautiful people. I hate how they exclude any overweight or "too ethnic looking" people. They might be in the article sections, but they are never in the fashion or beauty sections. Magazines should include models that are more realistic in their body type and in their race. I want to see magazines that reflect what I see on the street and at my school.

—Yvonne, fourteen years old

"The things that aren't perfect give you personality."

When I saw models in magazines, I used to think, "Oh, they're perfect! I'd like to be perfect too." Now I understand that I wouldn't like to be perfect. Why? Because the things that aren't perfect give you personality. I don't think the portrayal of models is realistic. Women aren't so perfect—it's not natural.

—Angela, sixteen years old

"It kills me to hear a girl say, 'I look so ugly.'"

I'm very satisfied with my looks; sometimes I think I'm vain. When I read magazines and they say how to put makeup on to accentuate your cheekbones or brighten your eyes, do this, do that, that is trying to make me feel like my cheekbones or my eyes aren't good enough. And I'm already happy with them. I'm not gorgeous, and I have bad hair days, bad skin days, bad everything days. But I'd be a fool to say I'm ugly, and it kills me to hear a girl say, "I look so ugly," because they don't. I don't think *anyone* looks really ugly.

—Jasmine, fourteen years old

Model Talk

The media make it seem as if models never have a bad day. All those glamorous locations, fancy clothes and oh-so-cool expressions. In reality modeling can be a tiring, pressured and competitive experience. Two models talk about what life is like in this "fast lane":

"You get tired of people critiquing you all the time."

Modeling is a constant reassurance that someone thinks you look good, and most people don't get that kind of approval. Every day it's like, "Well you're pretty enough to be in this magazine." It's kind of glamorous. You get to wear cute clothes and dress up. But at the same time you're constantly getting rejected and being told what's wrong with you: "You're too thin"; "You should stay the way you are"; "Your nose is too big"; "You have a nice ethnic look"; "Your eyes are too close together"; "Your eyes are too far apart." Everything. Sometimes you get really paranoid and think they're right. And you get tired of people critiquing you all the time. I want to shout, "Enough already. I'm sick of being torn apart." But you just have to step away from it and think, "Wait a second, it doesn't really matter." In the end you have to weigh it out, because some people will always think you look good and some people won't.

—Shannon, seventeen years old

"They don't realize that all the pictures they see are retouched."

The typical fashion magazines—*Vogue*, *Glamour*, *Mademoiselle*, *Seventeen*, *Elle*—are not realistic. The readers don't realize that all the pictures they see are retouched! That means if the model has a wrinkle, they smooth the wrinkle out, or if her eyes are red, they make them white. They can change your body too; like if there is a bulge of fat under your behind, they can just touch it up on the picture. The retouching and the light have so much to do with the outcome. I mean these models are sixteen and they never have pimples? Come on that's too strange. The girls are so skinny they have to twist and pin clothes behind their backs. It is dangerous because women who don't look like that think, "Oh, I have to look like that." They put so much makeup on us. The first thing everyone does is take it off; you would never recognize us!

If I could give advice to a girl just starting out in modeling, I would say, you can't trust too many people. Everyone wants something from you, especially if you are young. You also have to travel a lot, and it's so easy to say, "I love to travel," but it's not so easy when you have to leave your family and friends and go to a country where you don't know anyone or speak the language. It sounds fun but it's not easy.

—Vicki, eighteen years old

"I no longer had one idea of beauty, but lots of ideas of beauty."

In junior high I was into magazines and thought ideal beauty was tall, voluptuous, long hair and white skin. I was wanting something that I could never be because I'm not tall, I'm not voluptuous, and I'm not white. Watching TV also showed me that men want tall and voluptuous women. Then in high school it changed, and I thought women who looked more like me were beautiful: shorter and with dark hair. I no longer had one idea of beauty, but lots of ideas of beauty. Before I thought because I didn't look like the beauty standard, it meant that I wasn't beautiful. I realized that wasn't true and that I didn't have to fit a stereotypical beauty standard. Lots of people can be beautiful. I think the most attractive people have odd facial features, or are ugly and carry it off really well. Those are the most interesting and attractive people to me.

—Aiko, seventeen years old

"Magazines are so glamorous—I see it as fun."

I'm obsessed with fashion magazines, but it's more for the clothes than the models. Magazines are so glamorous—I see it as fun, someone else may see it as intimidating. I think it is enjoyable to pick up a magazine and see the newest lines. As opposed to, "Look how beautiful she is, I just have to look like that," I cut pictures out for the clothes or photography. I think the dresses are beautiful even though I could never wear them. Half the outfits they show on runways are not what they really have in the stores; it's to get you excited about the line.

—Soy, seventeen years old

Pretty Girl

I'm beautiful, I'm gorgeous
Don't try to tell me I'm not
I'm sassy, I'm smart

Don't try to make me change this
I've got class, I've got style
Don't try to make me deny this
Don't try to fix me—I'm not broken
Your pages dictate to me how I should look
How I should act, what I should wear
Your ads tell me what I should
Spend my money on to be better
Your photo shoots show me a glimpse
Of that perfection that I will never have
Well, I want to tell you something—so listen up
I don't want that perfection—I've got my own, thanks
And those rules and tips—I've got a brain
I don't want this "charity," these ideas
Because I love myself
I love my mind, I love my body
Don't try to change me, don't try to turn myself against myself.
Because I'll fight back. Hey Nikki, Cindy, Naomi!
Take a look over here. Here's a real
Pretty girl

—Lila, fourteen years old

BARBIE: THE PLASTIC QUEEN OF BEAUTY

Even our *toys* are focused on idealized beauty. One of the most popular toys ever is Barbie. Barbie was introduced in 1959 at the New York Toy Fair by Mattel Toys as "Barbie: a shapely teen-age fashion model. She's grown up!" She was a far cry from the cute, pudgy baby dolls girls usually played with—for starters, she had breasts.

In the past twenty-five years, over 250 million Barbie dolls have been sold. That's a doll population almost equal to the population of the United States! We can now buy Diamond Dazzle Barbie, Circus Star Barbie, Shopping Fun Barbie, Evening Extravaganza Barbie, Hula Hoop Barbie and many others. There's even a wheelchair Barbie, an admirable addition, except that when she's in the chair she can't fit in the door to the Barbie Dreamhouse. (Sorry, "imperfect" Barbie—*you* have to stay outside!) Each of these figures has Barbie's *amazing* proportions, which would be a forty-two-inch bust, eighteen-inch waist and thirty-three-inch hips if Barbie were a full-sized woman! The average *real* woman is roughly thirty-five (bust), twenty-six (waist), thirty-seven and a half (hips). Barbie, time to eat some donuts.

Barbie Tales

- The first talking Barbie doll—"Teen Talk Barbie," introduced in 1992—created controversy because one of her sentences was, "Math class is tough."

- The Barbie Liberation Organization, a group of concerned parents, feminists, and other activists, launched an effort to free Barbie from her traditional gender shackles. In 1989, they switched the voice boxes of three hundred talking Barbies and talking G.I. Joes so that Joe now asked, "Want to go shopping?" while Barbie warned, "Dead men tell no lies." (*Brillo* magazine website)
- In 1991 the High Self-Esteem Toys Corporation came out with a "Happy to Be Me" doll that was designed to reflect a more realistic female body type than Barbie. The doll, which had a wider waist, larger feet, and shorter legs, never took off in popularity. (*New York Times* Aug, 15, 1991)
- Mattel is gearing up to introduce a new Barbie with more realistic features (though still more model-like than "Happy to Be Me" doll). For example, the proportions are less dramatic, she has darker hair, and her nose is slightly bigger. Good luck new Barbie.

Girls admire Barbie's appearance and neat outfits. But boys don't seem to like Barbie's counterpart, Ken. They dig G.I. Joe over Ken, not because of Joe's cute camouflage outfits or his slick looks, but for his warrior abilities. When G.I. Joe was introduced, the creators refused to call him a doll, calling him an "action figure" instead. Girls, you've probably noticed, are not traditionally given "action figures," but *dolls* with an emphasis on appearance.

> Who would admire a Barbie doll? She is just skinny and blonde with big breasts.
>
> —Kimra, thirteen years old

> "This is my take on Barbie: She's not so bad, she has a cool pink car, a dream house, and Ken tags along on the side."

> They have ethnic Barbies now, which is cool. And there are career Barbies. There is room for improvement though, like they still need to make a plump Barbie.
>
> —Natalie, seventeen years old

FASHION TRENDS: THEY USED TO WEAR WHAT?

> If you want a girl to grow up gentle and womanly in her ways and her feelings, lace her tight.
>
> —One man's testimonial to the corset in the late Victorian press

Women's clothing is about much more than function and practicality—it's about the image that we're supposed to project. Last season, for example, fashion magazines stressed being feminine again, telling us, "Dress like a girl!" and "Curves are BACK!!!" But the silly thing about trying to look like the latest *Vogue* cover girl or MTV's newest soul queen is that the ideal image changes like the wind.

Fashion trends mirror what's going on around us—whether it's the end of a world war in the 1940s or a boom of women entering executive positions in the 1980s. The following is a look at beauty and fashion trends throughout the twentieth century. (This overview is outlined and fully described in *The Changing Face of Beauty* by Sharon Romm.) Each trend had a "personality" women were supposed to adopt along with the clothing. Watching old movies or period pieces, we might think, "How could women have worn that?" about styles that seem outrageous and impractical. Fifty years from now women may be saying the same thing about our current beauty and fashion ideals.

Late 1800s/Early 1900s: Corsets Create the "Perfect" Figure

After the conservative Victorian era ended, sexuality became an important part of the beauty standard. Women were supposed to focus on improving their appearance instead of their "far less useful intellect." The ideal figure had large breasts, a small waist and slim hips. To achieve the impossible figure of this period, women wore corsets and laced them so tightly that some fainted or had to see their doctors for crushed organs. People admired the beauty of older women, and a "willowy seventeen-year-old would have to wait her turn for the limelight."

The "Gibson Girl," an illustration drawn by Charles Dana Gibson, represented this era's standard of beauty. She was dark haired and "athletic but not manly." Her personality was modest and standoffish. The identity of the model for the Gibson Girl was kept a secret, and some wondered if she existed or not. The "Gibson Girl" was the last time that a beauty ideal was created by a single artist, rather than through media images.

1914–1918, World War I: Back to Natural Forms

During this period, women went to work for the war effort. Naturalness became an asset, and the ideal was "simple and sleek." Women's bodies were released from their corsets and allowed to relax into their natural form.

1920s: Short Skirts All the Rage by Mid-Decade

World War I was over, and new technology allowed for more leisure time. Women finally gained the right to vote. The flapper represented the "easy life" and greater independence, and became the new standard of beauty. She shed the layers of petticoats and for the first time wore shorter skirts that allowed easier mobility and showed off her legs. Prior to this time, a woman needed floor-length skirts, as showing her legs was "immodest, ungodly and sinful." The flapper's rebellious beauty style, including her newly bobbed hair, paralleled the women's movement, changing the established order. Cinema became a force for the first time, with wide-eyed actresses such as Mary Pickford and Clara Bow stepping into the limelight.

1930s: Women Welcome Pants

Fashion magazines began setting and creating the rules for beauty and fashion. The photographic model replaced the high-society woman as the standard for beauty. Good health and a more athletic build were part of being beautiful. For the first time it became acceptable for women to wear trousers. Wearing men's clothing was fashionable as long as women kept feminine accessories such as long hair, jewelry, and high heels. Greta Garbo, with her perfect skin and mysterious image, embodied the ideal that women were striving for.

1939–1945, World War II: The Pin-Up Girl Era

The American ideal of beauty was robust good health and "scrubbed smiling faces." The pin-up became popular among American soldiers. Rita Hayworth, with her long legs, ample buttocks and breasts and cute nose, epitomized the pin-up girl.

1950s: Hello, Marilyn

Two types of beauty were in the limelight during this decade. The first was an extremely voluptuous woman with a rougher quality than had been seen before. Movie actresses who represented this version of beauty were Ava Gardner and Jane Russell. The second type was a more childlike and passive woman. After the war, women were supposed to resume their roles as housewives, and a woman's greatest success was thought to be a happy marriage. Fashion ideals returned to small waists and full skirts. Girdles acted as modern corsets and were used to achieve the "perfect" figure. Movie actresses who represented this second type were Sandra Dee and Debbie Reynolds, women who "hid their sexuality under ponytails and bobby socks." Marilyn Monroe, the most famous actress from this decade, managed to embrace both categories of beauty by combining a childlike persona and sexiness.

1960s: Thin Is In (Thanks, Twiggy ...)

Beauty became as important as wealth and status. Models bragged about working-class backgrounds and everyone could be found in blue jeans. Youth reigned. Some women spent hours in front of mirrors trying to achieve the natural flower-child/hippie look. Ninety-two-pound fashion model Twiggy, with her long legs, thin waist and nonexistent hips and breasts, was idealized as the perfect beauty. Women became obsessed with being thin. As the civil rights movement unfolded, Black models broke into the all-white confines of the high-fashion world. Motown Records also introduced such Black beauties as Diana Ross and Aretha Franklin.

1970s: Feathered Hair, Lip Gloss and Charlie's Angels

Athletic women who were "wholesome yet erotic" became the ideal. Farrah Fawcett, Diana Ross (showing her staying power through the decades) and Cheryl Tiegs were examples of this decade's beauty goddesses. The interesting and unusual were sometimes in style. For example, Lauren Hutton's gapped teeth and Brooke Shields' shaggy eyebrows were part of their popularity. In the late seventies we saw the beginning of the "how to dress for success" campaigns.

1980s: Yuppies and Frou-Frou Dresses

The sale of women's suits soared between 1980 and 1987. Then suddenly, in 1987, Christian Lacroix introduced twenty-pound dresses of taffeta and hoops for "women who like to dress up like little girls"—but sales were disappointing. It seemed as though the advances women made in the business world were in direct proportion to the backward leaps of the fashion world. Some other looks seen in women's closets during this decade were athletic/spandex, androgynous, gothic, *Flashdance* and punk.

1990s: Retro

The nineties have seen the waif, grunge and retro-sixties looks come and go. Other retro hits, such as crimped hair, blue eye shadow, bell bottoms and platform shoes are deemed "back." Body piercing and tattoos are hot. As always, it's hard to keep up with the trends because they change seasonally. Within these trends, we continue to be given advice: "How to look professional, yet sexy," "How to dress to seduce but not look like a tramp," and let's not forget, "How to find a bathing suit that transforms your so-so bod into a '10'."

TRANSFORMING OUR LOOKS: THE BIG MAKEOVER

In the factory we make cosmetics. In the store we sell hope.

—Charles Revson, founder of Revlon cosmetics

She wants me to go to the mall
SHE wants ME
To put the pretty, pretty lipstick on
She wants me to be like her
She wants me to be like her
I want to kill her
But I'm afraid it might kill me

—Bikini Kill, "Alien She," *Pussy Whipped*

REBELLING: TRASHING THE BEAUTY STANDARD

Some of us are uncomfortable with the "pretty" mold and do everything to go against the "norm." We boycott the Gap, shave our heads, pierce various body parts, tattoo ourselves, dress in whatever is not "in" or ditch the "nice girl" attitude. Rebelling against the standard can be a statement that expresses our attitude about the world. Our belly-button ring and jet-black hair can say we don't care about looking like a fresh, young flower. Or our green lipstick may be a way to separate from (or be accepted by) the "gang." These days, an Izod shirt, loafers and a quilted skirt can be their own form of rebellion. We may rebel to make a point or to express our inner emotions—or maybe we are just sick and tired of seeing the mainstream look.

"I also wanted to destroy the possibility of looking beautiful."

I'm not your conventional Barbie doll/Miss America type. I shaved my head in January. I want people to know that I'm not trying to match their ideas of beauty, that I'm trying to match my own ideas of beauty. You know, girls are supposed to be pretty. I'm obsessed with beauty, and sometimes I think, "Oh, if I were beautiful like a model, everything would be great." Which is silly because I also don't want beauty to be the basis that people are judging me on. It scares me to look completely normal. In ninth grade I looked as strange as possible because I wanted people to know from the first that they couldn't judge me like they judge other girls. Then I grew up a little and thought, "Well, that's ridiculous." But it's still weird for me to walk down the street wearing jeans and a T-shirt looking like everyone else—I feel lost. In a lot of ways, that's bad because I should be confident enough about what's inside not to have to try and show it.

I hated high school. I was into this masochism thing because it's a quick release when you're feeling bad. I wanted to be beautiful all the time, but I also wanted to destroy the possibility of looking beautiful. I scratched my arms, and when my mom saw them, it was a big deal. So instead, I started piercing my ears. That was a more aesthetically pleasing way of destroying my body. I got my lip ring a week ago, and I like having it; it feels really good. I think it mirrors the chaos of moving from the suburbs to a new city. I feel like everything is kind of crazy, and this is something I can do to mark myself so I don't feel so lost.

—Tanya, seventeen years old

"I like to wear strange clothes."

Everyone dresses in jeans and a shirt, but I like unusual, dark clothes, mostly black. My parents and some other people ask, "Did someone die? When is the funeral?" Ha ha. A lot of girls worry if other people like what they wear. I don't. If I like it, I get it.

—Theresa, fifteen years old

"I went through my gothic stage in eighth grade."

I dyed my hair blue-black, wore really red lipstick and dark eyeliner. I decided I wanted to look unnatural. Then I dyed my hair fuchsia. For two years I went through pink, purple whatever. Finally I dyed it back to black and let it grow out. It was fun, but then I got bored with it. People thought I was trying to make some big statement with it, but I was like, "No, I just think it's fun."

—Dina, eighteen years old

PUTTING BEAUTY IN ITS PLACE

"What's on the outside isn't all there is."

It's not that how traditionally beautiful you are doesn't affect you at all. Certainly it does. If you are traditionally beautiful, what other people consider beautiful, then maybe it will seem like you have an easier time because people will want to be around you. But if you're beautiful and you have no thoughts of your own, people won't want to stay around you. And if you're not beautiful, but you do have thoughts of your own or you have a good character or if you have a great sense of humor or have interesting things to talk about, then eventually people are going to find you. I think that's part of growing up. People figure out, or I hope they figure out, that what's on the outside isn't all there is.

—Tara, sixteen years old

Beauty is fine, but it's not the solution to life. What if beauty were not such an important trait? If we were to grow up on a desert island, we might always feel wonderful about how we look, or we might not give it any thought. In our own isolated world, clothing might be worn just for warmth, pimples might be welcomed as beauty marks, and our own body type might symbolize perfection. Instead we live in a world that tells us what is beautiful and that, as girls, beauty is extremely important. Making things happen and living "happily ever after" is up to us, not our looks. We can take what we want from the beauty culture and throw out what makes us uncomfortable. Within the range of beauty possibilities there is freedom to be ourselves. We need to find, create, and *insist* on valuing other images of beauty. Variety is the spice of life.

"You shouldn't hurt yourself just to look a certain way."

Women in the media are perfect, thin people. But in real life no one looks that perfect. You shouldn't hurt yourself just to look a certain way; not everyone can be tiny. Be true to yourself. Girls shouldn't have to be beautiful to impress men and be a guy's little creature. We should dress to impress *ourselves*.

—Zoe, eighteen years old

39. Emi Koyama, "A New Fat-Positive Feminism: Why the Fat-Positive Feminism (Often) Sucks and How to Reinvent It," from http://eminism.org/readings/fatpositive.html

Excerpts from "A New Fat-Positive Feminism" (http://eminism.org/readings/fatpositive.html), May 5, 2004.

In this essay, influential and hard-hitting third-wave feminist activist Emi Koyama takes on the fat-positive movement from a third-wave perspective, arguing that the fat-positive movement is blind to race, class, and heterosexism when it describes fat as "the last oppression"—as if the mainstream is not still affected by these. The fat-positive feminist movement is unable to "address multiple layers of meanings the society attributes to fatness ... other ways in which human bodies are socially regulated." Koyama says that a "new fat-positive feminism focused on dissecting political and cultural values imposed on our diverse bodies" is needed.

A while back, I went through my entire 'zine library to decide which 'zines and chapbooks I want to keep and which ones I should give away or recycle, since the sheer volume of other people's DIY writings I've accumulated over the years began to overwhelm me.

My goal was to consolidate three medium-size cardboard boxes full of 'zines into one big box that would only contain those select 'zines that I am actually likely to read again. In the process, I've come across quite a few 'zines addressing the topic of fat oppression and women's self-esteem written by other girls who are, like me, fat, proud, and fierce.

Even though I've never been deeply involved in the "fat-positive" feminist movements, I've been around them long enough to know how much they have impacted fat girls like me, and how zine-making is the perfect medium to confront and contradict the anti-fat, pro-diet biases in the mainstream media and the anti-fat industries that finance them. Nonetheless, after skimming through several of these 'zines, I felt empty and ended up tossing many of them in the "give away or recycle" pile.

And I know that this is the same empty feeling I get after attending just about every "fat positive" workshop and event (and I've attended many) including even the otherwise fabulous "FatGirl Speaks!" event in which I performed a spoken-word piece last year. This essay is an attempt to verbalize the shallowness or emptiness that I frequently feel within the fat-positive feminist movement, and how we can reinvent it.

The greatest turn-off for me with fat-positive workshops—and it somehow manages to take place in just about every such workshop—is hearing the comment that "fat oppression is the last remaining socially acceptable oppression" or that "if this was done to Blacks (and it's always Blacks, or else other people of color), there'd be an outrage."

Sometimes, this is the premise that workshop presenters (almost always white) speak from, and other times these comments are made by regular participants (again, almost always white). And it is extremely rare that someone would point out how wrong it is to rank severity of various oppressions, or to assume that the mainstream society is no longer tolerant of racism (or classism, or heterosexism, or any other oppressions, for that matter) before I do. Or sometimes don't.

The view that the fat oppression is the only socially tolerated oppression negates the experiences of not just Blacks, but all people who are marginalized by various intersecting and overlapping systems of oppressions, while at the same time erasing the presence of fat people who are dealing with multiple oppressions. Together, these factors function to limit the appeal and the membership of the fat-positive feminist movement almost exclusively to the fat women who are relatively privileged otherwise.

This brings us to the second problem with the "fat-positive" feminist movement: the inability of fat-positive workshops and 'zines to address multiple layers of meanings the society attributes to fatness. Contrary to the idea that the fat oppression functions in some sort of socially accepted vacuum, the anti-fat attitudes and systems have everything to do with racial and class politics, not just the gender politics.

For example, the debate over the "welfare reform" has been intrinsically shaped by the fiscal conservatives' manipulation of the public perception of inner-city welfare recipients as fat, Black, lazy single mothers. Exploiting such perception, they managed to convince voters that the solution to the problem of poverty is to send the poor mothers back to work, nevermind the fact that few jobs today actually pay "family" wage. In order to counter such propaganda, it is not enough to criticize the use of fatness or fat stereotype as the symbol of laziness or unworthiness; we must take apart its anti-fat, sexist, racist, and classist overtones piece by piece until lies and bigotry are exposed as such.

Third, the fat-positive feminism must pay attention to many other ways in which human bodies are socially regulated. For example, there appears to be natural opportunities for the disability movement and fat-positive movement to work together as both movements challenge the society's definition of normal and acceptable bodies. However, this potential alliance is hindered by the fat-positive movement's oft-repeated insistence that fat people are healthy and productive.

These notions of health and productivity both assume a certain type of body to be "normal" based on its ability to participate in the capitalist labor market as it exists today, and deny the basic human dignity to those bodies deemed too "crippled" to participate in the workforce. However, it is not our physical differences that limit the ability of people with "crippled" bodies to fully participate in the society; it is the lack of accessibility and accommodation based on the limited view of humanity that does.

Also problematic is the fat-positive movement's disdain of people with "eating disorders," especially toward members of the so-called "pro-ana" movement (i.e., women who celebrate extreme dieting and purging as personally gratifying and empowering). Dieting and purging are often forms of self-help, two of many creative ways women cope with life and reclaim the sense of control in a society that robs from us genuine control over circumstances of our lives. If so, we could recognize that both fat-positive feminism and pro-ana movement are basically made up of women who are refusing the society's labeling of their bodily differences and coping methods as "unhealthy" or "maladaptive."

In fact, similarities between the two movements are many. Both groups are primarily made up of women who are considered sick and in need of "help" to alter who they are. Women from both groups report a strong sense of alienation and isolation prior to finding others with similar experiences. A common statement made toward someone who is anorexic is that "most men aren't attracted to fat women, but neither are they attracted to extremely thin women," as if that is all that matters in a woman's life.

Sure, dieting and purging could be, if not careful, harmful to one's health, but so is being fat: why do we need to judge or fight each other? Some fat-positive activists refer to those who diet and purge as "brainwashed" or as victims in need of our rescue, but how is that different from the society telling the fat women that we should lose weight for our own good? As we criticize the anti-fat element within the pro-ana movement, we must also confront the paternalistic and pathologizing gaze our movement sometimes imposes on other women.

Lastly, if I may entertain a little snobbism in me, I find a large portion of fat-positive personal essays and performance art boring. Too often, they provide such a simplistic and linear narrative of complete victimhood to complete pride that it is laughable. I find them devoid of human complexity and contradiction that make essays and art meaningful. The concept of fat pride is revolutionary when you hear it for the first time, but after third or fourth time I begin to yearn for something more real, something that I can relate to.

And most women in America simply do not relate to feeling completely proud and unashamed about their bodies, whether they are fat or not. It's just not realistic. Most women in America, myself included, struggle with our bodies. Or rather, we struggle with voices in our heads and outside telling us how dirty and ugly our bodies are, no matter how we look, and sometimes we end up agreeing with it. I'm not saying that this is right or wrong, but that is how it is.

Through the writings and performances like those I described above, the fat-positive feminism fosters a political climate that idolizes complete pride and shamelessness as an ideal. By doing so, however, we are in effect setting up yet another unattainable set of ideals that women are somehow expected to live up to, just like the "beauty myth" itself.

In such climate, women who feel ashamed of their bodies—that is, most American women at some point in their lives—are made to feel ashamed of their shame, and are thus doubly silenced, because an admission of body-shame or desire to be thinner is interpreted by those in the movement as the proof of their ideological impurity, or as the evidence that she is still under the patriarchal brainwashing and needs to be liberated further. We need arts that imitate and enrich life, not those that dictate or condemn perfectly reasonable life experiences of women living in an unjust society.

I envision a new fat-positive feminism that does more than just confronting fatphobia. We need to pay attention to many ways in which fat oppression is embedded not only in sexism, but also in racism, classism, heterosexism, ableism, and other oppressions. Instead of merely arguing that fat is normal and healthy, we need to challenge the concepts of normalcy and health altogether and question who is arbitrating these categories and who benefits.

In addition to the army of "fat and proud" women and activists we already have, a new fat-positive feminism needs to attract, not repel or patronize, weight watchers, pro-anorexics, women struggling with eating disorders (i.e., those who are not pro-ana), and ordinary women in America who are concerned about their weight either somewhat or great deal. And by that I am not talking about "liberating" them from their body image "pathologies" and converting them to be just like us; I am talking about starting from the assumption that other women's ways of coping with this woman-hating, body-hating society may be just as valid as our own.

Instead of belittling or condemning the vast majority of women, a new fat-positive feminism focuses on dissecting political and cultural values imposed on our diverse bodies. It will promote pro-women and pro-body attitudes by validating creative ways in which women cope with struggles of daily life and breaking the silence and isolation that separate us. The fat-positive feminist movement must take over the mainstream, rather than settling with the consolation of being the righteous fringe—and we can do so without compromising any of the key progressive values.

Along with the rampant violence against women, fat oppression is one of the oppressions targeting especially women that is so ubiquitous that it can be readily identified once one begins to notice it. This fact suggests that fat-positive feminism could be an entry point for millions of women to embrace a full range of progressive politics that seek to create a more just and equitable society.

So far, the fat-positive feminism has been able to enlist only a relatively small number of women—and from a relatively thin socioeconomic layer of the society—partly due to the problems discussed above. If we were to change how the society ranks and regulates our bodily differences, instead of secluding ourselves in the homogeneous enclaves of affinity groups who think and act just like us, we must seize this previously untouched opportunity and rally for it.

By combining the dedication of pro-anorexics, persistence of weight watchers, and, yes, our fierceness and pride, we will be able to bring millions of women and men (and people of other genders) into progressive social change movements. And then, the fat-positive feminism will become a new common sense in the American mainstream.

40. Evelyn Summerstein (Ophira Edut), "Absolutely Capitalist," from *Bitch* Magazine

Excerpts from "Absolutely Capitalist," by Ophira Edut, writing as Evelyn Summerstein, published in *Bitch* magazine, Vol. 2, No. 1 (Spring 1998). Reprinted with permission.

In an essay that both demonstrates third-wave sensibility and the cultural conditions that inform it, Ophira Edut, one of the publishers of *HUES* magazine, tells the story of her adventures in book publishing and the ways the mainstream publishing industry forces young feminists concerned with social change to "think less like a writer and more like a marketing associate." It is compelling commentary on the place of third-wave sensibility within the larger culture.

I never intended to write a book. Not a "real" book, anyway. Not, like, the bestselling kind that would land me a guest therapist spot on *Jenny Jones* and a national book-signing tour at Barnes and Noble Cafés. After all, I don't know any serial killers or celebrities. I've never had any good jury duty gigs. I'm not a Spice Girl.

Nay, my beginnings are much humbler, and go a little somethin' like this: Grew up in the Midwest. Publish a feminist zine in my basement. Responsible for large interest payments on various college and personal loans. Juggle six freelance and temp jobs to pay my bills. High moral standards. High monthly living expenses. High from the caffeine required to maintain this act.

When I found myself in the posh Manhattan office of a Real Live New York Literary Agent, six-figure visions danced in my head. I had more baggage than a fleet of Greyhound buses—financially speaking, anyway—and I was ready to make a drop-off. But I'm getting ahead of myself.

My plan was simple. I would exchange service industry livin' for full-on media whoredom, complete with paid assignments and the salary of a white-collar escort. TV appearances, infomercials—you name it and I was ready to perform the act. In no time, I'd be stackin' enough Benjamins to pay off my debts. Yet, it was in midtown Manhattan, the literary Hollywood Boulevard of the East Coast, that I damn near pimped out my soul by mistake.

Before I paint myself as some greedy, soulless faux feminist, let me explain. The book I intended to write was a modern feminist guide/manifesto, which I planned to call *Generation XX: Women Here and Now*, or something along those clever yet meaningful lines. Intelligent and articulate, my book would explore a new generation's approach to sisterhood, relationships, media, activism, politics, multiculturalism, and feminism. It would include the perspectives of women from a range of ethnicities, sexual orientations, religions, and identities. I even hoped to invite some cool celebrities and underground role models to write guest introductions to each chapter.

My deepest motive was not money, but conveying a healing message to young women. So much of the media being churned out by the mainstream sucks. It speaks to women's insecurities rather than to our intelligence. It tries to sell us the same old 6'10" 52-pound hetero blond girl prescription. Frankly, that shit is tired. Through my zine—and the book I envisioned—I hoped to in some small way counterbalance those wack messages, while still delivering a dose of pop culture and entertainment.

After all, I was no stranger to the harmful effects mainstream reading material can have on a girl's self-esteem. I grew up with my hungry snout buried in the feedbag of *Seventeen* and *Sweet Valley High*. Like so many young women, I bought into the bullshit, believing that my ethnic features were a curse and that my index finger had been separated from my throat at birth only to be reunited in a secret adolescent binge-and-purge ritual. After a painful college era spent recovering my self-esteem, I wanted to help other young women see that we have choices beyond self-hatred. I wanted to create a platform for young women to share real, honest stories that would inspire and support us and lead us back to our long-forgotten power.

Although big bucks weren't the major motivation for me, the way I see it, healing is real work, and I deserve to be paid for it. Why not? Women who work in healing professions are always undervalued. People assume that nurturing others is so intrinsic for women that it hardly takes a toll on us. In truth, it's incredibly draining. It requires us to remove the focus from ourselves and offer our vital energies and support to an outside force, instead of investing it back into our own energy banks. If I was gonna give this project my soul, then at least my bills could get paid, right?

My arrival in the world of mainstream publishing happened like this: Last year, a friend and fellow young zine publisher called me, excited. She'd just landed a $100,000 book deal with a major publishing house. Her agent, New York literary scene hotshot Linda Goodman, heard my friend on a radio show and called to solicit a proposal. The rest was six-figure history.

"And guess what?" my friend said. "Linda asked if I knew any other young women writers! Since my proposal went over so well, she thinks there's a really big market for us. I'm giving you her phone number now."

I took one look at the stack of unpaid bills gathering dust on my desk—credit cards, car payments, phone bills, student loans, rent—and decided my ship had come in. At that precise moment, something new and unfamiliar, something green and depositable into a commercial bank, gave my inspiration a swift kick-start. If my friend could make that kind of money just for being herself, so could I. Best of all, my friend's zine was highly intelligent, pro-woman, "alternative" in every good way. Her book would be based on her zine, which meant she'd get paid by "the man" without having to sell her soul to him.

Again I asked, Why not me, too? If my zine never became profitable, at least I'd be able to eat while I continued publishing. Besides, a book that was marketed by a major publishing house would help spread my positive, pro-woman message to the masses. Feminism and pop culture would unite at long last into something cool and financially viable.

I spent six weeks drafting my first proposal and sent it off to Linda in October 1996. It was a hodgepodge of chapters covering what I thought were important third-wave feminist topics—body image, race, dating, education and careers, general identity politics.

Admittedly, I felt vague about the whole book-writing thing, since my publishing experience was limited to magazines. Hell, I was only 23. Linda offered no guidance throughout the proposal process, but she did give me a copy of my friend's book proposal to use as a road map. In fact, she seemed annoyed when I called with questions. "You're not done yet?" she'd sigh with great exasperation.

The pressure, coupled with my inexperience, made for a proposal that elicited a curt, typed reply on Linda's letterhead:

> Your proposal seems to fall flat for a variety of reasons. The tone seems too bitter and defensive, and you spend too much energy on body image—The Beauty Myth was published about five years ago and this takes away from the freshness of what you should be writing. Obviously, we'll be open to looking at a rewrite.
>
> Kind regards,
> Linda

Ever the optimist, I moped around for a few hours then decided to step back up to bat. What did I have to lose? I knew I could add a lot more flavor and personality to the proposal. I called Linda again, hoping she'd actually offer some concrete advice this time.

"Make it fresh!" she screamed, in full-on New Yahwk character. "Just [*sigh*] ... I don't know [*annoyed sigh*] ... you're the young woman! What's Courtney Love talking about? What's Alanis doing? What do the Spice Girls have to say? [*Extremely annoyed, drawn-out sigh.*] Look, you're wasting my time. *Just. Make. It. Fresh.*" And with that, she slammed down the phone.

Mmm-kay. I was tempted to call back and ask Linda whether she wanted a second proposal or a new, turbo-powered douche. She was definitely giving me a not-so-fresh feeling. I imagined her age-defying cheeks, pulled taut by the hands of New York's most gifted plastic surgeons, crackling like a relief map of parched soil. Somehow, this soothed me. I was on a mission to get this deal, so I swallowed my tongue, focused on my mission, and resumed my flow.

I decided not to let Linda press me for time, and spent four months writing my new proposal. As promised, it was springtime-fresh and packed hella irreverence. Per Linda's request, I included a photo of myself with the neatly packaged proposal so potential buyers could judge whether I was "televisionworthy."

Something was a little different this time, though. I began to think less like a writer and more like a marketing associate. There were times when I could hardly express myself for fear I'd be "too serious" or "not fresh enough," and thus would lose the deal. "Will this sell?" a voice kept nagging, and light-'n'-airy phrases stumbled from my word processor. My new proposal was sassy, no doubt, but steeped in its own shocking irreverence (and the ensuing controversy that it would stir up) and less focused on making women feel soothed and supported. Linda and her associates loved the writing and sent the proposal to about twenty big publishers. She was certain we'd get crazy offers. I rode a premature high, psyched that I could attach my name to a flavorful, feminist book that would also pay my bills.

Then ... shock. Instead of fielding offers, Linda got a pile of rejection letters. One after another, the naysayers filed in, all with the same basic excuse: We love the writing, but ... there's just not a large enough mainstream market for it.

Linda was as disappointed as I was, mostly for economic reasons. Again, she was unable to articulate instructions, should I decide to take a third go-round. Instead, she faxed me a stream of rejection letters so I could see for myself. Excerpts follow:

> Thanks for letting me see Evelyn Summerstein's proposal, which I'll be passing on the opportunity to publish. Ms. Summerstein's voice is fun, spunky, and smart. Unfortunately, we didn't see a large mainstream audience for this book.

> What Summerstein has accomplished in her magazine is most impressive—smart, sunny, fresh, timely, and engaging—but I'm sorry to say that her book proposal struck those of us who read it simply as more of the same.

> Ms. Summerstein is sassy, young, and edgy. Unfortunately, this book seems more geared to teenage girls, rather than postfeminist young women.

> Evelyn Summerstein is entertaining and full of energy, but not enough to make me want to go out on a limb. Thanks so much for the look. She's a firecracker.

> I like Evelyn Summerstein's feisty style and her sense of humor. However, I don't feel that the material is focused enough to attract a large audience. If she was Ricki Lake or Queen Latifah, then this could sell. Forgive my cynicism, but it's my feeling that readers only care about the opinions of the famous.

I spent the rest of the day in bed, crying. Maybe I did suck. I didn't have what it took to be a bestseller. I wasn't even worthy of a modest print run. On and on went the self-deprecation, and my bills loomed larger than ever.

Then Linda called one last time. "A few of the young editors we solicited want to meet with you, and try to come up with some ideas together. They really like your writing," she told me. "You have to come out to New York right away, though. If you don't grab this while it's hot, they'll lose interest tomorrow!"

Apparently, there was still one more born-again sucker bone in me. I jumped in my car five days later, less than twenty-four hours after returning from a conference in New Mexico. I made the normally twelve-hour road trip to New York in just under nine and a half. Sprung for a hotel room and prayed I'd "earn it back" if I got the deal.

The next two days, Linda toted me around to four super-huge publishing houses, which shall remain nameless. At each, I met with a group of surprisingly cool women who were mostly between the ages of 25 and 35. They threw around the term *feminist* liberally, seemed to have more than a clue, and were very excited about my zine. It wasn't at all what I expected, and I felt hope renewed once again.

With the exception of one, where a 29-year-old editor decided that I was "too young to write a book," editors at each house offered to work one-on-one with me. I narrowed it down to one, and made plans to work with a hip, young editor named Pam.

Long story short, Pam and I went back and forth for a couple more months, crafting a new proposal that we hoped would sway the skeptics in the upper echelons. She was really excited about working with me and bent over backwards to help. At one point, we exchanged faxes every day, and clocked considerable long-distance minutes.

Nevertheless, Pam was still what Naomi Wolf might call a "power feminist"—if one could call her a feminist at all. She was living the dream that has been handed to young women today by our mothers' struggles: an impressive corporate position, a female boss, a closet full of self-purchased business suits from an impressive array of designers. Yet the more I worked with Pam, the more I realized how much a part of the "establishment" she really was. She still had to answer to the big boys and girls in marketing—which meant that she, too, was a part of that whole Linda Goodman-style douche conspiracy, trapped in the never-ending quest for an unnatural sense of freshness.

I'd been further clued in to the constraints of establishment feminism at a morning power-suit meeting at one of the houses I visited. Seated at the head of an oval table, I faced fifteen female editors and remarked, "Wow, there are a lot of women in book publishing." "Honey, it's about eighty-five percent women," laughed one thirtyish editor as she pushed back a lock of no-fuss hair. I wasn't surprised. By that time I'd met with about forty editors at four different houses. Not a single one was male. Only one had a man as its top decision-maker. The rest of the big kahunas signing the checks were women.

Like fashion magazines, many publishing houses have mostly female staffs, even women presidents and publishers. Yet they insist upon continuing traditions of reducing women, then reusing and recycling images that insult the piss outta us. Many of these women even consider themselves feminists, measuring their contributions to womankind by the balance column in their checkbooks after payday.

Well, it ain't enough for me. I could only conclude that changing the system from within the system was a dangerous game. Especially for a wide-eyed gal of 23 who'd bought one too many elevator passes in her day. I wasn't comfortable straddling both worlds, sittin' on Big Daddy's lap in a naughty piece of satin and whisperin' sweet nothings about the evil patriarchy. I had to pick a side.

Pam believed that she could help me "balance" my proposal enough to get it approved. I had to spell out my theme in ABCs and 123s for the publisher, effectively draining all the spunk and flavor out of it. Pam beat the thing into mainstream-ready submission, dividing my ideas into chapters like "Go for It, But Keep It in Check" and "Let's Get Real." Somehow, I ended up with a proposal for a how-to book on building a multicultural feminist movement, onto which Pam attached a kumbaya title. Although I suppose I could have written this joyless book, the outline was safe, oversimplified, and dangerously close to falling off the tightrope into an abyss of mainstream cheese.

And there was still one obstacle. Pam had to get the proposal past the hardcover and trade paperback publishers, and the marketing team. They were gonna be the toughest sell. In the end, the hardcover woman said she'd do it only if the paperback woman did too. The paperback woman sold me out.

It was June. I had spent nine months (significant?) on this project, and hadn't brought in a dime from it. My roommates were sick of watching my moods swing back and forth every time I got jerked around by what they now called "the Massengill Gang." I was so emotionally disoriented, I wasn't even sure what the hell *I* stood for anymore.

Fortunately, it didn't take me too long to remember. The episode turned into a big-time reality check. Linda and I parted ways, mutually. I faced the existential question of a broke-ass 24-year-old attempting to juggle ideology with a need to pay the bills: How far was I willing to bend—for money and for my beliefs?

Well, part of being a feminist, for me, at least, means having a soul. It means caring about the impact of my words, and speaking what my spirit tells me. My mistake was buying into the naive misconception that in the late '90s, feminism and corporate America could share crayons and color a happy world together. Clichéd as it sounds, telling the truth is a shield. If someone hates me for speaking my mind, I'm ok with that. My views may be more radical than what commercial publishing is ready to risk, and that's just how it is for now. I can only hope it will change in the next decade. They would have used me and my girl power to make as much money as they could, then dropped me as soon as the next craze came along. Frankly, I'm glad I didn't qualify.

I believe that a pop culture feminism can exist, but only if it grows organically. Ambitious young feminists need to dole our goods out carefully. We need to do our thing no matter what, and let the mainstream types come to us. Then we can decide if we want to be bothered with them.

After this fiasco, I decided I wanted to write a book anyway, even if I had to publish it myself. Even if I never made a dime off of it. I wanted to write it because I had something to say. I put together a proposal that truly reflected my beliefs and sent it on my own to a couple of feminist publishers. They responded with total support.

I won't be raking in the cheddar that a Linda Goodman deal would have brought (my publisher pays only royalties), but I'm over it. I have a contract and supportive editors who share my beliefs.

Seeing how I feel satisfied with that proves that the dangers of selling out are overrated. When I was working with the mainstream publishers, I could hardly express myself for fear I'd lose the deal. There was so much more at stake. If my first book didn't do well enough, I knew they'd dump me with a quickness—which would undoubtedly jeopardize my chance for a long-term writing career.

I offered the cream of my soul to mainstream publishing, only to be informed that everything on their shelves was freshness-dated. So I concluded that there's no price tag on my spirit. As for all those greedy folk who rejected me from the ranks of media whoredom? Well, I guess they can kiss my bottom line.

41. Jennifer Baumgardner and Amy Richards, *Manifesta: Young Women, Feminism, and the Future*

Excerpts from Jennifer Baumgardner and Amy Richards, *Manifesta* (New York: Farrar, Straus, and Giroux, 2000), 128–151. Reprinted with permission.

Baumgardner and Richards brought third-wave feminism to national attention with this book. In this piece, Baumgardner and Richards define what they mean by "girlie" culture and discuss the ways that it is both feminist and empowering. Arguing that "the difference between the First, Second, and Third Waves is our cultural DNA," Baumgardner and Richards address this culture and the use to which third-wavers have put it. With the proposition that "Girlie encompasses the tabooed symbols of women's feminine enculturation—Barbie dolls, makeup, fashion magazines, high heels—and says using them isn't shorthand for 'we've been duped,'" Baumgardner and Richards articulate a flashpoint of the third-wave debate and its engagement with popular culture.

One day in 1993, twenty-seven-year-old Lisa Silver took the Delta shuttle from New York to Washington, D.C., for a meeting of Second Wave feminists. The author and chronicler of male-female communication problems Deborah Tannen, CNN correspondent Judy Woodruff, inside-the-Beltway journalist Sally Quinn, political strategist Ann Lewis, and other luminaries had assembled to discuss the women's agenda for the Clinton era. "I walked into that room and was faced with all of these red blazers, brass buttons, and sensible high-heel shoes, and I was like, This is not me," Silver says, recalling the meeting in early 1999. "I thought, What am I doing here?"

Silver was working with Betty Friedan's Women, Men, and Media research group, which produced *The Front Page Report*. As a graduate student in journalism at New York University, she had been thrilled to hook up with Friedan

("I mean *Betty Friedan*!!"), the "mother of the movement." She began as an assistant on a staff of three and soon moved up to program director, the No. 2 spot. Silver was excited to be in the thick of feminist journalism, exposing the still-unequal situation for women. She respected Friedan and the troop of glass-ceiling shatterers at the D.C. meeting, but she also felt alienated from them. Some of the disconnect was simply generational. At twenty-seven, she was working with women ranging in age from their fifties to their seventies, And some of it was aesthetics; a conflict about style, approach, or even emotion: "There I am, going to this meeting with all of these women who are highly successful, but where's the excitement? Where's the spark?"

The backbone of feminism isn't so different from one generation to the next. We want to distinguish ourselves from doormats, as early twentieth-century feminist Rebecca West and her cohorts did, and as Betty Friedan's generation did. And our values are similar, although our tactics and style often differ. (Suffragist Alice Paul was surely horrified when some early Second Wave feminists, including Shulamith Firestone, wanted to stage an action in D.C. to give *back* the vote as part of a 1969 Vietnam protest.) The difference between the First, Second, and Third Waves is our cultural DNA. Each generation has a drive to create something new, to find that distinctive spark that Silver couldn't locate that day in D.C.

The word "generation" is an apt pun here, because what distinguishes one era from the next is what we generate—whether it's music, institutions, or magazines—and how we use what has already been produced. Marlo Thomas grew up on Toni dolls and Nancy Drew stories. In her mid-thirties, she created one of the Third Wave's first glimpses of feminist culture, the 1973 book and record *Free to Be ... You and Me*. When Thomas and Friends created this early manifesto of freedom, in which a football player sang about crying and girls wanted to be firemen, they couldn't have imagined the guys with earrings and girls with tattoos and shaved heads who would emerge a decade or two later—their former readers.

Thomas didn't choose to be influenced by Toni dolls any more than we chose to be influenced by *Free to Be*—or by MTV. Our generation watched powerful, fashionable private detectives solve crimes and bond together in prime-time sisterhood on *Charlie's Angels* but couldn't help noticing that they did all the work while a male voice, always out of reach, told them what to do. We were a generation in which many girls grew up thinking that *Playboy* was for them, too, to sneak peeks at while Mom and Dad were occupied, or to lead tours of neighborhood kids out to the garage for the unveiling of an old copy featuring Miss November 1972. As girls, we saw the culture reflect a bit of our particular vernacular: Valley Girls who shop and register pronouncements about the relative grodiness or radness of all things. We were a generation that was forced to experience equality when it came to the newly coed gym classes, and reveled in Title IX's influence on sports for girls. These products of culture are mundane to us, simply the atmosphere in our temporal tank.

The fact that feminism is no longer limited to arenas where we expect to see it—NOW, *Ms.*, women's studies, and red-suited congresswomen—perhaps means that young women today have really reaped what feminism has sown. Raised after Title IX and "William Wants a Doll," young women emerged from college or high school or two years of marriage or their first job and began challenging some of the received wisdom of the past ten or twenty years of feminism. We're not doing feminism the same way that the seventies feminist did it; being liberated doesn't mean copying what came before but finding one's own way—a way that is genuine to one's own generation.

For the generation that reared the Third Wave, not only was feminism apparent in the politics of the time but politics was truly the culture of the time—Kennedy, the Vietnam War, civil rights, and women's rights. For the Third Wave, politics was superceded by culture—punk rock, hip-hop, zines, products, consumerism, and the Internet. Young women in the early nineties who were breaking out of the "established" movement weren't just rebelling, they were growing up and beginning to take responsibility for their lives and their feminism.

The following is a sampling of what the Third Wave grew up with:

- In 1984, Madonna came out with the album *Like a Virgin*. Lying on her back on the album's cover photo, elbows propped, looking sexy, bored, and tough as hell, she wore fluffy crinolines, black eyeliner, and a belt that said "Boy Toy." She was bad, and looked at you like she wanted it bad. *She* wanted it. Then there were the dozens of incarnations that followed for the material girl. The video identities: stripper, pregnant girl from the neighborhood, dominatrix, men's-suit-wearing activist for female sexuality (*C'mon girls! Do you believe in love?*), and a kick-ass version of the vulnerable, victimized Marilyn Monroe. (Which is why, no doubt, Madonna's fans were mostly young women, while Marilyn's were mostly men.) And Madonna's off-camera identities: strongest thighs in all pop music, bitch, best friend to all the fabulous lesbians, "serious" actress with affected English accent, beatific single mother, and most powerful performer in all the pop firmament. Throughout all this she was sending a message, teaching by example: Be what you want to be, then be something else that you want to be. (And earn a billion bucks while you're at it.)
- In 1988, when *Seventeen* had just been liberated from being run by an ex-nun, and *YM* still stood for *Young Miss* (rather than the current *Young & Modern*), a revolutionary new teen magazine debuted for girls. It was called *Sassy*, and it managed to put on makeup and fashion without prescribing it and created a camp aesthetic for girls. It took the pressure off beauty and fashion by turning away from *Go from So-So to Sexy!* and toward wardrobes donned simply because they were pleasurable: *Dye your hair with Jell-O! Dress like a mod from the sixties! Wear a*

little Catholic schoolgirl outfit with a down vest! Wear a furry hat with mouse ears! Wheeeee! Writer Christina Kelly's two-page pastiche, called "What Now" (essentially an archive of Kelly's taste), vaulted this teen fashion magazine into the counterculture. "What Now" profiled a zine of the month, legitimizing the DIY (do-it-yourself) publications at a time when zines were the only place where people who were too young, punk, or weird, such as Riot Grrrls, could publish. Bands like Jon Spencer Blues Explosion and Guided by Voices got their first teen or women's press in *Sassy*'s "Cute Band Alert." For once, a teen magazine was actually in touch with youth culture. But the salient point here is not so much that the *Sassy* creators were hip, although they were, as that they were hip to feminism. They told girls to get their own guitars, that it's okay to be a lesbian, and that it's even okay *not* to go to the prom. (*Ms.* may have believed this, too, but *Ms.* wasn't written with teenage girls in mind.) The *Sassy* editors were drawing from wells that were below the radar of *Ms.* and over the heads of nonfeminist competitors *Seventeen*, *Teen*, and *YM*.

- In 1991, twenty-eight-year-old Naomi Wolf published *The Beauty Myth*. This book analyzed body image and the consumer trappings of femininity—magazines and makeup and, by extension, porn—from the perspective of a new generation. Wolf was writing for us, and she was one of us: a woman reared in the wake of the Second Wave. Gorgeous and articulate, she drew the reader in the way a fashion magazine did—with pretty pictures (at least, in the Scavullo portraits that accompanied interviews)—and then got you mad with her feminist research. Her critique was one that young women conversant in the coded language of eating disorders could recognize (six glasses of water and hard-boiled egg whites from the salad bar for every dinner equals anorexic masquerading as fitness fanatic; pointer fingers with scratches equals bulimic), as could the girls who felt hostile and ugly when they looked at magazines and porn. As one of the first itinerant feminists of the Third Wave, Wolf traveled to college campuses across the United States, talking to young women. This touring led her to conclude that "girls are still understood more clearly as victims of culture and sexuality than as cultural and sexual creators," so she set out to change that assumption. Her next book, *Fire with Fire: How Power Feminism Will Change the 21st Century*, told women to embrace power, and *Promiscuities* recast the slut as a rebel.
- In 1991, a loose-knit group of punk-rock girls in Olympia, Washington, and Washington, D.C., rescued feminism from two hazards: one, the male-dominated punk-rock scene; and two, their own cohorts, women who didn't use the term *feminist*. Seizing radicalism and activism from the dump in which they thought it had slumped since the mid-seventies, Riot Grrrls weren't pushing a rational feminism. They scrawled *slut* on

their stomachs, screamed from stages and pages of fanzines about incest, rape, being queer, and being in love. They mixed a childish aesthetic with all that is most threatening in a female adult: rage, bitterness, and political acuity. In bands such as Bikini Kill, Bratmobile, Huggy Bear, and Heavens to Betsy, these Grrrls shot up like flames, influencing countless girls and showing them feminism before dissipating, seemingly, around the mid-nineties.

- In 1993, a xerox-and-staple zine of fewer than twenty pages called *Bust* presented an embraceable, nourishing reflection of young women and their lives—and called it girl culture. "The Booty Myth" was a *Bust* story about black women's sexuality, "Elektra Woman and Dyna-Girl" was fiction about two young white girls who staged play-date rapes, "I Was a Teenage Mommy" was self-explanatory, as was "Blow Job Tips for Straight Women from a Gay Man." These articles were juxtaposed with buxom images from vintage soft-core porn, images now in the control of women. In *Bust*, porn was demystified, claimed for women, debated. Vibrators tried and tried again. Childhood heroines revisited (Judy Blume! Farrah! Cynthia Plaster Caster!). Seventies artists and writers with varying degrees of credentials were recast as Second Wave sheroes (such as sex revolutionaries and authors Erica Jong and Nancy Friday). "We're not apologizing for the culture we've been raised with and not overvaluing masculine culture," said Debbie Stoller, the co-editor of *Bust*. "Barbies, for example, are seen by the main culture as kind of dumb, and playing with trucks is more important—but, in fact, when we played with Barbies it was complicated and interesting, and it's something we should tell the truth about." Rock critic Ann Powers codified Stoller's definition in the fall 1997 Girl issue of *Spin*: "Girl Culture girls have transformed what it means to be female in the nineties. Unlike conventional feminism, which focused on women's socially imposed weaknesses, Girl Culture assumes that women are free agents in the world, that they start out strong and that the odds are in their favor."

All of this Girlie culture, from Madonna to *Bust*, is different from the cultural feminism of the seventies. It promoted a gynefocal aesthetic (as a form of politics), too, but sometimes in the service of a "separate but equal" alternative world. (In keeping with the previously proposed Femitopia.) Cultural feminism put the *y* in *womyn* and brought us women-owned Diana publishing, the aforementioned Olivia Records, and all-ladies collectives such as the Michigan Womyn's Music Festival, which has been going strong annually since 1976 and allows males only under the age of six to grace "the Land" (as the nature preserve upon which everyone camps is always called, with reverence). But for this generation, having or loving our own culture isn't the same as cultural feminism—a separate ghetto (or utopia) for women—it's just feminism for a culture-driven generation. And if feminism aims to create a world where our standard of measurement doesn't start with a white-male heterosexual nucleus, then believing that feminine things are weak means that we're believing our own bad press. Girlies say, through actions and attitudes, that you don't have to make the feminine powerful by making it masculine or "natural"; it is a feminist statement to proudly claim things that are feminine, and the alternative can mean to deny what we are. *You were raised on Barbie and soccer? That's cool.* In a way, establishing a girl culture addresses what Gloria Steinem was trying to identify when she wrote *Revolution from Within*—the huge hole that grows in a woman who is trying to be equal but has internalized society's low estimation of women. "It was as if the female spirit were a garden that had grown beneath the shadows of barriers for so long," she wrote, "that it kept growing in the same pattern, even after some of the barriers were gone."

What does the Third Wave garden look like? Planted near Madonna, *Sassy*, Wolf, Riot Grrrls, and *Bust* are influential xerox-and-staple zines such as *I (heart) Amy Carter*, *Sister Nobody*, *I'm So Fucking Beautiful*, *Bamboo Girl*; the glossy-but-still-independent zines such as *HUES*, *Roller Derby*, *Bitch*, *Fresh and Tasty*, *WIG*; chickclick and estronet Web sites like Disgruntled Housewife, Girls On, gURL; webzines such as *Minx and Maxi*; feature films like *Clueless*, *Go Fish*, *All Over Me*, *The Incredibly True Adventure of Two Girls in Love*, *Welcome to the Dollhouse*, *High Art*; art films by Elisabeth Subrin, Sadie Benning, Pratibha Parmar, and Jocelyn Taylor; musicians such as Ani DiFranco, Brandy, Luscious Jackson, Courtney Love as the slatternly, snarly singer, Courtney Love as the creamy Versace model, Erykah Badu, Me'shell Ndege'ocello, Bikini Kill, Missy Elliott, the Spice Girls, Salt-N-Pepa, TLC, Gwen Stefani, Team Dresch, Foxy Brown, Queen Latifah, Indigo Girls, and all those ladies featured at Lilith Fair; products galore, Urban Decay, Hard Candy, MAC, Manic Panic; on the small screen, *Wonder Woman* (in comic-book form, too), *Buffy the Vampire Slayer*, *My So-Called Life*, *Xena*, *Felicity*, and Alicia Silverstone in Aerosmith videos; Chelsea Clinton; the New York club Meow Mix and other joints with female go-go dancers getting down for women; funny girls loving Janeane Garofalo and Margaret Cho; angry women loving Hothead Paisan and *Dirty Plotte* comics; Jenny McCarthy, who somehow satirized being a pinup even as she was one; controversial books like *Backlash* and *The Morning After*; uncontroversial ones like *The* Bust *Guide to the New Girl Order* and *Listen Up*; the West Coast mutual-admiration society of sex writers Lisa Palac and Susie Bright; Monica Lewinsky; the Women's World Cup; the WNBA; and hundreds more films, bands, women, books, events, and zines.

We, and others, call this intersection of culture and feminism "Girlie." Girlie says we're not broken, and our desires aren't simply booby traps set by the patriarchy. Girlie encompasses the tabooed symbols of women's feminine enculturation—Barbie dolls, makeup, fashion magazines, high heels—and says using them isn't shorthand for "we've been duped." Using makeup isn't a sign of our sway to the marketplace and the male gaze; it can be sexy, campy, ironic, or simply decorating ourselves without the loaded issues (à la dye your hair with Jell-O!). Also, what we loved as girls was good and, because of feminism, we know how to make girl stuff work for us. Our Barbies had jobs and sex lives and friends. We weren't staring at their plastic figures and Dynel tresses hoping to someday attain their pneumatic measurements. Sticker collections were no more trivial than stamp collections; both pursuits cultivated the connoisseur in a young person.

While it's true that embracing the pink things of stereotypical girlhood isn't a radical gesture meant to overturn the way society is structured, it can be a confident gesture. When younger women wearing "Girls Rule" T-shirts and carrying Hello Kitty lunch boxes dust off the Le Sportsacs from junior high and fill them with black lipstick and green nail polish and campy sparkles, it is not as totems to an infantilized culture but as a nod to our joyous youth. Young women are emphasizing our real personal lives in contrast to what some feminist foremothers anticipated their lives would—or should—be: that the way to equality was to reject Barbie and all forms of pink-packaged femininity. In holding tight to that which once symbolized their oppression, Girlies' motivations are along the lines of gay men in Chelsea calling each other "queer" or black men and women using the term "nigga."

In creating a feminism of their own, though, Girlies are repeating a pattern as old as the patriarchy: rebelling against their mothers. For instance, Debbie Stoller, who was quoted calling Gloria Steinem a dinosaur in the dumb and now defunct Gen-X magazine *Swing* or Katie Roiphe writing books that seem to be a direct response to her seventies-feminist mother Anne Roiphe. In the same way that Betty Friedan's insistence on professional seriousness was a response to every woman in an office being called a girl, this generation is predestined to fight against the equally rigid stereotype of being too serious, too political, and seemingly asexual. Girlie culture is a rebellion against the false impression that since women don't want to be sexually exploited, they don't want to be sexual; against the necessity of brass-buttoned, red-suited seriousness to infiltrate a man's world; against the anachronistic belief that because women could be dehumanized by porn (and we include erotica in our definition), they must be; and the idea that girls and power don't mix.

Although rebelling appears to be negative, we think it's natural—and the result leads to greater diversity and, in turn, produces a stronger feminist movement. For example, it's important that Andrea Dworkin identify herself as "a feminist, not the fun kind," but if it was ever implied that she was the *only* kind, the movement might feel a little Antioch, as in rigid. Similarly, the Spice Girls make for a pretty thin definition of *feminist* because they are only the fun kind. And yet preteen girls dancing around freely in their living rooms or at concerts singing "Wannabe," rock music made just for them, can be nothing short of empowering.

Girlie doesn't so much identify different issues for young women as say that this generation of feminists wants its own institutions and a right to its own attitudes and interpretations. Familiarity with porn, sexual aggressiveness, and remaining single and childless until pretty late in life play out in their take on issues such as censorship, date rape, and day care. The fact that most of the Girlies are white, straight, work outside the home, and belong to the consumer class provides some explanation for why they chose to promote certain issues. The Second Wave, our mothers, had *Ms.* (and *Sojourner* and *Lilith* and *Our Bodies, Ourselves*) and NOW and the fight for the ERA. We have *Bust* (and *Bitch* and the now defunct *HUES* and web-zines and fanzines) and the Third Wave Foundation, Riot Grrrls and Queen Latifah and Lilith Fair and, well, we still have the fight for the ERA, and *Ms.*, *Sojourner*, and *Our Bodies, Ourselves*.

Where Girlie stops short of being the path to a forceful movement is that it mistakes politics for a Second Wave institution as well, rather than seeing it as inherent feminism. This disconnect—politics versus culture—was on display at the 1997 Media and Democracy Forum, where Girlie debuted as a topic of conversation.

At a conference devoted to alternative journalism and leftist politics, "Girl Power: Progress ... or the Selling of Feminism Lite?" was one of the few women-oriented panels. The panelists—Debbie Stoller of *Bust*, Ophira Edut of *HUES*, Erin Aubry of *L.A. Weekly*, Susan Douglas, the author of *Where the Girls Are* and *Listening In: Radio and the American Imagination* (and the token older feminist), and Tara Roberts, the former lifestyle editor of *Essence* and author of *Am I the Last Virgin?*—grappled with the meaning of Girlie before an auditorium filled half with earnest and frizzy old-school feminists and half with the pierced and tattooed new-girl feminists. To the audience, this panel of great women seemed scattered and oppositional. The confused debate that occurred produced three overarching conclusions. One, Girlie is pretty much an all-white phenomenon, and black women have never made such a big deal about the implications of wearing nail polish or makeup; two, the more you talk to Second Wave feminists about nail polish, the less they want to hear anything you're saying; and three, Girlie is both "progress" *and* the "selling of feminism lite."

Although she was asked to moderate this panel, twenty-nine-year-old Tara Roberts confessed that she didn't relate to Girlie per se. Nonetheless, she was able to draw some connections to her own experience. "Girl power—this tough, sexy woman who is speaking her mind—is not something that's new to black women," Roberts said. "When I was fourteen, Salt-N-Pepa rappers were definitely out there saying, 'I'm a sexual being, and I'm not gonna be taken advantage of.' The people in my high school that had the juice, the props, the respect, were the girls who were tough, who were sexy, who had their hair fly, their nails done, but you didn't mess with them." Bringing up the nearly opposite point, Erin Aubry asserted that black women's bodies, specifically their butts, have been seen only as sex machines and workhorses to such a profane degree that the simple act of trying to buy a pair of jeans becomes a metaphor for not fitting into the white patriarchy and its notions of feminine bodies.

In an effort to reclaim her booty and her body, Aubry had written an article called "The Butt" for *L.A. Weekly* and had her posterior photographed for the cover in a pair of tight blue jeans. Many in the black community were outraged. The butt was associated with the racist sexual objectifying of black women into hungry, haveable pieces of ass, and there she was promoting the stereotype. "It's like we've already decided what sexual images are in our community: bad," Aubry said. "They *are* bad. But, I'm trying to argue, part of me is me as a woman. But [the woman side and the black woman side] almost don't coexist."

In a racist and sexist society, Aubry is divided against herself in at least two ways. American culture has a history of slave rape and forced (on black women) miscegenation coursing through it like the white blood of the slave owners. During the plantation era, white women often did—or could do—little to protect female slaves from the unwanted advances of the master. It's true that some white wives left their husbands or joined the abolition underground. It is also true that some mistresses were threatened by the attention—albeit unwanted—that black women received, and were sometimes more punishing and cruel than the masters. This history is one of the reasons that black women sometimes feel more betrayed by white women than by white men. This was a betrayal that happened again, but in reverse, during the civil-rights movement, when some black male leaders began sleeping with white women, thus nudging out black women as sexual beings. The complex relationship continues, as Roberts pointed out with her Salt-N-Pepa comment—white Girlies appear to be borrowing, consciously or not, from black women in popular culture when they talk about femininity and strength. Think of actress Pam Grier, activist Faye Wattleton, or radical Angela Davis. (Of course, the "strong black woman" is a stereotype, too, and black women aren't hardwired to be powerhouses or to never let the black male forget that he's a man. But black women have more pop culture examples of sexy women who are also tough.)

Moments later, Debbie Stoller took the conversation in a different direction, vociferously arguing that painting one's nails is a feminist act because it expands the notions of what a feminist is allowed to do or how she may look. "Maybe we *should* be painting our nails in the boardroom," she concluded, in order to bring our Girlie-ness into male-defined spaces. In other words, not being allowed to wear a miniskirt is the same as being forced to wear a miniskirt. A Second Waver in the audience, outraged, countered that her generation fought to free women from the traps of femininity. While everything that Stoller said is true, the implication of painting one's nails in the boardroom is, best-case scenario, that you are claiming that space as your own. (Another implication is that you aren't quite ready for a job and are, therefore, unlikely to be in the boardroom in the first place.) Compared to the act of owning one's body as a black woman, nail-polish activism seems very silly. Or at least apolitical. Even with varying holds on the reins of political consciousness, what drove each woman on the panel was the same key issue—being able to claim that we are sexual ladies as feminists, as black women, or as whoever we happen to be.

The point is that the cultural and social weapons that had been identified (rightly so) in the second wave as instruments of oppression—women as sex objects, fascist fashion, pornographic materials—are no longer being exclusively wielded against women and are sometimes wielded by women. Girlie presumes that women can handle the tools of patriarchy and don't need to be shielded from them. Protective labor laws that were part of the original ERA limited the jobs women could do. They were changed by seventies feminists to promote egalitarian labor laws, which presumed that women could really do the police, car-assembly, and late-night work that men could do. Similarly, Girlie is replacing protective cultural "rules" with a kind of equality. "These days putting out one's pretty power, one's pussy power, one's sexual energy for popular consumption no longer makes you a bimbo," wrote Elizabeth Wurtzel in her 1998 glory rant *Bitch*. "It makes you smarter." Madonna is control of her sexual power, rather than a victim of it; she wields it the way she could a gun or a paintbrush or some other power tool that is usually the province of men. And she *is* enjoying it, which is her luxury and her strength. When Riot Grrrls screamed versions of *IlovefuckingIhatedanger* from rock clubs and fanzines and song lyrics in the early nineties, or when women rappers like Lil' Kim "objectified" men's bodies right down to their dicks, they presumed some sort of strength in the social arena. But where did that strength come from?...

In 1991, Tali Edut, an eighteen-year-old University of Michigan student, applied to be art director on the second reader-produced issue of *Sassy* magazine. Chosen, she spent the summer in Manhattan, at the 230 Park Avenue office, putting the issue together. Stories included "These Skinheads Aren't Racist" (about anti-racist skinheads, obviously) and a piece on the importance of female friendships. Once she was back at UMich with her identical twin, Ophira, and her best friend, Dyann Logwood, and having been inspired by her summer at the fresh teen magazine, Tali decided to put together a magazine for her introductory women's studies class. They named it *HUES*, the acronym for Hear Us Emerging Sisters, which also signaled its multicultural mission. "We incorporated all of the stuff we talked about among ourselves and got our friends in the dorm to write," Ophira says. "So the first issue featured vending-machine snacks and late-night philosophical discussions." Because they themselves were the publishers and they weren't tied to any advertisers, the three would not have to conform to any less-than-cool compromises. (For instance, women of color weren't on many *Sassy* covers. The staff had to fight with the publisher when the girl who won the magazine's Sassiest Girl in America contest happened to be black—horror, according to myth, for the newsstand bottom line.) Furthermore, *HUES* wouldn't emulate *Sassy*'s ultraskinny model requirements (also advertiser-imposed, and thus required by its money-hungry publisher). A fashion story might be called "PMS Fashion." The bathing-suit issue featured size 10 and up.

HUES debuted in April 1992, and self-published eight issues over the next five years. This multi-culti independent women's magazine started off with such a bang that, upon graduating, Ophira Edut took out a $30,000 loan and attempted to expand the magazine. (By 1997, it proved to be too much work to keep going, so the Edut sisters and Dyann Logwood began looking for a buyer. *New Moon*, the Duluth-based girls-empowerment magazine, purchased *HUES* that same year. It was unable to make *HUES* profitable enough to keep it going, however, and published only five more issues before putting the magazine to sleep in early 1999.)

At the same time that Tali was interning at *Sassy*, Debbie Stoller and Marcelle Karp, both in their late twenties, were working at boring jobs for Nickelodeon, the cable-television channel for children. They met and soon realized they were both interested in "woman stuff and we both read *Sassy*," Karp recalls. They bonded over their infatuation with this teen magazine and its creators, women who were from their generation and who were doing what they wanted to do; namely, making a cultural product to which they could relate. They both thought that what was great about *Sassy* was that the staff talked to their female readership the way they talked to each other, not as if the reader was younger or less sophisticated than they were. "I thought *Sassy* caught on that it wasn't just about giving girls a good role model, and it was not just about the negative things that need to be changed about being female in this society," Stoller says. "*Sassy* realized that you had to embrace the positive stuff, and that would go a long way toward empowering people. It made me laugh, and it made me like being a girl." But despite all its kudos and adult fans, *Sassy* was still a teen magazine. Unlike Karp and Stoller, the average reader was just a few years into menstruating and had to be home before midnight.

Karp and Stoller would talk about how odd it was that they read only *Details* and *Sassy*, and how they didn't read *Ms.*, even though they were big feminists. "I was disappointed in *Ms.* I didn't understand why the Riot Grrrls weren't on the cover of that magazine. Here this was a new wave of feminism and *Ms.* seemed so disconnected," said Stoller, who had graduated from Yale with a Ph.D. in the psychology of women and had as her goal the creation of new media for women. Stoller was a fabulous typist—long a mixed blessing for women. She began temping at Nickelodeon, hoping to get in on the ground floor of MTV, which was owned by the same company. "In my late twenties, I wasn't living a lifestyle so different from that of a teenage girl," says Stoller. "Most single girls were living in our own apartments and cooking our own food, but we were also buying records, finding cute boys—sort of a chronic teenagerhood."

Stoller and Karp talked about doing their own magazine, a sort of *Sassy* senior for girls like them who weren't on a mommy track or a career track but cared about sex and brains and rock 'n' roll and feminism. Walking to the subway one morning, Stoller had an epiphany: "There should be a magazine for us, and it should not suck and it should be cool and funny and smart and we should call it *Bust*." She liked the way this aggressive double entendre made you think of tits *and* of making through barriers. It reminded her of a Dutch women's magazine she read during a stay in the Netherlands called *Opziy*, which means both "step aside" and "about her." Karp had just been fired from her too-menial job as a production assistant at Nick, and thus was freed up to realize their dream. So, one freezing spring day in 1993, the two met in Tompkins Square Park and hammered out what *Bust* would be. Karp recalls:

> We were so organized. It's incredible to think about it because we didn't even know what we were doing. Next thing we knew, we were getting a P.O. Box and a *Bust* E-mail account, and a checking account for the two of us. I called up the zine bible god, *Fact Sheet Five*, and they sent us the computer guide, the printer guide, and the retail-store thing. In the first four issues, it was me doing money and business, and Debbie getting stories. We did the editors' letter together and she did the editing. We read submissions together, and laid it out together, and took copyediting classes together—we did it all together. Gradually, we were getting the hang of being *Bust* girls, of being women in charge of our own thing. For that first issue, we went to Debbie's office at night and xeroxed and stapled the issue ourselves. For the second issue, I had made so much money on a project that I bankrolled the whole thing, and we upgraded and went to newsprint, two color. It was forty-eight pages, and I was so excited. We got Laurie Henzel involved as designer. Somebody told me about advertising, because I didn't know that revenue could really be generated that way. And then someone else said you can get money up front if you put a subscription page in. With every issue, people would give publishing cues, and we would take their advice and implement it and figure stuff out.

Five years after *Bust* debuted as a xerox-and-staple zine, Karp, Stoller, and Henzel were doing print runs of 35,000. (To give you a sense of that accomplishment, *Bamboo Girl*, another successful glossy zine with ads, was printing about 2,000 with each issue.)

Meanwhile, after years of boycotts, losing ad money, losing readership because of censorship by advertisers, and the cowardice of its corporate parent, *Sassy* died in 1995. Actually, it was sold to Petersen Publishing, which also published *Guns & Ammo*, moved to L.A., and was made over as a *YM* clone. Within a year, that pale substitute was put out of its misery. *Jane* debuted in 1997 with the same creative duo that was behind the iconic teen magazine: Christina Kelly and Jane Pratt. *Jane* is doing a lot of what *Sassy* did, except the ethos is the single independent woman rather than the single independent girl. The food column is called "Eat," and the editorial content is in marked contrast to *Cosmo*'s "big pyramid," where all articles lead to landing a man. The "What Now"-type column in *Jane* is called "Dish" and is edited by Kelly.

"*Jane* is feminist," says Pratt. The feminism is tucked into stories like going undercover at the Aryan Nation and profiling the female astronauts who should have gone up with John Glenn, a story done by *Ms.* two decades earlier. There are many other feministy stories that seemed to be recycled from *Ms.* (a reversal of *Ms.*'s old reliance on *Sassy*). It's also a fashion magazine that courts fashion ads. So, while the stylists incorporate cheap pieces from Kmart and secondhand shops, *Jane* doesn't critique the skinny models wearing expensive clothes, or the preponderance of editorial directly related to advertising. Pratt is aware that this may seem like a cop-out, but she wants her magazine to have more "mall appeal," as in girls who aren't urban hipsters. "I wouldn't have gotten *Bust* when I was in high school at Andover," says Pratt. "I like seducing people with something that looks like it might be one thing and then actually giving them something a lot harder, stronger, more empowering than they might have expected it to be." But by her own admission, there is no way that *Jane* could have the impact that the original *Sassy* had. "By the time you are in your twenties your relationship to a magazine is so different. You are never going to need it in the same way—it's never going to be your lifeline," says Pratt.

Of course, adult women's magazines can be just as much of a lifeline if the content is honest and speaks to women beyond their wallets. *Ms.* magazine has been a connection to feminism for thousands of women (and still is, to some). Still, the original *Sassy* did something crucial for feminism that *Ms.* couldn't. Beyond treating girls with respect, *Sassy* talked about women's rights and politics cloaked in culture and inspired *Bust* and *HUES* to do the same. Together, they pushed feminist institutions to acknowledge the power of the next generation and its culture. These magazines recognized Girlie culture and promoted it. Concurrently, they provided new avenues into feminism for women who might not have found their way to a NOW meeting. For instance, a college student at the University of Michigan might pick up *Sassy* to make fun of Joey Lawrence but could end up reading about how racist it can be when you go car shopping.

The *Bust* and *HUES* girls saw a gaping hole in feminism; they felt connected to the movement, but they didn't relate to the existing institutions and saw an opportunity to create their own. They in turn sparked women such as San Francisco writer Lisa Miya-Jervis and Andi Zeisler to found *Bitch* as a xerox-and-staple journal of media criticism in 1995. In it, she declares: "This magazine is about thinking critically about every message the mass media sends; it's about loudly articulating what's wrong and what's right with what we see. This magazine is about speaking up. Will that make us bitchy? Yeah. *You wanna make somethin' of it?*" The next year in San Francisco, Janelle Brown, a twenty-two-year-old tech journalist for *Hotwired* (*Wired*'s on-line magazine), decided to start *Maxi*. "It grew out of an interest in fashion magazines—I always devoured them and hated them at the same time—and I was getting into feminist zines," she says. "I wanted to write something smart about women who are interested in feminism and politics and the personal day-to-day hazards of growing up female. There was nothing on-line for women at that point."

What these zines and culture-makers had in common was that they were proving that it was okay to speak one's mind and that they didn't have to depend on advertising and its attendant censorship and shaping of editorial content. Each drew its critique from their and their readers' own experiences. Even if they weren't liberated enough to change anything, they were liberated enough to complain, celebrate, and generally jump into the media fray.

Even those women who weren't reading *Sassy* or *Bust* were picking up the reverberations of a new feminist voice—the explosion of women in rock, or the success of TV shows such as *Ally McBeal*, *Buffy*, and *Living Single*, which featured women for whom feminism was just a part of life.

In some ways, these magazines and TV shows were presenting old feminism with a new spin, and the process that each of these culture-creators went through is a feminist one. The magazines were the result and a manifestation of a nineties version of consciousness raising—honest talk that spawns more feminism, making connections between women—kind of like a dinner party in print or on the Web....

42. Leora Tanenbaum, "Introduction," from *Slut!: Growing Up with a Bad Reputation*

Excerpts from "Introduction," by Leora Tanenbaum, published in *Slut* (New York: Harper Perennial, 2000), xiii–xix. Reprinted with permission.

Using the third-wave strategy of taking a derogatory term aimed at women and turning it on its head, in the introduction to *Slut* Tanenbaum exposes the terms of the sexual double standard and shows how it is still used to intimidate and control women and keep them from fully expressing themselves. "Slut-bashing," Tanenbaum argues, "is uniquely damaging—and not only to teenage girls but to all women ... the cultural assumptions behind slut-bashing implicate us all."

Julie arrives for our meeting, at a diner across the street from her college campus, dressed for comfort: faded jeans, untucked denim shirt, olive-green army-surplus jacket. She slides opposite me into the windowed booth. I offer her a menu, but she shakes it away: she already knows she wants the French fries. Julie's face is round and friendly, her manner relaxed. But as Julie unfolds her story, I learn that she wasn't always as self-assured as she is today, at nineteen. Back in junior high in New Jersey, she was easily intimidated. Her greatest ambition in life was just to fit in. But she didn't fit in. Julie was something of an outsider in her solidly Catholic, Irish-Italian neighborhood. Her family was the only one in town that didn't attend church. She hadn't gone to the same middle school her friends had attended. And she was pudgy, a bit overweight. Too eager to conform yet too different, Julie was an easy target.

One evening when she was thirteen, Julie tells me, her soft brown eyes meeting mine squarely, she and her friends were hanging out as usual at one of their houses. They were drinking beers. Julie had recently begun to drink more and more: Alcohol enabled her to push aside the fact that her parents were sleeping in separate beds and not talking to each other. Besides, some older guys had joined them this evening, and Julie figured that it made her seem cool if she drank. That night she drank until she passed out unconscious. When she regained consciousness semiclothed and with a dull pain, she realized that someone had had sex with her. Julie pulled herself together and asked one of her friends what had happened. The guy who did it, she was informed, had been drinking with the group that night—a classmate she only slightly knew. Julie understood that she had been raped.

By Monday morning a friend of the rapist, who had witnessed the event, had spread the news that his friend and Julie had had sex. In a matter of hours, Julie tells me, she was known as a slut. "They'd call out 'slut' to me in the halls. There was graffiti. I got calls in the middle of the night, at four a.m.: 'Fat slut.' Behind the junior high school there was a playground with a handball court, and people would write graffiti there in shaving cream." Everybody in school knew about her. Even today, years later, Julie's reputation as a slut is known to each new crop of incoming high school students.

Julie's story of being singled out as a slut is much more common than you might think. Indeed, you would be hard-pressed to find a high school in the United States in which there is no designated slut. Two out of five girls nationwide—42 percent—have had sexual rumors spread about them, according to a 1993 poll conducted for the American Association of University Women (AAUW) on sexual harassment in schools. ("Sexual rumor" sometimes means speculation that a classmate is gay, but more often it is a polite way of saying "slutty reputation.") Three out of four girls have received sexual comments or looks, and one in five has had sexual messages written about her in public areas.

Slut-bashing—as I call it—is one issue that affects every single female who grows up in this country because any preteen or teenage girl can become a target. "Slut" is a pervasive insult applied to a broad spectrum of American adolescent girls, from the girl who brags about her one-night stands to the girl who has never even kissed a boy to the girl who has been raped. Some girls are made fun of because they appear to have a casual attitude about sex (even if, in reality, they are no more sexual than their peers). Many others are picked on because they stand out in some way—being an early developer, new in school, an ethnic or class minority, overweight, or just considered "weird" for whatever reason. Some are called "sluts" because other girls dislike or envy them, and spread a sexual rumor as a form of revenge. While a girl can almost instantly acquire a "slut" reputation as a result of one well-placed rumor, it takes months, if not years, for the reputation to evaporate—if it does at all.

Being called a slut sounds like a sexy topic: All of my male friends joked that they wanted to help me with the research for this book. But in truth the "slut" label doesn't necessarily have anything to do with sex. Very often the label is a standin for something else: the extent to which a girl fails to conform to the idea of "normal" appearance and behavior.

A girl's sexual status is a metaphor for how well she fits into the American ideal of femininity. Boys who don't conform to the masculine role are similarly judged on a phantom sexual scale—the short boy with a slight build who strikes out whenever he's up to bat is called a fag, even though his ability in sports says nothing about his sexual orientation. Yet a "fag" can overcome his status through bench-pressing; there is little a "slut" can do to erase her stigma. Magnified by sexual metaphor, her social difference defines everything about her. She represents soiled femininity.

Looking and behaving and dressing like everyone else is a classic American tradition, possibly attributable to the melting-pot ideal for ethnic groups, the Protestant work ethic, and the capitalist drive to be accepted into the centrist middle class. Fitting into America requires adherence to gender roles: girls and women must act one way, boys and men must act another way. Girls and women are expected to lack sexual desires; boys and men are presumed to be ruled by them. Sexuality and gender roles, then, become intertwined—and easily confused.

The "slut" label carries a set of class associations. Regardless of her family's actual economic status, the "slut" is thought to be "low class" and "trampy," the kind of girl who wears gobs of makeup and whose voluptuous curves threaten to explode the fabric of her tight clothes. She lacks the polish of the "good" girl, who keeps her sexuality reigned in and discreet (beneath a blazer, a belt, some nude panty-hose), and who will no doubt one day marry a nice middle-class man and raise a nice middle-class family. The "slut" is thought to be a girl without a future.

Being known as the school slut is a terrifying experience. In school, where social hierarchy counts for everything, the school "slut" is a pariah, a butt of jokes, a loser. Girls and boys both gang up on her. She endures cruel and sneering comments—*slut* is often interchangeable with *whore* and *bitch*—as she walks down the hallway. She is publicly humiliated in the classroom and cafeteria. Her body is considered public property: She is fair game for physical harassment. There is little the targeted girl can do to stop the behavior. I was surprised to learn that teachers, generally speaking, do not intervene; they consider this behavior normal for teenagers.

I know what it feels like. I, too, was a "slut" in my high school. In the spring of 1984, when I was in the ninth grade, I fooled around with a guy whom a popular friend of mine had her eye on. In retaliation, she spread the word that I was a "slut." For many months I was snubbed by girls as well as guys, called names to my face, and whispered about behind my back. Gossip shadowed me through the rest of my high school years, and I felt alienated and insecure up until the day of graduation. For years afterward I thought that I alone had been called a slut, and I never discussed it with anyone. I sliced off the experience from my memory when I went away to college, where no one knew.

It was only in 1993, when the AAUW poll revealed the prevalence of hurtful sexual rumors about teenage girls, that I came to terms with my own history. It was then that the enormity of slut-bashing really sank in. I understood that slut-bashing is a form of verbal sexual harassment and a classic illustration of the sexual double standard: the idea that there is one set of sexual rules for men and boys, and another, unequal one for women and girls....

Adolescence, we can all recall, is perhaps more than anything else a time of social jostling and petty cruelties. Isn't slut-bashing, then, just part of the fabric of adolescence? Isn't it, to some extent, normal and therefore acceptable? No. Slut-bashing is uniquely damaging—and not only to teenage girls but to all women. Fearful of being considered a "slut," many girls and women don't carry or use contraception, leading to unplanned and unwanted pregnancies and life-threatening diseases. Worried about seeming sexually aggressive, many girls and women remain silent in ambivalence rather than say yes or no, which leads to murky sexual scenarios that are neither completely consensual nor completely coerced but somewhere in between. The cultural assumptions behind slut-bashing implicate us all: Knowing that being sexually promiscuous stigmatizes a girl, many of us assume that a girl who reports that she was raped is lying in order to cover up a regretted sexual encounter.

Slut-bashing shows us that sexism is still alive and that as boys and girls grow up, different sexual expectations and identities are applied to them. Slut-bashing is evidence of a sexual double standard that should have been eliminated decades ago, back when abortions were illegal, female office assistants were called "gal Fridays," and doctors were men and nurses were women. Slut-bashing sends the message to all girls, no matter how "pure" their reputations, that men and boys are free to express themselves sexually, but women and girls are not.

43. Leora Tanenbaum, "Introduction," from *Catfight: Women and Competition*

Excerpts from "Introduction," by Leora Tanenbaum, published in *Catfight* (New York: Harper, 2002), 13–35. Reprinted with permission.

Continuing the cultural work she performed with *Slut*, in this introduction to *Catfight*, Tanenbaum explores the issue of competitiveness between women, focusing on women's "confused place in society" that fuels it: "at the same time we are gaining liberties, we are expected to conform, more or less, to a narrow role." Rather than being "natural enemies," as the old social stereotype would say, women's competitiveness with each other is fueled by structural inequalities, and they need to resist it. They "must begin celebrating each other, and, in doing so, take the reigns of real, raw, raging power."

Competitiveness between women is a fact. It has a history and function in American society that does not benefit women. So why does it persist? And can we make it go away? Before tackling these questions we need to understand the role of competitiveness on a personal level.

I've long been fascinated by the issue of competitiveness between women because I've long been, well, competitive with other women. Growing up I wanted not only to get A's, but to get more A's than others. In junior high, when I developed an hourglass figure, I felt awkward about my burgeoning physique, but also good about getting more attention from the boys than the other girls did. In college I lived with a woman who possessed many traits I wanted in a friend—she was smart, witty, reflective, adventurous—but her beauty made her a magnet for men, plus she was talented as a journalist, a career I wished for myself. All of which led my envy to trump our friendship. My loss.

Another college friend now lives just blocks away from me, on Manhattan's West Side. We each have young children and we work in similar professions. Only her apartment is a *Friends*-worthy "classic six" with a terrace overlooking Central Park; her little girls rarely fuss or whine; and her career (travel writer) is glamorous and gives her the opportunity to take expenses-paid vacations around the world. And, oh yes, she is beautiful; wears gorgeous, perfectly fitting, up-to-the-minute clothes; has a good-looking, successful husband; and never has a chipped manicure. She seems so ... perfect. I find it difficult to spend time with her.

When I was thirty, my husband and I decided to have a child, and I became pregnant. My status as Mother-To-Be was considered open for discussion by every woman I knew. Even strangers on supermarket checkout lines felt totally at ease asking me: would I have an epidural, would I breast-feed, would I continue to work? My answers—yes, I'm not sure, yes—elicited judgmental eyebrow raises, if not outright condemnations. Labor is *supposed* to feel like you're being ripped in two! Breast milk is best! Only a negligent mother would *think* of working before her child enters first grade, and even then a mother should only work part time! Feeling under attack, I began obsessing about the choices that other mothers made. To protect my fragile ego, I imagined that anyone who diverged from my path was a mindless baby machine without an ounce of ambition.

It was actually the most trivial part of my pregnancy that held particular fascination: the rate and size of my weight gain. I had gained too much too fast, I was told. Or, I hadn't gained enough—was I one of those crazy, misguided women who actually *diets* while pregnant, thereby harming the health of the fetus?! I couldn't win with anyone. When you're pregnant and wearing the same five outfits over and over, it would be nice for others to compliment you on your looks, even if they don't really mean it. Of course, lots of women (and men) did indeed tell me that I looked glowing and happy and wonderful. But just as often, I experienced exchanges like this one, with a colleague:

"You look so big; how far along are you?"

"Five and a half months," I mumbled.

"You're only *five and a half* months? Hmmm ... You know, my daughter gained only nine pounds during her entire pregnancy."

I declined to mention that with three and a half months to go, I had already surpassed her daughter's total gain. Instead, I went immediately to the nearest women's room, which fortunately had a full-length mirror, stared at my out-of-control belly, and pondered my options if I outgrew my maternity clothes. Later, on the street, I saw another, larger pregnant woman. I reckoned the number of pounds *she* had gained, and felt better.

As you can see, I measure myself against other women. I constantly need to prove my worth, show everyone (especially myself) that I am capable, deserving, a woman who should be paid attention to. At some level, this is an expression of inadequacy. I worry I can never measure up. I am not smart, fashionable, thin, savvy, or maternal enough. The success of another woman translates into my failure. And my success translates into her failure—which makes my success all the more sweet. Although I am a feminist, committed to the idea that every woman should be given the opportunity to succeed in whatever endeavor she chooses, there is also a part of me that feels reassured if a woman on the same playing field stumbles. Such behavior is damaging. It never soothes my anxieties and always wields the potential to harm my relationships with others.

Why don't I feel competitive with men? I discount them as true rivals because, in most arenas, they either have more power than I (such as in their ability to earn more money or to rise in their professions) or they're not striving for the same things I am (such as being a good mother). I don't regard men as rivals because their successes in life have more to do with their privilege than with my failure.

For my own sanity, I needed to inspect the roots of my competitiveness. But I found that it was not my problem alone. Essayist Anne Taylor Fleming has perfectly expressed this problem faced by so many contemporary American women:

> Whenever I enter a room of people these days, I am conscious that it is the women, not the men, who give me the once-over, a quick, slightly veiled, not entirely ungenerous instant appraisal. I look back at these women across the room as if it were empty of men. Who are you, our eyes say to one another, what joys and sorrows have you known, what do you do, where do you work, where do you buy your clothes, but mostly, mostly, we ask one another, are you successful, do you have what you want, do you have what I want? There then ensues a kind of amiable grilling, a sizing up, a comparing of husbands, children, children's schools, numbers of miles run that day: the underlying question always: is she farther ahead than I?...

Envy and competitiveness are close cousins, but they are not the same thing. Both stem from societal inequality and an ensuing psychological sense of inadequacy. But envy—the feeling that I want what she has—leaves open the possibility of cooperation. I may covet what she has, but that doesn't make her a better person and it doesn't mean that we can't work together. I can usually rise above my envy because I recognize that cooperation has the potential of eliminating the inequalities that bred the envy in the first place. Competitiveness, however—the feeling that I want to surpass her—usually precludes cooperation. When women feel competitive, we want to feel superior and we want our rivals to be inferior. As a result, we do not believe we have anything to gain in cooperating because we want to perpetuate the inequality between us.

A person can feel envious but still be content. We live in a world filled with inequalities, and we all recognize that some people possess attributes or things that we would also like to possess, but do not. It is possible to long for these attributes or things yet remain fulfilled. Being envious isn't fun—it is, fundamentally, the recognition of the unfairness of inequality—but it isn't, in and of itself, destructive. (Besides, though I may envy what she has, I may possess something she lacks, so there is a sense of balance to our worlds.) Competitiveness is different. It is envy transformed into a destructive feeling of one-upmanship.

Sometimes, of course, competitiveness can be a positive thing—if it is out in the open rather than covert. A rival can spur a person to achieve heights she might not achieve on her own. When I swim laps at the Y, I always swim harder and faster when there is another, better swimmer in the lane with me. If a friend lands an assignment to write an article for a high-paying, prestigious magazine, I am encouraged to try to get such an assignment myself. My ambition is kindled by others who become, unintentionally, my rivals. Without realizing it, they show me what is possible and attainable.

... It is precisely the negative side to competition that is also undiscussed and unresolved. Much of the time, our competitiveness is tacit, underground. The covert desire to surpass another necessarily becomes bound up with resentment, bitterness, pettiness, and, in some cases, all-consuming obsession. One does not feel fulfilled with her lot. What she has is not enough. She needs more. She needs to be better than others.

What does she gain from being competitive? Initially, a woman feels a sense of purpose, even excitement. It feels good to have a goal. But when that goal is at the expense of another woman, fulfillment is usually short-lived. For as long as competitiveness continues, the insecurities that sparked it will continue to gnaw at her and destroy any sense of self-worth. She will also become divided from other women.

We feel competitive with one another because of our confused place in society. On the face of it, we are equal to men. Thanks to the tireless work of women's-movement activists in the late 1960s and 1970s, and to the continuing work of feminists today, we live lives far different from those of our mothers and grandmothers. We can have sex with far less anxiety about having an unwanted child, work in many of the same professions as men, and see ourselves represented in national sports leagues and rock bands, as well as among television news anchors. Many of us don't have to wear hose, heels, and girdles if we don't want to. We cannot legally be fired from jobs when we become pregnant or when we rebuff the sexual advances of a boss. We have attained high positions on the Supreme Court, in Congress, in presidential cabinets. Having been born in 1969, I can take all of these achievements for granted. Yet I also know that without these gains, my life would be intolerable.

And yet ... at the same time that we are gaining liberties, we are also expected to conform, more or less, to a narrow role. According to the contemporary, middle-class American feminine script, we are supposed to attain the highest educational level possible, develop a meaningful career, get married, quit or slow down our career to have children, stay at home with them, return five or seven years later to work in a job that lets us get home in time to make dinner (and that therefore tends to go nowhere), and some-how always manage to look sexy. This script is conveyed in subtle and blatant ways. Our First Lady is proud that she lacks career ambition and is content to glide on her husband's coattails. The legal right (and, depending on where you live, the logistical ability) to terminate an unwanted or dangerous pregnancy, already precarious, is eroding at a steady clip. Mothers do not have earning parity with fathers, nor do they typically achieve the professional heights that fathers do. Most women continue to work in the so-called pink ghetto as secretaries, cashiers, maids, clerks, waitresses, hospital and nursing home aides, and elementary school and day-care teachers—jobs characterized by pitifully low wages and little, if any, prestige. The national media tell us that all child care provided by anyone other than the mother is deficient and that mothers should stay home with their young children. Mothers mistakenly believe they have to raise their children without assistance from anyone; to ask for help is evidence that one has failed as a mother. Keeping one's home reasonably clean and organized is no longer enough; authors like Cheryl Mendelson (*Home Comforts*) and icons like Martha Stewart instruct middle-class women on the joys of excessive domesticity. Women's fashions are at their clingiest, with low-rider, belly-button-baring outfits the norm, while men's fashions are at their baggiest. (Could it be, as many feminists have suggested, that women's fashions become more feminized the more power women accrue?)

Given the freedoms that women have attained over the last three decades, the traditional female role seems outdated. Many women, therefore, either defy it, ignore it, or just fall out of it. But its allure snares most of us eventually in some capacity. Besides, whether we end up following the American feminine script or thumbing our noses at it, it exacts a toll on our attitude toward other women: We become divided from one another and competitive with each other. This is because femininity and competition go hand in hand. By definition, the female role is something a woman "wins" at. Being feminine entails being attractive (more than other women); dating, living with, or marrying a "good catch" (who earns more money or is better-looking than other women's men); and having faultless children (who are smarter, cuter, more creative, and better behaved than her peers' children). If she works in a career surrounded by men, she has to do a better job than the other women so that she can be the perfect token female who is almost as good as the guys. When women's traditional role is exalted, a woman feels pressured to "win" at being the most feminine woman possible.

Yet when we think about competition, we hold a double standard. Men by their nature are supposedly ambitious and competitive; women by their nature are supposedly devoid of ambition and competitiveness. Women are caught in an impossible bind: We need to be competitive in order to be truly feminine, yet we can't be competitive because that would make us unwomanly. The only way out, as we will see, is for a woman to be competitive but to *pretend* that she is not. Covert competition, in my opinion, is unhealthy competition. This state of affairs explains why few women are willing to discuss their competitiveness. Even if we are self-aware enough to recognize our competitive feelings, we don't like to admit that we have them.

To understand and analyze their conditioning as women, members of Redstockings, an influential, early feminist activist group, developed the idea of consciousness-raising: In a group, women shared personal experiences. They discovered that others experienced the same hardships, and they analyzed the roots of their problems. "The personal"—problems that had seemed private and exclusive to oneself—were in fact "political"—linked to wider social forces. For instance, if a woman endured cruel comments from her husband—she was fat, needed to go on a diet, and was not sexually attractive to him—she internalized the belief that she was indeed ugly and unfeminine. But when she discovered that other women, who were far from unattractive, were experiencing the same abuse, she came to realize that restrictive beauty standards, combined with men's expectations—not her physical appearance—were the real problems. Women's eyes and minds were opened to the fact that their oppression was connected with their conditioning and that they were not alone. They found liberation through linking with other women, through their shared astonishment at how they were being manipulated to comply with what society wished them to do or be.

We could still benefit from consciousness-raising. We rarely, if ever, acknowledge how competitive we still are. Ashamed of our behavior, we refuse to discuss it openly, or we place blame on another woman—"*She's* competitive with *me*" or "Sure I'm competitive, but only with *myself*." But today, consciousness-raising has devolved into recovery-movement-style sharing. The energy created by the awareness that "the personal is political" has been replaced by an emphasis on personal challenges for improvement; the political element has largely disappeared. (At my local Barnes & Noble bookstore, ten bookcases are devoted to "Self-Improvement." Four are filled with books on "Women's Studies.") Yet an emphasis on self-improvement—rather than group improvement—serves to keep women isolated from one another. It makes everyone's problem appear individual, not collective or societal. This isolation compounds our inclination to compare ourselves with others and find ourselves lacking.

Today, pockets of feminist activism exist, but it is generally rare to find collaboration among women trying to advance the interests of women as a class of people. Notable exceptions include young "third wave" feminist activists, who continue the momentous battles for abortion rights and protection from sexual violence but who are only beginning to collide with the challenge of having children and working and therefore generally (and understandably) have not focused on bread-and-butter issues like subsidized child care. There are also religious women who are making amazing strides in chipping away at sexism in religious life but who limit their struggle for women's rights to their narrow milieu. More typical is the collaboration of mothers who join forces not to press for women's rights but to assert their moral authority as mothers on an unrelated social issue such as gun control. The mothers who participated in the Million Mom March on Washington in 2000, for instance, only reinforced our country's perception of women's traditional role as the moral guardians of our youth.

Does the idea of universal sisterhood have validity? On one hand, all women share a fundamental commonality and understanding of one another because we all experience (or have the potential to experience) menstruation, birthing, nursing, and the cultural expectations of being a woman. But when taken to an extreme, this thinking loses focus: Does a poor black married woman in Somalia share any common ground with a white lesbian Internet editor in San Francisco? Still, there is some basis of commonality among women. All women, after all, experience sexism. We are all defined by our reproductive capacity because so many cultures equate having a uterus with being a mother. Even if we do not give birth or become adoptive mothers, we are expected to "mother" others through nurturing or enabling behavior (taking care of an elderly parent, preparing meals for our families). We are all subjected to the sexual double standard: Any one of us could be called to task for our sexuality. And without effective, safe, cheap, easy, and widely available contraception, our reproductive biology impedes our physical safety and social mobility, whether we are heterosexual or lesbian.

Yet, as we will see, women—even those of similar backgrounds—do not automatically understand each other and empathize with one another simply by virtue of experiencing these hardships....

The truth is, women remain divided. On some level, we are trained—by mothers, fathers, friends, religions, the media—to value male opinion and attention, even at the expense of sisterhood. As feminist theorist bell hooks has observed, "We are taught that women are 'natural' enemies, that solidarity will never exist between us because we cannot, should not, and do not bond with one another." Sadly, many females—even "you go, girl" types who otherwise are the first to show support for feminist causes—can be very quick to malign other girls and women. Our secret hope is to raise our own value. But in the face of competition with other women, do any of us feel better about ourselves? Of course not. We are left feeling envious, resentful, and inadequate. And yet, it doesn't take long before we're competing again. In a sense, we cooperate in our own subordination.

Whose interests are served by our relentless compulsion to belittle other women? By and large, a small number of privileged, individual women benefit from this state of affairs. They reap the rewards of "winning" at femininity. They remain at the top of the feminine social pecking order. Still, even the stature of these fortunate few is quite limited when compared with the stature of the group that truly benefits from our situation—men in power. Because of competition among women, men in power, usually white, get to safeguard their high-echelon jobs in business, medicine, law, government, and the military. Unless they are single fathers, they get to have children without doing half the scut work. They can afford to be choosy about whom they marry, if they marry at all. They get to ogle women in revealing outfits on the street and in their offices without having to expose a proportionate amount of their own physiques. They get to earn more money. They can divorce knowing that, most of the time, their standard of living won't drop dramatically. They can keep their jobs after having a baby without worrying that they are negligent parents. The elevation of the traditional female role, and the ensuing division of women from one another, serves a society run primarily by men. While women are shopping for a new outfit, on the Stairmaster, or dragging their three-year-old from music class to art class, men in power are making decisions that ensure their place at the top of the social order.

There is no reason to put down every facet of traditional femininity. I enjoy wearing makeup, high heels, low-cut camisoles. There's nothing I find more relaxing than getting a manicure. I love taking care of my young sons; indeed, I often find it impossible to concentrate on my work knowing that they are in the next room, their delicious, plump legs just begging to be squeezed. But I enjoy these things precisely because I have chosen them. If they were mandatory, I would feel oppressed. And, in fact, I do feel oppressed that I earn so much less money than my husband, even though I work equally hard. I do feel oppressed that my character alone is judged on the basis of the achievements of our sons. I do feel oppressed that if, God forbid, I were to become widowed or divorced, I would be in really big financial trouble. I do feel oppressed that when we attend a formal event, my husband gets to wear the same suit he always wears, while I have to coordinate a not-worn-too-many-times dress with shoes, hose, jewelry, and handbag. I do feel oppressed that, even though I'm married, I still feel the need to be at least a little flirtatious and even a bit deferential with men—otherwise I am considered too serious, too uptight, or a bitch. I do feel oppressed that I have to go to the gym three times a week to stay in shape, lest I be condemned as a woman who has "let herself go."

Women are not inherently more competitive than men. Rather, our restrictive gender roles, combined with our relatively new liberties, create a confusing environment that sets us up as adversaries—and we have to compete with each other if we're ever going to succeed according to the rules of the mixed-up game we are living. And when we do compete, we tend to be more underhanded and personal in our attacks than men are. "There is data suggesting that males are much more direct expressors," says Solomon Cytrynbaum, Ph.D., a psychiatry and behavioral sciences professor at Northwestern University who has studied the relationship between gender and authority in groups for more than twenty-five years. "They compete more directly; they go head to head. If they undercut someone, they tend to do it more directly. Women are much more behind the scenes, much more subtle. If you ask women in the workplace about issues that trouble them, this is among the most frequent concerns they report."

In part women are more "behind the scenes" because we have few, if any, legitimate arenas in which we *can* openly compete—forcing our ambitions for power, money, and control underground. As writer Elizabeth Wurtzel puts it, "Women, you see, like any other group obstructed from paths to power, tend to get their action on the sly." Men, on the other hand, have many opportunities to compete and excel. A male friend hits the nail on the head when he jokes, "I watch *Jerry Springer* for the catfights. If I want to see men fight, I'll watch the news."

Being competitive, catty, and cunning are part of the stereotype of femininity. At the same time, however, women are said to cooperate in gentle sisterhood and to shun any ambition that might pit one against another. These stereotypes contradict each other, providing girls and women with clashing messages. But it's the former stereotype—the ruthlessly competitive woman—that has captured more attention throughout the centuries....

Twentieth-century cinema served up, again and again, representations of women who are ruthless and cunning in every aspect of their lives. Classics like *The Women* (1939) and *All About Eve* (1950) portrayed cartoon-like predatory females circling each other. *Rich and Famous* (1981) and the French film *Mina Tannenbaum* (1993) thoughtfully and seriously explored the complexities of women's friendships and seriously explored the complexities of women's friendships and the undercurrent of competitiveness and envy flowing through them. *Working Girl* (1988) gave us the portrayal of a secretary who struggles for her big break on Wall Street at the expense of her (conniving) female boss. *The Hand That Rocks the Cradle* (1992) showed us that a woman who dares to leave her child with a nanny deserves what she gets: a psychotic and jealous female caregiver. *The First Wives Club* (1996) and *Stepmom* (1998) exposed antagonisms between first and second wives.

The noun *catfight*, used in a mocking, derogatory way to describe a vicious clash between women, dates back to 1919 but only became popular in the

1970s. Cultural historian Susan Douglas describes how the national news media, in an effort to downplay the women's liberation movement, portrayed it not as a dignified struggle for women's rights but as a silly squabble between homely hippies and happy housewives. But the noun *cat*, according to the Oxford English Dictionary, has been used as a term of contempt for a spiteful or backbiting woman as far back as the early 1600s, while the adjective *catty* to describe a woman who denigrates another woman in a malicious way dates back to 1886. In the United States, *cat* was also used as a term of vulgarity to refer to a vulva or vagina; it was sometimes a synonym for a sexually promiscuous woman or prostitute. Beginning in the early 1900s, the term *cat-fit* was used to describe a fit of anger or hysteria that was expected from a child or woman.

Today, pop culture teems with references to backbiting "other women." In one week alone in May 2001, I watched an episode of *The Sopranos*, in which Tony Soprano cheats on his wife with an "other woman," and went to the movies to see *Bridget Jones's Diary*, in which Bridget discovers that the man she pines for is sleeping with another woman. I also sat through the off-Broadway production of *Cinderella*, in which stepsisters fight over whose foot fits in the glass slipper, and listened to the Ani DiFranco song "32 Flavors," which includes the lyrics "everyone harbors a secret hatred/for the prettiest girl in the room."

Advertising agencies, magazines, and television screenwriters continue to exploit the stereotype to the fullest. An ad for Aquafina bottled water shows two women in a boutique viciously grabbing for the same pair of shoes. (That's right, it's an ad for *water*.) The spring 1999 Louis Vuitton ad campaign showcased young models, fierce determination in their eyes and posture, fighting each other over the designer handbags. *New York* magazine recently ran a profile of a beautiful socialite scorned by other women in her social milieu because she is a Latina from Queens, as opposed to a white, uppercrust Wasp, while the cover of *W* magazine's June 2002 issue trumpeted, "Meow! Fashion's Best Catfights."

Meanwhile, the characters on *Sex and the City* blithely refer to young, beautiful women as "bitches"; Carrie buys five-hundred-dollar Manolo Blahnik mules and a Bergdorf's dress costing her a month's rent in order to outdress the organizer of an arts luncheon, who happens to be the wife of her ex-boyfriend. *Ally McBeal* was similarly rife with women's jealousies; Ally was for a number of seasons in love with a married ex-boyfriend who was a colleague at her Boston law firm (and whose wife was another colleague). In one episode, Ally and the wife, Georgia, who had finally attempted to become friends, took a kickboxing class together and almost killed each other after a friendly sparring session escalated, their unresolved aggression pouring out. But Ally's competitiveness with Georgia was surpassed by her competitiveness with just about every other woman with whom she crossed paths. Typical episode: Ally tells everyone that the opposing counsel on a case, a beautiful woman, is a "bitch";

after the commercial break, said bitchiness is confirmed when the lawyer says to Ally, her saccharine-sweet smile belying her hostility: "Ally, forgive me for saying this. But don't you think it's a little inappropriate to wear such a short skirt in a courtroom?"...

... Tempting though it may be to dismiss the stereotype as part of a sexist plot or backlash, it doesn't do anyone, least of all women, any good to do so. Rather, we must confront the stereotype. We must be honest about the fact that, to some extent, American women *are* guilty of occasional acts of covert competition. Of course, we tend to be more subtle than the cinema's Eve Harringtons or television's Ally McBeals—we are more likely to make a cutting comment here, a sizzling scowl there. But let's face it: feeling insecure, many of us really do resort to backstabbing and other manipulative behaviors as a pitiful way to make ourselves feel, however fleetingly, more powerful. And, with the media-generated, highly exaggerated images of competitive women everywhere around us, it can become difficult for women to maintain a sense of which behaviors are appropriate in daily life.

Today, American women have more power than in the past. Shouldn't we be grateful? Aren't we lucky in comparison to past generations of women? Yes and yes—but the fact is that we still do not have enough power. No matter how high a woman may rise, there is almost always a man above her who makes the final, bottom-line decisions. Condoleezza Rice may have risen to National Security Advisor, but it's men such as Secretary of State Colin Powell and Defense Secretary Donald Rumsfeld who step in to make the *real* decisions about the war. No wonder women's insecurity today is so complex and volatile. It is fraught with contradictions....

44. Laurel Gilbert and Crystal Kile, "Surfergrrrls FAQ," from *Surfergrrrls: Look Ethel! An Internet Guide for Us!*

Excerpts from Laurel Gilbert and Crystal Kile, eds., *Surfergrrrls* (Seattle: Seal Press 1996), 3–25. Reprinted by permission of Seal Press.

One of the first girl-friendly guides to the Internet, excerpts from this short piece written by third-wavers Gilbert and Kile tell why girls need to be technically savvy. The authors see cyberspace as an important activist arena for the third wave.

... [W]omen are a kicking, amazing, important part of Internet culture, not anomalies.... Women are using the Internet in personally and economically empowering ways, and their examples can inspire other women.... Even though women and girls from many walks of life are doing extremely fun, fabulous and useful stuff on the Internet, this myth still persists that the Net is a "guy thing" or a "geek thing" or a "white thing" or something only for the affluent, the businessman, or those interested only in the alt.sex newsgroup hierarchy....

... So much of the way we think about the Internet has been determined by "manly" metaphors (the frontier, the highway) and by cyberpunk (we dig it, but it's not really a female-friendly vision in a lot of ways), that we decided it was time to take a look at the visions suggested by women's spaces on the Net, our participation in online culture, and the sites and creations women offer to the developing Net at large.

... We're not against men online, or against men, period. No matter what you've heard on the playground, that's not what feminism is about. Moreover, sexism on the Internet is no worse than it is anywhere else, and, thankfully, the number of cool, nice guys is at *least* equal to the number of jerks and trolls with hair-trigger keyboards and or perpetual virtual hard-ons (um, actually those guys tend to talk mostly to one another, usually in alt.sex.whatever on Usenet). We've met some rad guys out there: on the other hand, we've also been involved in a few flame wars where we've been baited and attacked as "fucking feminists." We've also received some unwanted and crude solicitations and an occasional unwarranted "read the manual, you dumb bitch," but we prefer to look at these incidents as instructive. After all, it's good to know what folx really think of you, and the relative anonymity of the Internet inspires people to really let go and vent. Besides, sticks and stones may break your bones, but words you can *answer*! We're totally down with the geekgirl motto: "A keyboard is a greater equalizer than a Glock .45." What this means to us is that the Internet can be a powerful tool for communication and for dissemination of information that can help women and all peoples in the struggle for self-determination. The flip side of "divide and conquer" is, of course, "network and resist with every resource available to you."

The unprecedented thing about cyberspace is that it is a forum in which there is, theoretically, more than enough room for everybody. Women have to insist on and work for that reality, get technology in the hands of people who haven't had it before, and get our ideas, perspectives, art, priorities, and information out there! Call us utopian, but the more the Net swells with the sound of many different voices, the more we'll all enjoy it and learn from it, and the more representative it'll be.

WHAT'S WITH THE "GRRRL" THING?

"Grrrl," a word coined by Bikini Kill singer and activist Kathleen Hanna, is a spontaneous young-feminist reclamation of the word "girl." It has proud analogies among many groups of women; in fact, "grrrl" was at least partially derived from a phrase of encouragement popularized by young American black women in the late 1980s: "You go, *guuuurlll!*" As we all know, when it is not being used to describe a woman under sixteen, the word "girl" often takes on pejorative, infantilizing overtones, suggesting silliness, weakness or insubstantiality.

"Grrrl" puts the growl back in our pussycat throats. "Grrrl" is intended to recall the naughty, confident, and curious ten-year-olds we were before society made it clear it was time to stop being loud and playing with boys and concentrate on learning "to girl," that is, to be a proper lady so that boys would like us.

Riot Grrrl is a loosely affiliated group of young, generally punkish, take-no-prisoners feminists who publish zines, play in bands, make art, produce radio shows, maintain mailing lists, create Websites and sometimes just get together and talk about our lives and being women in contemporary society. "Grrrlishness" is at once cuddly and fierce, Hot-head Paisan *and* Hello Kitty, Lynda Barry's Marlys and Maybonne *and* Tank Girl, Susan Faludi *and* Winona LaDuke, Queen Latifah *and* Courtney Love!...

... We've coined a new grrrl-word, CyborGrrrl, in homage to the ways that feminist Donna Haraway, author of "A Cyborg Manifesto," prompts us to think about our online selves, the gendering of technology, and our common cyberfuture.

BUT DOESN'T THAT BEACH BOYS SONG "SURFER GIRL" REPRESENT EVERYTHING YOU OPPOSE?

Well, yeah. That's the idea behind culture-jamming the song and all those sixties beach movies and eighties surfpunk movies and making a place for women in the cybersurfing metaphor. Surfer girls are all those chicks in bikinis who hang around on the beach and cheer and glom all over the surfer boys when they return from riding the big bad waves. Surfer *grrrls*, however, are us: the hot-chix, out-there, in the water, on the board, standin' up and gettin' wet. We are rad, we are bad, and we are on the boards (or modems) with the best of the boys. We *rock*. And we're not just surfer grrrls, we're *CyborGrrrls*, too. We actively negotiate what it means to be grrrls with computers ... making the waves we surf. *SurferGrrrls*' theme song is the cover of "Surfer Girl" by Cub, a Canadian grrrl-pop band. You can find it on their first album, *Betti-Cola* (Mint Records).

SO WHO ARE YOU, AND WHAT'S YOUR PERSONAL INTEREST IN THIS BOOK?

Crystal: I started messing around with computers when I was in the seventh grade, way back in the disco era. Before school I used to hang out in the math room and play on the (get this) TRS-80 with 16K RAM and a cassette tape drive! Ahhh, 1979! One couldn't do much with that TRS-80—write a few BASIC programs, play backgammon or blackjack—but I was hooked. Somehow I even talked my math teacher into letting me take the computer home on weekends. That winter my parents enrolled me in a Saturday morning computer class at the University of Tennessee at Chattanooga where I learned more BASIC and met my first mainframe. I learned a lot, but I was the only girl in both of those classes and felt really out of place, like a crasher in some sacred boy-space.

Not only were most of the boys older than I was, but I wasn't into science fiction or role-playing games and had already manifested a real dislike for so-called progressive bands like Rush. I wasn't particularly interesting to boys, nor was I willing to suck up to them. A twelve-year-old girl, however smart or cool or interested, had no chance to participate fully in the overwhelmingly homosocial teen-boy would-be-hacker subculture of that time, nor was there anyplace else for her to go. *Blah.* So I spent a lot of time working alone at the terminals in the library, messing around with whatever interested or amused me.

Laurel: I started messing with computers in junior high, too, but didn't get serious about the whole thing until college....

We learned BASIC, a programming language, in junior high. That "goto loop" was *sooo* endlessly fascinating. I mean, I could get the computer to talk to me; I could program it to have a conversation ... granted, it had to be the same conversation over and over because I couldn't change the format or the machine would freak out. But I could teach it to interact on a really crude level. It was *interactive.* I noticed even then that the guys in the lab (and, it wasn't—oddly enough—all, or even mostly, guys in the computer labs in junior high) were trying to program shoot-em-up games while the girls were trying to make interactive games. Our assignment might have been to develop an educational game for younger kids; the guys would make "Asteroid Alphabet" while the girls would make "Bob Bunny Counts Carrots." It was my first introduction to the different ways gender impacts computer use.

Crystal: By the time I got to high school, the culture-wide emphasis on computer literacy had emerged. We had a great computer lab full of Apple II + machines, BASIC programming classes (but no Advanced Placement programming classes) and learned how to use word-processing programs. We had a lot of machines, but very little in the way of software and computer-savvy teachers (still a common problem in many schools), so there were limits to what we could do and explore. I was discouraged that even among my girl friends who dug computers (yes, finally!), crude role-playing games like Wizardry and Hitchhiker's Guide to the Galaxy were choice computer distractions.

I got my first computer—an Apple II + with an ImageWriter printer—in tenth grade and started programming crude graphics and sound creations. I'll never forget pulling my first all-nighter, staying up to write a report on my beloved new machine, then waking up the house with curses and howls the millisecond after oh-so-geeked and exhausted me turned the computer off without saving the document! That's how I used my machine: I wanted to be able to write with it, make art with it....

... I was turned on by the new Macintoshes popping up in friends' dorm rooms and labs. Around 1987 a friend bought an early IBM-PC clone and a modem (!) that he used to access the online service Prodigy. I was impressed, but didn't really foresee a day when I'd be able to afford to go online. I knew nothing about bulletin board systems (BBSs)....

Laurel: When I went to college, I got totally hooked on computers and discovered the world of cyberspace. The guy I was living with was really into computers, and it didn't take very long before I was lost in my own right in the late-night-online world of BBSs. I adopted the name "novice" because, well, I was one, and because when I had to make up my first alias, I had a "best novice debater" trophy on the wall in front of me. I had some (guy) friends who really pushed me along unknowingly ... I was adamant about never, ever showing my ignorance in front of them. Early on, if one of them would start talking about computer stuff I didn't understand, I'd nod and go "uh-huh" and then figure out what they were talking about on my own. Not the easiest way to learn, for sure! These guys would be up until two, three in the morning doing "computer stuff," and I felt sort of left out. So finally, one boring afternoon, I sat down at *his* computer, fired up the communications program, dialed the number for my first BBS, and instantly became an addict. Soon, *I* was the one up until two or three in the morning. *I* was the one talking about people I'd never met as though they were my closest friends, and so on.

Crystal: Even though it was woefully "antique," my Apple II + got me through my masters program in popular culture studies and through the first year of my doctoral course work before it gave up the ghost. I turned it off one night after I finished writing a paper and it went into a coma. Using extreme measures, I managed to get it to power up a couple of times after that and was able to make hard copies of most of my writings, but its little power-pack was juiced out. *Sob. My baby*! Then I got a Mac LC II and a modem and discovered a whole new world. It was June 1992.

Laurel: It wasn't until I got to graduate school in 1992 that I discovered the Internet. I knew more about computers than most people around me, so I started focusing on them. At first I had some ... not problems, exactly, but a couple of male computer geeks in my department seemed to feel that because I wasn't as interested in the traditional canon of cyberpunk stuff as they were, I wasn't a *real* computer/cyberspace geek.

Crystal: I'd been reading here and there about the Internet, so I was totally geeked to get online. A friend loaned me her printout of that classic guide by Brendan Kehoe, *Zen and the Art of Internet*. After reading it and finally managing to log on to one of the university mainframes, I determinedly pestered a computer guru in one of the campus labs until he helped me. Within a couple of weeks of my first connection, I was fully functional ... and totally addicted.

For a grrrl who'd grown up perversely thrilled by libraries and book and record/CD stores, the Internet (even then!) was absolutely mind-blowing! And being able to access libraries around the world 24/7 was a grad student's dream come true. My experiences on the Net were totally in sync with a lot of the reading I was doing at the time: Foucault, Avital Ronell's *The Telephone Book*, Donna Haraway's "A Cyborg Manifesto," and *Mondo 2000*. Far freakin' out! Crystal was goooooonnnne, baby—gone through the mirror into the raging electron sea that birthed her e-alter ego, PopTart. Truly, I knew then how Batgirl must have felt the first time she zipped up her bitchin' Bat-boots and elbowed Robin out of her way! So from that point, I set about turning on all my friends, professors, and students. In my Batgirl-as-Timothy Leary phase, I concentrated especially on my women friends, many of whom were technophobically hesitant at first, but who totally dug it after they made it over that initial hurdle.

Laurel: It's kind of like a religious cult or the whole Deadhead thing. If you're already into computers and the Net, you know what I'm talking about. You've felt the quickening heartbeat at the sound of modems connecting. If you aren't yet into computers but want to be, you might feel poised on the edge of a community of cyborgs—half human, half machine—that constantly beep and buzz. Are they unfriendly, or are they just preoccupied? If you're not interested in computers and don't know what all the fuss is about, you might suspect (and rightfully so) that it's all a sick and twisted phenomenon, and that the masses of techno-geeks out there are totally brainwashed by being plugged in.

I've made it my mission in life (this stage of it, anyway) to get as many grrrls as possible using the Internet and thinking about how it can help them in whatever they do. My hands-down-most-fabulous experience has been getting my own mom wired. I left her alone with my computer and many pages of handwritten notes explaining how to get Netscape up and working, and when I came back ... *bam!* I discovered my mother had fallen prey to the seductive whir of the hard drive and the glow of the monitor. *Sigh.* When I left her, she was unsure about the whole double-clicking business, and if the machine got a little too friendly with beeping or flashing lights she had to immediately take a smoking break on the porch to recover. But the last time I talked to her—and it was through e-mail—she had just discovered yet another fabulous Web site and was sending me the address. Yup, my mom has joined the ranks of women enamored with the screen....

45. Rosamund Else-Mitchell and Naomi Flutter, "Introduction," from *Talking Up: Young Women's Take on Feminism*

Excerpts from Rosamund Else-Mitchell and Naomi Flutter, eds., *Talking Up: Young Women's Take on Feminism* (Melbourne: Spiniflex Press, 1998), xi–xxiii. Reprinted with permission.

In this essay, the authors, voices from Australia's third wave, discuss conditions in Australia that inform third-wave feminism and how their book was meant to address these conditions from a specifically third-wave perspective. The essay gives a broader sense of third wave beyond the confines of the United States.

... In *Generation f: Sex, Power & the Young Feminist*, Virginia Trioli eloquently captures the impact of feminism on many dimensions of young women's lives today. She examines the significance of the 1994 AGB McNair telephone poll in which seventy per cent of young women polled in Sydney and Melbourne said they would not call themselves feminists. Trioli highlighted the paradox implicit in these numbers. Of course they believe in equal pay, a fair justice system, harassment-free workplaces and sexual freedom. This then raises several questions. What do the seventy per cent call these beliefs, if not feminism? And amongst the thirty per cent who "identify" as feminists, what else (if anything) do they see as feminist?... It seems as though the term is up for grabs. If we and many of our contemporaries were simply "taking feminism for granted", as has been the accusation of many "older" (read "real") feminists, especially since *The First Stone* was published, what then did, in fact, it mean we were doing?

In her book, Trioli answers some of these questions. *Talking Up* provides further reassurance that "feminism ... in the hands of the next generation is alive and well, and as crucial as ever" ... Trioli interviewed hundreds of young women and in using their stories, revealed their nous and strategic vision, their unsung community activism and their commitment to ideals of equity and justice. She paved the way for this collection of emerging voices. In giving the microphone to these women, we intend to dispel the idea that feminism is irrelevant in the 1990s, recently punitive or only about criticism. Instead, we want to illustrate that its principles and promotion, its goals and debates, are still part of many women's lives, including at their workplaces, in conversation, at home and in their relationships.

Equally important to the genesis of this anthology was Kathy Bail's *DIY Feminism* (1996). In some ways as a collection of articles by young women it is not dissimilar to this one, but for its premise that feminism was "about individual practice and taking on personal challenges".... It *sounds* very edgy. Let's face it, marketing feminism with groovy fonts, a funky layout and some pictures makes it palatable and digestible to a populist post-modern world. But it doesn't necessarily equate with social transformation, it isn't a call to action.

Multi vocal, savvy, with rock chicks, grunge and riot grrls: feminism pitched as sexy. *DIY* was so well-tuned for media take-up that despite the impressive range of contributors, it became a soundbite take-away. Its stumbling point is its marketing strength—truckloads of attitude. Are "fun and feisty" our only credentials these days? ... If you are a woman with attitude, does this then make you a feminist? Much of do-it-yourself feminism just didn't wash with many of the women involved in this book. What if we can't do-it-ourselves? What if I can't? What if you can't? It is easy to assume that if we couldn't get on our modems, play in a band or be a bit wicked, then we wouldn't cut it. Bail sets up more politicised ideas of feminism as rigid, "dowdy, asexual" ... With this stereotype entrenched once again, it is hardly surprising that she asserts that "women like me ... are still less likely to make an issue of gender"...

We do not want to pit ourselves ... against the DIY images, nor co-opt humourless, separatist stereotypes; but this anthology does not see feminism as either individualised; "disorganised" or even as much fun....

... We are reminded of the reception of Naomi Wolf's second and third books, particularly *Fire with Fire* (1993) in which she was said to be refuting many of her views about female "victimhood" in *The Beauty Myth* (1990). So too Germaine Greer's visit to Melbourne in 1997 when, following her impassioned speech, questioning the nature of sexual liberation today, she was derided for changing her mind about women's sexual freedom, in spite of asserting that she still believed everything she wrote in *The Female Eunuch*.... These critical responses are underpinned by a belief that feminist behaviours are static, fixed, and prescriptive. But if our political and social values are in any way informed by our experiences, then our philosophies, our ideas, our actions, and how we live out our feminism must inevitably evolve....

As Misha Schubert points out, feminism is not, despite its impact, an institution. It has various institutional and legislative manifestations—such as democratic representation, educational and employment opportunities, anti-discrimination, affirmative action and sexual harassment legislation, abortion rights, even no-fault divorce enshrined in the *Family Law Act* of 1975—all thanks to extraordinary lobbying and campaigning by first- and second-wave feminists. Kate Lundy confesses to her late realisation ten years ago that without the *Sex Discrimination Act* of 1984, she would not have been given her first job on a building site. Her reflections on her responsibilities as a federal senator remind us that often our visions about a better world begin with issues that impact on our day-to-day lives. But with support and via active participation we can channel our concerns into social change....

The growth of Women's Studies and feminist revisionism within the Academy in the 1970s and 1980s has provided our generation of graduates—including interested men—the opportunity to read hidden histories, to develop ideas about gender relations, to explore feminist approaches to other disciplines, and consequently, to acquire new ways of seeing the world....

High-profile British feminist, Natasha Walter in *The New Feminism* (1998), extols a bright new future for feminism, based on increased access to material wealth and power, the reorganisation of homes and workplaces and support for women experiencing violence. Although Walter advocates an "unpicking of the tight link between the personal and the political" and implies the importance of public policy to force change, she acknowledges "that personal freedom can be aligned to political equality".... She paints a feminism which is inclusive and one which includes men. Jo Dyer reaches a similar conclusion highlighting the importance of dialogue when negotiating relationships between women and men, and suggesting that the bedroom is not necessarily the best place to be redressing political imbalance. And, Anita Harris' revisiting of heterosexual sex is more about self-honesty and self-rescue, than setting out prescriptive sexual behaviours and rules for feminists....

Relationships with our mothers both actual and political is a frequent preoccupation ... We can grow in experience and vision as we age, and that in ten years time some of us may be more moderate, or more radical. However, we do resent being typecast as unfeminist or anti-feminist, even postfeminist, by those who assert ownership (and imply invention) of the term. Herein lie the contentions that exist between older and younger women: that feminists are this, and not that. But to say "we are" should not mean "they aren't", nor that one is a greater truth than the other. Understanding, consciousness raising, and activism take many forms....

It is commonplace to attribute feminism's divisiveness in Australia to the media—that most amorphous and evasive of creatures. It is endlessly frustrating to see that a "good story" is one based on conflict; and there's nothing better than two prominent feminists "having it out" in public. Maybe this explains much of the coverage of the United Nations Fourth World Conference on Women held in Beijing in 1995. The Conference was variously billed as a middle-aged talk-fest and an east-meets-west, rich-trammels-poor clash of absurd proportions....

Often the best "hook" for young feminists looking for media profile is to trash the past, claiming our reinvention....[Yet] to support feminism, build on its legacies where they exist, and envision a more just world is, in fact, where courage lies:

> If only the whole gang of them hadn't been so afraid of life
> —*The First Stone*, Helen Garner: 1995, p. 222.

46. Misha Schubert, "The Strategic Politics of Organisation," from *Talking Up: Young Women's Take on Feminism*

Excerpts from Rosamund Else-Mitchell and Naomi Flutter, eds., *Talking Up: Young Women's Take on Feminism* (Melbourne: Spiniflex Press, 1998), 217–228. Reprinted with permission.

In an essay that examines her experiences as a third-wave feminist Australian activist, as well as the experiences of her mother in an earlier feminist generation, Misha Schubert discusses her tactics for political activism and how she and her fellow third-wavers have implemented third-wave politics.

From the Girlpower Diary.
April 1997
86 Nicholson Street, Fitzroy

> A gang of twentysomethings, mostly women, sit sprawled around a lounge room littered with pizza boxes and Diet Coke cans. This time the occasion isn't Melrose Night. They've been invited to discuss the government's Constitutional Convention on the Republic.
>
> In this room are the political upstarts who will soon form their own youth ticket for the event and take on the well-resourced forces of the baby-boomers.
>
> The discussion switches from small talk into strategy.
>
> "Do you have any idea how many votes we'll need to get elected?" someone asks rhetorically. "At the bare minimum, 100 000."

> There's a long pause as the scope of the dream sets in.
>
> "Shit." someone mutters.
>
> But within weeks a campaign has taken shape—focus groups will research views and test opinions, we'll build a web site, start fundraising through events and grant applications, complete email and snail mail contact lists, generate media coverage, enlist some prominent supporters, recruit like crazy, train volunteers, run a public forum and make a television advertisement.
>
> All in a day's work for the daughters of modern feminism.

It was no accident that a network of young women had the political vision and the skills to run an independent youth ticket for the nation's Constitutional Convention in the late 1990s. Our capacity to do so attests to the progress of feminism.

As we gathered a group of campaigners and started planning a political presence, we drew from precocious experience. Some came with a history of running student election campaigns at university, others with management skills gleaned as volunteers in women's organisations like the YWCA and the Women's Electoral Lobby. Some were communications kids—students of the media and public relations, while others came to their first political experience armed only with almost boundless energy. Across this diversity, we were unified by a vision of political participation. We knew the significance of the opportunity presented by the Convention, both as an historical event and as a forum in which to train young women in electoral politics.

Our political instinct for the task was no coincidence. More than any generation of women before us, the "FemXers" were groomed to dream audaciously and to realise our ambitions. We were schooled to think, plan and manage our way into political power, thanks largely to our mothers' groundbreaking activism. We are the daughters of modern feminism the students and recipients of its evolution. And now we have a role as feminism's strategists.

We grew up watching our mothers lobby for public policy reform and battle inequality in the paid work force. My mother was a teacher and resigned voluntarily during her pregnancy with me, before her marriage eleven months following my birth. Had she not done so, she would have been forced to resign, only to be offered reinstatement as a casual employee after her wedding. Around the same time, her friend Charmaine McEachern, wanted to keep her maiden name post-marriage, but was informed by the education department that she would only be paid if she used her married name.

Teachers like my mother and Charmaine educated my generation of girls, and their feminist values and working-class roots imbued us with a strong social justice ethic. Their intellects won them teaching bursaries and, later, middle-class salaries, making them supremely conscious of the capacity of formal education to enhance fortunes and bring about social change....

Many aspects of my mother's story are representative of her feminist generation. Women of her generation were advocates, counsellors and community-builders. They ran committees, lobbied for political reform and fostered the confidence and ambition of the young women they taught. If they felt that their own ambition had been stifled, they were determined that their daughters would not be discouraged. These women built a broadly accepted platform and created a culture in which feminism could come of age....

Few of us have employers who allow activism to be an intergrated part of our work day. So the day-to-day activities of organised feminism tend to be run by paid part-time staff in women's organisations with a small, committed volunteer base. Some might argue that a lack of time or resources is nothing new for the Women's Movement. But feminism's achievements have been disproportionate to its resources. It still amazes me to hear the stories behind impressive public policy wins, especially where a campaign was conducted by just a handful of well-organised women. Feminists have achieved a great deal for many women in a relatively short period of time.

It is because of its phenomenal success that feminism has begun to be viewed as an institutional power. Having permeated the bureaucracy and academies, feminist thought has in many instances become common sense, rather than radical doctrine. It is now accepted that women should not be forced to resign from their jobs when they marry, should not have to endure domestic violence, nor should they be subjected to sexual harassment at work. High profile Australian feminists like Patricia Turner at ATSIC, Sandra Yates at Saatchi and Saatchi and Ann Sherry at Westpac hold positions of significant influence in the public and private sectors. Feminist authors like Anne Summers and Helen Garner are among the baby boomers who exercise clout in the world of publishing and ideas.

With this level of influence, it is unsurprising that critics from inside and outside the Movement have begun to generalise about the capacities, potential and failings of organised feminism. Recently, I was in the news room after the committal hearing of a man charged with murdering his girlfriend's child. Media reports portrayed the accused's girlfriend as a deeply insecure young woman who lacked opportunities, ambition and independence. A senior writer in the bureau looked at the article and said to me (as a public feminist, you are invariably responsible for the entire history of feminism) "Feminism has done nothing for women like her". I thought about the comment for a while before I responded, saying it was a tough call to blame feminism for what it hasn't done, as though it were some kind of omnipresent institutional force. This construction of feminism assumes levels of resources and coordination which simply do not exist. A grassroots movement is seldom centrally coordinated or planned. Individual women tend to work on the issues they know locally or personally, not as a matter of self-interest, but rather because of expertise. Many women feel (rightly) uncomfortable about advocating for others where it may be seen as paternalistic. Thus, the more recent approach has been to provide personal or organisational support to women of diverse backgrounds as they advocate their own issues.

So, to the critics I return the challenge. If you want feminism to be or do something it is not, then the best way to make it happen is to take up the issue yourself. Feminism is not, despite its impact, an institution. It is a loose-knit collection of non-government organizations (NGOs) and individual women, most of whom could do with an injection of time, money and energy. The most effective way to influence the priorities of the Movement is to throw yourself into the fray or assist others who do so with time and/or resources.

Meanwhile, women's NGOs continue to be a much-needed legislative lobby, vocally monitoring government-friendliness to women. As Hillary Rodham Clinton pays tribute:

> Time and again we have seen that it's NGOs who are responsible for making progress in any society ... who have charted the real advances for women and children. It is the NGOs who have pressured governments ... down the path to economic, social and political progress, often in the face of overwhelming hostility.

Younger women are not only involved in these organisations—they lead them. At the helm of the YWCA of Australia—Australia's oldest existing women's organisation—are several strategic young women. Joint Presidents Susan Brennan and Lynda Poke are twenty-eight and thirty-two, while Acting Executive Officer Michelle Beg is twenty-four. Hardly yesterday's women. As leaders, they bring great skill to the organisation, applying their professional talents to non-paid work. Susan is barrister with an awesome attention to detail. During her last term on the National Executive, she rewrote the policy manual of the organisation (and, in the process, bolstered its feminist platform). Lynda runs her own accountancy practice and was the National Treasurer for two years before her election as President. She now oversees an ethical investment trust for the Association. Michelle is a journalism graduate whose writing skills are matched by her visual flair for layout and design. Through her efforts, the publications of the organisation are slick, professional productions.

As sites of power evolve and shift, feminist practice has expanded its agenda. In the 1970s and 1980s, the Women's Movement focused its attention on the role of the state. This reflected the strong influence of government in almost all aspects of women's lives. The gamut of issues from pay equity to childcare, discrimination to health care, fertility control to affirmative action were regulated by legislation. These days we must be vigilant about the "old" rights in addition to providing a feminist presence in new spheres of influence, including the bastions of the private sector. Feminists are now required to be active on more fronts than ever before, in an era characterised by the extremes of work and a deepening sense of time poverty. These days we struggle to find time for relaxation, let alone activism. Thus, the professionalisation of feminism has been both a boon and a frustration. The grassroots activists of the 1970s became the femocrats of the 1980s and the consultants or managers of the 1990s—highly skilled women with strong networks and finances, but little time for lobbying.

If, as some commentators have suggested, some young women reject the collective, many others recognise its strategic vantage. Many find a stronger guarantee of gender equality in structural change than in the precedents of a solitary trailblazer. We know that our freedoms depend on legal rights which were won by well-coordinated lobbying campaigns. Rights can only be retained through their exercise and organised vigilance. And as this year's abortion debate in Western Australia demonstrated, those legal rights can be threatened at any time. So we still need a commitment to organised politics if we are to secure our gains....

Today, our brave new world requires us to translate important feminist concepts into soundbites, rather than lectures. These days the way to reach decision-makers is to influence markets. Accordingly, we need the skills to reach mass audiences with short messages, cultivating public sympathy or endorsement for our causes. That's why I rang the producers of *A Current Affair* in December, 1997 and challenged the Victorian President of the RSL, Bruce Ruxton to a televised debate about the republic and the flag. A successful electoral strategy for our youth ticket was dependent upon broad commercial audiences, as well as our conventional alliances, if we were to make a difference.

This logic has also encouraged me over the past five years, to play "feminist" to my friend and talk-show host, Neil Mitchell at 3AW, the highest-rating morning show in metropolitan Melbourne. With a great deal of humour, we have discussed sexual harassment, sexist advertising on billboards, identifying discrimination and the need for women's organisations. Neil enjoys presenting the feminist position as unreasonable, prudish or petty to see what reaction he can provoke. I've found sustained humour and some jokes about insecure men of a certain age, with a paunch and facial hair to be effectively disarming.

My political training came from three invaluable years in the student union movement, which taught me everything from writing a press release to running an election campaign, from negotiating to debating, from accosting strangers to understanding organisational processes. Those experiences didn't just give me a skillset for my professional life, they also provided a strong, close network of female friends. Many of the women who worked together on campus have continued to seek each other out, to work together on projects in the broader Women's Movement. Our friendships are fuelled by a similar interest in politics, although our party sympathies and memberships vary. We learn from each other constantly; giving feedback on public speeches, editing each other's published work and helping one another to strategise in our professional or political situations. And still very few social commentators recognise this new breed of feminists.

Throughout this decade many observers have declared feminism's death, gleefully reporting young women's hesitation to describe themselves as feminists. But their proclamations are wilfully ignorant. A generation schooled in symbolism knows both the power and constraints of labels. We'll use them when it's smart but downplay them in more hostile forums. We are aware of the power of language to advocate but also to stereotype, to limit and dismiss. We understand the power of the *f* word to connect us with our history and take pleasure in its loaded meanings and the hoary old stereotypes. When we first take on the mantle we tend to be earnest to a fault. Which of us can't recall ourselves ensconsed in an impossible argument, using the particularly adament tone of one who knows she is right? Later we learn to temper the gravity and to laugh at our detractors.

Social change demands organisation. No great feat has ever been achieved without strategy and coordination. Whether we are talking electoral politics or popular culture, the lessons are translatable: influence comes with a strategy for its acquisition, no matter how effortless power appears. At the end of the day, a girl's gotta have a plan. We can't afford to be naive if we are going to take our rightful share of power. We need to learn the skills of public influence if we hope to retain and exercise our rights. And we need to move from the politics of influence to the politics of governance. We must make the move from training lobbyists to grooming feminists for electoral power. In essence, we need to be coordinated, streetsmart and hard-nosed in our politics.

Meanwhile in the girlpower diary...

February, 1998
Old Parliament House, Canberra

> After nine months of obsession, we took our places in history. I was one of the 152 delegates to the nation-shaping forum of the century, with a brief to speak for young Australians. The odds had been slim but we'd known enough about proportional representation to secure preferences across the field of candidates. I was still pinching myself to check it was real.
>
> And what a reality it was—the elder statespeople of Australian politics alongside novices, athletes and authors, war veterans and television producers, cattle farmers and clergy. All here to discuss the future shape of the nation.
>
> Two weeks of passionate dream-selling, story-telling and raw emotion. The indigenous intersecting the colonial, the aspirational meeting the nostalgic.
>
> And through the clamour rang the clear, articulate voices of young Australia, diverse in vision, but homogenous in passion. The young women, outnumbering the young men by two to one, gave us a taste of female power beyond the individual icon. Strong, sassy and streetsmart. Girlpower in action. Get used to it.

47. Suzette Mitchell, "Lines of Demarcation: Beijing 1995," from *Talking Up: Young Women's Take on Feminism*

Excerpts from Rosamund Else-Mitchell and Naomi Flutter, eds., *Talking Up: Young Women's Take on Feminism* (Melbourne: Spiniflex Press, 1998), 183–192. Reprinted with permission.

In this essay, Australian third-wave feminist Suzette Mitchell discusses her experiences at the United Nations Fourth World Conference in Beijing in 1995 and how categories of "youth" and child labor laws often apply to the increase of child labor in "a post-industrial free market system." For Mitchell this is a primary third-wave issue, and Beijing provided her with an "understanding of working toward feminist goals at an international level." This lively, personal essay provides a down-to-earth perspective on why the third wave needs to be transnationally inclined.

> We represent more than half of the world's population, but our voices are rarely heard in the halls of power. War, violence and environmental degradation leave a legacy of destruction for future generations. If we are to inherit these and other problems, then we want to share responsibility now for their solutions. Therefore, we must be allowed to participate actively and effectively at all levels of decision making
>
> United Nations Fourth World Conference on Women: Youth Declaration.

For me, as a young Australian feminist, nothing has been as intellectually, emotionally, or logistically exciting as my involvement in the preparations and staging of the United Nations (UN) Fourth World Conference on Women in Beijing and associated Non-Government Organisation (NGO) Forum in the (not so) nearby town of Huairou in 1995.

The Beijing Women's Conference stands as illustration that the much-hyped "generational debate" is largely mythical, constructed by the media to give good copy. As I saw it, Australian women worked together towards Beijing, unconcerned about age, ethnic background, sexual preference, religion and economic status. Indeed, the whole process revealed that young Australian feminists sometimes have more in common with older Australian women, than with our youthful feminist colleagues overseas. Nevertheless, the knowledge and wisdom we gained from working alongside motivated and intelligent young, feminist women from around the world, has strengthened the international perspectives of young Australian feminists....

During the UN Youth Consultation for the Asia Pacific Region, we spent several days drafting a supplement to the regional UN document, which would be discussed at the regional governmental conference in Jakarta. At a UN meeting, language is critical, with days and sometimes weeks spent deliberating over the choice of words for regional or international documents. Regional youth lobbied for the inclusion of issues related to young women and HIV/AIDS, poverty, education and employment opportunities, sexual and reproductive health and family planning, self-esteem and consumerism, amongst others. We were taken seriously, having developed the "tools" (language) for effective lobbying. The result was a regional plan with many references to youth issues and the particular effects of more general issues on young women. This set the scene for other regional meetings, and also the Beijing Conference itself.

Prior to the Beijing Conference, the Australian Young Women's Christian Association (YWCA) received funding to identify the key concerns of young Australian women. This project, "Young Women Say", was developed and implemented by young women around the country. It involved local consultations with twenty-two groups and organisations in sixteen communities, distribution of 600 questionnaires and almost 500 street interviews. The final report states that "much social research obscures the reality of women, and in the youth sector there has been an ongoing struggle to hear the voice of young women."

The "Young Women Say" project sought to document the views of young Australian women—many of which rarely receive attention in the media. When asked "what was the most important issue relating to young women?", more than half replied equal pay for equal work, followed by personal safety when out after dark, freedom of speech and respect for their views. The majority of women interviewed agreed that their lives hold more opportunities than was the case for previous generations, particularly in the paid workforce. When asked to identify the negative aspects of being a young woman, they identified their key concerns as sexism in the workplace and on the sports field, discrimination in job opportunities and sexual harassment. The survey also suggested that women appear to be more vulnerable to media misrepresentation than older women. However, younger feminists are learning media skills and creating alternative outlets for their views, particularly through new information technologies which involve no external editing or other forms of censorship.

The results of the "Young Women Say" project highlight the differences between young Australian women and our Asian and Pacific counterparts. Unsurprisingly, they parallel many of the priorities for young women in the USA and Europe. They are very similar to the views of older Australian women, although our generation seems to have chosen different mechanisms for addressing these concerns.

The Australian preparations for the Beijing Conference brought together feminists of all ages. The mobilisation of the Australian Women's Movement at this time was astounding. I have never before seen so many national and international networks working together to agree on the international language for women's rights. In Australia, many groups actively participated in preparations, including the YWCA, the Older Women's Network (OWN), Australian Women in Sport, the Country Women's Association (CWA), the Coalition of Activist Lesbians (COAL), Amnesty International, the Girl Guides Association, and the Catholic Women's League. Young Australian women were active in most of these groups.

For me, the Beijing Women's Conference and NGO Forum were phenomenal events which assembled a rich diversity of women. Over 30,000 other women from around the world joined a conversation about women's issues and concerns. After years of preparation, Australia was represented by some 500 women.

Young women were particularly well represented at Beijing, with more youth delegates than at any UN Conference ever staged. When the proceedings began, many of the young women had already met one another and formed caucuses at regional meetings. We had developed our own Declaration and suggested language amendments to the *International Platform for Action*, the official document produced by the Conference. We worked with women of all ages to ensure that this document represented the needs and concerns of all women, from the girl-child to the elderly. Young women were involved in all the activities at the conference. We led workshops, caucused and built alliances between different groups, negotiated with heads of state, addressed the plenary, testified as victims of war, covered the proceedings as journalists. Young women became a force with which to be reckoned, as we talked and strategised on every issue, from poverty to pornography into the early hours.

The Beijing Conference received a great deal of media attention, much of which unfortunately, did not focus on the issues discussed at either the Conference or the NGO Forum. Instead, the media covered the "sensations" of Chinese security, "clashes" between the North and South (rich and poor) countries, and the "splits" between fundamentalist and progressive delegates on issues such as reproductive rights.

Speaking at the NGO Forum, a young Australian feminist commented on the media's portrayal of the generational divide. She argued that while young and older women have different styles of activism, these differences are never as stark as made out by journalists. "[T]he debate in Australia", she continued, "has been led by a school of thought that argues that because young women aren't in the media, therefore they aren't actively organising as feminists in the community." Of course, no journalists picked up this statement!

Some older, high-profiled women aware of the media's obsession with "big names" declined to attend the Beijing Conference. The American feminist icon, Gloria Steinem, was one such. Instead, she wrote a letter to participants, stating that "perhaps the world media will introduce more new women to their readers and viewers at home if some of us golden oldies aren't around". Thanks Gloria, but no such luck. In fact, apart from the prominent feminists such as Betty Friedan, Bella Abzug, Jane Fonda, Hillary Clinton and Sally Field (white, middle-class, middle-aged American women), very few individual women were featured by the media.

Many Australian media commentators reflected on the differences between women's issues in the North and South. This point was made time and time again and was typified in a cartoon showing middle-class Australian activists on one side of the Great Wall of China, and poor Chinese "peasant" women on the other. Yet, this polarisation was totally artificial and absent from both the Conference and NGO Forum. Women from different regions and cultures disagreed on some issues and agreed on many others. And wealth and class were significant axes across which positions varied, with wealthy women from Southern countries having more in common with Northern feminists, than with poor women from their own countries.

In Beijing and Huairou, feminist infighting was not the focus, in spite of what was reported in the newspapers. While I understand why the media depicted the Conference and NGO Forum in this way, I am frustrated at the misrepresentation. I guess it just doesn't sell papers to cover stories of intergenerational and international solidarity. Jackie May, an ABC correspondent, commented:

> One of the most disheartening things for me as a journalist on location in Beijing was to be shown some of the vitriolic and misogynistic rubbish generated by male columnists in Australia. These so called "think" pieces refer[red] to the "middle-aged women's talk-fest" ... I can't imagine a men's conference being similarly belittled.

This view from inside the media illustrates some of the difficulties faced by young feminist journalists. Thoughtful pieces were juxtaposed in newspapers with articles which ridiculed, scorned or trivialised the event, encouraging readers to question the legitimacy or success of the event. Calling the Conference a "middle-aged talk-fest" ignores the record-breaking presence of young women, and derides middle-aged women for their assumed domination. It also ignores the Conference's outcomes generated by workshops and plenary sessions, as well as the UN document signed by the majority of the world's nation states.

Given the overall calibre of media coverage, it is telling that the International Platform for Action should identify "increase[d] participation ... expression and decision making in and through the media and new technologies of communication" and "promot[ion] of a balanced and non-stereotyped portrayal of women in the media."

Young feminists have a double burden in obtaining mainstream media coverage from an industry dominated by middle-aged men. Young women's feminist issues will not be accurately portrayed in our newspapers, magazines and television shows until more feminists, who are supportive of other women, gain access to decision-making in the Australian media industry.

In Beijing, I came to understand the importance of working towards feminist goals at an international level. Young Australian women lobbied effectively to establish an international legal framework for women's human rights. We focused our attention on the rights that Australian women have fought for during three generations: the right to vote, the right to equal pay, the right to education, and the right to be free from violence and harassment. The "Beijing experience" internationalised and strengthened Australia's feminist movements. We learned from the experience of other women, and they learned from ours. This was especially so for young women. Importantly, we developed relationships and connections with women from around the world. And, in this age of increasing technology, these links are being maintained as we continue our lobbying and campaigning.

If only because of our sheer numbers, young women are becoming a powerful force. Today, half the world's population is under twenty-five—youth represent a majority. Increasingly, the social and political agenda will be influenced by young minds. In Beijing, you couldn't help but stand back and be inspired, watching them take the floor—articulating the issues of the future and moulding the agenda—across boundaries of nations and ages.

48. Guerrilla Girls, "Introduction," from *The Guerrilla Girls' Bedside Companion to the History of Western Art*

An illustrated introduction to the position of women artists in art history, this essay is art history in a flash, bringing a funny and definitively third-wave perspective to the discussion of art.

THERE IS A GOOD PRINCIPLE, WHICH CREATED ORDER, LIGHT, AND MAN, AND AN EVIL PRINCIPLE, WHICH CREATED CHAOS, DARKNESS, AND WOMEN.
–PYTHAGORAS, 6TH CENTURY B.C.

GIRLS BEGIN TO TALK AND TO STAND ON THEIR FEET SOONER THAN BOYS BECAUSE WEEDS GROW MORE QUICKLY THAN GOOD CROPS.
–MARTIN LUTHER, 1533

INSTEAD OF CALLING THEM BEAUTIFUL, THERE WOULD BE MORE WARRANT FOR DESCRIBING WOMEN AS THE UNESTHETIC SEX. NEITHER FOR MUSIC, NOR FOR POETRY, NOR FOR FINE ART, HAVE THEY REALLY AND TRULY ANY SENSE OR SUSCEPTIBILITY.
–ARTHUR SCHOPENHAUER, 1851

Forget the stale, male, pale, Yale textbooks, this is Art Herstory 101!

If you were to believe what many of us were taught in school and museums, you would think a clear line of achievement links one genius innovator to the next. For example, Michelangelo paves the way for Caravaggio. Or, a few hundred years later, Monet begets Cézanne, who influences Picasso, who brings us to Pollock. This is the canon that–until recently–most of us took for granted as the history of Western art. It reduced centuries of artistic output to a bunch of white male masterpieces and movements, a world of "seminal" and "potent" art where the few women you hear about are white, and even they are rarely mentioned and never accorded a status anywhere near the big boys. Now, the Guerrilla Girls admire the old "masters"–and lots of young ones, too. But we also believe–along with most contemporary scholars–that the time has come, once and for all, for the canon to be fired.

The famous query by feminist artists and art historians goes, "Why haven't there been more great women artists throughout Western history?" The Guerrilla Girls want to restate the question: "Why haven't more women been *considered* great artists throughout Western history?" And we have a lot more questions (see below), because even though making it as an artist isn't easy for *anyone,* the history of art has been a history of discrimination.

Look at the attitudes toward women emanating from some of the most celebrated male minds of Western culture (quotations, above). Notice how little these attitudes

GEORGIA O'KEEFFE

EDMONIA LEWIS

ARTEMISIA GENTILESCHI, *GUERRILLA AND THE ELDERS,* 1610, SCHLOSS WEISSENSTEIN, POMMERSFELDEN

Who are the Guerrilla Girls?

We are a group of women artists and arts professionals who fight discrimination. We're the consicence of the art world, counterparts to the mostly male tradition of anonymous do-gooders like Robin Hood, Batman, and the Lone Ranger. We have produced over 80 posters, printed projects, and actions that expose sexism and racism in the art world and the culture at large. We wear gorilla masks to keep the focus on the issues rather than our personalities. We use humor to prove that feminists can be funny. Our work has been passed around the world by kindred spirits who consider themselves Guerrilla Girls too. We could be anyone; we are everywhere.

GARDNER'S
WHITE MALE ART THROUGH THE AGES
FIFTH EDITION

H. W. JANSON
HISTORY OF MOSTLY MALE ART

changed from the 6th century B.C. to the 19th century A.D. (Remember, women didn't even get the vote in the U.S. until 1919, in France until 1945.) With misogyny and racism the ideologies of the day, backed up with repressive laws, it is amazing that any women became artists at all, especially when you realize that until this century, women were rarely allowed to attend art schools, join artists' guilds or academies, or own an atelier. Many were kept from learning to read or write. For most of history, women have, by law, been considered the property of their fathers, husbands, or brothers, who almost always believed women were put on earth to serve them and bear children.

The truth is that, despite prejudice, there have been lots of women artists throughout Western history. From ancient Greece and Rome there are accounts of women painters who earned more than their male counterparts. In the Middle Ages, nuns made tapestries and illuminated manuscripts. In the Renaissance, daughters were trained to help in their fathers' ateliers; some went on to have careers of their own. In the 17th and 18th centuries, women excelled at portraiture and broke new ground in the scientific observation of plants and animals. In the 19th century, women cross-dressed for success or lived in exile, far enough from home to behave as they pleased. In the 20th century, the ranks of white women artists and women artists of color swelled. These artists were part of every 20th-century "ism" and started a few of their own, too.

But even after overcoming incredible obstacles, women artists were usually ignored by critics and art historians–who claimed that art by white women and people of color didn't meet their "impartial" criteria for "quality." These impartial standards place a high value on art that expresses white male experience and a low

A WOMAN BY ANY OTHER NAME...

For years the Guerrilla Girls have been using the label "women and artists of color" to describe the "others" we represent. But we've always felt the phrase was inadequate because it's unclear where women of color fit in: they are BOTH women AND artists of color. Furthermore, the history of Western art is primarily a history of white Europeans in which people of color have been excluded and marginalized. So, while we declare that when we use the word "women" we mean ALL women, we wish there was a better term to express the diverse experiences of Asians, blacks, Latinas, Native Americans, etc.

Why is The Museum of Modern Art more interested in African art than in art by African-Americans?

ALMA THOMAS

Why did so few male art historians mention me in their survey books?

ARTEMISIA GENTILESCHI

value on everything else. Twentieth-century art historians have worse records vis-à-vis women than their earlier counterparts: Pliny the Elder in the 1st century A.D., Boccaccio in the 14th, and Vasari in the 16th acknowledged more women artists than Meyer Schapiro, T.J. Clark and H.W. Janson in the 20th.

Luckily, in recent decades feminist art historians, most of whom are–surprise!–women, have resurrected and revalued hundreds of women artists from the past. Whenever an art history survey, like Janson's *History of Art* or Gardner's *Art Through the Ages* adds a female author, the number of women artists included–white and of color–miraculously increases. The Guerrilla Girls have gratefully benefited from the ideas and research of these scholars, several of whom have secretly helped us write this book.

THE ADVANTAGES OF BEING A WOMAN ARTIST:

Working without the pressure of success.
Not having to be in shows with men.
Having an escape from the art world in your 4 free-lance jobs.
Knowing your career might pick up after you're eighty.
Being reassured that whatever kind of art you make it will be labeled feminine.
Not being stuck in a tenured teaching position.
Seeing your ideas live on in the work of others.
Having the opportunity to choose between career and motherhood.
Not having to choke on those big cigars or paint in Italian suits.
Having more time to work when your mate dumps you for someone younger.
Being included in revised versions of art history.
Not having to undergo the embarrassment of being called a genius.
Getting your picture in the art magazines wearing a gorilla suit.

A PUBLIC SERVICE MESSAGE FROM **GUERRILLA GIRLS** CONSCIENCE OF THE ART WORLD
532 LaGUARDIA PLACE, #237 • NY, NY 10012
Email: guerrillagirls@voyagerco.com

POSTER BY THE GUERRILLA GIRLS, 1986

The Guerrilla Girls' Bedside Companion to the History of Western Art isn't a comprehensive survey of women artists in history. It doesn't include all the cultures of the world. It's not a list of the most significant women artists. It wasn't written for experts who already know all this stuff. Writing about women artists in Western history is complicated. There are lots of contradictory positions and theories. We have opted to stay out of the theory wars, and present our irreverent take on what life was like for some females in the West who managed, against all odds, to make art. It's ammunition for all the women who are–or will become–artists.

OFFICIAL DISCLAIMER: A GRAVE APPROACH TO ART HISTORY

WE'VE RESTRICTED THE BOOK TO DEAD ARTISTS BECAUSE WE DON'T BELIEVE IN EVALUATING OR EXCLUDING OUR PEERS. EVEN SO, IT'S BEEN HARD TO DECIDE WHOM TO WRITE ABOUT. THERE ARE MANY WOMEN ARTISTS WHO DESERVE TO BE IN THIS BOOK AND WOULD BE IF WE HAD MORE ROOM.

HARRIET POWERS

PAN YULIANG

FRIDA KAHLO

CLAUDE CAHUN

49. Guerrilla Girls, "Today Women Are Equal, Right?" from *The Guerrilla Girls' Bedside Companion to the History of Western Art*

Known for their humorous commentary on sexism in art history, in this concluding essay the Guerrilla Girls sum up what is good, bad, and ugly about what is happening for women artists today.

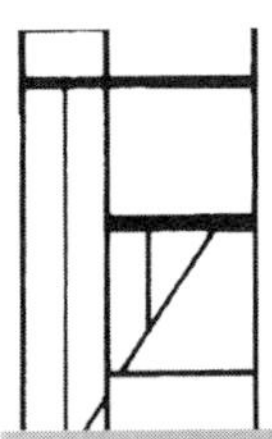

TODAY WOMEN ARE EQUAL, RIGHT?

In our introduction, many pages back, you probably remember that we decided not to write about living women artists in this *Bedside Companion,* because we didn't want to put ourselves in the position of having to evaluate (or exclude) our peers. We think of ourselves as representing all women artists, not just a few. But this doesn't mean we can't discuss the collective accomplishments of our contemporaries, which have been enormous. How's it going for women artists today? Well...

GUERRILLA GIRLS, POSTER, 1989

WHEN RACISM & SEXISM ARE NO LONGER FASHIONABLE, WHAT WILL YOUR ART COLLECTION BE WORTH?

The art market won't bestow mega-buck prices on the work of a few white males forever. For the 17.7 million you just spent on a single Jasper Johns painting, you could have bought at least one work by all these women and artists of color:

Bernice Abbott
Anni Albers
Sofonisba Anguisolla
Diane Arbus
Vanessa Bell
Isabel Bishop
Rosa Bonheur
Elizabeth Bougereau
Margaret Bourke-White
Romaine Brooks
Julia Margaret Cameron
Emily Carr
Rosalba Carriera
Mary Cassatt
Constance Marie Charpentier
Imogen Cunningham
Sonia Delaunay
Elaine de Kooning
Lavinia Fontana
Meta Warwick Fuller
Artemisia Gentileschi
Marguérite Gérard
Natalia Goncharova
Kate Greenaway
Barbara Hepworth
Eva Hesse
Hannah Hoch
Anna Huntingdon
May Howard Jackson
Frida Kahlo
Angelica Kauffmann
Hilma af Klimt
Käthe Kollwitz
Lee Krasner
Dorothea lange
Marie Laurencin
Edmonia lewis
Judith Leyster
Barbara Longhi
Dora Maar
Lee Miller
Lisette Model
Paula Modersohn-Becker
Tina Modotti
Berthe Morisot
Grandma Moses
Gabriele Münter
Alice Neel
Louise Nevelson
Georgia O'Keeffe
Meret Oppenheim
Sarah peale
Liubov Popova
Olga Rosanova
Nellie Mae Rowe
Rachel Ruysch
Kay Sage
Augusta Savage
Varvara Stepanova
Florine Stettheimer
Sophie Taeuber-Arp
Alma Thomas
Marie Robusti
Suzanne Valadon
Remedios Varo
Elizabeth Vigée Le Brun
Laura Wheeling Waring

A PUBLIC SERVICE MESSAGE FROM GUERRILLA GIRLS CONSCIENCE OF THE ART WORLD
532 LaGUARDIA PLACE, #237• NY, NY 10012
(Email: guerrillagirls@voyagerco.com

It's been good...

- More women's art has been exhibited, reviewed, and collected than ever before. Dealers, critics, curators, and collectors are fighting their own prejudices and practicing affirmative action for women and artists of color. (The GG's take some of the credit for this.)
- Everyone except a few misogynist diehards believe there are–and have been–great women artists. Finally, women can benefit from role models and mentors of their own gender.
- Feminists have transformed the fields of art, history, and philosophy, making room for the point of view of the "other" (that's us, girls). They have made people aware that what most of us learned as objective reality was actually white male reality.
- Recently, there have been shows of openly gay and lesbian artists, and shows that attempt to explore homosexual sensibility.
- The age of the isms is over. Few art historians still cling to the idea that there is a mainstream, that art develops in a linear direction from artist A to artist B. In the current postmodern era, more kinds of art practice and more kinds of artists are accepted and written into the historical record. This is creating a truer, richer picture of the present and the past.

It's been bad...

- Women artists still get collected less and shown less. The price of their work is almost never as high as that of white males. Women art teachers rarely get tenure and their salaries are often lower than those of their male counterparts.
- Museums still don't buy enough art by women, even though it's a bargain! Our 1989 poster "When racism and sexism are no longer fashionable..." pointed out that for the amount of money spent at auction on a single painting by Jasper Johns, an art collector could have bought a work of art by every woman in this book!
- There's still a materials hierarchy, with oil paint on canvas at the top. Other media–like sculpture, drawing, photography, installation, and performance–are not quite as prestigious. Ironically, this has made it easier for women to make it in these fields.
- Museums and galleries in Europe and New York are the worst. All our research shows that the farther you get from New York and Western Europe, the better it gets for women and artists of color.
- Although the West has lost some of its cultural hegemony, the art of Asia, Africa and the Americas is still not accorded equal status with European art, or taught as often.

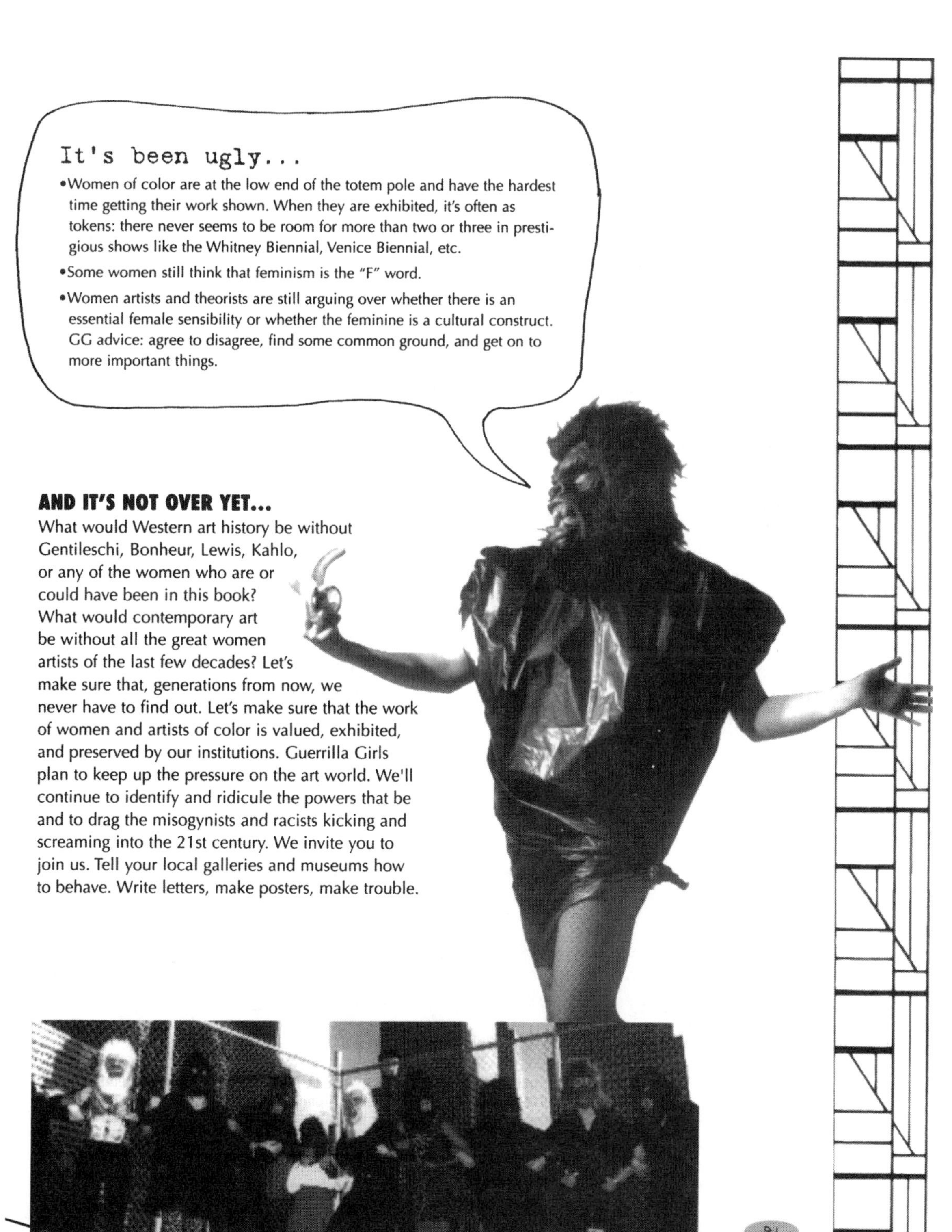

It's been ugly...

- Women of color are at the low end of the totem pole and have the hardest time getting their work shown. When they are exhibited, it's often as tokens: there never seems to be room for more than two or three in prestigious shows like the Whitney Biennial, Venice Biennial, etc.
- Some women still think that feminism is the "F" word.
- Women artists and theorists are still arguing over whether there is an essential female sensibility or whether the feminine is a cultural construct. GG advice: agree to disagree, find some common ground, and get on to more important things.

AND IT'S NOT OVER YET...

What would Western art history be without Gentileschi, Bonheur, Lewis, Kahlo, or any of the women who are or could have been in this book? What would contemporary art be without all the great women artists of the last few decades? Let's make sure that, generations from now, we never have to find out. Let's make sure that the work of women and artists of color is valued, exhibited, and preserved by our institutions. Guerrilla Girls plan to keep up the pressure on the art world. We'll continue to identify and ridicule the powers that be and to drag the misogynists and racists kicking and screaming into the 21st century. We invite you to join us. Tell your local galleries and museums how to behave. Write letters, make posters, make trouble.

91

50. Trina Robbins, "Grrrlz' Comix: The 1990's," from *From Girls to Grrrlz: A History of Women's Comics from Teens to Zines*

An illustrated look at the best grrrl comics from the zine scene, which in the 1990s was widely recognized as a powerful site for third-wave feminist activism, Robbins' essay provides a good selection from these zines. Her interpretation of and commentary on the zines provide a powerful sense of this aspect of third-wave feminist cultural production.

In 1992, *Wimmen's Comix* finally removed the word men from its name and became *Wimmin's Comix*. By then, though, it no longer mattered. Young women had started to reclaim the word girl, just as the gay movement had reclaimed the word queer, and they were using the previously forbidden word in the titles of their comics: *Real Girl*, *Action Girl*, *Deep Girl*, *Girl Hero*, *Girltalk*, *Girljock*, *Rude Girls and Dangerous Women*. (It's interesting to note here that throughout the 1990s, "bad girl" comics the kind produced for adolescent and teenaged boys and starring hypersexualized women with large breasts and little clothing are often preceded by the word lady, as in *Lady Death*, *Lady Justice*, and *Lady Rawhide*, while the feminist comics have the word girl in their titles.)

Real Girl, the first of the "girl" comics, started with the new decade in 1990, Editor Angela Bocage subtitled it "The Sex Comik for All Genders and Orientations by Artists Who Are Good in Bed." True to its title, *Real Girl* features artists of both genders, and emphasizes comics that deal with every variation of sex, positive and negative: abortion, harassment, AIDS, lesbians, cross dressers, and paper dolls of people like Gertrude Stein and Alice B. Toklas or Valerie Solanis, author of the *SCUM Manifesto* and would-be assassin of Andy Warhol.

In an article in Real Girl no. 1. Rebecka Wright defines girl as opposed to woman:

"Perhaps you're wondering why *Real Girl?* Why not *Real Woman?* Isn't "girl" a patronizing term for an adult female? Listen, junior, while it's true that this form of address is best reserved for intimates, some of the best people around call themselves girls. Quite a few call *themselves* women. The twain often meet even in the same person, but there are some philosophical differences.

"Sex, just to choose an example at random, has certain, well, serious and lasting connotations for women that just don't apply to girls. A 'fallen woman' is ruined: a 'bad girl' is only naughty....

"Not that it's all a game for girls, but there don't seem to be quite so many lurking consequences for them. There is a certain amount of freedom of action accorded adult girls, as succinctly put by this popular bumpersticker: "Good girls go to heaven. Bad girls go everywhere." Times had changed and that feminist warhorse *Wimmin's Comix*, after going through three publishers and twenty years, put out its last issue in 1992. Past issues had highlighted such themes as men, little girls, and work ... there had even been a 3-D issue ... but this last one was the "kvetch issue." In her editorial kvetch, Caryn Leschen echoed the frustrations of too many women cartoonists while explaining why there would be no more issues of the longest-lasting women's anthology comic:

"This book has been printed on cheap paper which will turn yellow in a few years. The print run was too small and all the stores, as usual, will sell out, but they won't reorder because 'Women don't buy comix.' Bullshit. How did they sell out in the first place? It's always like that. What a waste of time and energy. Forget it."

After the close of their longtime home at *Wimmin's Comix*, some cartoonists moved on to *Twisted Sisters*, under the editorship of Diane Noomin. *Twisted Sisters*, which began as a two-issue comic book in the 1970s, was revived in 1991 as a book, collecting earlier work by fourteen women cartoonists, much

Real Girl, 1992. Cover by Roxxie.

The last issue of Wimmin's Comix, 1992. Cover by Caryn Leschen.

of it from *Wimmin's Comix*. After that, Noomin edited four more issues as a comic book, expanded to include the work of newer, younger women cartoonists. And there were definitely enough to choose from; throughout the 1990s, scads of women cartoonists emerged on the pages of anthologies and their own comic books. *Twisted Sisters* exemplifies the tendencies of contemporary women cartoonists to produce autobiographical stories. Issue no. 3, from 1994, is typical; of four stories in the book, three are literally "true confessions." The main difference between these and the earlier love comics is that *Twisted Sisters'* confessions all deal with sex: the high school girl protagonist of Debbie Drechsler's "Sixteen" is raped; in Caryn Leschen's "Dutch Treat," a bride honeymooning in Europe sleeps with an old boyfriend; and Phoebe Gloeckner spins the unsettling tale of a fifteen-year-old runaway in a world of bad drugs and worse sex.

Like the old love comics, these stories are narrated in first person, but in the case of *Twisted Sisters*, we believe them to be true. Unlike the old love comics, with their tacked-on happy endings, many of the newer women's comic autobiographies range from mildly to extremely depressing.

But it's not all true confessions for the women who produce girl comics; they share a strong political and feminist awareness that they're not ashamed to talk about, and none of them are likely to boast of being politically incorrect.

"Nina's Wonderful World of P.M.S.", from **Wimmin's Comix**, 1992. Art and story by Nina Paley.

Many of the women in *Girltalk* also contributed to *World War 3*, an unapologetically radical comic book put together by a collective of both male and female New York artists. In their 1992 special issue on sexism, Sabrina Jones wrote:

"Today most women expect to enjoy certain hard-won rights of the feminist movement, while disavowing feminism itself. They're afraid to alienate the men in their lives, who still hold most of the power. The male-dominated editorial board of *World War 3* considers itself variously leftist/radical/progressive/anarchist ... and therefore open to feminism. In spite of these good intentions, the few feminist pieces we accepted just didn't seem to fit in."

The editorial board's answer, Jones continues, was to produce a special issue on sexism, but she has her doubts: "The material will be ghettoised—men won't read it, and then when we get more work on the topic, you'll say, 'We already covered that.'" *Girltalk*, which started three years later, would seem to have been the answer to Jones's problem. The editors define girl talk as "a safer haven that can handle anything from delirium to despair." But not all the contributors are women. One of the more powerful pieces in issue no. 2 is "Six Single Mothers," by Lance Tooks. His grim parody of a child's rhyme starts: "One single mother/ Rougher side of town/ had to take a second job/ To keep expenses down/ Can't afford a safer street/ Living in a dive/ Came home late one Friday night/ Then there were five." The last verse is the most tragic: "One forgotten mother/ Bare and callused feet/ Paid her taxes regular/ And wound up on the street/ Fought so hard to fix her life/ Until they took her son/ Strain turned out to be too much/ Then there were none."

Some of the girl heroes in Megan Kelso's comic book, *Girl Hero*, are Animata, Bottlecap, and Yolanda, three superpowered factory workers fomenting revolution against the corporate rulers of a near-future dystopia. But despite the often grim messages in her book, Kelso includes paper dolls of her characters, a tradition left over from the girl comics of the forties.

Paper dolls are also a regular feature of *Action Girl*, an anthology comic book that combines feminism with an upbeat girls-just-wanna-have-fun attitude. In her editorials for *Action Girl* comics, Sarah Dyer describes her book's upbeat philosophy ("girl-positive and female-friendly—never anti-boy"), and proceeds to give the reader a political pep talk:

"Remember—ACTION IS EVERYTHING! Our society, even when it's trying to be 'alternative' usually just promotes a consumerist mentality. Buying things isn't evil, but if that's all you do, your life is pretty pointless. Be an ACTION GIRL (or boy)! ... go out and do something with all that positive energy!"

Merely reclaiming the word *girl* was not enough for some women cartoonists, who went still further, following the tradition of *Tits 'n' Clits*. These women reclaim some seriously objectionable words in comics like Mary Fleener's *Slutburger*, Molly Kiely's *Saucy Li'l Tart*, the anthology *On Our Butts*, Roberta Gregory's *Naughty Bits* (starring Bitchy Bitch), and Julie Doucet's *Dirty Plotte* (*plotte* is French Canadian slang for a woman's naughty bits). Such in-your-face

ACTION GIRL COMICS
$2.75
ISSUE TWELVE
Action
Girl
COMICS
SLG

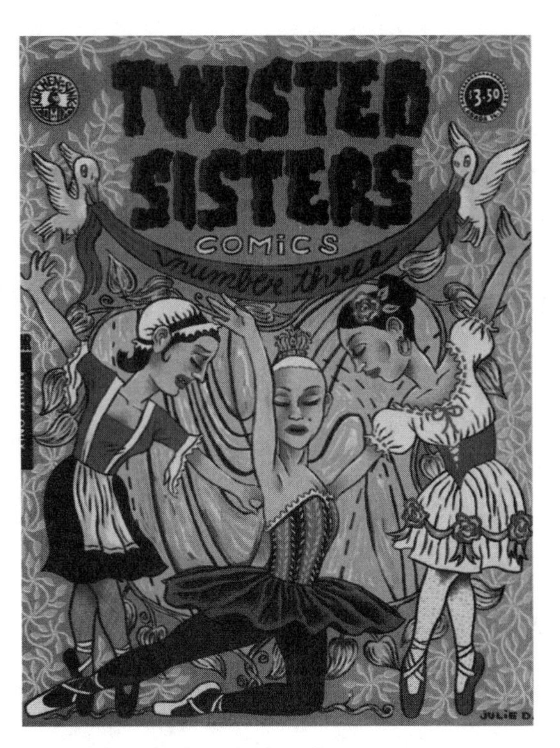

Twisted Sisters. Cover by Julie Doucet.

"Minnie's 3rd Love," from **Twisted Sisters**, 1994. Art and story by Phoebe Gloeckner.

titles are a symbolic bird defiantly flipped at the reader. "Sure," says the artist, "I'm a slut, a bitch. *Je suis une plotte*. You got a problem with that?"

Other women cartoonists go to the opposite extreme and turn sweetness inside out. Dame Darcy (*Meatcake*) and Christine Shields (*Blue Hole*) might well be the love children of Edward Gorey and Drusilla, the vampire from the television cult favorite *Buffy the Vampire Slayer*. Their comic books are 100 percent girl, but with a dark twist: sugar and spice and arsenic, and antique dolls in bloodstained lace bonnets. On the pages of both books, girls in thrift shop dresses (I, for one, strongly suspect they resemble the artists), drift through disturbing, dreamlike Victorian universes. Darcy's main character is a girl named Richard Dirt, who, with her long blond hair and granny boots, looks like a warped Alice in Wonderland. She and her Siamese-twin girlfriends Hindrance and Perfidia look like little darlings from some fin de siècle photo album, but they guzzle their booze right from the bottle. In *Blue Hole*, Shields relates the true story of a tragic San Francisco double murder, carried out Romeo and Juliet style. Her heroine, Ruby, also takes her rotgut straight, and in the company of pirates, no less. Yet both comics are so darn cute! Except for the aforementioned Edward Gorey, it would be hard to imagine any man drawing comics like these.

"Sixteen," from **Twisted Sisters**, 1994. Art and story by Debbie Drechsler.

Girltalk, 1995. Cover by Ann Decker.

Girl Hero, 1994. Paper doll cover by Megan Kelso.

If Christine Shields and Dame Darcy turn sweetness inside out, Linda Medley stands the Brothers Grimm on their heads with her self-published book, *Castle Waiting*. Drawing in the style of a classic fairy tale illustrator, Medley interweaves the frog prince, Rumplestiltskin, the Brementown musicians, and every other fairy tale our mothers lulled us to sleep with. The castle itself is

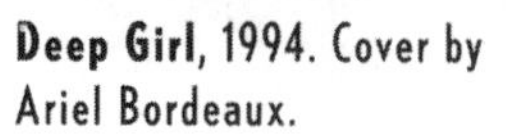

Deep Girl, 1994. Cover by Ariel Bordeaux.

Girljock, 1995. Cover by Trina Robbins.

Slutburger, 1992. Cover by Mary Fleener.

Saucy Li'l Tart, 1996. Cover by Molly Kiely.

Naughty Bits, 1991, with cover girl Bitchy Bitch. Art by Roberta Gregory.

Dirty Plotte, 1997. Cover by Julie Doucet.

A strip from **Action Girl**, 1995. Art and story by Patty Leidy.

BUT SHE KNOWS THAT ONE DAY, MOTOR-CYCLE BOY WOULD BE BACK, AND HE'D BE HERE TO TAKE HER AWAY FROM ALL OF THIS...

WITH JUST A THIN COAT AND THREE CLOVE CIGARETTES TO KEEP HER WARM...

SHE LIT THE THIRD CIGARETTE ~ THE STREETLIGHTS FAILED.

Panels from **On Our Butts**, 1994. Clockwise, from the top: "Motorcycle Boy," Fawn Gehweiler; Lisa Onomoto's gothic homage to Edward Gorey, "Little Goth Girl"; untitled by Anna Costa.

Sleeping Beauty's old home, still surrounded by its brambly fence years after the princess departed with her prince, leaving the other inhabitants (including a curious bird-headed creature called Rackham, named after the great fantasy artist Arthur Rackham) waiting for travelers who have stories of their own.

Still other women cartoonists use the word *girl,* but spell it with three Rs.

In the summer of 1991 a girls' movement was created in America with the odd merging of Washington, D.C., and Washington State. That was when two all-girl punk bands, Bikini Kill and Bratmobile, both from Olympia, Washington, came to D.C. for an extended stay. Our nation's capital had long been the

Naughty Bits, 1991. Roberta Gregory explains the creation of Bitchy Bitch.

Blue Hole, 1997. Art and story by Christine Shields.

The mosh pit experience from a girl's point of view. **Repressed in Portland**, 1996. Art and story by Mara Siciliano.

scene of a flourishing punk movement, which was predominantly male. The few women in the punk scene were angry at the increasingly macho violence of the male punkers, which kept them out of the scene, sometimes with real physical threats. The result of their anger was a revival of feminism—1990s-style "third wave feminism."

Many of the young women, most in their teens and twenties, had been brought up in nonsexist and nontraditional ways by mothers who had themselves been part of the "second-wave feminism" of the 1970s. (The first wave is considered to be the early suffragettes.) The daughters of these women grew up understanding the concept of sexism, and taking for granted many of the gains made by that earlier movement. Along came the backlash, and young women found their security rudely shattered by threats to their reproductive rights, and by a new wave of sexism and homophobia. They were still not free to walk down the street without being harassed. They were mad as hell and they weren't going to take it.

The girls of Bikini Kill and Bratmobile got together, coming up with such slogans as "Revolution girls style now," and the term *Riot Grrrl.* Two of them, Allison Wolte and Molly Neuman, put together the first Riot Grrrl zine, using that name, and the movement was born. "Grrrl" combined that reclaimed word *girl* with a defiant growl—these were no well-mannered, pink-ribboned "nice girls."

Within a year, the first Riot Grrrl convention took place in D.C., and chapters formed all over the country. As with the "Women's Lib" movement

Meatcake, 1997. Art and story by Dame Darcy.

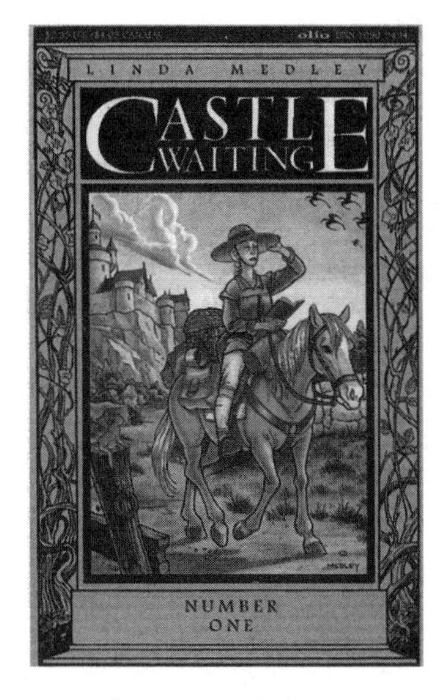

Castle Waiting, 1997. Cover by Linda Medley.

"Identity Crisis," from **Rude Girls and Dangerous Women**, 1994. Art and story by Jennifer Camper.

twenty years earlier, the national media was quick to cover it and slow to understand it. Riot Grrrlz were stereotyped as lesbians and/or violent man-haters. Actually, one of the first Riot Grrrl actions was to protest violence in a traditionally feminist collective way, by reclaiming the mosh pit, that crushing and frightening all-male area in front of the band at concerts. To make a space for themselves, the girls formed packs and forced their way to the front en masse, each protecting the other.

As much as the Riot Grrrl movement was about music, it was also about zines, self-published photocopied mini-magazines with print runs ranging anywhere from thirty to five hundred copies. Riot Grrrlz didn't invent fanzines, nor did the punk movement. The fanzine goes as far back as the early 1930s, when young science-fiction fans reproduced their own small magazines on messy mimeographs and even messier hectographs, crude precursors to today's more accessible photocopy machines. Many of the young fans who produced them eventually became professional writers and editors. The early zines, much as their later counterparts, were often letters in mini-magazine form, illustrated or not, featuring news and reviews of the latest science-fiction book or chatty

personal information. And like today's zines, they could be traded for other zines or they were available through the mail for anything from a postage stamp to a couple of quarters.

The next group to utilize zines were comic fans in the early 1960s. Some of the earliest underground comix were hardly more than zines produced with only slightly more sophisticated printing equipment, and some of today's well-known comics professionals started in their pages. The advent of cheap photocopying in the 1980s liberated the zine. Anyone with something to say could afford to self-publish. By the 1990s, women, feeling the need to communicate with each other and empowered by Riot Grrrlz, adopted the zine as the perfect medium in which to share their personal life stories, rants, philosophies, humor, poetry—and comics.

Like the early science-fiction and comic fans, some of today's well-known women cartoonists, like Diane DiMassa, Mary Fleener, Ariel Bordeaux, and Jessica Abel, started by publishing their own zines. Although their drawing styles are miles apart, both Abel's *Artbabe* and Bordeaux's *No Love Lost* (her zine was called *Deep Girl*) typify the mildly depressing autobiographical genre so often found in women's and grrrlz' zines and comics. Not much happens, and what does, happens in "real time." Girls agonize over boys, attend concerts, sit in cafes, discuss their relationships with their girlfriends. No real conclusions have been reached by the end of the book.

No Love Lost, 1997. Cover by Ariel Bordeaux.

So many women's autobiographical comics are depressing, and so many are about dysfunctional families, that it becomes tempting to believe that dysfunctional families breed women cartoonists. Luckily, there is Ellen Forney. In her self-published comic, *I Was Seven in '75*, Forney tells a warm, upbeat story about growing up in the 1970s with hippie parents. Not that bad things don't happen in the stories—Forney's brother gets five stitches when he hits his head on a chair, the kids manage to set fire to their new microwave, and her parents survive a pot bust when the baby-sitter turns them in to the cops—but these are your average everyday bad things. No one gets abused, raped, or permanently robbed of their self-esteem by rotten parents. Forney's parents are, in fact, terrific; she and her brother are normal, happy kids. Her book is sweet, funny, and refreshing.

Artbabe, the zine, 1995. Cover by Jessica Abel.

Artbabe, the comic book, 1997.

Diane DiMassa's *Hothead Paisan, Homicidal Lesbian Terrorist*, the angriest woman in comics since Bitchy Bitch, doesn't get depressed either—she acts, and acts violently. While Roberta Gregory's Bitchy Bitch (and her lesbian counterpart, Butchy Butch) is guaranteed to go postal several times in each issue of *Naughty Bits*, once the fit passes she's left as wretched as before. Hothead's rage, on the other hand, is cathartic—for the reader as well—and makes for some of the happiest violence you ever saw.

Hothead and Daphne, the girl she's madly in love with, sit on a park bench, happy together in the sunshine, when a huge man sits down next to them, spreading out his legs and invading their space the way huge men who spread their legs and invade your space have a way of doing. You gotta hand it to her, Hothead gives him a chance. She stares at the leg and says, "Uh, pardon me ...," but the guy mutters, "Whatcher problem?" With a demonic grin, Hothead produces a hatchet out of nowhere, chops off the offending leg, and hands it to him. "This!" she announces. "This is my problem! Does this belong to you? Because if it does, I found it way over here in MY space!"

Hothead and Daphne go to the movies and a seriously tall dude, wearing a baseball cap, sits right in front of Hothead. Again, she gives him a chance first. "Yoo-hoo, Mr. Total eclipse of the sun ..." she says. "You're twelve feet tall and you wear a hat to the movies? And ya sit in front? Why didn't ya wear a COWBOY hat??? Whatta gonna do next? Open up an UMBRELLA??" Naturally, the tall guy ignores her and continues to sit, legs spread apart (of course), revealing the sentences, "Me a big boy, me have special rights" written on the crotch of his jeans. Again, Hothead grins maniacally and while Daphne applauds, produces a chain saw from thin air and saws the guy in half. "He was in my way," she explains, "I couldn't accept that."

Besides, Hothead has a really cute cat named Chicken, who wears a fez.

Zine art ranges from amazingly excellent to mondo scratcho, but the not-very-good artists don't care if their work is crude. They're simply following the advice Sarah Dyer gives in *Action Girl*: "Don't think you can do comics? Try anyway, even if it's just for yourself!" They're producing illustrated letters, not art galleries to be sent through the mail. As with letters, they share their days, their friends, and their fun with the reader.

In *Ducks in a Row*, Bonni Moeller fits lists of her friends' one hundred favorite things ("1. Beer, 2. The Ramones, 3. Good shoes, 4. Burritos ...") between pages of delicately crosshatched comics. Carrie McNinch's art style is the complete opposite of Moeller's; she uses heavy, solid blacks and strong, woodcut-like outlines. But she's just as chatty. On the first page of *The Assassin and the Whiner* she shares with the reader her delight at finding the original ship used in *Gilligan's Island*, her favorite cooking show on PBS, her grandfather's funeral, her family's reaction to her coming out as a lesbian, her enjoyment of Ellen DeGeneres's "coming out episode," and her appreciation of the guy in her local comic-book store, who gives her discounts. In *Cone of Silence*, Kelly Renee shares with her readers "Men That Have Made Me Feel Wanton," a

Roberta Gregory's Bitchy Bitch goes postal.

I Was Seven in '75, 1997. Art and story by Ellen Forney.

Hothead Paisan, 1994. Art by Diane DiMassa.

Chicken the cat receives his fez and loves it. **Hothead Paisan**, 1994. Art and story by Diane DiMassa.

list that includes her high school crush, her grade school dream boy, and The Fonz. Tina, one of three grrrlz who produce *Buffy and Jody's Guide to the Galaxy*, tells us about the best friends she had in school, and in another issue the girls (Tina, Ami, and Alexis; no last names supplied) supply the recipe for deep-fried spaghetti ("serve with garlic bread and cherry kool aide"). Beth Templeton plays on the 1970s desire to "share." She produces postcards that read, "Sure, I'll share," and her zines ask, "Want Some of My Insomnia?", "Want Some of the Crap I Carry Around?"

After all this cheerful sharing, the bite in the zines comes as a shock, until we remember that grrrl is part growl. Canadian zine artist Patti Kim writes letters on Hello Kitty stationary and peppers her zines with cute Japanese cartoon characters, but when you turn a page, you come to this declaration:

"FIRST MOURN ... THEN WORK FOR CHANGE ...

On December 6, 1989, 14 women were murdered in Montreal. Women of every race and class are abused and killed by men they know. We mourn, and work for change ..."

One topic dealt with in a majority of zines is women's bodies, and our obsession with weight. Beth Templeton draws a comic about her breast reduction operation, commenting, "Why couldn't I be satisfied with my body? Why did one asshole doctor's controlled and surgically accepted violence on my body make such a difference?"

A gynecology lesson from **Maxine**, 1996. Art and story by Sari Wilson and Josh.

In *Cone of Silence*, Kelly Renee draws a disturbing comic about bulimia, "Living On Empty." As the bulimic waits in line at the supermarket to buy the junk food she'll devour, then throw up, "An image of the sainted Princess Diana sticking a lovely, manicured finger down her royal throat comes to mind. It is comforting. She would know. She would understand."

Following the comic is a parody of all those "Now You Are a Woman" pamphlets our mothers gave us, but instead of instructions on the use of sanitary napkins, it's a manual on how to be a bulimic. Some helpful tips: "Running water is an effective way to disguise sounds of gagging or retching." "Remember: you can learn to purge quietly!"

"My Amazing Secret," in *Buffy and Jody's Guide to the Galaxy*, provides another parody on weight loss, using copy from real ads: "*Suddenly—for the first time in my life—I started to lose weight!!!!* It was a miracle! The fat seemed to just melt away. I *finally* discovered *the Secret* to losing weight! It was all so simple … so easy! So I just kept doing it. And I kept getting thinner and thinner." In Tina's accompanying art, the protagonist becomes a living skeleton. Finally, in the last panel, she reveals "the Secret"—a crack pipe, a lighter, and rocks of crack, with accompanying directions, "1. Put rock in pipe. 2. Light the pipe. 3. Smoke pipe."

Madison Clell and Kim Hecht put out the most serious zine of all, but even here, there's room for humor. *Cuckoo* is subtitled "One Woman's True Stories of Living with Multiple Personality Disorder." Madison Clell draws a

A gallery of zine art. Top row, left to right: **Ducks in a Row**, Bonni Moeller; **Want Some?**, Beth Templeton; **Ab Inspector**, Patti Kim; bottom row, left to right: Untitled comic by Carrie McNinch, from **Asswhine**; "Helga's Life," by Helga Romoser, from **Happy Hour**; "Mimi's Adventure in Wonderland," by Tina, from **Buffy and Jody's Guide to the Galaxy**.

"The Magic of Spontaneous Combustion," from **Cone of Silence**, 1997. Kelly Renee finds another answer to the problem that plagued Hothead Paisan.

Cuckoo, 1997. The artist's "alters" come out for Christmas. Art and story by Madison Clell.

delighted psychology major, pointing with pride at the "multiple" she's discovered—Clell herself, turned into a giant furry guinea pig. She calls this "Guinea Pig Syndrome." Sometimes ironic, sometimes dead serious, sometimes with rage, Clell, using an expressionistic brush style, introduces us to the different people, whom she calls "alters," sharing her body. One is eight-year-old Melanie, who was raped as a child. "There's a technical term for what was inflicted on Melanie," Clell writes. "Phrases for clarity in courtrooms and doctor's notes. Names to tame monstrous actions. Sodomy. Rape. Child molestation. BULLSHIT! Words can never describe the reality."

Mystery Date, 1997. This mini-comic had a print run of thirty! Art and story by Carla Speed McNeil.

The Mysterious Tea Party, 1997. Art and story by Kalah Allen.

Cuckoo is not for kids or for those looking for a laugh. It's strong stuff, and it's important stuff.

Not much, actually, *is* out there for kids these days in the way of comics. The unsinkable *Archie* stands alone. *Pep*, the comic that started it all back in 1941, was finally canceled in 1989, but the *Archie* line is still going strong. In the 1990s, a character was added to Archie's crowd of pals and gals—Cheryl Blossom, a redhead who's twice as rich and three times as bitchy as Veronica—and in 1997, *Sabrina the Teenage Witch* became the latest in a long string of hit television series based on *Archie* characters. *Archie*'s only competition during the entire 1990s was *Barbie* comics, published by Marvel from 1990 through 1995. Currently, if little girls want to read a comic, their only choice is the *Archie* group.

Mainstream love comics have fared even worse. There *are* no mainstream love comics. However, the genre keeps getting revived by smaller publishers. Lea Hernandez combines romance with *manga*, the Japanese comic style, and a form of science fiction known as "steam punk," in her graphic novel *Cathedral Child*. Steam punk stories take place in some alternate past that has modern technology. Thus, Hernandez's story takes place in 1897; her heroine wears granny shoes, but she works with an *analytical engine*—their term for a computer.

All those old "nurses in love" comics are taken one step further by Jimmie Robinson in his comic-book sendup of the *ER*-style soaps, *Code Blue*. Jayeen "Chicken" Michaels is head of staff at Highland, a low-end, crumbling county

Archie in the nineties. Top, left to right: Sabrina; Cheryl Blossom; bottom, left to right: Josie and the Pussycats; Betty and Veronica, same as they ever were.

Lovers' leap, from **Cathedral Child**, 1998. Art and story by Lea Hernandez.

hospital. In her words, "We handle the homeless, runaways, addicts, you name it." On an average day, Jayeen deals with emergencies ranging from a mad bomber to the hunky head doctor of pricey, high-tech Northridge Hospital on the other side of town. She helps subdue the bomber and saves the doctor's life when he's brought in after a traffic pileup. But when he tries to date her, she's too resentful to admit she likes him: "I'd hate to deprive that fancy chrome building of its head doctor. The thought of some middle-aged woman missing out on her tummy-tuck and hip-suck ... it brings shivers down my spine." Readers wondering when the cute doctor will conquer Jayeen's foolish pride must wait for the next issue to find out.

The most traditionally campy romance comic of the 1990s is *Eternal Romance*, Janet Hetherington's blend of Roy Lichtenstein paintings and vampire stories. Perfectly parodying the traditional love comics style, Hetherington tells true confessions with a 1990s edge. In the first issue of her book, subtitled "*Love! Heartache! Vampires!*," the romantic leads, like the love comics genre, refuse to stay dead. They are all vampires. In later issues, Hetherington widens her scope to include anyone good-looking and supernatural. The love interest in "Mummy's Boy" is obvious. In "Once Bitten, Twice Shy," Joey's ex-girlfriend, Rochelle, suddenly pops back into his life, much to the dismay of his current girlfriend, Joyce. When the two finally come to blows over him, Rochelle reveals she's a vampire, but they're evenly matched—Joyce is a witch.

"NO! sob! I CAN NEVER marry you!" sobs Lin, the heroine of "Kiss of Death," also in the third issue of *Eternal Romance*. "My family is ... CURSED!" And indeed, one kiss transforms her into a rather cute werewolf. But it turns out that her fiancé is a werewolf, too, and the couple is free to howl at the moon together, happily ever after.

Obviously, men can create girl comics, too, as they have since the 1940s. Terry Moore's *Strangers in Paradise* is probably the best 1990s successor to *Love and Rockets*, which is no longer being published. Girls who once graduated from Betty and Veronica to Maggie and Hopy can now go straight to Francine and Katchoo. Moore's art is excellent, his stories moving and funny, his characters real. Like Maggie from *Love and Rockets*, Moore's pleasingly plump Francine proves that one doesn't have to be an anorexic supermodel to be absolutely adorable.

One of the best graphic novels of the 1990s, if not of the century, is Bryan Talbot's *The Tale of One Bad Rat*, a sensitive, beautifully drawn story of childhood sexual abuse. Helen, a teenage runaway, has fled from an abusive father and a cold, uncaring mother. As she begs on the streets of London, sleeping in alleys and abandoned buildings, her only companions are her pet rat and the Beatrix Potter books she has loved since childhood. When a cat kills her rat, Helen begins a pilgrimage to Beatrix Potter's home which will eventually lead to her own healing. The rat, which has become a kind of giant spirit guide visible only to her, accompanies Helen on her odyssey.

With all the wonderful girl comics out there, one would think that women and girls of all ages have all the comics they could want, and that the comics

Barbie, 1994. Story by Barbara Slate, art by Mary Wilshire and Trina Robbins. On this prophetic page, editor Hildy Mesnik (center) tells the **Barbie** crew that the comic has been canceled. In the story it turns out to be an April Fools' joke, but the book was canceled a year later.

Doctors in love, from **Code Blue**, 1998. Art and story by Jimmie Robinson.

Strangers in Paradise, 1994. Francine explains the title. Art and story by Terry Moore.

creators are in paradise, expressing themselves on paper and making a decent living doing so. This could not be further from the truth. The average woman cartoonist has a day job. Her books are hard to find. Zines, of course, are usually only available through the mail, but with few exceptions, even the better-selling girls' comics usually have a small print run compared to mainstream superhero comics, and very few comic book stores bother to carry them. Beth Templeton describes the situation perfectly in *Want Some?*:

"These days when I stake out a comic-book store. I'm looking for comics by women, or local self-published things … It's not hard to find stores devoid of both. No 'Artbabe,' 'Hothead Paisan,' 'Dirty Plotte,' or 'Dykes to Watch Out For' but, they would be 'happy to order something in for you,' "Uh, no thanks. If I can't browse from a great selection, how will I find anything new?"

A girl and her rat, from **The Tale of One Bad Rat, 1995**. Art and story by Bryan Talbot.

The result, of course, is that comparatively few women even know these comics exist. To further compound the irony, self-published or small-press black-and-white comics are usually priced higher than mainstream, full-color superhero comics, yet women earn less than men, and have less buying power.

It's a sorry situation, and in 1993, women decided to do something about it. During the San Diego comics convention, a group of women who worked in comics met at a coffeehouse to discuss the problems of working in such a male-dominated industry. The result of the meeting was the formation of Friends of Lulu, a national organization named for the plucky little girl who never gave up on her attempts to crash the boys' club. Their stated purpose is "to promote and encourage female readership and participation in the comic book industry." In February 1997, Friends of Lulu held their first annual conference, and in August of that year, they honored women creators and women-friendly comic books at their first annual Lulu awards ceremony.

As we come to the close of the twentieth century, the comic industry, such a vital art and communication form for over sixty years, is in real trouble. In fact, the industry has never been in worse shape.

Comic-book sales are at their lowest in fifty years. There was a time when one in three periodicals sold in the United States was a comic book. *Walt Disney's Comics and Stories* sold over four million issues every month. Other titles, including some westerns, crime comics, and the Simon and Kirby romance comics, sold more than one million copies per issue. Ninety percent of the nation were regular comics readers. Today that number is less than 1 percent. In fact, if 1 percent of the population read comics today, the industry would be considered healthy. The average mainstream superhero comic sells from forty thousand to sixty thousand copies. (And, of course, the average mainstream comic book is always a superhero comic!) The average black-and-white, independently published comic book sells about three thousand copies.

This had all happened before, although not on such a disastrous scale, when superhero comics, the biggest sellers during World War II, lost their popularity after the war, and were replaced by other genres, including teen comics and love comics. Tastes change and pendulums swing. The pendulum, which swung back to superhero comics in the 1960s, has reversed itself again.

Comic-book editors, publishers, and retailers like to blame television for the decline in their field, but people have not stopped reading. A 1998 survey by *Publishers Weekly* found that readers were buying three times as many books as they had bought the year before. The survey also found that they're young, under thirty-five, and that 58 percent of them are women, as opposed to 42 percent men. Obviously, there are books out there—lots of them—that women want to read. Women make up 52 percent of the population, and they like to read. It doesn't take a rocket scientist to figure out that they would also like to read comics, if publishers would only produce comics for them to read.

Diane DiMassa's Hothead says it all. **Hothead Paisan**, 1994.

The motto of Friends of Lulu is "Here To Save Comics." Once upon a time there was a woman named Ginger Rogers who could dance as well as Fred Astaire, only backwards and in high heels. If a woman could do that, saving comics ought to be a snap.

51. Rachel Fudge, "The Buffy Effect, or, a Tale of Cleavage and Marketing," from *Bitch* Magazine

Excerpts from "The Buffy Effect, or, a Tale of Cleavage and Marketing," by Rachel Fudge, published in *Bitch* magazine, No. 10 (Summer 1999). Reprinted with permission.

A perfect example of third-wave sensibility, this article explains the Buffy phenomenon for those who love her and know her, and for those who do not. This is classic third-wave thinking demonstrating the tension between enjoyment of and engagement with popular culture, and a critical distance from it.

In the early 1990s, vampire mythology, horror revival, teen angst, and kick-ass grrlness congealed in a new figure in the pop culture pantheon of the paranormal: the vampire slayer. Not just any vampire hunter, mind you, but Buffy, the Valley-dwelling teenage slayer. Before Buffy, Vampire stories and horror movies alike focused primarily on the male monster antagonists who preyed on innocent nubile young things. But in 1992, *Buffy the Vampire Slayer*'s eponymous protagonist kickboxed her way, via the big screen, into our heroine-starved, media-junkie feminist hearts, along the way reconfiguring the popular vampire/horror text.

Buffy was explicitly conceived as a feminist re-imagining of the horror genre: Screenwriter/TV producer Joss Whedon has said in interviews that his very inspiration for Buffy came from years of watching horror movies in which "bubbleheaded blondes wandered into dark alleys and got murdered by some creature." Whedon wanted to make a movie where the blonde "wanders into a dark alley, takes care of herself, and deploys her powers" to kill the monster. Buffy's exploits implicate the audience in a witty defiance of genre conventions: Instead of shouting, "Don't go in there!" to the naive gal traipsing through the darkened vacant house, we shout, "Go, girl!" as Buffy enters the dark alley to dispatch the monster of the moment with her quick thinking and martial-arts prowess.

Buffy the movie didn't quite live up to these noble intentions. A poorly reviewed, little-seen, campy one-liner—albeit an amusing one, with a kung fu–fighting heroine to boot—it told the story of a Southern California cheerleader in "the lite ages" who discovers that she has been fated to become a vampire slayer even though she would rather just go shopping. Full of Valley talk, workin'-hard-now training montages, an arena-rock soundtrack, cheesily sardonic vampires (courtesy of Paul Reubens), and an incongruous Luke Perry as the sensitive boy, the first incarnation of *Buffy* was more self-parody than wish-fulfillment vehicle for would-be feminist freedom fighters.

A scant few years later, however, the girl-power mantra had sung its spicy way through the ranks of pop culture. *Scream* revitalized the slasher genre in one ironic fell swoop, while teen-oriented TV solidified a lucrative market niche for savvy media-makers. The time seemed ripe to resuscitate Buffy and restore a little of her dignity. With Joss Whedon in full creative control as producer (and head writer), *Buffy the Vampire Slayer* debuted on the WB network in 1996. Buffy is still the chosen one, the "girl born once in every generation with the strength and skill to hunt vampires." But this time we get a bit more background: Because her hometown of Sunnydale sits upon a portal to hell, an unusual number of vampires and other assorted underworld denizens congregate there. It's Buffy's job to slay them one and all.

She's not without help, though: Buffy is under the care and training of her Watcher (who doubles as the school librarian) and is often assisted by her geek-chic pals Xander and Willow. No one else seems to be much concerned about the large number of bizarre, unexplained killings in Sunnydale—Buffy's career-focused single mom doesn't wise up to her daughter's vocation until the end of the show's second season, the teachers are all but oblivious, and the mayor himself is in league with the undead.

It's not surprising that a character like Buffy would surface in this particular pop cultural moment, saturated as it is with mixed messages about feminism and femininity, all tied up in the pretty bow of marketability. Buffy could be the poster girl for an entire decade of girl-oriented mass media/culture. For better and most certainly for worse, she's *Sassy* incarnate, an angsty alternateen with a penchant for Delia*s-style slip dresses. She's feisty and moody and won't let anyone push her around. Her ever-present tank tops showcase her rack quite efficiently. She has a passion for justice and goodness—even when it means killing her boyfriend, Buffy performs with martyr-like grace. Her makeup is impeccable, her eyebrows well-groomed. She's a girl's girl, fiercely loyal to her best girlfriend. She may have returned from a night of heavy slaying, but her frosted hair is still in its pigtails, her sparkly makeup intact.

Imagine the boardroom pitch for such a show: "It's all about a girl who trains in martial arts and the use of deadly weapons. She and her friends explore the powers of witchcraft. Every week she'll confront and conquer a new foe, all while rebelling against paternalistic authority, sticking up for sisterhood, and saving the fate of the world." Just add girl power and stir. For added appeal, toss in a cute star with a hot bod and rilly cool clothes. A kickboxing, demon-slaying, wisecracking teenage TV heroine—sounds promisingly subversive. But is Buffy really an exhilarating post–third-wave heroine, or is she merely a caricature of '90s pseudo–girl power, a cleverly crafted marketing scheme to hook the ever-important youth demographic?

Clearly, unlike other eponymous TV heroines, who spend more time gazing at their navels than thinking about injustice, Buffy has the sort of social conscience that appeals to the daughters of feminism's second wave. For many of us born in the post-*Roe* era, a certain awareness of gender and power is ingrained and inextricably linked to our sense of identity and self-esteem—call it feminism's legacy. The impulse that propels Buffy out on patrols, night after night, forgoing any semblance of "normal" teenage life, is identical to the one that compels us third-wavers to spend endless hours discussing the feminist potentials and pitfalls of prime-time television. Armed with the knowledge that the world is ours to make—and that no one else will make it for us—we can't simply sit back and watch the show: We have to try to change the ending. Buffy, for her part, is resolute in her conviction that the world can be a better place, and that she can help forge it.

Buffy is an ongoing lesson in this sisters-doing-it-for-themselves ideology: She never claims to be "just a girl." She never denigrates herself, nor is her girlhood ever depicted as a detraction. By contrast, it's the very source of her strength. *Buffy*'s small-screen cosmology—which suggests not only that the most powerful person in town is a petite, wisecracking Valley Girl with blond locks and pink-passion lips, but also that the source of this slayer's power is her teenage fallibility, her spunky girlness—has deeply feminist potential. Her anti-authority stance, her refusal to be intimidated by more powerful figures (whether the school principal or an archdemon)—these are her most important assets, the ones that make her more successful than previous generations of slayers.

While she may not be your typical feminist activist, Buffy's birthright is to do good and fight for the weak. Unlike the (anti)heroines of other high-school-in-hell creations (*Heathers*, *The Craft*), Buffy is fighting to *save* her school and her classmates from total destruction. Despite her pastel goth tendencies toward alienation and disaffection, Buffy is actually trying to maintain order in Sunnydale-on-Hellmouth. True, Buffy's enemies are more often demons than date rapists, vampires than patriarchal politicians. Buffy's not a riot grrl renegade out slaying frat-boy harassers or destroying all vestiges of sexism—at least not literally. But evil in Sunnydale often takes a nicely metaphoric slant.

Critics writing about the show have been quick to pinpoint the parallels between *Buffy*'s demonology and real-life high school horrors, focusing heavily on the high-school-as-hell metaphor: Demons are the gangs; the transformation of gullible kids, victimized and "turned" by demons, represents the effects of drugs; the helplessness of grown-ups in the face of all this, well, that's just life (according to *Psychology Today*). Then there are the parallels to *real* teenage life—as opposed to parents' fears about drugs and gangs. You can't bring your boyfriend home to meet your parents 'cause they just won't understand (or, well, he's a recovering vampire); the boy you lose your virginity to turns mean and nasty the morning after (vampires, even recovering ones, don't respond well to human bliss); your parents will never understand you or your problems (they may even try to burn you at the stake for being a witch). It's no accident that most of the demons are male and adult, or that the teenage demons often look a lot like those we all know, such as the "nice guy" whose science experiments have turned him into a possessive Mr. Hyde who beats the shit out of his girlfriend. Buffy even gets to survive her sexual mistake, both defying the horror-film convention dictating that virgins are the only ones who ever get out alive and alluding to the all-too-real emotional turmoil of that first failed relationship.

Buffy also earns feminist points for her martial arts proficiency (and penchant for nasty weapons), which pays homage equally to the women's self-defense collectives of the '70s and to '90s collegiate date-rape awareness training seminars. Unlike other such prime-time displays of "self-defense" (who can forget Tori Spelling smacking a purse snatcher while yelling "No! No! No!" on *90210*?), Buffy really means it. And while her incredible strength may seem unlikely for a girl of her stature, she isn't endowed with superpowers. Buffy wasn't chosen for her strength and fightin' skills—being chosen revealed strengths she never knew she possessed.

Physical prowess, and a real knack for turning ordinary items into deadly weapons, is certainly a big part of it, but Buffy's verbal slaying abilities are no less celebrated. Indeed, the first thing you learn in women's self-defense class is the power of a loud, confident voice: The ability to yell and talk back to sleazy would-be attackers could save your life. Even cheerleader-cum-megabitch Cordelia taps into the power of words to scare the pants off a hillbilly vampire, proving you don't have to be the chosen one to get rid of the nasties. Slaying could well become a grassroots movement.

In a distinctive nod to the feminist battle cry to reclaim the public realm as a space for women's participation, Buffy eschews the domestic sphere for the public one. With her preternatural strength and supreme confidence, she can literally go wherever the hell she pleases. Her domain is a traditionally male, conventionally dangerous one: the darkened streets, abandoned buildings, and stinking alleys that girls have long been cautioned to beware of. She refuses to remain in the house, and in fact rarely appears at home. While her peers impassively dance to bands performing at an all-ages nightclub, Buffy never seems to linger for more than a few minutes—she's always got somewhere else to be, some fight to pick or supernatural crisis to avert. It's many a girl/woman's dream: to be able to walk down any street of any town at any hour of the day or night, knowing she can defeat any monster who crosses her path.

In keeping with the parameters of contemporary girl culture, Buffy's strength doesn't negate her exaggerated femininity. She's no scarred, deep-in-shit Tank Girl—this slayer's tank tops are pastel and pristine, revealing plenty of creamy, unmarred cleavage. Her scars are internal only; that chip may never leave her shoulder, but you can bet it'll be color-coordinated. Yup, she's strong and sassy all right, but she's the ultimate femme, never disturbing the delicate definition of physical femininity. Unlike the high school coven of *The Craft*, whose members become markedly less "feminine" as their powers grow, the Buffster, for all her bravado and physical strength, is a girly girl through and through.

Herein lie the limitations inherent in the *Buffy* phenom: "Girl power" as articulated in the mass media (and mass marketing) is often misrepresented as de facto feminism, when in fact it's a diluted imitation of female empowerment. Indeed, for some people, it's a way to bypass the complexities of feminism—it's a lot easier to wear a "girls kick ass" t-shirt than to learn how to defend yourself physically. The problem with girl power is that all too often it relies on style over substance, baby tees over action. While girl power and the accompanying mania for girl culture has certainly helped spread pro-feminist, pro-female messages throughout the land, it also threatens to turn empowerment into yet another product. Like those clothes Buffy wears? Or how 'bout Willow's incense burner? Now you can go to the megamall and buy them, thanks to cross-marketing from the WB and clothing retailer Hot Topic. Or you can follow *Glamour*'s exhortations to "get Buffy's buff butt"—with actress Sarah Michelle Gellar's gluteal-toning secrets, not Buffy's martial-arts prowess.

Buffy constantly treads the fine line between girl-power schlock and feminist wish-fulfillment, never giving satisfaction to either one. Producer Whedon acknowledges this very intention: "If I can make teenage boys comfortable with a girl who takes charge of a situation without their knowing that's what's happening, it's better than sitting down and selling them on feminism." Call her a Hard Candy–coated feminist heroine for the girl-power era. And it isn't just the pubescent boys who like their heroines sweet: This pastel veneer might just be the necessary spoonful of sugar to make the pro-feminist message palatable to network honchos, the marketing crew, and teen viewers alike.

It's a point well-taken, but Buffy's unreconstructed, over-the-top girliness in the end compromises her feminist potential. Though this excessive femininity veers toward the cartoonish, in the end it's too earnest—too necessary—to be self-parody. We're never allowed to forget that Buffy is a girl—indeed, the show's hook relies on the "joke" of a petite cheerleader being chosen to save the world from evil. If the slayer had been quirky, brainy Willow rather than pert 'n' pastel Buffy, the show would never have gotten off the drawing board. Despite the fact that Willow is a much more likely feminist role model (super-smart Wicca-practicing computer whiz—be still my heart!) and has become the fave of many hard-core *Buffy* fans (male and female alike), she lacks the babe quotient necessary to forge a hit show. It may be wrong, but it's true nonetheless: Just as the girl-power phenomenon created a market for the show, the show's viability and commercial success depend upon this narrow definition of femininity and sex appeal.

Within the context of mass culture, however, we may be able to look past her girly foibles. While Buffy is most definitely a babe, and this is certainly part of her mass audience appeal (not to mention a great reason for magazines like *Rolling Stone* to put her on the cover), her babeification is confined to the marketing realm. As cute and perky and scantily clad as she is, she's not overtly sexualized *within* the show, which is a pretty dramatic shift from the jiggle-core of most other kung fu–fighting women on TV (Xena, Wonder Woman, you may sit down). In spite of the obvious sexual-predator symbolism, the vampires are not (for the most part) leering, drooling lechers who ogle Buffy before they get kickboxed and staked. Instead, they generally respect her position as the slayer, her power and strength.

In the end, it's precisely this contextual conflict that sets Buffy apart from the rest and makes her an appealing icon. Frustrating as her contradictions may be, annoying as her babe quotient may be, *Buffy* still offers up a prime-time heroine like no other. Caught between demands that initially appear to be in conflict—be pretty, be smart; be homecoming queen, be savior of the world—Buffy finds a balance, a middle ground that may be lonely but is undeniably empowering. Femininity—girlness—is a slippery slope, and at least *Buffy* honors our intelligence enough to allow us these contradictions and even occasionally poke fun at them.

PART IV

Producing Third-Wave Identities, Naming Names

The documents in this section look at third-wave feminist attempts to name and create specifically feminist identities that make sense to them. The third-wavers are negotiating cultural institutions related to sexuality, marriage, and motherhood and the ways these are complicated by racial, religious, and ethnic identities.

52. Merri Lisa Johnson, "Jane Hocus, Jane Focus: An Introduction," from *Jane Sexes It Up: True Confessions of Feminist Desire*

Excerpts from "Jane Hocus, Jane Focus," by Merri Lisa Johnson, ed., published in *Jane Sexes It Up: True Confessions of Feminist Desire* (New York: Four Walls, Four Windows, 2002), 1–11. Reprinted with permission.

In "Jane Hocus, Jane Focus," the introduction to *Jane Sexes It Up* by Lisa Johnson, an outspoken third-wave feminist whose work centers around the sex-positive wing of the movement, argues for women's right to their own sexual expressions. Critical of feminisms that police sexuality and prescribe "correct" actions, Johnson wants to "forge a feminist sexual identity informed (not imprisoned) by the women whose writing came before us ... feminist writing that weds resistance with joy to create a sexuality that pleases and a world we can live with."

> Sexuality, in all its guises, has become a kind of lightening rod for this generation's hopes and discontents (and democratic vision) in the same way that civil rights and Vietnam galvanized our generation in the 1960s.
>
> —Nan Bauer Maglin & Donna Perry, *"Bad Girls"/"Good Girls": Women, Sex & Power in the Nineties*

GENERATION X DOES THE SEX WARS

The word polices women—even now in this so-called postfeminist era—into silence about sex, constructed modesty, and self-regulating repression of behavior and fantasy....

Young feminists in particular feel the edges of feminist history grind against the conservative cultural contexts in which our lives unfold; we live inside the contradiction of a political movement that affirms and encourages expressions of female and/or alternative sexualities, and the "real world" of workplaces, families, and communities that continue to judge women harshly for speaking of sex, much less expressing one's "deviant" acts and complex erotic imagination....

When I first imagined this project, I thought that in writing it I would force feminism's legs apart like a rude lover, liberating her from the beige suit of political correctness. I wanted feminism to be *bad like me*. A young feminism, a sexy feminism. I found myself saying things like, "I'm not *that kind* of feminist," all sly innuendo and bedroom eyes. Early in my research, however, I discovered that *that kind of feminist* is mostly a media construct—oversimplification spiced with staged cat fights.

... At the now infamous Barnard Conference on April 24, 1982, "The Scholar and the Feminist,"... a conflict over what kinds of topics should and should not be covered turned into a long, divisive, legislative, media-mediated war over feminism's position of sex. The feminist Sex Wars that ensued got snagged once more on the seeming impasse of women fighting *for* sexual pleasure or *against* sexual danger.

PRO-SEX OR ANTI-SEX

Carole Vance's *Pleasure and Danger: Exploring Female Sexuality*, an anthology of essays from the conference, would have been our template—if we'd ever heard of it. But revolutionary ideas about sexual politics are consistently misrepresented or simply "disappeared" in most narratives of U.S. history. This face of feminism—the *smart-ass take-no-shit anarcha-orgasmic feminist persona* Gen X-ers thought we invented—is suppressed in the mainstream media. (I can only *begin* to imagine the ways corporate sponsors, women's tenuous positions as news reporters and anchors, and dominant American "family values" in the air like a toxic odorless gas converge to eclipse this unruly body of political thought.) Whatever conflicts exist within feminism, the first lesson for each generation must be about the politics of representation (which histories are handed over, which are not, and why); for it is frequently against "representations" of feminism as puritanical or anti-male or just plain crazy—not against feminism itself—that many young women posit our sexy "new" brand of bravado.

Rather than forcing ourselves on feminism, then, the *Jane* generation means to reconnect with our movement. The women who confess their messy desires in the following pages diverge purposefully from the path of "patriarchy's prodigal daughters" (young women trading on *chic* renunciations of feminism) to forge a feminist sexual identity informed (not imprisoned) by the women whose writing came before us. Feminism—often addressed by young women as a strict teacher who *just needs to get laid*—is a name we want to reclaim for the intersection of *smart* and *sexy* within each of us....

Vance's introduction to *Pleasure and Danger* bears repeating in this context, as we resist with her the loss of sexual pleasure as the "great guilty secret among feminists":

> The truth is that the rich brew of our experience contains elements of pleasure and oppression, happiness and humiliation. Rather than regard this ambiguity as confusion or false consciousness, we should use it as a source-book to examine how women experience sexual desire, fantasy, and action.

... [I] hold tightly to this belief that individual women's stories, narrow in scope and deep in reflection, aid in advancing the complexity of feminist social theory.

Young women define our politics in part by the second wave feminist legacy of sexual freedom—disrupting norms surrounding the body, unsettling rigid gender roles, and observing few, if any, boundaries on our speech as erotic creatures. Germaine Greer may have grown out of her "Lady, Love Your Cunt" days, but we are smack dab in the middle of ours. Yet sex-positive spokeswomen, often antiintellectual in tone, fail to give women new ways of thinking about fucking, new ways of understanding what's happening in our beds and to our bodies.

In a 1999 roundtable discussion with the bright lights of sex-positive feminism—Betty Dodson, Susie Bright, Sallie Tisdale, and Nancy Friday—*Nerve.com*, an enormously popular e-zine of "literate smut," asked, "How do you reconcile your feminism (or whatever you choose to call your convictions about sex and gender) with the more traditional feminine roles, behaviors, fantasies, positions, and exclamations that you may engage in (and perhaps even enjoy) in the bedroom?"—Susie Bright (a.k.a. Susie Sexpert, a regular columnist for *Playboy*) answers,

> What a weird question. I think you are trying to say, How can you be a feminist in the boardroom and a submissive in the bedroom? Is that it? I don't have to "reconcile feminism," how ridiculous—I challenged feminism and demanded that it get a grip and come to terms with human sexuality. My whole written legacy is about that. I don't sit in bed with my dildo trying to rationalize anything!

Sallie Tisdale makes a similar response: "Once upon a time, I thought to be a feminist meant to eliminate all thoughts of submission. I couldn't—I didn't. I enjoy submissive postures and play sometimes—I don't see it as an issue or anything needing analysis anymore."

Seductive, this image of throwing feminism across the room like a pair of bottom-cupping panties. But as brave and brash as these women are, as alluring as their model of uncritical sexual freedom may be, their perception of sexuality "not needing analysis anymore" stems, I conjecture, from the wisdom of experience rather than widespread cultural change; in fact, they gloss over a very real conflict in many women's lives—especially those of us living far from big-city sex-positive cultures, even more so for a generation that was still in middle school in 1982 when the Bernard Conference touched off the first skirmishes over sexual correctness among second wave feminists. Crazy as it may sound, the feminists of Generation X *are* sitting in bed rationalizing our dildos.

Yet in feminist writing about sexuality, you get *either* the critique *or* the clit—not both—reproducing the mind/body split of masculinist Western philosophy that feminists fight in every imaginable arena in the world—except this one. Conversely, the sex-negative critique—what's *wrong* with fucking—has been creatively imagined and forcefully argued. Reading Andrea Dworkin unquestionably opens new ways of seeing sex, prompting a click in one's mind—marking that moment when something that has gnawed just below the surface or your consciousness, just below the level of language, emerges into plain sight. Sex-positive writers have established no corresponding framework for understanding what we—as women, as feminists—*like* about sex. Or how to manage the relationship between what we like and what leaves us less enamored....

53. Patricia Payette, "The Feminist Wife: Notes from a Political 'Engagement,'" from *Jane Sexes It Up: True Confessions of Feminist Desire*

Excerpts from Patricia Payette, "The Feminist Wife," published in *Jane Sexes It Up*, ed. Merri Lisa Johnson (New York: Four Walls, Four Windows, 2002), 139–167. Reprinted with permission.

Patricia Payette's essay focuses on the tendency in media to "portray women either as domesticated victims of male patriarchy or angry, man-hating feminists," a tendency that she says "doesn't permit the nuances of real women's lives to come into clear view, just as the assumption that single women who long to be married must be 'unfeminist' obscures a more complete picture of contemporary women's psyches." Her essay explores the sometimes contradictory desires of third-wave feminists in their relationship to traditional institutions like marriage. It's not either/or: one can be both feminist and married, Payette says, as well as other combinations. "A woman can choose to be a wife, a mother, a scholar, and a feminist ... these roles are optional and the boundaries between and around these loaded terms are fluid and flexible."

Can one be within the framework of a marriage?

—May Sarton, *Journal of a Solitude*

... During the nine months I spent as a fiancée, I documented my emotional journey to the altar in a computer journal I simply named "engaged." Reading over the journal a year after my engagement, I see now that while I was writing, I was actively "engaged" in a process of sorting through the meaning of marriage and the significance of wedding traditions. I experienced waves of varying emotions—excitement, astonishment, chagrin, ambivalence, confidence—as a self-proclaimed feminist about to engage in one of the most traditional feminine rites of all.

My story as an independent, feminist woman who also desired to be married and struggled with that desire, is not an uncommon one. Stacey D'Erasmo, writing in the *New York Times Magazine*, observes the abundance of contemporary tales tracing the single woman's search for a husband, as evidenced by the television shows *Sex and the City* and *Ally McBeal* and the fiction bestsellers *Bridget Jones's Diary* and *The Girls' Guide to Hunting and Fishing*. D'Erasmo writes: "In nearly every medium, the marital quest of the fashionable, sexually well-traveled, thirty-something woman has become so popular as to seem like the dominant narrative of life on earth right now." Noting the "melodrama" and "misadventure" that follow these single heroines as they pursue a husband, D'Erasmo believes these narratives prove that feminism is "over" and has "failed." Her reasoning suggests that yearning for marriage is not only incompatible with feminist beliefs, the fact that the desire exists proves feminism is dead. My experience proves feminism isn't dead; it's merely undergoing a transformation at the hands of young women like myself who are refusing to submit to outmoded paradigms that tell us what we should and shouldn't desire for ourselves. The abundance of contemporary narratives about outspoken single women questing for satisfying personal and professional lives is a testament to our determination to speak truthfully about our generation's unique needs and desires. Hundreds of women like myself are struggling with age-old prejudices in order to reinvent the meaning of single life and the matrimonial urge.

The second wave adage "A woman without a man is like a fish without a bicycle" doesn't serve women or men in coming to terms with the thorny issues surrounding equality, mutuality, and marriage in this nation and historical moment. Portraying women as either domesticated victims of male patriarchy or angry, man-hating feminists doesn't permit the nuances of real women's lives to come into clear view, just as the assumption that single women who long to be married must be "unfeminist" obscures a more complete picture of contemporary women's psyches. I endorse a new approach to the marriage bond that undermines the power dynamics of male-female relationships in which we must choose between being master or slave, as Jessica Benjamin describes relationships in *The Bonds of Love: Psychoanalysis, Feminism and the Problems of Domination*. Benjamin concludes that the only way to avoid becoming trapped in a dualism of our relationships is to embrace the paradox "posed by our simultaneous need for recognition and independence," to sit comfortably with the desire to be both autonomous and to be connected.

I grew into feminism as I grew up. Like many third-wave feminists who grew up in the 1970s and 1980s, I was raised in a familial atmosphere of feminist ideals nurtured by my mother and my aunts. I learned a great deal from my female relatives through the example they set in their lives. My mother worked part-time during part of my growing up years, first as a dental hygienist when my brother and sister and I were very young, and then later, when we reached school age, she earned an MA in education and was a lab instructor in anatomy and physiology at the college in the small town where we lived. She was the first woman elected to the water board in that town and later was active in the League of Women Voters. My mother's scope of activities and interests has always ranged outside the home.

Even my mother's mother has been a dynamic role model for me, for she was, and is, a lively, active, and witty grandmother who treated me and my siblings to solo vacations with her to special places. While growing up, I learned as well that men could be feminists when my father, an auto dealer, supported women's equality in his traditionally male-dominated field by hiring women managers and even promoting a woman to general manager of his dealership. For the past twenty years, his dealership has sponsored a free workshop called "Women's Day" to help women become more comfortable buying and maintaining their cars....

In fifth grade, I questioned the gym teacher, Mr. Lando, about why he chose only boys to serve as team captains. Although I don't remember his response, I do remember that after I challenged him, he sent me to the office to fetch his coffee. Later, in high school, I got better results when I gently corrected my civics teacher—"congressperson"—aloud in class. He thanked me and corrected himself. Shortly after that, he and his wife began hiring me to baby-sit for their daughter.

... These events did not seem unusually significant to me at the time, but I now understand [my younger sister] Maggie and I were granted "permission" to be the kind of girls we wanted to be.

Nevertheless, I became self-conscious of those moments in life when the values of feminism appeared to be at odds with my own desires and impulses. During my undergraduate years at the University of Michigan, I was thrilled to find like-minded feminists among my peers, both men and women. Although we sometimes dressed and acted the part of "feminine" women and "masculine" men, we were acutely aware of our social conditioning as gendered subjects and often mocked our conformist impulses with sarcastic humor. If I broke a nail, I expressed displeasure and made fun of my reaction at the same time. We acted upon our sexual freedoms, but sometimes felt bound by ancient dating rituals and found prefeminist sexual assumptions hard to shake. Even though we knew we could make our own rules, my girlfriends and I wondered what it *meant* if we slept with a man on the first or second date.

In *Third Wave Agenda: Being Feminist, Doing Feminism*, Leslie Heywood and Jennifer Drake describe the third wave movement as "feminisms" that grew out of the social context of the late 1970s through the late 1980s: "Because our lives have been shaped by struggles between various feminisms as well as by cultural backlash against feminism and activism, we argue that contradiction—or what looks like contradiction, if one doesn't shift one's point of view—marks the desires and strategies of third wave feminists." The second wave generation of the 1960s frequently constructed the freedoms of feminism in opposition to the social strictures of femininity, but I have consistently sought balance between what I saw as the feminine and feminist sides of myself, precisely because I do not see them as contradictory.

Although "third wavers" hold strong to the belief that men are not the enemy, we take a cautious stance toward the twenty-something wedding mania as witnessed in pop culture portrayals of young women like Monica on the popular sitcom *Friends*. During my college years, and throughout my twenties, I savored a sense of emotional and financial independence that grew over the years. Time enough later for marriage, I told myself as I became absorbed by getting my M.A. and cultivated a strong connection to friends, family, and various community activities. I never eliminated the possibility of meeting Mr. Right during those dating years, but the search for a marriageable man didn't dominate my life. My single friends and I discovered that a happy and successful life didn't require a husband, or even a boyfriend.

This attitude toward marriage is commonplace among the third wave generation. Journalists and sociologists are sitting up and taking notice of the growing number of women staying single longer, and the abundance of "never married" women and their stereotype-shattering lives. In a 1996 issue of *Psychology Today*, Anatasia Toufexis dispels the popular assumptions about "never-married" women as "unloved, unwanted, unhealthy" by citing the numerous healthy, happy, successful single women buying houses, running companies, and having children on their own. I read Toufexis' article the year I turned thirty, and I identified with her "single woman as heroine of her own life" thesis, yet I also found myself more and more longing to be in a committed relationship.

Gradually, the freedoms that I had cherished in my twenties began to lose their charm, not because I felt incomplete without a man, but because I finally felt ready to take on a serious, loving, committed relationship with a man. I witnessed the settled homes and shared happiness that many of my peers, including my younger sister, had found with a mate, and I felt increasingly impatient with my charmingly noncommittal boyfriends, yet I still resented the frequented, worrisome questioning from my parents and others regarding my persistent single status. Why did they find that topic so much more pressing than the promising academic career in English literature I recently embarked upon? What happened to my feminist parents who raised me to cherish independence, but now pestered me about settling down with one of my male friends? Although I didn't perceive myself as one of the "never marrieds" for whom Toufexis advocates, I strongly related to her assertion that single women "have been staging a quiet revolution, battling social prejudice, family expectations, and their own apprehensions to set a new standard for what it means to be successful, fulfilled, and content women." The article helped me realize, for the first time, that a lot of my worries stemmed from internalizing the "social prejudice" and "family expectations" Toufexis names. Regardless of their intellectual commitment to women's independence, my parents had no personal experience to help them imagine what it was like to be a "never-married" thirtysomething adult with a fulfilling life. Marrying in their early twenties and then turning their attention immediately to raising children, they had no idea what life was like for a woman in my situation. I mailed them a copy of Toufexis' article. They seemed relieved.

I met my future husband, Ed, just as I was preparing to turn thirty-one. I was enjoying an intellectually active and socially engaging life, and on top of that, I often felt gratitude for the peaceful solitude of living alone and experienced relief when the occasional "socially free" weekend rolled around. But as happy and busy as my life felt, it also felt as if a piece of the puzzle, in the form of a loving partner, was missing. I wondered why it mattered to me that I was not attracting, or was not attracted to, the "right man." Was I merely brainwashed by my society's assumption that successful, single women just aren't successful enough unless they have a man to come home to? Was my mental preparation for a future with children (as a single mother, if necessary) just evidence that I was buying into the "biological clock" cliché? Meeting and dating Ed, just as I was preparing to turn thirty-one, nudged these questions out of my mind, as I started paying attention to the present moment; later these questions would come into sharp relief when our relationship grew more serious....

Spring 1997, Ed and I are spending every weekend together as we get to know each other. One Saturday afternoon, we are quietly sharing the love seat in his bedroom, academic books open in front of us. We've been dating for three months and I am thrilled to have found a lively intellectual partner whose interests encompass gender roles and women's history. As two doctoral students with similar liberal politics and social views, we were in complete intellectual agreement that women and men ought to be equal partners in a relationship. However, on this day I am thinking about marriage, specifically, I want to find out his reaction to my determination to retain my last name (or at least take on a hyphenated surname) after I marry. Somehow, I bring up the topic of marriage. "I know lots of women who kept their last names after getting married, including two of my aunts," I say and try to sound as casual as possible, afraid I might scare him off. Ed is still half-focused on the book in front of him, but nods and agrees, "Well, yes, all women should have the right to make that choice." While I am relieved to hear this, I feel disappointed that he isn't more passionate about the issue. I secretly hoped he would profess his desire that, no question, his future wife would keep her name. The conversation continues, and although I do not remember all the details, I do recall that we conclude our talk by tentatively agreeing that marriage is a definite goal, sooner rather than later, in each of our lives. "I'm impressed," I say to him that day. "We're talking about marriage and you're not screaming and running from the room." Ed smiles. I was never able to reach this kind of comfortable conversation about marriage with any other man I've dated. Much later, while planning our wedding, I declare my intention to keep my last name after marriage. I anticipate the subtle disapproval I will feel from some family members, friends, random store clerks, and even Ed, but it never materializes.

Despite my rational commitment to equality in a marriage partnership, I find that sometimes old stereotypes die hard for me. A year after our conversation on the love seat, our relationship is now serious. Our couplehood feels comfortably established as we discuss our plans for careers and a family. On the way home from the video store one night, I acknowledge my ambition to land a high-profile academic position, wondering exactly how this fits in with his picture of our future together. Ed admits that he, for one, would be happy with a less prestigious teaching position at a community college. When I point out that our different career paths might dictate that he will spend more time taking care of children and household obligations, he agrees. I am surprised at my relief—why am I clinging to old stereotypes that assume a man will resent his wife for being on a more ambitious career track? Is part of me uncomfortable with this imagined scenario, and had I been projecting this onto Ed?

According to a survey by Prudential Securities, women still hesitate to take the main bread-winning role in the family. Only 34 percent of men felt it would be problematic of their wives earned more money on the job than they did, whereas 53 percent of the women said they thought this scenario would create a problem. Clearly, I was one of those women who still needed to shed my assumptions about the undesirability of ambitious women. I had unconsciously held on to some anxieties about how far I could move outside a traditional partnership and still be acceptable....

As the first anniversary of our relationship arrives, Ed and I begin talking about moving in together later that year. Yet I start wondering: are things "too" comfortable between us, too settled? Other days I'm wondering how we will overcome our personality differences. Over the phone I voice my concern to my sister: "Is he truly the one for me, or have I just wanted him to be Mr. Right so badly that I've chosen to overlook certain problems?" She directs me to trust in the process of sharing my fears and concerns with Ed honestly and openly. Ed and I begin to discuss our differences more directly, including my desire to get engaged and his need for more time. We examine and study our personalities and disparate preferences and attempt to find the meaning of it all: how do we really know if this is a marriage-worthy relationship?...

Later that year, Ed and I prepare to rent a house together. Our decision provokes a great deal of anxiety in my parents. I am taken aback at their disapproval—after all, Ed and I are adults in our thirties. My sister translated my mother's concerns as the old cliché: "Why should he buy the cow when he is getting the milk for free?" In other words, Ed would have all the benefits of a marriage—including a convenient sex partner—without actually having to marry me. I pause and consider the truth of this. This assumption on their part skews our relationship, painting me as the commitment-crazy woman and him as the commitment-phobic, sex-crazy man. What about the fact that

I would also be enjoying the benefits of living with my partner, including sex? Not to mention the fact that we'd still be having sex even if we weren't living together....

Although staying single is a viable choice for more and more women, it's still not a completely comfortable choice. "[S]ingle women," Elizabeth Wurtzel declares, "are not societally sanctioned in their singleness." She adds, "No matter what clever tricks feminism has come up with, it has not quite succeeded at truly legitimizing an unmarried woman as an autonomous being, as a person in a chosen living arrangement and not as someone whose life is in abeyance." The nagging worries and insecurities on my thirtieth birthday surely betray my failure, despite long-held feminist leanings, to overcome the feeling that my life was "in abeyance" until I married. Paradoxically, moving in with Ed was both a declaration of my social autonomy and one step closer to marriage.

After a month of living together, and twenty months into the relationship, Ed produces a diamond ring over a special dinner in our rented duplex and asks me to marry him. The scene certainly sounds traditional, but we did not arrive at this point through a conventional courtship. I had voiced my readiness for marriage about six months earlier and was dismayed when he needed more time. I tried to relax because the last thing I wanted to do was pressure him to marry me before he was ready. On good days I appreciated the slow, thorough consideration he gave to life decisions. His proposal was not about a man inviting a woman to be his helpmate; it was about Ed making himself ready for couplehood, the mutual engagement we had been working toward together....

Two women I know, both doctoral students and recently married, congratulate me and then add ruefully: "You know, you won't get *anything* done on your dissertation before the wedding." I feel slightly panicky, for they had tapped my secret fear: my wedding would suddenly take over my life, which was up to now focused on completing my degree. I worry about becoming one of those women who gets a ring on her finger and suddenly talks of nothing but tulle and place settings.

I am determined that wedding planning will not interfere with my dissertation progress or my teaching assistantship. Ed and I decide on the location and date of the wedding, and after that I allow myself to complete one or two wedding tasks in a small chunk of time each week. While both Ed and I are increasingly excited about the July 3 wedding weekend, I feel contempt for the bridal magazines that build this day up as the "most important day of my life" and the day on which I need to be "my most beautiful." As if living a happy life on my own and supporting myself and then working toward my Ph.D. were mere side trips toward the most important journey—down the aisle into the arms of a man! While many people warn me about the stressors of dealing with family and fiancé during the wedding planning, I am unprepared to meet the stress of confronting my own mixed feelings about each piece of the process, feeling dreamy and at the same time indignant....

Before my engagement, I never truly appreciated the purely social construction of marriage. I now witness the "thin, permeable membrane" that Clements says separates those couples who are married and those who are not, and I see the social hierarchies in place. Two people could live together for years, buy a house, raise children, be active in their community, yet never be viewed, from some perspectives, as fully "mated." Only marriage, regardless of its day-to-day quality, completes the relationship. Our union was being celebrated by our family and friends, and we were touched by their support and approval, but it was also a source of wonder for me. What had we really accomplished that was worthy of this fuss, other than just living our lives together?...

I felt some relief when I read bell hooks's reflections on this topic in *Wounds of Passion: A Writing Life*:

> I decide that the issue is not sameness, that equality cannot be measured this way. That we all have to map our journeys according to our own desires. If I hate taking out the garbage and don't want to, and he does not mind, then that can be his chore even though it has always been defined as the male chore (at least in our family). And in our case I hate to do the shopping so he does. I love to clean so I do most (not all) of the cleaning. So we begin with equality in that we both have the skills to do the same chores, then we break them down according to desire making sure that everything balances out in the end.

This passage allowed me to rethink my own assumptions about chores. There was nothing *wrong* with what we had devised. I was enjoying the cooking and I preferred to be in charge of the laundry and Ed preferred doing the dishes and taking out the trash. As far as equality with regards to skills, I knew we could work on that. Ed could show me how to use the power drill and I could teach him how to cook for two. Additionally, during this period, I came to agree with hooks's assertion that we each must "map our own journeys according to our own desires." In other words, my feminist beliefs evolved and I became more comfortable with my role as a politically conscious bride-to-be.

As spring passes and early summer arrives, the wedding details double and Ed and I spend more and more time on preparations. I also spend more time on my dissertation, attempting to get the first chapter done and approved before the wedding. I am determined to focus on academic work—and not exclusively to the wedding—which I had accomplished in the first seven months of the engagement. With the arrival of May and the end of the semester, I turn in the next-to-final draft of my chapter and allow myself to enjoy the last two months of wedding planning. I spend some time at home with my mother working on wedding banners for the church, and Ed and I prepare and mail out all 175 invitations. Meanwhile, I finish my dissertation chapter on time and I no longer worry that I'm a woman whose life revolves only around her wedding day.

Dozens of wedding details swirl around us that spring, and I am disturbed by how frequently the wedding day is framed as a day of closure—when the bride "seals the deal"—rather than a day that begins a new chapter for the couple. Ed and I agreed early on that getting married could not be our central relationship goal; that king of thinking would erroneously make the wedding seem "proof" of our compatibility. We needed to see it as just one point, a special and unique point, on a longer continuum that represents our ongoing commitment and growth together. I knew this to be the truth of any marriage, but I still found myself half-anticipating the romantic atmosphere of "happily ever after" that would settle around us magically as we arrived hand in hand at the reception. Would things really be different—or feel different for us—starting on that day? Would the contours of our everyday world begin to smooth themselves out naturally?...

When our wedding finally arrives, I savor each moment: getting ready with my closest girlfriends and female family members, walking down the aisle with my dad with tears in our eyes, carefully and lovingly delivering each word in my vows to Ed, and as a couple, dancing, kissing, hugging our way through the reception with our nearest and dearest. For a woman who felt a great deal of anxiety over the engagement months and the wedding ceremony, I feel no fear about my transition into wifehood.

Who decided that successful, smart, and savvy women are weak and "unliberated" if they desire a mate? Our feminist foremothers didn't fight for our right to seek fulfillment only by living life solo, but to be free—to feel liberated—to make meaningful personal choices: a career, or a mate, or children, or all three at once. Can a feminist be a wife? In order to answer yes, the trick is to stop considering a wife as one who must obey certain rules, take on expected duties, or measure up to particular standards. We need to stop seeing *wife* as primarily a service role. Instead, we need to let our attitudes, personalities, and lifestyles expand the definition of what a *wife* can be. Marriage is not a sign of the failed feminist, it's the healthy recognition that a loving partner can make a sweet life sweeter. The key to a "feminist engagement" is to be truly engaged with one's own developing sense of marriage, gender roles, and personal desires.

POSTSCRIPT—JANUARY 2001

It's been a year and half since Ed and I married. Being a married couple has not magically transformed our relationship or our lives as individuals—for better or for worse. The most notable shifts in our relationship took place during that first year of living together and planning our wedding as we hashed out the details of our shared life: juggling expenses and bills, keeping the house clean, setting a comfortable rhythm for weekends. My concerns about how to be both a feminist and a wife are pushed to the back of my mind amid the flurry of tasks and minutiae of everyday life. Ideally, I wanted a marriage in which Ed and I would sometimes "trade off" those traditionally gendered tasks in order to strike a balance of equality around the house. At the same time, I wanted us both to be able to embrace those interests and concerns that make us who we are, regardless of whether they seem conventional or not. Achieving a comfortable balance is easier said than done.

What I've discovered is that it is much easier to just be ourselves—for me to do the lion's share of the cooking because I enjoy it and for Ed to attend to the automobile maintenance because he has more experience in that area. Additionally, I've continued to be the one taking the driver's seat, initiating plans and goals for us, and Ed is continually flexible and agreeable to these efforts. We work as a team, and if I want a game plan it is up to me to pull out the calendar or clipboard. It's true that this makes me uncomfortable sometimes, for it doesn't live up to my feminist ideals, but life runs much more smoothly when we play to our strengths and don't try to be something we are not. Or is this just what I tell myself when I am feeling too lazy to move outside of my relationship comfort zone? After all, it would be very practical for me to know how to use the jumper cables in case my car breaks down—it's not simply a feminist move.

Initiating healthy change and growing as a person—and a couple—takes energy and commitment. Most days, I have to admit, I don't have a lot of energy and focus to spare. So right now I settle for appreciating the little moments that assure me we are growing as individuals and as a couple: when Ed encourages me to spend time alone with my friends, when I take the time to deepen my relationship with his family members, when we reach for each other's hand during a movie.

So, if we maintain love and trust in our relationship, does it really matter who takes out the garbage? I am reconsidering this question since my daughter Molly was born last month. I want her to grow up in a household where her parents share the chores, the decisions, the child-rearing duties. Yet raising Molly in the feminist spirit in which I was raised means that Ed and I must freely be ourselves and encourage her to develop her own unique identity. I know that when it comes to being true to the feminist spirit, rigid politics and policies do not need to dictate the details of one's personal life. At the same time, it is important that we—as a family—make conscious choices that allow our actions to reflect our larger principles and beliefs. This tension can be productive and informative if we allow it to be.

Right now, however, I am focused on learning to be a mother to Molly without rendering my former life unrecognizable. Just as the women in my family demonstrated to me the many ways a woman's life can be meaningful, I want to model for Molly one way in which a woman can choose to be a wife, a mother, a scholar, and a feminist. I want her to know that these roles are optional and the boundaries between and around these loaded terms are fluid and flexible. I wish for her to become her own person, to name her desires and concerns, and perhaps claim her place in the flow from one wave of feminism to the next.

54. Ariel Gore, "Introduction," from *The Essential Hip Mama*

In this piece, *Hip Mama* founder Ariel Gore describes the way she came to start this zine, which put the question of motherhood on the map for third-wave feminists. A humorous look at the contradictions of motherhood in the third wave, this essay shows what it is like to be a young mother today trying to juggle academic training, career, and motherhood, and how one might bring a third-wave feminist sensibility to all of these.

In the fall of my senior year of college, I had a problem.

I'd been working insanely—baby on my back or crawling through the aisles of my lecture hall classes—for four years. I'd completed nearly all of my college credits, kept my growing daughter fed, made the honor roll, helped organize student moms to demand affordable daycare and a safe playground on campus, and managed to survive on an average of three-and-a-half hours' sleep a night. But one assignment stood between my high school-dropout self and college graduation … a senior project.

I listened to my classmates describe plans for complex theses on communication theory and documentary films about race and class in America. Folks were heading off to New York to do research internships and planning for endless hours in the library. All I could think was: *Where am I gonna get a babysitter for this one?* I'd mastered the art of all-night essay writing and studying after my toddler had fallen asleep, but this grand finale assignment was no 10-page sociology paper or statistics test cramming session. I was completely freaked out. So I did what I'd always done when I couldn't wrap my mind around something: I tried to forget about it.

As my classmates' plans for earth-shattering investigations into media distortions became more and more involved, I hid behind the latest issues of *Ms.*, *Parenting*, *Bust*, and the *Utne Reader*, concocting schemes to land a job or make a living as a freelance journalist when I got out of school. Whenever my postgraduation thoughts morphed into thoughts of *if* I got out of school, I put the magazines down and focused my energy on cleaning up finger-painting mishaps or making spaghetti for the throngs of disheveled children who ran through our family student-housing complex.

And, as always, I drank coffee. I drank *a lot* of coffee.

My best friend and radical mama ally, Julie Bowles, was studying psychology at the time, and together we lamented the removal of "caffeine-induced organic mental disorder" from the American Psychiatric Association's list of official insanities. We were both obviously suffering from the disorder, and now we'd never be able to get insurance to cover it—even if we ever *did* manage to graduate and find jobs with psychiatric benefits.

Anyway, I must have been having one of my caffeine-induced organic episodes the night Julie made dinner for us all, and her youngest had thrown half of it across the living room floor. The older preschoolers played outside in a sprinkler, muddying up their freshly laundered clothes, while Julie's partner quietly recycled all the stupid parenting magazines they'd gotten free from their pediatrician. Julie was doing the dishes and I was boiling water for more coffee when she turned to me and asked, casually, what I'd come up with for my senior project. My proposal was due in the morning, wasn't it?

I laughed uneasily, surveyed the chaos around us, and joked, "I'm gonna make a *real* parenting magazine—the kids are gonna be a mess, half the moms are gonna be single, and no 'experts.' All the writers are gonna be in the trenches. In my zine, mamas will tell the *truth* about this shit. You'll be able to hear the baby screaming right through the middle of it."

Julie's partner cackled. He said, "What's it gonna be called? *Espresso Is My Co-Pilot?*"

"No, man. I'm gonna call it *Hip Mama*."

Julie place a mug in the dish rack, looked me up and down, and couldn't help but laugh: my ripped jeans, my stained T-shirt, my messed-up whitey-afro. Not exactly the picture of an early '90s hipster.

Just then my daughter hit her son over the head with the hose—or somebody hit somebody—and all hell broke loose outside. Screaming, muddy, cold, drenched chaos.

I got up early the next morning, made myself a cup of coffee, typed up a proposal for my half-baked idea for a *real* parenting zine, threw on a clean T-shirt but didn't bother to change out of the sweats I'd slept in, delivered my newly potty-trained daughter to preschool, stopped at the college café for a quick double shot of espresso, and headed across the green-grass campus to my communications senior seminar, hoping I'd be able to present my project plan with a straight face.

Sitting under the fluorescent lights, reading over my notes for *Hip Mama*, listening to the other proposals in which my classmates described their plans to deconstruct 200 years of feminist theory or prove that the advertising industry was directly responsible for alcoholism in low-income communities and potentially legally liable for it, I felt like such a dork. I was planning to collect a bunch of articles with titles like "Barbie's Liberation" and "The Chaos Theory of Parenting" and "Mothers Don't Fart." My professors and peers had put up with me nursing my daughter through lectures when I couldn't find childcare, turning in papers with scribbles in the margins, and habitually slipping into baby talk when discussing economic theory or media monopolies. Surely *this* would be the limit. I wracked my brain for a spur-of-the-moment substitute idea. Something that would prove I'd really been digesting all that information from my textbooks, teachers, research projects, and class discussions. Something *serious*. I drew a blank. *Four years of higher education and what was I qualified to dissect?* My classmates had phrases like "postmodern media globalization" and "paradigm shifting." *What did I have? Postmodern diapering?* But it was my turn, so I stood up, and tried not to make eye contact with anyone as I began. *What was I going to say, anyway?* I opened my mouth and, miraculously, a quote right out of one of those boring communications textbooks fell from my lips: "It was the legendary press critic A. J. Liebling who said, 'Freedom of the press is guaranteed only to those who own one.'"

That last double shot of espresso did not fail me, and I rolled through my academic-sounding preamble before laying it out for everyone: In *Hip Mama,* parenting would get cutting-edge treatment.

The weird thing was, when I put it that way, it didn't sound like a joke anymore. I'd deconstruct Disney, expose the infant-formula marketing industry, speak the truth about the fact that I hadn't had a good night's sleep in years. I'd heard parenting belittled in theory discussions and the media alike. Maybe I'd felt like a dork only because I'd believed all the people who scoffed at motherhood. But now, I explained, I would exercise my right to freedom of the press: I'd own one.

"Desktop publishing," my cowboy hat-wearing professor nodded.

"Actually, I don't have a desk," I admitted. I'd somehow managed to get through nearly four years of school without even owning a computer. "Kitchen counter publishing."

A smirk and a nod. Project proposal approved.

Clichéd but true: If, on my way to my next class that bright morning in late fall 10 years ago, anyone had stopped to warn me that I'd just signed up for a career that would last at least a decade, I'd have rolled my eyes: *Yeah, right.* That I would put together the first issue of *Hip Mama* for my senior project and then produce another and another. That the mainstream press would write stories about the zine. That I'd be invited to debate then-Speaker of the House Newt Gingrich on MTV. That I'd write parenting books and one day get calls from national TV talk show producers looking to me as the "expert" on everything from potty training to getting through school with a baby on your back. That Julie and I would host a "Hip Mama Hour" on Free Radio Berkeley. That the coffee-inspired zine would in turn inspire Web sites, community groups, and annual gatherings of radical moms. That I would one day get a call from a reporter at the *Los Angeles Times* asking me how it felt to have founded a "movement." That my little zine would be called groundbreaking, lifesaving, kick-ass awesome. I would have thought my fortune-teller was suffering from "caffeine-induced organic mental disorder" herself. But that's the way it happened. I never got a real job after college—or grad school. I made *Hip Mama* my job. Low pay. Long hours. No insurance. Still headquartered in my kitchen. But mine. It's a free press because I own it.

These days, I get at least one letter a day from some mama somewhere telling me that *Hip Mama* saved her sanity, changed her life, inspired her to get real and not check her personality at the door just because she was a mother now. But I could just as easily say that *Hip Mama* saved *my* sanity, changed *my* life. It earned me a college degree and inspired me to get and stay real. I don't know what it feels like to have founded a "movement" because I didn't. I founded a zine. And the parents who sent me their essays and their art and their exposés and their own chaos theories taught me that I wasn't alone even when the mainstream parenting mags made me feel freakish and marginalized.

What was true when I was trying to come up with a senior project and what is true today: Motherhood has been my defining life experience. It is no small thing. When I started to write about that experience 10 years ago, the only other writers I read who admitted to sharing similar feelings seemed to be antifeminist "family values" wives who believed that women without children were somehow unfeminine, that a woman's worth could and should be measured by what she produced from her womb. The feminist writings I could find waxed philosophical about the institution of motherhood and explored real and deep truths about women's ambivalence, but too often harped on the oppression of it all rather than the powerful and shit-kicking good times. The magazine articles, when they weren't written by those so-called experts telling me what to do and when, described organic earth-mama perfection or Kodak moments in nuclear two-minivan families.

What I couldn't find back then were the voices of women like me and my radical mama allies—independent women who are raising their kids with love and fierceness, who could admit to their imperfections and fears, who cared to deconstruct Disney or who fell in love with Mister Rogers, whose feelings about motherhood ran from horror to joy on any given day, who could admit, as one writer did in issue 13 of *Hip Mama*,

> I dearly love my children and do not wish them gone. As a matter of fact it is precisely the love I feel for these people, a complex, many-faceted love unparalleled by any other I have known, that makes the condition of motherhood so unbearable. That I can never do right by them, that they can never live a pain-free existence, that I unthinkingly caused some of their pain, than the world I brought them into isn't good enough for them—all these are sources of anguish to me.

What I couldn't find were the voices of the mamas who worried about sexism in cartoons, who struggled to hang on to their own identities while allowing themselves to be defined by their roles as mothers, who appreciated the ambiguity of it all, who found themselves sometimes alienated from both the minivan set and the granola-eaters, and who, if given a platform, would be willing to tell their truths.

When I started *Hip Mama*, I had been a teen mom, a welfare mom, a single mom, a college mom. I was young, poor, urban. The plan from the start was that the zine would be reader-written, so I expected to receive essay submissions form other young and poor moms. I thought the zine would attract readers and writers like myself. But I discovered, almost immediately, that telling the truth about our experiences as mothers doesn't necessarily attract others like us—it attracts people who want to tell *their* truths about motherhood, no matter how different those experiences may be. The readers of *Hip Mama* are as diverse a group as the writers: There are teen moms and fifty-something moms, single moms and married moms, straight moms and queer moms, college moms and rural moms, midwives and bank tellers.

The zine has always had a political bent, so let's face it: *Hip Mama* can only count a handful of Republicans among its loyal readers. Diversity does have its limitations. But for me, the parental and the political have always been inextricably entwined. There are morals and values espoused in every fairy tale. *Sesame Street* is a political television show. If the Speaker of the House wants to blame young mothers for the nation's economic problems, I consider it my duty to be willing to show up and make my humble attempt to take him to task for that. Whether or not the president decides to send 100,000 children to fight his next war matters to me as a mother. Child support, family leave acts, domestic violence initiatives, and public education funding are more than faraway bills in Congress. They affect our daily lives, the ways in which we can support our children. They are political issues, but they begin and end in our living rooms and nurseries.

Looking back through 10 years of *Hip Mama*, I realize that the zine has grown and changed in ways both predictable and unexpected. I was a 23-year-old college senior in Oakland, California, when I published the first issue. My daughter had just turned four. Now I'm a 33-year-old editor, writer, and teacher in Portland, Oregon. And my baby is a cheerleader. The zine has followed my interests as a mother and an editor. Stories on weaning abounded when I was trying to get my daughter off the tit. The question of public education versus homeschooling took center stage as I struggled to find the right place for Maia to start school. Essays on family court seemed most relevant during my seven-year odyssey as a perpetual litigant. And as Maia enters adolescence, I search for the voices of the soulful mothers of teenagers who have come before me.

When the journalists and producers call me as an "expert," I have to laugh. Whenever I've needed parenting advice, I've put out a call for submissions.

The contributors and readers of *Hip Mama* have taught me how to be a mother, not the other way around. From Julie, I learned to accept chaos and laugh through the insanity. From Opal Palmer Adisa, I learned what it means to be soulful and confident, and that attachment parenting is applicable even after we've sent the kids off to college. From Nina Hagen, I learned to stay faithful and not worry about being too freakin' weird. To try to list everyone and their contributions to my sanity as a mom would be to become super-dork—one of those people with a crumpled list at the Academy Awards, shouting random names long after the get-off-the-stage music has been cranked up.

My point is that *Hip Mama* has been as much of a lifesaver for me as it has been for anyone. Occasionally through the years, I've considered quitting. Ceasing publication and getting a real job. But if I stopped publishing *Hip Mama* where would I read about Barbie's liberation and the ever-expanding chaos theory of parenting? Where would I read the truth about the defining experience of my life? As we learned in Communication 101, "Freedom of the press is guaranteed only to those who own one." And so I'll own my free press. And if I do my work well, so will you—groundbreaking, lifesaving, kick-ass awesome mamas, all.

55. Hillary Carlip, "Jocks," from *Girl Power: Young Women Speak Out*

Title IX, the Education Act of 1972 that mandated equal funding for men's and women's sports at any institution receiving federal funds, is widely credited with the explosion of women's participation in sports. In 1972, one in twenty-seven women participated in high school or college sports, while today the figure is one in three. Women's sports is a focus for the third wave because of the ways female athletes break down the distinctions between masculinity and femininity, and the stereotype that men are stronger, more aggressive, and more focused and directed than women. "Jocks" is a key third-wave piece that includes the voices of many female athletes who speak about how playing sports makes them feel, often giving them more self-esteem and a sense of power and achievement. Anyone interested in disproving gender stereotypes based on physical ability should read this piece.

Softball. Basketball. Volleyball. Football. Soccer. Track. Rowing. Ice Hockey. Field Hockey. BMX Racing. Wrestling. Lacrosse.

Girls are doing it all.

> It took moving to a larger city, and an athletically competitive school, to build up my confidence. Since I started school, I had been teased by a lot of people. My ability to stand up to people was almost non-existent. I would often come home from school and then I would have a comeback. An hour after each put-down I would imagine myself beating the people who beat me, just like Rocky. My quest has always been to come back and see those people and make them see how good I am.... I excelled in gym, but never enough. People called me a tomboy because I liked gym ... I was laughed at because I was tough, and I never did good enough.
>
> Then one day we had something called track and field day.... I won the 400 yard dash. From then on, things began to click....

What began to click in fourteen-year-old Paula Barkman from Pittsburgh, Pennsylvania, was an increase in self-esteem that many girls have found through participating in sports.

> My name is Laura Prinzer. I am a junior on the Kiski Area Girls Cross-Country and Track teams. We have finished our fourth undefeated season, and have just advanced to the W.P.I.A.L. final meet. There, we will try to qualify for the state meet.
>
> I think athletics has helped me tremendously. Being a part of a team is a great feeling, especially when it is a hardworking and successful one.... I have become a much more confident and independent person. I know that if I work hard enough at something, I can do it. Without sports, I don't think I would have ever achieved this confidence.

During her first field hockey game where she "started as sweeper," Hannah Duffy, age fifteen, from Rindge, New Hamsphire, experienced the gamut of emotions. She writes about herself from the point of view of her hockey stick:

> ... She's trembling again, but this time it's from excitement, and she's not afraid anymore. And I can't help feeling my own pleasure at assisting her, at helping her improve her self-esteem. For we have it now, a surge of power that bonds us together, that makes me hers. Together, we are unstoppable. And we both know it. I've felt her frustration and anger, her pride and happiness. I've taken on her sweat and tears, her weariness and euphoria. I complete her and she completes me, we are one and as the game goes on, her hands are dry and steady, and she makes no mistakes.

Yana Shteyn, age eighteen, who qualified for the Junior Olympics in table tennis, found strength by overcoming many obstacles on the way:

> Originally I come from former Soviet Union, Odessa, Ukraine.... Table tennis in Russia differs greatly from the sport here in America. For five years I trained in a sport school, in a special class for table tennis. There were twenty kids in my class, every one of us lived table tennis....
>
> Out of all those kids, I didn't stand out very much. I was a skinny, young girl. My coach didn't believe in me very much for two big reasons. I was a novice girl plus I was a daughter of a woman who worked for him.
>
> When I turned thirteen, my life completely changed, because I came to the United States. I didn't arrive to Colorado, New York or California, instead I came to a small city of Jacksonville, Florida, where table tennis is ping-pong, a fun game....

Yana and her mother found competitions and Yana started winning. She baby-sat to make money to buy tickets to the competitions, and often had to travel to other cities, sometimes spending the night in the car with her family before games.

Yana's dream finally came true. She became the number-one girl in Florida and qualified for the Junior Olympics. However, her joy was short-lived. She was banned from play on a technicality. She had come to America two months too late to be eligible for the competition.

> As I look back, I have no regrets. Everything that happened to me, all I had to go through, has made me a better player, but most of all a very strong person.

Fifteen-year-old Dana J. Battese Turdell ... has been running since the age of six. In 1993, she was the South Dakota TAC Junior Olympic female cross-country champion:

> When I run I get a lot of power. I pray and I think about things. I pray that I may do the best that I can. It's like running through time. To run the dream makes me more powerful within.

Like Cowgirls and Surfers, some Jocks, such as fifteen-year-old Sarah Janicke from Merriam, Kansas, find a sense of escape in their sport:

> ... Volleyball is an important part of my life. It is one of the few sports that I don't feel embarrassed playing. When I am out there on the court, all my worries, shyness and problems dissolve from my life.
>
> The only thing I think about when I'm playing is what I need to think about: where I'm supposed to be on the court, my skills and my opponents. All my usual thoughts like "Do I look okay? Does he like me? Are my grades good enough? Am I popular?" never taunt me when I'm involved in a game.

Jenny Buttolph, age thirteen, who plays volleyball and basketball in Pleasant Hill, Oregon, has a similar experience:

> One of the main reasons I play and enjoy sports is for me to forget about my personal problems and to set aside my feelings. It seems that I have quite a lot of problems but sports lets me set them aside.

Yet Jenny also feels disturbed and troubled by "the sexism that's involved" in sports. She continues:

> ... For example, a men's college basketball game gets a lot of people to watch them whereas a women's basketball game gets a considerable amount less. Women are just as good as men if not better! I don't mean to sound conceited but I don't think it is very fair to cheer on men and forget about women just because of their sex. I mean, where is a women's professional basketball team? All I see is women's college but men can go on to the N.B.A. One main thing that I believe in is giving *everyone* a fair chance.

This concern is evident in most of the girl's writing. Many share how daunting it is to immerse themselves fully in their sport knowing that, since there are basically no professional women's teams, they are not able to have a playing future. Most feel continually unacknowledged and dismissed.

Jessica Trybus, age sixteen, from Gibsonia, Pennsylvania, has been written up in countless local newspaper articles. Almost each week an article appears focusing on a different sport she excels in, including softball, tennis, swimming, golf, basketball, skiing, baseball, and football. With accomplishments like that, I was surprised to read about this experience:

> When I was fourteen years old, I tried out for one of my high school's boys ice hockey teams. I was the first ever and only girl to try out for this prestigious school.... During the clinics before the tryouts, I was the only one of my group to be asked to be moved up to practice with the Junior Varsity until tryouts.... I made first "cuts" and played well throughout tryouts. I thought that I was clearly better than at least 90% of the guys. So when second tryouts came along, I gave it all that I had. I even remember diving along the blue line to keep the puck on sides—and just as I did so, the whistle blew signaling the end of tryouts....

Jessica had to wait a week until the teams were posted. She, along with her family and friends, was confident that she would make it. On her birthday, she found out the results:

> I didn't speak a word for two whole days. Every time someone tried to comfort me, it just made matters worse. After supplying myself with ample time to think things over, I decided that these people who cut me aren't done with me, because I'll get them next time. I turned right around the next week and made the Bantam A team of a local amateur league and really learned a lot with that group. My ultimate high school goal is to make the Varsity ice hockey team my senior year at North Allegheny Senior high school. If I feel I'm skilled and in shape enough to try out, I expect to be judged fairly as a player.

Fourteen-year-old Jenny Olson, from Pleasant Hill, Oregon, addresses the same issue:

> Being a girl in the 90's is no easy task. Being an athletic woman is even harder. Almost everybody thinks that men are better at everything, and is an image that is imprinted unconsciously from day one. This is unfortunate because girls can achieve so much if they are given support instead of being ridiculed.

It wasn't until 1972 that girls were even allowed a fair shot at participating in high school sports. With the passing of the highly controversial law referred to as Title IX, schools were forbidden to discriminate against girls in sports. The law was revolutionary.

However, according to the girls I met and heard from, being legally allowed to play on boys' teams does not protect them from mockery and disdain from their fellow teammates.

Yet many young women, like Margaret LeGates, have prevailed, earning much respect and becoming role models for other girls:

> The smell of the mats, the roar of the crowd, I love it all. So why does this make me weird? Why do people stare when I enter the gym? I guess it's because girls aren't supposed to do certain things even if we enjoy them.
>
> I, Margaret LeGates, am the only girl wrestler on the boys wrestling team at Libertyville Community High School. I was the first girl to participate on the high school level in Illinois. At 17, I've been wrestling for two years now at 103 pounds. This will be my third and final season, and I'm hoping my best. I would say wrestling has been one of the greatest experiences of my life....

In eighth grade, Margaret decided to join the wrestling team. She was told she could not. She was again turned away in the ninth grade. She contacted the Women's Wrestling Federation and learned that under Title IX, she could not be blocked from participating. Once the school superintendent was informed of the law, she made the team.

After intensive training, which left her exhausted and in bed by 8:00 every night and bruised from head to toe, Margaret finally got to compete.

> ... None of the other schools knew I was wrestling until the end of November when we had our first meet. Wrestlers and fans alike were surprised to see me there. That night I received two forfeits because the other teams didn't have anyone at 103 on the sophomore level. As the season progressed, I got more of the same treatment. Stares and gasps greeted me as I entered the room. Eventually, I chalked up seven more forfeits, four from boys who didn't want to wrestle me.
>
> I won one match that season. In December at a multiple school tournament, I was in a close match, and tied with a young man 7-7 at the end of regulation time. I pinned him in overtime. Everyone was cheering for me, and my coach, Matt Leone, was so proud, I felt all the obstacles had been worth it. It was really exciting!
>
> My junior season I also won one match, but on the varsity level. I pinned the boy in 4:20. This win gave me a seventh place title out of twelve teams....

Margaret was forced to make concessions. She had to purchase a specially designed uniform and cut her hair. She also found herself faced with negative attitudes and prejudices from her male opponents and teammates.

But for Margaret it was all worth it:

> Wrestling experiences, however, have given me more gains than losses. I have gained self-respect, and respect for others' opinions. I have gained strength, and will power which will stay with me for life. I have gained respect from others, especially my peers....
>
> I've been called a pioneer, and I guess in some ways I am. Since I started wrestling I know a few other girls have joined the teams at their school.... It makes me feel proud to know that I may have influenced other girls to follow their wishes....

From Dumfries, Virginia, sixteen-year-old Nicky Croteau writes of the time when she was alone shooting baskets on a public basketball court in Pompano Beach, Florida. When other players—all men—showed up, every one of them avoided Nicky:

> ... More and more pour in; they begin to crowd up the courts. I still have my basket to myself. The baskets are now over-crowded. They've started up a couple of games on half-courts with groups sitting near waiting to play, and I STILL have my hoop to myself. This is ridiculous! The ones in line could play a game at my basket ... if I play, too. So I decide to show them my stuff. Maybe if they see I can play, they'll join me. So I do some fancy dribbling that I've been working on for awhile and pop a few shots. Still—no reaction. Maybe this is a step ahead for women. Maybe it's good they're not assuming they can just take the basket from me. Maybe I'm getting really annoyed, too. The game next to me ends. I grab my ball, walk over to the nearest guy and say, "May I play?", realizing I sound really stupid; no one else asks like that. The guy says sure, and I followed him onto the court. I felt pretty damn uncomfortable I'd like to add. There were nine black guys standing there looking at me. (By the way, I'm a not so tall white girl).
>
> "Hi." I said.
>
> Another great comment. A couple of them smiled. (Possibly laughing at me to themselves). But no one responded. They just began shooting around. I joined them....

But, to no surprise, Nicky was the last person picked for a team. The game began and Nicky made a basket quickly. It was apparent, however, that the men had let her score with little or no defense. She confronted them and asked them to play seriously. Then they went all out, "stuffing" her three times in a row, with no middle ground.

> I got used to it though. Eventually, as the game went on, I got better. I made a couple of shots, and I even made the winning point for my team. After the game, a few of the guys asked me where I was from, where I played, etc.... I answered them, talked for awhile, grabbed my

> ball and walked away. I did manage to hear some comments on the way to the car.
>
> "Damn. She was pretty good. I've never played against a girl before," said one of the players. "These are the 90's, better get used to it," responded one of my teammates. That really made my day.
>
> I've been back to the courts a few times since then, and you'd be surprised how much respect I've earned. I'm never the last one picked anymore.

Some girls, like Shona Williams, age thirteen, find that playing on coed teams, with all the teasing and the "smart comments," makes for a more competitive game:

> I played tackle football last season. All boys were on my team and I think I was the only girl on our league.... My first game I played I could hear boys making smart comments and stuff. And to tell you the truth I kinda liked it because they were making fun of me, but when the game started I gave them the beating of their life. Most of my games I heard smart comments, but they really didn't realize that they were just making me stronger by saying that rude stuff. I liked playing with guys though because they know more about football.

Fourteen-year-old Jacylyn De Board's frustration in an all-girl softball league forced her to choose the only option she felt she could:

> I made the all-star team every year I played. After my second year of league I stopped playing because I had become the best pitcher in league and I didn't have any kind of competition.

In addition to social pressures and physical pain, girl Jocks, with their rigorous and time-consuming practices, tryouts, and competitions, must sacrifice the social life other teens seem to crave. What keeps them going?

> It's the feeling you get after you've run your ten billionth lap, after you've shot your 100,000 free throws, after you practiced your spike approach approximately 4,800 times. If you could describe the feeling in a word it would be euphoria or pain. But that feeling that every muscle in your body is aware of, makes everything worthwhile. I can do anything. I know it because I *have* run ten billion laps and shot 100,000 free throws. Because I've heard the laughs and the "girls can't play sports" jokes. Well guys, you better check your bucks because the next time you're streaking down the court for a lay-in, the hand that stuffs the ball down your throat might just belong to a girl. And you can bet that she'll be feeling that euphoria.
>
> —Chelsea McAlister, age 14

Nineteen-year-old rower Jessica Smith competes in the Foot of Charles regatta in Boston, the novice equivalent of the Head of Charles—the biggest regatta in the United States, held annually in Boston on the Charles River.

She's a coxswain, the "captain" of her boat. It is up to her to manage eight rowers—steering, giving directions, and motivating each girl to race her best race.

> ... "Okay, taking it up. Full pressure, full steam ahead crossing the starting line. Let's go! We've worked hard for this day, let's show them how it's done! Pushing off, remembering your body angles ... make every stroke your best stroke. Keep it going, keep it going! Let's show some power! We're a powerhouse, we're looking great and working hard! Power ten on this one!" And so we rowed our hardest and our best ever. The steering came as naturally to me as breathing. I hardly thought about my next words to the rowers. It all came from within, from somewhere deep in my subconscious. All my hard work, reading articles and manuals, taking comments form the rowers and advice from the coach, listening to the varsity coxswains and pumping them for information, stressing, worrying, sleepless nights and morning rows—it was all paying off.
>
> We sailed under the Weeks Bridge and around the sharp corner as if we had wings. Suddenly, the finish line was on us. So soon? I was almost disappointed. I called a power ten—ten of the hardest, best possible strokes—for the finish line and we flew across. We didn't come in first, but no one had passed us either. We paddled for about fifty yards beyond the finish line, and weigh-'nuffed. We had done it! We were incredible! The adrenalin in that boat could have rowed the whole race over again, backwards, eight arms tied behind eight backs of the eight rowers who had pulled us through the water like a hot knife slicing through butter. (I, of course, would need both hands to steer.) ...

Of African-Italian descent, seventeen-year-old runner Danielle Purfey lives in Allison Park, Pennsylvania. Among other numerous achievements, Danielle is a seven-time National Junior Olympian, and was named Athlete of the Year in 1990 and 1988 by the USA Track and Field Southern Region.

I KNOW THE ANSWER

We trot to the starting position like thoroughbreds
The Others pawing and prancing.
There's one last moment of hesitation,
One last forced breath and, in the split second I wonder ...
Why am I here?
The terror
The smoke
The gun

BANG!

I'm in my own world now, with just enough room for me.
A pack of 15 girls is what reality pushes,
While solidarity is what I imagined,

Instead I'm all alone on this icy blue colored track.
I see no one else.
I hear no one else.
I run this race for me and only me ...
While giving much thanks to all who have helped me climb this steep mountain of success.
I have completed my second lap in moments ...
Right on schedule.
The third lap begins to wrestle with me but
I stay strong and claim the victory.
I cry tears of pain,
... yet shed tears of joy.
I'm down to the last 100 meters.
Every step represents everything I've worked for
And the uncountable hours of sacrifice.
Every step seems like another day—a lifetime ...
just waiting to pass.
I can see the bright white line now
I'm so anxious to cross.
I raise my arms in ecstasy
And no longer ask
Why am I here?
I know the answer.

Danielle writes of "giving much thanks" to all who have helped her "climb this steep mountain of success."

Many girls have received much support and valuable insight from those around them. Heather K. Ehrman, nineteen years old, is from Merrimack, New Hampshire:

> My parents, teachers, coaches and friends encouraged me to believe that I can achieve whatever I choose to accomplish due to my ambition, hard work, and desire for happiness. This is an important discovery between leaving a childhood and becoming an adult. A little girl would be frightened to think of the uncertainty that lay in her future. As a young woman, her fear remains but it has evolved into the excitement of unknown possibilities....

Other times, what is intended as support can actually feel like pressure, and instill self-doubt:

> I am fifteen years old and I am a fast pitch softball player. I have had a glove on my hand since I was a little girl. My father got me started because of his love for the game.
>
> Because my father was a pitcher, I am a pitcher. I started this position two years ago. My father says I have great potential but I just have to

> develop and go through the transition every pitcher goes through. He also tells me to practice just a little bit harder. Believe me, I do practice. I play from March to August and practice and condition from September to February.
>
> My problem is, my father was a great pitcher. He expects it all to come naturally to me, but sometimes I have a hard time with it. In the last season I have come very close to the strike zone, but not right on.
>
> It is very frustrating for me. I love pitching, I could do it for hours, I just wish I could be as good as I want to be. I do expect a lot from myself. I just realized that this season. I expected it to all come together. I told myself that this would be my season. Well, it turned out to be a horrible season. Except for a few games which I pulled through that made me proud of myself, I felt like my father felt differently.
>
> It seems like whenever I do something good he's not there to see it, but when I do something bad he is and I don't hear the end of it. I always feel like he's disappointed or let down. That's what I get though for having a softball dad.
>
> My plan for the future is to practice a lot harder. I am very ambitious. Soon I am going to have what it takes. I did make a promise to my father though, some day I will strike him out!
>
> —Sarah Fritz Zimmerman, Minnesota

There are many demands on teenage girls in sports as they struggle to fulfill their own personal goals amidst the expectations of others.

Jami Strinz is a fifteen-year-old all-around jock from Pleasant Hill, Oregon. She's played volleyball, soccer, and basketball. In softball, her underhand fast pitch puts many boys to shame. Three years ago, at twelve years old, her pitch clocked in at fifty-five miles per hour. She hasn't been timed since, but is certain it's only gotten faster. She writes:

> It really doesn't matter how old you are, you'll always have pressure on you, due to sports. I've learned that you have to take control, and if you think you can't, you better find another line of work.

Fifteen-year-old Tara Koenig from Elk River, Minnesota, experienced just too much pressure:

> Since I was young, I've never been one to sit around. I've always been busy, busy, busy. I became extremely active after I entered junior high with maintaining a straight A average and also competing in sports. But, somehow, I always ended up being able to handle all the stress ... until this year....
>
> My schedule was filled with swimming and weightlifting in the mornings, which meant getting up at 5:00 A.M. After practice, I went directly to school. Following school, I headed back to the pool for a practice

> usually lasting until 5:15. I worked as a lifeguard until around 7:00. When I finally arrived home, I always seemed to be loaded down with homework. Unable to put it off, I'd stay up until 1:00 or 2:00 A.M. just to wake up and do it over again. With swim meets on Thursdays and Saturdays, my week was filled. Loss of sleep, exhaustion, and stress took its toll.

Indeed, Tara became sick and was diagnosed with mononucleosis. Her life immediately had to change as she could no longer swim and could only attend school for three hours a day while she recuperated. The days were full of emotion and upset, impatience and frustration. She continues:

> ... Sometimes I wish that I could go back to when I was a child and my biggest worry was if I'd have to clean up the dishes after supper. Life was so carefree back then. The most magical thing was to wake up with a bright new morning to greet you. But I know there is no way to go back. So, with me, the stress keeps building up more and more until something gives. This Fall, it was my health.

Many Jocks feel, as the Teen Queens will tell us, that there is a fine line between encouragement from well-meaning parents and teachers, and persuading a girl to persist after her desire fades:

> As a teenage girl, I have had a lot of pressure in sports. Not only from my friends around me at school, but from my family, and especially my coach. I started playing soccer as a little first grader, not knowing how I would like it. As years past, it became my favorite sport. I was an average soccer player, until one coach came into the picture. He started teaching me skill. A few years later, I was what you called naturally talented in soccer. At age twelve, I had already been on two varsity soccer teams, and made an advanced out-of-school team.
>
> When I finally became a teenager, I started having a social life, with a boyfriend. I was playing an instrument, and trying to keep straight A's. With all this, and soccer, it was too much. My soccer coach wanted me to drop everything else, and just concentrate on soccer. I didn't drop everything but soccer was at the top of my list, along with good grades. I wasn't happy with this decision because it didn't feel like my own. Pressure from my parents and coaches was what made up my mind.
>
> It seemed like everybody was happy about me playing soccer because I was good at it. My love for this sport wasn't, or didn't seem like it was there anymore. I wasn't going to quit soccer because I had a talent for it. I wasn't going to give a talent up that could excel me in life.
>
> My coach always calls me before a tryout to make sure I don't have doubts about going. If I do, he'll put in the right words to make me

> go. He doesn't make the decision for me, but the pressure is so strong that I feel I have to tryout, or else I won't get a scholarship, and go on with soccer. I don't know if I like it or not. I'm at a point in my life where I feel I have to go along with it, and if I don't, I won't have an alternative for the rest of my life.
>
> People around me think that I love soccer, and I do, but the pressure draws me away from the love for it, and makes me feel as though I'm playing for everybody else, not me. For me to love a sport, I have to be playing for myself, not everybody else.
>
> —Karli Holob, age 13

Coaches can make an indelible impression on a young girl's life, both positively and negatively. Morgan Holbrook, age thirteen, was greatly affected by the behavior of her coach:

> A few years ago I was on a softball team and the coach only picked 3 or 4 girls to pitch and no one else and I even practiced a lot at pitching and showed him, but he didn't care. He just had the girls that he picked pitch no matter what. My friend thought the same way, she and I both thought they weren't very good so I don't think it was very fair. Also, when he was throwing us grounders just because I didn't catch it he started yelling at me and literally told me I sucked and made me feel so bad. That's why I didn't play softball for a year.

Jenny Olson, age fourteen, understands the profound effects a coach can have on girl's experience in athletics and in life:

> I really enjoy sports, yet at the same time, I find that it pushes my stress level to the max. I think that the area where most of the stress is produced is from the coaches. I personally do like to win, but the most important part of the game is to enjoy it. Some coaches are the win-no-matter-what-it-takes type of coaches. This is very unfortunate because it teaches the players low self-esteem.

Fortunately, there are also those coaches whose encouragement, insight, and support have greatly inspired those on their teams. Seventeen-year-old Shannon Elliot from Pittsburgh, Pennsylvania, has been swimming competitively for thirteen years. The past two years she has been state champion in the 200-yard Freestyle. Last year, she placed second in the 500 Freestyle. Shannon writes of her relationship with her coach:

> Even if he does have insatiable expectations of his swimmers and strenuously trains them like no other, I would not trade him for anyone. He helps me learn to make decisions, handle peer pressure and cope with my personal problems. He handles my uncompromising moods, my opinionated disposition and my unwavering stubbornness. Not only

> does he tolerate me, but he is making me a better person. We have our fair share of disagreements and fights, but we also experience victory and success together. I spend more time with this person, during the swim season, than I do with my parents. As I look at my state medals, framed and hanging on the wall, they represent Corky Semler, my swim coach, role model and second father....
>
> He is able to motivate teenagers through reason, not fear. He is also able to instill discipline while having fun.... Corky also teaches me to be fair and not to judge others too quickly.... He has also made me realize I need to balance work and fun.

Another pressure that is inherent in sports is the intensity of competition. It is expected between teams—after all, that's what makes a game. But Lisa Hope Barclay, age sixteen, from Brownsville, Oregon, found herself face-to-face with an unusual circumstance, another sort of competition she was not prepared for:

> ... I participate in a sport called BMX (Bicycle Motorcross.) I started BMX at the early age of 7 in 1985. My nickname at the track was "Sleeper." I was called this because I would wait until the last half of the track to make my move.
>
> In my early years of racing BMX, I struggled to beat my twin sister, Lori.... I had a hard time racing against my sister all of the time because she usually won. She is younger than me but started racing 4 months earlier than me. The weird thing about this is at Nationals I would usually beat Lori. When it came to the pressure, I could handle it better.
>
> One Saturday my sister and I were racing in Corvallis Indoor. We both raced for the same team at this time, so we were more competitive than ever. Going into the main event, I had first sewn up. To get second, I had to finish third. The girl in third was very slow. There was no way I could finish third! When we were staging up to the gate my sister, Lori, said that she wished she would win because she is one of the four on the team sheet. For our team to get first over all, she needed to get first. I felt bad (in my mind I wanted our team to finish first, first to me was no big deal) ... and gave up the race.
>
> Our team got first that night, but got accused of cheating to get our team to win. I lied and said that my ankle hurt because of a crash earlier in the week. One other team tried to fight us, and I turned on the tears so they would think that it really hurt. To this very day you are the only person I have told this to. It was one of the greatest pressures of my life.

Joan J. Ryoo, an eighteen-year-old Korean-American, is now on the varsity water polo team at Harvard University. For many years, she swam competitively, and won, by focusing only on herself:

> ... By the fourth meet of the season, I had learned the art of seclusion in a crowd, of separating myself from the clamor and excitement of swim competitions by building walls so thick and soundproof, only the gun of the referee could penetrate the woven silence of my universe. *Inside, it was only me and the race ahead....*
>
> However, little did I realize that with all I gained in erecting psychological partitions, I also lost group support and cut off the encouragement I could offer my fellow swimmers, two cherished advantages of participating in team sports. Fortunately, those artificial barriers—which shut out more than they let in—were to be broken early on, but not without the help of a complete stranger.

At one meet, a friendly girl swimming in the lane next to Joan smiled and reached out to her. Joan relates that the girl's charm and warmth broke through her barriers of seclusion:

> ... Even after such a lovely demonstration of genuine goodwill, the old and stereotypic ideas surrounding athletic competition did not fail to surface. This time, though, I looked at the principles a little differently, began to question the validity and value of having to always win, win, win, or of constantly viewing the opponents as "the enemy." For as much as I'm ashamed to say it, I'll admit that I blindly accepted those notions in concept, though I may not have had the guts or natural talent to put those "ideals" fully into practice. Of course, it was to the strange and wonderful girl next to me that I owed this gradual awakening, and exhausted though I was at the end of the race, I was still quite eager to talk to her....

And they did talk, the girl being particularly complimentary of Joan's skills, as Joan beat her, though only by a "hair's breadth." It was unmistakable that this was a turning point in Joan's life, one that set off a chain reaction of reexamination and transformation of previous beliefs.

> Everyone deserves a measure of respect and trust, and the best way to keep an atmosphere of good faith in competition is while we're practicing and competing. Thus, all of a sudden, I also figured out that I was not alone, that I belonged on a team who put sportsmanly ideals into action everyday by supporting each other, building team camaraderie, developing good rapport—all things which can be extended to the community at large.

I heard from many girls like Joan that teamwork has changed their view of living in the world. The support and camaraderie they experience builds and sturdy foundation for relationships.

> One learns to support a teammate like a friend, a sister, a brother. Teammates lean on one another for support and are always there to back each other up. They pull together to achieve a common goal. As a team, we learned not only skills, but determination, intensity and desire to succeed. We played with our bodies, our minds, our hearts and our souls. We felt that as long as we stayed together we could conquer the world.... I pity my children because I have this feeling that I'll talk about my high school soccer team like old men do war stories....
>
> —Heather Ehrman

Throughout the Jocks' writings, I discovered another attribute that has changed many girls' points of view, like seventeen-year-old Anette Pham, from Colonia, New Jersey:

> She said that we had to be strong—to assert ourselves on the court. After all, basketball is a contact sport and the most successful team is the team that outhustles the other team and remains aggressive throughout the entire thirty-two minutes. Consequently, being assertive on and off the court is my key to success.

Yet is this quality just another pressure that is imposed on a girl? Fourteen-year-old Ronee Cochrane from Princeton, Idaho, seems to think so:

> "BE AGGRESSIVE"
>
> I would describe myself as a tall, quiet A student that is very easy-going and maybe even too nice. "What exactly do you mean?" you might ask. Well, put in more detail, I am a girl that may say "sorry" when she is tripped and just smiles when she is upset. A girl that lets people take advantage of her easy-going nature....
>
> Basketball is a sport that I have played and enjoyed since the fifth grade. I love the thrill of making a point, assisting in a great play, or getting compliments from the crowd, team, or coach. The one thing that I thoroughly hate about basketball is the phrase that I constantly hear: "be aggressive." I hear it from every coach I ever had, the crowd, team, and my family. When I come on and off of the court I hear the coach say, "You've got to get aggressive, get mean. Throw some elbows!" My only response is the nodding of my head and a short "O.K." This is my response on the outside, but in the inside I am shouting wildly, "I'm trying! What exactly do I have to do to fit 'aggressive'? Is there somewhere that I can get a set of instructions?"
>
> The reason that "aggressive" is such a hateful word in my eyes, is because I don't feel that I will ever learn how. I don't believe that I will ever find it in me. I was born to be generous, giving, and nice, not aggressive and mean; not even on the court.

Perhaps the intention behind the idea of being aggressive is to experience one's power and alleviate fear. In Hannah's story, told through her hockey stick, she expands this notion:

> ... On the outside she seems confident, ready, but on the inside she's unsure, terrified of making a mistake. Then the ball is passing the links, passing the halfbacks, heading straight for us. The tension is mounting, can she handle the pressure? She's frozen in place, fear emanating from her entire body. Her hands are slippery now. She shakes her head slightly, as if to shake off the fear, then runs towards the ball, all terror gone, because it has to be. We've worked too hard for this moment to let that little round ball go by....

And coxswain Jessica Smith battles with fear and uncertainty as well:

> ... I made some excuse to my friend and went up to my room and burst into tears. Later that day we were leaving for Boston and what was I doing? Crying! Me, tell the big, mean rowers what to do? Me, motivate them and soothe their fears and tell them there was nothing to worry about and smile blithely when I was scared shitless? Me, steer us around a tricky race course with a number of turns, including one at the notorious Weeks Bridge where, if navigated incorrectly, one could either crash the boat into the bridge or run aground because the river made a ninety-degree turn? No way!

In the face of fear many girls, like seventeen-year-old Melani Lowman from Sidney, Montana, push through with determination. Her story is reminiscent of surfer Kelly who competed in Tahiti, despite feeling quite sick and having her feet all cut up:

> ... Having a fractured foot the last part of the track season, it was an accomplishment in itself to be competing at State. Fighting my pain and tears I set a new Montana State record in the triple jump, but it was recorded as wind-aided (the jump was not my personal best so my goal is to break that record with my personal best jump.) I also went on to place in the long jump and the 1600m relay. Eve though I am still suffering from a fractured bone and the doctors say it was a mistake to compete, I wouldn't have had it any other way. For myself it was a great challenge because I knew I had enough courage and pride to compete....

The bravery displayed by the following group of girls is inspiring. Proficient in a variety of sports, these athletes refuse to let anything, including physical disability, stop them.

There are many sports organizations for the disabled. According to NHS (National Handicapped Sports), of the 60,000 who participate in sports programs, 20 percent are women.

> As the recess bell rang, the large doors burst open with shrieks of delight from the school children. Children ran to the yellow diamond in anticipation of the daily kick-ball game. One by one the children were picked by the two opposing sides, until only two girls remained standing on the yellow line; both wishing to be picked before the other; but the little girl left over was the one who had the brace....

That girl was Julie Wolfe from Lafayette, Indiana, who, despite having to wear a brace from the effects of cerebral palsy and still having to endure periodic operations to correct the problems with her right leg, has gone on to become the athlete representative in the board of directors for the United Cerebral Palsy Athletic Association. She broke eight national records, winning eight gold medals in various swimming events at the 1994 USCPAA National Championship Games. Julie competed in the 1988 Paralympic games in Seoul, South Korea, and the '92 Paralympics in Barcelona.

> ... I had never before realized the intensity required of an Olympic athlete. I began a rigorous training regimen full of many challenges. I was training for victory. As each day passed my focus was to stand on the gold medal platform and hear the national anthem as I felt the gold medal being placed around my neck. Gone were the days of skipping practice to be with my friends; I knew I had taken on a responsibility—to win a gold in Seoul for my country.... The day before my trip began, I was surprised by a pep rally in my honor. The day had finally arrived when handicapped people were praised, not pitied. My dreams had come true....

Julie had the time of her life in Seoul, signing autographs, being treated like a star, swimming in the same pool where world record holders Matt Biondi and Janet Evans had won just two weeks earlier. To the Korean people, Julie was an American hero.

Yet at the last minute, her events were canceled. Paralympic rule requires that at least four countries be represented in each event, and in Julie's events, only three countries had competitors. Julie never had the opportunity even to try to realize her dream of the gold medal being placed around her neck. She came home disappointed, but not daunted:

> I gained the confidence I lost as a child. I felt whole in Korea. Growing up I felt as if a part of me was missing. The part that needed to know if I was good athletically compared to people with a similar degree of disability. I had to prove to the world that I don't have to be picked last. It made me realize I was special ... and it is not in a negative way.

Julie finally was able to compete in the 1992 games in Barcelona, and placed sixth, eighth, tenth, and twelfth in various events. She is currently training for the world championships in Malta, and holds two world records: one in the 100 Freestyle and one in the 400 Freestyle.

Growing up with a rare congenital heart defect that nearly killed her, at the age of eleven Danielle Cafferata finally received a heart transplant. Shortly thereafter, due to a degenerative disease that was affecting her eyesight, Danielle lost her vision entirely, as well as a portion of her hearing. She now must wear hearing aids. With courage and determination, Danielle, now eighteen, has only grown stronger, and more accomplished:

> Since my heart transplant and knowing how close I was to not being here at all, I decided to try whatever I can in life. One month after my heart transplant, I competed in the Braille Olympics being able to run for the very first time in my life without getting tired. Since then, I've competed in other track and field events for the blind and visually impaired.... Another sport I recently tried was downhill skiing. Wow! What an experience, although I wasn't so sure at first that I would like it. But being the way that I am, I am always willing to give something a try! ... I hope some of my life story can help other girls who might just be a little afraid of taking a chance to fulfill their dreams. Believe me I'm going to continue to fill mine.

Beating the odds and overcoming physical and other limitations, striving for and achieving goals, feeling camaraderie and forming friendships through teamwork, and simply experiencing the joy of competing and playing—these are reasons why girls play sports.

And despite the hardships many female athletes endure, it is clear that girls will continue to be "Willing to Dream":

> The Dream: Conquer and Defeat
> My hard work will carry me to my destination
> while my determination will fight my battle
> when I cry out, "I can't do it!"
> I slowly begin to drown in that dreadful word:
> self-doubt.
> But, I must protect what I cherish
> So, my hope will act as Superwoman
> and throw me a life jacket before I drown.
> I desperately grab for it
> so I can keep my dream alive.
> Whether I win or lose this scary battle
> I don't think it really matters
> what matters is that I was willing to dream.
>
> —Danielle Purfey

And there are those who might not have survived if not for athletics—those who were nurtured and cared for by sports. Kelo R. Le'Igiro, age fifteen, from

North Little Rock, Arkansas, is one such girl. Here is an excerpt from her piece "Yes, I've Felt All This":

> … Some say I don't have a lot to be thankful for. All my life people have come and gone stripping parts of my heart away from me as they chose new paths. Paths on which I would not stand. But out of all these memories, all the hate and unforgiving, all the sadness and hurt, there was something. Something that pulled me through each time. Then, I didn't know exactly what it was or how much it meant to me. But now I understand, grown up enough I can grasp the idea.
>
> It wasn't voluntary. My mom got me started and everytime made me finish. At first it was only one lap around lake #3. Only .9 mile once everyday. Then after a while it was three laps; 2.7 miles everyday. The family would pile in the car, go to the lake and run, everyday. Some faster than others, some even walking, but it always got done. Everyday until my older brother, Brandon, moved out. Meredith and Brent quit but I ran even more. It was because Brandon had been accused of selling and using drugs. Misunderstandings and anger were plentiful in my thoughts.
>
> Yes, I've felt all this.
>
> I ran for help concentrating, trying to understand. I was too young, I didn't know. Mom and I ran. We ran and ran. That was the only thing we could do to escape: run and pretend it never happened or was not happening. Mom understood, but I couldn't. Brandon was my big brother, the guy I was supposed to try to make myself be like. I was supposed to grow into his life with admiration, respect and adoration. Trying to understand, I ran more. I ran my first half marathon the day after I turned twelve in 2 hours and twenty minutes. Of course Mom ran with me. Victory, accomplishment, relief.
>
> Yes. I've felt all this….

Kelo's challenges continued as her sister, whom she adored, walked out, never to return. She describes her sister: "When my siblings fought in such rages, she would hide me away under the sink to protect me from their fury. She was my hiding place, my first and last resort, my childhood Jesus."

Once again, running was an essential element in Kelo's finding escape and solace.

> … All my life I've turned to writing, to running and to God to solve everything. Writing changed my world to the way I wanted it, running relieved me from my deepest pressures, and God moved it all out of my way so I could achieve my highest goals, to be all I could be.

Happiness, despair, victory, loss, fulfillment, emptiness, and the breath of God across my face.

Yes, I have felt all this.

56. Summer Wood, "Freedom of 'Choice': Parsing the Word that Defined a Generation," from *Bitch* Magazine

Excerpts from "Freedom of Choice: Parsing the Word that Defined a Generation," by Summer Wood, published in *Bitch,* No. 24 (Spring 2004). Reprinted with permission.

In this essay, Wood discusses how ideas about "choice" have affected the third-wave feminist movement for better and worse, where the rhetoric of choice most powerfully emerged. Intersections between ideas about "choice," consumer culture, and feminism have often functioned to make feminism complicit in practices that might otherwise be questionable, such as the idea that the "choice" to obtain cosmetic surgery is a feminist act. The way "choice" in consumer practices overlaps with the idea of "choice" in reproductive rights has trivialized the struggle for reproductive rights. "Choice" also sometimes functions as a mask for situations in which there is actually little choice.

"You can bake your cake and eat it, too!" declares Julia Roberts, playing bohemian Wellesley art-history professor Katherine Watson in the period chick flick *Mona Lisa Smile*. She eagerly proffers an armful of law-school applications, standing on the doorstep of the imposingly tony house where Joan (played by Julia Stiles), one of her best students, resides. But it's too late, Joan replies. She has eloped, and now that she has her M.R.S., she won't be getting that law degree after all. "This is my choice," she says earnestly, but her character, like most of the others in the film, is written so flatly that it's impossible to tell whether we're supposed to believe her. The filmmakers clearly meant for women in the audience to breathe a sigh as we watched Roberts's signature grin crumble on hearing the news—a sigh of pity for those poor, repressed Wellesley girls, and a sigh of relief that women today are free of such antiquated dilemmas as having to choose between work and family.

Fast-forward 50 years, however, and the media is full of stories of real-life Joans: intelligent, ambitious women, educated at the country's top schools, trading in their M.B.A.s and Ph.D.s for SUVs with car seats. Sylvia Ann Hewlett claimed to have revealed an epidemic of "creeping nonchoice" in her much-publicized 2002 book, *Creating a Life: Professional Women and the Quest for Children*, while Lisa Belkin last year tagged a related trend "The Opt-Out Revolution" in a *New York Times Magazine* cover story. While Hewlett profiles high-powered women who "chose" to put their careers first and postpone childbearing, only to find out their ovaries hadn't gotten the memo, Belkin focuses on impeccably credentialed younger women preempting the challenges of balancing career and family by dropping out of the rat race soon after it begins.

Neither writer bothers to examine the ways in which decisions to work or stay home are rarely made solely as a function of free will, but rather are swayed by underlying socioeconomic forces. But both Hewlett's book and Belkin's article do illustrate something crucial—namely, the deep, complex, and uneasy relationship between the ideology of feminism and the word "choice."

The significance of "choice" in the feminist lexicon has fluctuated over time and with the various priorities of feminist movements, but for the past 30 years, it has been most strongly associated with abortion rights. Indeed, since the mid-'80s, "choice" has all but eclipsed "abortion" in the ongoing discourse about reproductive rights. In *Beggars and Choosers: How the Politics of Choice Shapes Adoption, Abortion, and Welfare in the United States*, historian Rickie Solinger traces the evolution of "choice" in the context of reproductive rights back to Mother's Day, 1969, when the National Abortion Rights Action League (recently renamed NARAL Pro-Choice America) held its first national action, calling it Children by Choice. These rallies gave NARAL an opportunity to market-test "choice" as the movement's new watchword. After Justice Harry Blackmun repeatedly referred to abortion as "this choice" in his majority opinion in *Roe v. Wade*, writes Solinger, choice was cemented as "the way liberal and mainstream feminists could talk about abortion without mentioning the 'A-word.'" Wary of alienating moderate supporters by claiming that women had an absolute right to abortion, movement leaders adopted a more pragmatic rhetorical strategy: "Many people believed that 'choice'—a term that evoked women shoppers selecting among options in the marketplace—would be an easier sell," writes Solinger.

Substituting "choice" for "rights" as both a legal framework and a common language indeed proved successful in attracting some libertarians and conservatives to vote for the "pro-choice" position in numerous state-level abortion contests during the '80s. Because "choice" is, in essence, an empty word, people with vastly divergent political viewpoints can be united under its banner. In retrospect, this is both the word's greatest strength and its ultimate weakness. As various constituencies brought their own political prerogatives and definitions of "choice" to the negotiating table, parents, physicians, husbands, boyfriends, and religious leaders all came to be included as rightful participants in making the abortion choice, significantly weakening the idea that women have a right to make this decision on their own. Solinger identifies the linguistic shift from abortion rights to "the individualistic, marketplace term 'choice'" as deeply problematic, on both a philosophical and a practical level.

The word's primacy in the arena of reproductive rights has slowly caused the phrase "It's my choice" to become synonymous with "It's a feminist thing to do"—or, perhaps more precisely, "It is anti-feminist to criticize my decision." The result has been a rapid depoliticizing of the term and an often misguided application of feminist ideology to consumer imperatives, invoked not only for the right to decide whether to terminate a pregnancy, but also for the right to buy all manner of products marketed to women, from cigarettes to antidepressants to diet frozen pizzas. It seems that if you can slap a purple or pink label that says "for women" on a product, choosing to buy it must be a feminist act.

The marriage of convenience between feminist rhetoric and the language of purchasing power has caused the word "choice" to lose steam even in areas where its nonreproductive use once resonated. When *Sex and the City*'s Charlotte decided to quit her job a few seasons back, for instance, she summoned feminism in her defense: "The women's movement is supposed to be all about choice, and if I choose to quit my job, that is my choice," she tells a disgruntled Miranda, who's busy getting ready for work. After suggesting that Charlotte's "choice" to drop out of the workforce has been unduly influenced by her then-husband, Trey, Miranda hangs up on Charlotte, leaving her shouting, "I choose my choice, I choose my choice," over and over, as if to convince herself that she really does.

Elsewhere in American culture, one of the newest, and arguably most controversial, intersections between "choice," consumer culture, and feminism is the argument that undergoing cosmetic surgery can be a feminist exercise. The leading proponent of this theory is Kathy Davis, a women's studies lecturer at the University of Utrecht in the Netherlands. In *Embodied Practices: Feminist Perspectives on the Body*, Davis decries feminist critiques of plastic surgery, contending that "the paternalistic argument against choice rests on the assumption that women who want cosmetic surgery need to be protected—from themselves (their narcissistic desire for beauty) or from undue influence from others."

For many young feminists, "choice" has become the very definition of feminism itself—illustrated by the standard-bearing right to choose abortion and supported by the ever-advertised notion that they have choice in everything else in life as well. The cult of choice consumerism wills us to believe that women can get everything we want out of life, as long as we make the right choices along the way—from the cereal we eat in the morning to the moisturizer we use at night, and the universe of daily decisions, mundane and profound, that confront us in between. But when things fall apart, as they tend to do from time to time, women's individual choices are always to blame. "If only I had purchased that new personal digital assistant, it would somehow have given me the superhuman power to be in two places at once," we're meant to say, and vow to be more compliant consumers next time.

However, at a time when the language of choice is at an all-time popular high, when it comes to abortion, young women may have the least choice of all, especially if they are minors residing in one of the 33 states requiring the consent of at least one parent in order to undergo the procedure. Some reproductive-rights activists have suggested that third-wavers don't turn out in large numbers at the polls—only 52 percent voted in the 2000 presidential election—because they've become complacent about the right to choose their foremothers worked so hard to win.

Though NARAL Pro-Choice America is now courting young women with a web-based "Generation Pro-Choice" campaign featuring the specter of an overturned *Roe* if Bush is elected for a second term, the current administration's opponents have paid little attention to issues affecting women's other life choices, from the wage gap, healthcare, and education access to the dearth of quality, affordable childcare or federal policies designed to ease the burdens often faced by working parents of either sex. While paying lip service to "choice" in its narrowest definition—i.e., preserving *Roe*—politicians donning the pro-choice mantle continue to neglect the full significance of choice in women's lives, and the underlying social and economic conditions that constrain or empower us to do much more than choose whether to bake a cake, eat it, or both.

Such an uncritical language of choice doesn't even work in the movies: At the end of *Mona Lisa Smile*, Katherine Watson has little to show for the choices she makes—no tenure-track job at Wellesley, and no guy, either (assuming, as this is Hollywood, that she was supposed to desire both). The fact that Katherine chooses to leave Wellesley—whether motivated by her pedagogical clashes with older female faculty, her reluctance to become part of the elite academic establishment, or having her heart bruised by the swarthy Italian professor who turns out to be from New Jersey—plays like a pretty unhappy ending for a character who has spent the past two hours trying to convince her students that, at last, women really can have it all.

57. Riki Wilchins, "Queerer Bodies: When I Was in Gender and You Were the Main Drag," from *GenderQueer: Voices from beyond the Sexual Binary*

Excerpts from Riki Wilchins, "Queerer Bodies," published in *GenderQueer: Voices from beyond the Sexual Binary,* Joan Nestle, Clare Howell, and Riki Wilchins, eds. (Los Angeles: Alyson Publications, 2002), 33–44. Reprinted with permission.

This is an important essay to third-wave thinking and an example of third-wave thinking in its demonstration of how gender, the categories of masculine and feminine, cannot be simply opposed. Wilchins argues that "the way we think about bodies needs to be changed." Many bodies and people simply do not fit the language of "male" and "female," and each person, rather than accepting reductive social labels, needs to think beyond "gender as a system of language that shapes our experience of our bodies."

Somewhere inside yourself, you just know.
—nontransgendered lesbian explaining how she knows she's a woman

Inside, I just know.
—transgendered lesbian explaining how she knows she's a woman

Nothing in man—not even his body—is sufficiently stable to serve as the basis for self-recognition, or for understanding other men.
—Michel Foucault, presumably explaining how he doesn't know if he's a man or a woman, *Language, Counter-Memory, and Practice*, 1997

When it comes to gender, each of us, in our own private way, is an implicit philosopher. For instance, you probably believe that your body is male or female, that you are gay or straight (or bi), that feminism is distinct from gay rights, that physical sex is genetic but gender learned and that sexual orientation is distinct from other kinds of gendered behavior. These beliefs probably feel to you like "just common sense." But that is only because philosophical beliefs, aged in the keg, and widely enough accepted, are promoted to common sense. None of these concepts is just "out there." We think them because we think about bodies and the world in very particular ways. If you spoke about these thoughts a lot, people would call you a theorist, and if you spoke about really big thoughts, people would call you a bigamist.

In this section, I want to encourage you to think those big thoughts. This is an anthology of personal narratives written by some very exceptional people, often living very painful lives, and I hope it's accessible to readers on an emotional level. But that's not all. While the exceptionalism and the pain are important, for me, they are not the point of this book. The real importance lies in how these writers' lives show that the ways we think about bodies is broken, is frequently oppressive, and needs to be changed.

And I don't just mean changed in the sense of being more tolerant and inclusive, although that is important. Nor do I mean better ways of thinking about gender, although that's important too. I mean changed in the largest sense: revising how we think about things like language and meaning, truth and difference, knowledge and power. Especially the political effects of these things on people, when they suppress individual experience, discourage difference, and prevent new forms of knowledge from emerging.

These are big themes. But of all the things we know in the world, the most fundamental is our bodies. If the ways we have of knowing don't work there, I can see only two conclusions: Either these are bodies that have "failed" or the ways we have of knowing about them have failed—and, by extension, the ways we have of knowing about all bodies and many other things have failed as well.

These stories point the way to a new kind of freedom. Not an ultimate freedom, because I doubt that exists, but a different kind of freedom nonetheless. Whatever we are, whatever that fuzzy thing called "self" may be, I think these stories point to the way toward being more of that self in a deeper and fuller sort of way.

Every model of reality has margins where it begins to run out of explanatory steam, where we can see its problems and limitations. This anthology is about the people at those margins and thus about those who have found their bodies the target of discrimination because they transcended narrow stereotypes, because they were perceived as too old, young, black, short, fat, disabled, deaf, hairy, ill, butch, flamboyant, or any of a thousand other things. In short, this is about all of us.

We're not the ones who are broken. It's the model that's broken. The model of Western thought about bodies itself, and much more besides. So, welcome to my breakdown.

A FLUID ANALOGY

What is knowledge? Consider something simple and familiar: bodily fluids. We'll check someplace objective and scientific, perhaps several medical textbooks.

We begin with menstrual blood. "Menstruation entails the discharge from the body of a couple of teaspoons of lukewarm fluid. This discharge occurs about once a month for a number of years, and women's bodies lose perhaps 500 gametes slowly over about 40 years."

As a bodily fluid, menstrual blood is a loser. It symbolizes—there's no kind way to say this—waste, weakness, loss, passivity—all the general ills associated with a feminine disposition. Young girls are often properly appalled to learn this, spending hours staring in shamed silence at their bodies, imagining all the little potential human beings leaking out, perhaps even at that very moment.

We move on to ejaculation. "Ejaculation entails the discharge from the body of a couple of teaspoons of lukewarm fluid. This discharge occurs—oh, up to five times a day it seems—for a number of years. Men's bodies lose perhaps two gazillion (the number is imprecise here) gametes each time: potential little human beings sprayed onto the carpet, handkerchiefs, rolled pieces of liver, and hollowed-out pumpkins."

As a bodily fluid, semen is the Man. It symbolizes—there's no unkind way to say this—dominance, strength, activity, vitality, potency—all the general benefits associated with a masculine disposition. Young boys are often properly proud to learn this, spending hours in rapt contemplation of their own pubescent, potent crotches.

"WITH A CAPITAL P/AND THAT RHYMES WITH T/AND THAT STANDS FOR ..."

Bodies bear an enormous weight of cultural meaning. While acknowledging that bodies are "really there," one can reasonably question the meanings we give them. Anything but the barest facts—weight, mass, height—seems to go well beyond knowledge into the politics of meaning. I don't mean politics here with a capital P, as in civil rights and political parties. I mean "small p" politics: the power to say and track and even control different things about bodies.

For instance, when I shaved my legs and put on my first dress, everyone wondered what it meant. When I yearned for surgery, everyone thought it meant I was crazy. I thought it meant I really wanted to wear a dress and have a more feminine body. There wasn't anything else to know, any more than there was something to know about my inexhaustible craving for chocolate.

While my wearing dresses has resulted in my being diagnosed with a mental illness (gender identity disorder), it never occurred to anyone to ask whether my choco-cravings constituted a mental disorder, because we don't regulate or politicize attraction to chocolate. If we did, not doubt the nation's therapy couches would be filled with "cross-chocolaters," disgorging their deepest, darkest, semisweet secrets. ("And you were how old when *your mother* gave you your first piece of chocolate? Well! First, let's try something we call 'behavioral therapy.' Just put your foot in this warm clamp here, hold on to this electrode while I plug in your chair, and we'll watch some *nice* pictures of chocolate together.")

CASHING IN ON KNOWLEDGE IN A DIFFERENT REGISTER

Maybe that seems silly. But not as silly when you consider that while our taste for specific foods passes without comment, our taste in specific bodies and pleasures seldom does. People immediately start asking what it means.

Why do men want to wear women's clothes? Why would a femme, who could have a "real man," instead want a wife-beater tank-top, strapit-on butch? Why do some men want to become women? The only reason to track such things about bodies as their sex, genders, and desires is because we want to *do* something with them. Knowledge about bodies does not stand passively by, awaiting discovery by an objective and dispassionate Science.

Beyond measurable facts, knowledge about bodies is something we create. We go looking for it, and we fashion it in ways that respond to cultural needs and aims. We create the idea of binary genders because it marks something we want to track and control about bodies' appearance and behavior. We create gender identity disorders (GIDs) because we want to control sex and discourage the desire to change the body's sexual characteristics. We create the knowledge of sexual orientation and study it exhaustively because we want to know and control the individual's capacity to contribute to reproduction. There is not bright-line separation here between knowledge and politics. Knowledge marches to the beat of power. Specific kinds of knowledge *about* bodies enable us to exercise specific kinds of power *over* them. Such knowledge is not "disinterested." It is *very* interested, it is purposeful, it has aims.

For instance, when I went in for a nose job, the doctors were agreeable, quick, and friendly. But when I went in for that groin job, my whole life went to hell. Everything came under fire: my upbringing (probably failed), my mother (probably overbearing), my father (probably distant), and the demands of modern manhood (obviously threatening). I'm really a man (I'm still Arnold), finally a woman (but I look like Brooke), basically homo (news to my girlfriend), and actually a transvestite (news to my tailor).

Luckily for me, here come the professionals. Doctors, lawyers, psychiatrists on one hand and theorists, academics, and writers on the other. Not to mention gender's Holy Trinity: Sally, Jerry, and Oprah.

The fact that many of us prefer different bodies, genders or pleasures is clearly knowledge in the same register as the meaning of those bodies, genders and pleasures. In fact, I would go a step further. The propagation of norms for things like pleasure and gender, and the pursuit and categorization of divergence from such norms, are also knowledge in a different register. And the realm in which that knowledge lives is not Science but Politics.

IF YOU'RE NOT PART OF THE PROBLEM, YOU'RE NOT PART OF THE SOLUTION

> Prefer what is positive and multiple: difference over uniformity, flows over unities, mobile arrangements over systems. Believe that what is productive is not sedentary but nomadic.
>
> —Michel Foucault, *Language, Counter-Memory, and Practice*, 1977

There is a huge and ongoing current critique of Western knowledge—sometimes called "postmodernism"—that is questioning what we know, how we know it, and what effect it has on those we know it about. And of all the things we know, indeed feel we *must* know, none is more fundamental than our own bodies. If that knowledge is showing cracks, then what else might be faulty as well? It is this nexus—the models of how we think and the problems posed by bodies that don't fit the model—that has led to the explosion of interest in genderqueerness and "gender studies."

Whenever I wanted to feel feminine, I couldn't because I was a boy, too tall, too wide-shouldered, not "real." Later, when I sometimes wanted to feel masculine, I couldn't because I had breasts, I was too curvy, I was no longer a "real" man. And when I wanted to feel something that was neither—well, that was impossible. It doesn't matter that some of these were things other people said about me and others things I said silently to myself. What matters is that the way in which we think—and especially the way we "think the body"—has too often become an off-the rack, one-size-fits-all approach. One that favors that which is universal, known, stable, and similar. But my experience of my body and my place in the world was exactly the opposite: mobile, private, small, often unique, and usually unknown. These are places familiar to many people on knowledge's margins where many of us wish to go. And these stories, standing just beyond the sexual binary, point a way.

TRUTH CORRUPTS, ABSOLUTE TRUTH CORRUPTS ABSOLUTELY

> "Let's assume you're right ..."
>
> "No, let's not assume I'm right. Let's assume there are lots of different 'rights' out there and this is just one of them."
>
> —exchange in a gender seminar

> The philosophical tradition, at least from Plato on, has always favored the concept of the same; i.e., the aim of philosophical thought has been to reveal the essential characteristics that two things hold in common.
>
> —Newton Garver, *Wittgenstein and Derrida*, 1994

Why are we so frightened of difference and multiplicity? Perhaps it is the Western belief in the One True God? Strength, goodness, and truth are properties of our God's oneness. And all those tribes with multiple gods, tribes that were slaughtered by the ancient Hebrews, must have been weak, false, evil, and duplicitous.

Probably we fear that the alternative to the universal is not plurality but an endless abyss, a chaos where no person's knowing is any more (or less) right than any other's. And if all this reminds you of the revolt against queer bodies as well as the "threat" of multiculturalism, then go to the front of the class.

Some cultures accommodate, even exalt, difference. Yet in the West we pursue unity, we believe in singularity, we worship not only our God but final Truths. If it's not true somewhere, then it's not really true. There is no room for what is private or unique. To seek the Truth—always capital T—is to seek what is universal and perfect.

Unfortunately, such an approach is a kind of intellectual fascism that squeezes out individual truths. As the exchange quoted above illustrates, valuing of difference can cause real confusion in my presentations.

Good modernists that they are, my students assume that there is a (single) right answer about things like gender and the meaning of bodies. Our job is arguing over the right one. It's a winner-take-all approach to knowledge. But where gender and meaning is concerned, there are lots of little truths. The way you understand your hips, your chest, your hair. How you feel when your lover holds you, gets on top, makes you come. The rush when you dress up, dress down, put on silk or leather. These are immensely small and private experiences. They are among our most intimate experiences of ourselves in the world. And they are precisely what is lost when we propound and pursue singular and monolithic Truths about bodies, gender, and desire.

We have "centered" all such knowledge over a binary of masculine/feminine. Body hair must mean masculine. Breasts must be feminine and passive. Hips are maternal, muscles masculine. An erect clitoris is vulnerable, an erect penis is commanding and strong. We need to de-center knowledge about the body. We need to allow other kinds of meanings to emerge, and other experiences of the body. We need room to find truths—always small t—that resonate with ourselves. To do this, many of us will need to transcend and transgress the kinds of knowledge that are out there. But that is how things change. That's why if you're not part of the problem, you're not part of the solution.

ONE TRUTH WITH NO TRIMMINGS, PLEASE

Counseling, NOT Cutting! Get Your Scalpels Off Our Bodies!
—Hermaphrodites With Attitude poster

Knowledge is not made for understanding; it is made for cutting.
—Michel Foucault, *Language, Counter-Memory, and Practice*, 1977

There is nothing abstract abut the power that sciences and theories have to act

materially and actually upon our bodies and our minds ...
—Monique Wittig, *The Straight Mind*, 1992

If multiplicity is a pinging under the hood, a "noise" in the system waiting to be found and fixed, then there's no louder *ping* than one that disrupts two perfect and complementary opposite sexes. Male and female are Nature's way, our highest physical Truth. But what if Nature doesn't oblige? What if She exasperates us by producing bodies that aren't "natural?" What if that pinging under the hood is the sound of genderqueer bodies that just ... don't ... fit?

I am speaking, of course, of intersexed infants. Such children, who are not clearly male or female, occur in about one in every 2,000 births. Because anything that is not male or female is not a true sex, we pronounce them "abnormal," fit them legally into male or female, and fit them physically into boy or girl by cutting them up at the rate of about five every day. Thus are "natural" males and females maintained. In the aphorism of the Intersex Society's Cheryl Chase, intersex is the sex that can't exist. Because by definition, every child must be male or female. Inside every intersex infant is a real boy or girl just waiting to come out.

For instance, in one segment of *Primetime*, a pediatrician showed color slides of intersex genitals while Diane Sawyer tried to guess their "real sex": That surreal change went something like this:

DS: That's a male, right?
Doctor: Nope. A female. And this one?
DS: A female.
Doctor: No. A male.
DS: Now, this is surely a male. That looks like a penis.
Doctor: Sorry, another female. This one?
DS: Female?
Doctor: Male.
DS: ***Shee-it!***

The surgeon's job is figuring out which sex the child really is "underneath" whatever sex they "appear" and to surgically restore them to what Nature intended. If Nature produces some kids that aren't "natural," well, even Nature stops now and then to down a brewski. Such doctors are not malicious or destructive. In fact, they are anything but. They are usually dedicated physicians and surgeons who are doing what they see as compassionate surgery for little, if any, fee.

But it is part of the peculiar tyranny of our taste for perfect and singular Truths that difference cannot be ignored but must be stamped out and made to fit the model. If the model and the body disagree, it is the body that must give way. And this is the case whether it's intersexed infants, cross-dressing teens, or genderqueer adults.

IT'S ALWAYS THE SAME MOVIE IF YOU DON'T CHANGE THE REALS

Part of the problem of applying notions of truth to the body is that lurking in the background is always the idea of what is real and authentic. Now, since I keep getting called "sir" these days, maybe I should create a whole new category called M-to-F-to-M, where I finally get to be Real:

You know you're a real M-to-F-to-M when...

- Your mother still calls you "Richard."
- You tell your boss you're transexual and he asks, "Which way did you go?"
- You look at your girlfriend's naked butt and wish you had a good strap-on.
- Your lesbian girlfriend looks at your naked crotch and wishes you had a good strap-on.

We're back to different orders of knowledge here. What can it mean to say that my sister's femininity is real but that of a drag queen, a cross-dresser, an effeminate little boy, or an M-to-F is not? Why do we say that the masculinity of a Sly Stallone is real but that of an F-to-M, a stone butch, or a woman bodybuilder is not?

This kind of knowledge is still politics going in drag. It's about power. By creating notions of realness and dividing bodies along a binary of real/false, bodies like mine are kept disempowered. And indeed, in places as diverse as my last job, the Michigan Womyn's Music Festival, my local women's events house in Miami, and the next women's room I have to use, I run smack up against the Real. Realness is not only about naturalness and the distinction between the groin you were born with and the one you bought yourself for Christmas. If gender is about language and meaning, then Realness is also about ownership, about who is allowed to use what meanings legitimately.

For instance, a drag queen is seen as appropriating women's symbols. No matter how convincing the illusion of femininity is, it's still an illusion, because by definition, the femininity is copied, not owned. The same is true for a transexual. No matter how "real" an M-to-F *looks*, she will never *be* Real.

Queer bodies are always defined by gender norms that are constructed in their absence. In fact, such norms are constructed only *by* their absence, because if they were there at the inception, the norm couldn't exist. It would be queered from the start.

It's particularly intriguing to hear charges of Realness coming from lesbians and feminists. Barely 100 years ago, suffragettes were not considered to be "real women" because they shunned passivity to invade men's social prerogatives. Only 40 years ago, lesbians were accused of not being "real women" because they didn't want to marry men and become mothers. Twenty years ago femmes were ridiculed for not being "real lesbians" because they looked like straight women—yet another kind of displacement that ceded femininity to heterosexuality.

And, of course, through it all, any man who slept with or desired the same sex gave up forever the hope of ever being a "real man." In fact, the United States may be the only country in the world where we are so insecure about gender that the words *man* and *woman* have no meaning unless they are preceded by *real*.

Realness circulates in so many different contexts because it is very politically effective. As a form of knowledge, it empowers some bodies, discourages others, and teaches all to stay within the lines.

DOUBLE VISION

"Can I ask you something—are you a man or a woman?"

—attendee at women's conference

"Not always, but sometimes I think I am."

—smart-ass author

What is it about binaries that so captivates our thinking: men/women, gay/straight, M-to-F/F-to-M, white/black, real/artificial, male/female, lesbian/feminist. Whoops ... sorry. Scratch that. If there are more than two genders, it's a cinch that, with our bifocal glasses, we'll never see them. Actually, that's backward. Two-ness is not something "out there" but a product of the way we see. We look for that twoness. Our categories assure that we see it. That's why no matter what gender I do, the only question is "Are you a man or a woman?" because that exhausts all the available possibilities.

When we pick up complex things—like desire or gender—with primitive mental tools like binaries, we lose nuance and multiplicity. Binaries don't give us much information. But then, they're not supposed to.

Quick: What is the meaning of masculinity? Mannish, not feminine, right? What about being straight? That means not being gay.

To say that I'm still really a man is only meaningful in terms of my not being a woman. I am feminine only to the exact degree that I am ... not masculine. I am gay only as much as I'm not straight or to the exact number of songs I've memorized from *The Sound of Music*.

There's really not very much meaning or information circulating here, because with only two possibilities, meaning is confined to what something is not. As a form of thinking, binaries prevent other kinds of information from emerging. That is why no other genders ever appear. Binaries are the black holes of knowledge. Nothing is allowed to escape, so we get the same answers every time.

TWO'S A CROWD

So in binaries all knowledge is broken down into two equal halves, right? Actually, no. Despite the name, binary thinking is not like two, like two halves of an aspirin you break down the middle.

At this point in my life, I have spoken to hundreds of people about my body. Some of them even standing up. In 20 years, not one has asked me anything about "gaining a vagina." If they mentioned my surgery at all, every one said something, often in the form of a crude joke that was related to my losing the big Magic Wand. Now, I'm as impressed with my genitals as the next person. Maybe more so. This is the same sort of question posed to F-to-Ms. It seems no matter what sex it is, it's about male.

At this point, it should surprise no one that binaries are about power, a form of doing politics through language. Binaries create the smallest possible hierarchy of one thing over another. They are not really about two things, but only one.

I'LL SEE IT WHEN I BELIEVE IT WHEN YOU'VE NAMED IT

But is the world really "right here?" Do words really describe the world accurately, exhausting what's "there"? Or are they limited only to what is repeatable and shared, and thus communicable? What about all those messy spaces between words and around their borders? Many of them are populated by our life's more profound experiences. Can language capture why you prefer wearing a nice dress to a new suit, why you want to penetrate instead of being penetrated, why you enjoy having a chest but don't want breasts, how you feel when you're stoned (not that the author has any experience here), or why you like Big Macs but hate sashimi (Japanese for "tastes like shit")?

Indeed, what about all those messy spaces between words like *feminine* and *masculine* and around the borders of words like *male* and *female* that are populated by bodies that don't fit the language? Or any of us whose gender experience confounds words when we transcend the narrow, outdated language of norms?

Words work well for things we can repeat, that we hold in common. What is unique or private is lost to language. But gender is a system of meanings that shapes our experience of bodies. Genderqueerness is by definition unique, private, and profoundly different. That's what makes it "queer." When we force all people to answer to a single language that excludes their experience of themselves in the world, we not only increase their pain and marginalization, we make them accomplices in their own erasure.

It is bad enough to render them silent, even worse to make them speak a lie, worse yet if speaking the lie erases them.

A recurrent theme of this anthology is writers struggling with language used about them and against them, even as it struggles back, twists in their hands, erases their sounds. All of us have those small, private experiences that we can never truly put into words. Our belief in language tells us that they aren't as real, as important, as the things we can say and share.

But I think it's just the opposite. For nowhere are we more ourselves than in those small, private moments when we transcend the common reality, when we experience ourselves in ways that cannot be said or understood or repeated. It is to those moments that we are called, and it is to those moments that we must listen.

58. Kristina Sheryl Wong, "A Big Bad Prank: Broadening the Definition of Asian American Feminist Activism," from *YELL-Oh Girls!: Emerging Voices Explore Culture, Identity, and Growing Up Asian American*

In an essay that describes exemplary third-wave feminist activism that uses the stereotypes and conventions of culture against itself, Wong describes the mock mail-order bride/Asian porn site spoof she created called www.bigbadchinesemama.com. She argues for the need to do the cultural work of "intercepting the overwhelmingly negative presence [Asian women] hold on the web," and to "stop waiting for other people to speak on our behalf and start building the spectrum of voices that actually exists." Wong's essay goes a long way toward that kind of building.

"I am an anti-geisha. I am not Japanese, I am Chinese. There is a difference between the two, you know. I have gigantic size 9 feet, crater zits that break out through my 'silky skin' before and after and during my period, and a loud mouth that screams profanities and insults and my mind. I have a little potbelly, I have an ass that needs to go to the gym. I have hangnails and calluses and blisters and baggage (emotional, historical, and whatever the hell else kind of baggage that is keeping HIM from taking a chance on someone who actually gives a shit about herself).... I am a beautiful animal." (From my "Memoirs of an Anti-Geisha" link on www.bigbadchinesemama.com.)

It all started because I was feeling like I never had ample means to represent myself. College graduation approached, the real world peering over the horizon. What was my college career but a mishmash of theory, half-read books, a dozen hangovers, papers written in one night, a bit of modern dance, and some daydreams about stardom hiding in the back of my head? I worried about my unhealthy fear of computers making me pretty unemployable. And my classes, which were winding down to the final few days, were driving me nuts. Asian American studies, which had previously been enlightening, had become repetitive and numbing. I was getting sick of dissecting Asian women stereotypes with the same classmates quarter after quarter. My senior project was approaching and I winced at the thought of writing one more paper in a night to be seen by only me and my professor, and to find its fate tossed away in a recycling bin. For my senior project, however, the medium was broadened from type and paper; I could create anything—a documentary, exhibition, research paper, or other medium that would reflect a culmination of my studies.

I was surfing through Asian women's Web sites for an Asian women's writing class. I noticed some Asian girl Web sites were bannering, "This is not an Asian porn site!" at the bottom of their splash pages. With the presence of Asian women on the Web probably being 97 percent Asian sex sites, statements like these were made in defiance to the cross-traffic from people who fell upon their sites in search of porn. Then I had an idea. To trick people mid-pursuit. Why not willingly intercept the efforts of nasty men and school them?

I wanted to skip academic rhetoric altogether and just screw with people. I would trick my audience into visiting me by marketing my site as porn! Slip in a little critical theory and social analysis—voilà! I would find the perfect audience, a mix of people who are and are not educated on Asian American and social justice issues, in an accessible, changeable, malleable, though, most of all, humorous format. I wanted to do more with my education. I wanted to spark a dialogue with people who might not choose to go to college or take Asian American studies and women's studies. I wanted to take a stand for myself. I wanted to debate with people, and for people to debate among each other. I chose to use the format of a mail-order-bride Web site as a response to the blatant racism, Western stereotyping of the East, and sexist attitudes that are typical of Asian sex sites.

If you have never been to one of these sites before, let me offer you a preview. First, generate a list of stereotypes for Asian and black women ("black" I say specifically because in the world of porn women are stripped of political identity). For black women, you might enter words like "Big Mama," "Big Booty," and "Rump Shaker" into a search engine. The results are usually all black porn sites. For Asian women, you might enter words like "exotic," "demure," and "petite" and get Asian porn sites. For Latina women I have found that entering "Latina" into the search engine yields enough Latina porn sites to skip the guesswork. Then examine the imagery and language used to describe black women in porn sites. The layouts are crude, the women are emphasized for their "big booty" and ability to "fuck like animals." And then look at sites featuring Asian women. They are described as "horny sluts," "sushi-to-go," and are featured alongside "chopstick" font and Chinese characters. East and West are almost overemphasized and in all the pictures the men are white and occasionally black. Take a tour of a mail-order-bride/Thailand-sex-tour site by entering "mail-order bride" into a search engine (by the way, here you will see my site listed too). Study the language and the sections of the site—how the women are said to be a "fantasy," "exotic," and "faithful." (This is why I picked the subversive title of "the Big Bad Chinese Mama"—to mix up racist expectations of pornography.) In particular, look at the "Frequently Asked Questions" section. The procurers of the site answer such pressing questions as "Why are Eastern women better wives for Western men?" and "Do these women speak English?"

It was a difficult process. Not only did I need to learn HTML with no background in computers, I was constantly asking myself how much of my life I should divulge to an audience that would be adverse to my site. I did not set out to praise "Asian American" identity, expose the hidden realities behind Southeast Asian women forced into the sex trade industry, or attack "the Man" as the root of the problem. My goal was only to satirize the blatant racism perpetuated by Orientalism and to spoof anger itself. However, I make a playful critique of all three of these and am often misconstrued as putting forth a brutal and confused argument. I spoof a mail-order-bride catalog in my link "The Harem of Angst," finishing it off with a "not so exotic" collection of "brides." I also answer "Frequently Unasked Questions"—questions from actual bride sites answered on my terms. I also spoof Orientalism in photo-shopped, two-headed china dolls, and present my take of Arthur Golden's *Memoirs of a Geisha* in my "Memoirs of an Anti-Geisha." There are also sound bites of prank calls to "Introduction Service," porn studios, and massage parlors. So much of putting up the site was getting over the fear of having my image seen by people who might be looking for porn and trying to predict my audience's reaction. Nevertheless, all the panic paid off.

My site launched, my professors were supportive, and the reaction has been tremendous. I have also done extensive guerrilla marketing to draw more traffic to my site. All of the tactics are intended to draw in both Asian audiences who may or may not feel camaraderie with my work, as well as non-Asian audiences. My tricky tactics include placing line ads in the adult classified section of the *New Times LA*, spamming to porn-swapping clubs, linking to Asian American organizations, intercepting the efforts of pants-down surfers in chat rooms, and sticker campaigns via my exhausted color printer. I keep an unedited guest book to monitor my feedback and reflect upon the reality of my audience. As anticipated, much of the feedback is negative. And every couple of weeks, a lone appreciative note of feedback will come and bury itself between "Fuck you, gook, shut up!" and "Asian women ARE sluts." Despite criticisms that my site shouldn't pass for academic material, some universities are eating it up and adding the site to their syllabi. Most of them are attracted to the radical way I am representing race and gender. Others are intrigued by the "no-fear" policy I have in addressing people who are and aren't in the community. And not just Asian American Studies classes, but media/journalism, art/design, and women's studies classes have all invited me to speak. I have given guest lectures in these classes and have been invited to speak on panels.

59. Sonia Shah, "Introduction: Slaying the Dragon Lady: Toward an Asian American Feminism," from *Dragon Ladies: Asian American Feminists Breathe Fire*

Excerpts from "Slaying the Dragon Lady," by Sonia Shah, published in *Dragon Ladies: Asian American Feminists Breathe Fire,* ed. Sonia Shah (Boston: South End Press, 1997), xii–xix. Reprinted with permission.

In a key essay that articulates what it means to be an Asian American feminist, Shah argues that a historical perspective must inform present politics and discusses what a specifically Asian American perspective has to offer to feminism today. "Neither the feminist movement or the Asian American movement have taken Asian American women's interests into consideration on their agendas," she writes, and Shah's essay aims to address these deficiencies. Although she may not call herself third wave, her insistence on developing a historical perspective that brings a previously silenced and invisible demographic into view is very much in alignment with third-wave goals.

... Works on Asian American women often take as their focal point their experiences, tacitly assuming *something* is similar or unifying in Asian American women's experiences, despite the obligatory disclaimers to the contrary. As critics and scholars have long pointed out, the experiences of Asian American women are fantastically diverse. We are a group of people with different nationalities, languages, religions, ethnicities, classes, and immigration status. I agree that there *is* something unifying in women's varying experiences. But in works on Asian American women, that something is left undefined—it is vaguely referred to, if at all, as something about being from Asia, or about stereotypes, foods, and career choices.

All of the above similarities do exist, to varying degrees. But, I think, in the end, that those similarities are only skin-deep, not enough to make relations between different Asian American women any more likely than relations between Asian women and any other group of people. Indeed, the differences are at times much bigger, more real, more visceral and emotionally laden than the similarities, which are so often abstract.

To critics who would then say, well then, how does it make sense to talk about Asian American women at all? I would respond: it makes as much sense as it does to talk about white people or black people or Latinos. These racial groups admit just as much, if not more, diversity within their ranks than they have similarities. In the end, they are historical constructs, kept in place by social and political institutions, in service of a hierarchical, racially biased society. White people include poor Irish Catholic illegal immigrant, rich WASPs, and Jewish intellectuals. They are at least as different as they are similar. But it makes sense to talk about them as a group because they all share the same rung on the racial hierarchy, which, in many areas of life, is the most significant determinant of their social status in the United States. More than their shared language, ethnic heritage, or class, their *whiteness* determines who they live with, who they go to school with, what kind of jobs they get, how much money they make, and with whom they start families.

Similarly, the reason to talk about Asian American women as a single group is because we all share the same rung on the racial hierarchy *and* on the gender hierarchy. It is not that our lives are so similar in substance, but that our lives are all monumentally shaped by three major driving forces in U.S. society: racism and patriarchy most immediately, and ultimately, imperial aggression against Asia as well. As long as those systems of distributing and exercising power continue to exist, it will continue to make sense to talk about Asian American women as a group (as well as other racial and gender groups).

... There is no *political* point in just talking about Asian American women's experiences, even as the very question rests upon the years of vital scholarship and creative work done on detailing that experience. What it makes *political* sense to talk about is how the forces or racism, patriarchy, and imperialism specifically affect Asian American women. And, most importantly, how Asian American women counter resistance to those forces. In *other* words, about a racially conscious, international feminism: Asian American feminism.

DRAGON LADIES: A BRIEF POLITICAL HISTORY

Empress Tsu-hsi ruled China from 1898 to 1908 from the Dragon Throne. The *New York Times* described her as "the wicked witch of the East, a reptilian dragon lady who had arranged the poisoning, strangling, beheading, or forced suicide of anyone who had ever challenged her autocratic rule." Decades later, scholars such as Sterling Seagrave attempted to balance this self-servingly racist caricature of Empress Tsu-hsi. But the shadow of the Dragon Lady—with her cruel, perverse, and inhuman ways—continued to darken encounters between Asian women and the West they flocked to for refuge: the 1996 Merriam Webster dictionary describes a dragon lady as "an over-bearing or tyrannical woman."

Far from being predatory, many of the first Asian women to come to the United States in the mid 1800s were disadvantaged Chinese women, who were tricked, kidnapped, or smuggled into the country to serve the predominantly male Chinese community as prostitutes. The impression that *all* Asian women were prostitutes, born at that time, "colored the public perception of, attitude toward, and action against all Chinese women for almost a century," writes historian Sucheng Chan. Police and legislators singled out Chinese women for special restrictions and opprobriums, "not so much because they wee prostitutes as such (since there were also many white prostitutes around plying their trade) but because—as Chinese—they allegedly brought in especially virulent strains of venereal diseases, introduced opium addiction, and enticed white boys to a life of sin." While Chinese men bought Chinese women's sex and displayed their bound feet to curious Americans (at the St. Louis World's Fair, for example), white women took to "saving" their disadvantaged sisters. Protestant missionary women brought policemen with hatchets to brothels to round up Chinese women into Mission Homes, where everything from personal mail to suitors was overseen by the missionary women. Chinese women who were not prostitutes ended up bearing the brunt of the Chinese exclusion laws that passed in the late 1800s, engendered by the missionaries' and other anti-Chinese campaigns.

During these years, Japanese immigration stepped up, and with it, a reactionary anti-Japanese movement joined established anti-Chinese sentiment. During the early 1900s, Japanese numbered less than 3 percent of the total population in California, but nevertheless encountered virulent and sometimes violent racism. The "picture brides" from Japan who emigrated to join their husbands in the United States were, to racist Californians, "another example of Oriental treachery," according to historian Roger Daniels.

U.S. immigration policy towards Asians has in large part been shaped by its perceived labor needs. Early Chinese and Japanese immigrants were actively recruited from the poorer classes to work as manual laborers on the railroads and elsewhere. As has been widely noted, before the immigration laws were radically changed in 1965, few Asian women emigrated to the United States. But it bears noting that despite the fact that they weren't in the country, Asian women shouldered much of the cost of subsidizing Asian men's labor. U.S. employers didn't have to pay Asian men as much as other laborers who had families to support, since Asian women in Asia bore the costs of rearing children and taking care of the older generation.

Asian women who did emigrate here in the pre-1960s years were also usually employed as cheap laborers. In the pre-World War II years, close to half of all Japanese American women were employed as servants or laundresses in the San Francisco area. The World War II internment of Japanese Americans made them especially easy to exploit: they had lost their homes, possessions, and savings when forcibly interned at the camps. Yet, in order to leave, they had to prove they had jobs and homes. U.S. government officials thoughtfully arranged for their employment by fielding requests, most of which were for servants.

The 1965 Immigration Act brought in a huge influx of immigrants from Asia to fill primarily professional positions in the United States. Asian engineers, physicians, students, and other professionals flocked to the country, drastically altering the face of Asian America and Asian American politics.

MAKING WAVES. BIG AND SMALL

The first wave of Asian women's organizing formed out of the Asian American movement of the 1960s, which in turn was inspired by the civil rights movement and the anti-Vietnam War movement. While many Asian American women are quick to note that women's issues are the same as men's issues—i.e., social justice, equity, human rights—history shows that Asian American men have not necessarily felt the same way. Leftist Asian women in Yellow Power and other Asian American groups often found themselves left out of the decision-making process and their ideas and concerns relegated to "women's auxiliary" groups that were marginal to the larger projects at hand. Some Asian male activists rationalized this by

> pointing to their own oppression, arguing that they had a "right" to the sexual services of "their" women, after years when Asian women were excluded from the country. Moreover, they saw services from women as "just compensation" for the sacrifices they were making on behalf of the "people."

As Asian American scholar Gary Okihiro notes, "Europe's feminization of Asia, its taking possession, working over, and penetration of Asia, was preceded and paralleled by Asian men's subjugation of Asian women." Asian women naturally gravitated together in response to men's patronizing attitudes and some formed ambitious, radical political projects. Eager to advance "the correct line," most of these early groups petered out over sectarian conflicts. They were unable to inspire large numbers of Asian or other women or to hammer out unity amongst themselves.

While earnest, hardworking, and vital, these early Asian women radicals couldn't compete with the growing reality that for many Asian American women, there was money to be made. The highly educated and affluent Asian immigrants who came to the United States after 1965 were eager to be incorporated into the U.S. economy, and could be treated as a sort of second-tier professional class by U.S. employers. Not surprisingly, large organizations of primarily middle-class East Asian women, such as Asian Women United and the Organization of Asian Women, flourished during these years. These groups devoted themselves to educational and service projects, rather than to directly resisting social injustices. Their popularity was at least partly affected by the fact that they helped professional Asian American women, in various ways, get and keep better jobs. The National Network of Asian and Pacific Women, founded in 1982 under the auspices of a federal grant, provides a case in point. As William Wei writes:

> It has been castigated for catering to middle-class women who are mainly interested in enhancing their employment opportunities.... [The Network believes that] it will be the professionals, rather than the workers, who will be in the vanguard of social change in the United States. Besides, its leaders claim, when it organizes activities that focus mainly on middle-class women, it is merely responding to the wishes of the majority of its members.

Whatever oppositional sparks organizers of these groups may have had were easily squelched by the triple pressure created by the growing model minority myth and multiculturalism's identity politics. Conservative and mainstream institutions who wanted to advance racialized theories supported model minority myth-making because it implied there was a "good" minority in tacit opposition to the "bad" minorities—African Americans and Latinos. At the same time, the model minority myth helped countless struggling Asian Americans start businesses and send their kids to Ivy League schools, and was thus consciously upheld by Asian American community leaders. The ongoing condemnation of white supremacy by African Americans and others was answered by liberals with the benign image of multiculturalism: a scenario in which white people don't exploit black people, but white, brown, yellow, black, and red live together harmoniously. White feminists and other liberals advanced this feel-good fantasy with celebrations of Asian American culture and people. The result was a triple pressure on Asian women to conform to the docile, warm, upwardly mobile stereotype liberals, conservatives, and their own community members all wanted to promote.

The political context of the 1990s is significantly different, and likewise colors Asian women's organizing in this decade. Today, Asian immigrant professionals are less vital to the labor market and are thus, in a familiar cycle, being forced down the status ladder. Affirmative action policies that benefited them are being dismantled. Laws that restrict their access to public assistance and legal rights have been enacted. China and Japan are once again being invoked as evil empires—due now to their financial strength—as a new Yellow Peril is sweeping the country.

At the same time, Asian immigration laws have changed such that the new Asian immigrant is not educated and professional but working-class or poor. Trade agreements such as NAFTA and GATT have broken down protections for workers and the environment in order to secure a free-wheeling capitalist global economy, and Asian workers in Asia and in the United States, especially women, are suffering the worst of it—laboring under worse working conditions and being forced to compete for the most degraded, worst-paying jobs. As Miriam Ching Louie points out, the U.S. workforce is "increasingly female, minority, and immigrant." For example, in San Francisco's garment industry—its largest manufacturing sector—90 percent of the workers are women: 80 percent of those are Chinese-speaking, and less than 8 percent are unionized.

Activists have responded to these new changes with a renewed labor movement and new worker campaigns that cross borders and industries. Asian women organizers have been at the forefront of these campaigns. Most significant among these is the groundbreaking campaign by Asian Immigrant Women Advocates (AIWA) to organize Asian seamstresses against a powerful fashion designer, Jessica McClintock. AIWA's Garment Workers Justice Campaign was launched in May 1992 to secure $15,000 in back wages for Asian immigrant seamstresses who had been stiffed by their employer, Lucky Sewing Company. Instead of going after the sewing shop, which had declared bankruptcy, AIWA aimed its campaign directly at the designer who used the shop's labor. (This was a vital strategic move, as manufacturers often seek to immunize themselves against workers' grievances by subcontracting with shops for whose working conditions they don't take responsibility.) Not only did this campaign, which in the end secured a generous settlement for the seamstresses, establish a vital precedent for labor organizing, it politicized hundreds of young Asian American women across the country. AIWA staff inspired the seamstresses to outrage by showing them McClintock's fancy boutiques and organized Asian American women college students to stage protests at McClintock stores nationwide.

With worker campaigns such as AIWA's, new issue-oriented organizations such as the National Women's Health Organization, and rejuvenated Asian battered women's organizations, a new generation of activists is springing up. They are uncovering the hidden history of previous generations of Asian women activists. With fewer and fewer class interests to divide them, they are shaping a new movement, one that goes beyond just agitating for our little piece of the ever-shrinking pie. They are putting poor immigrant and refugee Asian women at the forefront of their organizing, they are thinking globally, and they are making the connections among the politics of labor, health, environment, culture, nationalism, racism, and patriarchy: connections that have in the past eluded left activists.

An Asian American feminist movement is *the only movement* that will consistently represent Asian American women's interests.... [N]either the feminist movement nor the Asian American movement have taken Asian American women's interests into consideration on their agendas. But it's much more than that. An Asian American feminist movement is vital for the larger project of uncovering the social structure, with its built-in injustices and inequities that affect us all. In today's global economy, in which nothing is certain for anyone save the most elite of the elite, this is a project that vitally concerns the majority.

... Asian American women are already making their movement happen. A different sort of Dragon Lady is emerging—not a cold-blooded reptile, but a creature who breathes fire.

60. Delia D. Aguilar, "Lost in Translation: Western Feminism and Asian Women," from *Dragon Ladies: Asian American Feminists Breathe Fire*

Excerpts from "Lost in Translation," by Delia D. Aguilar, published in *Dragon Ladies: Asian American Feminists Breathe Fire*, ed. Sonia Shah (Boston: South End Press, 1997), 153–165. Reprinted with permission.

In a complicated, important essay that pinpoints some of the biggest problems within feminism today, Aguilar argues that, "identity or difference feminism has the paradoxical effect of ostensibly recognizing the 'other' at the same time that it conceals the material conditions underpinning that marginality." She argues for the need to "name the real world of capital/labor relations in a globalized economy," and how those relations affect Asian American women. The essay discusses her work with nonwhite women from countries other than the United States, and the ways their experiences show that "the pragmatic skepticism of feminists who herald difference often plays right into the hands of international monetary agencies and transnational corporations." Aguilar's essay is a good example of the future direction of the third wave, which has increasingly begun to consider the conditions of globalization.

Not too long after the inception of second-wave feminism, U.S. women of color and Third World women called attention to and repeatedly challenged exclusionary tendencies in feminist theory and practice. Now understood as the problem of universalization or essentialism, this ahistorical approach examines white, middle-class women's lives through the singular prism of gender and extends its findings to all womankind. It should be observed, however, that, racist as its effects undoubtedly were, essentialism had currency at a time when "progressive politics" meant, above all else, having a vision of an alternative society. Thus, women's subordination was contextualized in social formations whose relations of production were made explicit—capitalist, socialist, welfare state, feudal, etc.—and changes in gender relations situated within larger transformational agendas.

With the neoconservatism of the Reagan/Bush era, followed by the collapse of the Soviet Union and the establishment of a globalized order premised on capitalist triumphalism, progressives began to lose ground and vision. No longer certain about the tenability of socialist alternatives, not a few have turned to fashionable postmodern conceptualizations that reject perspectives striving to grasp the nature of society in its wholeness or totality. It is in this setting that essentialism has acquired something of the status of a bogey to be shooed away upon detection.

Displacing universalization is the postmodernist notion of "difference," where the formerly invisible "other" emerges and now speaks, presumably with a unified voice—a problematic formulation in that the Western self is thought to have become fragmentary and dislocated. Now, this is not to diminish the importance of the space within which specificities of the lives and identities of Asian American and other women of color are today accorded recognition. Indeed, with "difference feminism," women of color are now able to speak as they had not before. Bell hooks, for example, views the process of coming to voice as an act of resistance and a metaphor for self-transformation.

Perhaps here the key word is "self-transformation," for it must be noted that postmodern celebrations of difference and coming to voice transpire in the absence of an encompassing frame capable of revealing relations of power, particularly those rooted in the political economy. Consequently change, if it occurs at all, is discursive, cultural, and individual. With materially grounded politics effectively abolished, the "other" is either romanticized or seen as very different from the self, so as to preclude any possibility of genuine equality or even dialogue.

Identity or difference feminism, then, has the paradoxical effect of ostensibly recognizing the "other" at the same time that it conceals the material conditions underpinning that marginality. Refusing to name the real world of capital/labor relations in a globalized economy, much less to analyze it, what can the effect of such a feminist politics be on Asian American women? Is it enough that we are now seen in our tremendous diversity so that we can celebrate equally those among us who are in possession of property and those who are not? What sorts of struggles are made possible by this kind of politics, detached as it is from material reality? Who benefits? Who loses?

TEACHING FEMINISM TO ASIAN/PACIFIC WOMEN

With this feminist politics in mind, let me now turn to my experience teaching feminism to a group of Asian/Pacific women in Manila, Philippines, in 1992. Titled "Intercultural Course on Women and Society," this intensive program was offered by the Institute of Women's Studies in St. Scholastica's College. Seventeen women attended; they represented 13 countries, two of which fall outside the Asian/Pacific region. One woman came from Zambia, and two from the United States. Each year the Institute designates a few slots for women from the "First World" who must pay their own way. The rest of the women are on full scholarships, including travel and living expenses. While a requirement for admission calls for work experience with women, only two students (the ones from the United States) had taken classes in women's studies.

The objectives of the program can best be described as practical in thrust, with the enhancement of existing social movements as a major goal. Learning was not to be conducted solely for learning's sake. The women themselves, at the outset, declared their status as community workers in search of knowledge, skills, and strategies that they could utilize upon return to their home countries. By providing a place where women could live and study together, the Institute sought to develop a critical understanding of women's condition and to forge a sense of solidarity among Asian/Pacific women, with the hope of "exploring cooperative actions" in the context of "working toward a more just and egalitarian society."

My assignment was to introduce the women to "Feminist Analyses of the Woman Question" as these applied to the Asian/Pacific region. Before my section of the course, the group had shared their life stories and presented country reports documenting the position of women as encoded by custom and governmental policies. We had also gone on the first part of a series of "exposure tours," which brought into focus the jarring disjointedness and fragmentation that have become defining characteristics of urban life in developing societies.

These day trips within Manila and its vicinity included visits to an opulent mega-mall flaunting superfluous consumer items (an added attraction featured an exhibit on "the world's 'firsts,'" highlighted by a lecture from U.S. astronaut Eugene Cieman, who taught his Filipino listeners that the history of U.S. space exploration is "your history"); a slum dweller women's association; San Agustin church, an imposing 16th-century cathedral; garment factories producing winter coats for export; a ballpoint pen factory shut down by striking women workers who had pitched makeshift shelters outside. The glaring disparities of class everywhere on display as we took in the sights were surely familiar scenes to these Asian/Pacific women. Something in the manner in which juxtaposed symbols of wealth and poverty converged as if solely for our perusal gave us pause, and, throughout, served as a backdrop against which to interrogate women's lives. By the time I began my session, the ice had been broken and the groundwork laid for exploring the terrain of feminist thinking.

Still, an appreciation of feminism requires, at the very least, the naming of women's oppression. Even though the UN-declared Decade for Women opened people's eyes to the subordination of women worldwide, "feminism" remains taboo for many in developing countries. Seeing consciousness raising as my first task, I asked the group to bring up examples showing the ways in which women's experience differed from men's in the women's respective societies. The response was immediate and animated, and soon the discussion centered on traditional practices that threaten women's existence or constrain their behavior. The list was lengthy: dowry deaths, the taking of temple prostitutes, requiring proof of virginity on one's wedding night, female infanticide, taking multiple wives, women eating only after everyone else has been fed, submission to the husband's authority as "chief spirit of the household" (*Aing U Nut* in Burma), and so on and so forth. We also discovered in the process of assembling this cross-cultural inventory that "under the *saya*" (skirt), a taunt thrown at "henpecked" husbands, was a sexist phrase of common currency not only in the Philippines but also among Indians, Pakistanis, and Sri Lankans.

Prepared to meet some resistance, I was relieved not to encounter any. What I found most unusual was the enthusiasm, the vigorous flow of energy that generated this litany of misogynistic rituals and conventions. But even more intriguing was the relatively undisturbed state of mind maintained by the group as a whole. In my introductory women's studies courses in the United States, female students who first begin to glimpse the extent of women's oppression typically react with open rage. If not rage, one usually senses in the newly awakened a palpable tension, an impatience to extricate themselves from what all too suddenly has come to be a burdensome situation.

In contrast, here the response was calm, thoughtful, deliberate. Yasmin, a well-heeled Sri Lankan school principal, appropriately recognized her own victimization as being less pronounced than that of her subordinates: "What do I do with my maid? Should I raise her salary? Maybe I am oppressing teachers in my school, too." A few days after this discussion, Minah from Indonesia confided that she had written her parents, telling them how women's consignment to the chores of cooking, washing, cleaning, and childcare constitutes oppression. Pratima, a Nepali lawyer, reported that she had done the same. Ma Paw from Myanmar, who regularly got phone calls from her boyfriend stationed on a traveling commercial vessel, joked that she was not going to get married anymore. If I must sum up the overall sentiment of the group, however, I would say that it was best captured by Barbara's solemn matter-of-factness as she spoke to me across the lunch table: "I've been married 24 years. Now I know that I'm oppressed, and that women in my country are oppressed. In our organization [in Zambia] we believe we must change ourselves first and then change others. So I must change my relationship with my husband. But what am I to do? How do I do this without divorcing?" Then she added, "Battering is something we all say we don't want. But how about housework?"

INDIVIDUALISM VS. COMMUNITY

Without a doubt, the experiences and age range (21 to 46) of these women separate them from the average U.S. college student I teach in my women's studies classes. These factors alone can account for the difference in their responses. But another factor is the rootedness felt quite deeply by these Asian/Pacific women, their profound embeddedness in an intricate network comprised of family, clan, friends, workmates, acquaintances, and others in the community. Their identities, though inevitably influenced by the market (e.g., as workers and consumers), are not primarily defined by it. Subsequently, the discovery or "naming" of female oppression did not trigger the individualist impulse to escape that it often does among women in industrialized nations.

An example should serve to clarify my point. Bidya from Nepal, 25 and single, began to take a new look at arranged marriages as a result of our ongoing dialogue. Yet she continued to insist that, despite the freedom to choose allowed by her parents (she was, after all, a lawyer practicing in the city), she preferred not to take this route. "I don't have my parents' wisdom and judgment and wouldn't know on what basis to select," she explained. Afterward, she made quite clear her belief that families of origin are a solid anchor, implying that marriage is no more than a way of extending kinship connections. I did not get the impression that marriage might signal, as it could for some young people in the United States, a breaking away into adulthood and independence. "A husband is someone who is new to you, but you've known your family all your life," she declared, in a tone hinting that there was something strange in having to distinguish between an untested relationship and an established institution whose permanence ought to be taken for granted. As if foreseeing that her inexperience could lead to the wrong choice, she expressed anxiety over requesting her family's assistance should her marriage not work out: "I would really feel bad about that."

When I tell U.S. audiences about Bidya, what they almost invariably communicate back to me precisely proves my point. They consider her powerless—power being equated with the individual's ability to take action and choose freely, a market-impelled notion. For them, the possibility that arranged marriage may be beneficial to a kin system, the smooth functioning of which in turn ensures its members' survival and well-being, is an alien thought. (This is not to romanticize a custom that automatically cancels romance, or to propose cultural relativism.)

Given that individualism is a core Western value that neither class nor race appears amply capable of mitigating, it was hardly surprising that Ann, my U.S. student who enrolled in the course, found the dissonance in her new store of information unsettling. She told me how angry she was starting to feel about the distortion that U.S. policies, enacted through international monetary bodies, have foisted on the economies of developing countries. She was enraged to see with her own eyes the resulting havoc in people's lives. On the other hand, she also felt that her sympathy was somehow misplaced. In the face of her Asian/Pacific colleagues' seeming resignation to their fates, she "just could not imagine the lives of these women."

But, chances are, these women's lives were not as wretched as Ann imagined. They knew that although they were surely women, they were simultaneously many other things as well. Gender for them was not an autonomous category unaffected by other social relations, a point rather belabored in feminist writing in the United States and Britain. (Deconstructing the category "women," Denise Riley asks: "what does it mean to insist that 'women' are only sometimes 'women'?")

Like Asian American feminists and other women of color in the United States and Britain, it did not seem to take much for these women to be conscious of their multiple, shifting, fluctuating identities, to use postmodernist jargon. For what else would have led to Yasmin's perceptive comments, her concern about her subordinates? By considering her maid and teaching staff instead of herself, she demonstrated an instinctive understanding of class as a shaping influence of no lesser consequence than gender. (This constituted a radical switch from the gist of her country report, in which she claimed gender parity for Sri Lankan women on the basis of laws granting them equal economic rights.) Moreover, being rooted in a community means feeling responsible, in your diverse roles and capacities, for those around you. Replying to her own question about what is to be done, Barbara later stated that altering her marriage to any significant degree was no longer possible, but she assured us all that she would definitely use her newfound knowledge about gender inequality to educate her children and the families and couples she counsels in her job.

ANTI-WESTERN SENTIMENTS

Ironically, the powerlessness that U.S. audiences typically attribute to these women's equanimity, which supposedly derives from the absence of a viable alternative, is belied by what I saw as a keen awareness on my students' part of the existence of other worlds and other cultures. One can rarely say the same for many in the United States, who, presuming themselves to be situated in the hub of the universe, harbor little curiosity about anything outside. This is not to say that this group's ideas about other cultures were always accurate, but their interest was present and strong.

Let me explain what I mean. At breakfast one morning, Yasmin showed me an essay commending the protection afforded to women by Islamic religion. I assumed the author to be someone else, but on subsequent inquiry found out that she herself had written it "many years ago" as an address to teachers. The piece did not simply exhort women to be faithful to their domestic duties because doing so was valuable in itself, or because female piety would guarantee the stability of family life and, by extension, the society at large. Instead, it seized upon the social disruption plaguing the United States—worded in the well-worn conservative assertion that the untrammeled freedom of Western women has led to family breakdown which, in turn, is causing juvenile crime, drug addiction, wanton violence, and a pervasive moral collapse—and used that as a warning to keep Sri Lankan women in place.

At this point in the course I was convinced that Yasmin had taken hold of my feminist agenda and was mulling it over very carefully in her mind. So while there were two major points in her article, one anti-feminist and the other pro-Islam, it really was not feminism that she was against, nor was she necessarily urging conversion to Islam. Before long I began to realize that what Yasmin and others along with her had undertaken to staunchly defend was the matter of cultural pride, which, though now punctured by their cognizance of misogyny, remained over and above all a weapon to fight off a more feared specter—moral decadence and degeneration as they saw these manifested in the technologically advanced West.

This message was as explicit as it could be in the speech Yasmin wrote. Echoes of that sentiment resonated with others in the group, and, intoned again and again in various ways, this point of view simply could not be missed or misinterpreted. For example, I was shortly to learn from Gail (the other U.S. student) that she and Ann had received a tepid welcome from the start, in spite of the fact that everyone knew that the two of them had not received funding. As Gail was recounting events surrounding her arrival, I recalled a prior exchange during the country reports when her use of terms "First World" and "Third World" immediately drew sharp criticism from a number of women who questioned the basis for the implied ranking. Moreover, the women's impression of the Philippines as not only heavily "Westernized" but worse, suffering from a "lack of their own culture" (observations that are hard to contest), operated to aggravate simmering antagonisms between those from the North and from the South. Giving voice to these conflicts, as the more outspoken women began to do, was, in my opinion, a perfectly healthy sign.

When Vibha of Pakistan announced, "We are proud of our own culture; we do not look up to America as our model," she unmistakably meant it for Filipino ears. I was glad to hear her say this, because I felt that it was important for my compatriots in the class to hear directly from other Asians how we, as Filipinos, are viewed. I felt that such comments would compel constant alertness to the often confounding ramifications in a neocolonial formation like the Philippines, where feminist issues intersect with questions of national sovereignty at every single juncture. Interestingly enough, no one impugned the vibrancy of feminism in the Philippines as a symptom of its acquiescence to Western values. Perhaps it was inevitable, after I encouraged this drift—by asking for examples of what someone had referred to as "Western behavior" in Filipinos—that Luzviminda, a Filipina organizer of domestic workers in Hong Kong, was described to her face as a "dominating" person who "talks too much," conduct in women that is purportedly antithetical to Asian values. It was mentioned privately to me afterwards that Luzviminda's keeping company with the two U.S. women was interpreted as a sign that she looked up to them and had taken them for role models, their closeness in age having been discounted altogether as another explanation. Also brought in for questioning was the advice that Señora Carmen, director and founder of the Institute, told us she had dispensed to a woman who was an object of repeated battering. "We'd never advise a wife to leave her husband," Vibha volunteered, risking accuracy or veracity to insinuate that this was somehow out of tune with Asian folkways. Ann was perceived as "acting just like her country" when one Saturday morning she got out of bed and, still groggy, grouchily asked the three women chatting in the room across the hall to quiet down or move so she could resume her sleep. And at a session one afternoon, Gail and Ann found themselves abandoned in their request for a schedule change, a turnabout from the previous night, when everyone had supported their proposal.

IS SISTERHOOD GLOBAL?

This development effectively laid to rest a prior worry of mine. All indications up until then had led me to believe that my efforts at consciousness-raising around inequalities of gender had produced the reductive notion that, since women share a common oppression, all women are sisters. The fact is, there was a push for just this stand among some Filipina facilitators—a predisposition bound up, I suspect, with the exhilaration infusing a women's movement in its initial stages. Extolling universal sisterhood on the grounds that all women, regardless of class, race, or other structuring relations, are potential victims of male violence, a Filipina feminist at one point spiritedly asserted that "a victory for women anywhere is a victory for us." I queried the statement by asking everyone to consider who the women are who are inclined to celebrate which women's victories. How many British (or U.S., French, etc.) women have celebrated as their own triumph the successes won by Philippine slum dweller women, assuming Western women even hear about such campaigns? Although I thought that the criticism I was making was clear, I failed to get my point across. To my chagrin, moreover, I noted that, in a collective project to create murals depicting the women's vision of a better society, practically all the drawings iterated the same essentializing motif of global sisterhood.

To place this assumption of sisterhood in perspective, I sought to draw out women's similarities and differences by situating us Asian/Pacific women squarely within the international economic order. I summed up our common experiences as elaborated in the country reports each participant had delivered early on: massive rural to urban migration, ever-increasing poverty and homelessness, militarization, cash-crop production and production of consumer goods for export, dominance of multinationals, external debt, structural adjustment dictated by international lending agencies such as the International Monetary Fund and World Bank. Within this framework, we discussed how large numbers of women migrate overseas as domestics or, in the absence of an opportunity to leave, stay home to do backbreaking labor or work in the informal sector; how women's "nimble fingers" and "docility" ("genetic" credentials authenticated by a garment factory president we interviewed, who also cited women's ability to sit patiently) qualify them for low-paid employment on the assembly line; how women succumb to being mail-order brides or to working in the "entertainment industry" when limited options for a living wage are available. In short, it became sufficiently manifest that there was no way we could speak of Asian/Pacific women without at the same time implicating unequal power relations between the North and the South.

Having explored the above issues, I expected the women to now apprehend commonalities and differences in another light. This they did, as the anti-Western posture described earlier attests. Not only had they withdrawn subscription to a universal sisterhood with "women everywhere," but they also pushed ahead of me. When they articulated "difference," the tone was not celebratory, and not a soul proclaimed the wonders of diversity.

Because our meetings averaged six-and-a-half hours every day, I was constantly in search of some activity or exercise to vary the pace of our sessions. I decided to start one morning with a narration of how some women in a poor neighborhood in Lima, Peru, organized around wife abuse. All the women had purchased whistles that they agreed to blow whenever a beating occurred, a strategy meant to embarrass or shame the perpetrator, and ultimately to bring him in line. I admired the Peruvian women's ingenuity and assumed that everyone hearing the account would, too. Reinforced by a Filipina friend who informed me that village women in a southern Philippine province had devised a scheme like it, substituting the clanging of pots and pans for whistles, I was positive that the story would go over well. I was wrong. Leilani from Papua New Guinea, strong and unafraid to speak, just about roared: "No! In my country that won't work! If women did that, the man would gather his relatives and they would all go and beat up the whistleblowers!" Taken aback, I asked why. With a little prodding from me, others eventually spoke up to reject the strategy, reasoning that it could only backfire. "Why, that is like broadcasting the woman's failings as a wife to the entire neighborhood!"

My mistake was to carelessly lump together in my mind, under the unspoken rubric "Third World," Peruvian women of one specific neighborhood with the group of "Asian/Pacific women" in my midst. By rejecting my proposal, Leilani and the rest forced my recognition of the group as separate and identifiable from one community of Peruvian women. In addition, their objection compelled me to reckon with the tremendous diversity within the group itself—disparities along the lines of race, nationality/ethnicity, class, caste, and religion, among other things, that had been concealed by the convenient geographic label "Asian/Pacific."

And what about within their own societies? It was evident that they were not oblivious to diversity there, either. For example, after having presented feminist theories offering explanations of women's subordination (liberal, radical, Marxist/feminist), I asked the group which paradigms would prove most applicable or relevant in their own countries. Rather than speaking for "women back home" as a unified entity, or on their own behalf as individuals (which no one did), many of the participants gauged the theories' worth in terms of the sector addressed, thus: for middle-class and rich women in the city, liberal feminism; for the poor in the city and agricultural areas, Marxist/feminism, and so on. This sensitivity to women's diversity was likewise confirmed in the course evaluation, when several class members noted their appreciation of the reminder I issued to constantly refer back to women's lives in their own societies; this they found to be a good means to help clarify the explanatory potential of these feminist theories, and also to test their own understanding. I should have also asked, along with the reminder, "which women?"

What was most instructive for me in this experience that might also be useful for Asian Americans? Above all, it was heartening to see that women could have their eyes wide open to the cleavages separating women and still remain committed to the search for a common ground for feminist solidarity. Here awareness of multiple standpoints did not appear to weaken presumptions of mutual agreement; in effect, solidarity (indeed, solidarity as "Third World" people demarcated by the metropolis/periphery divide) as both a guiding principle and a goal was assumed, differences notwithstanding. It must be remarked that the program itself was designed so that this aim remained in sight throughout. To illustrate, the final assignment in the last module required every participant to draw up a concrete plan of action, which each woman then shared with the rest, for the express purpose of exploring the possibility of collaborative ventures in the region. The participants, furthermore, had target populations with whom they were already involved—unemployed youth, illiterate women, domestic helpers, church organizations, to mention a few—and could envision the outcomes they were seeking.

The women's locatedness, a kind of surefootedness, if you will, secured them—plural, heterogeneous identities and all—to the unembellished realities of their "Third World" contexts. This is why the decision to dump hoary practices such as arranged marriage, however oppressive, can be neither reached nor carried out in any facile fashion. I think it is exactly their location in the "Third World" that makes people like this group of Asian/Pacific women painfully aware of social conditions, whatever their station in life might be. I wish to emphasize this factor—the beneficent burden of being unable to deny or ignore social reality—because I believe that it is only in contraposition to prevailing material, social, and political realities that social change can even begin to be imagined. By social change I include those everyday practices that affect women's lives and are at the same time indissociable from policies enacted on an international level.

Given that, neither essentialism nor difference feminism holds much utility for the struggles of Asian/Pacific women or, for the matter, for Asian American feminists. Both approaches are ahistorical. The latter, by focusing mainly on the cultural, has given up the goal of redistributive justice in favor of mere recognition. Those of us on the margins cannot allow ourselves to be mesmerized by calls proclaiming the glories of difference when the material conditions shaping our lives are ignored or glossed over.

As the daily struggles of Asian/Pacific women testify, the basic contours of the world order have not undergone a transfiguration so profound during this so-called postmodern era that its systemic and hierarchical nature completely defies apprehension. My Asian/Pacific sisters consistently urged that relations of dominance and exploitation attendant on the world economic order be elucidated in order for emancipatory transformation to be at all conceivable. Unfortunately, the pragmatic skepticism of feminists who herald difference often plays right into the hands of international monetary agencies and transnational corporations who themselves in their daily operations cannot do without deploying a global, indeed totalizing, view of human affairs on a planetary scale.

61. Ana Castillo, "A Countryless Woman: The Early Feminista," from *Massacre of the Dreamers*

Excerpts from Ana Castillo, *Massacre of the Dreamers* (Albuquerque, NM: University of New Mexico Press, 1994), 21–41. Reprinted with permission.

In this clear, accessible, and beautifully written explication of the contradictions involved in her social location, Castillo explains why she has "more in common with a Mexican man than with a white woman ... [but] much more in common with an Algerian woman than I do with a Mexican man." She addresses the cultural conditions of what third-wave feminism and postcolonial theory call "hybridity"—the experience of oneself in terms of multiple identities and locations that often contradict each other. Castillo's essay shows in the strongest terms why third-wave feminism takes differences between women as a starting point for any kind of feminist activism.

> I would have spoken these words as a feminist who "happened" to be a white United States citizen, conscious of my government's proven capacity for violence and arrogance of power, but as self-separated from that government, quoting without second thought Virginia Woolf's statement in The Three Guineas that "as a woman I have no country. As a woman I want no country. As a woman my country is the whole world." This is not what I come [here] to say in 1984. I come here

> with notes but without absolute conclusions. This is not a sign of loss of faith or hope. These notes are the marks of a struggle to keep moving, a struggle for accountability.
>
> —Adrienne Rich, "Notes toward a Politics of Location," *Blood, Bread, and Poetry*

I CANNOT SAY I AM A CITIZEN OF THE WORLD as Virginia Woolf, speaking as an Anglo woman born to economic means, declared herself; nor can I make the same claim to U.S. citizenship as Adrienne Rich does despite her universal feeling for humanity. As a mestiza born to the lower strata, I am treated at best, as a second class citizen, at worst, as a non-entity. I am commonly perceived as a foreigner everywhere I go, including in the United States and in Mexico. This international perception is based on my color and features. I am neither black nor white. I am not light skinned and cannot be mistaken for "white"; because my hair is so straight I cannot be mistaken for "black." And by U.S. standards and according to some North American Native Americans, I cannot make official claims to being indian.

Socioeconomic status, genetic makeup, and ongoing debates on mestisaje aside, if in search of refuge from the United States I took up residence on any other continent, the core of my being would long for a return to the lands of my ancestors. My ethereal spirit and my collective memory with other indigenas and mestizo/as yearn to *claim* these territories as homeland. In the following pages, I would like to review our socioeconomic status, our early activism and feminismo, and to begin the overall discussion that moves toward a Xicanista vision.

IN THE 1980S, LEFTISTS AND LIBERALS recognized that atrocities of U.S. intervention in Central America, as similar sympathizers did with Viet Nam in the 1960s. Their sympathy is reminiscent of North American leftists and liberals who in the 1930s struggled against fascism during the Spanish Civil War. In each instance, there is the implication that these liberal individuals are not in any way responsible for the persecution, and that it is all their government's fault. These same humanists have vaguely and apologetically acknowledged the injustice done to the descendants of their country's former slaves and to the Native Americans who have been all but obliterated through genocide and dispossession.

Yet, mestizo/as, those who are Mexican citizens as well as those who are U.S. born, are viewed less sympathetically. We are advised to assimilate into white dominant society or opt for invisibility—as invisibility that we are blamed for because of our own lack of ability to take advantage of the supposedly endless opportunities available through acculturation.

Racism has been generally polarized into a black-white issue. U.S. mestizo/as of Mexican background, therefore, are viewed by many white people, by many African Americans, and yes, by some Native Americans as having the potential to "pass" for white, in theory, at will. This general view is based on the assumptions, lack of information and misinformation that accompanies policies, media control, and distorted historical documentation disseminated to the general populace by the white male dominated power system that has traditionally governed this country. The United States cannot deny its early history of importing Africans as slaves, which explains the presence of African Americans throughout the Americas. However, censorship continues regarding the extent of genocide of Native Americans. As for mestizo/as, we were identified as a mongrel race, a mixture of the dispensable Amerindian race and the lowly Spaniard. Little is known by the general public regarding how these attitudes caused ongoing persecution of Mexic Amerindians and mestizo/as in what was once Mexico and later became United States territory. For example, while it is well known that in the South there were lynchings and hangings of African Americans, it isn't common knowledge that Mexicans were also lynched and hung in Texas and throughout the Southwest.

Most people in the United States have little awareness of this government's ongoing dominant-subordinate relationship with Mexico since, of course, this is not taught in schools as part of United States history. The general public assumes that all Mexicans are immigrants and therefore *obligated* to assimilate just as European immigrants did and do.

Most members of dominant society have very little understanding of the numerous ways a country, especially one supposedly based on the free enterprise system and democracy, systematically and quite effectively disenfranchises much of its population. While some white members of society have an understanding of this from an economic and historical standpoint, they do not or will not recognize that there are, to this day, economic inequities based on racism. Many more do not understand or refuse to accept that today all women suffer, in one way or another, as a result of the prevalent misogyny legislated and expounded in this society.

For the last twenty years the leaders of the U.S. government have tried to convince its population that the Civil Rights Movement succeeded in creating a true democracy and that increasing poverty and unemployment are primarily a question of world economics. If indications of the growing frustration on the part of women and people of color who cannot overcome job and educational inequities based on race, gender, and limited economic resources were not evident enough to the federal government, the national riots after the Rodney King verdict serve as the final argument.

WHILE I HAVE MORE IN COMMON WITH A MEXICAN MAN than with a white woman, I have much more in common with an Algerian woman than I do with a Mexican man. This opinion, I'm sure, chagrins women who sincerely believe our female physiology unequivocally binds all women throughout the world, despite the compounded social prejudices that daily affect us all in different ways. Although women everywhere experience life differently from men everywhere, white women are members of a race that has proclaimed itself globally superior for hundreds of years. We live in a polarized world of contrived dualisms, dichotomies, and paradoxes: light vs. dark and good vs. evil. We as Mexic Amerindians/mestizas are the dark. We are the evil ... or at least, the questionable.

Ours is a world imbued with nationalism, real for some, yet tenuous as paper for others. A world in which, from the day of our births, we are either granted citizenship or relegated to the netherstate of serving as mass production drones. Non-white women—Mexicans/Chicanas, Filipinas, Malaysians, and others—who comprise eighty percent of the global factory work force, are the greatest dispensable resource that multinational interests own. The women are, in effect, represented by no country.

Feminists of color in the United States (and around the world) are currently arduously reexamining the very particular ways our non-Western cultures use us and how they view us. We have been considered opinionless and the invariable targets of every kind of abusive manipulation and experimentation. As a mestiza, a resident of a declining world power, a countryless woman, I have the same hope as Rich who, on behalf of her country aims to be accountable, flexible, and learn new ways to gather together earnest peoples of the world without the defenses of nationalism.

I WAS BORN, RAISED, AND SPENT MOST OF MY LIFE in one of the largest cities in the United States. Despite its distance from México, Chicago has a population of approximately a quarter of a million people of Mexican background. It is also the third most frequent U.S. destination of Mexican migrants after El Paso and Los Angeles. The greatest influx of Mexicans occurred during the first half of this century, when the city required cheap labor for its factories, slaughterhouses, and steel mill industry.

In an effort to minimize their social and spiritual alienation, the Mexican communities there developed and maintained solid ties to Mexican culture and traditions. This was reinforced by the tough political patronage system in Chicago, which was dependent upon ethnically and racially divisive strategies to maintain its power. Thus I grew up perceiving myself to be Mexican despite the fact that I was born in the United States and did not visit México until the age of ten.

Assimilation into dominant culture, while not impossible, was not encouraged nor desired by most ethnic groups in Chicago—Mexicans were no exception. We ate, slept, talked, and dreamed Mexican. Our parishes were Mexican. Small Mexican-owned businesses flourished. We were able to replicate Mexico to such a degree that the spiritual and psychological needs of a people so despised and undesired by white dominant culture were met in our own large communities.

Those who came up north to escape destitution in México were, in general, dark-skinned mestizos. In the face of severe racism, it's no wonder we maintained such strong bonds to each other. But even those who were not as outwardly identifiably Mexican were usually so inherently Mexican by tradition that they could not fully assimilate. Not a few refused to "settle in" on this side of the border with the pretense that they would eventually return to their home towns in México.

As I was growing up, Mexicans were the second largest minority in Chicago. There was also a fair size Puerto Rican community and a fair amount of Cubans and other Latin Americans. But in those years, before the blatant military disruption of Latin American countries such as Chile and El Salvador, a person with "mestiza" characteristics was considered Mexican. When one had occasion to venture away from her insulated community to say, downtown, impressive and intimidating with its tremendous skyscrapers and evidently successful (white) people bustling about, she felt as if she were leaving her village to go into town on official matters. Once there she went about her business with a certain sense of invisibility, and even hoped for it, feeling so out of place and disoriented in the presence of U.S. Anglo, profit-based interests, which we had nothing to do with except as mass-production workers. On such occasions, if she were to by chance to run across another mestiza (or mestizo), there was a mutual unspoken recognition and, perhaps, a reflexive avoidance of eye contact. An instantaneous mental communication might sound something like this:

> I know you. You are Mexican (like me). You are brown-skinned (like me). You are poor (like me). You probably live in the same neighborhood as I do. You don't have anything, own anything. (Neither do I.) You're no one (here). At this moment I don't want to be reminded of this, in the midst of such luxury, such wealth, this disorienting language; it makes me ashamed of the food I eat, the flat I live in, the only clothes I can afford to wear, the alcoholism and defeat I live with. You remind me of all of it.
>
> You remind me that I am not beautiful—because I am short, round bellied and black-eyed. You remind me that I will never ride in that limousine that just passed us because we are going to board the same bus back to the neighborhood where we both live. You remind me of why the foreman doesn't move me out of that tedious job I do day after day, or why I got feverish and too tongue-tied to go to the main office to ask for that Saturday off when my child made her First Holy Communion.
>
> When I see you, I see myself. You are the mirror of this despicable, lowly sub-human that I am in this place far from our homeland which scarcely offered us much more since the vast majority there live in destitution. None of the rich there look like us either. At least here we feed our children; they have shoes. We manage to survive. But don't look at me. Go on your way. Let me go on pretending my invisibility, so that I can observe close up all the possibilities—and dream the gullible dreams of a human being.

AT SEVENTEEN, I JOINED THE LATINO/CHICANO MOVEMENT. I went downtown and rallied around City Hall along with hundreds of other youth screaming, "¡Viva La Raza!" and "Chicano Power!" until we were hoarse. Our fears of being recognized as lowly Mexicans were replaced with socioeconomic theories that led to political radicalism. Yet our efforts to bring unity and courage to the majority of our people were short lived; they did not embrace us. Among the factors contributing to this were the ability of some to assimilate more easily on the basis of lighter skin color and the consumer-fever that overrides people's social needs. The temptations of the rewards of assimilation and the internalization of racism by the colonized peoples of the United States was and is devastating. Society has yet to acknowledge the trauma it engenders.

THE HISPANIC POPULATION IN THE U.S. totaled 22,354,509, according to the 1990 U.S. Department of Commerce report. 13,495,938 of that total were of Mexican origin. (We can estimate therefore that when we are discussing the woman of Mexican origin we are referring to a population of about seven million women in the United States.) According to the 1989 report immigration constituted half of the recent Hispanic population growth. I am personally glad to see the U.S. Department of Commerce gives this reason to explain the disproportionate growth of Hispanics as compared to non-Hispanics, as opposed to the 1987 Department of Labor Report, which states that there are so many Hispanics because Hispanic women tend to be more fertile than non-Hispanic women. These figures, of course, do not include the undocumented Latino population. The U.S. Immigration and Naturalization Service estimated 1.2 million apprehensions at the border in 1986.

Hispanic as the ethnic label for all people who reside in the U.S. with some distant connection with the culture brought by the Spaniards during the conquest of the Americas is a gross misnomer. The word promotes an official negation of people called "Hispanic" by inferring that their ethnicity or race is exclusively European rather than partly Native American (as are most Chicano/as), or African American (as are those descendants of the African slave trade along the Caribbean coasts).

The term Hispanic is a misnomer because one-fifth of South America—Brazil—does not speak Spanish. A large population of Guatemala speaks indigenous dialects as a first language and maintain its own indigenous culture. Chicano/as and Puerto Ricans may have little or no fluency in Spanish, having been brought up in an English-dominant society, having attended its monolingual schools, and having been discouraged, in general, from pursuing the language of their ancestors. In fact, despite the provisions made by the Treaty of Guadalupe Hidalgo of 1848 to allow Spanish speakers in the Southwest to retain their native tongue, Spanish was prohibited in schools and workplaces. The debate rages on among educators and government alike.

If Hispanic refers to all natives and descendants of Latin America, it is including no less than twenty countries—whose shared patterns of colonization may allow them to be called Pan-American, but whose histories and cultural attitudes are nevertheless diverse in very particular ways.

How can people from the Caribbean states, whose economies depended on slave trade, be generically called Hispanic? Is it because they are from states that are presently Spanish speaking or were once colonized by the Spaniards, although they may presently be under another country's dominion? In the Caribbean, Hispanic includes Puerto Ricans, Cubans, and Dominicans. While Cuba's official language has remained Spanish since Spanish rule, many of its people are of African ancestry. Citizens of the Dominican Republic are considered Hispanic because they speak Spanish, but the residents of the other side of their island, Haiti, speak French (and more commonly, as I understand, patois). Are there enough major racial differences between these two nationalities on the same island to justifiably classify one as Hispanic but not the other? The Philippines were once colonized by Spain and now have English as a dominant language, but they are not classified as Hispanic. They are placed in another catch-all group, Asian.

Hispanic gives us all one ultimate paternal cultural progenitor: Spain. The diverse cultures already on the American shores when the Europeans arrived, as well as those introduced because of the African slave trade, are completely obliterated by the term. Hispanic is nothing more than a concession made by the U.S. legislature when they saw they couldn't get rid of us. If we won't go away, why not at least Europeanize us, make us presentable guests at the dinner table, take away our feathers and rattles and civilize us once and for all.

This erroneous but nationally accepted label invented by a white supremacist bureaucracy essentially is a resignation to allow, after more than two hundred years of denial, some cultural representation of the conquistadors who originally colonized the Southwest. Until now, in other words, only Anglo-Saxons were legitimate informants of American culture.

To further worsen the supposition that we can be Hispanic—simply long forgotten descendants of Europeans just as white people are—is the horrific history of brutal and inhuman subjugation that not only Amerindians experienced under Spanish and other European rules in Mexico and throughout Latin America and the Caribbean, but all those of mixed blood. Indeed, shortly after the Conquest of Mexico, Spanish rule set up a complex caste system in which to be of mixed-blood virtually excluded you from full rights as citizens and protection by the law. Jews and Moors in that Catholic society also experienced racist attitudes. Just as with today's African-Americans, among mestizo/as and Amerindians, the result of such intense, legislated racism throughout centuries is demoralization. As one historian puts it regarding the Mexic Amerindian people, "Trauma and neuroses linger still, and may not be entirely overcome. For the Spaniards, in Mexico, did not commit genocide; they committed culturcide."

Among Latino/as in the United States today there is a universe of differences. There is a universe of difference, for example, between the experience of the Cuban man who arrived in the United States as a child with his parents after fleeing Castro's revolution and the Puerto Rican woman who is a third generation single mother on the Lower East Side. There is a universe of difference between the young Mexican American aspiring to be an actor in Hollywood in the nineties and the community organizer working for rent control for the last ten years in San Francisco, although both may be sons of farmworkers. There is a universe of difference between Carolina Herrera, South American fashion designer and socialite, and a Guatemalan refugee who has hardly learned to speak Spanish but must already adapt to English in order to work as a domestic in the United States. Picture her: She is not statuesque or blonde (like Ms. Herrera). She is short, squat, with a moon face, and black, oily hair. She does not use six pieces of silverware at the dinner table, but one, if any, and a tortilla. There is a universe of differences among all of these individuals, yet Anglo society says they all belong to the same ethnic group: Hispanic.

A study by the University of Chicago shows that deep divisions based on race exist between black Hispanics and white Hispanics in the United States. The black/white dichotomy of the United States causes black Hispanics to relate more to African Americans than to non-black Hispanics. It is also revealed that "black Hispanics are far more segregated from U.S. whites than are white Hispanics." *Color*, rather than saying simply ethnicity, in addition to class and gender, as well as *conscientización*, all determine one's identity and predict one's fate in the United States.

EXCEPT FOR THE HISTORICAL PERIOD CHARACTERIZED BY "MANIFEST DESTINY" fate is not part of United States Anglo Saxon ideology. But the United States does have a fate.

Sir John Glubb in his book *A Short History Of The Arab Peoples* suggests reviewing world history to see how frequently great empires reach and fall from their pinnacle of power, all within two hundred to three hundred years. According to Glubb, for example, the Greek Empire (330 B.C. to about 100 B.C.) lasted two hundred and thirty years; the Spaniards endured for (1556 to 1800) two hundred and forty four years; and the British Empire lasted two hundred and thirty years (1700 to 1930). It is sobering to note that no great power simply lost its position as number one slipping into second or third place, nor has any former great power ever resumed its original, unchallenged position. They all have ceased to exist as a world power. After the fall of the Roman Empire, Italy has been little more than the home of the Pope for the past fifteen centuries. Moreover, regarding his figures Glubb tells us, "It is not desired to insist on rigid numbers, for many outside factors influence the fates of great nations. Nevertheless, the resemblance between the lives of so many and such varied empires is extremely striking, and is obviously entirely unconnected with the development of those mechanical devices of which we are so proud." "Mechanical devices" means military might.

Signs of the decline of the United States as the leading world power are most apparent in the phenomenal growth of the public debt in the 1980s: during the Reagan-Bush years, the public debt of the United States went from

907.7 billion dollars in 1980 to over 3 trillion dollars in 1990 (as reported by the United States Department of the Treasury).

The United States, being a relatively young, therefore resilient country, can and eventually will allow for the representation of people of color in the institutions that influence and mandate peoples' lives—government, private industry, and universities, for example. It will gradually relent with its blatant refusal to fulfill its professed democratic ideals and include the descendants of its slave trade, the Native Americans, mestizo/as, and Asians (who also come from a wide variety of countries and social and economic backgrounds and who, due to various political circumstances, are immigrating to the United States at an exorbitant rate). It will do so because the world economy will not permit anything short of it. Nevertheless, most assuredly among those who will get further pushed down as the disparity between the few wealthy and the impoverished grows, will be our gente.

THE LARGEST MOVEMENT IN THE HISTORY OF THE UNITED STATES ever to force the government to reckon with its native Latino population was the Chicano/Latino Movement of the late 1960s and 1970s. Because of its force there is today a visible sector of Latinos who are college degreed, who have mortgages on decent houses, and who are articulate in English. (In Spanish, when a person has facility in a language to get by, we say we can "defend" ourselves; we now have a substantial number of Latinos who are defending themselves against Anglophile culture.) The generation that came of age in the 1980s was given the general message that acculturation can be rewarding. Yes, the status quo will always reward those who succumb to it, who serve it, and who do not threaten its well being.

In 1980 when the Republicans and the Reagan administration came to office, their tremendous repression quashed the achievements of the Chicano/Latino Movement, which has been based on collectivism and the retention of our Mexican/Amerindian culture. Community projects and grassroots programs dependent on government funding—rehabilitation and training, child care, early education and alternative schooling, youth counseling, cultural projects that supported the arts and community artists, rehab-housing for low income families, and women's shelters—shut down.

In their place the old "American Dream"—a WASP male philosophy on which this country was founded at the expense of third world labor—was reinstated. As in U.S. society before the Civil Rights Movement, material accumulation equaled self-worth.

The new generation of Chicanos and Latinos who came of age in the 1980s had a radically different attitude than the collective mentality of the 1970s activists, believing that after two hundred years of racist and ethnic exploitation, the age of the "Hispanic" had finally come. Their abuelos, tíos, parents (some who had been in the Chicano/Latino Movement) had paid the dues for the American Dream. Now they could finally claim their own place in society. They had acculturated.

Encouraged by media hype announcing our arrival in the 1980s as the "Decade of the Hispanic," for the first time in U.S. history, ad campaigns took the Latino/a consumer into consideration. Magazines, billboards and even television commercials (Coors comes to mind) showed young, brown, beautiful Latina models in flashy wear reaping some of the comforts and pleasures of a democracy based on free enterprise. Also, there was the unprecedented tokenism of Latino/as in visible and high-level government posts and private industry that further convinced many among the new generation that each individual indeed had the ability to fulfill his or her own great master plan for material success. The new generation was not alone. The previous generation became more conservative along with immigrating Latinos who also believed in the Republican administration and the trickle down theory of Reaganomics.

It is difficult to generalize why so many Latino/as moved toward conservative, if not overtly right wing, views. Personal disillusionment with leftist ideology may explain in part the change in attitude and goals for some. But for many, I believe it is basically a matter of desiring material acquisitions. It is difficult to maintain a collective ideology in a society where possessions and power-status equal self-worth.

Unfortunately, the continuous drop of the U.S. dollar in the world trade market caused the economy to worsen each year. In the 1980s, jobs were lost, companies closed down and moved out of the country, banks foreclosed on mortgages, and scholarships and grants once available to needy college students in the 1970s were taken away. These were only a few of the losses experienced not only by Latino/as but by much of the population.

Simultaneously, the cost of living went up. The much coveted trendy lifestyle of the white yuppie moved further away from the grasp of the young and upwardly mobile Reagan-Bush generation. The nineties ushered a new generation cognizant of the white hegemonic atmosphere entrenched in colleges and universities and with a vigor reminiscent of the student movements of two decades earlier, have begun protests on campuses throughout the country. The acceleration of gang violence in cities, drug wars, cancer on the rise, and AIDS continue to be the backdrop, while the new decade's highlights so far for living in these difficult times were the Persian Gulf War Espectáculo and the Rodney King riots that resounded throughout the world—sending out a message that this is indeed a troubled country.

EL MOVIMIENTO CHICANO/LATINO saw its rise and fall within a time span of less than two decades on these territories where our people have resided for thousands of years. El Movimiento (or La Causa) was rooted to a degree in Marxist oriented theory (despite the strong ties activists felt to their Catholic upbringings) because it offered some response to our oppression under capitalism. Socialist and communist theories which were based on late nineteenth century ideas on the imminent mass industrialization of society, did not foresee the high technology world of the late twentieth century—one hundred years later—or fully consider the implications of race, gender, and sexual-preference differences on that world. Wealth accumulation no longer simply stays within the genteel class but our aristocracy now includes athletes, rock stars, and Hollywood celebrities.

THE EARLY FEMINISTA, as the Chicana feminist referred to herself then, had been actively fighting against her socioeconomic subjugation as a Chicana and as a woman since 1968, the same year the Chicano Movement was announced. I am aware that there have been Chicana activists throughout U.S. history, but I am using as a date of departure an era in which women consciously referred to themselves as *feministas*.

An analysis of the social status of la Chicana was already underway by early feministas, who maintained that racism, sexism, and sexist racism were the mechanisms that socially and economically oppressed them. But, for reasons explained here, they were virtually censored. The early history of la feminista was documented in a paper entitled, "La Feminista," by Anna Nieto Gómez and published in *Encuentro Feminil: The First Chicana Feminist Journal*, which may now be considered, both article and journal, archival material.

The early feminista who actively participated in the woman's movement had to educate white feminist groups on their political, cultural, and philosophical differences. Issues that specifically concerned the feminista of that period were directly related to her status as a non-Anglo, culturally different, often Spanish-speaking woman of lower income. Early white feminism compared sexism (as experienced by white middle-class women) to the racism that African Americans are subjected to. But African American feminists, such as those of the Rio Combahee Collective, pointed out that this was not only an inaccurate comparison but revealed an inherent racist attitude on the part of white feminists who did not understand what it was to be a woman *and* black in America.

By the same token, brown women were forced into a position in which we had to point out similar differences as well as continuously struggle against a prevalent condescension on the part of white middle-class women toward women of color, poor women, and women whose first language is Spanish and whose culture is not mainstream American. *This Bridge Called My Back*, first published in 1981, as well as other texts by feminists of color that followed, serve as excellent testimonies regarding these issues and the experiences of feminists of color in the 1970s.

At the same time, according to Nieto Gómez, feministas were labeled as *vendidas* (sell-outs) by activists within *La Causa*. Such criticism came not solely from men but also from women, whom Nieto Gómez calls Loyalists. These Chicanas believed that racism, not sexism, was the greater battle. Moreover, the Loyalists distrusted any movement led by any sector of white society. The early white women's movement saw its battle based on sex and gender and did not take into account the race and class differences of women of color. The Loyalists had some reason to feel reluctant and cynical toward an ideology and organizing effort that at best was condescending toward them. Loyalists told the feministas that they should be fighting such hard-hitting community problems as police brutality, Viet Nam, and La Huelga, the United Farm Workers labor strike. But white female intellectuals were largely unaware of these issues. While the Chicana resided in a first world nation, indeed the most powerful nation at that time, she was part of a historically colonized people.

I am referring to the approximate period between 1968 through the 1970s. However, more than twenty years later, the Chicana—that is a brown woman of Mexican descent, residing in the United States with political consciousness—is still participating in the struggle for recognition and respect from white dominant society. Residing throughout her life in a society that systematically intentionally or out of ignorance marginalizes her existence, often stereotypes her when she does "appear," suddenly represented (for example by mass-media or government sources), and perhaps more importantly, relegates her economic status to among the lowest paid according to the U.S. Census Bureau, the Chicana continues to be a countryless woman. She is—I am, we are—not considered to be, except marginally and stereotypically, United States citizens.

Nevertheless, according to las feministas, feminism was "a very dynamic aspect of the Chicana's heritage and not at all foreign to her nature." Contrary to ethnographic data that portrays Chicanas as submissive followers who are solely designated to preserve the culture, the feminista did not see herself or other women of her culture as such. While the feminist dialogue remained among the activists in el Movimiento, one sees in *Encuentro Feminil* that there indeed existed a solid initiative toward Chicana feminist thought, that is, recognition of sexism as a primary issue, as early on as the late 1960s. Clarifying the differences between the needs of the Anglo feminist and the feminista was part of the early feminista's tasks.

And if the focus of the Chicano male-dominated movement with regard to women had to do with family issues, the feminista zeroed in on the very core of what those issues meant. For instance, the feministas believed that women would make use of birth control and abortion clinics if in fact they felt safe going for these services; that is, if they were community controlled. Birth control and abortion are pertinent issues for all women, but they were particularly significant to the Chicana who had always been at the mercy of Anglo controlled institutions and policies.

Non-consenting sterilizations of women—poor white, Spanish speaking, welfare recipients, poor women of color—women in prison among them—during the 1970s were being conducted and sponsored by the U.S. government. One third of the female population of Puerto Rico was sterilized during that period. The case of ten Chicanas (*Madrigal v. Quilligan*) against the Los Angeles County Hospital who were sterilized without their consent led to activism demanding release of the Health, Education and Welfare (HEW) guidelines for sterilizations. During that period, HEW was financing up to 100,000 sterilizations a year.

The feminista also wanted a bicultural and bilingual child care that would validate their children's culture and perhaps ward off an inferiority complex before they had a chance to start public school; traditionally, monolingual and anglocentric schools had alienated children, causing them great psychological damage.

The early feminista understood the erroneous conceptions of the White Woman's Movement that equated sexism to racism because she was experiencing its compounding effects in her daily life. The feministas were fighting against being a "minority" in the labor market. According to Nieto Gómez, more Anglo women had jobs than did women of color. We must keep in mind that most women of color in this country have always needed employment to maintain even a level of subsistence for their families.

According to the 1991 U.S. Dept. of Commerce Census Bureau Report, income figures for 1989 show that "Hispanic" women are still among the lowest paid workers in the United States, earning less than African American women:

WEEKLY INCOME
Hispanic women $269.00
Black women 301.00
White women 334.00
Hispanic men 315.00
Black men 348.00
All Other Women 361.00

The mestiza still ranks in the labor force among the least valued in this country. In Susan Faludi's bestselling *Backlash*, which focuses on the media's backlash against the white feminist movement, the only noteworthy observation of women of color refers to our economic status in the 1980s. Faludi states that overall income did not increase for the African American woman and for the Hispanic woman, it actually got worse.

CLASHING OF CULTURES We need not look very far back or for very long to see that we have been marginalized in every sense of the word by U.S. society. But an understanding of the U.S. economic system and its relationship to Mexico is essential in order that we may understand our inescapable role as a productive/reproductive entity within U.S./Mexican society for the past two hundred years.

The transnational labor force into which most of us are born was created out of Mexico's neocolonialist relationship to the United States. Throughout the history of the United States, Mexicans have served as a labor reserve controlled by U.S. policy. Mexico encourages the emigration of this labor force to alleviate its own depressed economy, and the United States all too willingly consumes this labor without giving it the benefits enjoyed by U.S. residents.

Contrary to the ideological claim of the United States that insists that all immigrants (which by legislature and action meant European) pay their dues before being able to participate fully in its melting pot economy, the underpaid Mexican worker is crucial to the survival of the profit-based system of the United States. The maquiladoras illustrate this point.

Since the late sixties, U.S. production has undergone a transfer of manufacturing to less industrialized nations, such as México. The U.S.-Mexican border has been an appealing site for such assembly operations. Unskilled women pressed with dire economic necessity serve as a reserve for these industries. A continuing influx of labor from the interior of México provides competition and keeps wages at a base minimum. Daily wage for a maquiladora *rose* to a mere $3.50 per day in 1988. An unofficial border source told me that that figure had risen to $3.75 per day in 1992. The outrageously low wages for working in dangerous and unregulated conditions are among the strongest arguments against the free-trade agreements between United States, Mexico, and Canada.

The cultural and religious beliefs that maintain that most Latinas on either side of the border are (and should be) dependent on their men for economic survival are not only unrealistic, evidence shows they do not reflect reality. On this side of the border, according to the 1987 Department of Labor Report, one million "Hispanic" households were headed by women. Their average income was $337.00 per week. Fifty-two percent of these households headed by women survive below poverty level.

Any woman without the major support of the father of her children and who has no other resources, must, in order to survive, commodify her labor. Even most Chicano/Latino men do not earn enough to support their families; their wives must go outside the home to earn an income (or bring it home in the form of piece work). Furthermore, statistics show that many mothers do not live with the father of their children and do not receive any kind of financial assistance from him.

MOST CHICANAS/LATINAS ARE NOT CONSCIENTICIZED. The majority of the populace, on either side of the border, in fact, is not actively devoted to real social change. That sense of inferiority, as when two people were confronted with their mexicanidad on the streets of downtown Chicago, permeates most Chicanas' self-perceptions. Lack of conscientización is what makes the maquiladora an ideal worker for the semi-legal, exploitative operations of multinational factory production.

At an early age we learn that our race is undesirable. Because of possible rejection, some of us may go to any length to deny our background. But one cannot cruelly judge such women who have resorted to negation of their own heritage; constant rejection has accosted us since childhood. Certain women indeed had contact early on in their lives with México and acquired enough identification with its diverse culture and traditions to battle against the attempts of white, middle class society to usurp all its citizens into an abstract culture obsessed with material gain.

But many women born in the United States or brought here during childhood have little connection with the country of our ancestors. The umbilical cord was severed before we could develop the intellectual and emotional link to México, to the astonishing accomplishments of its indigenous past, to its own philosophical and spiritual nature so much at odds with that of the WASP. Instead we flounder between invisibility and a tacit hope that we may be accepted here and awarded the benefits of acculturation.

Looking different, that is, not being white nor black but something in between in a society that has historically acknowledged only a black/white racial schism is cause for great anxiety. Our internalized racism causes us to boast of our light coloring, if indeed we have it, or imagine it. We hope for light-skinned children and brag no end of those infants who happen to be born güeros, white looking, we are downright ecstatic if they have light colored eyes and hair. We sometimes tragically reject those children who are dark.

On the subject of color and internal conflicts there are also those who, despite identification with Latino heritage are light-skinned because of their dominating European genes or because one parent is white. For some this may be an added reason for internalizing racism, particularly when young (since it is difficult to explain the world to yourself when you are growing up). But for others, while their güero coloring may cause them to experience less racial tension in broad society, it may cause tension for a variety of reasons in their home, chosen communities, and when politically active against racism.

Let us consider for a moment a woman who does not necessarily desire marriage or bearing children, and works instead to attain a higher standard of living for herself. She must still interact with and quite often be subordinate to white people, and occasionally African Americans. I do not want to elaborate on the dynamics of her relationships with African Americans since it is understood here that institutionalized racism has not allowed either race to have real domination over the other. My own experience has been one of cultural difference rather than a racial one since there are also "black hispanos." But I will note that she will in all likelihood still feel "foreign" with African Americans who have an acknowledged history in the United States. Because of slavery, white people *know* why African Americans are here. They also *know* why Native Americans are here, yet they *assume* mestizos have all migrated here for economic gain as their own people did.

To compound our anxiety over our foreign-like identity in the United States is the fact that Mexican Americans are also not generally accepted in México. We are derogatorily considered *pochos*, American Mexicans who are either among the traitors or trash of Mexico because we, or previous generations, made the United States home. Unlike the experiences that many African Americans have had in "returning" and being welcomed in Africa, many U.S.-born mestizo/as have found themselves more unwelcomed by mexicanos than white gringos.

Aside from skin color, language can add to the trauma of the Chicana's schizophrenic-like existence. She was educated in English and learned it is the only acceptable language in society, but Spanish was the language of her childhood, family, and community. She may not be able to rid herself of an accent; society has denigrated her first language. By the same token, women may also become anxious and self-conscious in later years if they have no or little facility in Spanish. They may feel that they had been forced to forfeit an important part of their personal identity and still never found acceptability by white society.

Race, ethnicity, and language are important factors for women who aspire to a decent standard of living in our anglocentric, xenophobic society. Gender compounds their social dilemma and determines the very nature of their lifestyle regardless of the ability to overcome all other obstacles set against them.

Feminism at its simplest has not ever been solely a political struggle for women's rights, i.e., equal pay for equal work. The early feminista's initial attempts at placing women-related issues at the forefront were once viewed with suspicion by Marxist-oriented activists as The Woman Question was seen to be separate from or less significant than race and class issues by most activists, and along with gay issues, even thought to be an indication of betrayal to La Causa. Along those lines, in the 1990s; while issues of sexuality have come to the forefront, most recently with the national debate of permitting gays in the military, there remains a strong heterosexist bias among Chicano/Hispanic/Latino based organizations and our varying communities.

With the tenacious insistence at integrating a feminist perspective to their political conscientización as Chicanas, feminist activistas, and intellectuals are in the process of developing what I call Xicanisma. On a pragmatic level, the basic premise of Xicanisma is to reconsider behavior long seen as inherent in the Mexic Amerindian woman's character, such as, patience, perseverance, industriousness, loyalty to one's clan, and commitment to our children. Contrary to how those incognizant of what feminism is, we do not reject these virtues. We may not always welcome the taxing responsibility that comes with our roles as Chicanas. We've witnessed what strain and limitations they often placed on our mothers and other relatives. But these traits often seen as negative and oppressive to our growth as women, as well as having been translated to being equal to being a drone for white society and its industrial interests, may be considered strengths. Simultaneously, as we redefine (not categorically reject) our roles within our families, communities at large, and white dominant society, our Xicanisma helps us to be self-confident and assertive regarding the pursuing of our needs and desires.

As brown-skinned females, often bilingual but not from a Spanish speaking country (not a Mexican citizen yet generally considered to not really be American), frequently discouraged in numerous ways from pursuing formal education, usually with limited economic means, therefore made to compete in a racist and sexist lower skilled work force, we continue to be purposely rendered invisibly by society except as a stereotype and in other denigrating ways. The U.S. Women's Movement, which in fact began long before the Civil Rights Movement and the ensuing Chicano Movement, is now incorporating a more expansive vision that includes the unique perceptions and experiences of all peoples heretofore excluded from the democratic promise of the United States. Until we are all represented, respected, and protected by society and the laws that govern it, the status of the Chicana will be that of a countryless woman.

62. Danya Ruttenberg, "Blood Simple: Transgender Theory Hits the Mikveh," from *Yentl's Revenge*

Excerpts from "Blood Simple: Transgender Theory Hits the Mikveh," by Danya Ruttenberg, published in *Yentl's Revenge*, ed. Danya Ruttenberg (Seattle: Seal Press, 2001), 77–87. Reprinted with permission.

In this compelling personal and theoretically informed essay, Ruttenberg discusses her ambivalent relationship with Jewish history and its customs—such as the mikveh (ritual cleansing)—regarding the female body. Using the lens of transgender theory, she strives to "help Jewish feminists solve the menstruation dilemma, and help us figure out how to save a great ritual that's been perverted by a wretched history." A refreshing reinterpretation of biology, spirituality, and gender, Ruttenberg's essay is a must-read for third-wavers of any orientation or tradition.

I blame it on my friend Karissa, really. Her spiritual shtick is of the eclectic, earth-based variety, and one day as she was playing show-and-tell with her ritual stuff, things got personal.

"... with the bear-tooth charm. I wear the cowrie shell on a cord around my waist when I have my period; the rest of the time, it lives in this bag here." She pointed to the bag.

Her custom was pretty simple, and subtle: Wear a thingy on certain days to mark that the body's doing something different than it does on a lot of other days. No major hoopla, she just notices and registers the shift.

To my own shock and surprise, I felt a twinge. I couldn't believe that a part of me was ... *ack*. It's true. Jealous. For the first time in my life, I felt compelled to do what had always seemed to me so weird and dorky, so totally passé—what people who I thought I was much cooler than would call "honoring the sacred feminine." Or something like that. That, you know, lavender, touchy-feely, hand-holdy womyn-y-stuff that always made me cringe. But suddenly I couldn't stop thinking about menstruation.

I'd been practicing Judaism for a few years by this point, but always, *always* with an egalitarian bent. I was glad that the previous generation had pointed out that the modesty laws were nasty and the rule against singing was a crock, but I assumed that the point of their efforts was to save us from having to do the same. "Sometimes we're not Jewish women," I wrote when I was about twenty-two. "Sometimes, we're just Jews."

The reason for my egal-orientation seemed obvious: Judaism, from its inception, made male normative and female derivative. So for the spiritual seeker looking for the most meaningful aspects of a long, valorous tradition, it made sense to get in on the boys' stuff, on the bits from which we were excluded back in the days of chattel and slavery. Simple logic, really: The good parts have traditionally been given to the boys. So, we should do them, because they're the good parts. Duh. It's not that I wasn't a feminist—my feminism long predated my Judaism, and every move I made was predicated on the assumption that all people have a right to the power, to the spiritual riches available in this amazing ritual system.

But as I slowly became more observant, I started to develop an increasingly strong awareness of nature's, and my body's, role in my spiritual life. I love the naturalistic aspect of Judaism—watching the sun slowly set at the end of Shabbat, celebrating major moments in the agricultural year, blessing food as it comes from the land, from the vine, from the tree. And certainly marking menstruation with ritual is in some ways just as earthy—noting the body's inherent rhythms, making holy the moment of differentiation between one state of being and another.

Of course a religion as nitpicky and thorough as Judaism has already addressed menses. The modern laws of *niddah*, or menstruation, dictate that a woman is forbidden to have sex with her husband for the duration of her period and, according to some, for seven "clean" (or "white") days after. At the end of the abstention period (either roughly seven or fourteen days, depending on which tradition she follows) she goes to the mikveh, the ritual bath, and immerses herself with a blessing, thus rendering herself once again able to hop back into the marital bed.

There are couples who say the no-sex thing allows them to have a second honeymoon every single month—thus making their connection stronger the rest of the time—and adds a dimension of the sacred into their sexual relationship. And whether or not you're in a relationship (and/or just sexually active), the age-old appeal of surrender in water is hard to ignore. Many have testified to the profound spiritual effect of the mikveh, to the way it can deep-clean your soul just like *that*.

Whoosh.

The appeal of a menstruation rite became clearer. Judaism, as a religious system, is designed to affect every aspect of a person's life. We mark the doors of our houses with prayer, we say a blessing upon seeing a rainbow or an old friend. It's *about* living, and to not mark the birth-death cycles of the reproductive system would seem, well, like an omission.

As I began to spend more time noticing trees and looking at constellations, the urge to mark my own monthly passage increased. I ... I actually *wanted* to go to the mikveh when my period was done.

Despite the allure, though, I couldn't go. I couldn't let myself.

Why?

I knew the history, and the history made me mad.

In the book of Leviticus, menstruation was only one of many things—including touching a corpse, leprosy and male ejaculation—rendering a person ritually impure vis-à-vis entering the ancient Temple. This in itself was not problematic; similar rules applied to both men and women. But when the Temple was destroyed in 70 CE, the Rabbis were forced to rework Judaism in a lot of different ways. Folks stopped observing the purity laws, but the injunction against sex with a menstruant fell into a different legal category, and thus had to be minded even with no Temple in town. However, once menstruation became the only "polluting" force (if you will), the guys making the decisions began to treat it in a totally different way—tacking on extra injunctions and restrictions that hadn't ever been necessary before. As Tirzah Meacham writes, the early Rabbis began a "trend of thinking in which the category of normal menstruation ... came to fall in the category of abnormal bleeding, *zavah*."

Perhaps you can see where this is headed?

As time passed, menstruation became a way to express misogynistic fears about female as danger, female as death, female as the scary dark power that must be controlled. The Rabbis ask, "Why was the precept of niddah given to [Eve]? Because she spilled the blood of Adam," and muse about the feminine charms with clever euphemisms: "Though a woman be a pot of filth whose mouth is full of blood ... all chase after her." Further, they posit, "If a menstruous woman passes between two [men]—if it is at the beginning of her menstruation, she will cause one to die; if it is at the end of her menstruation, she will bring strife between them."

By the Middle Ages, the menstruant's "nail parings and the dust upon which she trod were believed to cause boils. Since such casual contact could inflict bodily harm, it follows that ... having sexual relations with menstruants would give rise to leperous births in families for generations to come."

It's enough to make a girl give up on Judaism entirely. I've come close, a couple of times, wondering if these guys have tainted the water in the ritual pool enough to invalidate the whole system. There are a lot of folks who think we should just pitch the niddah laws because they've convinced so many people that women's bodies are dirty, impure. Yet I do believe that we've managed, somehow, to get over feminist roadblocks that were at least as serious, if not more so.

And besides the fact that throwing away the niddah laws means we don't get a nice cycles-of-nature spiritual opportunity, I also think to do so would be a copout. Over time I've grown to regard halakha not only as a series of unrelated challenges aimed at making me a nicer, stronger, more-aware-of-the-sacred person, but as a whole entity—imperfect yet all-encompassing, the metronome by which life can be better and more fully lived. In Judaism, you don't get to do the stuff that seems fun and forget the parts that make you work a little; it's an organic system. You don't cut off your foot because your ankle's broken—nor, however, it is helpful to pretend that nothing's wrong. What needs to happen, of course, is that you have to fix the ankle.

I believe that, like women's (former) exclusion from many ritual roles, the laws of niddah are ripe for transformation—and deserving of close scrutiny, especially given the number of questions they raise about gender.

Entire Pandora's boxes of gender have been opened up in the last ten or fifteen years. I know butch dykes who consider their gender box c) none of the above, and femme lesbians who identify more with drag queens than straight women. There are places in the United States where people believe that gender can be chosen—which can mean anything from "what we've been taught about 'girls' and 'boys' is a crock of hooey" to "I use words that resonate with my internal knowledge of myself" to "I need a change on the biological level." To say nothing of the possibly 2 percent of the population born as "intersex."

It's important to look at transgender theory for two reasons: First, the people who have chosen to live in the gray areas of sex and gender have a lot to tell us about how the construction of gender plays out in our society. Feminism needs trans thinkers to help push the envelope even further, especially when so many of us take in a million hidden influence and tiny gender-poisons, courtesy of the society in which we were raised and live. Trans folks can help us see even more clearly the assumption and biases of a gendered society, and the ways in which a world of binary gender hurts everyone. The work being done in the trans community may well hold the key to feminism's future; the ideas being worked through there may be exactly the tools feminists have been seeking for a long time. Certainly, they may help Jewish feminists solve the menstruation dilemma and help us figure out how to save a great ritual that's been perverted by a wretched history. More on that in a moment.

Second, not everyone wants to, or can, or should, live fully as a man fully as a woman or in the gender s/he was assigned at birth. Feminism is a movement working toward the freedom from gender oppression, from the belief that "biology equals destiny," so it's imperative that the needs and interests of transgendered people are understood and fought for. If "women" get rights but "transpeople" are still under constant attack, we as a society haven't accomplished a thing.

Though we've been raised in a binary system of "male" and "female," many, many cultures throughout time—including our own—have seen degrees in between.

Leslie Feinberg writes in *Transgender Warriors* that "although what we think about gender today has been expressed differently in diverse historical periods, cultures, regions, nationalities and classes, there appears to have always been gender diversity in the human population. And there is just as much evidence that sexes have not always been arbitrarily squeezed into hard-and-fast categories of woman and man, and that fluidity between the sexes is an ancient path." The book details fluctuations of gender expression—and gender-crossing—from traditional African cultures and ancient Greece through the Middle Ages into today, and shows how gender has been shaped and read over time.

It could be argued that Judaism has always worked on a binary system; that's what gendered halakha is all about (despite the fact that the Talmud records several "other" genders—people born with two sets of sexual characteristics, or none—and usually assigns them low status, sometimes as low as, say, women). Yes, the Torah includes an injunction against women wearing men's clothing and men wearing women's clothing. But if a woman wears an article of clothing, doesn't it become an article of women's clothing? And more to the point, what is "woman"? And what is "man"? And how do we know?

The beauty of Jewish law is that it's constantly evolving; the Talmud has never actually been completed. Every generation of rabbis offers a new opinion on everything from the most ancient of issues—defining kosher food, for example—to the most modern, such as *in vitro* fertilization. As philosopher Yeshayahu Leibowitz has said, "What characterizes Judaism as a religion of Mitzvoth is not the set of laws and commandments that was given out at the start, but rather the recognition of a system of precepts as binding, even if their specifics were often determined only with time."

Of course, there are nuances and subtleties (and serious rules) regarding the evolution of Jewish law in which I'm not fully versed; I don't purport that this essay is an ironclad *responsum* in any way. But the questions I'm raising will have to be answered, I think, because the system as it exists now does not completely reflect humanity as we are beginning to understand it. Rabbi Harold Schulweis once said, "I am not a halakhic scholar but I am convinced that morality played an important and conscious role in the halakhic tradition. And I do know as a Jew ... what seizes me about our tradition and makes my heart leap with joy. And it certainly is not the denigration of the human Jewish ethical sensibility." Halakha at the expense of our ability to be wholly who we are in the healthiest and holiest of respects is halakha in need of repair. And I'd argue that halakha that divides us into genders is, in this day and age, imperfectly rendered.

Feinberg's cross-cultural gender survey, much to my surprise, offers one possible solution to the niddah quandary: It seems that "the people we would call male-to-female transsexuals in ... early [communal] societies ritually menstruated and wore 'the leaves prescribed for women in their courses.'" Elsewhere, in North American Mohave culture, young men who undergo a male-to-female initiation ritual assume female names, find a husband and simulate menstruation, pregnancy and miscarriage. Men have, in other times and places, observed menstruation rituals as a way of marking their female identification.

Even on the slightly less gray ends of the spectrum, there's no such thing as "perfect gender." Not even those who identify as male or female—and are comfortable and happy with that identification—embody "perfect manhood" or "perfect womanhood." What would that be, exactly? A woman who is always demure and never outspoken? A man who is never a nurturer? A hundred and fifty years ago, the ideas of a woman in pants was downright shocking; now, even "women" wearing "men's" underwear doesn't really defy anybody's concept of gender.

Identity is a strange, mutable thing. As we shift and grow, we constantly change the way we see ourselves—and, consciously or not, the way we conceive of our gender, of ourselves as gendered, changes too. Change can be as simple as a renewed interest in lipstick or the acquisition of combat boots, or it can be much more complex.

Feinberg issues a battle cry: "Let's open the door to everyone who is self-identified as a woman, and who wants to be in women's space. (Not every woman wants that experience.) Let's keep the door unlocked."

Hey, why the heck not?

Why not allow for a more open understanding of gender in which we all might fit on the continuum, from female to female-masculine to androgynous to male-feminine to male and back again? What if we allow the words we use to describe ourselves—and the rituals we choose to observe—to reflect that shift? What if we allow our gender identity to ebb and flow with the rest of our sense of self? After all, isn't feminism supposed to be about the right to self-define?

When I think about the possible implications for gendered halakha, it seems absolutely radical. Almost too radical for me, to be honest. But at the same time, utterly freeing.

What if the aspects of Jewish law that address biological gender became as mutable as gender itself? What if we maintained the idea of the niddah laws—the monthly connection, the cycles of abstinence and reunion, the immersion into ritual water—but allowed our definition of "woman" to be more fluid? And didn't require those who didn't identify as "women" to participate?

Look, I'm not a moron; I know that the niddah laws are intended to address menstruation, not female identity. Post-menopausal women don't traditionally go to the mikveh, nor do pregnant women. But this particular rite has accrued such a tremendous power over the years, especially lately, as a "women's ritual." The Rabbis gave the female biological process unreasonably heavy sociocultural weight in a fairly evil way, enabling women to feel terrible about their bodies and, in the process, feel as if they're under patriarchal lock and key.

There's the Jewish women's custom of slapping her daughter at the time of first menses and telling her, "Now you know, a woman's life is hardship and pain." Why are all of the horrors of male domination located in that first moment of bleeding?

The niddah laws have become an icon of Jewish womanhood; for women on all sides of this discussion, they are about much more than a monthly ovarian delivery. Radical measures clearly need to be taken—to restore our right to define ourselves and to re-sanctify our bodies, on our own damn terms—if we're ever to get all of that mud out of the mikveh. I think it's vital to at least consider new ways of approaching the issues . . . and maybe through the age-old process of debate, we can forge our way to a new understanding.

Women are not technically obligated to pray three times a day, to wear a tallis or to lay tefillin—they're legally exempt from anything that is considered a "time-bound mitzvah." (Historically it was understood that caring for children might preclude, for example, saying the afternoon prayers on time.) However, since the advent of feminism some women have taken advantage of the right to obligate themselves to these "male" mitzvot; upon this declaration of obligation, their legal status in relation to those mitzvot is the same as that of men—just as binding.

Couldn't, then, someone not born a woman decide to obligate him or herself to the mitzvah of niddah observance? (Here, we might define the mitzvah as a week or two of abstinence a month, followed by immersion in the mikveh—whatever the gender and observance level of the participant and the participant's partner.) We could sanction the act whether the person in question is a male-to-female transgendered person (who can, by the way, take hormones to mimic a menstrual cycle) or a man who identifies as female, whether said person considers observance of the niddah laws an extension of a gender identity or whether s/he wants to use the niddah laws as a way of connecting his/her body to the cycles of the moon, the month, passing time. Like a woman announcing that she is duty-bound to lay tefillin everyday, someone who declares s/he is obligated to this mitzvah would be required to maintain its practice as long as the mitzvah remained concordant with the gender identity. Of course, this principle could also extend to women who don't menstruate every month—for reasons ranging from reproductive irregularity to chemotherapy—but would like to be a part of the holy cycle, the sacred bodily connection.

As for folks who menstruate but don't want to emphasize that aspect of themselves—whether female-to-male transgendered people, people who identify as butch, or women who have had problematic relationships with their biology—there are precedents for that, too. In the Middle Ages the rabbis asked this question: When the prophet Elijah turned into an angel in the book of Kings, was his wife permitted to remarry, even though he had neither divorced nor widowed her? Ultimately it was decided that a woman is barred from marrying so long as she is another man's wife, and this woman was married to an angel, not a man. Since angels have no gender, the marriage was, the rabbis decided, therefore annulled. It could certainly be argued, as an extension of this logic, that if a person gets to a point where s/he does not identify as a "woman"—if s/he changes gender, biologically or sociologically—then s/he would not be obligated to mitzvot to which "women" are obligated. A change in gender status results in a change of legal status, and even those who consider their gender to be "butch" could be regarded as exempt from, say, the niddah laws.

As I said, it's a radical idea. But the spirit of Jewish law as I understand it intends to transform the individual for the better, to give him or her opening points for a relationship with the sacred—not to keep people locked down in a place where they can find nothing holy. If people who do a "women's ritual" can decide for themselves if the ritual fits the body it circumscribes, then the ritual no longer forces certain bodies into certain boxes; our definitions of who must, who can, and who might be exempt would be utterly transformed. Men wouldn't choose the system for women; individuals would choose it for themselves.

The changes in Judaism created by the fall of the Second Temple were far more radical than the ideas outlined here. Feminism has been described (correctly, I think) as one of the greatest contemporary threats to the survival of Judaism. Isn't it time we took some drastic measures to ensure that we can keep going even without the altar of male domination?

Judaism's history is its strength; the many souls who have questioned, changed and upheld Jewish law have created a collective system greater than the sum of its parts. It's not about throwing away what's there—it's about creating air and space and breath so that those same mitzvot can pass into our age with renewed vigor and integrity. The beauty of Judaism—and, with the niddah laws, the beautiful problem—is that its rituals carry the breath of all who have considered, written about, thought about, and done them before, of thousands of years of history.

Perhaps it's time to exhale.

63. Eve Rosenbaum, "The Word," from *Yentl's Revenge*

Excerpts from "The Word," by Eve Rosenbaum, published in *Yentl's Revenge*, ed. Danya Ruttenberg (Seattle: Seal Press, 2001), 88–101. Reprinted with permission.

This beautiful essay written by a third-wave feminist considers questions of traditional religion and culture and her own identity as a feminist writer. Rosenbaum weaves together scenes from her life to bring out some of the tensions, pleasures, and contradictions in the world of a third-wave feminist.

The door to the church is closed but not locked. People have been going in and out, watching me as they reach the top step and make their way into the lit hallway. It's not snowing but the air holds promise, and I am pacing back and forth in front of the door of the First Baptist Church of Silver Spring, wishing I hadn't left my coat in the car, wishing I'd finished the poem and not thrown it away. I look at my watch, five to seven.

Ushers are supposed to meet at seven in the lobby, and my feet are not willing to step inside. It's just a building, it's just a building. Gabrielle has been to tons of churches. It's not a big deal, it's just a building. It's Friday night, it's after sunset. Driving on Friday is still difficult for me. I'm worried that I'll have an accident, the police will call my parents and my cover will be blown. They'll demand, "What were you doing at the First Baptist Church of Silver Spring on a Friday night, ushering for a concert of Christmas carols?" And really, will any explanation be good enough?

If I can keep my head low enough to the desk then Mrs. Leibman won't call on me and I can write my poem. I won't know the answer anyway, she knows it, the whole class knows it, it's no secret. She can call on Ahuva, who's sitting next to me, but calling on me would just be a disaster all around. She'll ask me a question in Hebrew, I'll stumble, turn red. She'll stop me halfway through and call on someone else who can give her the right answer. Then she'll want to talk to me after class, ask if I'm studying, and I'll tell her I am when we both know I'm not, that I don't care. But I'll pretend to care and she'll pretend to believe me and we'll continue on until the next time she looks over and sees me writing something in my notebook that doesn't go from right to left.

"Esther," she says in Hebrew, "can you read the Rashi and explain it?"

In school I go by my middle name. I don't lift my head. There's another Esther in the class. Ahuva pokes me. "It's you," she says. I cover my poem with my hand, pull my Humash closer to me on the desk. I have no idea where we are. I take too long and she calls on Tehilah, who answers in perfect Hebrew, perfect grammar. I go back to my poem.

Three weeks later I will turn in an almost blank test and Mrs. Leibman will turn it back to me with almost no red marks on it. "I didn't understand the questions," I'll say. "They're all in Hebrew." And she'll tell me to try harder. At the end of the term she'll pass me on my report card. All of the teachers will....

Mrs. Leibman calls me over after class and tells me to sit. "I'm looking for some good books to read," she says, "and I'd like to hear some suggestions."

"I'm not sure what kind of books." I don't read the books she thinks I read: What if she tells the principal and he expels me? I'm worried this is a test and I'm about to fail.

"Literature," she says. "You're always reading something. Tell me what you're reading."

The next day I give her my copy of Of Human Bondage *and an anthology of short stories. A week later she hands them back to me and asks how I can read such books. "These are not things Bais Yaakov girls should be reading."*

She's appalled, she says.

It's Wednesday afternoon and the door to Elizabeth's office is closed. She is at her desk, going through the proof pages of her book, and I am at her computer, typing up the index. The pages are due back to the publisher, and I'm helping her finish the last of it.

"Thanks for helping," she says. "You're a goddess."

I say that I'm not and we drift back into silence. There are moments of conversations, clarifications of a word or title, but we work mostly back to back. I feel comfortable in her office.

She hands me more pages to index and stretches, takes celery from the bag on the couch. She says, "I spoke to the head usher and he's going to e-mail you about our next concert."

"That's great," I say. "Thanks."

I say, "I've never been inside a church."

She can't believe it. "Never?" I shake my head. "Well," she says. "It's not a big deal. You'll be okay." We go back to silence.

I try to write a poem about churches, about sitting on the steps of a church debating whether to go inside. It's not working. I email it to Gabrielle and she says to put it away for a while, don't look at it. "I can't do that," I tell her.

It's midnight and we are an hour into a telephone conversation. I am in Washington, playing computer solitaire and not doing homework. She is packing up her New York apartment, wrapping canvases to be shipped to Israel. "I'm ushering next week and if the poem's not finished before then, well then I won't finish it." I am six days away from going into a church for the first time and trying to write about it. But it sounds hollow, boring.

"You know, going into a church isn't a big deal," Gabrielle says. "I've been to tons of churches. It's just a building."

"I know."

"It'll be fine, trust me." I throw away the poem.

It's Purim and I go to shul late, miss part of the Megillah reading. "If you don't hear the whole thing then it doesn't count," someone says to me. I walk with my mother and sister to the rabbi's house down the street and he reads the Megillah for people who missed it. His wife, the rebbetzin, *is talking to my mother, looking at me. I can't hear what they're saying but I'm sure I can guess. I'm right.*

"What did she say to you?" I ask my mother on the way home.

"She wanted to know if you were seeing anyone, if she can fix you up."

"No way," I say. "I'm seventeen. And I don't believe in marriage."

My mother sighs. We've had this conversation before. "I don't want to do this now," she says.

We walk through the gardens and Gabrielle says, "This is nothing. You should see the cathedrals in Europe, hundreds of years old, gardens you can get lost in. This is nice, but it was built in 1910. It's nice, but it's not Europe." Gabrielle is a cathedral freak. She is in D.C. for one day and we go to the National Cathedral because the facade amazes her. She has her camera, black and white film. She's leaving Tuesday for art school in Israel.

My father is playing with the car radio, looking for a good song. He stops at the oldies station. I groan, roll my eyes, and he starts singing along. "Can I give you a tape?" I ask. I pull open my bag, start looking around for something, anything that will make it stop.

Simon & Garfunkel come on, singing "The Sounds of Silence." My father sings with them. I contemplate jumping out of the car. It's only going eighty miles an hour, it's worth a shot. He reaches over and turns down the volume. "Did you know they're from New York?" he asks. "They both grew up religious and one Shabbos they turned the lights on to see if something would happen. They wanted to see if they would be struck by lightning, and nothing happened. After you turn the lights on once, it gets easier."

I'm looking out the window.

"Do you keep Shabbos?" he asks.

"Yes."

"That's good." My father is silent. He turns the radio back on. "Give me your tape." ...

"There's religion," Gabrielle says, "and there is spirituality. I don't think the two go together at all." I agree. It is August and we are sitting outside at

Cafe Dante in Manhattan's West Village, drinking iced coffee and eating artichoke hearts, watching people. It is a favorite pastime.

"Religion is a way of life. It's rules that tell you what to do and how to do it, how to be a person, how to interact with others. But there's nothing spiritual about it. And the only reason I believe in religion is because I believe that the Torah is real, that it was written by God. But I don't think it's necessarily a spiritual thing."

She drinks her coffee and gets up to chase a man with a cat on his shoulder. He stops and she takes his picture.

The weather report predicts a hurricane and I'm convinced my building is the only building in the D.C. area to lose power. My mother calls to check on me. "I have to go out," I tell her. "I need to buy candles before I go to class."

"You don't have candles?" she asks and I know I've slipped. "You told me you were lighting Shabbos candles every week. I guess you weren't telling the truth."

"I just ran out. I'm buying more today."

When Kate was sixteen she thought about suicide. She ran up the mountain near her house in Arizona and headed for the boulder by the edge of the cliff. 5:00 a.m. and the world was silent. She sat there crying, willing her body to throw itself into the ravine. She thought about the time a year earlier when she'd swallowed a bottle of aspirin and a bottle of whiskey. It didn't take. Her mother found her, and the emergency room pumped her stomach. But this time, this could be it. The ravine could be bottomless, she could fall through the earth.

She didn't do it. She started making her way back down the mountain, desperate to finish her morning run. She pushed her way back through the tangled brush and caught her foot on a branch, went flying. The ravine was not bottomless.

My brother calls me four times on Friday afternoon, fifteen minutes before Shabbos to make sure I'm home. I'm not. When I speak to him Saturday night I tell him I was in the shower, I was in the kitchen, I didn't hear the phone ring. Sorry.

I am at my parent's house for a week in winter and I visit the company where I used to work. Thomas takes me out to lunch. He is fifty and crazy in the way that artists sometimes are. He asks if my parents know what I do when I'm not home.

"Of course not," I say.

He tells me to be careful or my parents will lock me in the basement and try to brainwash me back into religion. I tell him I don't mind being the crazy woman locked away. "But," I say, "it's been done to death."

Once the tickets have been collected and the audience shown to their seats, I walk into the sanctuary through the side entrance and take a seat in the back pew near the rest of the ushers. I think, This place looks like a synagogue, except for the cross. The choir sings Christmas carols and I leave when the audience joins in. I don't know the words.

Kate signs my copy of her book. "To Eve: whose own writing and voice is so powerful even now at such a 'young age.' Keep with it and do not ever, ever let anyone else tell you what to think, do or say—follow your heart, because it's a strong one."

My father sees what she's written and looks at me, "What does she mean, don't let anyone tell you what to do?"

"It's nothing," I say. I take the book from his hands.

In tenth grade I fall in love with a new word: apikores. *I've heard it before, I know what it means. But this is the first time I've taken it for myself, felt the letters as they coat my tongue. I don't say it out loud—this is not the kind of word you can say when people are near you. It's the worst insult. It's the one thing you should never say to anyone.*

Mrs. Leibman talks about it in Humash class one Thursday. She says, "Girls, I don't want you to think a person who is an apikores is dumb. These people are smart by nature. They study the things we study and they have questions, they challenge the rabbis for answers and they choose not to believe. They don't fall out of religion because it's hard or because they're lazy. They move away from religion because they choose to. They are not satisfied with answers, they think there is a better truth waiting for them out there. They throw away religion because they are not satisfied with the answers we know to be true."

I want to be an apikores; I covet the word, the notion. It is not simply to be a nonbeliever. It is to consciously reject religion, to value one's own opinion over what should be taken as fact. An apikores is more dangerous than the average secular Jew. An apikores creates anarchy. I start to wonder if I'm smart enough to become one. Do I accept things too easily? Do I push for answers when I'm not satisfied? I can't ask Mrs. *Leibman these questions, she doesn't like me and this isn't the lesson I'm supposed to get from her lecture. I trace the word in my notebook, give it shape, texture. I cross it out when Ahuva looks over at my paper. I cover the letters with black ink.*

My brother calls on Saturday night. "Yeshiva was fun tonight. I learned with Kirschner and then we had Chinese food. I had sweet and sour chicken." He asks, "You went out?"

"Yeah, I was out."

"Where'd you go?"

"I went to church." I'm telling the truth. He thinks I'm kidding.

"Really, where'd you go?"

"Really, I went to church. It was fun."

"Very funny."

"I went out. I saw a movie."

I can hear his hesitation. He's debating whether he should lecture me about movies and how evil they are. He doesn't, because he knows I won't listen.

I can't tell him that I didn't see a movie, that really I ushered for a concert in a church and that I'm doing it again in three weeks.

"Tell me about school," I say and we talk for almost an hour.

Elizabeth comes over to me after the concert and we sit on the couch in the lobby. "That was great," I say. "Beautiful."

She asks, "How does it feel to be in church?"

"Fine," I say. "It feels fine."

"Just a building, right?"

I nod. We talk about finals and her trip to Paris.

Thomas suggests the Airmont Diner for lunch, halfway between my house and the office. I watch the cars as we walk to the door, hoping no one I know is watching. It's safer to go at night, when maybe no one will recognize my car in the dark. But I'm home for two days and this is the only time we could meet.

"The problem," I say once we're inside, "is that this place is right smack in the middle of town and everyone gets into everyone else's business. If someone sees me here then they'll tell my parents and maybe my parents' rabbi and then all hell breaks loose. Someone will tell my sister's principal and she'll get kicked out of school, my brother will get kicked out of school, no one will want to marry them and my parents will blame everything on me. I'm not sure one cup of coffee is worth all that."

Thomas thinks I'm insane....

Shira calls me Sunday night. She tells me about her children and says that she and her husband are getting audited by the IRS. "So, tell me about your life."

"I went out with some people," I say.

"To a kosher restaurant?"

"Of course. We went out Thursday night." Really, Saturday afternoon to an Italian restaurant in Georgetown, but I can't think of any reason to be honest.

"Do you go to shul?" she asks. "Do you have a lot of Jewish friends in Washington?"

I can't figure out how to answer this. She asks again.

"I don't know very many Jewish people," I say. "Actually, I know almost none. And I don't live near a shul."

"So what do you do all Shabbos?"

"Sleep and read, it's fine."

"You know, I'm so proud of you," she says. "You live in a city where you don't know any religious Jews and you keep to what you believe in. That shows you are really dedicated. That makes me happy." We talk for a few more minutes. When we hang up I want to rip out my tongue.

I'm going from bedroom to bedroom, collecting my clothes and books to pack after a week at home. I have things all over the house and my brother is following me. He's trying to start a debate about religion. "Not now, okay?

I can't do this now." I go through piles of laundry looking for my socks. It's almost midnight. "Don't you have to go to sleep?" he's not moving.

"I want to understand where you're coming from," he says. He sounds reasonable but I know this is just the introduction to a conversation that will take hours. We've been through this before. "I want to know how you could go from wanting to be a Bais Yaakov girl to how you are now."

I want to laugh. He doesn't know how I am; I don't tell him anything. He starts the standard debate, I try to make jokes, get him to say goodnight, goodbye and go to sleep.

"Are you an apikores?" he asks. "You're an apikores."

I pretend to get angry. Really I'm flattered. Out of my half-lies and altered stories he has formed an opinion of me. I want to sit him down and tell him everything. I want to tell him what I do, who I am, and then let him call me an apikores. I want to tell him that two weeks ago I spent Friday night in a church, ushering for a concert where I listened to Christmas carols, staring at a cross draped in purple fabric. I want to tell him that I drove on Shabbos, ripped tickets, lit candles, wrote in my journal. I want to watch his face.

But really I don't want to watch his face. Two days later he has forgotten our conversation and he makes jokes to me over the telephone.

Gabrielle and I walk through the Whitney Museum and she peers closely at the Mark Rothko paintings. "It's all layered," she says. "It looks like one color but there's such depth behind each brush stroke, it's like the different paints have collided and turned themselves into one color that represents the whole. But if you look close enough, you can see their differences."

I move closer to the wall.

"He's a genius," she says.

It is Arizona. I know it is Arizona the way I know the sound of my voice in echo. I run up trails that are familiar, but I know I've never been here. I know these trails, recognize the brush, I jump over the branches, I run past saguaros. My feet pound the earth, pack the brown soil of desert into something tame, something easily stepped on. She has been here, I think, she has pounded this earth in predawn the way I am tracing her footfalls by moonlight.

I see the boulder. I see her sitting, crying, waiting for the sun to come up over the town she has learned to call home. I want to wave as I run past, but she is only an outline: she is not flesh. The cliff pulls itself into focus before me and if I dilate my eyes I can see straight through the night, see the cliff on the other side of the ravine. I can jump it, I think. I can make it across. Her outline faces the other direction. She does not watch as my legs arch away from earth and I take flight.

But my aim is wrong. I'm flying, but straight down is not the direction I hoped for. Beneath me is water that rushes toward nowhere, content enough to churn. I fall into its fever. My feet don't touch bottom. My arms reach for something to grab on to. I don't want to die here, I think, I don't want to drown. My fingers find a branch and start to pull themselves out of the water, my feet take hold of the wall and I climb straight up the cliff. I reach the top bruised and bleeding but alive. I look over the ravine and see her outline on the boulder, still contemplating death. My feet find the rhythm of the trail and pound the desert in time with the rising of the sun.

I sit by myself in the back pew of the church, the other ushers a few rows up. In crimson ink I write the word "apikores" on my hand in Hebrew, sure no one around me will know what it means. I decide to write the word on my hand every day until I am sure.

My brother calls me an apikores. Shira called me an apikores on the phone two days ago and I didn't disagree. But I'm not sure. I want to know that I own the word, that I can become the letters, now red and seeping into my skin, and never look back. I want to write in permanent ink or not write it at all.

After the concert I walk out with Elizabeth. I put my hand in the pocket of my coat.

64. Rebecca Walker, *What Makes a Man: 22 Writers Imagine the Future*

Excerpts from Rebecca Walker, ed., *What Makes a Man* (New York: Riverhead, 2004).

In a piece that expresses some of the central ideas of third-wave feminism, Rebecca Walker argues for the necessity to include men and thinking about masculinity in a third-wave framework and discusses all the ways that traditional gender roles intersect with race, making boy's lives dangerous. It is a persuasive, moving argument about the need for social change for men and boys, and the need for feminism to include them.

While the first and second waves of the women's movement have successfully encouraged many women to abandon restrictive stereotypes of feminity and redefine the very foundation of their identities, men have yet to embark upon a similar mass reeducation. John Stoltenberg, Robert Allen, Robert Bly, William Pollack, Susan Faludi, bell hooks, and others have all exerted considerable effort toward the project of deconstructing masculinity, and yet we are a long way from men being able to safely abandon self-sacrifice and emotional stoicism as a way of life. In envisioning the Third Wave as a space/movement/paradigm which fully recognizes the importance of psychologically integrated and emotionally healthy men to the overall well being of women, families, and the world at large, it is my belief that men's liberation, and the role women play in it, is critical Third Wave domain.

I fully came to this understanding one night after a grueling conversation with my eleven-year-old son. He had come home from middle school unnaturally quiet and withdrawn, shrugging off my questions of concern with uncharacteristic irritability. Where was the sunny, chatty boy I dropped off that morning? What had happened to him in the perilous halls of middle school?

Later he sat on a sofa in my study and read his science book as I wrote at my desk. As we worked under the soft glow of paper lanterns, with the heat on high and our little dog snoring at his feet, my son began to relax. I could feel a shift in his energy as he began to remember, deep in his body, that he was home, that he was safe, and that he didn't have to brace to protect himself from the expectations of the outside world.

An hour or so passed like this before he announced that he had a question. He was lying down now, his head resting on the padded arm of the sofa. "I've been thinking that maybe I should play sports at school." I raised my eyebrows. "Any sport in mind, or just sports in general?" He shrugged. "Basketball maybe, or softball. I like softball." I cocked my head to one side. "What brought this on?" He scratched behind the dog's ears. "I don't know. Maybe girls will like me if I play sports."

Excuse me?

My boy is intuitive, smart, and creative beyond belief. At the time he loved animals, Japanese anime, the rap group Dead Prez and everything having to do with snowboarding. He liked to help both of his grandmothers in the garden. He liked to read science fiction. He liked to climb into bed with me and lay his head on my chest. He liked to build vast and intricate cities of Legos, and spent hours separating little multicolored pieces of plastic into piles. He was beginning what I thought was a lifelong love affair with chess.

Maybe girls would like him if he played sports?

Call me extreme, but I felt as if I had a brilliant eleven-year old daughter and she had come home and said, "Maybe boys will like me if I pretend I am dumb." Or, "Maybe the kids will like me if I pretend to be white."

I tried to stay calm as he illuminated the harsh realities of the sixth grade social scene. Basically the girls liked the jocks the best, and sometimes designed to give the time of the day to the other team, the computer nerds. My son said that since he wasn't allowed to play the violent computer games we forbade in our house, he was having trouble securing his place with the latter, hence the contemplation of assuming the identity of the former. When I asked about making friends based on common interests, rather than superficial categories, he grew flustered. "You don't understand," he said. "Boys talk about sports, like their games and who scored what and stuff, or they talk about new versions of computer games or tricks they learned to beat the game." Tears welled up in his eyes. "I don't have anything to talk about."

He was right, until that moment I had had no idea, but suddenly the truth of being a sixth grade boy in America crystallized before me. My beautiful boy and every other mother's beautiful boy had what essentially boiled down to two options: fight actually in sport, or fight virtually on the computer. Athlete, gladiator, secret agent, Tomb Raider. The truth of his existence, his many likes and dislikes, none of them having to do with winning or killing of any kind, had no social currency. He could compete and score, perform and win, or be an outcast or worse, invisible.

That night I went to sleep with several things on my mind: the conversation I planned to have with the head of my son's school about the need for a comprehensive interrogation of the contours of masculinity; the way girls find themselves drawn to more "traditional" displays of masculinity because they are more unsure than ever about how to experience their own feminity; and the many hours and endless creativity I would have to devote to ensuring that my son's true self would not be entirely snuffed out by the cultural imperative.

And then there was the final and most chilling thought of all:

A bat, a "joy stick." What's next, a gun?

It occurred to me that my son was being primed to pick up a gun. The first steps were clear: tell him that who he is authentically is not enough; tell him that he will not be loved unless he abandons his own desires and picks up a tool of competition; tell him that to really be of value he must stand ready to compete, dominate, and, if necessary, kill, if not actually then virtually, financially, athletically.

If one's life purpose is obscured by the pressure to conform to a generic type and other traces of self are ostracized into shadow, if connection is not found through emotionally rich connection to friends and family, and identity is not located in creative contribution to the betterment of the community, then how difficult *is* it to pick up a gun, metaphoric or literal, as a means of self-definition, as a way of securing what feels like personal power?

If I didn't get it that night, I got it after talking with all of the men who told me their stories as I shared my concerns about my son: there is war being waged on boys and it starts before they are born. It is a war against vulnerability, creativity, individuality and the mysterious unknown. It is a war against tenderness, empathy, grief, fear, longing, and feeling itself. It is a war against wholeness and psychological integration. In its determination to annihilate the authentic self, it is war against peace.

Over the last two years every man I know shared his own version of the same basic story: A few years filled with wonder and freedom cut short by the subtle and not so subtle demands of being a man, a sudden and often violent reduction of individuality into a single version of boyhood. In what seemed like a moment but what was actually a slow build up over time, an insidious and deceptively gradual occupation of psychic territory, young men were expected to change, to follow spoken and unspoken cues: don't feel, take control, be physically strong, find your identity in money and work, do not be afraid to kill, distrust everything that you see. Don't cry.

This war against what is considered feminine that is wounding our sons and brothers, fathers and uncles is familiar to women, but now we are able to recognize that it is killing the other half of the planet, too. But instead of dying of heartache and botched abortions and breast cancer and sexual trauma and low self-esteem, this half is dying of radiation from modern weaponry, suicidal depression, and a soul-killing obsession with the material. This half is dying of prostrate cancer and heart attacks and workaholism and an overwhelming sense of failure, of missing something exceedingly important that they cannot name, of disconnection from the source of life itself.

What they are missing is themselves, the unique expression that has been rerouted and suppressed in the name of work, war, and the arduous and absurd task of "being a man." This mandate to repress or obliterate anything and everything expansive or off the grid has defined generations, so much so that most men cannot even perceive the extent to which they have been robbed. Those men who have managed to survive more or less intact, the artists, healers, teachers, philosophers, and monks, are the ones with the most harrowing tales. Having challenged the status quo, they enjoy more freedom, but carry gruesome battle scars.

The good news is that things are changing as more and more men begin to interrogate limiting concepts of masculinity, and to break away from conventional social scripts. By reevaluating the messages they have been given, these contemporary revolutionaries dare to imagine what the world would be like if the men decided to put down the gun, literal and metaphoric, and women decided to let them. Struggling to make sense of the disturbing legacy of masculinity, they excavate the many aspects of their lives—violence, sexuality, fatherhood, work, money, privilege, friendship, marriage—and become aware of just how emotionally defended they have been forced to be. In the process they begin to transform themselves from one dimensional "men," into multidimensional beings.

But there is an equally urgent need for women to reflect deeply on their part in maintaining the male charade. If we want men to be different we must eroticize that difference, and stop saying we want a man who can talk about his feelings only to marry the strong, silent type who happens to be a good provider. As mothers we can't run for the karate school brochures when our sons tell us they want dance lessons, and we can't turn a blind eye to their fight to hold on to who they are in the face of a million messages telling them to change. Women must also look at how we too have abandoned our own tenderness and intuitive knowing, and come to rely more and more upon the empirical and the competitive when navigating the world around us, succeeding in the patriarchal paradigm but failing overall.

Whether we hold tightly to the fantasy of a knight in shining armor swooping down to save, protect, and provide for us, or we believe that by thinking logically and "winning the race" we will secure greater happiness for ourselves and our families, we are still looking outside ourselves for the answers and turning our backs on what can truly set us free. To know peace and have relationships in which we no longer look for completion or salvation in the other, men and women alike must face their existential fears and find their true purpose, separate from any societally sanctioned ideas about masculine and feminine.

65. Rebecca Walker, "Liberate Yourself from Labels: Bisexuality and Beyond," from *50 Ways to Support Lesbian and Gay Equality*

Excerpts from Rebecca Walker, "Liberate Yourself from Labels: Bisexuality and Beyond," published in *50 Ways to Support Lesbian and Gay Equality,* ed. Meredith Maran and Angela Watrous (Makawao, Maui, HI: Inner Ocean Publishing, 2005): 131–132.

Rebecca Walker's essay "Liberate Yourself from Labels" stands as the last word on third-wave feminism and questions of identity because of the ways it addresses all the complications of third-wavers' lives, and how they never fit neatly into any given box, be that male/female, gay/straight, black/white, rich/poor, First World/Third World. "Can you stop your mind," she writes, "from slicing the world into tiny, seemingly irreconcilable pieces? Can I?" This is, perhaps, the most essential question for third-wave feminism, which has to negotiate a world that now transverses all these divides. What are the steps toward true equality? Walker outlines those steps here, and getting beyond labels is what defines them.

People who love both genders are the subject of all kinds of misguided stereotypes: that all bisexual people are promiscuous; that we're incapable of monogamy; that we're not "really" gay or "really" straight. The truth is, the only difference between bi people and others is that we have the flexibility—whether by choice or design—to be sexual with both genders. We're a diverse group of people, just like any other segment of the population, and deserve to be recognized for who we are as individuals.

Instead of asking what gay and straight people should understand about being bisexual, I think we need to ask what gay, straight, bisexual and transgender people need to understand about permanent liberation from divisive thought itself. I would much rather work on dismantling the mental boundaries we have created in a misguided attempt to avert the truth of our interconnectedness. Homophobia and heterophobia are only the symptoms of the problem. Let's get to the root. Can you stop your mind from slicing the world into tiny, seemingly irreconcilable pieces? Can I?

Bisexual people need what everyone else needs: food, air, clear water. Freedom from persecution and the threat of annihilation. A reasonable way to make a living. As long as we're not hurting anyone, it would be nice to be able to move freely without having to explain ourselves and our choices. It would be nice to be free of both the heavy pronouncements of religious morality and the earnest judgmentalism of politically correct progressives.

This business of convincing each other, group by group, of our right to exist is taking so long, I'm not sure it's working. Our survival as a species may depend on our ability to change the way we see the world right now. Straight, gay, bisexual, transgender—what does it matter? Have you found ways to minimize territoriality, labeling, anger, jealousy in your own life? Have you found ways to address your own assumptions and judgments? These are the questions we must all pursue if we're ever going to join together as happy, confident, and integrated human beings.

Steps for Equality

- Avoid making judgments about people based on generalizations and stereotypes. While you're at it, avoid making judgments about people at all. Make up your mind about people based on your actual experiences with them.

- Try to let go of "us and them" thinking. We're all sexual beings, and this similarity is a much greater truth than any differences our culture has manufactured.
- Don't assume someone's sexuality based on appearances or what you think you know about bisexual people. A man dating a woman may be bisexual; a woman married to another woman may be bisexual. In the same way that heterosexual married couples still experience attraction to other members of the opposite sex, a bisexual person maintains his or her sexual identity even while in a monogamous relationship. Being in a committed relationship doesn't change our sexuality; it just focuses our various expressions of sexuality.

Index

Note: Volume numbers are in **bold** type. Page numbers for main entries or primary documents are in *italic* type.